# CIVIL LIBERTIES

## and

# THE CONSTITUTION

CASES AND COMMENTARIES

LUCIUS J. BARKER
*Edna Gellhorn University Professor of Public Affairs
and Political Science, Washington University*

TWILEY W. BARKER, JR.
*Professor of Political Science,
University of Illinois at Chicago Circle*

PRENTICE-HALL, INC.
*Englewood Cliffs, New Jersey*

*TO RUTH, VALERIE, MAUD, TRACEY, AND HEIDI*

*PRENTICE-HALL INTERNATIONAL, INC., London*
*PRENTICE-HALL OF AUSTRALIA, PTY. LTD., Sydney*
*PRENTICE-HALL OF CANADA, LTD., Toronto*
*PRENTICE-HALL OF INDIA PRIVATE LIMITED, New Delhi*
*PRENTICE-HALL OF JAPAN, INC., Tokyo*

# Preface

This book focuses on some basic issues in civil liberties: free exercise of religion and church-state relations; freedom of expression and association; rights of persons accused of crime; and problems related to racial justice. Each major problem area is treated first in an introductory commentary. These commentaries summarize the development of case law and provide historical perspective for examining and evaluating the issues presented. In short, this volume points up civil-liberties issues as they have been expounded by and in leading judicial decisions, primarily those of the Supreme Court. Judicial opinions concerning these decisions often demonstrate currents of opinion about the scope and nature of fundamental freedoms. And the fact that judges play so important a role in shaping public policies—especially those related to civil liberties—makes it even more crucial for us to see what judges say, not what we think they said or ought to have said. To let judges speak for themselves puts us in a much better position to interpret and analyze what they have said or to second-guess what they have done.

This book is developed along traditional and historical lines. But this should not lead more sophisticated readers, including teachers and students, to use it in a traditional manner. We would be most disappointed if they should. Our own earlier volume, *Freedoms, Courts, Politics* (Prentice-Hall, Inc., 1965), points up the wide range of activities and actors involved in the formation of policy, especially judicial policy dealing with civil liberties. We are keenly aware and deeply sensitive to the political, social, psychological, and economic dimensions of civil-liberties problems. But we are also aware and sensitive to the fact that what the courts have said and done constitutes a valuable resource from which to draw in order to better understand the scope and complexity of the problems involved. Thus, our hope is that this book will be supplemented by materials (or by the teacher himself) that focus on other facets and dimensions of the problems discussed here.

We acknowledge with gratitude the assistance of Professor J.W. Peltason of the University of Illinois, Urbana-Champaign, who read the introductory commentaries and offered many helpful suggestions on them and on our selection of cases. We are also grateful for the help given by our student assistants, Sherry Joseph and Jonathan Walton of the University of Illinois at Chicago Circle, and Neil Bradley of the University of Wisconsin at Milwaukee. They not only did the laborious job of typing much of the manuscript but offered helpful suggestions for editing some of the cases. For the errors, which somehow always appear after publication, we take full responsibility.

L.J.B.

T.W.B.

# Contents

# 1. Nationalizing the Bill of Rights

*Barron v. Baltimore*    *Palko v. Connecticut*
*Adamson v. California*

The framers of the Bill of Rights considered federal power the major threat to individual liberties. The injunction of the First Amendment, "Congress shall make no law . . . ," is indicative of that concern. But there were others who viewed the Bill of Rights as restricting state power as well. This view was urged in *Barron* v. *Baltimore*,[1] but the Supreme Court rejected such a construction. Speaking for a unanimous Court, Chief Justice John Marshall said:

The Constitution was ordained and established by the people of the United States for themselves, for their own government, and not for the government of the individual states. . . . The powers they conferred on this government were to be exercised by itself; and the limitations on power, if expressed in general terms are . . . necessarily applicable to the government created by the instrument. They are limitations of power granted in the instrument itself; not of distinct governments framed by different persons and for different purposes.

He concluded that if his propositions are correct, then the Fifth Amendment (and hence the Bill of Rights) must be understood as restraining the power of the national government and not that of the states.

This principle was reaffirmed in a number of cases prior to the Civil War and continued to be a guide for the Court in decisions following the adoption of the Fourteenth Amendment in 1868. Indeed, the Court heard several cases in which counsel argued that the Fourteenth Amendment had as one of its objectives the incorporation of the Bill of Rights. But the Court steadfastly refused to interpret the Fourteenth Amendment in this way.

Then in 1925, in a historic decision, *Gitlow* v. *New York* (268 U.S. 652, 1925), the Court said:

For present purposes we may and do assume that freedom of speech and of the press which are protected by the First Amendment from abridgement by Congress are among the fundamental personal rights and liberties protected by the due process clause of the Fourteenth Amendment from impairment by the States.

[1] Complete citations for decisions reprinted in this book appear at the beginning of each decision.

1

*Gitlow* v. *New York* was a case of major, almost revolutionary, significance, which turned the tide in favor of those who saw the provisions of the Bill of Rights as effective limitations on the states through the Fourteenth Amendment. Two years after *Gitlow,* for example, the Court reversed a conviction under a Kansas criminal syndicalism act, saying that the application of the act imposed "an arbitrary and unreasonable exercise of the police power of the State . . . in violation of the due process clause of the Fourteenth Amendment."[2] Four years later in *Near* v. *Minnesota* (283 U.S. 679, 1931), the Court struck down a Minnesota statute as an abridgement of freedom of the press. Chief Justice Charles Evans Hughes asserted in the opinion for the Court that "it is no longer open to doubt that the liberty of the press, and of speech, is within the liberty safeguarded by the due process clause of the Fourteenth Amendment from invasion by state action."

The Court continued this erosion of the *Barron* rule, at least as far as First Amendment freedoms were concerned, when in *De Jonge* v. *Oregon* it held peaceable assembly a right cognate to those of free speech and free press and hence protected against state impairment by the due process clause of the Fourteenth Amendment.

But any notion that this trend of decisions would lead to a reversal of *Barron* v. *Baltimore* and the total incorporation of the first eight amendments into the Fourteenth Amendment was dispelled by Justice Benjamin Cardozo in a decision handed down just eleven months after *De Jonge.* In *Palko* v. *Connecticut* the Court refused to apply the double jeopardy provision of the Fifth Amendment to a state criminal prosecution. Justice Cardozo argued that only those guarantees of the first eight amendments which are "implicit in the concept of ordered liberty" are to be construed as valid restrictions on state power through the Fourteenth Amendment. In effect, he enunciated a doctrine of "selective incorporation" of specific Bill of Rights guarantees into the Fourteenth Amendment based on the test of their essentiality to his concept of "ordered liberty."

In 1940 the "selective incorporation" process resulted in the Court's holding in *Cantwell* v. *Connecticut* (310 U.S. 296, 1940) that the free exercise of religion clause of the First Amendment is applicable to the states. In this case the Court struck down a state statute which allowed officials unfettered discretion in regulating religious advocacy and solicitation. In his opinion for a unanimous Court, Justice Owen Roberts contended:

The fundamental concept of liberty embodied in that [the Fourteenth] Amendment embraces the liberties guaranteed by the First Amendment . . . , [which] declares that Congress shall make no law respecting an establishment

2 *Fiske* v. *Kansas* (274 U.S. 380, 1927).

of religion or prohibiting the free exercise thereof. The Fourteenth Amendment has rendered the legislatures of the states as incompetent as Congress to enact such laws.

This expansive interpretation of the scope of the Fourteenth Amendment was followed by an application of the establishment clause of the First Amendment to the states in *Everson v. Board of Education*. In that case the Court considered the troublesome issues of public aid to parochial schools and held that the due process clause of the Fourteenth Amendment enjoins the states from rendering such aid just as the First Amendment restrains Congress.

The most comprehensive arguments supporting the total incorporation theory were made in *Adamson v. California*. Here the Court's five-man majority refused to upset a state conviction where the appellant argued that the state procedure infringed the Fifth Amendment guarantee against compulsory self-incrimination, which was made applicable to the states through the Fourteenth Amendment. The four dissenters— Justices Hugo Black, William O. Douglas, Frank Murphy and Wiley B. Rutledge—contended that all the specific guarantees of the first eight amendments should be read into the due process clause of the Fourteenth Amendment and made applicable to the states. Justice Black's dissenting opinion is most often cited in support of this thesis. He maintained that the legislative history of the Fourteenth Amendment, as well as the debates in the state legislatures ratifying it, clearly revealed that the Fourteenth Amendment was designed to make the Bill of Rights applicable to the states. In effect, his position was that the framers of the Fourteenth Amendment intended for the due process clause to be a shorthand restatement of the specific guarantees of the Bill of Rights, *but no more.*

In a concurring opinion, Justice Felix Frankfurter not only questioned Black's reading and interpretation of history but contended that incorporation of the specific guarantees of the Bill of Rights into the due process clause would import to it a far more expansive meaning than intended in some cases and a more restricted meaning than intended in others. To him, such a construction would also do violence to the principle of federalism upon which the Republic was founded. As he put it:

A construction which gives to due process no independent function but turns it into a summary of the specific provisions of the Bill of Rights would . . . tear up the fabric of law in the several States, and would deprive the States of the opportunity for reforms in legal process designed for extending the area of freedom. It would assume that no other abuses would reveal themselves in the course of time than those which had become manifest in 1791.

On the other hand, two of Black's fellow dissenters did not share his view of the limited protection afforded by the due process clause. It was their view that restricting the scope of the clause only to the Bill of Rights guarantees and *no more* fails to include enough. As Murphy contended in a separate opinion in which Rutledge joined:

Occasions may arise where a proceeding falls so far short of conforming to fundamental standards of procedure as to warrant constitutional condemnation in terms of lack of due process despite the absence of a specific provision in the Bill of Rights.

In subsequent cases, Justice Black reaffirmed his total incorporation position and continued to urge a "narrow" or "strict" interpretation of the specific guarantees of the Bill of Rights. In *Wolf* v. *Colorado,* for example, he concurred in the Court's action "selectively incorporating" the Fourth Amendment into the Fourteenth *without* the exclusionary rule. He contended that the rule, which holds that evidence obtained in violation of the Fourth Amendment is inadmissible in criminal prosecutions, "is not a command of the Fourth Amendment" but instead is a "judicially created" one. Justices Murphy and Rutledge were joined this time by Justice Douglas in taking issue with Black's narrow construction of the Fourth Amendment. In their view, not only does the Fourteenth Amendment incorporate the guarantees of the Fourth, but the exclusionary rule must be construed as embraced in the Amendment if its command is to be an effective sanction against the evil to which it is directed.

Though the "total incorporation" theory has never gained majority support, its proponents have virtually accomplished their goal. Note the forward thrust of incorporation since 1961: *Mapp* v. *Ohio,* where the exclusionary rule was made obligatory on the states, thereby making the Fourth Amendment an effective restraint on state action; *Malloy* v. *Hogan* and *Benton* v. *Maryland,* making the Fifth Amendment's self-incrimination and double jeopardy provisions applicable to the states; *Gideon* v. *Wainwright, Pointer* v. *Texas, Klopfer* v. *North Carolina,* and *Duncan* v. *Louisiana,* in which the Court incorporated into the Fourteenth Amendment the Sixth Amendment guarantees of counsel, confrontation, a speedy trial, and trial by jury for serious criminal offenses; and *Robinson* v. *California,* tying to the Fourteenth Amendment the Eighth Amendment's protection against cruel and unusual punishment.

As the Court ended its 1968 term, only a few provisions of the Bill of Rights had not been incorporated into the Fourteenth Amendment. These include the Second and Third Amendments (which have no practical significance for the states), the grand jury indictment requirement of the Fifth Amendment, the jury trial provision for civil suits guaranteed by the Seventh Amendment, and the provision prohibiting excessive bail and the imposition of excessive fines of the Eighth Amendment. For all practical purposes, however, imposition of excessive bail and fines by a state would violate the due process clause of the Fourteenth Amendment.

The opponents of the incorporation theory did not allow the gradual process of undermining *Barron* to proceed uncontested. To them it was just as offensive as total incorporation. For example, Justice John Harlan contended in *Malloy* v. *Hogan* (1964) that this approach "is in fact nothing more or less than 'incorporation' in snatches." Furthermore, it was his contention there that "if the Due Process Clause of the Fourteenth Amendment is something more than a reference to the Bill of Rights and protects only those rights which derive from fundamental principles . . . , it is just as contrary to precedent and just as illogical to incorporate the provisions of the Bill of Rights one at a time as it is to incorporate them all at once." Harlan echoed this same theme in *Pointer* v. *Texas* (1965) one year later while concurring in the Court's decision guaranteeing the right of confrontation in state cases. To him the confrontation guarantee was "implicit in the concept of ordered liberty," and the majority opinion incorporating the guarantee into the Fourteenth Amendment was simply "another step in the onward march of the long-since discredited 'incorporation' doctrine. . . ."

In *Duncan* v. *Louisiana* (1968), Justice Harlan launched another full-scale attack on the "total incorporation" doctrine. Here, the Court incorporated the Sixth Amendment guarantee of trial by jury and in doing so revised the Palko test. Instead of asking whether a particular guarantee is essential for a civilized society, the Court now asks whether such a guarantee is "necessary to an Anglo-American regime of ordered liberty." Harlan argued that "the Court's approach [to the case] and its reading of history are altogether topsy-turvy." Hence, he rejected the view that it was the intention of those who drafted the Fourteenth Amendment to incorporate the first eight amendments. To him Black's interpretation of the legislative history of the Fourteenth Amendment (as set forth in *Adamson* in support of the "total incorporation" doctrine) had been thoroughly discredited by Charles Fairman.[3] He noted that the evidence marshalled by Professor Fairman convincingly demonstrates that the Congressmen who drafted, and the state legislators who ratified, the Fourteenth Amendment did not think they were making the first eight amendments applicable to the states. "In short," he concluded, "neither history, nor sense, supports using the Fourteenth Amendment to put the states in a constitutional straight-jacket with respect to their own development in the administration of criminal or civil law." For Harlan, the "only one method of analysis that has any internal logic . . . is to start with the words 'liberty' and 'due process' and attempt to define

---

[3] Charles Fairman, "Does the Fourteenth Amendment Incorporate the Bill of Rights? The Original Understanding," 2 *Stanford L. Rev.* 5 (1949).

them in a way that accords with American traditions and our system of government."

Justice Black could not let this opportunity pass without defending and clarifying his historical analysis, which supported the incorporation theory advanced in *Adamson*. In a concurring opinion (primarily a rejoinder to Professor Fairman's attack), Black caustically referred to Fairman's emphasis on "what was *not* said in the Congress which proposed, and the state legislatures that passed on, the Fourteenth Amendment" as a kind of "negative pregnant." (Emphasis added.) Reemphasizing the correctness of his reading of history, he contended that his appraisal followed ten years of experience in the United States Senate which prepared him "to learn the value of what *is* said in legislative debates, committee discussions, committee reports, and various other steps taken in the course of passage of . . . proposed constitutional amendments." (Emphasis added.) In essence, what Black seems to imply is that because of his Senate experience his history is better than Professor Fairman's. Apart from the historical issue, Black was critical of Harlan's restatement of the *Twining* concept of due process—a concept which Black contends allows the Court "boundless power under 'natural law' periodically to expand and contract constitutional standards to conform to the Court's conception of what at a particular time constitutes 'civilized decency' and 'fundamental liberty and justice.' "[4] Black noted that such a view of due process was too loose and shifting, since its meaning would be "in accordance with judges' predilections and understandings of what is best for the country."

Whether, as a general rule, the provisions of the Bill of Rights which have been incorporated into the Fourteenth Amendment operate with equal force and impose the same standards upon the states as upon the federal government is still an unsettled question. Justices supporting total incorporation (never a majority) have, at one time or another, argued that the standard should be the same. For example, Justice Black in his dissenting opinion in *Adamson* referred to the "literal application" of the Bill of Rights to the states, and Justice Douglas, dissenting in *Beauharnis* v. *Illinois* (343 U.S. 250, 288, 1952), contended that there is no exception in the command of the First Amendment when applied to limit states via the Fourteenth Amendment. Douglas has also contended that the rights incorporated in the Fourteenth Amendment are not "watered-down versions" of what the Bill of Rights guarantees. Likewise, Justice Brennan, dissenting in *Cohen* v. *Hurley* (336 U.S. 117, 1961), argued that the "full sweep" of the privilege against self-incrimination is

4 In *Twining* v. *New Jersey* (211 U.S. 78, 1908), the Supreme Court rejected a self-incrimination claim and upheld a state criminal procedure which permitted the courts in their instructions to the jury to comment on the accused's failure to testify and contradict evidence presented against him. Justice Moody concluded, after extensive historical analysis, that the self-incrimination privilege was not inherent in due process of law.

applicable to the states through the Fourteenth Amendment. And Justice Tom Clark declared in *Mapp* v. *Ohio* that the Fourth Amendment's provisions are enforceable against the states "by the same sanction of exclusion as issued against the Federal Government." Furthermore, Justice Clark wrote an opinion in *Ker* v. *California* (374 U.S. 23, 1963), in which all the justices except Harlan agreed that the "standard of reasonableness of a search and seizure is the same under the Fourth and Fourteenth Amendments."

On the other hand, a minority of justices have rejected this kind of congruence argument. For example, Justice Jackson, while dissenting in *Beauharnis,* rejected the notion that the liberty which the Fourteenth Amendment protects against state impairment is the "literal and identical freedom of speech or of the press" which the First Amendment protects against federal abridgement. Justice John Harlan II has offered the most vigorous opposition to the "equivalence" position. In his dissent in *Mapp,* in which he was supported by Justices Frankfurter and Whittaker, he contended that it would be improper to impose "any precise equivalence, either as regards the scope of the right or the means of its implementation, between the requirements of the Fourth and Fourteenth Amendment."

The cases that follow examine the rationale for the *Barron* rule, the modification of it by the *Palko* doctrine, and leading arguments on incorporation of the Bill of Rights into the Fourteenth Amendment.

## BARRON v. BALTIMORE

7 Peters 242; 8 L. Ed. 672 (1833)

CHIEF JUSTICE MARSHALL *delivered the opinion of the Court.*

[This case was instituted by the plaintiff in error against the city of Baltimore . . . to recover damages for injuries to the wharf-property of the plaintiff, arising from the acts of the corporation. Craig and Barron, of whom the plaintiff is survivor, were owners of an extensive and highly productive wharf in the eastern section of Baltimore, enjoying, at the period of their purchase of it, the deepest water in the harbour.

[The city, in the asserted exercise of its corporate authority over the harbour, the paving of streets, and regulating grades for paving, and over the health of Baltimore, directed from their accustomed and natural course, certain streams of water which flow from the range of hills bordering the city, and diverted them. . . . These streams becoming very full and violent in rains, carried down with them from the hills and the soil over which they ran, large masses of sand and earth, which they deposited along, and widely in front of the wharf of the plaintiff. The alleged consequence was, that the water was rendered so shallow that it ceased to be useful for vessels of any important burthen, lost its income, and became of little or no value as a wharf.

. . .

[At the trial of the cause . . . the decision of Baltimore county court was against the defendants, and a verdict for four thousand five hundred dollars was rendered for the plaintiff. An appeal was taken to the court of appeals, which reversed the judgment of Baltimore county court, and did not remand the case to that court for a further trial. From this judgment the defendant in the court of appeals, prosecuted a writ of error to this court.]

The plaintiff in error contends that it comes within that clause in the fifth amendment to the Constitution, which inhibits the taking of private property for public use, without just compensation. He insists that this amendment, being in favor of the liberty of the citizen, ought to be so construed as to restrain the legislative power of a State, as well as that of the United States. If this proposition be untrue, the court can take no jurisdiction of the cause.

The question thus presented is, we think, of great importance, but not of much difficulty.

The Constitution was ordained and established by the people of the United States for themselves, for their own government, and not for the government of the individual States. Each State established a Constitution for itself, and, in that Constitution, provided such limitations and restrictions on the powers of its particular government as its judgment dictated. The people of the United States framed such a government for the United States as they supposed best adapted to their situation, and best calculated to promote their interests. The powers they conferred on this government were to be exercised by itself; and the limitations on power, if expressed in general terms, are naturally, and, we think, necessarily applicable to the government created by the instrument. They are limitations of power granted in the instrument itself; not of distinct governments, framed by different persons and for different purposes.

If these propositions be correct, the fifth amendment must be understood as restraining the power of the general government, not as applicable to the states. In their several constitutions, they had imposed such restrictions on their respective governments, as their own wisdom suggested; such as they deemed most proper for themselves. It is a subject on which they judge exclusively. . . .

The counsel for the plaintiff in error insists, that the constitution was intended to secure the people of the several states against the undue exercise of power by their respective state governments; as well as against that which might be attempted by their general government. In support of this argument he relies on the inhibitions contained in the tenth section of the first article. We think that section affords a strong, if not a conclusive, argument in support of the opinion already indicated by the court. The preceding section contains restrictions which are obviously intended for the exclusive purpose of restraining the exercise of power by the departments of the general government. Some of them use language applicable only to congress; others are expressed in general terms. The third clause, for example, declares, that "no bill of attainder or *ex post facto* law shall be passed." No language can be more general; yet the demonstration is complete, that it applies solely to the government of the United States. In addition to the general arguments furnished by the instrument itself, some of which have been already suggested, the succeeding section, the avowed purpose of which is to restrain state legislation, contains in terms the very prohibition. It declares, that "no State shall pass any bill of attainder or *ex post facto* law." This provision, then, of the ninth section, however comprehensive its language, contains no restrictions on state legislation.

The ninth section having enumerated, in the nature of a bill of rights, the limitations intended to be imposed on the powers of the general government, the tenth proceeds to enumerate those which were to operate on the state legislatures. These restrictions are brought together in the same section, and are by express words applied to the states. "No state shall enter into any treaty," etc. Perceiving that in a constitution framed by the people of the United States for the government of all, no limitation of the action of government on the people would apply to the state government, unless expressed in terms, the restrictions contained in the tenth section are in direct words so applied to the states.

It is worthy of remark, too, that these inhibitions generally restrain state legislation on subjects intrusted to the general government, or in which the people of all the states feel an interest. A state is forbidden to enter into any treaty, alliance, or confederation. If these compacts are with foreign nations, they interfere with the treaty-making power, which is conferred entirely on the general government; if with each other, for political purposes, they can scarcely fail to interfere with the general purpose and intent of the constitution. To grant letters of marque and reprisal, would lead directly to war; the power of declaring which is expressly given to congress. To coin money is also the exercise of a power conferred on congress. It would be tedious to recapitulate the several limitations on the powers of the states which are contained in this section. They will be found, generally, to restrain state legislation on subjects intrusted to the government of the Union, in which the citizens of all the states are interested. In these alone were the whole people concerned. The question of their application to states is not left to construction. It is averred in positive words.

If the original constitution, in the ninth and tenth sections of the first article, draws this plain and marked line of discrimination between the limitations it imposes on the powers of the general government, and on those of the states; if in every inhibition intended to act on state power, words are employed, which directly express that intent; some strong reason must be assigned for departing from this safe and judicious course, in framing the amendments, before that departure can be assumed. We search in vain for that reason.

Had the people of the several states, or any of them, required changes in their constitutions; had they required additional safeguards to liberty from the apprehended encroachments of their particular governments; the remedy was in their own hands, and could have been applied by themselves. A convention could have been assembled by the discontented state, and the required improvements could have been made by itself. The unwieldy and cumbrous machinery of procuring a recommendation from two-thirds of congress, and the assent of three-fourths of their sister states, could never have occurred to any human being, as a mode of doing that which might be effected by the state itself. Had the framers of these amendments intended them to be limitations on the powers of the state governments, they would have imitated the framers of the original constitution, and have expressed that intention. Had congress engaged in the extraordinary occupation of improving the constitutions of the several states by affording the people additional protection from the exercise of power by their own governments, in matters which concerned themselves alone, they would have declared this purpose in plain and intelligible language.

But it is universally understood, it is a part of the history of the day, that the great revolution which established the constitution of the United States was not affected without immense opposition. Serious fears were extensively entertained that those powers which the patriot statesmen, who then watched over the interests of our country, deemed essential to union, and to the attainment of those invaluable objects for which union was sought, might be exercised in a manner dangerous to liberty. In almost every convention by which the constitution was adopted, amendments to guard against the abuse of power were recommended. These amendments demanded security against the apprehended encroachments of the general government, not against those of the local governments. In compliance with a sentiment thus generally expressed, to quiet fears thus extensively entertained, amendments were proposed by the required majority in congress, and adopted by the states. These amendments contained no expression indicating an intention to apply them to the state governments. This court cannot so apply them.

We are of opinion, that the provision in the fifth amendment to the constitution, declaring that private property shall not be taken for public use without just compensation, is intended solely as a limitation on the exercise of power by the government of the United States, and is not applicable to the legislation of the states. We are therefore, of [the] opinion, that there is no repugnancy between the several Acts of the General Assembly of Maryland, given in evidence by the defendants at the trial of this cause, in the court of that state, and the constitution of the United States. This court, therefore, has no jurisdiction of the cause, and it is dismissed.

## *PALKO v. CONNECTICUT*

302 U.S. 319; 82 L. Ed. 288; 58 S. Ct. 149 (1937)

MR. JUSTICE CARDOZO *delivered the opinion of the Court.*

A statute of Connecticut permitting appeals in criminal cases to be taken by the state is challenged by appellant as an infringement of the Fourteenth Amendment of the Constitution of the United States. . . .

Appellant was indicted . . . for the crime of murder in the first degree. A jury found him guilty of murder in the second degree, and he was sentenced to confinement in the state prison for life. Thereafter the State of Connecticut, with the permission of the judge presiding at the trial, gave notice of appeal to the Supreme Court of Errors. This it did pursuant to an act adopted in 1886 which [provides that appeals from the rulings and decisions of the superior court or of any criminal court of common pleas, upon all questions of law arising on the trial of criminal cases, may be taken by the state, with the permission of the presiding judge, to the supreme court of errors, in the same manner and to the same effect as if made by the accused]. Upon such appeal, the Supreme Court of Errors reversed the judgment and ordered a new trial. . . . It found that there had been error of law to the prejudice of the state (1) in excluding testimony as to a confession by defendant; (2) in excluding testimony upon cross-examination of defendant to impeach his credibility, and (3) in the instructions to the jury as to the difference between first and second degree murder.

Pursuant to the mandate of the Supreme Court of Errors, defendant was brought to trial again. Before a jury was impaneled and also at later stages of the case he made the objection that the effect of the new trial was to place him twice in jeopardy for the same offense, and in so doing to violate the Fourteenth Amendment of the Constitution of the United States. . . . The jury returned a verdict of murder in the first degree, and the court sentenced the defendant to the punishment of death. The Supreme Court of Errors affirmed the judgment of conviction. . . .

1. The execution of the sentence will not deprive appellant of his life without the process of law assured to him by the Fourteenth Amendment of the Federal Constitution.

The argument for appellant is that whatever is forbidden by the Fifth Amendment is forbidden by the Fourteenth also. The Fifth Amendment, which is not directed to the states, but solely to the federal government, creates immunity from double jeopardy. No person shall be "subject for the same offense to be twice put in jeopardy of life or limb." The Fourteenth Amendment ordains, "nor shall any State deprive any person of life, liberty, or property, without due process of law." To retry a defendant, though under one indictment and only one, subjects him, it is said, to double jeopardy in violation of the Fifth Amendment, if the prosecution is one on behalf of the United States. From this the consequence is said to follow that there is a denial of life or liberty without due process of law, if the prosecution is one on behalf of the People of a State.

. . .

We have said that in appellant's view the Fourteenth Amendment is to be taken as embodying the prohibitions of the Fifth. His thesis is even broader. Whatever would be a violation of the original bill of rights (Amendment I to VIII) if done by the federal government is now equally unlawful by a state. There is no such general rule.

The Fifth Amendment provides,

among other things, that no person shall be held to answer for a capital or otherwise infamous crime unless on presentment or indictment of a grand jury. This court has held that, in prosecutions by a state, presentment or indictment by a grand jury may give way to informations at the instance of a public officer. *Hurtado* v. *California,* 110 U.S. 516. . . . The Fifth Amendment provides also that no person shall be compelled in any criminal case to be a witness against himself. This court has said that, in prosecutions by a state, the exemption will fail if the state elects to end it. *Twining* v. *New Jersey,* 211 U.S. 78, 106, 111, 112. . . . The Sixth Amendment calls for a jury trial in criminal cases and the Seventh for a jury trial in civil cases at common law where the value in controversy shall exceed twenty dollars. This court has ruled that consistently with those amendments trial by jury may be modified by a state or abolished altogether. *Walker* v. *Sauvinet,* 92 U.S. 90; *Maxwell* v. *Dow,* 176. . . .

On the other hand, the due process clause of the Fourteenth Amendment may make it unlawful for a state to abridge by its statutes the freedom of speech which the First Amendment safeguards against encroachment by the Congress, *De Jonge* v. *Oregon,* 299 U.S. 353, 364; *Herndon* v. *Lowry,* 301 U.S. 242, 259; or the like freedom of the press, *Grosjean* v. *American Press Co.,* 297 U.S. 233; *Near* v. *Minnesota ex rel. Olson,* 283 U.S. 697, 707; or the free exercise of religion, *Hamilton* v. *Regents,* 293 U.S. 245, 262 . . . ; or the right of peaceable assembly, without which speech would be unduly trammeled . . . ; or the right of one accused of crime to the benefit of counsel, *Powell* v. *Alabama,* 287 U.S. 45. In these and other situations im-

munities that are valid as against the federal government by force of the specific pledges of particular amendments have been found to be implicit in the concept of ordered liberty, and thus, through the Fourteenth Amendment, become valid as against the states.

The line of division may seem to be wavering and broken if there is a hasty catalogue of the cases on the one side and the other. Reflection and analysis will induce a different view. There emerges the perception of a rationalizing principle which gives to discrete instances a proper order and coherence. The right to trial by jury and the immunity from prosecution except as the result of an indictment may have value and importance. Even so, they are not of the very essence of a scheme of ordered liberty. To abolish them is not to violate a "principle of justice so rooted in the traditions and conscience of our people as to be ranked as fundamental." . . . Few would be so narrow or provincial as to maintain that a fair and enlightened system of justice would be impossible without them. What is true of jury trials and indictments is true also, as the cases show, of the immunity from compulsory self-incrimination. *Twining* v. *New Jersey, supra.* This too might be lost, and justice still be done. Indeed, today as in the past there are students of our penal system who look upon the immunity as a mischief rather than a benefit, and who would limit its scope, or destroy it altogether. No doubt there would remain the need to give protection against torture, physical or mental. . . . Justice, however, would not perish if the accused were subject to a duty to respond to orderly inquiry. The exclusion of these immunities and privileges from the privileges and immunities protected against the action of the states has not been arbitrary or casual. It has been dictated by a study and appreciation of the meaning, the essential implications, of liberty itself.

We reach a different plane of social and moral values when we pass to the privileges and immunities that have been taken over from the earlier articles of the federal bill of rights and brought within the Fourteenth Amendment by a process of absorption. These in their origin were effective against the federal government alone. If the Fourteenth Amendment has absorbed them the process of absorption has had its source in the belief that neither liberty nor justice would exist if they were sacrificed. . . . This is true, for illustration, of freedom of thought, and speech. Of that freedom one may say that it is the matrix, the indispensable condition, of nearly every other form of freedom. With rare aberrations a pervasive recognition of that truth can be traced in our history, political and legal. So it has come about that the domain of liberty, withdrawn by the Fourteenth Amendment from encroachment by the states, has been enlarged by latter-day judgments to include liberty of the mind as well as liberty of action. The extension became, indeed, a logical imperative when once it was recognized, as long ago it was, that liberty is something more than exemption from physical restraint, and that even in the field of substantive rights and duties the legislative judgment, if oppressive and arbitrary, may be overridden by the courts. . . .

Our survey of the cases serves, we think, to justify the statement that the dividing line between them, if not unfaltering throughout its course, has been true for the most part to

a unifying principle. On which side of the line the case made out by the appellant has appropriate location must be the next inquiry and the final one. Is that kind of double jeopardy to which the statute has subjected him a hardship so acute and shocking that our polity will not endure it? Does it violate those "fundamental principles of liberty and justice which lie at the base of all our civil and political institutions"? . . . The answer surely must be "no." What the answer would have to be if the state were permitted after a trial free from error to try the accused over again or to bring another case against him, we have no occasion to consider. We deal with the statute before us and no other. The state is not attempting to wear the accused out by a multitude of cases with accumulated trials. It asks no more than this, that the case against him shall go on until there shall be a trial free from the corrosion of substantial legal error. . . . This is not cruelty at all, nor even vexation in any immoderate degree. If the trial had been infected with error adverse to the accused, there might have been review at this instance, and as often as necessary to purge the vicious taint. A reciprocal privilege, subject at all times to the discretion of the presiding judge . . . has now been granted to the state. There is here no seismic innovation. The edifice of justice stands, its symmetry, to many, greater than before.

2. The conviction of appellant is not in derogation of any privileges or immunities that belong to him as a citizen of the United States. . . .

The judgment is

*Affirmed.*

MR. JUSTICE BUTLER *dissents.*

# ADAMSON v. CALIFORNIA

332 U.S. 46; 91 L. Ed. 1903; 67 S. Ct. 1672 (1947)

MR. JUSTICE REED *delivered the opinion of the Court.*

The appellant . . . was convicted, without recommendation for mercy, by a jury in a Superior Court of the State of California of murder in the first degree. . . . [T]he sentence of death was affirmed by the Supreme Court of the state. . . . The provisions of California law which were challenged in the state proceedings as invalid under the Fourteenth Amendment of the Federal Constitution . . . permit the failure of a defendant to explain or to deny evidence against him to be commented upon by court and by counsel and to be considered by court and jury. The defendant did not testify. As the trial court gave its instructions and the District Attorney argued the case in accordance with the constitutional and statutory provisions just referred to, we have for decision the question of their constitutionality in these circumstances under the limitations of Section 1 of the Fourteenth Amendment. . . .

The appellant was charged in the information with former convictions for burglary, larceny and robbery . . . [and] answered that he had suffered the previous convictions. This answer barred allusion to these charges of convictions on the trial. Under California's interpretation of [the statute], however, if the defendant, after answering affirmatively charges alleging prior convictions, takes the witness stand to deny or explain away other evidence that has been introduced "the commission of these crimes could have been revealed to the jury on cross-examination to impeach his

testimony." . . . This forces an accused who is a repeated offender to choose between the risk of having his prior offenses disclosed to the jury or of having it draw harmful inferences from uncontradicted evidence that can only be denied or explained by the defendant.

In the first place, appellant urges that the provision of the Fifth Amendment that no person "shall be compelled in any criminal case to be a witness against himself" is a fundamental national privilege or immunity protected against state abridgment by the Fourteenth Amendment or a privilege or immunity secured, through the Fourteenth Amendment, against deprivation by state action because it is a personal right, enumerated in the federal Bill of Rights.

Secondly, appellant relies upon the due process of law clause of the Fourteenth Amendment to invalidate the provisions of the California law . . . and as applied (a) because comment on failure to testify is permitted, (b) because appellant was forced to forego testimony in person because of danger of disclosure of his past convictions through cross-examination and (c) because the presumption of innocence was infringed by the shifting of the burden of proof to appellant in permitting comment on his failure to testify.

We shall assume, but without any intention thereby of ruling upon the issue, that permission by law to the court, counsel and jury to comment upon and consider the failure of defendant "to explain or to deny by his testimony any evidence or facts in the case against him" would in-fringe defendant's privilege against self-incrimination under the Fifth Amendment if this were a trial in a court of the United States under a similar law. Such an assumption does not determine appellant's rights under the Fourteenth Amendment. It is settled law that the clause of the Fifth Amendment, protecting a per-son against being compelled to be a witness against himself, is not made effective by the Fourteenth Amend-ment as a protection against state action on the ground that freedom from testimonial compulsion is a right of national citizenship, or because it is a personal privilege or immunity secured by the Federal Constitution as one of the rights of man that are listed in the Bill of Rights.

The reasoning that leads to those conclusions starts with the unques-tioned premise that the Bill of Rights, when adopted, was for the protection of the individual against the federal government and its provisions were inapplicable to similar actions done by the states. . . . The power to free defendants in state trials from self-incrimination was specifically deter-mined to be beyond the scope of the privileges and immunities clause of the Fourteenth Amendment in *Twin-ing* v. *New Jersey*. . . . This Court held that the inclusion in the Bill of Rights of this protection against the power of the national government did not make the privilege a federal pri-vilege or immunity secured to citizens by the Constitution against state ac-tion. . . . After declaring that state and national citizenship coexist in the same person, the Fourteenth Amendment forbids a state from abridging the privileges and immuni-ties of citizens of the United States. As a matter of words, this leaves a state free to abridge, within the

limits of the due process clause, the privileges and immunities flowing from state citizenship. This reading of the Federal Constitution has heretofore found favor with the majority of this Court as a natural and logical interpretation. It accords with the constitutional doctrine of federalism by leaving to the states the responsibility of dealing with the priv-ileges and immunities of their citi-zens except those inherent in their national citizenship. It is the construc-tion placed upon the amendment by justices whose own experience had given them contemporaneous knowl-edge of the purposes that led to the adoption of the Fourteenth Amend-ment. This construction has become embedded in our federal system as a functioning element in preserving the balance between national and state power. We reaffirm the conclusion of the Twining and Palko Cases that protection against self-incrimination is not a privilege or immunity of national citizenship.

Appellant secondly contends that if the privilege against self-incrimina-tion is not a right protected by the privileges and immunities clause of the Fourteenth Amendment against state action, this privilege, to its full scope under the Fifth Amendment, inheres in the right to a fair trial. A right to a fair trial is a right ad-mittedly protected by the due process clause of the Fourteenth Amendment. Therefore, appellant argues, the due process clause of the Fourteenth Amendment protects his privilege against self-incrimination. The due process clause of the Fourteenth Amendment, however, does not draw all the rights of the federal Bill of Rights under its protection. That con-tention was made and rejected in *Palko* v. *Connecticut*. . . . Nothing has been called to our attention that either the framers of the Fourteenth Amendment or the states that adopted it intended its due process clause to draw within its scope the earlier amendments to the Constitution. . . .

Specifically, the due process clause does not protect, by virtue of its mere existence, the accused's freedom from giving testimony by compulsion in state trials that is secured to him against federal interference by the Fifth Amendment. . . .

MR. JUSTICE FRANKFURTER, *concurring.*

. . .

For historical reasons a limited immunity from the common duty to testify was written into the Federal Bill of Rights, and I am prepared to agree that, as part of that immunity, comment on the failure of an accused to take the witness stand is forbidden in federal prosecutions. It is so, of course, by explicit act of Congress. . . . But to suggest that such a limitation can be drawn out of "due process" in its protection of ultimate decency in a civilized society is to suggest that the Due Process Clause fastened fetters of unreason upon the State. . . .

Between the incorporation of the Fourteenth Amendment into the Constitution and the beginning of the present membership of the Court—a period of seventy years—the scope of that Amendment was passed upon by forty-three judges. Of all these judges, only one, who may respectfully be called an eccentric exception, ever indicated the belief that the Fourteenth Amendment was a shorthand summary of the first eight Amendments theretofore limiting only the Federal Government, and that due process incorporated those eight Amendments as restrictions upon the powers of the

States. Among these judges were not only those who would have to be included among the greatest in the history of the Court, but—it is especially relevant to note—they included those whose services in the cause of human rights and the spirit of freedom are the most conspicuous in our history. It is not invidious to single out Miller, Davis, Bradley, Waite, Matthews, Gray, Fuller, Holmes, Brandeis, Stone and Cardozo (to speak only of the dead) as judges who were alert in safeguarding and promoting the interests of liberty and human dignity through law. But they were also judges mindful of the relation of our federal system to a progressively democratic society and therefore duly regardful of the scope of authority that was left to the States even after the Civil War. And so they did not find that the Fourteenth Amendment, concerned as it was with matters fundamental to the pursuit of justice, fastened upon the States procedural arrangements which, in the language of Mr. Justice Cardozo, only those who are "narrow or provincial" would deem essential to "a fair and enlightened system of justice." . . .

The short answer to the suggestion that the provision of the Fourteenth Amendment, which ordains "nor shall any State deprive any person of life, liberty, or property, without due process of law," was a way of saying that every State must thereafter initiate prosecutions through indictment by a grand jury, must have a trial by a jury of twelve in criminal cases, and must have trial by such a jury in common law suits where the amount in controversy exceeds twenty dollars, is that it is a strange way of saying it. It would be extraordinarily strange for a Constitution to convey such specific commands in such a roundabout and inexplicit way. After all, an amendment to the Constitution should be read in a " 'sense most obvious to the common understanding at the time of its adoption.' . . . For it was for public adoption that it was proposed." See Mr. Justice Holmes in *Eisner* v. *Macomber*, 252 U.S. 189, 220. Those reading the English language with the meaning which it ordinarily conveys, those conversant with the political and legal history of the concept of due process, those sensitive to the relations of the States to the central government as well as the relation of some of the provisions of the Bill of Rights to the process of justice, would hardly recognize the Fourteenth Amendment as a cover for the various explicit provisions of the first eight Amendments. . . . The notion that the Fourteenth Amendment was a covert way of imposing upon the States all the rules which it seemed important to Eighteenth Century statesmen to write into the Federal Amendments, was rejected by judges who were themselves witnesses of the process by which the Fourteenth Amendment became part of the Constitution. Arguments that may now be adduced to prove that the first eight Amendments were concealed within the historic phrasing of the Fourteenth Amendment were not unknown at the time of its adoption. A surer estimate of their bearing was possible for judges at the time than distorting distance is likely to vouchsafe. Any evidence of design or purpose not contemporaneously known could hardly have influenced those who ratified the Amendment. . . . Thus, at the time of the ratification of the Fourteenth Amendment the constitutions of nearly half of the ratifying States did not have the rigorous requirements of the Fifth Amendment for instituting criminal proceedings through a grand jury. It could

hardly have occurred to these States that by ratifying the Amendment they uprooted their established methods for prosecuting crime and fastened upon themselves a new prosecutorial system.

. . .

It may not be amiss to restate the pervasive function of the Fourteenth Amendment in exacting from the States observance of basic liberties. . . . The Amendment neither comprehends the specific provisions by which the founders deemed it appropriate to restrict the federal government nor is it confined to them. The Due Process Clause of the Fourteenth Amendment has an independent potency, precisely as does the Due Process Clause of the Fifth Amendment in relation to the Federal Government. It ought not to require argument to reject the notion that due process of law meant one thing in the Fifth Amendment and another in the Fourteenth. . . . Are Madison and his contemporaries in the framing of the Bill of Rights to be charged with writing into it a meaningless clause? To consider "due process of law" as merely a shorthand statement of other specific clauses in the same amendment is to attribute to the authors and proponents of this Amendment ignorance of, or indifference to, a historic conception which was one of the great instruments in the arsenal of constitutional freedom which the Bill of Rights was to protect and strengthen.

A construction which gives to due process no independent function but turns it into a summary of the specific provisions of the Bill of Rights would, as has been noted, tear up by the roots much of the fabric of law in the several States, and would deprive the States of opportunity for reforms in legal process designed for extending the area of freedom. It would assume that no other abuses would reveal themselves in the course of time than those which had become manifest in 1791. Such a view not only disregards the historic meaning of "due process." It leads inevitably to a warped construction of specific provisions of the Bill of Rights to bring within their scope conduct clearly condemned by due process but not easily fitting into the pigeon-holes of the specific provisions. It seems pretty late in the day to suggest that a phrase so laden with historic meaning should be given an improvised content consisting of some but not all of the provisions of the first eight Amendments, selected on an undefined basis, with improvisation of content for the provisions so selected.

. . .

MR. JUSTICE BLACK, *dissenting.*

. . .

This decision reasserts a constitutional theory spelled out in *Twining* v. *New Jersey* . . . that this Court is endowed by the Constitution with boundless power under "natural law" periodically to expand and contract constitutional standards to conform to the Court's conception of what at a particular time constitutes "civilized decency" and "fundamental liberty and justice." Invoking this *Twining* rule, the Court concludes that although comment upon testimony in a federal court would violate the Fifth Amendment, identical comment in a state court does not violate today's fashion in civilized decency and fundamentals and is therefore not prohibited by the Federal Constitution as amended.

. . . But I would not reaffirm the *Twining* decision. I think that decision and the "natural law" theory of the Constitution upon which it relies

degrade the constitutional safeguards of the Bill of Rights and simultaneously appropriate for this Court a broad power which we are not authorized by the Constitution to exercise. . . .

My study of the historical events that culminated in the Fourteenth Amendment, and the expressions of those who sponsored and favored, as well as those who opposed its submission and passage, persuades me that one of the chief objects that the provisions of the Amendment's first section, and as a whole, were intended to accomplish was to make the Bill of Rights applicable to the states. With full knowledge of the import of the *Barron* decision, the framers and backers of the Fourteenth Amendment proclaimed its purpose to be to overturn the constitutional rule that case had announced. This historical purpose has never received full consideration or exposition in any opinion of this Court interpreting the Amendment. . . .

. . . In my judgment [the legislative history of the Fourteenth Amendment] conclusively demonstrates that the language of [its] first section . . . taken as a whole, was thought by those responsible for its submission to the people, and by those who opposed its submission, sufficiently explicit to guarantee that thereafter no state could deprive its citizens of the privileges and protections of the Bill of Rights. Whether this Court ever will, or whether it now should, in the light of past decisions, give full effect to what the Amendment was intended to accomplish is not necessarily essential to a decision here. However that may be, our prior decisions, including *Twining,* do not prevent our carrying out that purpose, at least to the extent of making applicable to the states, not a mere part, as the Court has, but the full protection of the Fifth Amendment's provision against compelling evidence from an accused to convict him of crime. And I further contend that the "natural law" formula which the Court uses to reach its conclusion in this case should be abandoned as an incongruous excrescence on our Constitution. I believe that formula to be itself a violation of our Constitution, in that it subtly conveys to courts, at the expense of legislatures, ultimate power over public policies in fields where no specific provision of the Constitution limits legislative power. And my belief seems to be in accord with the views expressed by this Court, at least for the first two decades after the Fourteenth Amendment was adopted. . . .

I cannot consider the Bill of Rights to be an outworn 18th Century "strait-jacket" as the *Twining* opinion did. Its provisions may be thought outdated abstractions by some. And it is true that they were designed to meet ancient evils. But they are the same kind of human evils that have emerged from century to century wherever excessive power is sought by the few at the expense of the many. In my judgment the people of no nation can lose their liberty so long as a Bill of Rights like ours survives and its basic purposes are conscientiously interpreted, enforced and respected so as to afford continuous protection against old, as well as new, devices and practices which might thwart those purposes. I fear to see the consequences of the Court's practices of substituting its own concepts of decency and fundamental justice for the language of the Bill of Rights as its point of departure in interpreting and enforcing that Bill of

Rights. If the choice must be between the selective process of the *Palko* decision applying some of the Bill of Rights to the States, or the *Twining* rule applying none of them, I would choose the *Palko* selective process. But rather than accept either of these choices, I would follow what I believe was the original purpose of the Fourteenth Amendment—to extend to all the people of the nation the complete protection of the Bill of Rights. To hold that this Court can determine what, if any, provisions of the Bill of Rights will be enforced, and if so to what degree, is to frustrate the great design of a written Constitution.

. . .

It is an illusory apprehension that literal application of some or all of the provisions of the Bill of Rights to the States would unwisely increase the sum total of the powers of this Court to invalidate state legislation. The Federal Government has not been harmfully burdened by the requirement that enforcement of federal laws affecting civil liberty conform literally to the Bill of Rights. Who would advocate its repeal? It must be conceded, of course, that the natural-law-due-process formula, which the Court today reaffirms, has been interpreted to limit substantially this Court's power to prevent state violations of the individual civil liberties guaranteed by the Bill of Rights. But this formula also has been used in the past, and can be used in the future, to license this Court, in considering regulatory legislation, to roam at large in the broad expanses of policy and morals and to trespass, all too freely, on the legislative domain of the States as well as the Federal Government.

## SELECTED REFERENCES

Fairman, Charles. "Does the Fourteenth Amendment Incorporate the Bill of Rights? The Original Understanding," 2 *Stanford L. Rev.* 5 (1949).

Flack, Horace. *The Adoption of the Fourteenth Amendment* (Baltimore: The Johns Hopkins University Press, 1908), especially chaps. 2 and 5.

Frankfurter, Felix. "Memorandum on 'Incorporation' of the Bill of Rights into the Due Process Clause of the 14th Amendment," 78 *Harvard L. Rev.* 746 (1965).

Green, John R. "The Bill of Rights, the Fourteenth Amendment and the Supreme Court," 46 *Michigan L. Rev.* 869 (1948).

Henkin, Louis. "Selective Incorporation in the Fourteenth Amendment," 73 *Yale L. J.* 74 (1963).

Morrison, Stanley. "Does the Fourteenth Amendment Incorporate the Bill of Rights? The Judicial Interpretation," 2 *Stanford L. Rev.* 140 (1949).

Walker, Frank H., Jr. "Was It Intended That the Fourteenth Amendment Incorporate the Bill of Rights?" 42 *N. Carolina L. Rev.* 925 (1964).

# 2. Religious Liberty

*Everson v. Board of Education*

*Board of Education v. Allen*     *Engel v. Vitale*

*School District of Abington Township v. Schempp*

*McGowan v Maryland*     *Sherbert v. Verner*

*United States v. Seeger*

The framers of the Bill of Rights guaranteed religious liberty in the United States by proclaiming in the First Amendment that "Congress shall make no law respecting an establishment of religion, or abridging the free exercise thereof. . . ." Despite the potential for litigation in this area, only a few controversies raising issues under these provisions reached the Supreme Court in the century following the Amendment's adoption. And, for the most part, these cases were concerned with the scope and meaning of the "free exercise" clause.

## FREE EXERCISE OF RELIGION

*Watson* v. *Jones* (13 Wall, 670, 1872) was one of the earliest cases in which the Supreme Court discussed the nature of the religious liberty guaranteed by the First Amendment. It involved a factional dispute within a Presbyterian church congregation over control of church property. The Court disclaimed any power to decide independently which of the two factions represented the church. Rather, it held that the dispute would have to be settled by church authority and that such a decision, under the constitutional guarantee of religious liberty, would be binding on the courts. In his opinion for the Court, Justice Samuel Miller expressed the prevailing view on the religious liberty protected by the First Amendment:

In this country the full and free right to entertain any religious belief, to practice any religious principle and to teach any religious doctrine which does not violate the laws of morality and property, and which does not infringe personal rights, is conceded to all. The laws know no heresy, and are committed to the support of no dogma, the establishment of no sect. The right to organize voluntary religious associations to assist in the expression, and the dissemination of any religious doctrine . . . is unquestioned.

21

The free exercise issue was squarely before the Court for the first time six years later in *Reynolds* v. *United States* (98 U.S. 145, 1878). At issue was the validity of a federal law prohibiting polygamy in the territories of the United States. Reynolds was convicted for violating the law, but he argued for reversal on the ground that as a member of the Mormon Church he was required by its religious tenets to engage in polygamous relationships. Hence, he maintained that the law impaired his free exercise of religion as guaranteed by the First Amendment. In rejecting this contention and affirming the conviction, the Court made a distinction between religious beliefs and the actions based on such beliefs. The former were considered inviolable and beyond the reach of Congress by the First Amendment; the latter, however, could be regulated by Congress consistent with the First Amendment in restraining antisocial conduct. Chief Justice Morrison R. Waite said in his opinion for the Court: "Laws are made for the government of actions, and while they cannot interfere with mere religious beliefs and opinions, they may with practices." The Chief Justice concluded that to allow a man to excuse his illegal actions because of his religious beliefs "would be to make the professed doctrines of religious beliefs superior to the law of the land. . . ."

There was no appreciable increase in the number of religious liberty cases decided by the Supreme Court during the first four decades of the 20th century. Among the problems considered in the few cases that did reach the Court were the constitutional status of parochial schools, military obligations of conscientious objectors, and the use of public funds to provide books for children attending parochial schools.

The Court considered the first problem in *Pierce* v. *Society of Sisters of the Holy Name* (268 U.S. 510, 1925). At issue was the constitutionality of an Oregon statute which required all children to attend public schools for the first eight grades. The Society argued that the statute threatened the continued existence of its educational operations and the destruction of its property. It was further argued that the statute infringed the right of parents to choose schools where their children will receive appropriate mental and religious training. The Court agreed with these claims and struck down the statute. Although this case involved a religious order challenging governmental action alleged to be harmful to its activities, the religious liberty issue was neither raised by the Society nor considered by the Court. Rather, Justice James McReynolds declared that the "liberty" guaranteed by the Fourteenth Amendment protects the Society's business and property (its schools) from destruction by the state's actions.

The conflict between freedom of conscience and compulsory military conscription was first considered by the Court in the *Selective Draft Law Cases* (245 U.S. 366, 1918). Rejecting the religious liberty claims of several conscientious objectors, the Court held that there was no constitutional right to be relieved of military obligations because of religious convictions. Chief Justice Edward Douglas White observed that the privilege of exemption from such duty is at the discretion of Congress.

Another aspect of this problem was considered in *Hamilton* v. *Regents of the University of California* (293 U.S. 245, 1934). Here the Court rejected the claims of two Methodist students who, because of religious principles, challenged the compulsory military science and tactics requirement of all able-bodied male students. Probably because the religious clauses of the First Amendment had not been made applicable to the states, the case was argued and decided on other issues. However, Justice Benjamin Cardoza, in a concurring opinion, made the point that instruction in a military science and tactics course was too remotely related to the actual bearing of arms in warfare to claim exemption on religious grounds. Significantly, he forecast the trend of the Court's interpretation of the religious clauses when he said: "I assume for present purposes that religious liberty protected by the First Amendment against invasion by the [national government] is protected by the Fourteenth against invasion by the states."

In 1930, the Court was presented with an opportunity to make a significant pronouncement on the scope of restrictions contained in the establishment clause in *Cochran* v. *Louisiana State Board of Education* (281 U.S. 370, 1930). At issue was the constitutionality of a state statute which provided free textbooks for children attending both public and parochial schools. Those attacking the statute alleged that in providing free books for pupils attending parochial schools, the state was expending public funds for private use contrary to the due process clause of the Fourteenth Amendment. The Court rejected that contention, holding the appropriations to be for a public purpose. In taking this approach, the Court simply postponed the day when such problems would be considered as establishment issues.

The most significant decisions by the Supreme Court involving religious liberty issues have been handed down during the last three decades. Many of the cases in the first part of this period were brought by the Jehovah's Witnesses who vigorously contested state and local action which they thought infringed upon their religious liberty. In *Cantwell* v. *Connecticut* (310 U.S. 296, 1940) the Witnesses succeeded in getting the Court to strike down a statute which required persons soliciting or canvassing for religious and philanthropic causes to obtain prior approval from a local administrative official. The local official was also clothed with the authority to determine if the cause was of a bona fide religious nature. Justice Owen Roberts, in announcing the decision for a unanimous Court, maintained that the statute's defectiveness stemmed from the unfettered discretion which it granted the administering official. Such discretion, argued Roberts, "is to lay a forbidden burden upon the exercise of liberty protected by the Constitution." In striking down this regulation, the Court made the "free exercise" clause applicable to the states when Justice Roberts asserted: "Such censorship of religion as a means of determining its right to survive is a denial of liberty protected by the First Amendment and included in the liberty which is within the protection of the Fourteenth."

During the same term, however, Jehovah's Witnesses were rebuffed in their attempt to have the Court strike down the "flag-salute" ceremony of the Minersville, Pennsylvania school district. Essentially, this ceremony required all public school children, as a part of the daily opening exercises, to salute the United States flag and repeat the Pledge of Allegiance. Two children of a member of the Jehovah's Witnesses were expelled from school for refusing to participate in the ceremony. A federal district court agreed with the contention of the Witnesses that compulsory participation in the ceremony infringed upon their free exercise of religion and enjoined the school district from its continued use. Upon appeal the Supreme Court reversed. (*Minersville School District* v. *Gobitis,* 310 U.S. 586, 1940). Justice Felix Frankfurter, speaking for the eight-man majority, rejected the religious liberty claims and, instead, stressed the relationship between such symbolism and national unity. He maintained that "we live by symbols" and that "the flag is a symbol of our national unity, transcending all internal differences, however large, within the framework of the Constitution." In addition, Frankfurter urged judicial restraint in such matters of "educational policy." Justice Harlan F. Stone, the lone dissenter, stressed the need to protect the right of the individual to hold and to express opinions. He contended that the liberty protected by the Constitution from state infringement includes "the freedom of the individual from compulsion as to what he shall think and what he shall say, at least where the compulsion is to bear false witness to his religion."

Three years later, the Court did a complete about-face on the "flag-salute" issue in *West Virginia State Board of Education* v. *Barnette* (319 U.S. 624, 1943). Factors usually cited in explaining this turnabout include: (1) the addition of two new associate justices—Justice Robert H. Jackson filled the vacancy created by the retirement of Chief Justice Charles Evans Hughes in 1941 (Justice Harlan Fiske Stone was elevated to the Chief Justiceship), and Justice Wiley B. Rutledge replaced Justice James C. McReynolds in 1943; and (2) while dissenting in *Jones* v. *Opelika* (316 U.S. 584) a year earlier, the unusual admission of three justices of the *Gobitis* majority that they believed *Gobitis* was wrongly decided.

Justice Jackson's opinion for the six-man majority was not based on the Witnesses' assertions of religious liberty. Rather it stressed freedom of speech and conscience, and the implied right to remain silent.

Noting that "the compulsory flag salute and pledge requires affirmation of a belief and an attitude of mind," Jackson argued:

To sustain the compulsory flag salute we are required to say that a Bill of Rights which guards the individuals right to speak his own mind, left it open to public authorities to compel him to utter what is not in his mind.

In language obviously directed at Frankfurter's "national unity and patriotism" theme expressed in *Gobitis,* Jackson asserted:

To believe that patriotism will not flourish if patriotic ceremonies are voluntary and spontaneous instead of a compulsory routine is to make an unflattering estimate of the appeal of our institutions to free minds. We can have intellectual individualism and the rich cultural diversities that we owe to exceptional minds only at the price of occasional eccentricity and abnormal atittudes. When they are so harmless to others or to the State as those we deal with here, the price is not too great. But freedom to differ is not limited to things that do not matter much. That would be a mere shadow of freedom. The test of its subsance is the right to differ as to things that touch the heart of the existing order.

In an oft-quoted passage in defense of freedom of expression and conscience, Jackson concluded:

If there is any fixed star in our constitutional constellation, it is that no official, high or petty, can prescribe what shall be orthodox in politics, nationalism, religion, or other matters of opinion or force citizens to confess by word or act their faith therein. . . .

Cases initiated by Jehovah's Witnesses also led to the Court's rejection of local ordinances levying license fees on the distribution of literature. In *Murdock* v. *Pennsylvania* (319 U.S. 105, 1943) the Court reversed its decision in *Jones* v. *Opelika* and struck down a local ordinance requiring payment of a license fee by those selling literature. The Court reasoned that in applying the law to Jehovah's Witnesses, government was in reality taxing the dissemination of religious doctrines. Speaking for a 5–4 majority, Justice William O. Douglas said that "the hand distribution of religious tracts is an age-old form of missionary evangelism [which] occupies the same high estate under the First Amendment as do worship in the churches and preaching from the pulpit." Applying the ordinance to this kind of activity was patently unconstitutional because of its restraint on freedom of the press and the free exercise of religion.

In recent years members of the Black Muslims, a militant black separatist group, have encountered official restrictions which they allege infringe their free exercise of religion. While operating within the framework of a religious ritual embracing many of the traditional elements of orthodox religious groups, the Muslims advocate political, economic, and social separation from white America. Its religious meetings are often used as a platform for denouncing white America, and its status as a religious sect has frequently been questioned. This was

essentially the rationale used by some prison officials to deny to Black Muslim prisoners the privilege of purchasing and using their Bible (the Quran, a modification of the Moslem Koran) and other Muslim literature, including the official organ *Muhammad Speaks,* and of conducting worship services.

The official position that such restrictions are essential to the maintenance of prison discipline has been accepted by several lower courts. In *Williford* v. *California* (217 F. Supp. 245, 1963), for example, a federal district court held that prison officials did not infringe the free exercise of religion of Muslims by denying them the right to conduct services because freedom to act on religious belief can be regulated in the maintenance of prison discipline. Similarly, the California Supreme Court in *In re Ferguson* (361 P2d 417, 1961), held that it is not unreasonable to prohibit the "religious" activities of Black Muslims because the black supremacy doctrines eschewed lead to a reluctance to submit to white authority in prison administration.

Where lower courts have followed the view that the Black Muslim group is not a religious sect and have summarily dismissed free exercise claims, appellate courts have reversed, contending that a constitutional claim of discriminatory action by government based solely on religion requires a hearing on its merits. In *Sewell* v. *Pigelow* (291 F2d 196, 1961), after the Court of Appeals for the Fourth Circuit reversed and remanded with such directions, prison officials lifted the restrictions complained of and the case became moot. Likewise, in *Cooper* v. *Pate* (378 U.S. 546, 1964), the Supreme Court reversed a federal district court ruling (affirmed by the Court of Appeals) which dismissed a claim by a Black Muslim prisoner that Illinois officials, in denying him the privilege of obtaining his Bible and other Muslim literature, and of being visited by Black Muslim ministers and holding religious services, had discriminated against him because of his religious faith. The Court held that such a claim constituted a valid cause of action. Upon remand, the district court held that these restrictions could be constitutionally justified only if exercise of the privileges in question presented a "clear-and-present-danger to prison security."

Undoubtedly one of the most significant and far-reaching decisions of the Supreme Court on the free-exercise issue during the last decade was *Sherbert* v. *Verner.* The case resulted from a ruling of the South Carolina Unemployment Compensation Commission (sustained by the state supreme court) holding that a member of the Seventh-Day Adventist faith was ineligible for benefits because of her unwillingness to accept jobs which required work on Saturdays (her day of worship). In a 7–2 decision, the Court held that the state's action imposed an unconstitutional burden on the free exercise of religion. Justice William J. Brennan's opinion for the majority contained language that indicated a broadening scope of the free exercise guarantee and a more restricted state

regulatory authority. Setting forth what has been characterized as the "compelling state interest" rule, Brennan asserted that "no showing merely of a rational relationship to some colorable state interest would suffice [for] in this highly sensitive constitutional area, '[o]nly the gravest abuses, endangering paramount interests, give occasion for permissible limitation.'" In addition, Brennan indicated that in order to justify, constitutionally, a regulation which has such an impact on the free exercise of religion, the state must show that it has "no alternative forms of regulation" to combat the abuse.

Using this "paramount state interest–no alternative means" test, the Court, in *In re Jennison* (375 U.S. 14, 1963), reversed a Minnesota criminal contempt conviction where the petitioner had refused to serve as a juror because of religious scruples. Upon remand, the Minnesota Supreme Court held that the state failed to demonstrate that its interest in obtaining competent jurors would be jeopardized by exempting those opposed to jury service on religious grounds (267 Minn. 136, 125 N.W. 2d 588, 1963).

In recent years a few groups have asserted religious claims to protect their use of narcotics. These groups contend that certain drugs are as essential to their religious ritual as the bread and wine are to orthodox religious sects. In *People* v. *Woody* (394 P. 2d 813, 1964), for example, a group of Navajo Indians, members of the Native American Church of California, were convicted in a California court for using the drug peyote (described as a nonaddictive hallucinatory drug). The Supreme Court of California reversed the conviction on the grounds that peyote was central, as a sacramental symbol, to the worship services of the church. Citing *Sherbert* v. *Verner,* the court said the use of peyote under such circumstances did not "frustrate a compelling interest of the state."

Attempts of other groups to use the *Woody* ruling as a precedent have proven unsuccessful. In *State* v. *Bullard* (148 S.E. 2d 565, 1966), for example, the Supreme Court of North Carolina affirmed a conviction for use of peyote by a person who claimed membership in the Neo-'American Church, in which "peyote is [considered] most necessary and marijuana . . . most advisable" in the practice of its ritual. However, the court reasoned that in this instance religion was merely a subterfuge for the use of drugs. The court found that the use of drugs under the circumstances constituted a threat to the public safety, morals, peace, and order.

On the issue of use of psychedelics and the free exercise of religion, one of the most widely publicized cases involved Dr. Timothy Leary's conviction by a federal district court for illegal trafficking in marijuana. Dr. Leary, known as the high priest of LSD (League of Spiritual Discovery), has been a prolific publisher on the religious and scientific uses of psychedelic drugs. Leary claims membership in a Hindu sect (Brahmakrishna) in Massachusetts that considers the use of marijuana essential to illumination and meditation. In affirming the lower court ruling, the Court of Appeals for the Fifth Circuit rejected Leary's reliance on *Sherbert* v. *Verner* as misplaced and inapposite on the facts (*Leary* v. *United States,* 383 F. 2d 851, 1967). Instead, the court found that trafficking in marijuana poses a "substantial threat to public safety [and] order." Furthermore, the court rejected Leary's attempt to apply the *Woody* decision and reiterated the need to show that the drug plays a "central role" in the religious ceremony and practice. The Supreme Court granted certiorari. However, the Court did not include the free-exercise issue in its review, but reversed the conviction on self-incrimination and due process grounds. (395 U.S. 6, 1969).

Opposition to United States participation in the Vietnam war in the 1960s once again brought to the Court the religious liberty-compulsory military service question in which both free exercise and establishment issues have been raised. As draft eligible college students lost their student deferment classification (2-S), a number of them sought the conscientious-objector classification (1-O). Denials of their petitions usually returned them to 1-A and made them eligible for immediate induction. However, usually as a highlight of antiwar rallies, some students openly expressed opposition to war in general and the Vietnam war in particular and used the rallies to dramatically announce that they would not submit to induction. These actions resulted in a number of constitutional challenges to the conscientious-objector provision of the Universal Military Training and Service Act on its face and as applied.

In *United States* v. *Seeger* and two companion cases (*United States* v. *Jakobson* and *Peter* v. *United States*), for example, the constitutionality of the section that defines the term "religious training and belief" was at issue. While the appeals pressed both establishment and free-exercise challenges, the Court chose to sidestep them. Instead, it focused on the interpretation of the statutory provision and ruled that the Selective Service System had improperly interpreted the statute in denying the conscientious objector status claimed. The Court set forth the following test for determining if a claimant qualifies for exemption under the statute: "whether the belief is a sincere and meaningful belief occupying in the life of its possessor a place parallel to that filled by the God of those admittedly qualified for the exemption."

What the Court said in effect was that adherence to formal religious principles was no longer the sole grounds for granting conscientious-objector status. But the possibility that a large number of young men would escape serving their country by claiming conscientious-objector status under this liberal construction was already foreclosed by the provision of the Selective Service Act that authorizes local draft boards, under Presidential regulations, to assign such persons to "civilian work contributing to the maintenance of national health, safety or interest" for a period equivalent to that which is required of military inductees.

Congressional response to the decision was in the form of a 1967 amendment to the selective service law eliminating the clause that defines the term "religious training and belief" in terms of an individual's "belief in relation to a Supreme Being." However, the lawmakers retained the provision that "religious training and belief" does not include political, sociological, or philosophical views and personal moral codes.

However, just as the Vietnam conflict has continued so has the legal assault continued over grounds of conscientious objection. For example, the Court of Appeals for the Third Circuit (*United States* v. *Spiro,* 384 F. 2d 159, 1967) denied the contention of a Roman Catholic registrant that his religious principles forbade participation in a "particular war" that was not "just." Here the appellate court affirmed an interpretation of officials of the Selective Service System that the registrant's contention was contrary to the statutory requirement that a conscientious objector must be in "opposition to participation in war of any kind."

A 1969 decision (*United States* v. *Sisson,* 297 F. Supp. 902) by Federal District Judge Charles Z. Wyzanski, however, could lead the Supreme Court, Congress, and administrators to thoroughly reexamine the entire question of conscientious objection. Defendant Sisson explicitly disclaimed any religious objection but rather based his objection on what Judge Wyzanski called a "table of ultimate values" that was "moral and ethical." But Congress in selective service legislation has never recognized these grounds as bases for conscientious objection, a fact that Wyzanski attributed to the law's prejudice for religion. "In the draft act," said the Judge, "Congress unconstitutionally discriminated against atheists, agnostics, and men who are motivated by profound moral beliefs which constitute the central convictions of their beings." Consequently, Wyzanski said that "in granting to the religious conscientious objector but not to Sisson a special status, the [Universal Military Training and Service] act violates the provision of the First Amendment that 'Congress shall make no law respecting an establishment of religion.'"

The Judge concluded his opinion by referring to what he saw as a dangerous clash between law and morality:

When the State through its laws seeks to override reasonable moral commitments it makes a dangerously uncharacteristic choice. The law grows from the deposits of morality. Law and morality are, in turn, debtors and creditors of each other. The law cannot be adequately enforced by the courts alone, or by courts supported merely by the police and the military. The true secret of legal might lies in the habits of conscientious men disciplining themselves to obey the law they respect without the necessity of judicial and administrative orders. When the law treats a reasonable, conscientious act as a crime it subverts its own power. It invites civil disobedience. It impairs the very habits which nourish and preserve the law.

Through these and other comments, Judge Wyzanski's pioneering opinion is destined to foster debate and action over conscientious objection.

## ESTABLISHMENT CLAUSE PROBLEMS

The various decisions in the Jehovah's Witnesses cases of the 1930's and 1940's gave considerable clarity to the scope of the free-exercise clause of the First Amendment, but the meaning and sweep of the establishment clause remained unclear. As we have noted in the discussion of *Cochran* v. *Louisiana* (1930), the controversial question of public aid to parochial schools was involved, but the establishment issue was neither raised in the statutory challenge nor considered by the Court. Hence, it was not until *Everson* v. *Board of Education* (1947) that the establishment issue was placed squarely before the Supreme Court. At issue was the constitutionality of a New Jersey statute which permitted expenditure of public funds to defray the cost of transporting children to both public and parochial schools. In upholding the law as a valid "public welfare" measure, the Court construed the establishment clause as erecting a "wall of separation between Church and State." As Justice Hugo Black asserted for the 5–4 majority:

Neither a state nor the Federal Government can set up a church. Neither can pass laws which aid one religion, aid all religions, or prefer one religion over another. Neither can force nor influence a person to go to or to remain away from church against his will or force him to profess a belief or disbelief in any religion. No person can be punished for entertaining or professing religious beliefs or disbeliefs, for church attendance or non-attendance. No tax in any amount, large or small, can be levied to support any religious activities or institutions, whatever they may be called, or whatever form they may adopt to teach or practice religion. . . . In the words of Jefferson, the clause against establishment of religion by law was intended to erect "a wall of separation between Church and State."

The financial assistance provided for under the statute would appear to constitute the kind of aid prohibited in this construction of the establishment clause. However, Black felt otherwise. He emphasized the "child benefit" and "public welfare" aspects of the New Jersey legislation and concluded that while state power cannot be used to favor religions, neither can it be used to handicap them.

In his dissenting opinion in *Everson,* Justice Wiley B. Rutledge warned of the drive to introduce religious instruction in the public schools. Just one year after this warning, the Court was asked to determine the constitutionality of a "released time" religious education program in the public schools in *McCollum* v. *Board of Education* (333 U.S. 203, 1948). The program was conducted in the Champaign, Illinois public school system on a voluntary basis and provided classes for Protestants, Catholics, and Jews. Instruction was the responsibility of the religious authorities and took place during the regular school hours and in the school classrooms. Students not participating in the program were required to leave their regular classrooms and pursue their school activities elsewhere in the school building. On the other hand, students who volunteered to participate in the program were required to attend religious classes. The public school teachers assisted in several routine matters such as distribution of permission slips and keeping attendance records.

Eight members of the Court found this arrangement an outright violation of the strictures of the establishment clause as enunciated in *Everson*. Justice Black, whose opinion was supported by five other justices, maintained that the use of the public school classrooms to conduct religious instruction, the operation of the compulsory school attendance machinery to provide audiences for the propagation of sectarian dogma, and the close cooperation between religious and school authorities in promoting the program constituted "beyond all question a utilization of the . . . tax-supported public school system to aid religious groups to spread their faith."

Justice Felix Frankfurter wrote a concurring opinion in which he complained about the coercive nature of the program and its separatist impact on children at a highly impressionistic age. To him, the program "sharpen[ed] the consciousness of religious differences . . . among some of the children committed to [the care of the Champaign public school system]. Justice Jackson agreed with Frankfurter, but, in addition cautioned against too much judicial interference in school policy. He feared such a result could follow from Black's failure to include in the Court's opinion a more specific statement of legal principles to provide guidance in this area of public school policy. Only Justice Reed dissented and it was his contention that the framers of the First Amendment did not intend to exclude religious education from the public schools. Instead, their concern was to prevent the establishment of a state church.

The decision in *McCollum* met with widespread criticism since in communities across the country such programs were commonly accepted. It would appear that a majority of the justices were not oblivious to such reaction when they decided to limit the *McCollum* ruling four years later in *Zorach* v. *Clauson* (343 U.S. 306, 1952).

The only significant difference in the two programs was the place where the religious classes were conducted. In Champaign they were held inside the regular school classrooms; in New York they were conducted off school property. For the six-man majority, however, this difference was sufficient to save New York's program from constitutional infirmity. Justice William O. Douglas, writing the majority opinion, rejected the view of rigid and absolute separation of Church and State. He maintained that the First Amendment does not say that in all respects there must be a separation of Church and State, for if that thesis were accepted, "the state and religion would be alien to each other—hostile, suspicious, and even unfriendly." In an oft-quoted passage, Justice Douglas argued further:

We are a religious people whose institutions presuppose a Supreme Being. . . . When the state encourages religious instruction or cooperates with religious authorities by adjusting the schedule of public events to sectarian needs, it follows the best of our traditions. For it then respects the religious nature of our people and accommodates the public service to their spiritual needs. To hold that it may not would be to find in the Constitution a requirement that the government show a callous indifference to religious groups. That would be preferring those who believe in no religion over those who do believe.

He concluded that while "government may not finance religious groups . . . or blend secular and sectarian education," there is nothing in the Constitution that requires governmental opposition to "efforts to widen the scope of religious influence."

The dissenters—Justices Black, Frankfurter, and Jackson—saw no significant difference between the invalid Champaign program and that of New York. To them, the school authorities were rendering invaluable (and unconstitutional) aid to religious sects in getting them audiences for the propagation of their dogma. The element of coercion was too great, and as Justice Black concluded: "Government should not be allowed, under cover of the soft euphemism 'cooperation', to steal into the sacred area of religious choice."

The Court reexamined its *Everson* holding in *Board of Education* v. *Allen*. At issue was the validity of a 1965 New York statute which requires local school boards to provide a free loan service of textbooks to students in grades seven through 12, including those attending parochial and other private schools. In upholding the law, the Court reaffirmed the "general welfare" and "secular legislative purpose" doctrines enunciated in *Everson*. In addition, Justice Byron White, who wrote the Court's opinion, thought the law met the test (the purpose and primary effect of the enactment) laid down in *School District of Abington Township* v. *Schempp*. He contended that the purpose of the legislation was to expand educational opportunity by making available textbooks free of charge. Ownership of the books remains with the school board and no funds or books are given to the parochial schools. The financial benefit is to the student and the parent and not to the school. White conceded that there is a difference between buses and books, but argued that the control of the public school board over the books loaned and the statutory requirement that only *secular* books could be loaned, provided sufficient protection against public funds being used to purchase sectarian matter.

Both Black and Douglas in their separate dissents felt that the majority's reliance on *Everson* was grossly misplaced. Black charged that the law "is a flat, flagrant and open violation" of the establishment clause and does not meet the test that was laid down in *Everson*. Black warned that it would take "no prophet to foresee" that similar arguments could be used to support and uphold legislation funding parochial school construction and teachers' salaries.

Justice Douglas was troubled with the ideological bias possible in the selection of textbooks. He noted that the statute provides that the board may only provide a student with textbooks, which he is required to use, "in a particular class in the school he legally attends." Hence, the initial selection is in the hands of those who can exercise an ideological (sectarian) bias and, whatever the subsequent action of the public school board, the church-state problem is aggravated. In distinguishing this case from *Everson,* Douglas concluded that "there is nothing ideological about a bus . . . , a school lunch . . . , a public school nurse, nor a scholarship." But he contended that the textbook had a far more significant impact for "it is the chief . . . instrumentality for propagating a particular religious creed or faith."

In recent years, considerable attention has focused on shared-time programs as an arrangement to provide the required secular education of the student and, at the same time, allow him religious instruction without bridging the "wall of separation." Basically, it is an arrangement that provides for dual enrollment of pupils in parochial and public schools. The plan rests on the premise that parents have the option of enrolling their children in either public or parochial schools in complying with compulsory school attendance laws. This is coupled with the controversial claim that a child is legally entitled to enroll as a part-time student in the public schools while, at the same time, attending a private (usually parochial) school on a part-time basis. Such an arrangement allows the child to receive the desired religious training and instruction in the parochial school. The attractiveness of the plan, however, does not alone rest on that factor. Of equal, if not greater importance, is the resulting financial relief to the private school. The plans, as a matter of fact, usually provide for the subjects where instruction is most costly (i.e., the natural sciences and industrial arts) to be offered the shared-time pupil in the public school.

Against claims that this kind of arrangement is nothing but a subterfuge (and not a very good one) for public support of sectarian education contrary to the establishment clause, supporters contend that shared-time programs provide a constitutional means for resolving the continuous policy controversy over public aid to parochial schools. Furthermore, a significant benefit (secular education) accrues to the pupil. In fact, proponents of shared-time point to a number of provisions of the Elementary and Secondary Education Act of 1965 that authorize dual admission (pupils from public and private schools) to special classes for "educationally deprived children" as substantial recognition of the constitutionality of such programs.

Despite the continuing debate over the validity of shared-time, however, there has been very little litigation challenging its constitutionality. Only in Pennsylvania has there been a significant judicial holding on the issue. In *Commonwealth ex rel. Wehrle* v. *School District of Altoona* (88 Atl. 481, 1913), the Pennsylvania Supreme Court sustained a lower court decision in which a shared-time plan was upheld against a challenge that it violated the state constitutional provisions that prohibit the expenditure of public funds to support private and sectarian schools. The court said that "the benefits and advantages of [programs embraced in public elementary schools] are not restricted to pupils in regular attendance . . . and pursuing the entire prescribed . . . courses, but are intended to be free to all 'persons residing in [the school] district'. . . ." The court concluded that the statutory provision authorizing a pupil to enroll in courses or departments of public schools, although his "academic education" is being received in a non-public school, was within the constitutional authority of the legislature. Understandably, coming when it did, a First Amendment issue was not raised or considered. Only state issues involving compulsory school attendance laws have been raised in two other challenges to shared-time programs in St. Louis, Missouri and Chicago, Illinois.[1]

The establishment clause issue raised by shared-time programs is almost certain to be considered by the United States Supreme Court in the near future. *Flast* v. *Cohen* (392 U.S. 83, 1968) opens the way for challenges to such kinds of arrangements now operating in many school districts under the Elementary and Secondary Education Act of 1965 noted above.[2] In fact, *Flast* was originally a challenge to provisions of the Elementary and Secondary Education Act and was remanded to a federal district court for a hearing on the merits.

## ESTABLISHMENT AND FREE EXERCISE IN CONFLICT

Several emotion-packed public questions brought to the Supreme Court during the 1960's have embraced both establishment and free-exercise issues, and the Court's disposition of some of them suggests the difficulty of reconciling the two clauses. Some have contended, as did Justice Potter Stewart in *Sherbert* v. *Verner,* that "a mechanistic" application of the establishment clause may result in a decision which compels government to violate that clause in order to guarantee the free exercise of religion and vice versa. Stewart concluded in the *Sherbert* case that so long as this dilemma is unresolved, "consistent and perceptive" decisions in such cases will be "impeded and impaired."

The school prayer and Bible reading cases are illustrative of the

1 *Special District for Education and Training of the Handicapped* v. *Wheeler* (408 S.W. 2d 60, 1966); *Morton* v. *Board of Education* (216 N.E. 2d 305, 1966).

2 In *Flast,* the Court reversed the rule enunciated in *Frothingham* v. *Mellon* (262 U. S. 447, 1923), that prohibited suits challenging the constitutionality of federal statutes where the plaintiff's standing to bring the action rested solely on his status as a federal taxpayer.

establishment—free-exercise dilemma posed by some types of regulatory action in the religious field. This controversy reached the Supreme Court in *Engel* v. *Vitale* in 1962. At issue was the constitutionality of the use of a twenty-two word prayer (composed by the State Board of Regents of New York) in the public school daily opening exercises. Although participation in the "prayer-exercise" was voluntary and the prayer was characterized as nonsectarian, the Court declared its use an infringement of the establishment clause. Justice Hugo Black's opinion for the 6–1 majority stressed that it was not prayer but an "officially prescribed prayer" that was being condemned. He warned that in this country it is not the business of any government to compose official prayers for any group of people.

In dissent, Justice Potter Stewart focused on the conflict between the two clauses declaring that he could not "see how an 'official religion' is established by letting those who want to say a prayer say it." On the contrary, however, Stewart contended that to deny use of the prayer by children who desire it, "is to deny them the opportunity of sharing in the spiritual heritage of our Nation."

Though Justice Black stressed that it was not prayer but a governmentally prescribed prayer that the Court was condemning, many churchmen, public officials, and laymen were nevertheless outraged and chose to base their condemnation of the Court's action on a more sweeping interpretation of the decision. These critics warned that the Court should be checked now before it struck down other types of activities, which were considered a part of our heritage as a religious people. Members of Congress likewise expressed their concern by introducing a variety of proposals to amend the First Amendment and overturn the Court's decision, but these efforts came to naught.

The emotional outbursts in response to the *Engel* decision had hardly subsided when, just one year later, the Court dropped the other shoe in this "two-pronged" controversy. In companion cases arising from school districts in Pennsylvania and Maryland (*School District of Abington Township* and *Murray* v. *Curlett*), public school opening exercises utilizing the more traditional Lord's Prayer and readings from the Holy Bible were struck down as unconstitutional infringements of the establishment clause. Justice Tom Clark's opinion for the Court set forth the test of establishment violation in this manner:

[W]hat are the purpose and primary effect of the enactment? If either is the advancement or inhibition of religion then the enactment exceeds the scope of legislative power as circumscribed by the Constitution. . . .

Clark explained that to save an enactment from condemnation under the establishment clause there must be a showing of "a secular legislative purpose and a primary effect that neither advances nor inhibits religion."

Justice Arthur Goldberg's concurring opinion focused on the difficult and sensitive task [of delineating] the constitutionally permissible relationship between religion and government. Noting that the opening exercises at issue were clearly prohibited by the establishment clause under the doctrine of state neutrality toward religion, Goldberg nevertheless advanced this warning:

[U]ntutored devotion to the concept of neutrality can lead to invocation or approval of results which partake not simply of that noninterference and noninvolvement with the religious which the Constitution commands, but of a brooding and pervasive devotion to the secular and a passive, or even active, hostility to the religious.

He concluded that the religious commitment of a vast majority of the population cannot be ignored and that "under certain circumstances the First Amendment may require" cognizance of it.

In his dissent, Justice Potter Stewart advanced the view that the free exercise of religion is the central value embodied in the First Amendment. Consequently, he argued that the Court's action striking down the opening exercises constituted a denial of a substantial free-exercise claim of those desiring the exercises. To him, the statutes authorizing the ceremonies are no more than measures that make possible the free-exercise of religion.

The Sunday Closing Law controversy also illustrates the difficult problem of reconciling the establishment and free-exercise requirements of the First Amendment. Challenged in four cases decided by the Court in 1961 were the laws of Pennsylvania (*Two Guys from Harrison-Allentown* v. *McGinley,* 366 U.S. 582; *Braunfeld* v. *Brown,* 366 U.S. 599), Massachusetts (*Gallagher* v. *Crown Kosher Super Market,* 366 U.S. 617), and Maryland (*McGowan* v. *Maryland*). While upholding the constitutionality of all the statutes against allegations that they infringed upon the establishment, free exercise, and equal protection clauses of the First and Fourteenth Amendments, the great difficulty the justices had in resolving the issues is revealed by the eight opinions filed in the cases. Chief Justice Earl Warren wrote the majority, or leading, opinion in each of the cases and, while recognizing "the strongly religious origin" of Sunday closing laws, stressed the secular purpose of the present day legislation. Hence, in *McGowan,* he noted:

[T]he State seeks to set one day apart from all others as a day of rest, repose, recreation and tranquility—a day which all members of the family and community have the opportunity to spend and enjoy together, a day in which there exists relative quiet and disassociation from the everyday intensity of commercial activities, a day in which people may visit friends and relatives who are not available during working days.

The Chief Justice made it clear that such laws do not infringe the establishment clause merely because the day (Sunday) through which the secular purpose is to be accomplished "happens to coincide or harmonize with the tenets of some or all religions." And, he concluded, since "Sunday is a day apart from all others," it would be unrealistic to require a state to select as its designated day of "rest and relaxation" one different from that to which most people traditionally adhere.

Warren also rejected the free-exercise claim advanced by the Orthodox Jewish merchants challenging the Pennsylvania legislation in *Braunfeld*. They argued that the statutory compulsion to close their business on Sunday places them at an economic disadvantage because they closed their businesses on Saturdays in observance of their Sabbath. Hence, they are penalized because of their religious beliefs. The Chief Justice recognized the operational consequences of the statute as making their religious beliefs and practices "more expensive," but he contended that none of those beliefs and practices are made unlawful. In essence, his argument is that alleged economic injury cannot be translated into a constitutional claim. When a statute regulates conduct, he argued, the imposition of an indirect burden on the exercise of religion does not necessarily render it unconstitutional. It is only when the "purpose and effect" of such a statute is to impede religious observance or is to "discriminate invidiously between religions" that it is constitutionally invalid. The Chief Justice set the constitutional limits of state regulatory power in this area this way:

[I]f the State regulates conduct by enacting a general law within its power, the purpose and effect of which is to advance the State's secular goals, the statute is valid despite its indirect burden on religious observance unless the State may accomplish its purpose by means which do not impose such a burden. . . .

Only Justice William O. Douglas dissented in all four cases, with Justices William J. Brennan and Potter Stewart joining him in the *Gallagher* and *Braunfeld* cases. Essentially, they argued that such laws, in recognizing the Christian sabbath and in putting Sabbatarians to a choice between their religion and economic survival, infringed both the establishment and free-exercise clauses.

Some have charged, including Justices Potter Stewart, John Harlan II, and Byron White, that the Court's action in *Sherbert* v. *Verner* discussed *supra*, constituted a reversal of *Braunfeld*. They could not see any substantial difference between the choice of religion and economic survival to which Verner had been subjected (which the Court condemned) and that to which Braunfeld was put under the Sunday Closing Law which the Court approved. The decisions in these two cases illustrate well the difficulty of obtaining consistent rulings on these kinds of questions under the Court's current construction of the establishment clause. As Justice Stewart pointed out in *Sherbert*, "[t]o require South Carolina to so administer its laws as to pay public money to the appellant is . . . clearly to require the State to violate the establishment clause. . . ."

The cases that follow focus on some of the most significant issues reviewed in this commentary.

# EVERSON v. BOARD OF EDUCATION

330 U.S. 1; 91 L. Ed. 711, 67 S. Ct. 504 (1947)

MR. JUSTICE BLACK *delivered the opinion of the Court.*

A New Jersey statute authorizes its local school districts to make rules and contracts for the transportation of children to and from schools. The appellee, a township board of education, acting pursuant to this statute, authorized reimbursement to parents of money expended by them for the bus transportation of their children on regular busses operated by the public transportation system. Part of this money was for the payment of transportation of some school children in the community to Catholic parochial schools. These church schools give their students, in addition to secular education, regular religious instruction conforming to the religious tenets and modes of worship of the Catholic Faith. The superintendent of these schools is a Catholic priest.

The appellant, in his capacity as a district taxpayer, filed suit in a state court challenging the right of the Board to reimburse parents of parochial school students. He contended that the statute and the resolution passed pursuant to it violated both the State and Federal Constitutions. That court held that the legislature was without power to authorize such payments under the state constitution. . . . The New Jersey Court of Errors and Appeals reversed, holding that neither the statute nor the re-

solution passed pursuant to it was in conflict with the State Constitution or the provisions of the Federal Constitution in issue. . . . The case is here on appeal under 28 U.S.C. sec. 344(a). . . .

The only contention here is that the state statute and the resolution, insofar as they authorize reimbursement to parents of children attending parochial schools, violate the Federal Constitution in these two aspects, which to some extent overlap. *First.* They authorize the State to take by taxation the private property of some and bestow it upon others, to be used for their own private purposes. This, it is alleged, violates the due process clause of the Fourteenth Amendment. *Second.* The statute and the resolution forced inhabitants to pay taxes to help support and maintain schools which are dedicated to, and which regularly teach, the Catholic Faith. This is alleged to be a use of state power to support church schools contrary to the prohibition of the First Amendment which the Fourteenth Amendment made applicable to the states.

*First.* The due process argument that the state law taxes some people to help others carry out their private purposes is framed in two phases. The first phase is that a state cannot tax A to reimburse B for the cost of transporting his children to church schools. This is said to violate the due process clause because the children are sent to these church schools to satisfy the personal desires of their parents, rather than the public's interest in the general education of all children. This argument, if valid, would apply equally to prohibit state payment for the transportation of children to any non-public school, whether operated by a church or any other non-government individual or group. But, the New Jersey legislature has decided that a public purpose will be served by using tax-raised funds to pay the bus fares of all school children, including those who attend parochial schools. The New Jersey Court of Errors and Appeals has reached the same conclusion. The fact that a state law, passed to satisfy a public need, coincides with the personal desires of the individuals most directly affected is certainly an inadequate reason for us to say that a legislature has erroneously appraised the public need. . . .

It is much too late to argue that legislation intended to facilitate the opportunity of children to get a secular education serves no public purpose. *Cochran* v. *Louisiana State Board of Education,* 281 U.S. 340; Holmes, J., in *Interstate Ry.* v. *Massachusetts,* 207 U.S. 79, 87. See opinion of Cooley, J. in *Stuart* v. *School District No. 1 of Kalamazoo,* 30 Mich. 69, (1874). The same thing is no less true of legislation to reimburse needy parents, or all parents, for payment of the fares of their children so that they can ride in public busses to and from schools rather than run the risk of traffic and other hazards incident to walking or "hitchhiking." . . . Nor does it follow that a law has a private rather than a public purpose because it provides that tax-raised funds will be paid to reimburse individuals on account of money spent

by them in a way which furthers a public program. See *Carmichael* v. *Southern Coal & Coke Co.,* 301 U.S. 495, 518. . . .

*Second.* The New Jersey statute is challenged as a "law respecting an establishment of religion." The First Amendment, as made applicable to the states by the Fourteenth, *Murdock* v. *Pennsylvania,* 319 U.S. 105, commands that a state "shall make no law respecting an establishment of religion, or prohibiting the free exercise thereof. . . ." These words of the First Amendment reflected in the minds of early Americans a vivid mental picture of conditions and practices which they fervently wished to stamp out in order to preserve liberty for themselves and for their posterity. Doubtless their goal has not been entirely reached; but so far has the Nation moved toward it that the expression "law respecting an establishment of religion," probably does not so vividly remind present-day Americans of the evils, fears, and political problems that caused that expression to be written into our Bill of Rights. . . .

The meaning and scope of the First Amendment, preventing establishment of religion or prohibiting the free exercise thereof, in the light of the history and the evils it was designed forever to suppress, have been several times elaborated by the decisions of this Court prior to the application of the First Amendment to the states by the Fourteenth. The broad meaning given the Amendment by these earlier cases has been accepted by this Court in its decision concerning an individual's religious freedom rendered since the Fourteenth Amendment was interpreted to make the prohibitions of the First applicable to state action abridging religious freedom. There is every reason to give the same application and broad interpretation to the "establishment of religion" clause. The interrelation of these complementary clauses was well summarized in a statement of the Court of Appeals of South Carolina, quoted with approval by this Court in *Watson* v. *Jones,* 13 Wall. 679, 730: "The structure of our government has, for the preservation of civil liberty, rescued the temporal institutions from religious interference. On the other hand, it has secured religious liberty from the invasion of the civil authority."

The "establishment of religion" clause of the First Amendment means at least this: Neither a state nor the Federal Government can set up a church. Neither can pass laws which aid one religion, aid all religions, or prefer one religion over another. Neither can force nor influence a person to go to or to remain away from church against his will or force him to profess a belief or disbelief in any religion. No person can be punished for entertaining or professing religious beliefs or disbeliefs, for church attendance or non-attendance. No tax in any amount, large or small, can be levied to support any religious activities or institutions, whatever they may be called or whatever form they may adopt to teach or practice religion. Neither a state nor the Federal Government can, openly or secretly, participate in the affairs of any religious organizations or groups and *vice versa.* In the words of Jefferson, the clause against establishment of religion by law was intended to erect "a wall of Separation between church and State. . . ."

We must consider the New Jersey statute in accordance with the foregoing limitations imposed by the First Amendment. But we must not strike that state statute down if it is within the State's constitutional power even though it approaches the verge of that power. . . . New Jersey cannot consistently with the "establishment of religion" clause of the First Amendment contribute tax-raised funds to the support of an institution which teaches the tenets and faith of any church. On the other hand, other language of the amendment commands that New Jersey cannot hamper its citizens in the free exercise of their own religion. Consequently, it cannot exclude individual Catholics, Lutherans, Mohammedans, Baptists, Jews, Methodists, Non-believers, Presbyterians, or the members of any other faith, because of their faith, or lack of it, from receiving the benefits of public welfare legislation. While we do not mean to intimate that a state could not provide transportation only to children attending public schools, we must be careful, in protecting the citizens of New Jersey against state-established churches, to be sure that we do not inadvertently prohibit New Jersey from extending its general state law benefits to all its citizens without regard to their religious belief.

Measured by these standards, we cannot say that the First Amendment prohibits New Jersey from spending tax-raised funds to pay the bus fares of parochial school pupils as a part of a general program under which it pays the fares of pupils attending public and other schools. It is undoubtedly true that children are helped to get to church schools. There is even a possibility that some of the children might not be sent to the church schools if the parents were compelled to pay their children's bus fares out of their own pockets when transportation to a public school would have been paid for by the State. The same possibility exists where the state requires a local transit company to provide reduced fares to school children including those attending parochial schools, or where a municipally owned transportation system undertakes to carry all school children free of charge. Moreover, state-paid policemen, detailed to protect children going to and from church schools from the very real hazards of traffic, would serve much the same purpose and accomplish much the same result as state provisions intended to guarantee free transportation of a kind which the state deems to be best for the school children's welfare. And parents might refuse to risk their children to the serious danger of traffic accidents going to and from parochial schools, the approaches to which were not protected by policemen. Similarly, parents might be reluctant to permit their children to attend schools which the state had cut off from such general government services as ordinary police and fire protection, connections for sewage disposal, public highways and sidewalks. Of course, cutting off church schools from these services, so separate and so indisputably marked off from the religious function, would make it far more difficult for the schools to operate. But such is obviously not the purpose of the First Amendment. That Amendment requires the state to be a neutral in its relations with groups of religious believers and non-believers; it does not require the state to be their adversary. State power is no more to be used so as to handicap religions than it is to favor them.

This Court has said that parents may, in the discharge of their duty under state compulsory education laws, send their children to a religious rather than a public school if the school meets the secular educational requirements which the state

has power to impose. See *Pierce* v. *Society of Sisters,* 268 U.S. 510. It appears that these parochial schools meet New Jersey's requirements. The State contributes no money to the schools. It does not support them. Its legislation, as applied, does no more than provide a general program to help parents get their children, regardless of their religion, safely and expeditiously to and from accredited schools.

The First Amendment has erected a wall between church and state. That wall must be kept high and impregnable. We could not approve the slightest breach. New Jersey has not breached it here.

*Affirmed.*

MR. JUSTICE JACKSON, *dissenting.*

I find myself, contrary to first impressions, unable to join in this decision. I have a sympathy, though it is not ideological, with Catholic citizens who are compelled by law to pay taxes for public schools, and also feel constrained by conscience and discipline to support other schools for their own children. Such relief to them as this case involves is not in itself a serious burden to taxpayers and I had assumed it to be as little serious in principle. Study of this case convinces me otherwise. The Court's opinion marshals every argument in favor of state aid and puts the case in its most favorable light, but much of its reasoning confirms my conclusions that there are no good grounds upon which to support the present legislation. In fact, the undertones of the opinion, advocating complete and uncompromising separation of Church from State, seem utterly discordant with its conclusion yielding support to their commingling in educational matters. The case which irresistibly comes to mind as the most fitting precedent is that of Julia who, according to Byron's reports, "whispering 'I will ne'er consent,'—consented."

The Court sustains this legislation by assuming two deviations from the facts of this particular case; first, it assumes a state of facts the record does not support, and secondly, it refuses to consider facts which are inescapable on the record.

The Court concludes that this "legislation, as applied, does no more than provide a general program to help parents get their children, regardless of their religion, safely and expeditiously to and from accredited schools," and it draws a comparison between "state provisions intended to guarantee free transportation" for school children with services such as police and fire protection, and implies that we are here dealing with "laws authorizing new types of public services. . . ." This hypothesis permeates the opinion. The facts will not bear that construction.

The Township of Ewing is not furnishing transportation to the children in any form; it is not operating school busses itself or contracting for their operation; and it is not performing any public service of any kind with this taxpayer's money. All school children are left to ride as ordinary paying passengers on the regular busses operated by the public transportation system. What the Township does, and what the taxpayer complains of, is at stated intervals to reimburse parents for the fares paid, provided the children attend either public schools or Catholic Church schools. This expenditure of tax funds has no possible effect on the child's safety or expedition in transit. As passengers on the public busses they travel as fast and no faster, and are

as safe and no safer, since their parents are reimbursed as before.

In addition to thus assuming a type of service that does not exist, the Court also insists that we must close our eyes to a discrimination which does exist. The resolution which authorizes disbursement of this taxpayer's money limits reimbursement to those who attend public schools and Catholic schools. That is the way the Act is applied to this taxpayer.

The New Jersey Act in question makes the character of the school, not the needs of the children, determine the eligibility of parents to reimbursement. The Act permits payment for transportation to parochial schools or public schools but prohibits it to private schools operated in whole or in part for profit. Children often are sent to private schools because their parents feel that they require more individual instruction than public schools can provide, or because they are backward or defective and need special attention. If all children of the state were objects of impartial solicitude, no reason is obvious for denying transportation reimbursement to students of this class, for these often are as needy and as worthy as those who go to public or parochial schools. Refusal to reimburse those who attend such schools is understandable only in the light of a purpose to aid the schools, because the state might well abstain from aiding a profit-making private enterprise. Thus, under the Act and resolution brought to us by this case, children are classified according to the schools they attend and are to be aided if they attend private secular schools or private religious schools of other faiths. . . .

. . . .[T]his case is not one of a Baptist or a Jew or an Episcopalian or a pupil of a private school complaining of discrimination. It is one of a taxpayer urging that he is being taxed for an unconstitutional purpose. I think he is entitled to have us consider the Act just as it is written. . . .

If we are to decide this case on the facts before us, our question is simply this: Is it constitutional to tax this complainant to pay the cost of carrying pupils of Church schools of one specified denomination?

Whether the taxpayer constitutionally can be made to contribute aid to parents of students because of their attendance at parochial schools depends upon the nature of those schools and their relation to the Church. The Constitution says nothing of education. It lays no obligation on the states to provide schools and does not undertake to regulate state systems of education if they see fit to maintain them. But they cannot, through school policy any more than through other means, invade rights secured to citizens by the Constitution of the United States. *West Virginia States Board of Education* v. *Barnette* 319 U.S. 624. . . . One of our basic rights is to be free of taxation to support a transgression of the constitutional command that the authorities "shall make no law respecting an establishment of religion, or prohibiting the free exercise thereof. . . ."

It is no exaggeration to say that the whole historic conflict in temporal policy between the Catholic Church and non-Catholics comes to a focus in their respective school policies. The Roman Catholic Church, counseled by experience in many ages and many lands and with all sorts and conditions of men, takes what, from the viewpoint of its own progress and the success of its mission, is a wise estimate of the importance of education to religion. It does not leave the individual to pick up religion by

chance. It relies on early and indelible indoctrination in the faith and order of the Church by the word and example of persons consecrated to the task.

Our public school, if not a product of Protestantism, at least is more consistent with it than with the Catholic culture and scheme of values. It is a relatively recent development dating from about 1840. It is organized on the premises that secular education can be isolated from all religious teaching so that the school can inculcate all needed temporal knowledge and also maintain a strict and lofty neutrality as to religion. The assumption is that after the individual has been instructed in worldly wisdom he will be better fitted to choose his religion. Whether such a disjunction is possible, and if possible whether it is wise, are questions I need not try to answer.

I should be surprised if any Catholic would deny that the parochial school is a vital, if not the most vital, part of the Roman Catholic Church. If put to the choice, that venerable institution, I should expect, would forego its whole service for mature persons before it would give up education of the young, and it would be a wise choice. Its growth and cohesion, discipline and loyalty, spring from its schools. Catholic education is the rock on which the whole structure rests, and to render tax aid to its Church school is indistinguishable to me from rendering the same aid to the Church itself. . . .

. . . I agree that this Court has left, and always should leave to each state, great latitude in deciding for itself, in the light of its own conditions, what shall be public purpose in its scheme of things. It may socialize utilities and economic enterprises and make taxpayers' business out of what conventionally had been private business. It may make public business of individual welfare, health, education, entertainment or security. But it cannot make public business of religious worship or instruction, or of attendance at religious institutions of any character. There is no answer to the proposition, more fully expounded by Mr. Justice Rutledge, that the effect of the religious freedom Amendment to our Constitution was to take every form of propagation of religion out of the realm of things which could directly or indirectly be made public business and thereby be supported in whole or in part at taxpayers' expense. That is a difference which the Constitution sets up between religion and almost every other subject matter of legislation, a difference which goes to the very root of religious freedom and which the Court is overlooking today. This freedom was first in the Bill of Rights because it was first in the forefathers' minds; it was set forth in absolute terms, and its strength is its rigidity. It was intended not only to keep the states' hands out of religion, but to keep religion's hands off the state, and, above all, to keep bitter religious controversy out of public life by denying to every denomination any advantage from getting control of public policy or the public purse. Those great ends I cannot but think are immeasurably compromised by today's decision.

This policy of our Federal Constitution has never been wholly pleasing to most religious groups. They all are quick to invoke its protections; they all are irked when they feel its restraints. This Court has gone a long way, if not an unreasonable way, to hold that public business of such paramount importance as maintenance of public order, protection of the privacy of the home, and taxation may not be pursued by a state in a way that even indirectly will interfere with religious proselyting. See dissent in *Douglas* v. *Jeannette,* 319 U.S. 157,186. . . .

But we cannot have it both ways. Religious teaching cannot be a private affair when the state seeks to impose regulations which infringe on it indirectly, and a public affair when it comes to taxing citizens of one faith to aid another, or those of no faith to aid all. If these principles seem harsh in prohibiting aid to Catholic education, it must not be forgotten that it is the same Constitution that alone assures Catholics the right to maintain these schools at all when predominant local sentiment would forbid them. *Pierce* v. *Society of Sisters,* 268 U.S. 510. Nor should I think that those who have done so well without this aid would want to see this separation between Church and State broken down. If the state may aid these religious schools, it may therefore regulate them. Many groups have sought aid from tax funds only to find that it carried political controls with it. Indeed this Court has declared that "It is hardly lack of due process for the Government to regulate that which it subsidizes." *Wickard* v. *Filburn,* 317 U.S. 111, 131.

But in any event, the great purposes of the Constitution do not depend on the approval or convenience of those they restrain. I cannot read this history of the struggle to separate political from ecclesiastical affairs, well summarized in the opinion of Mr. Justice Rutledge in which I generally concur, without a conviction that the Court today is unconsciously giving the clock's hands a backward turn.

MR. JUSTICE FRANKFURTER *joins in this opinion.*

MR. JUSTICE RUTLEDGE, *with whom* MR. JUSTICE FRANKFURTER, MR. JUSTICE JACKSON, *and* MR. JUSTICE BURTON *agree, dissenting.*

This case forces us to determine squarely for the first time what was "an establishment of religion" in the First Amendment's conception; and by that measure to decide whether New Jersey's action violates its command. . . .

I

The Amendment's purpose was not to strike merely at the official establishment of a single sect, creed or religion, outlawing only a formal relation such as had prevailed in England and some of the colonies. Necessarily it was to uproot all such relationships. But the object was broader than separating church and state in this narrow sense. It was to create a complete and permanent separation of the spheres of religious activity and civil authority by comprehensively forbidding every form of public aid or support for religion. In proof the Amendment's wording and history unite with this Court's consistent utterances whenever attention has been fixed directly upon the question. . . .

II

. . . [T]oday, apart from efforts to inject religious training or exercises and sectarian issues into the public schools, the only serious surviving threat to maintaining that complete and permanent separation of religion and civil power which the First Amendment commands is through use of the taxing power to support religion, religious establishments, or establishments having a religious

foundation whatever their form of special religious function.

Does New Jersey's action furnish support for religion by use of the taxing power? Certainly it does, if the test remains undiluted as Jefferson and Madison made it, that money taken by taxation from one is not to be used or given to support another's religious training or belief, or indeed one's own. Today as then the furnishing of "contributions of money for the propagation of opinions which he disbelieves" is the forbidden exaction; and the prohibition is absolute for whatever measure brings that consequence and whatever amount may be sought or given to that end. . . .

Believers of all faiths, and others who do not express their feeling toward ultimate issues of existence in any creedal form, pay the New Jersey tax. When the money so raised is used to pay for transportation to religious schools, the Catholic taxpayer to the extent of his proportionate share pays for the transportation of Lutheran, Jewish, and otherwise religiously affiliated children to receive their non-Catholic religious instruction. Their parents likewise pay proportionately for the transportation of Catholic children to receive Catholic instruction. Each thus contributes to "the propagation of opinions which he disbelieves" in so far as their religions differ, as do others who accept no creed without regard to those differences. Each thus pays taxes also to support the teaching of his own religion, an exaction equally forbidden since it denies "the comfortable liberty" of giving one's contribution to the particular agency of instruction he approves.

New Jersey's action therefore exactly fits the type of exaction and the kind of evil at which Madison and Jefferson struck. Under the test they framed it cannot be said that the cost of transportation is no part of the cost of education or of the religious instruction given. That it is a substantial and a necessary element is shown most plainly by the continuing and increasing demand for the state to assume it. Nor is there pretense that it relates only to the secular instruction given in religious schools or that any attempt is or could be made toward allocating proportional shares as between the secular and the religious instruction. It is precisely because the instruction is religious and relates to a particular faith, whether one or another, that parents send their children to religious schools under the *Pierce* doctrine. And the very purpose of the state's contribution is to defray the cost of conveying the pupil to the place where he will receive not simply secular, but also and primarily religious, teaching and guidance. . . .

Finally, transportation, where it is needed, is as essential to education as any other element. Its cost is as much a part of the total expense, except at times in amount, as the cost of textbooks, of school lunches, of athletic equipment, of writing and other materials; indeed of all other items composing the total burden. . . . Without buildings, without equipment, without library, textbooks and other materials, and without transportation to bring teacher and pupil together in such an effective teaching environment, there can be not even the skeleton of what our times require. Hardly can it be maintained that transportation is the least essential of these items, or that it does not in fact aid, encourage, sustain and support, just as they do, the very process which is

its purpose to accomplish. . . .

For me, therefore, the feat is impossible to select so indispensable an item from the composite of total costs, and characterize it as not aiding, contributing to, promoting or sustaining the propagation of beliefs which it is the very end of all to bring about. Unless this can be maintained, and the Court does not maintain it, the aid thus given is outlawed. Payment of transportation is no more, nor is it any the less essential to education, whether religious or secular, than payment for tuitions, for teachers' salaries, for buildings, equipment and necessary materials.

.   .   .


IV

No one conscious of religious value can be unsympathetic toward the burden which our constitutional separation puts on parents who desire religious instruction mixed with secular for their children. They pay taxes for others' children's education, at the same time the added cost of instruction for their own. Nor can one happily see benefits denied to children which others receive, because in conscience they or their parents desire for them a different kind of training others do not demand.

But if those feelings should prevail, there would be an end to our historic constitutional policy and command. No more unjust or discriminatory in fact is it to deny attendants at religious schools the cost of their transportation than it is to deny them tuitions, sustenance for their teachers, or any other additional expense which others receive at public cost. Hardship in fact there is which none can blink. But, for assuring to those who undergo it the greater, the most comprehensive freedom, it is one written by design and firm intent into our basic law. . . .

That policy necessarily entails hardship upon persons who forego the right to educational advantages the state can supply in order to secure others it is precluded from giving. Indeed this may hamper the parent and the child forced by conscience to that choice. But it does not make the state unneutral to withhold what the Constitution forbids it to give. On the contrary it is only by observing the prohibition rigidly that the state can maintain its neutrality and avoid partisanship in the dissensions inevitable when sect opposes sect over demands for public moneys to further religious education, teaching or training in any form or degree, directly or indirectly. . . .

The problem then cannot be cast in terms of legal discrimination or its absence. This would be true, even though the state in giving aid should treat all religious instruction alike. Thus, if the present statute and its application were shown to apply equally to all religious schools of whatever faith, yet in the light of our tradition it could not stand. For then the adherent of one creed still would pay for the support of another, the childless taxpayer with others more fortunate. Then, too, there would seem to be no bar to making appropriations for transportation and other expenses of children attending public or other secular schools, after hours in separate places and classes for their exclusively religious instruction. The person who embraces no creed also would be forced to pay for teaching what he does not believe. Again, it was the furnishing of "contributions of money for the propagation of opinions which he disbelieves" that the fathers outlawed. That consequences and effect are not removed by multiplying to all-inclusiveness the sects for which support is exacted. The Constitution requires, not comprehensive identification of state with religion, but complete separation. . . .

Two great drives are constantly in motion to abridge, in the name of education, the complete division of religion and civil authority which our forefathers made. One is to introduce religious education and observances into the public schools. The other, to obtain public funds for the aid and support of various private religious schools. See Johnson, *The Legal Status of Church-State Relationships in the United States,* (1934); Thayer, *Religion in Public Education,* (1947); Note (1941) 50 Yale L. J. 917. In my opinion both avenues were closed by the Constitution. Neither should be opened by this Court. The matter is not one of quantity, to be measured by the amount of money expended. Now as in Madison's day it is one of principle, to keep separate the separate spheres as the First Amendment drew them; to prevent the first experiment upon our liberties; and to keep the question from becoming entangled in corrosive precedents. We should not be less strict to keep strong and untarnished the one side of the shield of religious freedom than we have been of the other. The judgment should be reversed.

# BOARD OF EDUCATION OF CENTRAL SCHOOL DISTRICT NO. 1 v. JAMES E. ALLEN, JR., AS COMMISSIONER OF EDUCATION OF NEW YORK

392 U.S. 236; 20 L. Ed. 2d 1060; 88 S. Ct. 1923 (1968)

MR. JUSTICE WHITE *delivered the opinion of the Court.*

A law of the State of New York requires local public school authorities to lend textbooks free of charge to all students in grades seven through 12; students attending private schools are included. This case presents the question whether this statute is a "law respecting the establishment of religion or prohibiting the free exercise thereof," and so in conflict with the First and Fourteenth Amendments to the Constitution, because it authorizes the loan of textbooks to students attending parochial schools. We hold that the law is not in violation of the Constitution.

. . . Beginning with the 1966–1967 school year, local school boards were required to purchase textbooks and lend them without charge "to all children residing in such district who are enrolled in grades seven to twelve of a public or private school which complies with the compulsory education law." The books now loaned are "text-books which are designated for use in any public, elementary or secondary schools of the state or are approved by any boards of education," and which—according to a 1966 amendment—"a pupil is required to use as a text for a semester or more in a particular class in the school he legally attends."

Appellants, [the members of the Board of Education of Central School District No. 1 in Rensselaer and Columbia Counties] . . . sought a declaration that Sec. 701 [of the state education law] was invalid, an order barring appellee Allen from removing appellants from office for failing to comply with it, and another order restraining him from apportioning state funds to school districts for the purchase of textbooks to be lent to parochial students. After answer, and upon cross-motions for summary judgment, the trial court held the law unconstitutional under the First and Fourteenth Amendments and entered judgment for appellants. . . . The Appellate Division reversed, ordering the complaint dismissed on the ground that appellant school boards had no standing to attack the validity of a state statute. . . . On appeal, the New York Court of Appeals concluded by a 4–3 vote that appellants did have standing but by a different 4–3 vote held that Sec. 701 was not in violation of either the State or the Federal Constitution. . . . The Court of Appeals said that the law's purpose was to benefit all school children, regardless of the type of school they attended, and that only textbooks approved by public school authorities could be loaned. It therefore considered Sec. 701 "completely neutral with respect to religion, merely making available secular textbooks at the request of the individual student and asking no question about what school he attends." Section 701, the Court of Appeals concluded, is not a law which "established a religion or constitutes the use of public funds to aid religious schools." . . .

*Everson* v. *Board of Education,*

[*supra*] is the case decided by this Court that is most nearly in point in today's problem. New Jersey re-imbursed parents for expenses incurred in bussing their children to parochial schools. The Court stated that the Establishment Clause . . . does not prevent a State from extending the benefits of state laws to all citizens without regard for their religious affiliation and does not prohibit "New Jersey from spending tax-raised funds to pay the bus fares of parochial school pupils as part of a general program under which it pays the fares of pupils attending public and other schools." . . .

. . . Based on *Everson, Zorach, McGowan,* and other cases, *Abington School District* v. *Schempp,* [*supra*] fashioned a test ascribed to by eight Justices for distinguishing between forbidden involvements of the State with religion and those contacts which the Establishment Clause permits:

The test may be stated as follows: what are the purpose and the primary effect of the enactment? If either is the advancement or inhibition of religion then the enactment exceeds the scope of legislative power as circumscribed by the Constitution. That is to say that to withstand the strictures of the Establishment Clause there must be a secular legislative purpose and a primary effect that neither advances nor inhibits religion. . . .

This test is not easy to apply, but the citation of *Everson* by the *Schempp* Court to support its general standard made clear how the *Schempp* rule would be applied to the facts of *Everson.* The statute upheld in *Everson* would be considered a law having "a secular legislative purpose and a primary effect that neither advances nor inhibits religion." We reach the same result with respect to the New York law requiring school books to be loaned free of charge to all students in specified grades. The express purpose of Sec. 701 was stated by the New York Legislature to be furtherance of the educational opportunities available to the young. Appellants have shown us nothing about the necessary effects of the statute that is contrary to its stated purpose. The law merely makes available to all children the benefits of a general program to lend school books free of charge. Books are furnished at the request of the pupil and ownership remains, at least technically, in the State. Thus no funds or books are furnished to parochial schools, and the financial benefit is to parents and children, not to schools. Perhaps free books make it more likely that some children choose to attend a sectarian school, but that was true of the state-paid bus fares in *Everson* and does not alone demonstrate an unconstitutional degree of support for a religious institution.

Of course books are different from buses. Most bus rides have no inherent religious significance, while religious books are common. However, the language of Sec. 701 does not authorize the loan of religious books, and the State claims no right to distribute religious literature. Although the books loaned are those required by the parochial school for use in specific courses, each book loaned must be approved by the public school authorities; only secular books may receive approval. . . .

The major reason offered by appellants for distinguishing free textbooks from free bus fares is that books, but not buses, are critical to the teaching process, and in a sectarian school that process is employed to teach religion. However this Court has long recognized that religious schools pursue two goals, religious instruction and secular education. In the leading case of *Pierce* v. *Society of Sisters*, [*supra*] the Court held that although it would not question Oregon's power to compel school attendance or require that the attendance be at an institution meeting State-imposed requirements as to quality and nature of curriculum, Oregon had not shown that its interest in secular education required that all children attend publicly operated schools. . . . Since *Pierce*, a substantial body of case law has confirmed the power of the States to insist that attendance at private schools, if it is to satisfy state compulsory-attendance laws, be at institutions which provide minimum hours of instruction, employ teachers of specified training, and cover prescribed subjects of instruction. Indeed, the State's interest in assuring that these standards are being met has been considered a sufficient reason for refusing to accept instruction at home as compliance with compulsory education statutes. These cases were a sensible corollary of *Pierce* v. *Society of Sisters*: if the State must satisfy its interest in secular education through the instrument of private schools, it has a proper interest in the manner in which those schools perform their secular educational function. Another corollary was *Cochran* v. *Louisiana State Board of Education*, [*supra*] where appellants said that a statute requiring school books to be furnished without charge to all students, whether they attended public or private schools, did not serve a "public purpose," and so offended the Fourteenth Amendment. Speaking through Chief Justice Hughes, the Court summarized as follows its conclusion that Louisiana's interest in the secular education being provided by private schools made provision of textbooks to students in those schools a properly public concern: "[The State's]

interest is education, broadly; its method, comprehensive. Individual interests are sided only as the common interest is safeguarded." . . .

Underlying these cases, and underlying also the legislative judgments that have preceded the court decisions, has been a recognition that private education has played and is playing a significant and valuable role in raising national levels of knowledge, competence, and experience. Americans care about the quality of the secular education available to their children. They have considered high quality education to be an indispensable ingredient for achieving the kind of nation, and the kind of citizenry, that they have desired to create. Considering this attitude, the continued willingness to rely on private school systems, including parochial systems, strongly suggests that a wide segment of informed opinion, legislative and otherwise, has found that those schools do an acceptable job of providing secular education to their students. . . .

Against this background of judgment and experience, unchallenged in the meager record before us in this case, we cannot agree with appellants either that all teaching in a sectarian school is religious or that the processes of secular and religious training are so intertwined that secular textbooks furnished to students by the public are in fact instrumental in the teaching of religion. . . . Nothing in this record supports the proposition that all textbooks, whether they deal with mathematics, physics, foreign languages, history, or literature, are used by the parochial schools to teach religion. . . . We are unable to hold, based solely on judicial notice, that this statute results in unconstitutional involvement of the State with religious instruction or that Sec. 701, for this or the other reasons urged, is a law respecting the establishment of religion within the meaning of the First Amendment.

Appellants also contend that Sec. 701 offends the Free Exercise Clause of the First Amendment. However, "it is necessary in a free exercise case for one to show the coercive effect of the enactment as it operates against him in the practice of his religion," . . . and appellants have not contended that the New York law in any way coerces them as individuals in the practice of their religion.

*The judgment is affirmed.*

Mr. Justice Harlan's *brief concurring opinion is not reprinted here.*

Mr. Justice Black, *dissenting.*

. . . I believe the New York law held valid is a flat, flagrant, open violation of the First and Fourteenth Amendments which together forbid Congress or state legislatures to enact any law "respecting an establishment of religion." . . . This, I am confident, would be in keeping with the deliberate statement we made in *Everson* v. *Board of Education,* [*supra*] and repeated in *McCollum* v. *Board of Education,* [*supra*]. . . .

The *Everson* and *McCollum* cases plainly interpret the First and Fourteenth Amendments as protecting the taxpayers of a State from being compelled to pay taxes to their government to support the agencies of private religious organizations the taxpayers oppose. To authorize a State to tax its residents for such church purposes is to put the State squarely in the religious activities of certain religious groups that happen to be strong enough politically to write their own religious preferences and prejudices into the laws. This

links state and churches together in controlling the lives and destinies of our citizenship—a citizenship composed of people of myriad religious faiths, some of them bitterly hostile to and completely intolerant of the others. It was to escape laws precisely like this that a large part of the Nation's early immigrants fled to this country. It was also to escape such laws and such consequences that the First Amendment was written in language strong and clear barring passage of any law "respecting establishment of religion."

It is true, of course, that the New York law does not as yet formally adopt or establish a state religion. But it takes a great stride in that direction and coming events cast their shadows before them. The same powerful sectarian religious propagandists who have succeeded in securing passage of the present law to help religious schools carry on their sectarian religious purposes can and doubtless will continue their propoganda, looking toward complete domination and supremacy of their particular brand of religion. And it nearly always is by insidious approaches that the citadels of liberty are most successfully attacked.

I know of no prior opinion of this Court upon which the majority here can rightfully rely to support its holding this New York law constitutional. In saying this, I am not unmindful of the fact that the New York Court of Appeals purported to follow *Everson* v. *Board of Education, supra*. . . .

. . . The First Amendment's bar to establishment of religion must preclude a State from using funds levied from all of its citizens to purchase books for use by sectarian schools, which, although "secular," realistically will in some way inevitably tend to propagate the religious views of the favored sect. Books are the most essential tool of education since they contain the resources of knowledge which the educational process is designed to exploit. In this sense it is not difficult to distinguish books, which are the heart of any school, from bus fares, which provide a convenient and helpful general public transportation service. With respect to the former, state financial support actively and directly assists the teaching and propagation of sectarian religious viewpoints in clear conflict with the First Amendment's establishment bar; with respect to the latter, the State merely provides a general and nondiscriminatory transportation service in no way related to substantive religious views and beliefs.

. . .

I still subscribe to the belief that tax-raised funds cannot constitutionally be used to support religious schools, buy their school books, erect their buildings, pay their teachers, or pay any other of their maintenance expenses, even to the extent of one penny. The First Amendment's prohibition against governmental establishment of religion was written on the assumption that state aid to religion and religious schools generates discord, disharmony, hatred, and strife among our people, and that any government that supplies such aids is to that extent a tyranny. And I still believe that the only way to protect minority religious groups from majority groups in this country is to keep the wall of separation between church and state high and impregnable as the First and Fourteenth Amendments provide. The Court's affirmance here bodes nothing but evil to religious peace in this country.

MR. JUSTICE DOUGLAS, *dissenting*.

. . .

Whatever may be said of *Everson,* there is nothing ideological about a bus. There is nothing ideological about a school lunch, nor a public nurse, nor a scholarship. The constitutionality of such public aid to students in parochial schools turns on considerations not present in this textbook case. The textbook goes to the very heart of education in a parochial school. It is the chief, although not solitary, instrumentality for propagating a particular religious creed or faith. How can we possibly approve such state aid to a religion? A parochial school textbook may contain many, many more seeds of creed and dogma than a prayer. Yet we struck down in *Engel* v. *Vitale,* [*infra*], an official New York prayer for its public schools, even though it was not plainly denominational. For we emphasized the violence done the Establishment Clause when the power was given religious-political groups "to write their own prayers into law." . . . That risk is compounded here by giving parochial schools the intiative in selecting the textbooks they desire to be furnished at public expense.

. . .

It will be often difficult, as Mr. Justice Jackson said, to say "where the secular ends and the sectarian begins in education." *McCollum* v. *Board of Education,* 333 U.S., at 237–238. But certain it is that once the so-called "secular" textbook is the prize to be won by that religious faith which selects the book, the battle will be on for those positions of control. . . . Others fear that one sectarian group, gaining control of the state agencies which approve the "secular" textbooks, will use their control to disseminate ideas most congenial to their faith. It must be remembered that the very existence of the religious school—whether Catholic or Mormon, Presbyterian or Episcopalian—is to provide an education oriented to the dogma of the particular faith.

. . .

The challenged New York law leaves to the Board of Regents, local boards of education, trustees, and other school authorities the supervision of the textbook program.

The Board of Regents (together with the Commissioner of Education) has powers of censorship over all textbooks that contain statements seditious in character, or evince disloyalty to the United States or are favorable to any nation with which we are at war. . . . Those powers can cut a wide swathe in many areas of education that involve the ideological element.

In general textbooks are approved for distribution by "boards of education, trustees or such body or officer as performs the function of such boards. . . ." N.Y. Educ. Law Sec. 701(1). These school boards are generally elected, Sections 2013, 2502(2), though in a few cities they are appointed. Sec. 2553. Where there are trustees, they are elected. Sections 1523, 1602, 1702. And superintendents who advise on textbook selection are appointed by the board of education or the trustees. Sections 1711, 2503(5), 2507.

The initiative to select and requisition "the books desired" is with the parochial school. Powerful religious-political pressures will therefore be on the state agencies to provide the books that are desired.

These then are the battlegrounds where control of textbook distribution will be won or lost. Now that "secular" textbooks will pour into religious schools, we can rest assured that a contest will be on to provide those books for religious schools which the dominant religious group concludes best reflect the theocentric or other philosophy of the particular church.

The stakes are now extremely high . . . to obtain approval of what is "proper." For the "proper" books will radiate the "correct" religious view not only in the parochial school but in the public school as well.

. . .

What Madison wrote in his famous Memorial and Remonstrance against Religious Assessments is highly pertinent here:

Who does not see that the same authority which can establish Christianity, in exclusion of all other Religions, may establish with the same case any particular sect of Christians, in exclusion of all other Sects? That the same authority which can force a citizen to contribute three pence only of his property for the support of any one establishment, may force him to conform to any other establishment in all cases whatsoever?

JUSTICE ABE FORTAS' *brief dissenting opinion is not reprinted here.*

# ENGEL v. VITALE

## 370 U.S. 421; 8 L. Ed. 2d 601; 82 S. Ct. 1261 (1962)

MR. JUSTICE BLACK *delivered the opinion of the Court.*

The respondent Board of Education of Union Free School District No. 9, New Hyde Park, New York, acting in its official capacity under state law, directed the School District's principal to cause the following prayer to be said aloud by each class in the presence of a teacher at the beginning of each school day:

Almighty God, we acknowledge our dependence upon Thee, and we beg Thy blessings upon us, our parents, our teachers and our Country.

This daily procedure was adopted on the recommendation of the State Board of Regents, a governmental agency created by the State Constitution to which the New York Legislature has granted broad supervisory, executive, and legislative powers over the State's public school system. These state officials composed the prayer which they recommended and published as a part of their "Statement on Moral and Spiritual Training in the Schools," saying: "We believe that this Statement will be subscribed to by all men and women of good will, and we call upon all of them to aid in giving life to our program."

Shortly after the practice of reciting the Regents' prayer was adopted by the School District, the parents of ten pupils brought this acting in a New York State Court insisting that use of this official prayer in the public schools was contrary to the beliefs, religions, or religious practices of both themselves and their children. Among other things, these parents challenged the constitutionality . . . of this particular prayer on the ground that these actions of official governmental agencies violate that part of the First Amendment of the Federal Constitution which commands that "Congress shall make no law respecting an establishment of religion"—a command which was "made applicable to the State of New York by the Fourteenth Amendment of the said Constitution." The New York Court of Appeals . . . sustained an order of the lower state courts which had upheld the power of New York to use the Regents' prayer as a part of the daily procedures of its public schools so long as the schools did not compel any pupil to join in the prayer over his or his parents' objections. We granted certiorari to review this important decision involving rights protected by the First and Fourteenth Amendments.

We think that by using its public school system to encourage recitation of the Regents' prayer, the State of New York has adopted a practice wholly inconsistent with the Establishment Clause. There can, of course, be no doubt that New York's program of daily classroom invocation of God's blessings as prescribed in the Regents' prayer is a religious activity. It is a solemn avowal of divine faith and supplication for the blessings of the Almighty. The nature of such a prayer has always been religious, none of the respondents has denied this and the trial court expressly so found:

The religious nature of prayer was recognized by Jefferson and has been concurred in by theological writers, the United States Supreme Court and State courts and administrative officials, including New York's Commissioner of Education. A committee of the New York Legislature has agreed.

The Board of Regents as *amicus curiae*, the respondents and intervenors all concede the religious nature of prayer, but seek to distinguish this prayer because it is based on our spiritual heritage. . . .

The petitioners contend among other things that the state laws requiring or permitting use of the Regents' prayer must be struck down as a violation of the Establishment Clause because that prayer was composed by governmental officials as a part of a governmental program to further religious beliefs. For this reason, petitioners argue, the State's use of the Regents' prayer in its public school system breaches the constitutional wall of separation between Church and State. We agree with that contention since we think that the constitutional prohibition against laws respecting an establishment of religion must at least mean that in this country it is no part of the business of government to compose official prayers for any group of the American people to recite as a part of a religious program carried on by government.

It is a matter of history that this very practice of establishing governmentally composed prayers for religious services was one of the reasons which caused many of our early colonists to leave England and seek religious freedom in America. . . .

It is an unfortunate fact of history that when some of the very groups which had most strenuously opposed the established Church of England found themselves sufficiently in control of colonial governments in this country to write their own prayers into law, they passed laws making their own religion the official religion of their respective colonies. Indeed, as late as the time of the Revolutionary War, there were established churches in at least eight of the thirteen former colonies and established religions in at least four of the other five. But the successful Revolution against English political domination was shortly followed by intense opposition to the practice of establishing religion by law. This opposition crystallized rapidly into an effective political force in Virginia where the minority religious groups such as Presbyterians, Lutherans, Quakers and Baptists had gained such strength that the adherents to the established Episcopal Church were actually a minority themselves. In 1785–1786, those opposed to the established Church, led by James Madison and Thomas Jefferson, who, though themselves not members of any of these dissenting religious groups, opposed all religious establishments by law on grounds of principle, obtained the enactment of the famous "Virginia Bill for Religious Liberty" by which all religious groups were placed on an equal footing so far as the State was concerned. Similar though less far-reaching legislation was being considered and passed in other States.

By the time of the adoption of the Constitution, our history shows that there was a widespread awareness among many Americans of the dangers of a union of Church and State. These people knew, some of them from bitter personal experience, that one of the greatest dangers to the freedom of the individual to worship in his own way lay in the Government's placing its official stamp of approval upon one particular kind of prayer or one particular form of religious services. They knew the anguish, hardship and bitter strife that could come when zealous religious groups struggled with one another to obtain the Government's stamp of approval from each King, Queen, or Protector that came to temporary power. The Constitution was intended to avert a part of this danger by leaving the government of this country in the hands of the people rather than in the hands of any monarch. But this safeguard was not enough. Our Founders were no more willing to let the content of their prayers and their privilege of praying whenever they pleased be influenced by the ballot box than they were to let these vital matters of personal conscience depend upon the succession of monarchs. The First Amendment was added to the Constitution to stand as a guarantee that neither the power nor the prestige of the Federal Government would be used to control, support or influence the kinds of prayer the American people can say—that the people's religions must not be subjected to the pressures of government for change each time a new political administration is elected to office. Under that Amendment's prohibition against governmental establishment of religion, as reinforced by the provisions of the Fourteenth Amendment, government in this country, be it state or federal, is without power to prescribe by law any particular form of prayer which is to be used as an official prayer in carrying on any program of governmentally sponsored religious activity.

There can be no doubt that New York's state prayer program officially establishes the religious beliefs embodied in the Regents' prayer. . . . Neither the fact that the prayer may be denominationally neutral nor the fact that its observance on the part of the students is voluntary can serve to free it from the limitations of the Establishment Clause, as it might from the Free Exercise Clause, of the First Amendment, both of which are operative against the States by virtue of the Fourteenth Amendment. Although these two clauses may in certain instances overlap, they forbid two quite different kinds of governmental encroachment upon religious freedom. The Establishment Clause, unlike the Free Exercise Clause, does not depend upon any showing of direct governmental compulsion and is violated by the enactment of laws which establish an official religion whether those laws operate directly to coerce nonobserving individuals or not. This is not to say, of course, that laws officially prescribing a particular form of religious worship do not involve coercion of such individuals. When the power, prestige and financial support of government is placed behind a particular religious belief, the indirect coercive pressure upon religious minorities to conform to the prevailing officially approved religion is plain. But the purposes underlying the Establishment Clause go much further than that. Its first and most immediate purpose rested on the belief that a union of government and religion tends to destroy government and to degrade religion. . . . The Establishment Clause thus stands as an expression of principle on the part of the Founders of our Constitution that religion is too personal, too sacred, too holy, to permit its "unhallowed perversion" by a civil magistrate. Another purpose of the Establishment Clause rested upon an awareness of the historical fact that governmentally established religions and religious persecutions go hand in hand. . . .

It has been argued that to apply the Constitution in such a way as to prohibit state laws respecting an establishment of religious services in public schools is to indicate a hostility toward religion or toward prayer. Nothing, of course, could be more wrong. The history of man is inseparable from the history of religion. And perhaps it is not too much to say that since the beginning of that history many people have devoutly believed that "More things are wrought by prayer than this world dreams of." It was doubtless largely due to men who believed this that there grew up a sentiment that caused men to leave the cross-currents of officially established state religions and religious persecution in Europe and come to this country filled with the hope that they could find a place in which they could pray when they pleased to the God of their faith in the language they chose. And there were men of this same faith in the power of prayer who led the fight for adoption of our Constitution and also for our Bill of Rights with the very guarantees of religious freedom that forbid the sort of governmental activity which New York has attempted here. These men knew that the First Amendment, which tried to put an end to governmental control of religion and of prayer, was not written to destroy either. They knew rather that it was written to quiet well-justified fears which nearly all of them felt arising out of an awareness that governments of the past had shackled men's tongues to make them speak only the religious thoughts that government wanted them to speak and to pray only to the God that government wanted them to pray to. It is neither sacrilegious nor antireligious to say that each separate government in this country should stay out of the business of writing or sanctioning official prayers and leave that purely religious function to the people themselves and to those the people choose to look to for religious guidance.

It is true that New York's establishment of its Regents' prayer as an officially approved religious doctrine of that State does not amount to a total establishment of one particular religious sect to the exclusion of all others—that, indeed, the governmental endorsement of that prayer seems relatively insignificant when compared to the governmental encroachments upon religion which were commonplace 200 years ago. To those who may subscribe to the view that because the Regents' official prayer is so brief and general there can be no danger to religious freedom in its governmental establishment, however, it may be appropriate to say in the words of James Madison, the author of the First Amendment:

[I]t is proper to take alarm at the first experiment on our liberties. . . . Who does not see that the same authority which can establish Christianity, in exclusion of all other Religions, may establish with the same ease any particular sect of Christians, in exclusion of all other Sects? That the same authority which can force a citizen to contribute three pence only of his property for the support of any one establishment, may force him to conform to any other establishment in all cases whatsoever?

The judgment of the Court of Appeals of New York is reversed and the cause remanded for further proceedings not inconsistent with this opinion.

*Reversed and remanded.*

# SCHOOL DISTRICT OF ABINGTON TOWNSHIP
## PENNSYLVANIA v. SCHEMPP
## MURRAY v. CURLETT

374 U.S. 203; 10 L. Ed. 2d 844; 83 S. Ct. 1560 (1963)

MR. JUSTICE CLARK *delivered the opinion of the Court.*

Once again we are called upon to consider the scope of the provision of the First Amendment to the United States Constitution which declares that "Congress shall make no law respecting an establishment of religion, or prohibiting the free exercise thereof. . . ." These companion cases present the issues in the content of state action requiring that schools begin each day with readings from the Bible. While raising the basic questions under slightly different factual situations, the cases permit of joint treatment. In light of the history of the First Amendment and of our cases interpreting and applying its requirements, we hold that the practices at issue and the laws respecting them are unconstitutional under the Establishment Clause, as applied to the states through the Fourteenth Amendment.

. . . [In] No. 142 [t]he Commonwealth of Pennsylvania by law, 24 Pa. Stat. Sec. 15–1516, as amended, . . . requires that "At least ten verses from the Holy Bible shall be read, without comment, at the opening of each public school on each school day. Any child shall be excused from such Bible reading, or attending such Bible reading, upon the written request of his parent or guardian." The Schempp family, husband and wife and two of their three children, brought suit to enjoin enforcement of the statute, contending that their rights under the Fourteenth Amendment to the Constitution of the United States are, have been, and will continue to be violated unless this statute be declared unconstitutional as violative of these provisions of the First Amendment. They sought to enjoin the appellant school district . . . from continuing to conduct such readings and recitation of the Lord's Prayer in the public schools of the district. . . . A three-judge statutory District Court for the Eastern District of Pennsylvania held that the statute is violative of the Establishment Clause of the First Amendment as applied to the States by the Due Process Clause of the Fourteenth Amendment and directed that appropriate injunctive relief issue. . . .

The appellees . . . are of the Unitarian faith . . . [and] they . . . regularly attend religious services. . . . The . . . children attend the Abington Senior High School, which is a public school operated by appellant district.

On each school day at the Abington Senior High School between 8:15 and 8:30 A.M., while the pupils are attending their home rooms or advisory sections, opening exercises are conducted pursuant to the statute. The exercises are broadcast into each room in the school building through an intercommunications system and are conducted under the supervision of a teacher by students attending the school's radio and television workshop. Selected students from this course gather each morning in the school's workshop studio for the exercises, which include readings by one of the students of 10 verses of the Holy Bible, broadcast to each room in the building. This is followed by the recitation of the Lord's Prayer, likewise over the intercommunications system, but also by the students in the various classrooms, who are asked to stand and join in repeating the prayer in unison. The exercises are closed with the flag salute and such pertinent announcements as are of interest to the students. Participation in the opening exercises, as directed by the statute, is voluntary. The student reading the verses from the Bible may select the passages and read from any version he chooses, although the only copies furnished by the school are the King James version, copies of which were circulated to each teacher by the school district. During the period in which the exercises have been conducted the King James, the Douay and the Revised Standard versions of the Bible have been used, as well as the Jewish Holy Scriptures. There are no prefatory statements, no questions asked or solicited, no comments or explanations made and no interpretations given at or during the exercises. The students and parents are advised that the student may absent himself from the classroom or, should he elect to remain, not participate in the exercises.

It appears from the record that in schools not having an intercommunications system the Bible reading and the recitation of the Lord's Prayer were conducted by the home-room teacher, who chose the text of the verses and read them herself or had students read them in rotation or by volunteers. . . .

At the first trial Edward Schempp and the children testified as to specific religious doctrines purveyed by a literal reading of the Bible "which were contrary to the religious beliefs which they held and to their familial teaching." . . . Edward Schempp testified at the second trial that he had considered having . . . [his children] excused from attendance at the exercises but decided against it for several reasons, including his belief that the children's relationships with their teachers and classmates would be adversely affected.

. . .

The trial court, in striking down the practices and the statute requiring them, made specific findings of fact that the children's attendance at Abington Senior High School is compulsory and that the practice of reading 10 verses from the Bible is also compelled by law. It also found that:

The reading of the verses, even without comment, possesses a devotional and religious character and constitutes in effect a religious observance. The devotional and religious nature of the morning exercises is made all the more apparent by the fact that the Bible reading is followed immediately by a recital in unison by the pupils of the Lord's Prayer. . . . The exercises are held in the school buildings and perforce are conducted by and under the authority of the local school authorities and during school sessions. Since the statute requires the reading of the "Holy Bible," a Christian document, the practice . . . prefers the Christian religion. . . .

[The facts in] no. 119 [show that] [i]n 1905 the Board of School Commissioners of Baltimore City adopted a rule pursuant to . . . [state law which] . . . provided for the holding of opening exercises in the schools of the city, consisting primarily of the "reading, without comment, of a chapter in the Holy Bible and/or the use of the Lord's Prayer." The petitioners, Mrs. Madalyn Murray and her son, William J. Murray III, are both professed atheists. Following unsuccessful attempts to have the respondent school board rescind the rule, this suit was filed for mandamus to compel its rescission and cancellation. It was alleged that William was a student in a public school of the city and Mrs. Murray, his mother, was a taxpayer therein; . . . that at petitioners' insistence the rule was amended to permit children to be excused from the exercise on request of the parent and that William had been excused pursuant thereto. . . .

The respondents demurred and the trial court, recognizing that the demurrer admitted all facts well pleaded, sustained it without leave to amend. The Maryland Court of Appeals affirmed, the majority of four justices holding the exercise not in violation of the First and Fourteenth Amendments, with three justices dissenting. . . .

It is true that religion has been closely identified with our history and government. . . . The fact that the Founding Fathers believed devotedly that there was a God and that the unalienable rights of man were rooted in Him is clearly evidenced in their writings, from the Mayflower Compact to the Constitution itself. This background is evidenced today in our public life through the continuance in our oaths of office from the Presidency to the Alderman of the final supplication, "So help me God." Likewise each House of the Congress provides through the Chaplain an opening prayer, and the sessions of this Court are declared open by the crier in a short ceremony, the final phrase of which invokes the grace of God. Again, there are such manifestations in our military forces, where those of our citizens who are under the restrictions of military service wish to engage in voluntary wor-

ship. Indeed, only last year an official survey of the country indicated that 64% of our people have church membership . . . while less than 3% profess no religion whatever. . . . It can be truly said, therefore, that today, as in the beginning, our national life reflects a religious people who, in the words of Madison are "earnestly praying, as . . . in duty bound, that the Supreme Lawgiver of the Universe . . . guide them into every measure which may be worthy of his [blessing . . .]"

Almost a hundred years ago in *Minor* v. *Board of Education of Cincinnati*, Judge Alphonzo Taft, father of the revered Chief Justice, in an unpublished opinion stated the ideal of our people as to religious freedom as one of:

absolute equality before the law of all religious opinions and sects. . . . The government is neutral, and while protecting all, it prefers none, and it *disparages* none. . . .

The wholesome "neutrality" of which this Court's cases speak thus stems from a recognition of the teachings of history that powerful sects or groups might bring about a fusion or a concert or dependency of one upon the other to the end that official support of the State or Federal Government would be placed behind the tenets of one or of all orthodoxies. This the Establishment Clause prohibits. And a further reason for neutrality is found in the Free Exercise Clause, which recognizes the value of religious training, teaching and observance and, more particularly, the right of every person to freely choose his own course with reference thereto, free of any compulsion from the state. This the Free Exercise Clause guarantees. Thus, as we have seen, the two clauses may overlap. As we have indicated, the Establishment Clause has been directly considered by this Court eight times in the past score of years and, with only one Justice dissenting on the point, it has consistently held that the clause withdrew all legislative power respecting religious belief or the exercise thereof. The test may be stated as follows: what are the purpose and primary effect of the enactment? If either is the advancement or inhibition of religion then the enactment exceeds the scope of legislative power as circumscribed by the Constitution. That is to say that to withstand the strictures of the Establishment Clause there must be a secular legislative purpose and a primary effect that neither advances nor inhibits religion. . . . The Free Exercise Clause, likewise considered many times here, withdraws from legislative power, state and federal, the exertion of any restraint on the free exercise of religion. Its purpose is to secure religious liberty in the individual by prohibiting any invasions thereof by civil authority. Hence it is necessary in a free exercise case for one to show the coercive effect of the enactment as it operates against him in the practice of his religion. The distinction between the two clauses is apparent—a violation of the Free Exercise Clause is predicated on coercion while the Establishment Clause violation need not be so attended.

Applying the Establishment Clause principles to the cases at bar we find that the States are requiring the selection and reading at the opening of the school day of verses from the Holy Bible and the recitation of the Lord's Prayer by the students in unison. These exercises are prescribed as part of the curricular activities of students who are required by law to attend school. They are held in the

school buildings under the supervision and with the participation of teachers employed in those schools. None of these factors, other than compulsory school attendance, was present in the program upheld in *Zorach* v. *Clauson*. The trial court in [*Schempp*] has found that such an opening exercise is a religious ceremony and was intended by the State to be so. We agree with the trial court's finding as to the religious character of the exercises. Given that finding the exercises and the law requiring them are in violation of the Establishment Clause.

There is no such specific finding as to the religious character of the exercises in [*Murray*], and the State contends (as does the State in [*Schempp*]) that the program is an effort to extend its benefits to all public school children without regard to their religious belief. Included within its secular purposes, it says, are the promotion of moral values, the contradiction to the materialistic trends of our times, the perpetuation of our institutions and the teaching of literature. The case came up on demurrer, of course, to a petition which alleged that the uniform practice under the rule had been to read from the King James version of the Bible and that the exercise was sectarian. The short answer, therefore, is that the religious character of the exercise was admitted by the State. But even if its purpose is not strictly religious, it sought to be accomplished through readings, without comment, from the Bible. Surely the place of the Bible as an instrument of religion cannot be gainsaid, and the State's recognition of the pervading religious character of the ceremony is evident from the rule's specific permission of the alternative use of the Catholic Douay version as well as the recent amendment permitting nonattendance at the exercises. None of these factors is consistent with the contention that the Bible is here used either as an instrument for nonreligious moral consideration or as a reference for the teaching of secular subjects.

The conclusion follows that in both cases the laws require religious exercises and such exercises are being conducted in direct violation of the rights of the appellees and petitioners. Nor are these required exercises mitigated by the fact that individual students may absent themselves upon parental request, for that fact furnishes no defense to a claim of unconstitutionality under the Establishment Clause. . . . Further, it is no defense to urge that the religious practices here may be relatively minor encroachments on the First Amendment. The breach of neutrality that is today a trickling stream may all too soon become a raging torrent and, in the words of Madison, "it is proper to take alarm at the first experiment on our liberties." . . .

It is insisted that unless these religious exercises are permitted a "religion of secularism" is established in the schools. We agree of course that the State may not establish a "religion of secularism" in the sense of affirmatively opposing or showing hostility to religion, thus "preferring those who believe in no religion over those who do believe." . . . We do not agree, however, that this decision in any sense has that effect. In addition, it might well be said that one's education is not complete without a study of comparative religion or the history of religion and its relationship to the advancement of civilization. It certainly may be said that the Bible is worthy of study for its literary and historic qualities. Nothing we have said here indicates that such study of the Bible or of religion, when presented objectively as part of a secular program of education, may not be effected consistent with the First Amendment. But the exercises here do not fall into those categories. . . .

Finally, we cannot accept that the concept of neutrality, which does not permit a State to require a religious exercise even with the consent of the majority of those affected, collides with the majority's right to free exercise of religion. While the Free Exercise Clause clearly prohibits the use of state action to deny the rights of free exercise to *anyone,* it has never meant that a majority could use the machinery of the State to practice its beliefs. Such a contention was effectively answered by Mr. Justice Jackson for the Court in *West Virginia Board of Education* v. *Barnette,* 319 U.S. 624, 638, 63 S. Ct. 1178, 1185, 87 L. Ed 1628, (1943):

The very purpose of a Bill of Rights was to withdraw certain subjects from the vicissitudes of political controversy, to place them beyond the reach of majorities and officials and to establish them as legal principles to be applied by the courts. One's right to . . . freedom of worship . . . and other fundamental rights may not be submitted to vote; they depend on the outcome of no elections.

The place of religion in our society is an exalted one, achieved through a long tradition of reliance on the home, the church and the inviolable citadel of the individual heart and mind. We have come to recognize through bitter experience that it is not within the power of government to invade that citadel, whether its purpose or effect be to aid or oppose, to advance or retard. In the relationship between man and religion, the State is firmly committed to a position of neutrality. . . .

*It is so ordered.*

Judgment in [*Schempp*] affirmed; judgment in [*Murray*] reversed and cause remanded with directions.

*The concurring opinion of* Mr. Justice Douglas *and* Mr. Justice Brennan *are not reprinted here.*

Mr. Justice Stewart, *dissenting.*

I think the records in the two cases before us are so fundamentally deficient as to make impossible an informed or responsible determination of the constitutional issues presented. Specifically, I cannot agree that on these records we can say that the Establishment Clause has necessarily been violated. But I think there exist serious questions under both that provision and the Free Exercise Clause . . . which require the remand of these cases for the taking of additional evidence.

. . . It is, I think, a fallacious oversimplification to regard these two provisions as establishing a single constitutional standard of "separation of church and state," which can be mechanically applied in every case to delineate the required boundaries between government and religion. We err in the first place if we do not recognize, as a matter of history and as a matter of the imperatives of our free society, that religion and government must necessarily interact in countless ways. Secondly, the fact is that while in many contexts the Establishment Clause and the Free Exercise Clause fully complement each other, there are areas in which a doctrinaire reading of the Establishment Clause leads to irreconcilable conflict with the Free Exercise Clause. A single obvious example should suffice to make the point. Spending federal funds to employ chaplains for the armed forces might be said to

violate the Establishment Clause. Yet a lonely soldier stationed at some faraway outpost could surely complain that a government which did not provide him the opportunity for pastoral guidance was affirmatively prohibiting the free exercise of his religion. And such examples could readily be multiplied. The short of the matter is simply that the two relevant clauses of the First Amendment cannot accurately be reflected in a sterile metaphor which by its very nature may distort rather than illumine the problems involved in a particular case.

. . .

That the central value embodied in the First Amendment—and, more particularly, in the guarantee of "liberty" contained in the Fourteenth —is the safeguarding of an individual's right to free exercise of his religion has been consistently recognized. . . .

It is this concept of constitutional protection embodied in our decisions which makes the cases before us such difficult ones for me. For there is involved in these cases a substantial free exercise claim on the part of those who affirmatively desire to have their children's school day open with the reading of passages from the Bible.

. . .

It might also be argued that parents who want their children exposed to religious influences can adequately fulfill that wish off school property and outside school time. With all its surface persuasiveness, however, this argument seriously misconceives the basic constitutional justification for permitting the exercises at issue in these cases. For a compulsory state educational system so structures a child's life that if religious exercises are held to be an impermissible activity in schools, religion is placed at an artificial and statecreated disadvantage. Viewed in this light, permission of such exercises for those who want them is necessary if the schools are truly to be neutral in the matter of religion. And a refusal to permit religious exercises thus is seen, not as the realization of state neutrality, but rather as the establishment of a religion of secularism, or at the least, as government support of the beliefs of those who think that religious exercises should be conducted only in private.

What seems to me to be of paramount importance, then, is recognition of the fact that the claim advanced here in favor of Bible reading is sufficiently substantial to make simple reference to the constitutional phrase of "establishment of religion" as inadequate an analysis of the cases before us as the ritualistic invocation of the nonconstitutional phrase "separation of church and state." What these cases compel, rather, is an analysis of just what the "neutrality" is which is required by the interplay of the Establishment and Free Exercise Clauses of the First Amendment, as imbedded in the Fourteenth.

. . .

I have said that these provisions authorizing religious exercises are properly to be regarded as measures making possible the free exercise of religion. But it is important to stress that, strictly speaking, what is at issue here is a privilege rather than a right. In other words, the question presented is not whether exercises such as those at issue here are constitutionally compelled, but rather whether they are constitutionally invalid. And that issue, in my view, turns on the question of coercion.

It is clear that the dangers of coercion involved in the holding of religious exercises in a schoolroom differ qualitatively from those presented by the use of similar exercises or affirmations in ceremonies attended by adults. Even as to children, however, the duty laid upon government in connection with religious exercises in the public schools is that of refraining from so structuring the school environment as to put any kind of pressure on a child to participate in those exercises; it is not that of providing an atmosphere in which children are kept scrupulously insulated from any awareness that some of their fellows may want to open the school day with prayer, or of the fact that there exist in our pluralistic society differences of religious belief.

. . .

. . . [I]t seems to me clear that certain types of exercises would present situations in which no possibility of coercion on the part of secular officials could be claimed to exist. Thus, if such exercises were held either before or after the official school day, or if the school schedule were such that participation were merely one among a number of desirable alternatives, it could hardly be contended that the exercises did anything more than to provide an opportunity for the voluntary expression of religious belief. On the other hand, a law which provided for religious exercises during the school day and which contained no excusal provision would obviously be unconstitutionally coercive upon those who did not wish to participate. And even under a law containing an excusal provision, if the exercises were held during the school day, and no equally desirable alternative were provided by the school authorities, the likelihood that children might be under at least some psychological compulsion to participate would be great. In a case such as the latter, however, I think we would err if we assumed such coercion in the absence of any evidence.

Viewed in this light, it seems to me clear that the records in both of the cases before us are wholly inadequate to support an informed or responsible decision. Both cases involve provisions which explicitly permit any student who wishes, to be excused from participation in the exercises. There is no evidence in either case as to whether there would exist any coercion of any kind upon a student who did not want to participate. . . .

. . . It is conceivable that these school boards, or even all school boards, might eventually find it impossible to administer a system of religious exercises during school hours in such a way to meet this constitutional standard—in such a way as completely to free from any kind of official coercion those who do not affirmatively want to participate. But I think we must not assume that school boards so lack the qualities of inventiveness and good will as to make impossible the achievement of that goal.

I would remand both cases for further hearings.

## McGOWAN v. MARYLAND

366 U.S. 420; 6 L. Ed. 2d 393; 81 S. Ct. 1101 (1961)

MR. CHIEF JUSTICE WARREN *delivered the opinion of the Court.*

The issues in this case concern the constitutional validity of Maryland criminal statutes, commonly known as Sunday Closing Laws or Sunday Blue Laws. . . . The questions presented are whether the classifications within the statutes bring about a denial of equal protection of the law, whether the laws are so vague as to fail to give reasonable notice of the forbidden conduct and therefore violate due process, and whether the statutes are laws respecting an establishment of religion or prohibiting the free exercise thereof.

Appellants are seven employees of a large discount department store located on a highway in Anne Arundel County, Maryland. They were indicted for the Sunday sale of a three-ring loose-leaf binder, a can of floor wax, a stapler and staples, and a toy submarine in violation of Md. Ann. Code, Art. 27, section 521. Generally, this section prohibited, throughout the State, the Sunday sale of all merchandise except the retail sale of tobacco products, confectioneries, milk, bread, fruits, gasoline, oils, greases, drugs and medicines, and newspapers and periodicals. Recently amended, this section also now excepts from the general prohibition the retail sale in Anne Arundel County of all foodstuffs, automobile and boating accessories, flowers, toilet goods, hospital supplies and souvenirs. It now further provides that any retail establishment in Anne Arundel County which does not employ more than one person other than the owner may operate on Sunday.

Although appellants were indicted only under section 521, in order properly to consider several of the broad constitutional contentions, we must examine the whole body of Maryland Sunday laws. Several sections of the Maryland statutes are particularly relevant to evaluation of the issues presented. Section 492 of Md. Ann. Code, Art. 27, forbids all persons from doing any work or bodily labor on Sunday and forbids permitting children or servants to work on that day or to engage in fishing, hunting and unlawful pastimes or recreations. The section excepts all works of necessity and charity. Section 522 of [that article] disallows the opening or use of any dancing saloon, opera house, bowling alley or barber shop on Sunday. However, in addition to the exceptions noted above, . . . Section 509, exempts, for Anne Arundel County, the Sunday operation of any bathing beach, bathhouse, dancing saloon and amusement park, and activities incident thereto and retail sales of merchandise customarily sold at, or incidental to, the operation of the aforesaid occupations and businesses. . . .

The remaining statutory sections concern a myriad of exceptions for various counties, districts of counties, cities and towns throughout the State. Among the activities allowed in certain areas on Sunday are such sports as football, baseball, golf, tennis, bowling, croquet, basketball, lacrosse, soccer, hockey, swimming, softball, boating, fishing, skating, horseback riding, stock car racing and pool or billiards. Other immunized activities permitted in some regions of the State include group singing or playing of musical instruments; the exhibition of motion pictures; dancing; the operation of recreation centers, picnic grounds, swimming pools, skating rinks and miniature golf courses.

. . .

Appellants argue that the Maryland statutes violate the "Equal Protection" Clause of the Fourteenth Amendment on several counts. First, they contend that the classifications contained in the statutes concerning which commodities may or may not be sold on Sunday are without rational and substantial relation to the object of the legislation. Specifically, appellants allege that the statutory exemptions for the Sunday sale of the merchandise mentioned above render arbitrary the statute under which they were convicted.

. . .

It would seem that a legislature could reasonably find that the Sunday sale of the exempted commodities was necessary either for the health of the populace or for the enhancement of the recreational atmosphere of the day—that a family which takes a Sunday ride into the country will need gasoline for the automobile and may find pleasant a soft drink or fresh fruit; that those who go to the beach may wish ice cream or some other item normally sold there, that some people will prefer alcoholic beverages or games of chance to add to their recreation; that newspapers and drug products should always be available to the public.

. . .

Secondly, appellants contend that the statutory arrangement which permits only certain Anne Arundel County retailers to sell merchandise essential to, or customarily sold at, or incidental to, the operation of bathing beaches, amusement parks et cetera is contrary to the "Equal Protection" Clause because it discriminates unreasonably against retailers in other Maryland counties. But we have held that the Equal Protection Clause relates to equality between persons as such, rather than between areas and that territorial uniformity is not a constitutional prerequisite. With particular reference to the State of Maryland, we have noted that the prescription of different substantive offenses in different counties is generally a matter for legislative discretion. We find no invidious discrimination here. . . .

Thirdly, appellants contend that this same statutory provision . . . violates the "Equal Protection" Clause because it permits only certain merchants within Anne Arundel County (operators of bathing beaches and amusement parks et cetera) to sell merchandise customarily sold at these places while forbidding sale by other vendors of this merchandise, such as appellants' employer. Here again, it would seem that a legislature could reasonably find that these commodities, necessary for the health and recreation of its citizens, should only be sold on Sunday by those vendors at the locations where the commodities are most likely to be immediately put to use. Such a determination would seem to serve the consuming public and at the same time secure Sunday rest for those employees, like appellants, of all other retail establishments. In addition, the enforcement problems which would accrue if large retail establishments, like appellants' employer, were permitted to remain open on Sunday but were restricted to the sale of the merchandise in question would be far greater than the problem accruing if only beach and amusement park vendors were exempted.

. . .

The final questions for decision are whether the Maryland Sunday Closing Laws conflict with the Federal Constitution's provisions for religious liberty. First, appellants contend here that the statutes applicable to Anne Arundel County violate the constitutional guarantee of freedom of religion in that the statutes' effect is to prohibit the free exercise of religion in contravention of the First Amendment, made applicable to the States by the Fourteenth Amendment. But appellants allege only economic injury to themselves; they do not allege any infringement of their own religious freedoms due to Sunday closing. In fact, the record is silent as to what appellants' religious beliefs are. Since the general rule is that "a litigant may only assert his own constitutional rights or immunities," . . . we hold that appellants have no standing to raise this contention. . . .

Secondly, appellants contend that the statutes violate the guarantee of separation of church and state in that the statutes are laws respecting an establishment of religion contrary to the First Amendment, made applicable to the States by the Fourteenth Amendment. . . .

The essence of appellants' "establishment" argument is that Sunday is the Sabbath day of the predominant Christian sects; that the purpose of the enforced stoppage of labor on that day is to facilitate and encourage church attendance; that the purpose of setting Sunday as a day of universal rest is to induce people with no religion or people with marginal religious beliefs to join the predominant Christian sects; that the purpose of the atmosphere of tranquility created by Sunday closing is to aid the conduct of church services and religious observance of the sacred day. In substantiating their "establishment" argument, appellants rely on the wording of the present Maryland statutes, on earlier versions of the current Sunday laws and on prior judicial characterizations of these laws by the Maryland Court of Appeals. Although only the constitutionality of section 521, the section under which appellants have been convicted, is immediately before us in this litigation, inquiry into the history of Sunday Closing Laws in our country, in addition to an examination of the Maryland Sunday closing statutes in their entirety and of their history, is relevant to the decision of whether the Maryland Sunday law in question is one respecting an establishment of religion. There is no dispute that the original laws which dealt with Sunday labor were motivated by religious forces. But what we must decide is whether present Sunday legislation, having undergone extensive changes from the earliest forms, still retains its religious character.

Sunday Closing Laws go far back into American history, having been brought to the colonies with a background of English legislation dating to the thirteenth century. . . .

(Here follows a summary of some of that legislation.)
. . . Observance of the . . . language [of those laws] . . . reveals clearly that the English Sunday legislation was in aid of the established church.

The American colonial Sunday restrictions arose soon after settlement. Starting in 1650, the Plymouth Colony proscribed servile work, unnecessary travelling, sports, and the sale of alcoholic beverages on the Lord's day and enacted laws concerning church attendance. The Massachusetts Bay Colony and the Connecticut and New Haven Colonies enacted similar prohibitions, some even earlier in the seventeenth century. The religious orientation of the colonial statutes was equally apparent. For example, a 1629 Massachusetts Bay instruction began, "And to the end the Sabbath may be celebrated in a religious manner. . . ." A 1653 enactment spoke of Sunday activities "which things

tend much to the dishonor of God, the reproach of religion, and the profanation of his holy Sabbath, the sanctification whereof is sometimes put for all duties immediately respecting the service of God. . . ." These laws persevered after the Revolution and, at about the time of the First Amendment's adoption, each of the colonies had laws of some sort restricting Sunday labor. . . .

But despite the strongly religious origin of these laws, beginning before the eighteenth century nonreligious arguments for Sunday closing began to be heard more distinctly and the statutes began to lose some of their totally religious flavor. . . . With the advent of the First Amendment, the colonial provisions requiring church attendance were soon repealed. . . .

More recently, further secular justifications have been advanced for making Sunday a day of rest, a day when people may recover from the labors of the week just passed and may physically and mentally prepare for the week's work to come. . . .

The proponents of Sunday closing legislation are no longer exclusively representatives of religious interests. Recent New Jersey Sunday legislation was supported by labor groups and trade associations. . . ; modern English Sunday legislation was promoted by the National Chamber of Trade, the Drapers' Chamber of Trade, and the National Union of Shop Assistants. . . .

Throughout the years, state legislatures have modified, deleted from and added to their Sunday statutes. . . . Almost every State in our country presently has some type of Sunday regulation and over forty possess a relatively comprehensive system. . . . Some of our States now enforce their Sunday legislation through Departments of Labor. . . .

Moreover, litigation over Sunday closing laws is not novel. Scores of cases may be found in the state appellate courts relating to sundry phases of Sunday enactments. Religious objections have been raised there on numerous occasions but sustained only once, in *Ex parte Newman*, 9 Cal. 502 (1858); and that decision was overruled three years later, in *Ex parte Andrews*, 18 Cal. 678. A substantial number of cases in varying postures bearing on state Sunday legislation have reached this Court. Although none raising the issues now presented have gained plenary hearing, language used in some of these cases further evidences the evolution of Sunday laws as temporal statutes.

. . .

Before turning to the Maryland legislation now here under attack, an investigation of what historical position Sunday Closing Laws have occupied with reference to the First Amendment should be undertaken. . . .

This Court has considered the happenings surrounding the Virginia General Assembly's enactment of "An act for establishing religious freedom," . . . written by Thomas Jefferson and sponsored by James Madison, as best reflecting the long and intensive struggle for religious freedom in America, as particularly relevant in the search for the First Amendment's meaning. . . . In 1776, nine years before the bill's passage, Madison co-authored Virginia's Declaration of Rights which provided, *inter alia,* that "all men are equally entitled to the free exercise of religion, according to the dictates of conscience. . . ." . . . Virginia had had Sunday legislation since early in the seventeenth century. . . . Madison had sought also to have the Declaration expressly condemn the existing Virginia establishment. This

hope was finally realized when "A Bill for Establishing Religious Freedom" was passed in 1785. In this same year, Madison presented to Virginia legislators "A Bill for Punishing . . . Sabbath Breakers" which provided in part:

If any person on Sunday shall himself be found labouring at his own or any other trade or calling, or shall employ his apprentices, servants or slaves in labour, or other business, except it be in the ordinary household offices of daily necessity, or other work of necessity or charity, he shall forfeit the sum of ten shillings for every such offence, deeming every apprentice, servant, or slave so employed, and every day he shall be so employed as constituting a distinct offence.

This became law the following year and remained during the time that Madison fought for the First Amendment in the Congress. . . . In 1799, Virginia pronounced "An act for establishing religious freedom" as "a true exposition of the principles of the bill of rights and constitution," and repealed all subsequently enacted legislation deemed inconsistent with it. 2 Shepherd, Statutes at Large of Virginia, 149. Virginia's statute banning Sunday labor stood.

. . .

. . . [Over the years this Court] has found that the First and Fourteenth Amendments afford protection against religious establishment far more extensive than merely to forbid a national or state church. . . .

However, it is equally true that the "Establishment" Clause does not ban federal or state regulation of conduct whose reason or effect merely happens to coincide or harmonize with the tenets of some or all religions. In many instances, the Congress or state legislatures conclude that the general welfare of society, wholly apart from any religious considerations, demands such regulation. Thus, for temporal purposes, murder is illegal. And the fact that this agrees with the dictates of the Judaeo-Christian religions while it may disagree with others does not invalidate the regulation. So too with the questions of adultery and polygamy. . . . The same could be said of theft, fraud, etc., because those offenses were also proscribed in the Decalogue.

. . .

In the light of the evolution of our Sunday Closing Laws through the centuries, and of their more or less recent emphasis upon secular considerations, it is not difficult to discern that as presently written and administered, most of them, at least, are of a secular rather than of a religious character, and that presently they bear no relationship to establishment of religion as those words are used in the Constitution of the United States. Throughout this century and longer, both the federal and state governments have oriented their activities very largely toward improvement of the health, safety, recreation and general well-being of our citizens. Numerous laws affecting public health, safety factors in industry, laws affecting hours and conditions of labor of women and children, week-end diversion at parks and beaches, and cultural activities of various kinds, now point the way toward the good life for all. Sunday Closing Laws, like those before us, have become part and parcel of this great governmental concern wholly apart from their original purposes or connotations. The present purpose and effect of most of them is to provide a uniform day of rest for all citizens; the fact that this day is Sunday, a day of particular significance for the dominant Christian sects, does not bar the State from achieving its secular goals. To say

that the States cannot prescribe Sunday as a day of rest for these purposes solely because centuries ago such laws had their genesis in religion would give a constitutional interpretation of hostility to the public welfare rather than one of mere separation of church and State.

We now reach the Maryland statutes under review. The title of the major series of sections of the Maryland Code dealing with Sunday closing—Art. 27, sections 492–534G—is "Sabbath Breaking"; section 492 proscribes work or bodily labor on the "Lord's day," and forbids persons to "profane the Lord's day" by gaming, fishing et cetera; section 522 refers to Sunday as the "Sabbath day." . . .

The predecessors of the existing Maryland Sunday laws are undeniably religious in origin. The first Maryland statute dealing with Sunday activities, enacted in 1649, was entitled "An Act concerning Religion." . . . A 1692 statute entitled "An Act for the Service of Almighty God and the Establishment of the Protestant Religion within this Province" . . . , after first stating the importance of keeping the Lord's Day holy and sanctified and expressing concern with the breach of its observance throughout the State, then enacted a Sunday labor prohibition which was the obvious precursor of the present section 492. There was a re-enactment in 1696 entitled "An Act for Sanctifying & keeping holy the Lord's Day Commonly called Sunday." . . . By 1723, the Sabbath-breaking section of the statute assumed the present form of section 492, omitting the specific prohibition against Sunday swearing and the patently religiously motivated title. . . .

There are judicial statements in early Maryland decisions which tend to support appellants' position. . . .

Considering the language and operative effect of the current statutes, we no longer find the blanket prohibition against Sunday work or bodily labor. To the contrary, we find that section 521 of Art. 27, the section which appellants violated, permits the Sunday sale of tobaccos and sweets and a long list of sundry articles . . . ; [it] permits the Sunday operation of bathing beaches, amusement parks and similar facilities; . . . [it] permits the Sunday sale of alcoholic beverages, products strictly forbidden by predecessor statutes; we are told that Anne Arundel County allows Sunday bingo and the Sunday playing of pinball machines and slot machines, activities generally condemned by prior Maryland Sunday legislation. Certainly, these are not works of charity or necessity. Section 521's current stipulation that shops with only one employee may remain open on Sunday does not coincide with a religious purpose. These provisions, along with those which permit various sports and entertainments on Sunday, seem clearly to be fashioned for the purpose of providing a Sunday atmosphere of recreation, cheerfulness, repose and enjoyment. Coupled with the general proscription against other types of work, we believe that the air of the day is one of relaxation rather than one of religion.

The existing Maryland laws [therefore] are not simply verbatim re-enactments of their religiously oriented antecedents. . . .

Finally, the relevant pronouncements of the Maryland Court of Appeals dispel any argument that the statutes' announced purpose is religious. In *Miller* v. *Maryland,* 124 Md. 385, 92 A. 842 (1914), the court had before it a Baltimore ordinance prohibiting Sunday baseball. The court said . . . in its decision in . . . [that]

case: "The legislative plan is plain. It is to compel a day of rest from work, permitting only activities which are necessary or recreational." . . . [W]e accept the State Supreme Court's determination that the statutes' present purpose and effect is not to aid religion but to set aside a day of rest and recreation.

But this does not answer all of appellants' contentions. We are told that the State has other means at its disposal to accomplish its secular purpose, other courses that would not even remotely or incidently give state aid to religion. On this basis, we are asked to hold these statutes invalid on the ground that the State's power to regulate conduct in the public interest may only be executed in a way that does not unduly or unnecessarily infringe upon the religious provisions of the First Amendment. . . . However relevant this argument may be, we believe that the factual basis on which it rests is not supportable. It is true that if the State's interest were simply to provide for its citizens a periodic respite from work, a regulation demanding that everyone rest one day in seven, leaving the choice of the day to the individual, would suffice.

However, the State's purpose is not merely to provide a one-day-in-seven work stoppage. In addition to this, the State seeks to set one day apart from all others as a day of rest, repose, recreation and tranquility—a day which all members of the family and community have the opportunity to spend and enjoy together, a day on which there exists relative quiet and disassociation from the everyday intensity of commercial activities, a day on which people may visit friends and relatives who are not available during working days.

Obviously, a State is empowered to

determine that a rest-one-day-in-seven statute would not accomplish this purpose; that it would not provide for a general cessation of activity, a special atmosphere of tranquility, a day which all members of the family or friends and relatives might spend together. Furthermore, it seems plain that the problems involved in enforcing such a provision would be exceedingly more difficult than those in enforcing a common-day-of-rest provision.

Moreover, it is common knowledge that the first day of the week has come to have special significance as a rest day in this country. People of all religions and people with no religion regard Sunday as a time for family activity, for visiting friends and relatives, for late sleeping, for passive and active entertainments, for dining out, and the like. . . . Sunday is a day apart from all others. The cause is irrelevant; the fact exists. It would seem unrealistic for enforcement purposes and perhaps detrimental to the general welfare to require a State to choose a common day of rest other than that which most persons would select of their own accord. For these reasons, we hold that the Maryland statutes are not laws respecting an establishment of religion.

. . .

Accordingly, the decision is
*Affirmed.*

*Separate opinion of* Mr. Justice Frankfurter, *whom* Mr. Justice Harlan *joins.*[1]

. . .

Innumerable civil regulations enforce conduct which harmonizes with religious canons. State prohibitions of

[1] This opinion applies also to *Two Guys From Harrison-Allentown, Inc.,* v. *McGinley*; *Braunfeld* v. *Brown*; and *Gallagher* v. *Crown Kosher Super Market, Inc.*

murder, theft and adultery reinforce commands of the decaloque. Nor do such regulations, in their coincidence with tenets of faith, always support equally the beliefs of all religious sects: witness the civil laws forbidding usury and enforcing monogamy. Because these laws serve ends which are within the appropriate scope of secular state interest, they may be enforced against those whose religious beliefs do not proscribe, and even sanction, the activity which the law condemns. . . .

This is not to say that governmental regulations which find support in their appropriateness to the achievement of secular, civil ends are invariably valid under the First or Fourteenth Amendment, whatever their effects in the sphere of religion. If the value to society of achieving the object of a particular regulation is demonstrably outweighed by the impediment to which the regulation subjects those whose religious practices are curtailed by it, or if the object sought by the regulation could with equal effect be achieved by alternative means which do not substantially impede those religious practices, the regulation cannot be sustained. . . .

Within the discriminating phraseology of the First Amendment, distinction has been drawn between cases raising "establishment" and "free exercise" questions. Any attempt to formulate a bright-line distinction is bound to founder. In view of the competition among religious creeds, whatever "establishes" one sect disadvantages another, and vice versa.

. . .

In an important sense, the constitutional prohibition of religious establishment is a provision of more comprehensive availability than the guarantee of free exercise, insofar as both give content to the prohibited fusion of church and state. The former may be invoked by the corporate operator of a seven-day department store whose State-compelled Sunday closing injures it financially—or by the department store's employees, whatever their faith, who are convicted for violation of a Sunday statute —as well as by the Orthodox Jewish retailer or consumer who claims that the statute prejudices him in his ability to keep his faith. But it must not be forgotten that the question which the department store operator and employees may raise in their own behalf is narrower than that posed by the case of the Orthodox Jew. Their "establishment" contention can prevail only if the absence of any substantial legislative purpose other than a religious one is made to appear.

. . .

It is urged, however, that if a day of rest were the legislative purpose, statutes, it is argued, would provide for one day's labor stoppage in seven, leaving the choice of the day to the individual; or, alternatively, would fix a common day of rest on some other day—Monday or Tuesday. But, in all fairness, certainly, it would be impossible to call unreasonable a legislative finding that these suggested alternatives were unsatisfactory. A provision for one day's closing per week, at the option of every particular enterpriser, might be disruptive of families whose members are employed by different enterprises. Enforcement might be more difficult, both because violation would be less easily discovered and because such a law would not be seconded, as is Sunday legislation, by the community's moral temper. More important, one-day-a-week laws do not accomplish all that is accomplished by Sunday laws. They provide only a periodic physical rest, not that atmosphere of entire community repose which Sunday has traditionally brought and which, a legislature might reasonably believe, is necessary to the welfare of those who for many generations have been accustomed to its recuperative effects.

The same considerations might also be deemed to justify the choice of Sunday as the single common day when labor ceases. For to many who do not regard it sacramentally, Sunday is nevertheless a day of special, long-established associations, whose particular temper makes it a haven that no other day could provide. The will of a majority of the community, reflected in the legislative process during scores of years, presumably prefers to take its leisure on Sunday. The spirit of many people expresses in goodly measure the heritage which links it to its past. Disruption of this heritage by a regulation which, like the unnatural labors of Cladius' shipwrights, does not divide the Sunday from the week, might prove a measure ill-designed to secure the desirable community repose for which Sunday legislation is designed. At all events, Maryland, Massachusetts and Pennsylvania, like thirty-one other States with similar regulations, could reasonably so find. Certainly, from failure to make a substitution for Sunday in securing a socially desirable day of surcease from subjection to labor and routine a purpose cannot be derived to establish or promote religion.

. . .

MR. JUSTICE DOUGLAS, *dissenting*.[2]

The question is not whether one day out of seven can be imposed by a State as a day of rest. The question is not whether Sunday can by force

[2] This opinion applies also to *Two Guys From Harrison-Allentown, Inc., v. McGinley*; *Braunfeld v. Brown*; and *Gallagher v. Crown Kosher Super Market, Inc.*

of custom and habit be retained as a day of rest. The question is whether a State can impose criminal sanctions on those who, unlike the Christian majority that makes up our society, worship on a different day or do not share the religious scruples of the majority.

If the "free exercise" of religion were subject to reasonable regulations, as it is under some constitutions, or if all laws "respecting the establishment of religion" were not proscribed, I could understand how rational men, representing a predominantly Christian civilization, might think these Sunday laws did not unreasonably interfere with anyone's free exercise of religion and took no step toward a burdensome establishment of any religion.

But that is not the premise from which we start, as there is agreement that the fact that a State, and not the Federal Government, has promulgated these Sunday laws does not change the scope of the power asserted. For the classic view is that the First Amendment should be applied to the states with the same firmness as it is enforced against the Federal Government. . . .

With that as my starting point I do not see how a State can make protesting citizens refrain from doing innocent acts on Sunday because the doing of those acts offends sentiments of their Christian neighbors.

The institutions of our society are founded on the belief that there is an authority higher than the authority of the State; that there is a moral law which the State is powerless to alter; that the individual possesses rights, conferred by the Creator, which government must respect.

. . .

The First Amendment commands government to have no interest in

theology or ritual; it admonishes government to be interested in allowing religious freedom to flourish—whether the result is to produce Catholics, Jews, or Protestants, or to turn the people toward the path of Buddha, or to end in a predominantly Moslem nation, or to produce in the long run atheists or agnostics. On matters of this kind government must be neutral. . . . The "establishment" clause protects citizens also against any law which selects any religious custom, practice, or ritual, puts the force of government behind it, and fines, imprisons, or otherwise penalizes a person for not observing it. The Government plainly could not join forces with one religious group and decree a universal and symbolic circumcision. Nor could it require all children to be baptized or give tax exemptions only to those whose children were baptized.

Could it require a fast from sunrise to sunset throughout the Moslem month of Ramadan? I should think not. Yet why then can it make criminal the doing of other acts, as innocent as eating, during the day that Christians revere?

Sunday is a word heavily overlaid with connotations and traditions deriving from the Christian roots of our civilization that color all judgments concerning it. . . .

The issue of these cases would therefore be in better focus if we imagined that a state legislature, controlled by orthodox Jews and Seventh-Day Adventists, passed a law making it a crime to keep a shop open on Saturdays. Would a Baptist, Catholic, Methodist, or Presbyterian be compelled to obey that law or pay a fine? Or suppose Moslems grew in political strength here and got a law through a state legislature making it a crime to keep a shop open on Fridays.

Would the rest of us have to submit under the fear of criminal sanctions?

. . .

It seems to me plain that by these laws the States compel one, under sanction of law, to refrain from work or recreation on Sunday because of the majority's religious views about that day. The State by law makes Sunday a symbol of respect or adherence. Refraining from work or recreation in deference to the majority's religious feeling about Sunday is within every person's choice. By what authority can government compel it?

Cases are put where acts that are immoral by our standards but not by the standards of other religious groups are made criminal. That category of cases, until today, has been a very restricted one confined to polygamy . . . and other extreme situations. . . .

These laws are sustained because, it is said, the First Amendment is concerned with religious convictions or opinion, not with conduct. But it is a strange Bill of Rights that makes it possible for the dominant religious group to bring the minority to heel because the minority, in the doing of acts which intrinsically are wholesome and not antisocial, does not deter to the majority's religious beliefs. . . .

The Court balances the need of the people for rest, recreation, late sleeping, family visiting and the like against the command of the First Amendment that no one need bow to the religious beliefs of another. There is in this realm no room for balancing. I see no place for it in the constitutional scheme. A legislature of Christians can no more make minorities conform to their weekly regime than a legislature of Moslems, or a legislature of Hindus. The religious regime of every group must be respected—unless it crosses the line of criminal conduct. But no one can be forced to come to a halt before it, or refrain from doing things that would offend it. That is my reading of the Establishment Clause and the Free Exercise Clause. Any other reading imports, I fear, an element common in other societies but foreign to us.

. . .

## SHERBERT v. VERNER

374 U.S. 398; 10 L. Ed. 2d 965; 83 S. Ct. 1790 (1962)

Mr. Justice Brennan *delivered the opinion of the Court.*

Appellant, a member of the Seventh-day Adventist Church, was discharged by her South Carolina employer because she would not work on Saturday, the Sabbath Day of her faith. When she was unable to obtain other employment because from conscientious scruples she would not take Saturday work, she filed a claim for unemployment compensation benefits under the South Carolina Unemployment Compensation Act. That law provides that, to be eligible for benefits, a claimant must be "able to work and . . . available for work"; and further, that a claimant is ineligible for benefits "[i]f . . . he has failed, without good cause . . . to accept available suitable work when offered him by the employment office or the employer. . . ." The appellee Employment Security Commission, in administrative proceedings under the statute, found that appellant's restriction upon her availability for Saturday work brought her within the provision disqualifying for benefits insured workers who fail, without good cause, to accept "suitable work when offered . . . by the employment office or the employer. . . ." The Commission's finding was sustained by the Court of Common Pleas for Spartanburg County. That court's judgment was in turn affirmed by the South Carolina Supreme Court, which rejected appellant's contention that, as applied to her, the disqualifying provisions of the South Carolina statute abridged her right to the free exercise of her religion secured under the Free Exercise Clause of the First Amendment through the Fourteenth Amendment. . . .

We turn first to the question whether the disqualification for benefits imposes any burden on the free exercise of appellant's religion. We think it is clear that it does. In a sense the consequences of such a disqualification to religious principles and practices may be only an indirect result of welfare legislation within the State's general competence to enact; it is true that no criminal sanctions directly compel appellant to work a six-day week. But this is only the beginning, not the end, of our inquiry. For "[i]f the purpose or effect of a law is to impede the observance of one or all religions or is to discriminate invidiously between religions, that law is constitutionally invalid even though the burden may be characterized as being only indirect." *Braunfeld* v. *Brown* (366 U.S. 607). Here not only is it apparent that appellant's declared ineligibility for benefits derives solely from the prac-

tice of her religion, but the pressures upon her to forego that practice is unmistakable. The ruling forces her to choose between following the precepts of her religion and forfeiting benefits, on the one hand, and abandoning one of the precepts of her religion in order to accept work, on the other hand. Governmental imposition of such a choice puts the same kind of burden upon the free exercise of religion as would a fine imposed against appellant for her Saturday worship.

Nor may the South Carolina court's construction of the statute be saved from constitutional infirmity on the ground that unemployment compensation benefits are not appellant's "right" but merely a "privilege." It is too late in the day to doubt that the liberties of religion and expression may be infringed by the denial of or placing of conditions upon a benefit or privilege. . . . In *Speiser* v. *Randall*, 357 U.S. 513, we emphasized that conditions upon public benefits cannot be sustained if they so operate, whatever their purpose, as to inhibit or deter the exercise of First Amendment freedoms. We there struck down a condition which limited the availability of a tax exemption to those members of the exempted class who affirmed their loyalty to the state government granting the exemption. While the State was surely under no obligation to afford such an exemption, we held that the imposition of such a condition upon even a gratuitous benefit inevitably deterred or discouraged the exercise of First Amendment rights of expression and thereby threatened to "produce a result which the State could not command directly." 357 U.S., at 526. "To deny an exemption to claimants who engage in certain forms of speech is in effect to penalize them for such speech." Id. 357 U.S., at 518. Likewise, to condition the availability of benefits upon this appellant's willingness to violate a cardinal principle of her religious faith effectively penalizes the free exercise of her constitutional liberties.

Significantly South Carolina expressly saves the Sunday worshipper from having to make the kind of choice which we here hold infringes the Sabbatarian's religious liberty. When in times of "national emergency" the textile plants are authorized by the State Commissioner of Labor to operate on Sunday, "no employee shall be required to work on Sunday . . . who is conscientiously opposed to Sunday work; and if any employee should refuse to work on Sunday on account of conscientious . . . objections he or she shall not jeopardize his or her seniority by such refusal or be discriminated against in any other manner." S.C. Code, par. 64–4. No question of the disqualification of a Sunday worshipper for benefits is likely to arise, since we cannot suppose that an employer will discharge him in violation of this statute. The unconstitutionality of the disqualification of the Sabbatarian is thus compounded by the religious discrimination which South Carolina's general statutory scheme necessarily effects.

We must next consider whether some compelling state interest enforced in the eligibility provisions of the South Carolina statute justifies the substantial infringement of appellant's First Amendment right. It is basic that no showing merely of a rational relationship to some colorable state interest would suffice; in this highly sensitive constitutional area, "[o]nly the gravest abuses, endangering paramount interests, give occasion for permissible limitation," *Thomas* v.

*Collins,* 323 U.S. 516, 530. No such abuse or danger has been advanced in the present case. The appellees suggest no more than a possibility that the filing of fraudulent claims by unscrupulous claimants feigning religious objections to Saturday work might not only dilute the unemployment compensation fund but also hinder the scheduling by employers of necessary Saturday work. But that possibility is not apposite here because no such objection appears to have been made before the South Carolina Supreme Court, and we are unwilling to assess the importance of an asserted state interest without the views of the state court. Nor, if the contention had been made below, would the record appear to sustain it; there is no proof whatever to warrant such fears of malingering or deceit as those which the respondents now advance. . . . For even if the possibility of spurious claims did threaten to dilute the fund and disrupt the scheduling of work, it would plainly be incumbent upon the appellees to demonstrate that no alternative forms of regulation would combat such abuses without infringing First Amendment rights. . . .

In these respects, then, the state interest asserted in the present case is wholly dissimilar to the interests which were found to justify the less direct burden upon religious practices in *Braunfeld* v. *Brown.* The Court recognized that the Sunday closing law which that decision sustained undoubtedly served "to make the practice of [the Orthodox Jewish merchants'] . . . religious beliefs more expensive," 366 U.S., at 605. But the statute was nevertheless saved by a countervailing factor which finds no equivalent in the instant case—a strong state interest in providing one uniform day of rest for all workers. That secular objective could be achieved, the Court found, only by declaring Sunday to be that day of rest. Requiring exemptions for Sabbatarians, while theoretically possible, appeared to present an administrative problem of such magnitude, or to afford the exempted class so great a competitive advantage, that such a requirement would have rendered the entire statutory scheme unworkable. In the present case no such justifications underlie the determination of the state court that appellant's religion makes her ineligible to receive benefits.

In holding as we do, plainly we are not fostering the "establishment" of the Seventh-day Adventist religion in South Carolina, for the extension of unemployment benefits to Sabbatarians in common with Sunday worshippers reflects nothing more than the governmental obligation of neutrality in the face of religious differences, and does not represent that involvement of religious with secular institutions which it is the object of the Establishment Clause to forestall. . . . Nor does the recognition of the appellant's right to unemployment benefits under the state statute serve to abridge any other person's religious liberties. Nor do we, by our decision today, declare the existence of a constitutional right to unemployment benefits on the part of all persons whose religious convictions are the cause of their unemployment. . . . Finally, nothing we say today constrains the States to adopt any particular form or scheme of unemployment compensation. Our holding today is only that South Carolina may not constitutionally apply the eligibility provisions so as to constrain a worker to abandon his religious convictions respecting the day of rest. This holding but reaffirms a principle that we announced a decade and a half ago,

namely that no State may "exclude individual Catholics, Lutherans, Mohammedans, Baptists, Jews, Methodists, Non-believers, Presbyterians, or the members of any other faith, *because of their faith, or lack of it,* from receiving the benefits of public welfare legislation." . . .

In view of the result we have reached under the First and Fourteenth Amendments' guarantee of free exercise of religion, we have no occasion to consider appellant's claim that the denial of benefits also deprived her of the equal protection of the laws in violation of the Fourteenth Amendment.

The judgment of the South Carolina Supreme Court is reversed and the case is remanded for further proceedings not inconsistent with this opinion.

*It is so ordered.*

MR. JUSTICE STEWART *wrote a concurring opinion which is not printed here.* MR. JUSTICE HARLAN, *whom* MR. JUSTICE' WHITE *joins, dissenting.*

Today's decision is disturbing both in its rejection of existing precedent and in its implications for the future. The significance of the decision can best be understood after an examination of the state law applied in this case.

South Carolina's Unemployment Compensation Law was enacted in 1936 in response to the grave social and economic problems that arose during the depression of that period. As stated in the statute itself:

Economic insecurity due to unemployment is a serious menace to health, morals and welfare of the people of this State; *involuntary unemployment* is therefore a subject of general interest and concern . . . ; the achievement of social security requires protection against this greatest hazard of our economic life; this can be provided by encouraging the employers *to provide more stable employment and by the systematic accumulation of funds during periods of employment to provide benefits for periods of unemployment,* thus maintaining purchasing power and limiting the serious social consequences of poor relief assistance. Sec. 68-38. (Emphasis added.)

Thus the purpose of the legislature was to tide people over, and to avoid social and economic chaos, during periods when *work was unavailable.* But at the same time there was clearly no intent to provide relief for those who for purely personal reasons were or became *unavailable for work.* In accordance with this design, the legislature provided, in Sec. 68-113, that "[a]n unemployed insured worker shall be eligible to receive benefits with respect to any week *only* if the Commission finds that . . . [h]e is able to work and is available for work. . . ." (Emphasis added.)

The South Carolina Supreme Court has uniformly applied this law in conformity with its clearly expressed purpose. It has consistently held that one is not "available for work" if his unemployment has resulted not from the inability of industry to provide a job but rather from personal circumstances, no matter how compelling. . . .

In the present case all that the state court has done is to apply these accepted principles. Since virtually all of the mills in the Spartanburg area were operating on a six-day week, the appellant was "unavailable for work," and thus ineligible for benefits, when personal considerations prevented her from accepting employment on a full-time basis in the industry and locality in which she had worked. The fact was wholly without relevance to the state court's application of the law. Thus in no proper sense can it be

said that the State discriminated against the appellant on the basis of her religious beliefs or that she was denied benefits *because* she was a Seventh-day Adventist. She was denied benefits just as any other claimant would be denied benefits who was not "available for work" for personal reasons.

With this background, this Court's decision comes into clearer focus. What the Court is holding is that if the State chooses to condition unemployment compensation on the applicant's availability for work, it is constitutionally compelled to *carve out an exemption*—and to provide benefits—for those whose unavailability is due to their religious convictions. Such a holding has particular significance in two respects.

*First,* despite the Court's protestations to the contrary, the decision necessarily overrules *Braunfeld* v. *Brown* . . . which held that it did not offend the "Free Exercise" clause of the Constitution for a State to forbid a Sabbatarian to do business on Sunday. The secular purpose of the statute before us today is even clearer than that involved in *Braunfeld.* And just as in *Braunfeld*—where exceptions to the Sunday closing laws for Sabbatarians would have been inconsistent with the purpose to achieve a uniform day of rest and would have required case-by-case inquiry into religious beliefs—so here, an exception to the rules of eligibility based on religious convictions would necessitate judicial examination of those convictions and would be at odds with the limited purpose of the statute to smooth out the economy during periods of industrial instability. . . .

*Second,* the implications of the present decision are far more troublesome than its apparently narrow dimensions would indicate at first glance. The meaning of today's holding, as already noted, is that the State must furnish unemployment benefits to one who is unavailable for work if the unavailability stems from the exercise of religious convictions. The State, in other words, must *single out* for financial assistance those whose behavior is religiously motivated, even though it denies such assistance to others whose identical behavior (in this case, inability to work on Saturdays) is not religiously motivated.

It has been suggested that such singling out of religious conduct for special treatment may violate the constitutional limitations on state action. See Kurland, Of Church and State and the Supreme Court, 29 U of Chi L Rev 1. . . . My own view, however, is that at least under the circumstances of this case it would be a permissible accommodation of religion for the State, if it *chose* to do so, to create an exception to its eligibility requirements for persons like the appellant. The constitutional obligation of "neutrality" . . . is not so narrow a channel that the slightest deviation

from an absolutely straight course leads to condemnation. There are too many instances in which no such course can be charted, too many areas in which the pervasive activities of the State justify some special provision for religion to prevent it from being submerged by an all-embracing secularism. . . . [T]here is, I believe, enough flexibility in the Constitution to permit a legislative judgment accomodating an unemployment compensation law to the exercise of religious beliefs such as appellant's.

For very much the same reasons, however, I cannot subscribe to the conclusion that the State is constitutionally *compelled* to carve out an exception to its general rule of eligibility in the present case. Those situations in which the Constitution may require special treatment on account of religion are, in my view, few and far between, and this view is amply supported by the course of constitutional litigation in this area. . . .

For these reasons I respectfully dissent from the opinion and judgment of the Court.

## *UNITED STATES v. DANIEL ANDREW SEEGER*

380 U.S. 163; 13 L. Ed. 2d 733; 85 S. Ct. 850 (1965)

MR. JUSTICE CLARK *delivered the opinion of the Court.*

These cases [U.S. v. Jakobson and Peter v. U.S. were consolidated with U.S. v. Seeger and are reported thereunder] involve claims of conscientious objectors under Sec. 6(j) of the Universal Military Training and Service Act, 50 U.S.C. App. Sec. 456(j) (1958 ed.), which exempts from combatant

training and service in the armed forces of the United States those persons who by reason of their religious training and belief are conscientiously opposed to participation in war in any form. The cases were consolidated for argument and we consider them together although each involves different facts and circumstances. The parties raise the basic question of the constitutionality of the section which defines the term "religious training and belief," as used in the Act, as "an individual's belief in a relation to a Supreme Being involving duties superior to those arising from any human relation, but [not including] essentially political, sociological, or philosophical views or a merely personal moral code." The constitutional attack is launched under the First Amendment's Establishment and Free Exercise Clauses and is twofold: (1) The section does not exempt non-religious conscientious objectors; and (2) it discriminates between different forms of religious expression in violation of the Due Process Clause of the Fifth Amendment. Jakobson . . . and Peter . . . also claim that their beliefs come within the meaning of the section. Jakobson claims that he meets the standards of Sec. 6(j) because his opposition to war is based on belief in a Supreme Reality and is therefore an obligation superior to one resulting from man's relationship to his fellow man. Peter contends that his opposition to war derives from his acceptance of the existence of a universal power beyond that of man and that this acceptance in fact constitutes belief in a Supreme Being, qualifying him for exemption. . . .

We have concluded that Congress, in using the expression "Supreme Being" rather the designation "God," was merely clarifying the meaning of religious training and belief so as to embrace all religions and to exclude essentially political, sociological, or philosophical views. We believe that under this construction, the test of belief "in a relation to a Supreme Being" is whether a given belief that is sincere and meaningful occupies a place in the life of its possessor parallel to that filled by the orthodox belief in God of one who clearly qualifies for the exemption.

Where such beliefs have parallel positions in the lives of their respective holders we cannot say that one is "in a relation to a Supreme Being" and the other is not. We have concluded that the beliefs of the objectors in these cases meet these criteria, and, accordingly, we affirm the judgments in [*Seeger* and *Jakobson*] and reverse the judgment in [*Peter*]. . . .

### THE FACTS IN THE CASES

. . . Seeger was convicted in the District Court for the Southern District of New York of having refused to submit to induction in the armed forces. He was originally classified 1-A in 1953 by his local board, but this classification was changed in 1955 to 2-S (student) and he remained in this status until 1958 when he was reclassified 1-A. He first claimed exemption as a conscientious objector in 1957 after successive annual renewals of his student classification. Although he did not adopt verbatim the printed Selective Service System form, he declared that he was conscientiously opposed to participation in war in any form by reason of his "religious" belief; that he preferred to leave the question as to his belief in a Supreme Being open, "rather than answer 'yes' or 'no' "; that his "skepticism or disbelief in the existence of God" did "not necessarily mean lack of faith in anything whatsoever"; that his was a "belief in and devotion to goodness and virtue for their own sakes, and a religious faith in a purely ethical creed." . . . He cited such personages as Plato, Aristotle and Spinoza for support of his ethical belief in intellectual and moral integrity "without belief in God, except in the remotest sense." . . . His belief was found to be sincere, honest, and made in good faith; and his conscientious objection to be based upon individual training and belief, both of which included research in religious and cultural fields. Seeger's claim, however, was denied solely because it was not based upon a "belief in a relation to a Supreme Being" as required by Sec. 6(j) of the Act. At trial Seeger's counsel admitted that Seeger's belief was not in relation to a Supreme Being as commonly understood, but contended that he was entitled to the exemption because "under the present law Mr. Seeger's position would also include definitions of religion which have been stated more recently," . . . and could be "accommodated" under the definition of religious training and belief in the Act. . . . He was convicted and the Court of Appeals reversed, holding that the Supreme Being requirement of the section distinguished "between internally derived and externally compelled beliefs" and was, therefore, an "impermissible classification" under the Due Process Clause of the Fifth Amendment. . . .

. . . Jakobson was also convicted in the Southern District of New York on a charge of refusing to submit to induction. On his appeal the Court of Appeals reversed on the ground that rejection of his claim may have rested on the factual finding, erroneously made, that he did not believe in a Supreme Being as required by Sec. 6(j). . . .

Jakobson was originally classified 1-A in 1953 and intermittently enjoyed a student classification until 1956. It was not until April 1958 that he made claim to noncombatant classification (1-A-O) as a conscientious objector. He stated on the Selective Service System form that he believed in a "Supreme Being" who was "Creator of Man" in the sense of being "ultimately responsible for the existence

of" man and who was "the Supreme Reality" of which "the existence of man is the *result.*" . . . (Emphasis in the original.) He explained that his religious and social thinking had developed after much meditation and thought. He had concluded that man must be "partly spiritual" and, therefore, "partly akin to the Supreme Reality"; and that his "most important religious law" was that "no man ought ever to wilfully sacrifice another man's life as a means to any end. . . ." In December 1958 he requested a 1-O classification since he felt that participation in any form of military service would involve him in "too many situations and relationships that would be a strain on [his] conscience that [he felt he] must avoid." . . . He submitted a long memorandum of "notes on religion" in which he defined religion as the *"sum and essence of one's basic attitudes to the fundamental problems of human existence,"* . . . (emphasis in the original); he said that he believed in "Godness" which was "the Ultimate Cause for the fact of the Being of the Universe"; that to deny its existence would but deny the existence of the universe because "anything that Is, has an Ultimate Cause for its Being." . . . The Board classified him 1-A-O and Jakobson appealed. The hearing officer found that the claim was based upon a personal moral code and that he was not sincere in his claim. The Appeal Board classified him 1-A. It did not indicate upon what ground it based its decision, i.e., insincerity or a conclusion that his belief was only a personal moral code. The Court of Appeals reversed, finding that his claim came within the requirements of Sec. 6 (j). Because it could not determine whether the Appeal Board had found that Jakobson's beliefs failed to come within the statutory definition, or whether it had concluded that he lacked sincerity, it directed dismissal of the indictment.

. . . Forest Britt Peter was convicted in the Northern District of California on a charge of refusing to submit to induction. In his Selective Service System form he stated that he was not a member of a religious sect or organization; he failed to execute section VII of the questionnaire but attached to it a quotation expressing opposition to war, in which he stated that he concurred. In a later form he hedged the question as to his belief in a Supreme Being by saying that it depended on the definition and he appended a statement that he felt it a violation of his moral code to take a human life and that he considered this belief superior to his obligation to the state. As to whether his conviction was religious, he quoted with approval Reverend John Haynes Holmes' definition of religion as "the consciousness of some power manifest in nature which helps man in the ordering of his life in harmony with its demands . . . [; it] is the supreme expression of human nature; it is man thinking his highest, feeling his deepest, and living his best." . . . The source of his conviction he attributed to reading and meditation "in our democratic American culture, with its values derived from the western religious and philosophical tradition." *Ibid*. As to his belief in a Supreme Being, Peter stated that he supposed "you could call that a belief in the Supreme Being or God. These just do not happen to be the words I use." . . . In 1959 he was classified 1-A, although there was no evidence in the record that he was not sincere in his beliefs. After his conviction for failure to report for induction the Court of Appeals, assuming arguendo that he was sincere, affirmed. . . .

### INTERPRETATION OF SEC. 6(j)

The crux of the problem lies in the phrase "religious training and belief" which Congress has defined as "belief in a relation to a Supreme Being involving duties superior to those arising from any human relation." In assigning meaning to this statutory language we may narrow the inquiry by noting briefly those scruples expressly excepted from the definition. The section excludes those persons who, disavowing religious belief, decide on the basis of essentially political, sociological or economic considerations that war is wrong and that they will have no part of it. These judgments have historically been reserved for the Government, and in matters which can be said to fall within these areas the conviction of the individual has never been permitted to override that of the state. . . . The statute further excludes those whose opposition to war stems from a "merely personal moral code," a phrase to which we shall have occasion to turn later in discussing the application of Sec. 6(j) to these cases. We also pause to take note of what is not involved in this litigation. No party claims to be an atheist or attacks the statute on this ground. The question is not, therefore, one between theistic and atheistic beliefs. We do not deal with or intimate any decision on that situation in these cases. Nor do the parties claim the monotheistic belief that there is but one God; what they claim (with the possible exception of Seeger who bases his position here not on factual but on purely constitutional grounds) is that they adhere to theism, which is the "belief in the existence of a god or gods, as opposed to atheism." Our question, therefore, is the narrow one: Does the term "Supreme Being" as used in Sec. 6(j) mean the orthodox God or the broader concept of a power or being, or a faith, "to which all else is subordinate or upon which all else is ultimately dependent"? Webster's New International Dictionary (Second Edition). In considering this question we resolve it solely in relation to the language of Sec. 6(j) and not otherwise.

In spite of the elusive nature of the inquiry, we are not without certain guidelines. In amending the 1940 Act, Congress adopted almost intact the language of Chief Justice Hughes in *United States* v. *Macintosh*.

The essence of religion is belief in a relation to *God* involving duties superior to those arising from any human relation. At 633-634 of 283 U. S. . . . (Emphasis added.)

By comparing the statutory definition with those words, however, it becomes readily apparent that the Congress deliberately broadened them by substituting the phrase "Supreme Being" for the appellation "God." And in so doing it is also significant that Congress did not elaborate on the form or nature of this higher authority which it chose to designate as "Supreme Being." By so refraining it must have had in mind the admonitions of the Chief Justice when he said in the same opinion that even the word "God" had myriad meanings for men of faith:

[P]utting aside dogmas with their particular conceptions of deity, freedom of conscience itself implies respect for an innate conviction of paramount duty. The battle for religious liberty has been fought and won with respect to religious beliefs and practices, which are not in conflict with good order, upon the very ground of the supremacy of conscience within its proper field. (At 634.)

Moreover, the Senate Report on the bill specifically states that Sec. 6(j) was intended to re-enact "substantially the same provisions as were found" in the 1940 Act. That statute, of course, refers to "religious training and belief" without more. Admittedly, all of the parties here purport to base their objection on religious belief. It appears, therefore, that we need only look to this clear statement of congressional intent as set out in the report. Under the 1940 Act it was necessary only to have a conviction based upon religious training and belief; we believe that is all that is required here. Within that phrase would come all sincere religious beliefs which are based upon a power or being, or upon a faith, to which all else is subordinate or upon which all else is ultimately dependent. The test might be stated in these words: A sincere and meaningful belief which occupies in the life of its possessor a place parallel to that filled by the God of those admittedly qualifying for the exemption comes within the statutory definition. This construction avoids imputing to Congress an intent to classify different religious beliefs, exempting some and excluding others, and is in accord with the well-established congressional policy of equal treatment for those whose opposition to service is grounded in their religious tenets. . . .

We recognize the difficulties that have faced the trier of fact in these cases. We hope that the test that we lay down proves less onerous. The examiner is furnished a standard that permits consideration of criteria with which he has had considerable experience. While the applicant's words may differ, the test is simple of application. It is essentially an objective one, namely, does the claimed belief occupy the same place in the life of the objector as an orthodox belief in God holds in the life of one clearly qualified for exemption?

Moreover, it must be remembered that in resolving these exemption problems one deals with the beliefs of different individuals who will articulate them in a multitude of ways. In such an intensely personal area, of course, the claim of the registrant that his belief is an essential part of a religious faith must be given great weight. . . . The validity of what he believes cannot be questioned. Some theologians, and indeed some examiners, might be tempted to question the existence of the registrant's "Supreme Being" or the truth of his concepts. But these are inquiries foreclosed to Government. As Mr. Justice Douglas stated in *United States* v. *Ballard*, 322 U.S. 78. (1944): "Men may believe what they cannot prove. They may not be put to the proof of their religious doctrines or belief. Religious experiences which are as real as life to some may be incomprehensible to others." Local boards and courts in this sense are not free to reject beliefs because they consider them "incomprehensible." Their task is to decide whether the beliefs professed by a registrant are sincerely held and whether they are, in his own scheme of things, religious.

But we hasten to emphasize that while the "truth" of a belief is not open to question, there remains the significant question whether it is "truly held." This is the threshold question of sincereity which must be resolved in every case. It is, of course, a question of fact—a prime consideration to the validity of every claim for exemption as a conscientious objector.

The Act provides a comprehensive scheme for assisting the Appeals Board in making this determination, placing at their service the facilities of the Department of Justice, including the Federal Bureau of Investigation and hearing officers. Finally, we would point out that in *Estep* v. *United States,* 327 U.S. 114, (1946), this Court held that:

The provision making the decisions of the local boards 'final' means to us that Congress chose not to give administrative action under this Act the customary scope of judicial review which obtains under other statutes. It means that the courts are not to weigh the evidence to determine whether the classification made by the local boards was justified. The decisions of the local boards made in conformity with the regulations are final even though they may be erroneous. The question of jurisdiction of the local board is reached only if there is no basis in fact for the classification which it gave the registrant. At 122-123.

APPLICATION OF SEC. 6(j) TO THE

INSTANT CASES

As we noted earlier, the statutory definition excepts those registrants whose beliefs are based on a "merely personal moral code." The records in these cases, however, show that at no time did any one of the applicants suggest that his objection was based on a "merely personal moral code." Indeed at the outset each of them claimed in his application that his objection was based on a religious belief. We have construed the statutory definition broadly and it follows that any exception to it must be interpreted narrowly. The use by Congress of the words "merely personal" seems to us to restrict the exception to a moral code which is not only personal but which is the sole basis for the registrant's belief and is in no way related to a Supreme Being. It follows, therefore, that if the claimed religious beliefs of the respective registrants in these cases meet the test that we lay down then their objections cannot be based on a "merely personal" moral code.

In Seeger, No. 50, the Court of Appeals failed to find sufficient "externally compelled beliefs." However, it did find that "it would seem impossible to say with assurance that [Seeger] is not bowing to 'external commands' in virtually the same sense as is the objector who defers to the will of a supernatural power." 326 F.2d at 853. It found little distinction between Jakobson's devotion to a mystical force of "Godness" and Seeger's compulsion to "goodness." Of course, as we have said, the statute does not distinguish between externally and internally derived beliefs. Such a determination would, as the Court of Appeals observed, prove impossible as a practical matter, and we have found that Congress intended no such distinction.

The Court of Appeals also found that there was no question of the applicant's sincerity. He was a product of a devout Roman Catholic home; he was a close student of Quaker beliefs from which he said "much of [his] thought is derived"; he approved of their opposition to war in any form; he devoted his spare hours to the American Friends Service Committee and was assigned to hospital duty.

In summary, Seeger professed "religious belief" and "religious faith." He did not disavow any belief "in a relation to a Supreme Being"; indeed he stated that "the cosmic order does, perhaps, suggest a creative intelligence." He decried the tremendous "spiritual" price man must pay for his willingness to destroy human life.

In light of his beliefs and the unquestioned sincerity with which he held them, we think the Board, had it applied the test we propose today, would have granted him the exemption. We think it clear that the belief in a traditional deity holds in the lives of his friends, the Quakers. . . .

It may be that Seeger did not clearly demonstrate what his beliefs were with regard to the usual understanding of the term "Supreme Being." But as we have said Congress did not intend that to be the test. We therefore affirm the judgment in [his case].

In Jakobson, . . . the Court of Appeals found that the registrant demonstrated that his belief as to opposition to war was related to a Supreme Being. We agree and affirm that judgment.

We reach a like conclusion in [Peter]. It will be remembered that Peter acknowledged "some power manifest in nature . . . the supreme expression" that helps man in ordering his life. As to whether he would call that belief in a Supreme Being, he replied, "you could call that a belief in the Supreme Being or God. These just do not happen to be the words I use." We think that under the test we establish here the Board would grant the exemption to Peter and we therefore reverse the judgment . . . [in his case].

*It is so ordered.*

Mr. Justice Douglas, *concurring.*

If I read the statute differently from the Court, I would have difficulties. For then those who embraced one religious faith rather than another would be subject to penalties; and that kind of discrimination, as we held in Sherbert v. Verner, 374 U.S. 398, would violate the Free Exercise Clause of the First Amendment. It would also result in a denial of equal protection by preferring some religions over others—an invidious discrimination that would run afoul of the Due Process Clause of the Fifth Amendment. . . .

The legislative history of this Act leaves much in the dark. But it is, in my opinion, not a tour de force if we construe the words "Supreme Being" to include the cosmos, as well as an anthropomorphic activity. If it is a tour de force so to hold, it is no more so than other instances where we have gone to extremes to construe an Act of Congress to save it from demise on constitutional grounds. In a more extreme case than the present one we said that the words of a statute may be strained "in the candid service of avoiding a serious constitutional doubt." *United States* v. *Rumely*, 345 U.S. 41. . . .

When the Congress spoke in the vague general terms of a Supreme Being I cannot, therefore, assume that it was so parochial as to see the words in the narrow sense urged on us. I would attribute tolerance and sophistication to the Congress, commensurate with the religious complexion of our communities. In sum, I agree with the Court that any person opposed to war on the basis of a sincere belief, which in his life fills the same place as a belief in God fills in the life of an orthodox religionist, is entitled to exemption under the statute. None comes to us an avowedly irreligious person or as an atheist; one, as a serious believer in "goodness and virtue for their own sakes." His questions and doubts on theological issues, and his wonder, are no more alien to the statutory standard than are the awe-inspired questions of a devout Buddhist.

## SELECTED REFERENCES

Carroll, William A., "The Constitution, the Supreme Court, and Religion," 61 *The American Political Science Review* 657 (1967).

Choper, Jesse H., "Establishment Clause and Aid to Parochial Schools," 56 *California Law Review* 260 (1968).

Douglas, William O., *The Bible and the Schools* (Boston: Little, Brown & Co., 1966).

Finer, J. J., "Psychedelics and Religious Freedom," 19 *Hastings Law Journal* 667 (1968).

"Free Exercise and the Police Power—Current Developments," 43 *Notre Dame Lawyer* 764 (1968).

Giannella, Donald A., "Religious Liberty, Nonestablishment, and Doctrinal Development," 80 *Harvard Law Review* 1381 (1967).

Griffiths, William E., *Religion, the Courts, and the Public Schools* (Cincinnati: The W. H. Anderson Co., 1966).

Hochstadt, Theodore, "The Right to Exemption from Military Service of a Conscientious Objector to a Particular War," 3 *Harvard Civil Rights—Civil Liberties Review* 1 (1967).

Jones, Edward L., editor, *War and Conscience in America* (Philadelphia: Westminster Press, 1967).

La Noue, George R., "Child Benefit Theory Revisited: Textbooks, Transportation and Medical Care," 13 *Journal of Public Law* 76 (1964).

Lowell, C. Stanley, *The Embattled Wall* (Washington: Americans United, 1966).

Morgan, Richard E., *The Politics of Religious Conflict* (New York: Pegasus, 1968).

Strong, George A., "Liberty, Religion and Flouridation," 8 *Santa Clara Lawyer* 37 (1967).

Sutherland, Arthur E., "Establishment of Religion—1968," 19 *Case Western Reserve Law Review* 469 (1968).

"The Controversy over the U. S. Supreme Court's School Prayer Decisions: Pro and Con," 43 *Congressional Digest* 257 (1964).

# 3. Freedom of Expression, Assembly, and Association

Feiner v. New York     Edwards v. South Carolina

Adderly v. Florida     De Jonge v. Oregon     NAACP v. Alabama

Thornhill v. Alabama     United States v. O'Brien

Ginzburg v. United States     Ginsberg v. New York

Freedman v. Maryland

Speech, press, assembly, and association represent rights that go to the heart of the democratic process. For without these guarantees that process becomes hollow. That process must ensure free exchange of ideas, ensure minorities the opportunity to challenge the majority and its prevailing policies with full opportunity to change those policies and the majority itself. This constant sifting and winnowing process—with constantly shifting majorities and minorities—is premised upon preserving and protecting the First Amendment rights of all of us. To put the matter starkly, this means that to keep the democratic process open and functioning, those we hate must be as fully protected in the exercise of their rights to free speech, press, association, and assembly as those we like. Even in periods of relative calm this is not an easy proposition. And given periods of great controversies, such as those involving civil rights and the Vietnam war—when the pressure on these constitutional rights is severe—the proposition becomes even more difficult to uphold. This applies to those who espouse unpopular causes, who participate in mass demonstrations and parades, who picket, who distribute literature that some think is obscene. Here is where First Amendment guarantees have met and are likely to meet some of their most severe tests. Substantial state interests, such as the preservation of peace and order invariably collide with substantial constitutional interests, viz., free speech, assembly, and association. The intensity of civil rights and the antiwar drives, coupled with the equally intense determination of law enforcement officials and others to maintain "law and order," has exacerbated the problem.

Moreover, as we begin the next decade, another group of Americans —university and college students—are using ideas and muscle to gain more student power, more freedoms, more relevant curricula and experiences, and more changes in academy. Student activists—seasoned by civil rights struggles and antiwar drives—have resorted to similar tactics such as demonstrations and sit-ins to achieve these goals. But faculty and administrators, governing boards, state legislatures, and others have resisted this attempted power grab or at the least they do not think that "coercive and disruptive actions" are the proper way to bring about change in the academic community. In any case, it is reasonably arguable that such conflicts—be they in or outside the halls of ivy—involve the exercise of First Amendment guarantees, such as freedom of speech and assembly. When these constitutional rights hang in the balance, sooner or later the courts—and ultimately the U.S. Supreme Court—become the arenas for resolving (or accommodating) the disputes. Let us take a look at what the courts, especially the U.S. Supreme Court, have done in these areas.

## SOME JUDICIAL GUIDELINES

Although the First Amendment guarantees are couched as absolutes, the Supreme Court has never interpreted them without limitations. The Court has long since tried to distinguish between speech that is protected by the Constitution and speech that is not. In doing so, the Court has developed several tests or doctrines to serve as guidelines. Though judges rather than "tests or doctrines" decide cases that come before them, a brief look at these "tests or doctrines" might help explain how the Court has gone about the difficult task of safeguarding First Amendment freedoms in the face of substantial societal interests, such as the preservation of peace and order.

Perhaps the first test to be adopted by the Court was the "clear-and-present-danger" test. "The question in every case," said Justice Holmes for a unanimous Court in *Schenck* v. *United States* (249 U.S. 47, 1919), "is whether the words used are used in such circumstances and are of such a nature as to create a clear and present danger that they will bring about the substantive evils that Congress has a right to prevent." Though destined to become a sort of "libertarian" test (see *Bridges* v. *California* 314 U.S. 252, 1941), its early effect was to restrict rather than broaden the scope of First Amendment freedoms.[1] Even since its formative years, however, the test has traveled a rather rocky road. This, of course, illustrates the fact that judges rather than doctrines decide cases.

Another judicial guideline used in dealing with free expression problems is the "preferred position" doctrine. Those who adhere to this

[1] For the development and early application of clear and present danger, see Chapter IV.

doctrine believe that the First Amendment freedoms are so important to the democratic process that they occupy—or should occupy—a preferred position in our constitutional hierarchy. Hence, legislation restricting First Amendment freedoms is presumed to be unconstitutional, and courts bear a heavy responsibility to scrutinize such legislation with care. While having roots in several cases in the late 1930s and early 40s, perhaps the first clear statement of the preferred position doctrine which commanded support of the Court majority occurred in *Thomas* v. *Collins* (323 U.S. 516, 1945):

> The case confronts us again with the duty our system places on this Court to say where the individual's freedom ends and the State's power begins. Choice on that border, now as always delicate, is perhaps more so where the usual presumption supporting legislation is balanced by the preferred place given in our scheme to the great, the indispensable democratic freedoms secured by the First Amendment. . . . That priority gives these liberties a sanctity and a sanction not permitting dubious intrusions. And it is the character of the right, not of the limitation, which determines what standard governs the choice. . . .

> For these reasons any attempt to restrict those liberties must be justified by clear public interest, threatened not doubtfully or remotely, but by clear and present danger. The rational connection between the remedy provided and the evil to be curbed, which in other contexts might support legislation against attack on due process grounds, will not suffice. These rights rest on firmer foundation. Accordingly, whatever occasion would restrain orderly discussion and persuasion, at appropriate time and place, must have clear support in public danger, actual or impending. Only the gravest abuses, endangering paramount interests, give occasion for permissible limitation.

The "preferred position" doctrine, thus stated, could be considered as an extension of the clear-and-present-danger doctrine to its outermost limits. In fact, of all the doctrines used by the court, it comes closest to an absolutist position with regard to First Amendment freedoms.

"Legislative reasonableness" or "bad tendency" has been the guideline used by the Court in some free speech cases, most notably in *Gitlow* v. *New York, supra.* Here, in effect, was the reasonable man theory, so widely applied in the economic field, now being applied to First Amendment freedoms. This doctrine or test gives great deference to the *legislative* determination that certain kinds of speech have a tendency to lead to substantive evils and therefore do not enjoy constitutional protection. In upholding a New York statute prohibiting certain kinds of utterances, the Court said:

> By enacting the present statute the State has determined, through its legislative body, that utterances advocating the overthrow of organized government by force, violence and unlawful means, are so inimical to the general welfare and involve such danger of substantive evil that they may be penalized in the exercise of its police power. That determination must be given great weight. Every presumption is to be indulged in favor of the validity of the statute. . . .

And the case is to be considered "in the light of the principle that the State is primarily the judge of regulations required in the interest of public safety and welfare"; and that its police "statutes may only be declared unconstitutional where they are arbitrary or unreasonable attempts to exercise authority vested in the State in the public interest." . . . That utterances inciting to the overthrow of organized government by unlawful means present a sufficient danger of substantive evil to bring their punishment within the range of legislative discretion is clear. Such utterances, by their very nature, involve danger to the public peace and to the security of the State. They threaten breaches of the peace and ultimate revolution. And the immediate danger is none the less real and substantial, because the effect of a given utterance cannot be accurately foreseen. The State cannot reasonably be required to measure the danger from every such utterance in the nice balance of a jeweler's scale. A single revolutionary spark may kindle a fire that, smouldering for a time, may burst into a sweeping and destructive conflagration. It cannot be said that the State is acting arbitrarily or unreasonably when in the exercise of its judgment as to the measures necessary to protect the public peace and safety, it seeks to extinguish the spark without waiting until it has enkindled the flame or blazed into the conflagration. It cannot reasonably be required to defer the adoption of measures for its own peace and safety until the revolutionary utterances lead to actual disturbances of the public peace or imminent and immediate danger of its own destruction; but it may, in the exercise of its judgment, suppress the threatened danger in its incipiency.

. . . We cannot hold that the present statute is an arbitrary or unreasonable exercise of the police power of the State unwarrantably infringing the freedom of speech or press; and we must and do sustain its constitutionality.

In effect the adoption in *Gitlow* of the earlier standard of judicial review, the reasonable-man test, brought it into conflict with the emerging clear-and-present-danger test. The latter gives the judiciary great latitude in determining whether the circumstances warrant restrictions on First Amendment freedoms while the former limits the judiciary to deciding whether a reasonable man could have reached the legislative conclusion that the statute was necessary to prevent substantive evils.

In general the Court has steadfastly held to the view that the First Amendment forbids *prior restraint* on the exercise of those freedoms. Government cannot prevent a speech or publication *before* the act takes place but can take such action as might be appropriate *after* the act. For example, in *Near* v. *Minnesota* (283 U.S. 697, 1931) the Court declared a state statute unconstitutional that allowed a newspaper to be enjoined from future publication on the ground that it constituted a "public nuisance" for engaging "in the business of regularly and customarily producing . . . a malicious, scandalous and defamatory newspaper, magazine or other periodical. . . ." The paper enjoined was a Minneapolis weekly, *The Saturday Press,* which had directed charges against law enforcement officers including the chief of police, county attorney, and mayor. In effect the paper charged these officials were allowing a

"Jewish gangster" to control illegal operations—gambling, bootlegging, racketeering—and were not "energetically performing their duties." Some, principally the chief of police, "was charged with gross neglect of duty, illicit relations with gangsters, and with participation in graft." But by a 5–4 decision, the Court thought the statute authorizing an injunction was an unconstitutional prior restraint on freedom of the press as protected by the First and Fourteenth Amendments. Chief Justice Hughes, speaking for the Court, found that the statute was directed not against publication of scandalous and defamatory statements about private citizens but at the continued publication of such matters against public officials. Moreover, the statute operated not only to suppress the offending publication but to put the publisher under effective censorship as well. The Court found this to be the essence of censorship, which is inconsistent with the constitutional guarantee of liberty of the press. The extent of that constitutional guarantee has been generally, if not universally, considered, said Hughes, to "prevent previous restraints upon publication." He quoted Blackstone with approval: "The liberty of the press is indeed essential to the nature of a free state; but this consists in laying no *previous* [italics theirs] restraints upon publications." Hughes said that "for whatever wrong the appellant has committed or may commit, by his publications, the state appropriately affords both public and private redress by its libel laws. However, the Chief Justice said that the protection against previous restraint is not "absolutely unlimited." "But," he contended, "the limitation has been recognized only in exceptional cases." The Chief Justice said:

No one would question but that a government might prevent actual obstruction to its recruiting service or the publicaton of the sailing dates of transports or the number and location of troops. On similar grounds, the primary requirements of decency may be enforced against obscene publications. The security of the community life may be protected against incitements to acts of violence and the overthrow by force of orderly government. . . . These limitations are not applicable here.

In dissent, Justice Butler made two major points. First, he said that the statute did not constitute prior restraint within the proper meaning of that phrase since "it does not authorize administrative control in advance such as was formerly exercised by the licensers and censors, but prescribes a remedy to be enforced by a suit in equity." Moreover, Butler felt that the state was not "powerless to restrain by injunction the business of publishing and circulating among the people malicious, scandalous, and defamatory periodicals that in due course of judicial procedure has been adjudged to be a public nuisance." Butler concluded:

The doctrine that measures such as the one before us are invalid because they operate as previous restraints to infringe freedom of press exposes the peace and good order of every community and the business and private affairs of every individual to the constant and protracted false and malicious assaults of any insolvent publisher who may have purpose and sufficient capacity to contrive and put into effect a scheme or program for oppression, blackmail or extortion.

Judges weigh a variety of factors in making their decisions. However, when some judges, such as the late Justice Frankfurter, and now Justice Harlan, began to articulate the weighing of interests in particular cases, the "balancing doctrine" began to take on a more special meaning. Those who espouse the "balancing doctrine" reject the notion that the First Amendment should be read in absolute terms—that those freedoms should stand on a higher plane or be preferred more than other constitutional freedoms. They view the judge's responsibility regarding the protection of First Amendment freedoms as no more or no less than that in any other area. Justice Frankfurter's concurring opinion in *Dennis* v. *United States* (339 U.S. 162, 1950) provides a good example of the "balancing doctrine" in operation.[2]

Justices Black and Douglas have been highly critical of "balancing" away First Amendment freedoms. As Black said in his dissent in *Barenblatt* v. *United States,* applying the balancing test is like reading the First Amendment to say "Congress shall pass no law abridging freedom of speech, press, assembly, and petition unless Congress and the Supreme Court reach the joint conclusion that on balance the interests of the Government in stifling these freedoms is greater than the interest of the people in having them exercised."


## SPEECHMAKING, SOLICITATIONS, AND DEMONSTRATIONS

The street corner speaker, the demonstrator, the distributor of handbills, the labor organizer who solicits members, and the man who uses the sound amplifier are all exercising what they consider their First Amendment freedoms. But sometimes these activities run counter to some state law or local ordinance designed to preserve peace and order or some other societal value. The crucial question then becomes how and under what conditions may a state control speechmaking, solicitation, or demonstrations in public places such as streets and parks.

Permit systems have been one way that state and local governments have attempted to cope with this problem. In *Hague* v. *CIO* (307 U.S. 496, 1939), the Court declared unconstitutional a Jersey City ordinance that prohibited public parades or public assemblies "in or upon the public streets, highways, public parks, or public buildings" without first securing a permit from the director of public safety. Here Jersey City,

---

[2] See Chapter IV. Consider also Justice Harlan's opinions in *Barenblatt* v. *United States* (360 U.S. 109, 1959) and *NAACP* v. *Alabama.*

under Mayor Hague, was preventing members of the CIO from distributing materials and holding a meeting to discuss the National Labor Relations Act. The ordinance enabled the Director of Safety "to refuse a permit on his mere opinion that such refusal will prevent riots, disturbances or disorderly assemblage." By investing such uncontrolled authority in the Director of Public Safety, said Justice Roberts, the ordinance can "be made the instrument of arbitrary suppression of free expression of views on national affairs, for the prohibition of all speaking will undoubtedly 'prevent' such eventualities."

It was in *Hague* that Justice Roberts made what has now become a classic comment on the use of public streets and parks for speechmaking, soliciting, and assembly:

Wherever the title of streets and parks may rest, they have immemorially been held in trust for the use of the public and, time out of mind, have been used for purposes of assembly, communicating thoughts between citizens, and discussing public questions. Such use of the streets and public places has, from ancient times, been a part of the privileges, immunities, rights, and liberties of citizens. The privilege of a citizen of the United States to use the streets and parks for communication of views on national questions may be regulated in the interest of all; it is not absolute, but relative, and must be exercised in subordination to the general comfort and convenience, and in consonance with peace and good order; but it must not, in the guise of regulation, be abridged or denied.

Though there was no majority opinion in *Hague* (some of the majority Justices acted on the due process clause, others on privileges and immunities), it was generally assumed in later decisions that the public had a basic constitutional right to use the streets and parks and other public places in the exercise of First Amendment freedoms subject to reasonable state regulations such as protecting public safety. In *Cox* v. *New Hampshire* (312 U.S. 569, 1941) the Court unanimously upheld convictions of Jehovah Witnesses who marched along downtown streets of Manchester without first securing a special permit (license) as required by state statute for "parades or processions" on public streets. Here the Court found that the statute as construed by the state supreme court provided for reasonable and non-discriminatory regulations with respect to the use of streets. Chief Justice Charles Evans Hughes, who delivered the opinion of the Court, defined further the problem of maintaining public order vis-à-vis the exercise of civil liberties. The Chief Justice said:

Civil liberties, as guaranteed by the Constitution, imply the existence of an organized society maintaining public order without which liberty itself would be lost in the excesses of unrestrained abuses. The authority of a municipality to impose regulations in order to assure the safety and convenience of the people in the use of public highways has never been regarded as inconsistent with civil liberties but rather as one of the means of safeguarding the good order upon which they ultimately depend. The control of travel on the streets of cities is the most familiar illustration of the recognition of social need. Where a restriction of the use of highways in that relation is designed to promote the public convenience in the interest of all, it cannot be disregarded by the attempted exercise of some civil rights which in other circumstances would be entitled to protection. One would not be justified in ignoring the familiar red traffic light because he thought it his religious duty to disobey the municipal command or sought by that means to direct public attention to an announcement of his opinions. As regulation of the use of the streets for parades and processions is a traditional exercise of control by local government, the question in a particular case is whether that control is exerted so as not to deny or unwarrantedly abridge the right of assembly and the opportunities for communication of thought and the discussion of public questions immemorially associated with resort to public places. . . .

In *Thomas* v. *Collins* (323 U.S. 516, 1945) the Court declared unconstitutional a Texas statute which forbade the solicitation of members for labor unions without first obtaining an organizer's card from the Secretary of State. The majority considered the registration device an interference with free speech and assembly because of the conditions imposed before these First Amendment freedoms could be exercised. Justice Rutledge, who spoke for the majority, said:

If the exercise of the rights of free speech and free assembly cannot be made a crime, we do not think this can be accomplished by the device of requiring previous registration as a condition for exercising them and making such a condition the foundation for restraining in advance their exercise and for imposing a penalty for violating such a restraining order. So long as no more is involved than exercise of the rights of free speech and assembly, it is immune to such a restriction. We think a requirement that one must register before he undertakes to make a public speech is quite incompatible with the requirements of the First Amendment.

During the 1950s the Court continued its close scrutiny of permit and licensing systems. In *Niemotko* v. *Maryland* (340 U.S. 268, 1951), for example, there was no statute or ordinance requiring a permit to use public parks and there were no established standards for granting permits. There was, however, a "custom" that required those desiring to use parks to first obtain permits from the Park Commissioner. In accordance with this practice, Jehovah Witnesses requested and were refused permission by the Commissioner and the City Council to use a public park for Bible talks. But the Witnesses used the park anyway and were arrested and convicted of disorderly conduct. However, there was no evidence of disorder; "on the contrary, there was positive testimony by police that each of the appellants had conducted himself beyond reproach." Here the Court was faced with a situation where there was "no ordinance or statute regulating or prohibiting the use of the park; all that is here is an amorphous 'practice' whereby all authority to grant permits . . . is in the Park Commissioner and the

City Council." There were no standards; "no narrowly drawn limitations; no circumscribing of this absolute power; and no substantial interests of the community to be served." Moreover, there was evidence that other groups had in the past sought and received permisson to use public parks. Under such circumstances, the Court found the practice of obtaining permits a *prior restraint* on the exercise of First Amendment freedoms, and "the completely arbitrary and discriminatory refusal to grant the permits was a denial of equal protection."

Likewise in *Staub* v. *Baxley* (355 U.S. 313, 1958) the Court held a city ordinance unconstitutional on its face as a prior restraint on freedom of speech. Here the ordinance made it unlawful to " 'solicit' citizens of the City (Baxley, Georgia) to become members of any 'organization, union, or society' which requires fees or dues from its members without first applying for and receiving from the Mayor and Council a 'permit.' " (A labor union organizer was convicted of violating the ordinance in the instance case.) In determining whether to grant the permit the Mayor and city council were to consider "the character of the applicant, the nature of the organization and its effect upon the general welfare." Similarly, in *Cantwell* v. *Connecticut, supra,* and *Kunz* v. *New York,* (340 U.S. 395, 1953), the Court found that permit requirements amounted to prior restraints on First Amendment freedoms. By contrast, the Court in *Poulos* v. *New Hampshire* (345 U.S. 395, 1953) upheld a city ordinance providing a permit system for "open air public meetings" on the ground that "by its construction of the ordinance the state left to the licensing officials no discretion as to granting permits, no power to discriminate, no control over speech."

Demonstrations may also be limited by court injunctions. Indeed, when Nobel Peace Prize Winner Martin Luther King and his followers deliberately violated a state court injunction forbidding them to participate in or encourage "mass street parades or mass processions" without a permit as required by a Birmingham city ordinance, the Supreme Court affirmed their convictions for criminal contempt (*Walker* v. *Birmingham,* 388 U.S. 307, 1967). Though Justice Stewart, who spoke for the 5–4 court majority, admitted that both the injunction and the city ordinance raised "substantial" constitutional questions, he nevertheless maintained that the petitioners should have followed the orderly procedures of the law rather than ignoring them altogether and carrying "their battle to the streets."[3] "One may sympathize with the petitioners' impatient commitment to their cause," said Stewart, "but respect for judicial process is a small price to pay for the civilizing hand of law, which alone can give

[3] However, in another case growing out of the same factual situation (*Shuttlesworth* v. *Birmingham,* 394 U.S. 147, 1969), the Court reversed a conviction for violating the permit ordinance because of the unfettered discretion allowed administrative officials in its application.

abiding meaning to constitutional freedom." However, Justice Brennan, in a dissent joined by Chief Justice Warren, and Justices Douglas and Fortas, bitterly assailed the majority for letting "loose a devastatingly destructive weapon [the injunction] for infringement of freedoms. . . ." "Convictions for contempt of court orders which invalidly abridge First Amendment freedoms," said Brennan, "must be condemned equally with convictions for violation of statutes which do the same thing."

An interesting contrast to *Walker* is afforded in *Carroll* v. *President and Commissioners of Princess Anne* (393 U.S. 175, 1968). There a "white supremacist" organization called the National States Rights Party was enjoined in *ex parte* proceedings from resuming a rally which had been held the night before. In his opinion for the Court, Justice Fortas described the nature of the first night's rally:

Petitioners' speeches, amplified by a public address system so that they could be heard for several blocks, were aggressively and militantly racist. Their target was primarily Negroes, and secondarily, Jews. It is sufficient to observe with the court below, that the speakers engaged in deliberately derogatory, insulting, and threatening language, scarcely disguised by disclaimers of peaceful purposes; and that listeners might well have construed their words as both a provocation to the Negroes in the crowd and an incitement to the whites. The rally continued for something more than an hour. . . . The crowd listening to the speeches increased from about 50 at the beginning to about 150 of whom 25% were Negroes.

In the course of the proceedings it was announced that the rally would be resumed the following night. . . .

It was against the resumption of the rally the second night that law enforcement officials in Princess Anne and Somerset County, Maryland sought and obtained a restraining order in *ex parte* proceedings from the county circuit court. The order, originally issued for ten days and later extended for ten months, sought to restrain petitioners from holding rallies "which . . . tend to disturb and endanger the citizens of the County." No notice was given to the petitioners, and apparently as Justice Fortas observed, no effort was made to otherwise communicate with them as was "expressly contemplated under Maryland law." In any case, the petitioners obeyed the injunction and took their battle to the courts.

The Maryland Court of Appeals subsequently upheld the ten-day injunction but reversed the ten-month order on the ground that "the period of time was unreasonable and that it was arbitrary to assume that a clear and present danger of civil disturbance and riot would persist for ten months." However, on certiorari, Justice Fortas speaking for the U.S. Supreme Court brushed aside the ten-day order "because of a basic infirmity in the procedure by which it was obtained." "There is no place within the area of basic freedoms guaranteed by the First Amendment for [ex parte] orders," said Fortas, "where no showing is made that it is impossible to serve or to notify the opposing parties and to give them an opportunity to participate." Earlier in his opinion Fortas noted that unlike *Walker* the petitioners here had pursued orderly judicial procedures to challenge the injunction.

What about political or religious speechmaking in public places with the use of sound amplifiers? Here is an attempt by the speechmaker to reach a wider audience, but what about the unwilling listener, those who do not wish to be disturbed? In *Saia* v. *New York* (334 U.S. 558, 1948) the Court was faced with a city ordinance that forbade use of sound amplification devices except "public dissemination through radio loud speakers of items of news and matters of public concern . . . provided that the same be done under permission obtained from the Chief of Police." Here the appellant, a Jehovah's Witness, was refused a new permit since complaints had been received concerning his speeches and sermons delivered under an earlier permit. Nevertheless, the lack of a permit did not keep the appellant from delivering speeches over a loud speaker in a small public park used primarily for recreational purposes. He was subsequently tried and convicted for violating the ordinance. By a 5–4 majority, the Supreme Court held the ordinance unconstitutional on its face as a prior restraint on freedom of speech. Said Justice William O. Douglas, speaking for the majority:

Any abuses which loud speakers create can be controlled by narrowly drawn statutes. When a city allows an official to ban them in his uncontrolled discretion, it sanctions a device for suppression of free communication of ideas. In this case a permit is denied because some persons were said to have found the sound annoying. In the next one a permit may be denied because some people find the ideas annoying. Annoyance at ideas can be cloaked in annoyance at sound. The power of censorship inherent in this type of ordinance reveals its vice.

Justice Felix Frankfurter, joined by Justices Stanley Reed and Harold Burton, dissented. "The native power of human speech," said Frankfurter, "can interfere little with the self-protection of those who do not wish to listen." But modern devices for amplifying the range and volume of the noise, continued Frankfurter, "afford easy, too easy, opportunities for aural aggression," and "if uncontrolled the result is intrusion into cherished privacy."

In a subsequent case (*Kovacs* v. *Cooper*, 336 U.S. 77, 1949), however, the Court retreated and upheld a Trenton, New Jersey, loudspeaker ordinance that prohibited use of sound trucks and similar amplifying devices that emit "loud and raucous noises." Justice Reed announced the judgment of the 5–4 majority and, in an opinion joined by Chief Justice Vinson and Justice Burton, accepted the state supreme court's construction of the ordinance to apply only to vehicles with sound amplifiers emitting "loud and raucous noises." Said Justice Reed:

City streets are recognized as a normal place for the exchange of ideas by speech or paper. But this does not mean the freedom is beyond all control. We think it is a permissible exercise of legislative discretion to bar sound trucks with broadcasts of public interest, amplified to a loud and raucous volume, from the public ways of municipalities. On the business streets of cities like Trenton, with its more than 125,000 people, such distractions would be dangerous to traffic at all hours useful for the dissemination of information, and in the residential thoroughfares the quiet and tranquility so desirable for city dwellers would likewise be at the mercy of advocates of particular religious, social or political persuasions. We cannot believe that rights of free speech compel a municipality to allow such mechanical voice amplification on any of its streets. The right of free speech is guaranteed every citizen that he may reach the minds of willing listeners and to do so there must be opportunity to win their attention. This is the phase of freedom of speech that is involved here. We do not think the Trenton ordinance abridges that freedom.

Justices Douglas, Black, Rutledge, and Murphy dissented. Justice Black, in an opinion supported by Douglas and Rutledge, thought the ordinance on its face and as applied constituted "an absolute and unqualified prohibition of amplifying devices on any of Trenton's streets at any time, at any place, for any purpose, and without regard to how noisy they may be." Black said that he was "aware that the 'blare' of this new method of carrying ideas is susceptible of abuse and may under certain circumstances constitute an intolerable nuisance." "But," he continued, "ordinances can be drawn which adequately protect a community from unreasonable use of public speaking devices without absolutely denying to the community's citizens all information that may be disseminated or received through this new avenue for trade in ideas."

What about persons who ride on public streetcars? May music, news announcements, and advertisements be piped in beyond the control of unwilling listeners? How much privacy can one have in public? These questions were raised in *Public Utilities Commission* v. *Pollak* (343 U.S. 451, 1952). Here Capital Transit Company, with the approval of the Public Utilities Commission of the District of Columbia, arranged with an FM station for special programs to be piped in over streetcar radios. The special programs consisted of about 90 per cent music, 5 per cent news announcement, and 5 per cent commercial advertisements. Two passengers thought that this practice infringed upon their constitutional right to privacy under the Fifth Amendment. But Justice Burton, speaking for the Court majority said:

This position wrongly assumes that the Fifth Amendment secures to each passenger on a public vehicle regulated by the Federal Government a right of privacy substantially equal to the privacy to which he is entitled in his own home. However complete his right of privacy may be at home, it is substantially limited by the rights of others when its possessor travels on a public thoroughfare or rides in a public conveyance.

Justice Douglas dissented and Justice Black dissented in part. Justice Frankfurter did not participate in the case since "[his] feelings [were] so strongly engaged as a victim of the practice in controversy. . . ." Justice Douglas' dissent emphasized "the right to be let alone," which he argued, "is . . . the beginning of all freedom." Said Douglas:

The present case involves a form of coercion to make people listen. The listeners are of course in a public place; they are on streetcars traveling to and from home. In one sense it can be said that those who ride streetcars do so voluntarily. Yet in a practical sense they are forced to ride, since this mode of transportation is today essential for many thousands. Compulsion which comes from circumstances can be as real as compulsion which comes from a command. . . .

When we force people to listen to another's ideas, we give the propagandist a powerful weapon. . . . Once a man is forced to submit to one type of radio program, he can be forced to submit to another. It may be but a short step from a cultural program to a political program.

How much privacy can one have in his own home? The door-to-door canvasser has long been a constant irritant to the late sleeper, the night shift worker, the fearful housewife, or the person who just wants to be let alone. Some door-to-door canvassing is protected by the First Amendment, but not all. Noncommercial canvassing, for example, would appear to come within First Amendment guarantees. In *Martin* v. *Struthers* (319 U.S. 141, 1943) the Court was faced with an ordinance that made it unlawful "for any person distributing handbills, circulars or other advertisements to ring the doorbell, sound the doorknocker, or otherwise summon the inmate or inmates to the door for the purpose of receiving such handbills, circulars or other advertisements they or any person with them may be distributing." When a Jehovah Witness was convicted under this ordinance for distributing advertisements for a religious meeting, the Supreme Court declared the ordinance invalid as a denial of free speech and press. Justice Black, who delivered the opinion for a 5–4 majority said:

The ordinance does not control anything but the distribution of literature, and in that respect it substitutes the judgment of the community for the judgment of the individual householder. . . .

Freedom to distribute information to every citizen wherever he desires to receive it is so clearly vital to the preservation of a free society that, putting aside reasonable police and health regulations of time and manner of distribution, it must be fully preserved. The dangers of distribution can so easily be controlled by traditional legal methods, leaving to each householder the full right to decide whether he will receive strangers as visitors, that stringent prohibition can serve no purpose but that forbidden by the Constitution, the naked restriction of the dissemination of ideas.

Justice Reed, for himself and Justices Roberts and Jackson, dissented. Reed said:

If the citizens of Struthers desire to be protected from the arrogance of being called to their doors to receive printed matter, there is to my mind no constitutional provision which forbids their municipal council from modifying the rule that anyone may sound a call for the householder to attend his door. It is the council which is entrusted by the citizens with the power to declare and abate the myriad nuisances which develop in a community. Its determination should not be set aside by the Court unless clearly and patently unconstitutional.

. . . The ordinance seems a fair adjustment of the privilege of distributors and the rights of householders.

On the other side of the ledger, Court decisions also suggest that commercial canvassing is clearly subject to local regulation (*Green River* v. *Bunger,* 58 P. 2d 456; *Bunger* v. *Green River,* 300 U.S. 638, 1937); and (*Breard* v. *Alexandria,* 341 U.S. 622, 1951). The Court held to this view in *Breard* despite the free speech and free press problem raised by an Alexandria, Louisiana, city ordinance against door-to-door commercial canvassing as applied in this instance to magazine solicitors. Justice Reed, who dissented in *Struthers,* now spoke for the Court majority in *Breard.* To Reed, the constitutionality of the ordinance turned on "a balancing of the conveniences between some householders' desires for privacy and the publisher's right to distribute publications in the precise way that those soliciting for him think brings the best results." But Justice Black, in an opinion joined by Justice Douglas, dissented on the strength of the free press guarantee of the First Amendment. Said Black:

The constitutional sanctuary for the press must necessarily include liberty to publish and circulate. In view of our economic system, it must also include freedom to solicit paying subscribers. Of course homeowners can if they wish forbid newsboys, reporters or magazine solicitors to ring their doorbells. But when the homeowner himself has not done this, I believe that the First Amendment interpreted with due regard for the freedoms it guarantees, bars laws like the present ordinance which punish persons who peacefully go from door to door as agents of the press.

Government also seeks to preserve public peace and order through laws relating to unlawful assembly, breach of the peace, disorderly conduct and incitement to riot. But the enforcement of these laws may, and sometimes do, collide with the exercise of constitutional guarantees. Governmental restrictions on unpopular speakers, streetcorner preachers, picketers, protesters, and demonstrators has produced an almost endless stream of Supreme Court cases.

Two of the early cases in this area involved Jehovah's Witnesses. In *Cantwell* v. *Connecticut, supra,* a Jehovah's Witness approached two men in the street, asked and received permission to play, and played a phonograph record entitled "Enemies," which contained a vitriolic attack on organized religion and the Catholic Church. Coincidentally, both men were Catholics and were incensed by the contents of the record. They testified that they were tempted to strike Cantwell, but on being told to be on his way he left their presence. There was no evidence that Cantwell was personally offensive or entered into any argument with the persons he stopped. Cantwell was charged and convicted of inciting a breach of the peace. The Supreme Court reversed the conviction, as Justice Roberts, who wrote the majority opinion, declared:

The offense known as breach of the peace embraces a great variety of conduct destroying or menacing public order and tranquility. It includes not only violent acts but acts and words likely to produce violence in others. No one would have the hardihood to suggest that the principle of freedom of speech sanctions incitement to riot or that religious liberty connotes the privilege to exhort others to physical attack upon those belonging to another sect. When clear and present danger of riot, disorder, interference with traffic upon the public streets, or other immediate threat to public safety, peace, or order, appears, the power of the State to prevent or punish is obvious. Equally obvious is it that a State may not unduly suppress free communication of views, religious or other, under the guise of conserving desirable conditions. Here we have a situation analogous to a conviction under a statute sweeping in a great variety of conduct under a general and indefinite characterization, and leaving to the executive and judicial branches too wide a discretion in its application. . . .

Although the contents of the record not unnaturally aroused animosity, we think that, in the absence of a statute narrowly drawn to define and punish specific conduct as constituting a clear and present danger to a substantial interest of the State, the petitioner's communication, considered in the light of the constitutional guarantees, raised no such clear and present menace of public peace and order as to render him liable to conviction of the common law offense in question.

In *Chaplinsky* v. *New Hampshire* (315 U.S. 568, 1942) another Jehovah's Witness was convicted under a state law for calling a city marshal a "God damned racketeer" and a "damned Fascist." The state law made it a crime for any person to address "any offensive, derisive or annoying word" to another person or call him by "any offensive or derisive name. . . ." In an opinion by Justice Murphy, the Supreme Court affirmed the conviction stating that" . . . it is well understood that the right of free speech is not absolute at all times and under all circumstances." Said Justice Murphy:

There are certain well-defined and narrowly limited classes of speech, the prevention and punishment of which have never been thought to raise any Constitutional problem. These include the lewd and obscene, the profane, the libelous, and the insulting or "fighting" words—those which by their very utterance inflict injury or tend to incite an immediate breach of the peace. It has been well observed that such utterances are no essential part of any exposition of ideas and are of such slight social value as a step to truth that any benefit that may be derived from them is clearly outweighed by the social interest in order and morality.

Another case that could have extended or clarified the "fighting words" doctrine of *Chaplinsky* was *Terminiello* v. *Chicago* (337 U.S. 1, 1947). However, the Court decided the case on another basis. Terminiello, a defrocked Catholic priest, was well known for his vicious attacks on Jews, Negroes, Communists, and others. The instant case arose when he spoke in a Chicago auditorium to a crowd of about 800. An even larger crowd gathered outside picketing the auditorium, throwing ice picks, stones and bottles, and attempting to storm the doors. In his speech Terminiello condemned the conduct of the crowd outside and bitterly criticized various political, racial, and religious groups whose activities he denounced as "inimical to the welfare of the nation." Terminiello was arrested and convicted under a breach of the peace ordinance. The Supreme Court, however, reversed the conviction on a basis that neither party brought to the Court—the trial judge's charge to the jury. The trial judge charged the jury that "breach of the peace" includes "misbehavior" (or speech) which "stirs the public to anger, invites dispute, brings about a condition of unrest, or creates a disturbance, or if it molests the inhabitants in the enjoyment of peace and quiet by arousing alarm." Justice Douglas, who spoke for the majority, read this construction of the breach of the peace ordinance as "part of the ordinance" itself and binding upon the Court. Consequently, Douglas and the majority of his colleagues ignored completely the facts or circumstances of the situation and rested their decision on the fact that the ordinance, as construed by the trial judge in his charge to the jury, was too broad and might encompass speech that is constitutionally protected. Said Justice Douglas:

. . . [A] function of free speech under our system of government is to invite dispute. It may indeed best serve its high purpose when it induces a condition of unrest, creates dissatisfaction with conditions as they are, or even stirs people to anger. Speech is often provocative and challenging. It may strike at prejudices and preconceptions and have profound unsettling effects as it presses for acceptance of an idea. . . .

The ordinance as construed by the trial court seriously invaded this province. It permitted conviction of petitioner if his speech stirred people to anger, invited public dispute, or brought about a condition of unrest. A conviction resting on any of those grounds may not stand.

Justice Jackson, in a dissent joined by Justices Frankfurter and Burton, sharply criticized the majority for ignoring the facts of the highly explosive situation that existed in *Terminiello* and for not giving sufficient weight to the importance of order in the enjoyment of liberty. Said Jackson: "The choice is not between order and liberty. It is between liberty with order and anarchy without either. There is danger that, if the Court does not temper its doctrinaire logic with a little practical wisdom, it will convert the constitutional Bill of Rights into a suicide pact."

Though in *Terminiello* the Court avoided the problem of free speech when a threat to public peace and order is imminent, the problem was before the Court again a short time later in *Feiner* v. *New York*. Feiner, a Syracuse University student, spoke from a large box placed on the sidewalk and used loudspeakers fixed on his car. He was protesting the revocation of a speaker's permit which his organization, the Young Progressives of America, had obtained, and he was also publicizing the new place where the YPA would hold its public meeting. A crowd gathered to hear him, along with two policemen who were sent to the scene because there was a "disturbance." In the course of his speech, Feiner made some critically sharp references to the mayor, the city administration, the American Legion, the President of the United States, and others. After listening for about 20 minutes, the two policemen on the scene, upon hearing some angry muttering throughout the crowd of about 75 people, concluded that the situation had become volatile and ordered Feiner to stop speaking. His refusal to do so led to his arrest and eventual conviction under a breach of the peace statute. The conviction was affirmed by the Supreme Court as Chief Justice Fred Vinson, who spoke for the 6–3 majority, declared:

> We are well aware that the ordinary murmurings and objections of a hostile audience cannot be allowed to silence a speaker, and are also mindful of the possible danger of giving overzealous police officials complete discretion to break up otherwise lawful public meetings. . . . But we are not faced here with such a situation. It is one thing to say that the police cannot be used as an instrument for the suppression of unpopular views, and another to say that, when as here the speaker passes the bounds of argument or persuasion and undertakes incitement to riot, they are powerless to prevent a breach of the peace. . . .

Justices Black, Douglas, and Minton dissented. Black issued a particularly sharp dissent saying that he was convinced that Feiner was convicted for his unpopular views, nothing more.

The *Feiner* case was only a prelude to a number of cases the Court faced in the 1960s when civil rights demonstrators and protesters took to the streets and other public places to press their causes. In *Edwards* v. *South Carolina* the Supreme Court reversed breach of peace convictions of 187 Negro student demonstrators who had marched in small groups to the South Carolina State House grounds to protest segregation practices. A crowd of some 200 onlookers gathered, but there was no disturbance or obstruction of any kind. Accordingly, the Court found insufficient evidence to support breach of the peace convictions. "The Fourteenth Amendment," said Justice Stewart speaking for the majority, "does not permit a state to make criminal the peaceful expression of unpopular views." While Stewart attempted to distinguish *Edwards* from *Feiner,* Justice Tom Clark, in dissent, did not see such distinction. Said Clark: "We upheld a breach of the peace in a situation (in *Feiner*) no more dangerous than found here." Nevertheless, the Court continued to support its *Edwards* position in several subsequent cases. (Cf. *Fields* v. *South Carolina,* 375 U.S. 44, 1963; *Henry* v. *Rock Hill,* 376 U.S. 776, 1964; and *Gregory* v. *City of Chicago,* 394 U.S. 111, 1969.)

Far more difficult questions reached the Court in 1965 in two cases (*Cox* v. *Louisiana,* No. 24; and *Cox* v. *Louisiana,* No. 49, 379 U.S. 536, 1965), arising out of the same set of facts. In 1961 over 2,000 Southern University students converged on downtown Baton Rouge, Louisiana, and conducted a protest rally near the Old State Capitol Building in the vicinity of the Courthouse. They were protesting against segregation practices generally as well as the arrest the day before of 23 of their fellow students who had been picketing downtown stores that maintained segregated lunch counters. The leader of the group, an ordained Congregational minister, the Reverend Mr. B. Elton Cox, was arrested and convicted on three charges: (1) disturbing the peace under Louisiana's breach of the peace statute; (2) obstructing public passages; and (3) picketing before a Courthouse. The Supreme Court reversed convictions on all three charges. The first two charges were heard in *Cox* No. 24, the third in *Cox* No. 49.

The Court voted unanimously to reverse the breach of the peace conviction saying that it infringed on Cox's rights of free speech and free assembly. The Court relied on grounds similar to those in *Edwards,* and as in *Edwards,* found the situation a "far cry from *Feiner.*" The Court held that not only was there insufficient evidence to support the breach of the peace charge but also that the statute as interpreted by the Louisiana Supreme Court was unconstitutionally broad in scope.

The Court next considered Cox's conviction on the "obstructing public passages" charge, and voted 7–2 for reversal. The relevant Louisiana statute provided in part:

No person shall wilfully obstruct the free, convenient and normal use of any public sidewalk, street, highway, bridge, alley, road or other passageway, or the entrance, corridor or passage of any public building, structure, water craft or ferry, by impeding, hindering, stifling, retarding or restraining traffic or passage thereon or therein.

Providing however nothing herein contained shall apply to a bona fide legitimate labor organization or to any of its legal activities such as picketing, lawful assembly or concerted activity in the interest of its members for the purpose of, accomplishing or securing more favorable wage standards, hours of employment and working conditions.

Speaking for five members of the Court, Justice Goldberg said that "although the statute . . . on its face precludes all street assemblies and parades, it has not been so applied and enforced by the Baton Rouge authorities." Goldberg said that "city officials who testified for the State clearly indicated that certain meetings and parades are permitted in Baton Rouge, even though they have the effect of obstructing traffic, provided prior approval is obtained." Goldberg continued:

The statute itself provides no standards for the determination of local officials as to which assemblies to permit or which to prohibit. Nor are there any administrative regulations on this subject which have been called to our attention. From all the evidence before us it appears that the authorities in Baton Rouge permit or prohibit parades or street meetings in their completely uncontrolled discretion.

The situation is thus the same as if the statute itself expressly provided that there could only be peaceful parades or demonstrations in the unbridled discretion of local officials. The pervasive restraint on freedom of discussion by the practice of authorities under the statute is not any less effective than a statute expressly permitting such selective enforcement. . . .

Consequently Goldberg concluded that the practice of allowing such "unfettered discretion" in local officials in the regulation of the use of the streets for peaceful parades and meetings [was] an unwarranted abridgement of the appellant's freedom of speech and assembly. . . ." Justices Black and Clark concurred on the basis that the Louisiana statute ran afoul of the equal protection clause of the Fourteenth Amendment by expressly permitting picketing for the publication of labor union views while forbidding picketing for other purposes.

In *Cox* No. 49 the Court, by a narrow 5–4 majority, also reversed the appellant's conviction on the third charge of picketing before a Courthouse. The relevant state law prohibited picketing or parading "in or near" a building housing a state court "with the intent of interfering with, obstructing, or impeding the administration of justice or with the intent of influencing any judge, juror, witness, or court officer in the discharge of his duty. . . ." Justice Goldberg again spoke for the majority. He found that the state statute was precise, well drawn and that its purpose of protecting the state's judicial system was wholly within the legitimate interest of the state. In general, Goldberg's opinion supported the proposition that the state had a right to forbid what the demonstrators had done. "There can be no question," said Goldberg, "that a state has a legitimate interest in protecting its judicial system from pressures which picketing near a courthouse might create." Despite the principled rhetoric, however, Goldberg and a majority of his colleagues reversed Cox's conviction on the ground that:

[T]he highest police officials of the city, in the presence of the Sheriff and Mayor, in effect told the demonstrators that they could meet where they did, 101 feet from the courthouse steps, but could not meet closer to the courthouse. In effect, appellant was advised that a demonstration at the place it was held would not be one 'near' the courthouse within the terms of the statute.

Goldberg concluded that "under all the circumstances of this case, after the public officials acted as they did, to sustain appellant's later conviction for demonstrating where they told him he could, would be to sanction an indefensible sort of entrapment by the State—convicting a citizen for exercising a privelege which the State had clearly told him was available to him. The Due Process Clause does not permit convictions to be obtained under such circumstances."

Justice Black, along with Justices Clark, White, and Harlan dissented. In his dissent, Black said that he could not "understand how the Court can justify the reversal of these convictions [in No. 49] because of a permission which testimony in the record denies was given, which could not have been authoritatively given anyway, and which even if given was soon afterward revoked." What of mass demonstrations and protest that take place on public properties other than streets? The Court considered this question in two cases decided in 1966. In *Brown* v. *Louisiana* (383 U.S. 131, 1966), the demonstrations did not take place on the streets but in a public library. When the five Negro demonstrators refused to leave, they were arrested and convicted for violating Louisiana's "breach of the peace" statute, the same statute involved in *Cox*. By a 5–4 decision, the Supreme Court reversed the convictions on the ground that there was, in fact, no violation of the statute. As Justice Abe Fortas said for the majority, there was no disorder, no intent to provoke a breach of the peace and no circumstances indicating a breach might be occasioned by petitioners actions. They were merely exercising their constitutional right to protest unconstitutional segregation. However, Justice Black, joined by Justices Clark, Harlan, and Stewart issued a strong dissent. Black said that he did not believe that the First Amendment guarantees to any person "the right to use someone else's property, even that owned by government and dedicated to other purposes, as a stage to express dissident ideas," especially in a library where tranquility is of the highest priority.

Black did not have to wait long for his views to gain majority support. In *Adderley* v. *Florida* the Court upheld the convictions of student demonstrators under a state trespass statute. The demonstrators, students at Florida A. & M. University, had marched to the jailhouse to protest segregation, including segregation of the jail. But Justice Black, now speaking for the majority, emphasized the significant difference between this case and *Edwards*. In *Edwards,* the demonstrators went to the state capitol grounds whereas in this case they went to the jail. Traditionally state capitol grounds are open to the public, said Black, but jails, built for security purposes, are not. The Constitution does not prevent Florida, Black continued, from "evenhanded enforcement of its general trespass statute . . . to preserve the property under its control for the use to which it is lawfully dedicated." People who wish to propagandize protests or views do not have a constitutional right to do so "whenever and however and wherever they please."

Justice Douglas wrote a dissenting opinion in which Chief Justice Warren and Justices Brennan and Fortas joined. To Douglas, the jailhouse, just as an executive mansion, legislative chamber, or a statehouse, is one of the seats of government and when it "houses political prisoners or those whom many think are unjustly held, it is an obvious center for protest."

Are public universities and colleges "obvious centers of protest"? To what extent may university officials regulate student demonstrations and protests on campus without running afoul of constitutional guarantees? In essence these were the questions that faced a California state court in *Goldberg* v. *Regents of The University of California* (248 C.A. 2d 867; 57 Cal. Rptr. 462), a case resulting from the "Free Speech" movement at Berkeley in the spring of 1965. Here the state court upheld the suspensions and dismissal of several students for the use and display of filthy language (four letter words) during protest rallies and demonstrations on campus. This behavior, according to University officials, was against university regulations requiring students to "adhere to acceptable standards of conduct and good taste." While the authority of a public university to regulate student conduct raises a number of constitutional issues, especially those involving procedural due process (see Ch. V, *infra*), the exercise of First Amendment rights in an academic setting is spelled out cogently in the following excerpt from the *Goldberg* decision:

Plaintiffs first contend that they were engaged in the exercise of their First Amendment rights of free speech and assembly in protesting . . . and that the University's disciplinary action taken as the result of their conduct . . . constituted a denial of these rights. Their argument has as its major unarticulated premise that since their purpose was to protest, they had a constitutional right to do so whenever, however, and wherever they pleased. That concept of constitutional law was vigorously and forthrightfully rejected by the United States Supreme Court in *Adderley* v. *Florida* and *Cox* v. *Louisiana*. . . . These cases recognize that it is not enough for the plaintiffs to assert they are exercising a "right" to claim absolute immunity against any form of social control or discipline, for it is well recognized that individual freedoms and group interests can and do clash. . . .

. . . [R]easonable restrictions on the freedoms of speech and assembly are recognized in relation to public agencies that have a valid interest in maintaining good order and proper decorum. . . . Conduct, even though intertwined with expression and association, is subject to regulation. . . . As the purposes and functions of a public university are markedly different from the public institutions involved in the cases mentioned above, we must examine the interest the University was protecting in disciplining the plaintiffs.

Broadly stated, the function of the University is to impart learning and to advance the boundaries of knowledge. This carries with it the administrative responsibility to control and regulate that conduct and behavior of the students which tends to impede, obstruct or threaten the achievements of its educational goals. Thus, the University has the power to formulate and enforce rules of student conduct that are appropriate and necessary to the maintenance of order and propriety, considering the accepted norms of social behavior in the community, where such rules are reasonably necessary to further the University's educational goals.

Unquestionably, the achievement of the University's educational goals would preclude regulations unduly restricting the freedom of students to express themselves. . . .

Historically, the academic community has been unique in having its own standards, rewards and punishments. Its members have been allowed to go about their business of teaching and learning largely free of outside interference. To compel such a community to recognize and enforce precisely the same standards and penalties that prevail in the broader social community would serve neither the special needs and interests of the educational institutions, nor the ultimate advantages that society derives therefrom. Thus, in an academic community, greater freedoms and greater restrictions may prevail than in society at large, and the subtle fixing of these limits should, in a large measure, be left to the educational institution itself.

The question here is whether the University's requirement that plaintiffs conform to the community's accepted norms of propriety with respect to the loud, repeated public use of certain terms was reasonably necessary in furthering the University's educational goals. We note that plaintiffs were not disciplined for protesting . . . but for doing so in a particular manner. The qualification imposed was simply that plaintiffs refrain from repeated, loudly and publicly using certain terms which, when so used, clearly infringed on the minimum standard of propriety and the accepted norm of public behavior of both the academic community and the broader social community. . . . The conduct of plaintiffs thus amounted to coercion rather than persuasion.

The association with an educational institution as a student requires certain minimum standards of propriety in conduct to insure that the educational functions of the institution can be pursued in an orderly and reasonable manner. The limitation here imposed was necessary for the orderly conduct of demonstrations, not unlike reasonable restrictions on the use of loudspeakers (*Kovacs* v. *Cooper*). The irresponsible activity of plaintiffs seriously interfered with the University's interest in preserving proper decorum in campus assemblages. . . . Conduct involving rowdiness, rioting, the destruction of property, the reckless display of impropriety or any unjustifiable disturbance of the public order on or off campus is indefensible whether it is incident to an athletic event, the advent of spring, or devotion, however sincere, to some cause or ideal.

We hold that in this case, the University's disciplinary action was a proper exercise of its inherent general powers to maintain order on the campus and to exclude therefrom those who are detrimental to its well being. . . .

An unusual and controversial state action directed against Vietnam War protests was brought to the Supreme Court in *Bond* v. *Floyd* (385 U.S. 116, 1966). At issue was the Georgia legislature's refusal to seat Julian Bond, a newly elected black legislator and an officer of the Student Nonviolent Coordinating Committee (SNCC), because of statements he made supporting SNCC's opposition to the draft and United States involvement in the war. A unanimous Court rejected the legislature's reasoning that Bond's statements rendered him incapable of taking in "good faith" the required oath of office to support the constitutions of the United States and Georgia, and held that Bond was entitled to his seat. Chief Justice Earl Warren's opinion for the Court focused on the First Amendment. Citing *New York Times* v. *Sullivan,* Warren noted that the "central commitment of the First Amendment is that 'debate on public issues should be uninhibited, robust, and wide-open,' [and that] just as erroneous statements must be protected to give freedom of expression the breathing space it needs to survive," so must expression criticizing public policy be extended similar protection. He concluded that "the manifest function of the First Amendment in a representative government requires that legislators be given the widest latitude to express their views on issues of policy."

## ASSEMBLY AND ASSOCIATION: DEVELOPING THE STANDARDS

In *DeJonge* v. *Oregon* the Supreme Court made it clear that the "right of peaceable assembly is a right cognate to those of free speech and free press and equally fundamental." *DeJonge* was indicted for violating the state criminal syndicalism law. He was charged and convicted with assisting in the conduct of a meeting called under the auspices of the Communist Party. The fact that nothing unlawful took place at the meeting was immaterial, since the indictment was not concerned with conduct at the meeting in question but rather with the fact that *DeJonge* assisted in the conduct of a public meeting held under the auspices of the Communist Party. The Supreme Court reversed the conviction saying that "peaceable assembly for lawful discussion cannot be made a crime." Chief Justice Hughes, in his strongly worded opinion for the Court, hit hard at the "broad reach" of the statute and said that "the question, if the rights of free speech and peaceable assembly are to be preserved, is not as to the auspices under which the meeting is held but as to its purposes; not as to the relations of the speakers, but whether their utterances transcend the bounds of the freedom of speech which the Constitution protects."

The right of assembly of DeJonge was greatly bolstered in 1958 when the Court in *National Association for the Advancement of Colored People* v. *Alabama* clearly recognized that the First Amendment protected freedom of association.[4] Here the Court overturned Alabama's attempt to compel the NAACP to disclose its membership list. Speaking for a unanimous Court, Justice Harlan said:

[4] This associational freedom has been quite relevant in the context of cases dealing with the Communist Party and loyalty oaths. See Chapter IV.

Effective advocacy of both public and private points of view, particularly controversial ones, is undeniably enhanced by group association, as this Court has more than once recognized by remarking upon the close nexus between the freedoms of speech and assembly. . . . It is beyond debate that freedom to engage in association for the advancement of beliefs and ideas is an inseparable aspect of the "liberty" assured by the Due Process Clause of the Fourteenth Amendment, which embraces freedom of speech. . . .

The Court said that the NAACP had uncontrovertedly shown that in the past, revealing the identity of rank and file members had resulted in "economic reprisals, loss of employment, threat of physical coercion, and other manifestations of public hostility." Under such circumstances, the Court thought, compelled disclosure of membership would be likely to effect the petitioner's freedom of association adversely.

Following *NAACP* v. *Alabama*, in *Shelton* v. *Tucker* (364 U.S. 479, 1960) the Court declared unconstitutional an Arkansas statute on the ground that it violated the "associational freedom" of the First Amendment. The statute required every teacher, as a condition of employment in a state supported school or college, to file annually an affidavit listing without limitation every organization to which he has belonged or regularly contributed within the preceding five years." Unlike the *NAACP* case, the Court acknowledged that Arkansas had a legitimate interest to inquire into the fitness and competence of its teachers. Nevertheless, the Court thought the statute went "far beyond what might be justified in the exercise of the state's legitimate inquiry and thus greatly interfered with associational freedom. Said Justice Stewart for the 5–4 majority:

The question is whether the State can ask every one of its teachers to disclose every single organization with which he has been associated over a five-year period. The scope of the inquiry required by [the statute] is completely unlimited. The statute requires a teacher to reveal the church to which he belongs, or to which he has given financial support. It requires him to disclose his political party, and every political organization to which he may have contributed over a five-year period. It requires him to list, without number, every conceivable kind of associational tie—social, professional, political, avocational, or religious. Many such relationships could have no possible bearing upon the teacher's occupational competence or fitness.

In a series of decisions this Court has held that, even though the governmental purpose be legitimate and substantial, that purpose cannot be pursued by means that broadly stifle fundamental personal liberties when the end can be more narrowly achieved. The breadth of legislative abridgement must be viewed in the light of less drastic means for achieving the same basic purpose.

Justice Frankfurter, who spoke for himself and the other dissenting justices, thought the statute provided a reasonable means for a school board to inquire into the nature and quality of its teachers' outside activities as these might relate to their school work. If information collected is misused—such as terminating a teacher's employment solely on the basis of membership in "unpopular" organizations—said Frankfurter, "it will be time enough . . . to hold the application of the statute unconstitutional."

## PICKETING AND SYMBOLIC SPEECH

When Alabama banned all peaceful picketing regardless of purpose, the Supreme Court declared the law unconstitutional as an invasion of freedom of speech. The statute swept too broadly. Speaking for the Court in *Thornhill* v. *Alabama,* Justice Frank Murphy contended:

The freedom of speech and of the press guaranteed by the Constitution embraces at the least the liberty to discuss publicly and truthfully all matters of public concern without previous restraint or fear of subsequent punishment. . . . Freedom of discussion, if it would fulfill its historic function in this nation, must embrace all issues about which information is needed or appropriate to enable the members of society to cope wtih the exigencies of their period.

In the circumstances of our times the dissemination of information concerning the facts of a labor dispute must be regarded as within that area of free discussion that is guaranteed by the Constituiton. . . . The merest glance at State and Federal legislation on the subject demonstrates the force of the argument that labor relations are not matters of mere local or private concern.

This glowing language of *Thornhill,* however, has since been narrowed in subsequent Court decisions. Thus, even peaceful picketing can be constitutionally enjoined if it prevents the effectuation of valid state policies. (See for example, *Hughes* v. *Superior Court of California* 339 U.S. 460, 1950, and *International Brotherhood of Teamsters* v. *Vogt* 354 U.S. 284, 1957). Indeed picketing, the traditional method used by workers to convey their views to the public, involves more than speech; it involves elements of speech and conduct. And the Court indicated in *Hughes* and *Vogt* that "because of the intermingling of [these] protected and unprotected elements, picketing can be subjected to controls that would not be constitutionally permissible in the case of pure speech." But in *Amalgamated Food Employees Local 590* v. *Logan Valley Plaza, Inc.* (391 U.S. 308, 1968) Justice Thurgood Marshall rejected the notion that "the nonspeech aspects of peaceful picketing are so great as to render the provisions of the First Amendment inapplicable to it altogether."

Is the communication of an idea by conduct protected by the First Amendment? In other words, what about symbolic speech? The issue was raised when four persons stood on the steps of the South Boston Courthouse on March 13, 1966, and burned their draft cards as a way of expressing opposition to the Vietnam War. They were tried and convicted under a 1965 Congressional law which made it a crime to knowingly destroy or mutilate draft cards. But burning draft cards, they argued, was "symbolic speech" or "communication of ideas by conduct," all of which are protected by the First Amendment. But the Supreme Court disagreed. In *United States* v. *O'Brien* the Court by a 7–1 vote said it could not accept the position that an "apparently limitless variety of conduct can be labelled 'speech' whenever the person engaging in the conduct intends thereby to express an idea." Moreover, continued Chief Justice Warren who spoke for the majority, when "speech" and "non-speech" elements are "combined in the same course of conduct, a sufficiently important governmental interest in regulating the non-speech element can justify incidental limitations on First Amendment freedoms." The Court found that the governmental regulation as imposed by the 1965 law was sufficiently justified. Justice Douglas, the lone dissenter, thought that the basic question in the case was "whether conscription is permissible in the absence of a declaration of war." He argued that the Court should make a ruling on it.

In 1969 the Supreme Court faced yet another symbolic speech case focusing on the Vietnam war (*Tinker* v. *Des Moines Independent Community School District* 393 U.S. 503, 1969). Here public school officials, under the claim of maintaining orderly processes and decorum, suspended students who persisted in wearing black armbands to express opposition to United States involvement in Vietnam. Justice Fortas, speaking for the Court, viewed the black armbands as peaceful expression of political opinion and thus protected by the First Amendment. The students' behavior did not cause disorder or disruption of school activities, observed Fortas, and "undifferentiated fear or apprehension of disturbance is not enough to overcome the right to freedom of expression." In any event, since school officials had permitted students in Des Moines to wear other symbols, e.g., political campaign buttons, Fortas saw the prohibition against armbands as a method to suppress opposition to the Vietnam War. "In our system," said Fortas, "students may not be regarded as closed-circuit recipients of only that which the state chooses to communicate." Thus, for the first time in its history, the Court ruled that public school students are entitled to free speech guarantees of the First Amendment. However, Fortas was careful to point out that the Court's decision pertained only to "symbolic speech" or speech itself and did not extend to protest demonstrations.

Nonetheless, Justice Hugo Black issued a sharp dissent. He complained that the Court's decision ushers in "a new revolutionary era of permissiveness in this country in which the power of school officials to control pupils is substantially weakened." Black took judicial notice of the timing of the decision and noted that "groups of students all over the land . . . [were] running loose, conducting break-ins, sit-ins, lie-ins, and smash-ins." Decisions like *Tinker,* warned Black, "subject all the public schools in the country to the whims and caprices of their loudest-mouthed, but maybe not their brightest students." He was certain that students were not wise enough to run the public school system.

In *Street* v. *New York* (394 U.S. 577, 1969), a case similar to *O'Brien*, the Court skirted the question of whether a person could be punished for burning or defacing an American flag. After learning that James Meredith had been shot from ambush in Mississippi in 1966, Street, a Brooklyn black, in apparent disgust, burned the American flag that he had always displayed on national holidays. When encountered by a police officer, Street remarked: "We don't need no damn flag." He was convicted under a New York law that makes it a crime to "publicly mutilate, deface, defile or defy, trample upon or cast contempt upon either by word or act" the state or national flag. By a 5–4 majority the Court voted to set aside Street's conviction. Justice John Marsall Harlan delivered the Court's opinion and emphasized the overbreadth of the statute under which Street was convicted. Harlan noted that the judge (Street was tried before a judge without a jury) did not make a distinction between the actual act of burning and the contemptuous remarks about the flag. Consequently, he held that the statute "was unconstitutionally applied [to Street] because it permitted him to be punished merely for [his] defiant or contemptuous words about the flag"—words which, Harlan contended, were constitutionally protected. Even assuming that the conviction could have been based solely on the act of burning the flag, Harlan argued that the conviction should be reversed because a guilty verdict ensued from the indictment, which charged the commission of a crime by use of words and the act of flag burning without elucidation and it is possible that the trial judge could have considered the two acts as "intertwined . . . , [resting] the conviction on both together." Harlan concluded that while "disrespect for our flag is to be deplored no less in these vexed times than in calmer periods of our history," a conviction that may have been based on a form of expression that the Constitution protects cannot be sustained. For, he continued, "the 'right to differ as to things that touch the heart of the existing order,' encompass[es] the freedom to express publicly one's opinions about our flag, including those opinions which are defiant or contemptuous."

The dissenters took sharp exception to the majority's avoidance of the crucial constitutional issue presented in the case. To them, this case was not one in which constitutionally protected expression had been sacrificed to protect the flag; rather, at issue was whether the deliberate act of burning the American flag is symbolic expression protected by the Constitution. In his dissent, Chief Justice Earl Warren noted that the record below indicated clearly that all parties focused on the "flag burning as symbolic expression" issue and so did the state appellate court. Warren argued that where a constitutonal issue is presented to the Court, as this one had been, the Court has the "responsibility to confront [it] squarely and resolve it." He warned that facing the flag burning and desecration issue was particularly pressing because the "flag has increasingly become an integral part of public protests." Indicating his belief that Federal and state governments have the power to protect the flag from desecration, he thought that the Court would have concluded likewise if it had faced the issue.

## DAMAGE TO REPUTATION

In his opinion in *Near* v. *Minnesota,* Chief Justice Charles Evans Hughes emphasized the need for "a vigilant and courageous press" to focus attention on malfeasance and corruption of unfaithful public officials. But when does comment on official conduct lose its character as constitutionally protected expression and become subject to the sanctions of state libel laws? The Supreme Court supplied the answer in *New York Times* v. *Sullivan* (376 U.S. 254, 1964) in reversing a half-million dollar judgment against the New York Times Publishing Company which had been awarded to a local public official by an Alabama court. Paradoxically, the allegedly defamatory publication did not deal with the traditional subjects on which there has been criticism of official conduct, e.g., alliances with criminal elements and malfeasance in office. Instead, the publication was an editorial advertisement on the civil rights movement in the South.

In setting aside the judgment, the Supreme Court applied the brakes to southern public officials who try to stifle comment critical of their conduct in actions involving race relations. Thus, Sullivan's allegation that the advertisement contained a number of inaccuracies and was injurious to his reputation as a public official was rejected. Justice William J. Brennan, who wrote the opinion for the Court, noted that the case must be considered "against the background of a profound national commitment to the principle that debate on public issues should be uninhibited, robust, and wide open, and that it may well include vehement, caustic, and sometimes unpleasant sharp attacks . . . on public officials." With this principle in mind, Brennan held that the crucial question is whether the advertisement forfeited its status as constitutionally protected expression because it contained some false statements and allegedly defamed the respondent. Advancing the proposition that "erroneous statement is inevitable in free debate and . . . must be protected if the freedoms of expression are to have the 'breathing space' that they 'need . . . to survive,' " he concluded that "neither factual error nor defamatory content" nor "the combination of the two elements" can justify removal of "the constitutional shield from criticism of official conduct" unless there is proof of "actual malice."

Jusitce Hugo Black's concurring opinion, supported by Justice William O. Douglas, set forth the absolutist position that the *Times* and the

sponsors of the ad had an "unconditional constitutional right to publish
. . . their criticisms of the Montgomery agencies and officials."

One year later, the Court extended its *New York Times* rule to limit
state power to impose criminal sanctions for criticism of the official conduct of public officials. In *Garrison* v. *Louisiana* (379 U.S. 64, 1964) a
unanimous Court reversed the conviction of District Attorney Jim Garrison of Orleans Parish (County), Louisiana, on a charge of criminal
defamation based on his criticism of the official conduct of judges of the
parish's Criminal District Court. In an opinion supported by five members of the Court, Justice Brennan rejected the contention that because
"criminal libel laws serve distinct interests from those secured by civil
libel laws" they should not be subject to the limitations laid down in the
*New York Times* case. Said Brennan, "[t]he *New York Times* rule is not
rendered inapplicable merely because an official's private reputation, as
well as his public reputation, is harmed. . . . [A]nything which might
touch an official's fitness for office is relevant." He concluded that "even
where the utterance is false, the great principles of the Constitution . . .
preclude attaching adverse consequences to any except the knowing or
reckless falsehood."

Just as in *New York Times,* the concurring opinions of Justices Black
and Douglas once again emphasized that the absolutist position is the
only rule which makes sense.

The Court examined further the scope of the term "public official"
and the meaning of "malice" in *Rosenblatt* v. *Baer* (383 U.S. 75, 1966).
Here the Court reversed a state libel judgment against a newspaper col-
umnist for using defamatory falsehoods in commentary about the performance of a supervisor of a county recreation area. Justice William J.
Brennan held that since the position of "Supervisor of the Belknap
County Recreation Area" was embraced within the term "public official"
as construed in *New York Times,* the instructions to the jury (which
permitted the jury to find that negligent misstatement of fact would
abrogate the commentary's privileged status) were defective.

Regarding "malice," Brennan contended that the state court definition,
which includes "ill will, evil motive [and] intention to injure," was
"constitutionally insufficient where discussion of public affairs is concerned." It did not square with the definition set forth in *New York
Times* which requires a showing that the statement was made with knowledge of its falsity or "reckless disregard of whether it was false or not."

In another dimension of the defamation issue, the Court, in *Time, Inc.*
v. *Hill* (385 U.S. 374, 1967) applied the *New York Times* rule in holding
that a New York "Right of Privacy" statute was unconstitutionally applied to redress false reports of matters of public interest in the absence
of proof of actual malice. The case involved a *Life* magazine article

in which the fictionalized play "The Desperate Hours" was portrayed as a reenactment of the ordeal of a family held captive by three escaped convicts. Taking cognizance of the "exposure of one's self to others [as] a concomitant of life in a civilized community," Justice William J. Brennan contended that such a risk "is an essential incident of life in a society which places a primary value on freedom of speech and of press." He argued that "[e]rroneous statement[s]" are just as inevitable in commentary on "newsworthy" private citizens and events as in commentary on "public affairs." Consequently, Brennan concluded, erroneous statements in both categories, "if innocent or merely negligent, . . . must be protected if the freedoms of expression are to have the 'breathing space' that they 'need . . . to survive.'"

In the companion cases of *Curtis Publishing Co.* v. *Butts,* and *Associated Press* v. *Walker* (338 U.S. 130, 1967) the Court considered whether its ruling in *New York Times* extended to libel actions brought by "public figures" who are "involved in issues in which the public has a justified and important interest." The *Butts* case involved a federal district court libel judgment of $460,000 against the Curtis Publishing Company for publication of an article in *Saturday Evening Post* in which Wally Butts, longtime football coach and athletic director of the University of Georgia, was accused of plotting to fix a football game between his school and the University of Alabama. The *Walker* case was an appeal from a state court libel judgment of $500,000 against the Associated Press for publication of news stories describing the role of retired Major General Edwin A. Walker in the campus disorders accompanying the enrollment of James Meredith at the University of Mississippi.

In examining the constitutional issues presented by these cases, Justice Harlan, who wrote the leading opinion, counseled against "blind application" of the *New York Times* rule. He stressed that "none of the particular considerations involved in *New York Times"* were present in *Butts* and *Walker.* Hence, it was necessary to formulate a new rule of libel which he stated as follows:

[A] "public figure" who is not a public official may . . . recover damages for a defamatory falsehood whose substance makes substantial danger to reputation apparent, on a showing of highly unreasonable conduct constituting an extreme departure from standards of investigation and reporting ordinarily adhered to by responsible publishers.

Applying this new rule to the cases, Harlan concluded that there was enough evidence to support the judgment in *Butts* but that the evidence was insufficient to prove "a severe departure from accepted publishing standards" in *Walker.*

## OBSCENITY

Justice William J. Brennan noted in his opinion in *Roth* v. *United States,* that "sex . . . has indisputably been a subject of absorbing interest through the ages . . . ," and as Professors Lockhart and McClure contend, the subject "has always occupied too important and dominant a place in literature and in human interest to be excluded from the [protection of the] First Amendment. . . ."[5] The portrayal of sex in books, magazines, motion pictures, the legitimate theater, and television is now commonplace. Sex and obscenity are not synonymous, but the various media have the potential for portraying sex in an obscene manner. Hence, governments have instituted various types of regulatory actions to protect the public morals. Statutes have been enacted to prohibit the publication, production, sale, and exhibition of obscene books, magazines, motion pictures, and other matter. Administrative agencies have been established to review and license motion pictures prior to their exhibition. Postal and customs authorities have exercised regulatory powers in prohibiting dissemination of obscene materials thru their channels. Enforcement of such regulations has raised many troublesome questions involving the federal constitutional guarantees of freedom of speech and freedom of the press—questions that have inevitably ended up in the Supreme Court for resolution.

The Court first considered the difficult problem of defining obscenity in 1957. In companion cases arising under the federal obscenity statute (*Roth* v. *United States,* 354 U.S. 476) and the California obscenity code (*Alberts* v. *California*), the Court sustained convictions (in *Roth*) for use of the mails to disseminate obscene matter, and (in *Alberts*) for possession of obscene matter for sale by mail order. In his opinion for the Court, Justice William J. Brennan emphasized that ideas with the "slightest redeeming social importance" must be accorded the full protection of the First Amendment. But since obscene matter is "utterly without redeeming social importance," it is not protected expression. The test, said Brennan, is "whether to the average person, applying contemporary community standards, the dominant theme of the material taken as a whole appeals to prurient interest." While this test was considered an improvement over the earlier Hicklin test that allowed material to be judged "by the effect of an isolated [passage] upon particularly susceptible persons," in practice it opened up a Pandora's box of questions for law enforcement officials and the lower courts. What does the term "prurient interest" mean? Who is "the average person"? What is "redeeming social importance"? Who determines "contemporary community standards" and what is the "relevant community"?

5 William B. Lockhart and Robert C. McClure, "Literature, the Law of Obscenity, and the Constitution," 38 *Minn. L. Rev.* 358–359 (1954).

In subsequent decisions the Court has provided some answers to these questions. In *Manual Enterprises* v. *Day* (370 U.S. 478, 1962), the Court narrowed the sweep of its "prurient interest" test by holding that to be adjudged obscene, material must not only have "prurient interest" appeal but its "patent offensiveness" must be demonstrated. Furthermore, Justice Harlan held that the two elements "must conjoin" to support a finding of obscenity. Applying this test to reverse an obscenity finding of postal authorities, Harlan contended that the magazines in question (containing photographs of nude males), while "dismally unpleasant, uncouth, and tawdry," were not "under any permissible constitutional standard . . . beyond the pale of contemporary notions of rudimentary decency."

*Jacobellis* v. *Ohio* (378 U.S. 184, 1964) was used by Justice William J. Brennan to expand upon the "redeeming social importance" concept. In that case, a state court obscenity conviction for exhibiting the movie *Les Amants* was reversed by the Court and Justice Brennan stressed that obscene material is that which is "utterly without redeeming social importance." Conversely, he argued, if material "has literary or scientific or any other form of social importance [it] may not be branded as obscenity. . . ." Brennan also focused attention on the "contemporary community standards" concept. The "relevant community," he held, must be construed in the broad sense of "society at large."

The significance of the "redeeming social importance" test is well illustrated in *A Book Named "John Cleland's Memoirs of a Woman of Pleasure* v. *Attorney General of Massachusetts* (383 U.S. 413, 1966). The controversial novel *Fanny Hill,* in which a prostitute reviews her life's experiences, was adjudged obscene by Massachusetts courts. The Supreme Court reversed that holding and, in the opinion for the Court, Justice Brennan emphasized that, although a book may have "prurient interest" appeal and is "patently offensive," it may not be held obscene unless it is "utterly without redeeming social value." To him, each of these criteria is to be applied independently, but material must have all three qualities to be proscribed as obscene. Hence, because the trial court found that *Fanny Hill* contained at least "a modicum of social value" its obscenity finding was erroneous.

A further criterion for determining obscenity was set forth in *Ginzburg* v. *United States.* Apparently frowning on the "sordid business" of commercializing sex engaged in by some publishers under the guise of freedom of expression, the Court affirmed a federal obscenity conviction on the basis of the publisher's motives as revealed by his advertising and promotion methods. Conceding that the materials under "a different setting" might not be obscene, Justice Brennan, speaking for the majority, made it clear that "where the purveyor's sole emphasis is on the sexually provocative aspects of his publications, that fact may be decisive in the determination of obscenity. Furthermore, he assumed that the prosecution could not have succeeded otherwise.

The obvious difficulty with Brennan's opinion is that it provides for the evaluation of the substantive content of a work partly on the basis of the use to which it is put. Actually, Brennan was focusing on "pandering" and in doing so, as Justice Harlan pointed out, the conviction was affirmed upon something quite different from that on which Ginzburg was charged and tried. Harlan contended that if there is any validity in adding the "pandering" dimension to the existing obscenity tests, then the least the Court could do would be to remand the case so Ginzburg could "have his day in court" on the "amended" charges.

The Court continued to recognize the need for more legislative flexibility in dealing with obscenity when it held in *Ginsberg* v. *New York* that what may be obscene for minors may not be for adults. Speaking for the Court, Justice Brennan accepted the state's "variable obscenity" standard and held that government can impose stricter standards on materials sold to juveniles than on that sold to adults. "The state has an independent interest in the well-being of its youth," said Brennan, and can constitutionally accord them "a more restricted right than that assured to adults." But even the "variable obscenity" doctrine does not give states unfettered discretion to move against minors. In *Interstate Circuit, Inc.* v. *Dallas* (390 U.S. 676, 1968), for example, the Court held void for vagueness a city ordinance that empowered a board to ban from exhibition for persons under 16 years of age motion pictures in which the portrayal of brutality and sex would tend to incite crime and encourage sexual promiscuity among youth. Justice Thurgood Marshall, who wrote the Court's opinion, pointed out that the inclusion of such undefined terms as "sacrilegious" and "sexual promiscuity" rendered the ordinance fatally defective. Such loose language, said Marshall, left the censors free to apply their own mores in regulating the film fare of others.

Various methods used by state and local government to control dissemination of obscene matter have resulted in considerable litigation producing a number of significant Supreme Court decisions. With regard to books and other printed matter, the Court has: (1) approved a New York statute authorizing limited injunctive proceedings against the sale of obscene books (*Kingsley Books* v. *Brown,* 354 U.S. 436, 1957, reaffirmed in *A Quantity of Copies of Books* v. *Kansas,* 378 U.S. 205, 1964); (2) declared a Michigan statute unconstitutional that made it a crime to sell to the general public materials, which tended to "incite minors to violent or depraved or immoral acts, manifestly tending to the corruption of the morals of youth" (*Butler* v. *Michigan,* 352 U.S. 380, 1957); (3) invalidated a city ordinance because it did not contain "scienter"—a provision that the bookseller knowingly offered an obscene book for sale

(*Smith* v. *California,* 361 U.S. 147, 1959); (4) declared the "informal practices" of a Rhode Island Statutory Commission to Encourage Morality in Youth unconstitutional as a form of prior restraint abridging freedom of the press (*Bantam Books* v. *Sullivan,* 372 U.S. 58, 1963); and (5) invalidated the search and seizure procedures of a Kansas law because the procedures lacked sufficient safeguards for the protection of non-obscene materials and allowed law enforcement officials too much discretion to determine which publication should be seized (*Marcus* v. *Search Warrant,* 376 U.S. 717, 1961).

The Court has also held that mere possession of obscene matter in the home for personal use is not a crime. In *Stanley* v. *Georgia* (394 U.S. 557, 1969) a unanimous Court overturned a Georgia conviction for possession of obscene matter where law enforcement officers raided Stanley's home searching for gambling paraphernalia and in the process discovered and seized three reels of "stag movies" from a desk drawer in the bedroom. These movies were used as evidence to support the obscenity conviction. In overturning the conviction, Justice Thurgood Marshall emphasized the constitutional right of an individual "to satisfy his intellectual and emotional needs in the privacy of his own home." "If the First Amendment means anything," said Marshall, "it means that a state has no business telling a man sitting alone in his own house, what books he may read or what films he may watch."

Motion pictures, unlike books and other printed matter, were long considered entertainment and not a medium for the communication of ideas protected by the First Amendment. Justice Joseph McKenna stated the principle in *Mutual Film Corporation* v. *Industrial Commission of Ohio* (236 U.S. 230, 1915) when he said that the production and exhibition of motion pictures is "a business, pure and simple," and is not "to be regarded . . . as part of the press of the country, or as organs of public opinion." As such, and recognizing the medium's "capacity for evil," the Court approved state censorship of motion pictures. By 1948, however, a change in the judicial attitude on the subject was indicated in the antitrust case of *United States* v. *Paramount Pictures, Inc.* (334 U.S. 131, 1948) when Justice Douglas remarked: "We have no doubt that moving pictures like newspapers and radio, are included in the press whose freedom is guaranteed by the First Amendment." Four years later in *Burstyn* v. *Wilson* (343 U.S. 495, 1952), the controversy over New York's banning of the Italian film *The Miracle* put the constitutional issue squarely before the Court. The Court struck down the New York ban and in so doing overruled the *Mutual* precedent. There can be no longer any doubt, said the Court, "that motion pictures are a significant medium for the communication of ideas." However, because the New York statute contained vague and meaningless standards, the Court found it unnecessary to rule on whether censorship would be valid under a narrowly drawn statute directed at obscene films.

The Court reemphasized the need for definitive standards in clearly drawn statutes in *Kingsley International Pictures* v. *Regents of State University of New York* (360 U.S. 684, 1959). In his opinion for the Court, Justice Potter Stewart said that the manner in which the state court construed the movie licensing statute "struck at the very heart of constitutionally protected liberty." The state court had sustained a ban on the movie *Lady Chatterly's Lover* because it advocated the unorthodox idea that adultery may be proper behavior under certain circumstances. While Justice Stewart was careful to indicate that this case was not an occasion to consider the scope of state power of censor movies, two concurring justices—Black and Douglas—did. They expressed the view that prior censorship of motion pictures was just as offensive to the First and Fourteenth Amendments as is prior censorship of newspapers and books.

A full examination of the extent of state movie censorship authority came two years later in *Times Film Corporation* v. *City of Chicago* (365 U.S. 43, 1961). In question was the constitutionality of the Chicago movie censorship ordinance, which required submission of motion pictures to a censorship agency before exhibition. No issue of standards was raised. The distributor applied for a permit, paid the license fee, but refused to submit the film *Don Juan* for screening by the censors. He urged on the Court an absolute privilege against prior restraint, thereby challenging the basic authority of the censor. A closely divided Court (5–4) rejected that claim and held that motion picture censorship per se was not necessarily unconstitutional. Justice Tom Clark's majority opinion recognized the motion picture medium's "capacity for evil" as a relevant factor "in determining the permissible scope of community control." Consequently, he argued, since the Court had held in *Burstyn* that motion pictures were not "necessarily subject to the precise rules governing any other particular method of expression," states should not be limited in the selection of the remedy it considered most effective to deal with the problem. In exercising such authority, however, Justice Clark warned against regulations that allowed censors unfettered discretion.

Chief Justice Earl Warren, writing the major dissent (in which Justices Black, Douglas, and Brennan joined), contended that the majority's action amounted to approval of unlimited motion picture censorship by an administrative agency and could also subject other media—newspapers, books, television, radio—to the same type of unlimited censorship.

Four years later, in 1965 (*Freedman* v. *Maryland*) the Court restricted its *Times Film* ruling and outlined certain specific and permissible constitutional standards that must be included in laws calling for prior submission of all films to a review board. These standards, printed in *Freedman* (pp. 172–176), were reaffirmed in *Teitel Film Corporation* v. *Cusak* (390 U.S. 139, 1968) in which the Court invalidated the Chicago motion picture censorship ordinance because of the lengthy administrative licensing process (50 to 75 days) required before initiation of judicial proceedings.

Of course, censorship of films and books may be imposed by means other than formal action (through laws). Informal actions (sanctions) taken by religious and civic groups prove much more effective (or damaging to free expression) than formal means. (See selected references.)

The cases that follow focus on some of the significant issues reviewed in this commentary.

## FEINER v. NEW YORK
### 340 U. S. 315; 95 L. Ed. 295; 71 S. Ct. 303 (1951)

MR. CHIEF JUSTICE VINSON *delivered the opinion of the Court.*

Petitioner was convicted of the offense of disorderly conduct, a misdemeanor under the New York penal laws,* in the Court of Special Sessions of the City of Syracuse and was sentenced to thirty days in the county penitentiary. The conviction was affirmed by the Onondaga County Court and the New York Court of Appeals. . . . The case is here on certiorari, . . . petitioner having claimed that the conviction is in violation of his right of free speech under the Fourteenth Amendment.

In the review of state decisions where First Amendment rights are

* [Sec. 722 of the Penal Law of New York provides:]
  Any person who with intent to provoke a breach of the peace, or whereby a breach of the peace may be occasioned, commits any of the following acts shall be deemed to have committed the offense of disorderly conduct:
  1. Uses offensive, disorderly, threatening, abusive or insulting language, conduct or behavior;
  2. Acts in such a manner as to annoy, disturb, interfere with, obstruct, or be offensive to others;
  3. Congregates with others on a public street and refuses to move on when ordered by the police; . . . .

drawn into question, we of course make an examination of the evidence to ascertain independently whether the right has been violated. Here, the trial judge who heard the case without a jury rendered an oral decision at the end of the trial setting forth his determination of the facts upon which he found the petitioner guilty. His decision indicated generally that he believed the state's witnesses, and his summation of the testimony was used by the two New York courts on review in stating the facts. Our appraisal of the facts is, therefore, based upon the uncontroverted facts and, where the controversy exists, upon that testimony which the trial judge did reasonably conclude to be true.

On the evening of March 8, 1949, petitioner Irving Feiner was addressing an open-air meeting at the corner of South McBride and Harrison Streets in the City of Syracuse. At approximately 6:30 p.m., the police received a telephone complaint concerning the meeting, and two officers were detailed to investigate. One of these officers went to the scene immediately, the other arriving some twelve minutes later. They found a crowd of about seventy-five or eighty people, both Negro and white, filling the sidewalk and spreading out into the street. Petitioner, standing on a large wooden box on the sidewalk, was addressing the crowd through a loud-speaker system attached to an automobile. Altough the purpose of his speech was to urge his listeners to attend a meeting to be held that night in the Syracuse Hotel, in its course he was making derogatory remarks concerning President Truman, the American Legion, the Mayor of Syracuse, and other local political officials.

The police officers made no effort to interfere with petitioner's speech, but were first concerned with the effect of the crowd on both pedestrian and vehicular traffic. They observed the situation from the opposite side of the street, noting that some pedestrians were forced to walk in the street to avoid the crowd. Since traffic was passing at the time, the officers attempted to get the people listening to petitioner back on the sidewalk. The crowd was restless and there was some pushing, shoving and milling around. One of the officers telephoned the police station from a nearby store, and then both policemen crossed the street and mingled with the crowd without any intention of arresting the speaker.

At this time, petitioner was speaking in a "loud, high-pitched voice." He gave the impression that he was endeavoring to arouse the Negro people against the whites, urging that they rise up in arms and fight for equal rights. The statements before such a mixed audience "stirred up a little excitement." Some of the onlookers made remarks to the police about their inability to handle the crowd and at least one threatened violence if the police did not act. There were others who appeared to be favoring petitioner's arguments. Because of the feeling that existed in the crowd both for and against the speaker, the officers finally "stepped in to prevent it from resulting in a fight." One of the officers approached the petitioner, not for the purpose of arresting him, but to get him to break up the crowd. He asked petitioner to get down off the box, but the latter refused to accede to his request and continued talking. The officer waited for a minute and then demanded that he cease talking. Although the officer had thus twice requested petitioner to stop over the course of several minutes, petitioner not only ignored him but continued talking. During all this time, the crowd was pressing closer around petitioner and the officer. Finally, the officer told petitioner he was under arrest and ordered him to get down from the box, reaching up to grab him. Petitioner stepped down, announcing over the microphone that "the law has arrived, and I suppose they will take over now." In all, the officer had asked petitioner to get down off the box three times over a space of four or five minutes. Petitioner had been speaking for over a half hour.

. . .

We are not faced here with blind condonation by a state court of arbitrary police action. Petitioner was accorded a full, fair trial. . . . The exercise of the police officers' proper discretionary power to prevent a breach of the peace was . . . approved by the trial court and later by two courts on review. The courts below recognized petitioner's right to hold a street meeting at this locality, to make use of loud-speaking equipment in giving his speech, and to make derogatory remarks concerning public officials and the American Legion. They found that the officers in making the arrest were motivated solely by a proper concern for the preservation of the general welfare, and that there was no evidence which could lend color to a claim that the acts of the police were a cover for suppression of petitioner's views and opinions. Petitioner was thus neither arrested nor convicted for the making or the content of his speech. Rather, it was the reaction which it actually engendered.

. . . The findings of the New York courts as to the condition of the crowd and the refusal of petitioner to obey the police requests, supported as they are by the record of this case, are persuasive that the conviction of petitioner for violation of public peace, order and authority does not exceed the bounds of proper state police action. This Court respects, as it must, the interest of the community in maintaining peace and order on its streets. . . . We cannot say that the preservation of that interest here encroaches on the constitutional rights of this petitioner.

We are well aware that the ordinary murmurings and objections of a hostile audience cannot be allowed to silence a speaker, and are also mindful of the possible danger of giving overzealous police officials complete discretion to break up otherwise lawful public meetings. . . . But we are not faced here with such a situation. It is one thing to say that the police cannot be used as an instrument for the suppression of unpopular views, and another to say that, when as here the speaker passes the bounds of argument or persuasion and undertakes incitement to riot, they are powerless to prevent a breach of the peace. Nor in this case can we condemn the considered judgment of three New York courts approving the means which the police,

faced with a crisis, used in the exercise of their power and duty to preserve peace and order. The findings of the state courts as to the existing situation and the imminence of greater disorder coupled with petitioner's deliberate defiance of the police officers convince us that we should not reverse this conviction in the name of free speech.

*Affirmed.*

MR. JUSTICE FRANKFURTER *concurs in the result in an opinion which is not printed here.*

MR. JUSTICE BLACK, *dissenting.*

The record before us convinces me that petitioner, a young college student, has been sentenced to the penitentiary for the unpopular views he expressed on matters of public interest while lawfully making a street-corner speech. . . . Today's decision, however, indicates that we must blind ourselves to this fact because the trial judge fully accepted the testimony of the prosecution witnesses on all important points. Many times in the past this Court has said that despite findings below, we will examine the evidence for ourselves to ascertain whether federally protected rights have been denied; otherwise review here would fail of its purpose in safeguarding constitutional guarantees. Even a partial abandonment of this rule marks a dark day for civil liberties in our Nation.

But still more has been lost today. Even accepting every "finding of fact" below, I think this conviction makes a mockery of the free speech guarantees of the First and Fourteenth Amendments. The end result of the affirmance here is to approve a simple and readily available technique by which cities and states can with impunity subject all speeches, political or otherwise, on streets or elsewhere, to the supervision and censorship of the local police. I will have no part or parcel in this holding which I view as a long step toward totalitarian authority.

. . .

The Court's opinion apparently rests on this reasoning: The policeman, under the circumstances detailed, could reasonably conclude that serious fighting or even riot was imminent; therefore he could stop petitioner's speech to prevent a breach of peace; accordingly, it was "disorderly conduct" for petitioner to continue speaking in disobedience of the officer's request. As to the existence of a dangerous situation on the street corner, it seems far-fetched to suggest that the "facts" show any imminent threat of riot or uncontrollable disorder. It is neither unusual nor unexpected that some people at public street meetings mutter, mill about, push, shove, or disagree, even violently, with the speaker. Indeed, it is rare where controversial topics are discussed that an outdoor crowd does not do some or all of these things. Nor does one isolated threat to assault the speaker forebode disorder. Especially should the danger be discounted where, as here, the person threatening was a man whose wife and two small children accompanied him and who, so far as the record shows, was never close enough to petitioner to carry out the threat.

Moreover, assuming that the "facts" did indicate a critical situation, I reject the implication of the Court's opinion that the police had no obligation to protect the petitioner's constitutional right to talk. The police of course have power to prevent breaches of the peace. But if, in the name of preserving order, they ever

can interfere with a lawful public speaker, they first must make all reasonable efforts to protect him. Here the policeman did not even pretend to try to protect petitioner. According to the officers' testimony, the crowd was restless but there is no showing of any attempt to quiet it; pedestrians were forced to walk into the street, but there was no effort to clear a path on the sidewalk; one person threatened to assault petitioner but the officers did nothing to discourage this when even a word might have sufficed. Their duty was to protect petitioner's right to talk, even to the extent of arresting the man who threatened to interfere. Instead, they shirked that duty and acted only to suppress the right to speak.

Finally, I cannot agree with the Court's statement that petitioner's disregard of the policeman's unexplained request amounted to such "deliberate defiance" as would justify an arrest or conviction for disorderly conduct. On the contrary, I think that the policeman's action was a "deliberate defiance" of ordinary official duty as well as of the constitutional right of free speech. For at least where time allows, courtesy and explanation of commands are basic elements of good official conduct in a democratic society. Here petitioner was "asked" then "told" then "commanded" to stop speaking, but a man making a lawful address is certainly not required to be silent merely because an officer directs it. Petitioner was entitled to know why he should cease doing a lawful act. Not once was he told. I understand that people in authoritarian countries must obey arbitrary orders. I had hoped that there was no such duty in the United States.

In my judgment, today's holding means that as a practical matter, minority speakers can be silenced in any city. Hereafter, despite the First and Fourteenth Amendments, the policeman's club can take heavy toll of a current administration's public critics. Criticism of public officials will be too dangerous for all but the most courageous. . . .

MR. JUSTICE DOUGLAS, *with whom* MR. JUSTICE MINTON *concurs, dissenting.*

Feiner, a university student, made a speech on a street corner in Syracuse, New York. . . . The purpose of the speech was to publicize a meeting of the Young Progressives of America to be held that evening. A permit authorizing the meeting to be held in a public school auditorium had been revoked and the meeting shifted to a local hotel.

. . .

The speech was mainly devoted to publicizing the evening's meeting and protesting the revocation of the permit. It also touched on various public issues. The following are the only excerpts revealed by the record:

"Mayor Costello (of Syracuse) is a champagne-sipping bum; he does not speak for the negro people."

"The 15th Ward is run by corrupt politicians, and there are horse rooms operating there."

"President Truman is a bum."

"Mayor O'Dwyer is a bum."

"The American Legion is a Nazi Gestapo."

"The negroes don't have equal rights; they should rise up in arms and fight for their rights."

There was some pushing and shoving in the crowd and some angry muttering. That is the testimony of the police. But there were no fights and no "disorder" even by the standards of the police. There was not even any heckling of the speaker.

But after Feiner had been speaking about 20 minutes a man said to the police officers, "If you don't get that son of a bitch off, I will go over and get him off myself." It was then that the police ordered Feiner to stop speaking; when he refused, they arrested him.

Public assemblies and public speech occupy an important role in American life. One high function of the police is to protect these lawful gatherings so that the speakers may exercise their constitutional rights. When unpopular causes are sponsored from the public platform there will commonly be mutterings and unrest and heckling from the crowd. When a speaker mounts a platform it is not unusual to find him resorting to exaggeration, to vilification of ideas and men, to the making of false charges. But those extravagances . . . do not justify penalizing the speaker by depriving him of the platform or by punishing him for his conduct.

A speaker may not, of course, incite a riot any more than he may incite a breach of the peace by the use of "fighting words." . . . But this record shows no such extremes. It shows an unsympathetic audience and the threat of one man to haul the speaker from the stage. It is against that kind of threat that speakers need police protection. If they do not receive it and instead the police throw their weight on the side of those who would break up the meetings, the police become the new censors of speech. Police censorship has all the vices of the censorship from city halls which we have repeatedly struck down. . . .

# EDWARDS v. SOUTH CAROLINA

372 U. S. 229; 9 L. Ed. 2d 697; 83 S. Ct. 680 (1963)

MR. JUSTICE STEWART *delivered the opinion of the Court.*

The petitioners, 187 in number, were convicted in a magistrate's court in Columbia, South Carolina, of the common-law crime of breach of the peace. Their convictions were ultimately affirmed by the South Carolina Supreme Court. . . . We granted certiorari . . . to consider the claim that these convictions cannot be squared with the Fourteenth Amendment of the United States Constitution.

There was no substantial conflict in the trial evidence. Late in the morning of March 2, 1961, the petitioners, high school and college students of the Negro race, met at the Zion Baptist Church in Columbia. From there, at about noon, they walked in separate groups of about 15 to the South Carolina State House grounds, an area of two city blocks open to the general public. Their purpose was "to submit a protest to the citizens of South Carolina, along with the Legislative Bodies of South Carolina, our feelings and our dissatisfaction with the present condition of discriminatory actions against Negroes, in general, and to let them know that we were dissatisfied and that we would like for the laws which prohibited Negro privileges in this State to be removed."

Already on the State House grounds when the petitioners arrived were 30 or more law enforcement officers, who had advance knowledge that the petitioners were coming.* Each group of petitioners entered the grounds through a driveway and parking area known in the record as the "horse-shoe." As they entered, they were told by the law enforcement officials that "they had a right, as a citizen, to go through the State House grounds, as any other citizen has, as long as they were peaceful." During the next half hour or 45 minutes, the petitioners, in the same small groups, walked single file or two abreast in an orderly way† through the grounds, each group carrying placards bearing such messages as "I am proud to be a Negro" and "Down with segregation."

During this time a crowd of some 200 to 300 onlookers had collected in

---

* The Police Chief of Columbia testified that about 15 of his men were present, and that there were, in addition, "some State Highway Patrolmen; there were some South Carolina Law Enforcement officers present and I believe, I'm not positive, I believe there were about three Deputy Sheriffs."

† The Police Chief of Columbia testified as follows:
"Q. Did you, Chief, walk around the State House Building with any of these persons?
"A. I did not. I stayed at the Horseshoe. I placed men over the grounds.
"Q. Did any of your men make a report that any of these persons were disorderly in walking around the State House Grounds?
"A. They did not.
"Q. Under normal circumstances your men would report to you when you are at the scene?
"A. They should.
"Q. Is it reasonable to assume then that there was no disorderly conduct on the part of these persons, since you received no report from your officers?
"A. I would take that for granted, yes."
The City Manager testified:
"Q. Were the Negro college students or other students well demeaned? Were they well dressed and were they orderly?
"A. Yes, they were."

the horseshoe area and on the adjacent sidewalks. There was no evidence to suggest that these onlookers were anything but curious, and no evidence at all of any threatening remarks, hostile gestures, or offensive language on the part of any member of the crowd. The City Manager testified that he recognized some of the onlookers, whom he did not identify, as "possible trouble makers," but his subsequent testimony made it clear that nobody among the crowd actually caused or threatened any trouble.‡ There was no obstruction of pedestrian or vehicular traffic within the State House grounds. . . . Although vehicular traffic at a nearby street intersection was slowed down somewhat, an officer was dispatched to keep traffic moving. There were a number of bystanders on the public sidewalks adjacent to the State House grounds, but they all moved on when asked to do so, and there was no impediment of pedestrian traffic. Police protection at the scene was at all times sufficient to meet any foreseeable possibility of disorder.

‡ "Q. Who were those persons?
"A. I can't tell you who they were. I can tell you they were present in the group. They were recognized as possible trouble makers.
"Q. Did you and your police chief do anything about placing those people under arrest?
"A. No, we had no occasion to place them under arrest.
"Q. Now, sir, you have stated that there were possible trouble makers and your whole testimony has been that, as City Manager, as supervisor of the City Police, your object is to preserve the peace and law and order?
"A. That's right.
"Q. Yet you took no official action against people who were present and possibly might have done some harm to these people?
"A. We took no official action because there was none to be taken. They were not creating a disturbance, those particular people were not at that time doing anything to make trouble but they could have been."

In the situation and under the circumstances thus described, the police authorities advised the petitioners that they would be arrested if they did not disperse within 15 minutes. Instead of dispersing, the petitioners engaged in what the City Manager described as "boisterous," "loud," and "flamboyant" conduct, which, as his later testimony made clear, consisted of listening to a "religious harangue" by one of their leaders, and loudly singing "The Star Spangled Banner" and other patriotic and religious songs, while stamping their feet and clapping their hands. After 15 minutes had passed, the police arrested the petitioners and marched them off to jail.

Upon this evidence the state trial court convicted the petitioners of breach of the peace, and imposed sentences ranging from a $10 fine or five days in jail, to a $100 fine or 30 days in jail. In affirming the judgments, the Supreme Court of South Carolina said that under the law of that State the offense of breach of the peace "is not susceptible of exact definition," but that the "general definition of the offense is as follows:

In general terms, a breach of the peace is a violation of public order, a disturbance of the public tranquility, by an act or conduct inciting to violence . . . , it includes any violation of any law enacted to preserve peace and good order. It may consist of an act of violence or an act likely to produce violence. It is not necessary that the peace be actually broken to lay the foundation for a prosecution for this offense. If what is done is unjustifiable and unlawful, tending with sufficient directness to break the peace, no more is required. Nor is actual personal violence an essential element in the offense. . . .
By "peace," as used in the law in this connection, is meant the tranquility enjoyed by citizens of a municipality or community where good order reigns

among its members, which is the natural right of all persons in political society.

It has long been established that . . . First Amendment freedoms are protected by the Fourteenth Amendment from invasion by the States. . . . The circumstances in this case reflect an exercise of these basic constitutional rights in their most pristine and classic form. The petitioners felt aggrieved by laws of South Carolina which allegedly "prohibited Negro privileges in this State." They peaceably assembled at the site of the State Government and there peaceably expressed their grievances "to the citizens of South Carolina, along with the Legislative Bodies of South Carolina." Not until they were told by police officials that they must disperse on pain of arrest did they do more. Even then, they but sang patriotic and religious songs after one of their leaders had delivered a "religious harangue." There was no violence or threat of violence on their part, or on the part of any member of the crowd watching them. Police protection was "ample."

This, therefore, was a far cry from the situation in *Feiner* v. *New York*. . . . And the record is barren of any evidence of "fighting words." See *Chaplinsky* v. *New Hampshire*, 315 U.S. 568 (1942). . . .

We do not review in this case criminal convictions resulting from the evenhanded application of a precise and narrowly drawn regulatory statute evincing a legislative judgment that certain specific conduct be limited or proscribed. If, for example, the petitioners had been convicted upon evidence that they had violated a law regulating traffic, or had disobeyed a law reasonably limiting the periods during which the State House grounds were open to the public, this would be a different case. . . . These petitioners were convicted of an offense so generalized as to be, in the words of the South Carolina Supreme Court, "not susceptible of exact definition." And they were convicted upon evidence which showed no more than that the opinions which they were peaceably expressing were sufficiently opposed to the views of the majority of the community to attract a crowd and necessitate police protection.

The Fourteenth Amendment does not permit a State to make criminal the peaceful expression of unpopular views. "[A] function of free speech under our system of government is to invite dispute. It may indeed best serve its high purpose when it induces a condition of unrest, creates dissatisfaction with conditions as they are, or even stirs people to anger. Speech is often provocative and challenging. It may strike at prejudices and preconceptions and have profound unsettling effects as it presses for acceptance of an idea. That is why freedom of speech . . . is . . . protected against censorship or punishment, unless shown likely to produce a clear and present danger of a serious substantive evil that rises far above public inconvenience, annoyance, or unrest. . . . There is no room under our Constitution for a more restrictive view. For the alternative would lead to standardization of ideas either by legislatures, courts, or dominant political or community groups." *Terminiello* v. *Chicago*, 337 U.S. 1 (1949). . . . As in the Terminiello Case, the courts of South Carolina have defined a criminal offence so as to permit conviction of the petitioners if their speech "stirred people to anger, invited public dispute, or brought about a condition of unrest. A conviction resting on any of these grounds may not stand."

. . .

For these reasons we conclude that these criminal convictions cannot stand.

*Reversed.*

MR. JUSTICE CLARK, *dissenting.*

. . . Petitioners, of course, had a right to peaceable assembly, to espouse their cause and to petition, but in my view the manner in which they exercised their rights was by no means the passive demonstration which this Court relates; rather, as the City Manager of Columbia testified, "a dangerous situation was really building up" which South Carolina's courts expressly found had created "an actual interference with traffic and an imminently threatened disturbance of the peace of the community." Since the Court does not attack the state courts' findings and accepts the convictions as "binding" to the extent that the petitioners' conduct constituted a breach of the peace, it is difficult for me to understand its understatement of the facts and reversal of the convictions.
. . . [T]he petitioners were arrested, as they apparently planned from the beginning, and convicted on evidence the sufficiency of which the Court does not challenge. The question thus seems to me whether a State is constitutionally prohibited from enforcing laws to prevent breach of the peace in a situation where city officials in good faith believe, and the record shows, that disorder and violence are imminent, merely because the activities constituting that breach contain claimed elements of constitutionally protected speech and assembly. To me the answer under our cases is clearly in the negative.

Beginning, as did the South Caro-

lina courts, with the premise that the petitioners were entitled to assemble and voice their dissatisfaction with segregation, the enlargement of constitutional protection for the conduct here is as fallacious as would be the conclusion that free speech necessarily includes the right to broadcast from a sound truck in the public streets. *Kovacs* v. *Cooper,* 336 U.S. 77. . . . Here the petitioners were permitted without hindrance to exercise their rights of free speech and assembly. Their arrests occurred only after a situation arose in which the law-enforcement officials on the scene considered that a dangerous disturbance was imminent. The County Court found that "the evidence is clear that the officers were motivated solely by a proper concern for the preservation of order and the protection of the general welfare in the face of an actual interference with traffic and an imminently threatened disturbance of the peace of the community." In affirming, the South Carolina Supreme Court said the action of the police was "reasonable and motivated solely by a proper concern for the preservation of order and prevention of further interference with traffic upon the public streets and sidewalks." . . .

In *Cantwell* v. *Connecticut* . . . this Court recognized that "[w]hen clear and present danger of riot, disorder, interference with traffic upon public streets, or other immediate threat to public safety, peace, or order, appears, the power of the State to prevent or punish is obvious." And in *Feiner* v. *New York* . . . we upheld a conviction for breach of the peace in a situation no more dangerous than that found here. There the demonstration was conducted by only one person and the crowd was limited to approximately 80, as compared with the present lineup of some 200 demonstrators and 300 onlookers. There the petitioner was "endeavoring to arouse the Negro people against the whites, urging them that they rise up in arms and fight for equal rights." . . . Only one person—in a city having an entirely different historical background—was exhorting adults. Here 200 youthful Negro demonstrators were being aroused to a "fever pitch" before a crowd of some 300 people who undoubtedly were hostile. Perhaps their speech was not so animated but in this setting their actions, their placards reading "You may jail our bodies but not our souls" and their chanting of "I Shall Not Be Moved," accompanied by stamping feet and clapping hands, created a much greater danger of riot and disorder. It is my belief that anyone conversant with the almost spontane-

ous combustion in some Southern communities in such a situation will agree that the City Manager's action may well have averted a major catastrophe.

The gravity of the danger here surely needs no further explication. The imminence of that danger has been emphasized at every stage of this proceeding, from the complaints charging that the demonstrations "tended directly to immediate violence" to the State Supreme Court's affirmance on the authority of Feiner. This record, then, shows no steps backward from a standard of "clear and present danger." But to say that the police may not intervene until the riot has occurred is like keeping out the doctor until the patient dies.

. . .

I would affirm the convictions.

## ADDERLEY v. FLORIDA

385 U. S. 39; 17 L. Ed. 2d 149; 87 S. Ct. 242 (1966)

MR. JUSTICE BLACK *delivered the opinion of the Court.*

Petitioners, Harriett Louise Adderley and 31 other persons, were convicted by a jury in a joint trial . . . on a charge of "trespass with a malicious and mischievous intent" upon the premises of the county jail contrary to section 821.18 of the Florida statutes set out below.* Petitioners, apparently all students of the Florida A. & M. University in Tallahassee, had gone from the school to the jail

* "Every trespass upon property of another, committted with a malicious and mischievous intent, the punishment of which is not specially provided for, shall be punished by imprisonment not exceeding three months, or by fine not exceeding one hundred dollars." Fla. Stat. section 821.18 (1965).

about a mile away, along with many other students, to "demonstrate" at the jail their protests because of arrests of other protesting students the day before, and perhaps to protest more generally against state and local policies and practices of racial segregation, including segregation of the jail. The county sheriff, legal custodian of the jail and jail grounds, tried to persuade the students to leave the jail grounds. When this did not work, he notified them that they must leave or he would arrest them for trespassing, and notified them further that if they resisted arrest he would arrest them for resisting arrest as well. Some of the students left but others, including petitioners, remained and they were arrested. On appeal the convictions were affirmed by the Florida [appellate courts]. . . . [P]etitioners applied to us for certiorari contending that, in view of petitioners' purpose to protest against jail and other segregation policies, their conviction denied them "rights of free speech, assembly, petition, due process of law and equal protection of the laws as guaranteed by the Fourteenth Amendment to the Constitution of the United States." On this "Question Presented" we granted certiorari. . . .

Petitioners have insisted from the beginning of these cases that they are controlled and must be reversed because of our prior cases of *Edwards* v. *South Carolina,* 372 U.S. 229, . . . and *Cox* v. *Louisiana,* 379 U.S. 536. . . . We cannot agree.

The *Edwards* case, like this one, did come up when a number of persons demonstrated on public property against their State's segregation policies. They also sang hymns and danced, as did the demonstrators in this case. But here the analogies to this case end. In Edwards, the demonstrators went to the South Carolina State Capitol grounds to protest. In this case they went to the jail. Traditionally, state capitol grounds are open to the public. Jails, built for security purposes, are not. The demonstrators at the South Carolina Capitol went in through a public driveway and as they entered they were told by state officials there that they had a right as citizens to go through the State House grounds as long as they were peaceful. Here the demonstrators entered the jail grounds through a driveway used only for jail purposes and without warning to or permission from the sheriff. More importantly, South Carolina sought to prosecute its State Capitol demonstrators by charging them with the common-law crime of breach of the peace. This Court in

*Edwards* took pains to point out at length the indefinite, loose, and broad nature of this charge. . . . The South Carolina breach-of-the-peace statute was thus struck down as being so broad and all-embracing as to jeopardize speech, press, assembly and petition. . . . And it was on this same ground of vagueness that in *Cox* v. *Louisiana* . . . , the Louisiana breach-of-the-peace law used to prosecute Cox was invalidated.

The Florida trespass statute under which these petitioners were charged cannot be challenged on this ground. It is aimed at conduct of one limited kind, that is for one person or persons to trespass upon the property of another with a malicious and mischievous intent. There is no lack of notice in this law, nothing to entrap or fool the unwary.

Petitioners seems to argue that the Florida trespass law is void for vagueness because it requires a trespass to be "with a malicious and mischievous intent. . . ." But these words do not broaden the scope of trespass so as to make it cover a multitude of types of conduct as does the common-law breach-of-the-peace charge. On the contrary, these words narrow the scope of the offense. The trial court charged the jury as to their meaning and petitioners have not argued that this definition, set out below,† is not a

---

† 'Malicious' means wrongful, you remember back in the original charge, the State has to prove beyond a reasonable doubt there was a malicious and mischievous intent. The word 'malicious' means that the wrongful act shall be done voluntarily, unlawfully, and without excuse or justification. The word 'malicious' that is used in these affidavits does not necessarily allege nor require the State to prove that the defendant had actual malice in his mind at the time of the alleged trespass. Another way of stating the definition of 'malicious' is by 'malicious' is meant the act was done know-

reasonable and clear definition of the terms. The use of these terms in the statute, instead of contributing to uncertainty and misunderstanding, actually makes its meaning more understandable and clear.

Petitioners in this Court invoke the doctrine of abatement announced by this Court in *Hamm* v. *City of Rock Hill,* 379 U.S. 306. . . . But that holding was that the Civil Rights Act of 1964 . . . which made it unlawful for places of public accommodation to deny service to any person because of race, effected an abatement of prosecutions of persons for seeking service in establishments covered by the Act. It involves only an alleged trespass on jail grounds—a trespass which can be prosecuted regardless of the fact that it is the means of protesting segregation of establishments covered by the Act.

Petitioners next argue that "petty criminal statutes may not be used to violate minorities' constitutional rights." This of course is true but this abstract propostion gets us nowhere in deciding this case.

Petitioners . . . contend that "[their] convictions are based on a total lack of relevant evidence." If true, this would be a denial of due process under *Garner* v. *Louisiana,* 368 US 157 . . . , and *Thompson* v. *City of Louisville,* 362 U.S. 199. . . . Both in the petition for certiorari and in the brief on the merits petitioners state that their summary of the evidence "does not conflict with the facts contained in the Circuit Court's opinion" which was in effect affirmed by

the District Court of Appeals. . . .

In summary both these statements show testimony ample to prove this: Disturbed and upset by the arrest of their schoolmates the day before, a large number of Florida A. & M. students assembled on the school grounds and decided to march down to the county jail. Some apparently wanted to get themselves put in jail too, along with the students already there. A group of around 200 marched from the school and arrived at the jail singing and clapping. They went directly to the jail door entrance where they were met by a deputy sheriff, evidently surprised by their arrival. He asked them to move back, claiming they were blocking the entrance to the jail and fearing that they might attempt to enter the jail. They moved back part of the way, where they stood or sat, singing, clapping and dancing, on the jail driveway and on an adjacent grassy area upon the jail premises. This particular jail entrance and driveway were not normally used by the public, but by the sheriff's department for transporting prisoners to and from the courts several blocks away and by commercial concerns for servicing the jail. Even after their partial retreat, the demonstrators continued to block vehicular passage over this driveway up to the entrance of the jail. Someone called the sheriff who was at the moment apparently conferring with one of the state court judges about incidents connected with prior arrests for demonstrations. When the sheriff returned to the jail, he immediately inquired if all was safe inside the jail and was told it was. He then engaged in a conversation with two of the leaders. He told them that they were trespassing upon jail property and that he would give them 10 minutes to leave or he would arrest them.

---

ingly and willfully and without any legal justification.

'Mischievous,' which is also required, means that the alleged trespass shall be inclined to cause petty and trivial trouble, annoyance and vexation to others in order for you to find that the alleged trespass was committed with mischievous intent. R74.

Neither of the leaders did anything to disperse the crowd, and one of them told the sheriff that they wanted to get arrested. A local minister talked with some of the demonstrators and told them not to enter the jail, because they could not arrest themselves, but just to remain where they were. After about 10 minutes, the sheriff, in a voice loud enough to be heard by all, told the demonstrators that he was the legal custodian of the jail and its premises, that they were trespassing on county property in violation of the law, that they should all leave forthwith or he would arrest them, and that if they attempted to resist arrest, he would charge them with that as a separate offense. Some of the group left. Others, including all petitioners, did not leave. Some of them sat down. In a few minutes, realizing that the remaining demonstrators had no intention of leaving, the sheriff ordered his deputies to surround those remaining on jail premises and placed them, 107 demonstrators, under arrest. The sheriff unequivocally testified that he did not arrest any person other than those who were on the jail premises. Of the three petitioners testifying, two insisted that they were arrested before they had a chance to leave, had they wanted to, and one testified that she did not intend to leave. The sheriff again explicitly testified that he did not arrest any person who was attempting to leave.

Under the foregoing testimony the jury was authorized to find that the State had proven every essential element of the crime, as it was defined by the state court. That interpretation is, of course, binding on us, leaving only the question of whether conviction of the state offense, thus defined, unconstitutionally deprives petitioners of their rights to freedom of speech, press, assembly or petition. We hold it does not. The sheriff, as jail custodian, had power, as the state courts have here held, to direct that this large crowd of people get off the grounds. There is not a shred of evidence in this record that this power was exercised, or that its exercise was sanctioned by the lower courts, because the sheriff objected to what was being sung or said by the demonstrators or because he disagreed with the objectives of their protest. The record reveals that he objected only to their presence on that part of the jail grounds reserved for jail uses. There is no evidence at all that on any other occasion had similarly large groups of the public been permitted to gather on this portion of the jail grounds for any purpose. Nothing in the Constitution of the United States prevents Florida from even-handed enforcement of its general trespass statute against those refusing to obey the sheriff's order to remove themselves from what amounted to the curtilage of the jailhouse. The State, no less than a private owner of property, has power to preserve the property under its control for the use to which it is lawfully dedicated. For this reason there is no merit to the petitioners' argument that they had a constitutional right to stay on the property, over the jail custodian's objections, because this "area chosen for the peaceful civil rights demonstration was not only 'reasonable' but also particularly appropriate. . . ." Such an argument has as its major unarticulated premise the assumption that people who want to propagandize protests or views have a constitutional right to do so whenever and however and wherever they please. . . . We reject [that concept]. . . . [T]he United States Constitution does not forbid a State to control the use of its own property for its own lawful nondiscriminatory purpose.

*These judgments are Affirmed.*

MR. JUSTICE DOUGLAS, *with whom the* CHIEF JUSTICE, MR. JUSTICE BRENNAN, *and* MR. JUSTICE FORTAS *concur, dissenting.*

. . . With all respect, the Court errs in treating the case as if it were an ordinary trespass case or an ordinary picketing case.

The jailhouse, like an executive mansion, a legislative chamber, a courthouse, or the statehouse itself . . . is one of the seats of government whether it be the Tower of London, the Bastille, or a small county jail. And when it houses political prisoners or those whom many think are unjustly held, it is an obvious center for protest. The right to petition for the redress of grievances has an ancient history and is not limited to writing a letter or sending a telegram to a congressman; it is not confined to appearing before the local city council, or writing letters to the President or Governor or Mayor. . . . Conventional methods of petitioning may be, and often have been, shut off to large groups of our citizens. Legislators may turn deaf ears; formal complaints may be routed endlessly through a bureaucratic maze; courts may let the wheels of justice grind very slowly. Those who do not control television and radio, those who cannot afford to advertise in newspapers or circulate elaborate pamphlets may have only a more limited type of access to public officials. Their methods should not be condemned as tactics of obstruction and harassment as long as the assembly and petition are peaceable, as these were.

There is no question that petitioners had as their purpose a protest against the arrest of Florida A. & M. students for trying to integrate public theatres. The sheriff's testimony indicates that he well understood the purpose of the rally. The petitioners who testified unequivocally stated that the group was protesting the arrests, and state and local policies of segregation, including segregation of the jail. This testimony was not contradicted or even questioned. The fact that no one gave a formal speech, that no elaborate handbills were distributed, and that the group was not laden with signs would seem immaterial. Such methods are not the sine qua non of petitioning for the redress of grievances. The group did sing "freedom" songs. And history shows that a song can be a powerful tool of protest. . . . There was no violence; no threats of violence; no attempted jail break; no storming of a prison; no plan or plot to do anything but protest. The evidence is uncontradicted that the petitioners' conduct did not upset the jailhouse routine; things went on as they normally would. None of the group entered the jail. Indeed, they moved back from the entrance as they were instructed. There was no shoving, no pushing, no disorder or threat of riot. It is said that some of the group blocked part of the driveway leading to the jail entrance. The chief jailer to be sure testified that vehicles would not have been able to use the driveway. Never did the students locate themselves so as to cause interference with persons or vehicles going to or coming from the jail. Indeed, it is undisputed that the sheriff and deputy sheriff, in separate cars, were able to drive up this driveway to the parking places near the entrance and that no one obstructed their path. Further, it is undisputed that the entrance to the jail was not blocked.

And wherever the students were requested to move they did so. If there was congestion, the solution was a further request to move to lawns or parking areas, not complete ejection and arrest. The claim is made that a tradesman waited inside the jail because some of the protestants were sitting around and leaning on his truck. The only evidence supporting such a conclusion is the testimony of a deputy sheriff that the tradesman "came to the door and then did not leave." His remaining is just as consistent with a desire to satisfy his curiosity as it is with a restraint. Finally the fact that some of the protestants may have felt their cause so just that they were willing to be arrested for making their protest outside the jail seems wholly irrelevant. A petition is nonetheless a petition, though its futility may make martyrdom attractive.

We do violence to the First Amendment when we permit this "petition for redress of grievances" to be turned into a trespass action. It does not help to analogize this problem to the problem of picketing. Picketing is a form of protest usually directed against private interests. I do not see how rules governing picketing in general are relevant to this express constitutional right to assemble and to petition for redress of grievances. In the first place the jailhouse grounds were not marked with "NO TRESPASSING!" signs, nor does respondent claim that the public was generally excluded from the grounds. Only the sheriff's fiat transformed lawful conduct into an unlawful trespass. To say that a private owner could have done the same if the rally had taken place on private property is to speak of a different case, as an assembly and a petition for redress of grievances run to government not to private proprietors.

. . .

. . . When we allow Florida to construe her "malicious trespass" statute to bar a person from going on property knowing it is not his own and to apply that prohibition to public property, we discard *Cox* and *Edwards*. Would the case be any different if, as is common, the demonstration took place outside a building which housed both the jail and the legislative body? I think not.

There may be some public places which are so clearly committed to other purposes that their use for the airing of grievances is anomalous. There may be some instances in which assemblies and petitions for redress of grievances are not consistent with other necessary purposes of public property. A noisy meeting may be out of keeping with the serenity of the statehouse or the quiet of the courthouse. No one, for example, would suggest that the Senate gallery is the proper place for a vociferous protest rally. And, in other cases it may be necessary to adjust the right to petition for redress of grievances to the other interests inherent in the uses to which the public property is normally put. . . . But this is quite different than saying that all public places are off-limits to people with grievances. . . . And it is farther yet from saying that the "custodian" of the public property in his discretion can decide when public places shall be used for the communication of ideas, especially the constitutional right to assemble and petition for redress of grievances. . . . For to place such discretion in any public official, be he the "custodian" of the public property, or the local police commissioner . . . is to place those who assert their First Amendment rights at his mercy. It gives him the awesome power to decide whose ideas may be expressed and who shall be denied a place to air their claims and petition their government. Such power is out of step with all our decisions prior to today where we have insisted that before a First Amendment right may be curtailed under the guise of a criminal law, any evil that may be collateral to the exercise of that right must be isolated and defined in a "narrowly drawn" statute . . . lest the power to control excesses of conduct be used to suppress the constitutional right itself. . . .

That tragic consequence happens today when a trespass law is used to bludgeon those who peacefully exercise a First Amendment right to protest to government against one of the most grievous of all modern oppressions which some of our States are inflicting on our citizens.

. . .

Today a trespass law is used to penalize people for exercising a constitutional right. Tomorrow a disorderly conduct statute, a breach of the peace statute, a vagrancy statute will be put to the same end. It is said that the sheriff did not make the arrests because of the views which petitioners espoused. That excuse is usually given, as we know from the cases involving arrests of minority groups for breaches of the peace, unlawful assemblies, and parading without a permit. The charge against William Penn, who preached a nonconformist doctrine in a street in London, was that he caused "a great concourse and tumult of people" in contempt of the King and "to the great disturbance of the peace." That was in 1670. In modern times also such arrests are usually sought to be justified by some legitimate function of government. Yet by allowing these orderly and civilized protests against injustice to be suppressed, we only increase the forces of frustration which the conditions of second-class citizenship are generating amongst us.

## DE JONGE v. OREGON

### 299 U. S. 353, 81 L. Ed. 278, 57 S. Ct. 255 (1937)

MR. CHIEF JUSTICE HUGHES *delivered the opinion of the Court.*

Appellant, Dirk De Jonge, was indicted . . . for violation of the Criminal Syndicalism Law of . . . [Oregon]. The Act . . . defines "criminal syndicalism" as "the doctrine which advocates crime, physical violence, sabotage or any unlawful acts or methods as a means of accomplishing or effecting industrial or political change or revolution." With this preliminary definition the Act proceeds to describe a number of offenses, embracing the teaching of criminal syndicalism, the printing or distribution of books, pamphlets, etc., advocating that doctrine, the organization of a society or assemblage which advocates it, and presiding at or assisting in conducting a meeting of such an organization, society or group. The prohibited acts are made felonies, punishable by imprisonment for not less than one year nor more than ten years, or by a fine of not more than $1,000, or both.

We are concerned with but one of the described offenses and with the validity of the statute in this particular application. The charge is that appellant assisted in the conduct of a meeting which was called under the auspices of the Communist Party, an organization advocating criminal syndicalism. The defense was that the meeting was public and orderly and was held for a public purpose; that while it was held under the auspices of the Communist Party, neither criminal syndicalism nor any unlawful conduct was taught or advocated at the meeting either by appellant or by others. Appellant moved for a a direction of acquittal, contending that the statute as applied to him, for merely assisting at a meeting called by the Communist Party at which nothing unlawful was done or advocated, violated the due process clause of the Fourteenth Amendment of the Constitution of the United States.

This contention was overruled. Appellant was found guilty . . . and was sentenced to imprisonment for seven years. The judgment was affirmed by the Supreme Court of the State. . . . The case comes here on appeal.

The record does not present the evidence adduced at the trial. The parties have substituted a stipulation of facts. . . .

The stipulation, after setting forth the charging part of the indictment, recites in substance the following: That on July 27, 1934, there was held in Portland a meeting which had been advertised by handbills issued by the Communist Party; that the number of persons in attendance was variously estimated at from 150 to 300; that some of those present, who were members of the Communist Party, estimated that not to exceed ten to fifteen per cent of those in attendance were such members; that the meeting was open to the public without charge and no questions were asked of those entering, with respect to their relation to the Communist Party; that the notice of the meeting advertised it as a protest against illegal raids on workers' halls and homes and against the shooting of striking longshoremen by Portland police; that the chairman stated that it was a meeting held by the Communist Party; that the first speaker dwelt on the activities of the Young Communist League; that the defendant De Jonge, the second speaker, was a member of the Communist Party and went to the meeting to speak in its name; that in his talk he protested against conditions in the county jail, the action of city police in relation to the maritime strike then in progress in Portland and numerous other matters; that he discussed the reason for the raids on the Communist headquarters and workers' halls and offices; that he told the workers that these attacks were due to efforts on the part of the steamship companies and stevedoring companies to break the maritime longshoremen's and seamen's strike; that they hoped to break the strike by pitting the longshoremen and seamen against the Communist movement; that there was also testimony to the effect that defendant asked those present to do more work in obtaining members for the Communist Party and requested all to be at the meeting of the party to be held in Portland on the following evening and to bring their friends to show their defiance to local police authority and to assist them in their revolutionary tactics; that there was also testimony that defendant urged the purchase of certain communist literature which was sold at the meeting; that while the meeting was still in progress it was raided by the police; that the meeting was conducted in an orderly manner; that defendant and several others who were actively conducting the meeting were arrested by the police and that on searching the hall the police found a quantity of communist literature.

The stipulation then set forth various extracts from the literature of the Communist Party to show its advocacy of criminal syndicalism. The stipulation does not disclose any activity by the defendant as a basis for his prosecution other than his participation in the meeting in question. Nor does the stipulation show that the communist literature distributed at the meeting contained any advocacy fo criminal syndicalism or of any unlawful conduct. It was admitted by the Attorney General of the State in his argument at the bar of this Court that the literature distributed in the meeting was not of that sort and that the extracts contained in the stipulation were taken from communist literature found elsewhere. Its introduction in evidence was for the purpose of showing that the Communist Party as such did advocate the doctrine of criminal syndicalism, a fact which is not disputed on this appeal.

. . . The indictment charged as follows:

"The said Dirk De Jonge, Don Cluster, Edward R. Denny and Earl Stewart on the 7th day of July A. D., 1934, in the county of Multnomah and state of Oregon, then and there being, did then and there unlawfully and feloniously preside at, conduct and assist in conducting an assemblage of persons, organization, society and group, to wit: The Communist Party, a more particular description of which said assemblage of persons, organization, society and group is to this grand jury unknown, which said assemblage of persons, organization, society and group did then and there unlawfully and feloniously teach and advocate the doctrine of criminal syndicalism and sabotage, contrary to the statutes in such cases made and provided, and against the peace and dignity of the state of Oregon."

On the theory that this was a charge that criminal syndicalism and sabotage were advocated at the meeting in question, defendant moved for acquittal insisting that the evidence was insufficient to warrant his conviction. The trial court denied his motion and error in this respect was assigned on appeal. The Supreme Court of the State put aside that contention by ruling that the indictment did not charge that criminal syndicalism or sabotage was advocated at the meeting described in the evidence, either by defendant or by anyone else. The words of the indictment that "said assemblage of persons, organization, society and group did then and there unlawfully and feloniously teach and advocate the doctrine of criminal syndicalism and sabotage," referred not to the meeting in question, or to anything then and there said or done by defendant or others, but to the advocacy of criminal syndicalism and sabotage by the Communist Party in Multnomah County. . . .

In this view, lack of sufficient evidence as to illegal advocacy or action at the meeting became immaterial. Having limited the charge to defendant's participation in a meeting called by the Communist Party, the state court sustained the conviction upon that basis regardless of what was said or done at the meeting.

We must take the indictment as thus construed. Conviction upon a charge not made would be sheer denial of due process. It thus appears that, while defendant was a member of the Communist Party, he was not indicted for participating in its organization, or for joining it, or for soliciting members or for distributing its literature. He was not charged with teaching or advocating criminal syndicalism or sabotage or any unlawful acts, either at the meeting or elsewhere. He was accordingly deprived of the benefit of evidence as to the orderly and lawful conduct of the meeting and that it was not called or used for the advocacy of criminal syndicalism or sabotage or any unlawful action. His sole offense as charged, and for which he was convicted and sentenced to imprisonment for seven years, was that he had assisted in the conduct of a public meeting, albeit otherwise lawful, which was held under the auspices of the Communist Party.

The broad reach of the statute as thus applied is plain. While defendant was a member of the Communist Party, that membership was not necessary to conviction on such a charge. A like fate might have attended any speaker, although not a member, who "assisted in the conduct" of the meeting. However innocuous the object of the meeting, however lawful the subjects and tenor of the addresses, however reasonable and timely the discussion, all those assisting in the conduct of the meeting would be subject to imprisonment as felons if the meeting were held by the Communist Party. . . . Thus if the Communist Party had called a public meeting in Portland to discuss the tariff, or the foreign policy of the Government, or taxation, or relief, or candidates for the offices of President, members of Congress, Governor, or state legislators, every speaker who assisted in the conduct of the meet-

ing would be equally guilty with the defendant in this case, upon the charge as here defined and sustained. The list of illustrations might be indefinitely extended to every variety of meetings under the auspices of the Communist Party although held for the discussion of political issues or to adopt protests and pass resolutions of an entirely innocent and proper character.

While the States are entitled to protect themselves from the abuse of the privileges of our institutions through an attempted substitution of force and violence in the place of peaceful political action in order to effect revolutionary changes in government, none of our decisions go to the length of sustaining such a curtailment of the right of free speech and assembly as the Oregon statute demands in its present application. . . .

. . . The right of peaceable assembly is a right cognate to those of free speech and free press and is equally fundamental. As this Court said in *United States* v. *Cruikshank* (92 U.S. 542, 552) . . . : "The very idea of a government, republican in form, implies a right on the part of its citizens to meet peaceably for consultation in respect to public affairs and to petition for a redress of grievances." The First Amendment of the Federal Constitution expressly guarantees that right against abridgment by Congress. For the right is one that cannot be denied without violating those fundamental principles of liberty and justice which lie at the base of all civil and political institutions,—principles which the Fourteenth Amendment embodies in the general terms of its due process clause. . . .

These rights may be abused by using speech or press or assembly in order to incite to violence and crime. The people through their legislatures may protect themselves against that abuse. But the legislative intervention can find constitutional justification only by dealing with the abuse. The rights themselves must not be curtailed. The greater the importance of safeguarding the community from incitements to the overthrow of our institutions by force and violence, the more imperative is the need to preserve the constitutional rights of free speech, free press and free assembly in order to maintain the opportunity for free political discussion, to the end that government may be responsive to the will of the people and that changes, if desired, may be obtained by peaceful means. Therein lies the security of the Republic, the very foundation of constitutional government.

It follows from these considerations that, consistently with the Federal Constitution, peaceable assembly for lawful discussion cannot be made a crime. The holding of meeting for peaceable political action cannot be proscribed. Those who assist in the conduct of such meetings cannot be branded as criminals on that score. The question, if the rights of free speech and peaceable assembly are to be preserved, is not as to the auspices under which the meeting is held but as to its purpose; not as to the relations of the speakers, but whether their utterances transcend the bounds of the freedom of speech which the Constitution protects. If the persons assembling have committed crimes elsewhere, if they have formed or are engaged in a conspiracy against the public peace and order, they may be prosecuted for their conspiracy or other violations of valid laws. But it is a different matter when the State, instead of prosecuting them for such offenses, seizes upon mere participation in a peaceable assembly and a lawful public discussion as the basis for a criminal charge.

. . .

We hold that the Oregon statute as applied to the particular charge as defined by the state court is repugnant to the due process clause of the Fourteenth Amendment. The judgment of conviction is reversed. . . .

MR. JUSTICE STONE *took no part in the consideration or decision of this case.*

# NATIONAL ASSOCIATION FOR THE ADVANCEMENT OF COLORED PEOPLE *v.* STATE OF ALABAMA EX REL. JOHN PATTERSON

357 U. S. 449; 2 L. Ed. 2d 1488; 78 S. Ct. 1163 (1958)

MR. JUSTICE HARLAN *delivered the opinion of the Court.*

We review from the standpoint of its validity under the Federal Constitution a judgment of civil contempt entered against petitioner, the National Association for the Advancement of Colored People, in the courts of Alabama. The question presented is whether Alabama, consistently with the Due Process Clause of the Fourteenth Amendment, can compel petitioner to reveal to the State's Attorney General the names and address of all its Alabama members and agents, with regard to their positions or functions in the Association. The judgment of contempt was based upon petitioner's refusal to comply fully with a court order requiring in part the production of membership lists. Petitioner's claim is that the order, in the circumstances shown by this record, violated rights assured to petitioner and its members under the Constitution.

Alabama has a statute similar to those of many other States which requires a foreign corporation, except as exempted, to qualify before doing business by filing its corporate charter with the Secretary of State. . . . The statute imposes a fine on a corporation transacting intrastate business before qualifying and provides for criminal prosecution of officers of such a corporation. . . . The National Association for the Advancement of Colored People is a non-profit membership corporation organized under the laws of New York. Its purposes, fostered on a nationwide basis, are those indicated by its name and it operates through chartered affiliates which are independent unincorporated associations, with membership therein equivalent to membership in petitioner. The first Alabama affiliates were chartered in 1918. Since that time the aims of the Association have been advanced through activities of its affiliates, and in 1951 the Association itself opened a regional office in Alabama, at which it employed two supervisory persons and one clerical worker. The Association has never complied with the qualification statute, from which it considered itself exempt.

In 1956 the Attorney General of Alabama brought an equity suit in the State Circuit Court, Montgomery County, to enjoin the Association from conducting further activities within, and to oust it from, the State. Among other things the bill in equity alleged that the Association had opened a regional office and had organized various affiliates in Alabama; had recruited members and solicited contributions within the State; had given financial support and furnished legal assistance to Negro students seeking admission to the state university; and had supported a Negro boycott of the bus lines in Montgomery to compel the seating of passengers without regard to race. The bill recited that the Association, by continuing to do business in Alabama without complying with the qualification statute, was ". . . causing irreparable injury to the property and civil rights of the residents and citizens of the State of Alabama for which criminal prosecution and civil actions of law afford no adequate relief. . . ." On the day the complaint was filed, the Circuit Court issued ex parte an order restraining the Association, *pendente lite,* from engaging in further activities within the State and forbidding it to take any steps to qualify itself to do business therein.

Petitioner demurred to the allegations of the bill and moved to dissolve the restraining order. It contended that its activities did not subject it to the qualification requirements of the statute and that in any event what the State sought to accomplish by its suit would violate rights to freedom of speech and assembly guaranteed under the Fourteenth Amendment to the Constitution of the United States. Before the date set for a hearing on this motion, the State moved for the production of a large number of the Association's records and papers, including bank statements, leases, deeds, and records containing the names and addresses of all Alabama "members" and "agents" of the Association. It alleged that all such documents were necessary for adequate preparation for the hearing, in view of petitioner's denial of the conduct of intrastate business within the meaning of the qualification statute. Over petitioner's objections, the court ordered the production of a substantial part of the requested records, including the membership lists, and postponed the hearing on the restraining order to a date later than the time ordered for production.

Thereafter petitioner filed its answer to the bill in equity. It admitted its Alabama activities substantially as alleged in the complaint and that it had not qualified to do business in the State. Although still disclaiming the statute's application to it, petitioner offered to qualify if the bar from qualification made part of the restraining order were lifted, and it submitted with the answer an executed set of the forms required by the statute. However petitioner did not comply with the production order, and for this failure was adjudged in civil contempt and fined $10,000. The contempt judgment provided that the fine would be subject to reduction or remission if compliance were forthcoming within five days but otherwise would be increased to $100,000.

At the end of the five-day period petitioner produced substantially all the data called for by the production order except its membership lists, as to which it contended that Alabama could not constitutionally compel disclosure, and moved to modify or vacate the contempt judgment, or stay its execution pending appellate review. This motion was denied. While a similar stay application, which was later denied, was pending before the

Supreme Court of Alabama, the Circuit Court made a further order adjudging petitioner in continuing contempt and increasing the fine already imposed to $100,000. Under Alabama law . . . the effect of the contempt adjudication was to foreclose petitioner from obtaining a hearing on the merits of the underlying ouster action, or from taking any steps to dissolve the temporary restraining order which had been issued ex parte, until it purged itself of contempt. . . .

The State Supreme Court thereafter twice dismissed petitions for certiorari to review this final contempt judgment.

. . .

The Association both urges that it is constitutionally entitled to resist official inquiry into its membership lists, and that it may assert, on behalf of its members, a right personal to them to be protected from compelled disclosure by the State of their affiliation with the Association as revealed by the membership lists. We think that petitioner argues more appropriately the rights of its members, and that its nexus with them is sufficient to permit that it act as their representative before this Court. In so concluding, we reject respondent's argument that the Association lacks standing to assert here constitutional rights pertaining to the members, who are not of course parties to the litigation.

To limit the breadth of issues which must be dealt with in particular litigation, this Court has generally insisted that parties rely only on constitutional rights which are personal to themselves. . . . This rule is related to the broader doctrine that constitutional adjudication should where possible be avoided. . . . The principle is not disrespected where constitutional rights of persons who are not immediately before the Court could not be effectively vindicated except through an appropriate representative before the Court. . . .

If petitioner's rank-and-file members are constitutionally entitled to withhold their connection with the Association despite the production order, it is manifest that this right is properly assertable by the Association. To require that it be claimed by the members themselves would result in nullification of the right at the very moment of its assertion. Petitioner is the appropriate party to assert these rights, because it and its members are in every practical sense identical. The Association, which provides in its constitution that "[a]ny person who is in accordance with [its] principles and policies . . ." may become a member, is but the medium through which its individual members seek to make more effective the expression of their own views. The reasonable likelihood that the Association itself through diminished financial support and membership may be adversely affected if production is compelled is a further factor pointing towards our holding that petitioner has standing to complain of the production order on behalf of its members. . . .

We thus reach petitioner's claim that the production order in the state litigation trespasses upon fundamental freedoms protected by the Due Process Clause of the Fourteenth Amendment. Petitioner argues that in view of the facts and circumstances shown in the record, the effect of compelled disclosure of the membership lists will be to abridge the rights of its rank-and-file members to engage in lawful association in support of their common beliefs. It contends that governmental action which, although not directly suppressing association, nevertheless carries this consequence, can be justified only upon some overriding valid interest of the State.

Effective advocacy of both public and private points of view, particularly controversial ones, is undeniably enhanced by group association, as this Court has more than once recognized by remarking upon the close nexus between the freedoms of speech and assembly. . . . It is beyond debate that freedom to engage in association for the advancement of beliefs and ideas is an inseparable aspect of the "liberty" assured by the Due Process Clause of the Fourteenth Amendment, which embraces freedom of speech. . . . Of course, it is immaterial whether the beliefs sought to be advanced by association pertain to political, economic, religious or cultural matters, and state action which may have the effect of curtailing the freedom is subject to the closest scrutiny.

. . .

It is hardly a novel perception that compelled disclosure of affiliation with groups engaged in advocacy may constitute as effective a restraint on freedom of association as the forms of governmental action in the cases above were thought likely to produce upon the particular constitutional rights there involved. This Court has recognized the vital relationship between freedom to associate and privacy in one's associations. When referring to the varied forms of governmental action which might interfere with freedom of assembly, it said in *American Communications Asso.* v. *Douds, supra* (339 U.S. 402): "A requirement that adherents of particular religious faiths or political parties wear identifying arm-bands, for example, is obviously of this nature." Compelled disclosure of membership in an organization engaged in advocacy of particular beliefs is of the same order. Inviolability of privacy in group association may in many circumstances be indispensable to preservation of freedom of association, particularly where a group espouses dissident beliefs. . . .

We think that the production order, in the respects here drawn in question, must be regarded as entailing the likelihood of a substantial restraint upon the exercise by petitioner's members of their right to freedom of association. Petitioner has made an uncontroverted showing that on past occasions revelation of the identity of its rank-and-file members has exposed these members to economic reprisal, loss of employment, threat of physical coercion, and other manifestations of public hostility. Under these circumstances, we think it apparent that compelled disclosure of petitioner's Alabama membership is likely to affect adversely the ability of petitioner and its members to pursue their collective effort to foster beliefs which they admittedly have the right to advocate, in that it may induce members to withdraw from the Association and dissuade others from joining it because of fear of exposure of their beliefs shown through their associations and of the consequences of this exposure.

It is not sufficient to answer, as the State does here, that whatever repressive effect compulsory disclosure of names of petitioner's members may have upon participation by Alabama citizens in petitioner's activities follows not from *state* action but from *private* community pressures. The crucial factor is the interplay of governmental and private action, for it is only after the initial exertion of state power represented by the pro-

duction order that private action takes hold.

We turn to the final question whether Alabama has demonstrated an interest in obtaining the disclosures it seeks from petitioner which is sufficient to justify the deterrent effect which we have concluded these disclosures may well have on the free exercise by petitioner's members of their constitutionally protected right of association. . . .

It is important to bear in mind that petitioner asserts no right to absolute immunity from state investigation, and no right to disregard Alabama's laws. As shown by its substantial compliance with the production order, petitioner does not deny Alabama's right to obtain from it such information as the State desires concerning the purposes of the Association and its activities within the State. Petitioner has not objected to divulging the identity of its members who are employed by or hold official positions with it. It has urged the rights solely of its ordinary rank-and-file members. This is therefore not analogous to a case involving the interest of a State in protecting its citizens in their dealings with paid solicitors or agents of foreign corporations by requiring identification.

. . .

. . . [W]e think it apparent that New York ex rel. *Bryant* v. *Zimmerman,* 278 U.S. 63 . . . cannot be relied on in support of the State's position, for that case involved markedly different considerations in terms of the interest of the State in obtaining disclosure. There, this Court upheld as applied to a member of a local chapter of the Ku Klux Klan, a New York statute requiring any unincorporated association which demanded an oath as a condition to membership to file with state officials copies of its ". . . constitution, by-laws, rules, regulations, and oath of membership, together with a roster of its membership and a list of its officers for the current year." NY Laws 1923, ch 664, sections 53, 56. In its opinion, the Court took care to emphasize the nature of the organization which New York sought to regulate. The decision was based on the particular character of the Klan's activities, involving acts of unlawful intimidation and violence, which the Court assumed was before the state legislature when it enacted the statute, and of which the Court itself took judicial notice. Furthermore the situation before us is significantly different from that in *Bryant,* because the organization there had made no effort to comply with any of the requirements of New York's statute but rather had refused to furnish the State with any information as to its local activities.

We hold that the immunity from state scrutiny of membership lists which the Association claims on behalf of its members is here so related to the right of the members to pursue their lawful private interests privately and to associate freely with others in so doing as to come within the protection of the Fourteenth Amendment. And we conclude that Alabama has fallen short of showing a controlling justification for the deterrent effect on the free enjoyment of the right to associate which disclosure of membership lists is likely to have. Accordingly, the judgment of civil contempt and the $100,000 fine which resulted from petitioner's refusal to comply with the production order in this respect must fall.

. . .

*Reversed.*

## THORNHILL v. ALABAMA

310 U. S. 88; 84 L. Ed. 1093; 60 S. Ct. 736 (1940)

MR. JUSTICE MURPHY *delivered the opinion of the Court.*

Petitioner, Byron Thornhill, was convicted . . . of . . . violati[ng] . . . Section 3448 of the [Alabama] Code . . . [which] reads as follows:

. . . Loitering or picketing forbidden —Any person or persons, who, without a just cause or legal excuse therefore, go near to or loiter about the premises or place of business of any other person, firm, corporation, or association of people, engaged in a lawful business, for the purpose, or with the intent of influencing, or inducing other persons not to trade with, buy from, sell to, have business dealings with, or be employed by such persons, firm, corporation, or association, or who picket the works or place of business of such other persons, firms, corporations, or associations of persons, for the purpose of hindering, delaying, or interfering with or injuring any lawful business or enterprise of another, shall be guilty of a misdemeanor; but nothing herein shall prevent any person from soliciting trade or business for a competitive business.

The complaint against petitioner, . . . is phrased substantially in the very words of the statute. The first and second counts charge that petitioner, without just cause or legal excuse, did "go near to or loiter about the premises" of the Brown Wood

Preserving Company with the intent or purpose of influencing others to adopt one of enumerated courses of conduct. In the third count, the charge is that petitioner "did picket" the works of the Company "for the purpose of hindering, delaying or interfering with or injuring its lawful business." Petitioner demurred to the complaint on the grounds, among others, that Section 3448 was repugnant to the Constitution of the United States in that it deprived him of "the right of peaceful assemblage," "the right of freedom of speech," and "the right to petition for redress." The demurrer, so far as the record shows, was not ruled upon, and petitioner pleaded not guilty. . . . The Circuit Court . . . found petitioner "guilty of Loitering and Picketing. . . ." The judgment was affirmed by the Court of Appeals. . . . A petition for certiorari was denied by the Supreme Court of the State. The case is here on certiorari. . . .

The proofs consist of the testimony of two witnesses for the prosecution. It appears that petitioner on the morning of his arrest was seen "in company with six or eight other men" "on the picket line" at the plant of the Brown Wood Preserving Company. Some weeks previously a strike order had been issued by a Union, apparently affiliated with The American Federation of Labor, which had as members all but four of the approximately one hundred employees of the plant. Since that time a picket line with two picket posts of six to eight men each had been maintained around the plant twenty-four hours a day. . . . There is no testimony indicating the nature of the dispute between the Union and the Preserving Company, or the course of events which led to the issuance of the strike order, or the nature of the efforts for conciliation.

The Company scheduled a day for the plant to resume operations. One of the witnesses, Clarence Simpson, who was not a member of the Union, on reporting to the plant on the day indicated, was approached by petitioner who told him that "they were on strike and did not want anybody to go up there to work." None of the other employees said anything to Simpson, who testified: "Neither Mr. Thornhill nor any other employee threatened me on the occasion testified to. Mr. Thornhill approached me in a peaceful manner, and did not put me in fear; he did not appear to be mad." "I then turned and went back to the house, and did not go to work." The other witness, J. M. Walden, testified: "At the time Mr. Thornhill and Clarence were talking to each other, there was no one else present, and I heard no harsh words and saw nothing threatening in the manner of either man." For engaging in some or all of these activities, petitioner was arrested, charged, and convicted as described.

The freedom of speech and of the press, which are secured by the First Amendment against abridgment by the United States, are among the fundamental personal rights and liberties which are secured to all persons by the Fourteenth Amendment against abridgment by a state.

The safeguarding of these rights to the ends that men may speak as they think on matters vital to them and that falsehoods may be exposed through the processes of education and discussion is essential to free government. Those who won our independence had confidence in the power of free and fearless reasoning and communication of ideas to discover and spread political and economic truth. Noxious doctrines in those fields may be refuted and their evil averted by the courageous exercise of the right of free discussion. Abridgment of freedom of speech and of the press, however, impairs those opportunities for public education that are essential to effective exercise of the power of correcting error through the processes of popular government.

. . .

Section 3448 has been applied by the State courts so as to prohibit a single individual from walking slowly and peacefully back and forth on the public sidewalk in front of the premises of an employer, without speaking to anyone, carrying a sign or placard on a staff above his head stating only the fact that the employer did not employ union men affiliated with the American Federation of Labor; the purpose of the described activity was concededly to advise customers and prospective customers of the relationship existing between the employer and its employees and thereby to induce such customers not to patronize the employer. . . . The statute as thus authoritatively construed and applied leaves room for no exceptions based upon either the number of persons engaged in the proscribed activity, the peaceful character of their demeanor, the nature of their dispute with an employer, or the restrained character and the accurateness of the terminology used in notifying the public of the facts of the dispute.

The numerous forms of conduct proscribed by Section 3448 are subsumed under two offenses: the first embraces the activities of all who "without just cause or legal excuse" "go near to or loiter about the premises" of any person engaged in a lawful business for the purpose of influencing or inducing others to adopt any of certain enumerated courses of action; the second, all who "picket" the place of business of any such person "for the purpose of hindering, delaying or interfering with or injuring any lawful business or enterprise of another." It is apparent that one or the other of the offenses comprehends every practicable method whereby the facts of a labor dispute may be publicized in the vicinity of the place of business of an employer. The phrase "without just cause or legal excuse" does not in any effective manner restrict the breadth of the regulation; the words themselves have no ascertainable meaning either inherent or historical. . . . The courses of action, listed under the first offense, which an accused—including an employee—may not urge others to take, comprehends those which in many instances would normally result from merely publicizing, without annoyance or threat of any kind, the facts of a labor dispute. An intention to hinder, delay or interfere with a lawful business, which is an element of the second offense, likewise can be proved merely by showing that others reacted in a way normally expectable of some upon learning the facts of a dispute. The vague contours of the term "picket" are nowhere delineated. Employees or others, accordingly, may be found to be within the purview of the term and convicted for engaging in activities identical with those proscribed by the first offense. In sum, whatever the means used to publicize the facts of a labor dispute, whether by printed sign, by pamphlet, by word of mouth or otherwise, all such activity without exception is within the inclusive prohibition of the statute so long as it occurs in the vicinity of the scene of the dispute.

We think that Section 3448 is invalid on its face.

The freedom of speech and of the press guaranteed by the Constitution embraces at the least the liberty to discuss publicly and truthfully all matters of public concern without previous restraint or fear of subsequent punishment. . . . Freedom of discussion, if it would fulfill its historic function in this nation, must embrace all issues about which information is needed or appropriate to enable the members of society to cope with the exigencies of their period.

In the circumstances of our times the dissemination of information concerning the facts of a labor dispute must be regarded as within that area of free discussion that is guaranteed by the Constitution. . . . It is recognized now that satisfactory hours and wages and working conditions in industry and a bargaining position which makes these possible have an importance which is not less than the interests of those in the business or industry directly concerned. The health of the present generation and of those as yet unborn may depend on these matters, and the practice in a single factory may have economic repercussions upon a whole region and affect widespread systems of marketing. The merest glance at State and Federal legislation on the subject demonstrates the force of the argument that labor relations are not matters of mere local or private concern. Free discussion concerning the conditions in industry and the causes of labor disputes appears to us indispensable to the effective and intelligent use of the processes of popular

government to shape the destiny of modern industrial society. The issues raised by regulations, such as are challenged here, infringing upon the right of employees effectively to inform the public of the facts of a labor dispute are part of this larger problem. We concur in the observation of Mr. Justice Brandeis, speaking for the Court in Senn's Cases (301 U.S. at 478) . . . , "Members of a union might, without special statutory authorization by a State, make known the facts of a labor dispute, for freedom of speech is guaranteed by the Federal Constitution."

. . .

The range of activities proscribed by Section 3448 . . . embraces nearly every practicable, effective means whereby those interested . . . may enlighten the public on the nature and causes of a labor dispute. The safeguarding of these means is essential to the securing of an informed and educated public opinion with respect to a matter which is of public concern. It may be that effective exercise of the means of advancing public knowledge may persuade some of those reached to refrain from entering into advantageous relations with the business establishment which is the scene of the dispute. Every expression of opinion on matters that are important has the potentiality of inducing action in the interests of one rather than another group in society. But the group in power at any moment may not impose penal sanctions on peaceful and truthful discussion of matters of public interest merely on a showing that others may thereby be persuaded to take action inconsistent with its interests. Abridgment of the liberty of such discussion can be justified only where the clear danger of substantive evils arises under circumstances affording no opportunity to test the merits of ideas by competition for acceptance in the market of public opinion. We hold that the danger of injury to an industrial concern is neither so serious nor so imminent as to justify the sweeping proscription of freedom of discussion embodied in Section 3448.

The State urges that the purpose of the challenged statute is the protection of the community from the violence and breaches of the peace, which, it asserts, are the concomitants of picketing. The power and the duty of the State to take adequate steps to preserve the peace and to protect the privacy, the lives, and the property of its residents cannot be doubted. But no clear and present danger of destruction of life or property, or invasion of the right of privacy, or

breach of the peace can be thought to be inherent in the activities of every person who approaches the premises of an employer and publicizes the facts of a labor dispute involving the latter. We are not concerned with picketing en masse or otherwise conducted which might occasion such imminent and aggravated danger to these interests as to justify a statute narrowly drawn to cover the precise situation giving rise to the danger. . . . The danger of breach of the peace or serious invasion of rights of property or privacy at the scene of a labor dispute is not sufficiently imminent in all cases to warrent the legislature in determining that such place is not appropriate for the range of activities outlawed by Section 3448.

*Reversed.*

## UNITED STATES v. O'BRIEN, O'BRIEN v. UNITED STATES

391 U. S. 367; 20 L. Ed. 672; 88 S. Ct. 1673 (1968)

Mr. Chief Justice Warren *delivered the opinion of the Court.*

On the morning of March 31, 1966, David Paul O'Brien and three companions burned their Selective Service registration certificates on the steps of the South Boston Courthouse. A sizable crowd, including several agents of the Federal Bureau of Investigation, witnessed the event. . . . After he was advised of his right to counsel and to silence, O'Brien stated to FBI agents that he had burned his registration certificate because of his beliefs, knowing that he was violating federal law. He produced the charred

remains of the certificate, which, with his consent, were photographed.

For this act, O'Brien was indicted, tried, convicted, and sentenced in the United States District Court for the District of Massachusetts. He did not contest the fact that he had burned the certificate. He stated in argument to the jury that he burned the certificate publicly to influence others to adopt his antiwar beliefs, as he put it, "so that other people would reevaluate their positions with Selective Service, with the armed forces, and reevaluate their place in the culture of today, to hopefully consider my position."

The indictment upon which he was tried charged that he "wilfully and knowingly did mutilate, destroy, and change by burning . . . [his] Registration Certificate (Selective Service System Form No. 2); in violation of Title 50, App., United States Code, Section 462(b)." Section 462(b) is part of the Universal Military Training and Service Act of 1948. Section 462(b)(3) . . . was amended by Congress in 1965, 79 Stat. 586 (adding the words italicized below), so that at the time O'Brien burned his certificate an offense was commited by any person,

who forges, alters, *knowingly destroys, knowingly mutilates,* or in any manner changes any such certificate. . . . (Italics supplied.)

In the District Court, O'Brien argued that the 1965 Amendment prohibiting the knowing destruction or mutilation of certificates was unconstitutional because it was enacted to abridge free speech, and because it served no legitimate legislative purpose. The District Court rejected these arguments, holding that the statute on its face did not abridge First Amendment rights, that the court was not competent to inquire into the motives of Congress in enacting the 1965 Amendment, and that the Amendment was a reasonable exercise of the power of Congress to raise armies.

On appeal, the Court of Appeals for the First Circuit held the 1965 Amendment unconstitutional as a law abridging freedom of speech. At the time the Amendment was enacted, a regulation of the Selective Service System required registrants to keep their registration certificates in their "personal possession at all times." . . . Wilful violations of regulations promulgated pursuant to the Universal Military Training and Service Act were made criminal by statute. . . . The Court of Appeals, therefore, was of the opinion that conduct punishable under the 1965 Amendment was already punishable under the nonpossession regulation, and consequently that the Amendment served no valid purpose; further, that in light of the prior regulation, the Amendment must have been "directed at public as distinguished from private destruction." On this basis, the Court concluded that the 1965 Amendment ran afoul of the First Amendment by singling out persons engaged in protests for special treatment. The Court ruled, however, that O'Brien's conviction should be affirmed under the statutory provision, 50 U.S.C. App. Sec. 462(b)(6), which in its view made violation of the nonpossession regulation a crime, because it regarded such violation to be a lesser included offense of the crime defined by the 1965 Amendment.*

The Government petitioned for certiorari . . . arguing that the Court of Appeals erred in holding the statute unconstitutional, and that its decision conflicted with decisions by the Court of Appeals for the Second†

---

* The Court of Appeals nevertheless remanded the case to the District Court to vacate the sentence and resentence O'Brien. In the Court's view, the district judge might have considered the violation of the 1965 Amendment as an aggravating circumstance in imposing sentence. The Court of Appeals subsequently denied O'Brien's petition for a rehearing, in which he argued that he had not been charged, tried, or convicted for nonpossession, and that nonpossession was not a lesser included offense of mutilation or destruction. *O'Brien* v. *United States,* 376 F. 2d 538, 542 (C.A. 1st Cir. 1967).

† *United States* v. *Miller,* 367 F. 2d 72 (C.A. 2d Cir. 1966), cert. denied, 386 U.S. 911 (1967).

and Eighth Circuits‡ upholding the 1965 Amendment against identical constitutional challenges. O'Brien cross-petitioned for certiorari, . . . arguing that the Court of Appeals erred in sustaining his conviction on the basis of a crime of which he was neither charged nor tried. We granted the Government's petition to resolve the conflict in the circuits, and we also granted O'Brien's cross-petition. We hold that the 1965 Amendment is constitutional both as enacted and as applied. We therefore vacate the judgment of the Court of Appeals and reinstate the judgment and sentence of the District Court without reaching the issue raised by O'Brien in [his cross-petition].

. . .

. . . We note at the outset that the 1965 Amendment plainly does not abridge free speech on its face, and we do not understand O'Brien to argue otherwise. Amended Sec. 12(b) (3) on its face deals with conduct having no connection with speech. It prohibits the knowing destruction of certificates issued by the Selective Service System, and there is nothing necessarily expressive about such conduct. The Amendment does not distinguish between public and private destruction, and it does not punish only destruction engaged in for the purpose of expressing views. . . . A law prohibiting destruction of Selective Service certificates no more abridges free speech on its face than a motor vehicle law prohibiting the destruction of drivers' licenses, or a tax law prohibiting the destruction of books and records.

O'Brien nonetheless argues that the 1965 Amendment is unconstitutional in its application to him, and is un-

‡ *Smith* v. *United States,* 368 F. 2d 529 (C.A. 8th Cir. 1966).

constitutional as enacted because what he calls the "purpose" of Congress was "to suppress freedom of speech." We consider these arguments separately.

O'Brien first argues that the 1965 Amendment is unconstitutional as applied to him because his act of burning his registration certificate was protected "symbolic speech" within the First Amendment. His argument is that the freedom of expression which the First Amendment guarantees includes all modes of "communication of ideas by conduct," and that his conduct is within this definition because he did it in "demonstration against the war and against the draft."

We cannot accept the view that an apparently limitless variety of conduct can be labeled "speech" whenever the person engaging in the conduct intends thereby to express an idea. However, even on the assumption that the alleged communicative element in O'Brien's conduct is sufficient to bring into play the First Amendment, it does not necessarily follow that the destruction of a registration certificate is constitutionally protected activity. This Court has held that when "speech" and "nonspeech" elements are combined in the same course of conduct, a sufficiently important governmental interest in regulating the nonspeech element can justify incidental limitations on First Amendment freedoms. To characterize the quality of the governmental interest which must appear, the Court has employed a variety of descriptive terms: compelling; substantial; subordinating; paramount; cogent; strong. Whatever imprecision inheres in these terms, we think it clear that a government regulation is sufficiently justified if it is within the constitutional power of the government; if it furthers an important or substantial governmental interest; if the governmental interest is unrelated to the suppression of free expression; and if the incidental restriction on alleged First Amendment freedom is no greater than is essential to the furtherance of that interest. We find that the 1965 Amendment to Sec. 462(b)(3) of the Universal Military Training and Service Act meets all of these requirements, and consequently that O'Brien can be constitutionally convicted for violating it.

The constitutional power of Congress to raise and support armies and to make all laws necessary and proper to that end is broad and sweeping. . . . The power of Congress to classify and conscript manpower for military service is "beyond question." . . . Pursuant to this power, Congress may establish a system of registration for individuals liable for training and service, and may require such individuals within reason to cooperate in the registration system. The issuance of certificates indicating the registration and eligibility classification of individuals is a legitimate and substantial administrative aid in the functioning of this system. And legislation to insure the continuing availability of issued certificates serves a legitimate and substantial purpose in the system's administration.

O'Brien's argument to the contrary is necessarily premised upon his unrealistic characterization of Selective Service certificates. He essentially adopts the position that such certificates are so many pieces of paper designed to notify registrants of their registration or classification, to be retained or tossed in the wastebasket according to the convenience or taste of the registrant. Once the registrant has received notification, according to

this view, there is no reason for him to retain the certificates. O'Brien notes that most of the information on a registration certificate serves no notification purpose at all; the registrant hardly needs to be told his address and physical characteristics. We agree that the registration certificate contains much information of which the registrant needs no notification. This circumstance, however, leads not to the conclusion that the certificate serves no purpose but that, like the classification certificate, it serves purposes in addition to initial notification. Many of these purposes would be defeated by the certificates' destruction or mutilation. Among these are:

1. The registration certificate serves as proof that the individual described thereon has registered for the draft. The classification certificate shows the eligibility classification of a named but undescribed individual. Voluntarily displaying the two certificates is an easy and painless way for a young man to dispel a question as to whether he might be delinquent in his Selective Service obligations. Correspondingly, the availability of the certificates for such display relieves the Selective Service System of the administrative burden it would otherwise have in verifying the registration and classification of all suspected delinquents. . . .

2. The information supplied on the certificates facilitates communication between registrants and local boards, simplifying the system and benefiting all concerned. . . .

3. Both certificates carry continual reminders that the registrant must notify his local board of any change of address, and other specified changes in his status. The smooth functioning of the system requires that local boards be continually aware of the

status and whereabouts of registrants, and the destruction of certificates deprives the system of a potentially useful notice device.

4. The regulatory scheme involving Selective Service certificates includes clearly valid prohibitions against the alteration, forgery or similar deceptive misuse of certificates. The destruction or mutilation of certificates increases the difficulty of detecting and tracing abuses such as these. Further, a mutilated certificate might itself be used for deceptive purposes.

The many functions performed by Selective Service certificates establish beyond doubt that Congress has a legitimate and substantial interest in preventing their wanton and unrestrained destruction and assuring their continuing availability by punishing people who knowingly and wilfully destroy or mutilate them. And we are unpersuaded that the pre-existence of the nonpossession regulations in any way negates this interest.

. . .

We think it apparent that the continuing availability to each registrant of his Selective Service certificates substantially furthers the smooth and proper functioning of the system that Congress has established to raise armies. We think it also apparent that the Nation has a vital interest in having a system for raising armies that functions with maximum efficiency and is capable of easily and quickly responding to continually changing circumstances. For these reasons, the Government has a substantial interest in assuring the continuing availability of issued Selective Service certificates.

It is equally clear that the 1965 Amendment specifically protects this substantial governmental interest. We perceive no alternative means that would more precisely and narrowly assure the continuing availability of issued Selective Service certificates than a law which prohibits their wilful mutilation or destruction. . . . The 1965 Amendment prohibits such conduct and does nothing more. In other words, both the governmental interest and the operation of the 1965 Amendment are limited to the noncommunicative aspect of O'Brien's conduct. . . . When O'Brien deliberately rendered unavailable his registration certificate, he wilfully frustrated this governmental interest. For this noncommunicative impact of his conduct, and for nothing else, he was convicted.

. . .

O'Brien finally argues that the 1965 Amendment is unconstitutional as enacted because what he calls the "purpose" of Congress was "to suppress freedom of speech." We reject this argument because under settled principles the purpose of Congress, as O'Brien uses that term, is not a basis for declaring this legislation unconstitutional.

It is a familiar principle of constitutional law that this Court will not strike down an otherwise constitutional statute on the basis of an alleged illicit legislative motive.

. . .

Since the 1965 Amendment to Sec. 12(b)(3) of the Universal Military Training and Service Act is constitutional as enacted and as applied, the Court of Appeals should have affirmed the judgment of conviction entered by the District Court. Accordingly, we vacate the judgment of the Court of Appeals, and reinstate the judgment and sentence of the District Court. This disposition makes unnecessary consideration of O'Brien's claim that the Court of Appeals erred in affirming his conviction on the basis of the nonpossession regulation.

*It is so ordered.*

MR. JUSTICE MARSHALL *took no part in the consideration or decision of these cases.*

MR. JUSTICE HARLAN's *brief concurring opinion is not reprinted here.*

MR. JUSTICE DOUGLAS, *dissenting.*

. . . The underlying and basic problem in this case . . . is whether conscription is permissible in the absence of a declaration of war. That question has not been briefed nor was it presented in oral argument; but it is, I submit, a question upon which the litigants and the country are entitled to a ruling. . . . It is time that we made a ruling. This case should be put down for reargument and heard with *Holmes* v. *United States* and with *Hart* v. *United States* . . . in which the Court today denies certiorari.

The rule that this Court will not consider issues not raised by the parties is not inflexible and yields in "exceptional cases" . . . to the need correctly to decide the case before the court. . . .

## GINZBURG v. UNITED STATES

383 U. S. 463; 16 L. Ed. 2d 31; 86 S. Ct. 942 (1966)

MR. JUSTICE BRENNAN *delivered the opinion of the Court.*

A judge sitting without a jury in the District Court for the Eastern District of Pennsylvania convicted petitioner Ginzburg and three corporations controlled by him upon all 28 counts of an indictment charging violation of the federal obscenity statute, 18 U.S.C. 1461*. . . . The Court of

* The statute provides in pertinent part:
Every obscene, lewd, lascivious, indecent, filthy or vile article, matter thing device, or substance; and

. . .

Every written or printed card, letter, circular, book, pamphlet, advertisement, or notice of any kind giving information, directly or indirectly, where, or how, or from whom, or by what means of such mentioned matters . . . may be obtained.

. . .

Is declared to be nonmailable matter and shall not be conveyed in the mails or delivered from any post office or by any letter carrier.

Appeals for the Third Circuit affirmed. . . . We granted certiorari. . . . We affirm. Since petitioners do not argue that the trial judge misconceived or failed to apply the standards we first enunciated in *Roth* v. *United States.* . . . the only serious question is whether these standards were correctly applied.

In the cases in which this Court has decided obscenity questions since *Roth,* it has regarded the materials as sufficient in themselves for the determination of the question. In the present case, however, the prosecution charged the offense in the context of the circumstances of production, sale, and publicity and assumed that, standing alone, the publications themselves might not be obscene. We agree that the question of obscenity may include consideration of the setting in which the publications were presented as an aid to determining the question of obscenity, and assume without deciding that the prosecution could not have succeeded otherwise. As in . . . and as did the courts below, . . . we view the publications against a background of commercial exploitation of erotica solely for the sake of their prurient appeal. . . .

The three publications were EROS, a hard-cover magazine of expensive format; Liaison, a bi-weekly newsletter; and THE HOUSEWIFE'S HANDBOOK ON SELECTIVE PROMISCUITY (hereinafter called the HANDBOOK), a short book. The issue of EROS specified in the indicament, Vol. 1, No. 4, contains 15 articles and photo-essays on the subject of love, sex, and sexual relations. The specified issue of Liaison, Vol. 1, No. 1, contains a prefatory "Letter from the Editors" announcing its dedication to "keeping sex an art and preventing it from becoming a science." The remainder of the issue consists of digests of two articles concerning sex and sexual relations which had earlier appeared in professional journals and a report of an interview with a psychotherapist who favors the broadest license in sexual relationships. As the trial judge noted, [w]hile the treatment is largely superficial, it is presented entirely without restraint of any kind. According to defendants' own expert, it is entirely without literary merit. . . . The Handbook purports to be a sexual autobiography detailing with complete candor the author's sexual experiences from age 3 to age 36. The text included, and prefatory and concluding sections of the book elaborate, her views on such subjects as sex education of children, laws regulating private consensual adult sexual practices, and the equality of women in sexual relationships. It was claimed at trial that women would find the book valuable, for example as a marriage manual or as an aid to the sex education of their children.

Besides testimony as to the merit of the material, there was abundant evidence to show that each of the accused publications was originated or sold as stock in trade of the sordid business of pandering—"the business of purveying textual or graphic matter openly advertised to appeal to the erotic interest of their customers. *Eros* early sought mailing privilege from the postmasters of Intercourse and Blue Ball, Pennsylvania. The trial court found the obvious, that these hamlets were chosen only for the value their names would have in furthering petitioners' efforts to sell their publications on the basis of salacious appeal; the facilities of the post offices were inadequate to handle the anticipated volume of mail, and the privileges were denied. Mailing privileges were then obtained from the postmaster of Middlesex, New Jersey. . . .

The "leer of the sensualist" also permeates the advertising for the three publications. The circulars sent for EROS and Liaison stressed the sexual candor of the respective publications, and openly boasted that the publishers would take full advantage of what they regarded an unrestricted license allowed by law in the expression of sex and sexual matters. . . . The solicitation was indiscriminate, not limited to those, such as physicians or psychologists, who might independently discern the book's therapeutic worth. Inserted in each advertisement was a slip labeled "GUARANTEE" and reading, "Documentary Books, Inc. unconditionally guarantee full refund on the price of THE HOUSEWIFE'S HANDBOOK ON SELECTIVE PROMISCUITY if the book fails to reach you because

of U.S. Post Office censorship interference." Similar slips appeared in
the advertising for EROS and Liaison; they highlighted the gloss petitioners put on the publications,
eliminating any doubt what the
purchaser was being asked to buy.

This evidence, in our view, was
relevant in determining the ultimate
question of "obscenity" and, in the
context of this record, serves to resolve all ambiguity and doubt. The
deliberate representation of petitioners' publication as erotically arousing,
for example, stimulated the reader to
accept them as prurient; he looks for
titillation, not for saving intellectual
content. . . . And the circumstances
of presentation and dissemination of
material are equally relevant to determining whether social importance
claimed for material in the courtroom
was, in the circumstances, pretense or
reality—whether it was the basis upon
which it was traded in the marketplace or a spurious claim for litigation purposes. Where the purveyor's
sole emphasis is on the sexually provocative aspects of his publications,
that fact may be decisive in the determination of obscenity. Certainly in a
prosecution which, as here, does not
necessarily imply suppression of the
materials involved, the fact that they
originate or are used as a subject of
pandering is relevant to the application of the *Roth* test. . . .

A similar analysis applies to the
judgment regarding the *Handbook*.
The bulk of the proofs directed to
social importance concerned this publication. Before selling publication
rights to petitioners, its author had
it printed privately; she sent circulars
to persons whose names appeared on
membership lists of medical and psy-
chiatric associations, asserting its value
as an adjunct to therapy. Over 12,000
sales resulted from this solicitation,

and a number of witnesses testified
that they found the work useful in
their professional practices. The Government does not seriously contest
the claim that the book has worth in
such a controlled, or even neutral,
environment. Petitioners, however,
did not sell the book to such a limited
audience, or focus their claims for it
on its supposed therapeutic or educational value; rather, they deliberately
emphasized the sexually provocative
aspects of the work, in order to catch
the salaciously disposed. They proclaimed its obscenity; and we cannot
conclude that the court below erred
in taking their own evaluation at its
face value and declaring the book as
a whole obscene despite the other
evidence. . . .

We perceive no threat to First
Amendment guarantees in thus holding that in close cases evidence of
pandering may be probative with respect to the nature of the material
in question and thus satisfy the *Roth*
test. No weight is ascribed to the fact
that petitioners have profited from
the sale of publications which we have
assumed but do not hold cannot themselves be adjudged obscene in the
abstract; to sanction consideration of
this fact might induce self-censorship,
and offend the frequently stated principle that commercial activity, in
itself, is no justification for narrow-
ing the protection of expression
secured by the First Amendment. . . .
All that . . . [is] determined is that
questionable publications are obscene
in a context which brands them as
obscene as that term is defined in
*Roth*—a use inconsistent with any
claim to the shelter of the First
Amendment. "The nature of the materials is, of course, relevant as an
attribute of the defendant's conduct,
but the materials are thus placed in
context from which they draw color

and character. A wholly different result might be reached in a different setting." *Roth* v. *United States,* 354 U.S., at 495, 77 S. Ct., at 1315 (Warren, C. J. concurring).

It is important to stress that this analysis simply elaborates the test by which the obscenity vel non of the material must be judged. Where an exploitation of interests in titillation by pornography is shown with respect to material lending itself to such exploitation through pervasive treatment or description of sexual matters, such evidence may support the determination that the material is obscene even though in other contexts the material would escape such condemnation. . . .

*Affirmed.*

MR. JUSTICE BLACK, *dissenting.*

Only one stark fact emerges with clarity out of the confusing welter of opinions and thousands of words written in this and two other cases today. [*Mishkin* v. *State of New York* and *A Book Named John Cleland's Memoirs of A Woman of Pleasure* v. *Attorney General of Massachusetts.*] That fact is that Ginzburg, petitioner here, is now finally and authoritatively condemned to serve five years in prison for distributing printed matter about sex which neither Ginzburg nor anyone else could possibly have known to be criminal. Since, as I have said many times, I believe the Federal Government is without any power whatever under the Constitution to put any type of burden on speech and expression of ideas of any kind (as distinguished from conduct), . . . I would reverse Ginzburg's conviction on this ground alone. Even assuming, however, that the Court is correct in holding today that Congress does have power to clamp official censorship on

some subjects selected by the Court in some ways approved by it, I believe that the federal obscenity statute as enacted by Congress and as enforced by the Court against Ginzburg in this case should be held invalid on two other grounds.

Criminal punishment by government, although universally recognized as a necessity in limited areas of conduct, is an exercise of one of government's most awesome and dangerous powers. Consequently, wise and good governments make all possible efforts to hedge this dangerous power by restricting it within easily identifiable boundaries. Experience, and wisdom flowing out of that experience, long ago led to the belief that agents of government should not be vested with power and discretion to define and punish as criminal past conduct which had not been clearly defined as a crime in advance. To this end, at least in part, written laws came into being, marking the boundaries of conduct for which public agents could thereafter impose punishment upon people. . . .

I agree with my Brother Harlan that the Court has in effect rewritten the federal obscenity statute and thereby imposed on Ginzburg standards and criteria that Congress never thought about, or if it did think about them certainly did not adopt them. Consequently, Ginzburg is, as I see it, having his conviction and sentence affirmed upon the basis of a statute amended by this Court for violation of which amended statute he was not charged in the courts below. Such an affirmance we have said violates due process. . . . Quite apart from this vice in the affirmance, however, I think that the criteria declared by a majority of the Court today as guidelines for a court or jury to determine whether Ginzburg or anyone else can be punished as a common criminal for publishing or circulating obscene material are so vague and meaningless that they practically leave the fate of a person charged with violating censorship statutes to the unbridled discretion, whim and caprice of the judge or jury which tries him. . . .

The first element considered necessary for determining obscenity is that the dominant theme of the material taken as a whole must appeal to the prurient interest in sex. It seems quite apparent to me that human beings, serving either as judges or jurors, could not be expected to give any sort of decision on this element which would even remotely promise any kind of uniformity in the enforcement of this law. What conclusion an individual, be he judge or juror, would reach about whether the material appeals to "prurient interest in sex" would depend largely in the long run not upon testimony of witnesses such as can be given in ordinary criminal cases where conduct is under scrutiny, but would depend to a large extent upon the judge's or juror's personality, habits, inclinations, attitudes and other individual characteristics. In one community or in one courthouse a matter would be condemned as obscene under this so-called criterion but in another community, maybe only a few miles away, or in another courthouse in the same community, the material could be given a clean bill of health. In the final analysis the submission of such an issue as this to a judge or juror to assert his own personal beliefs about whether the matter should be allowed to be legally distributed. Upon this subjective determination the law becomes certain for the first and last time.

The second element for determining obscenity as it is described by my Brother Brennan is that the material must be "patently offensive because it affronts contemporary community standards relating to the description or representation of sexual matters. . . ." Nothing that I see in any position adopted by a majority of the Court today and nothing that has been said in previous opinions for the Court leaves me with any kind of certainty as to whether the "community standards" referred to are world-wide, nation-wide, section-wide, state-wide, country-wide, precinct- or township-wide. But even if some definite areas were mentioned, who is capable of assessing "community standards" on such a subject? Could one expect the same application of standards by jurors in Mississippi as in New York City, in Vermont as in California? So here again the guilt or innocence of a defendant charged with obscenity must depend in the final analysis upon the personal judgment and attitudes of particular individuals and the place where the trial is held. And one must remember that the Federal Government has the power to try a man for mailing obscene matter in a court 3,000 miles from his home.

A third element which three of my Brethren think is required to establish obscenity is that the material must be "utterly without redeeming social value." This element seems to me to be as uncertain, if not even more uncertain, than is the unknown substance of the Milky Way. If we are to have a free society as contemplated by the Bill of Rights, then I can find little defense for leaving the liberty of American individuals subject to the judgment of a judge or jury as to whether material that provokes thought or stimulates desire is "utterly without redeeming social value. . . ." Whether a particular treatment of a particular subject is with or without social value in this evolving, dynamic society of ours is a question upon which no uniform agreement could possibly be reached among politicians, statesmen, professors, philosophers, scientists, religious groups or any other type of group. A case-by-case assessment of social values by individual judges and jurors is, I think, a dangerous technique for government to utilize in determining whether a man stays in or out of the penitentiary.

My conclusion is that certainly after the fourteen separate opinions handed down in these three cases today no person, not even the most learned judge much less a layman, is capable of knowing in advance of an ultimate decision in his particular case by this Court whether certain material comes within the area of "obscenity" as that term is confused by the Court today. . . . As bad and obnoxious as I believe governmental censorship is in a Nation that has accepted the First Amendment as its basic ideal for freedom, I am compelled to say that censorship that would stamp certain books and literature as illegal in advance of publication or conviction would in some ways be preferable to the unpredictable book-by-book censorship into which we have now drifted. . . .

I would reverse this case.

MR. JUSTICE HARLAN, *dissenting.*

I believe that under this statute the Federal Government is constitutionally restricted to banning from the mails only "hardcore pornography," . . . Because I do not think it can be maintained that the material in question here falls within that narrow class, I do not believe it can be excluded from the mails.

The Court recognizes the difficulty of justifying these convictions; the majority refuses to approve the trial judge's "exegesis of *Roth*" . . . ; it declines to approve the trial court's "characterizations" of the Handbook "outside" the "setting" which the majority for the first time announces to be crucial to this conviction. . . . Moreover, the Court accepts the Government's concession that the Handbook has a certain "worth" when seen in something labeled a "controlled, or even neutral environment" . . . ; the majority notes that these are "publications which we have assumed . . . cannot themselves be adjudged obscene in the abstract." . . . In fact, the Court in the last analysis sustains the convictions on the express assumption that the items held to be obscene are not, viewing them strictly, obscene at all. . . .

This curious result is reached through the elaboration of a theory of obscenity entirely unrelated to the language, purposes, or history of the federal statute now being applied, and certainly different from the test used by the trial court to convict the defendants. While the precise holding of the Court is obscure, I take it that the objective test of *Roth,* which ultimately focuses on the material in question, is to be supplemented by another test that goes to the question whether the mailer's aim is to "pander" to or "titillate" those to whom he mails questionable matter.

Although it is not clear whether the majority views the panderer test as a statutory gloss or as constitutional doctrine, I read the opinion to be in the latter category. The First Amendment, in the obscenity area, no longer fully protects material on its face non-obscene, for such material must now also be examined in the light of the defendant's conduct, attitude, motives. This seems to me a mere euphemism for allowing punishment of a person who mails otherwise constitutionally protected material just because a jury or a judge may not find him or his business agreeable. Were a State to enact a "panderer" statute under its police power, I have little doubt that—subject to clear drafting to avoid attacks on vagueness and equal protection grounds—such a statute would be constitutional. Possibly the same might be true of the Federal Government acting under its postal or commerce powers. What I fear the Court has done today is in effect to write a new statute, but without the sharply focused definitions and standards necessary in such a sensitive area. Casting such a dubious gloss over a straightforward 101-year-old statute (see 13 Stat. 507) is for me an astonishing piece of judicial improvisation. . . .

If there is anything to this new pandering dimension to the mailing statute, the Court should return the case for a new trial, for petitioners are at least entitled to a day in court on the question on which their guilt has ultimately come to depend. . . .

If a new trial were given in the present case, as I read the Court's opinion, the burden would be on the Government to show that the motives of the defendants were to pander to "the widespread weakness for titillation by pornography." . . .

In the past, as in the trial of these petitioners, evidence as to a defendant's conduct was admissible only to show relevant intent. Now evidence not only as to conduct, but also as to attitude and motive, is admissible on the primary question of whether the material mailed is obscene. I have difficulty seeing how these inquiries are logically related to the question whether a particular work is obscene. In addition, I think such a test for obscenity is impermissibly vague, and unwarranted by anything in the First Amendment or in 18 U.S.C. Section 1461.

I would reverse the judgment below.

MR. JUSTICE STEWART, *dissenting.*

The petitioner has been sentenced to five years in prison for sending through the mail copies of a magazine, a pamphlet, and a book. There was testimony at his trial that these publications possess artistic and social merit. Personally, I have a hard time discerning any. Most of the material strikes me as both vulgar and unedifying. But if the First Amendment means anything, it means that a man cannot be sent to prison merely for distributing publications which offend a judge's esthetic sensibilities, mine or any other's.

Censorship reflects a society's lack of confidence in itself. It is a hallmark of an authoritarian regime. Long ago those who wrote our First Amendment charted a different course. They believed a society can be truly strong only when it is truly free. In the realm of expression they put their faith, for better or for worse, in the enlightened choice of the people, free from the interference of a policeman's intrusive thumb or a judge's heavy hand. So it is that the Constitution protects coarse expression as well as refined, and vulgarity no less than elegance. A book worthless to me may convey something of value to my neighbor. In the free society to which our Constitution has committed us, it is for each to choose for himself. . . .

Because such is the mandate of our

Constitution, there is room for only the most restricted view of this Court's decision in *Roth* v. *United States*, . . . The Court there characterized obscenity as that which is "utterly without redeeming social importance," . . . "deals with sex in a manner appealing to prurient interest," . . . and "goes substantially beyond customary limits of candor in description or representation of such matters." . . . In *Manual Enterprises* v. *Day*, . . . I joined Mr. Justice Harlan's opinion adding "patent indecency" as a further essential element of that which is not constitutionally protected.

There does exist a distinct and easily identifiable class of material in which all of these elements coalesce. It is that, and that alone, which I think government may constitutionally suppress, whether by criminal or civil sanctions. I have referred to such material before as hardcore pornography, without trying further to define it. . . .

For me, . . . there is another aspect of the Court's opinion in this case that is even more regrettable. Today the Court assumes the power to deny Ralph Ginzburg the protection of the First Amendment because it disapproves of his "sordid business." That is a power the Court does not possess. For the First Amendment protects us all with an even hand. It applies to Ralph Ginzburg with no less completeness and force than to G. P. Putnam Sons. In upholding and enforcing the Bill of Rights, this Court has no power to pick or to choose. When we lose sight of that fixed star of constitutional adjudication, we lose our way. For then we forsake a government of law and are left with government by Big Brother.

I dissent.

## GINSBERG v. NEW YORK

390 U. S. 629; 20 L. Ed. 2d 195; 88 S. Ct. 1274 (1968)

Mr. Justice Brennan *delivered the opinion of the Court.*

This case presents the question of the constitutionality on its face of a New York criminal obscenity statute which prohibits the sale to minors under 17 years of age of material defined to be obscene on the basis of its appeal to them whether or not it would be obscene to adults.

. . . Appellant was prosecuted under two informations, each in two counts, which charged that he personally sold a 16-year-old boy two "girlie" magazines on each of two dates in October 1965, in violation of Sec. 484-h of the New York Penal Law.

He was tried before a judge without a jury . . . and was found guilty on both counts. The judge found (1) that the magazines contained pictures which depicted female "nudity" in a manner defined in subsection 1(b) . . . and (2) that the pictures were "harmful to minors" in that they had, within the meaning of subsection 1(f) ". . . that quality of . . . representation . . . of nudity . . . [which] . . . (i) predominantly appeals to the prurient, shameful or morbid interest of minors, and (ii) is patently offensive to prevailing standards in the adult community as a whole with respect to what is suitable material for minors, and (iii) is utterly without redeemable social importance for minors." He held that both sales to the 16-year-old boy therefore constituted the violation [of the statute]. . . . The conviction was affirmed without opinion by the Appellate Term, Second Department, of the Supreme Court. Appellant was denied leave to appeal to the New York Court of Appeals and then appealed to this Court. . . . We affirm.

The "girlie" magazines involved in the sales here are not obscene for adults, *Redrup* v. *New York,* 386 U.S. 767. But Sec. 484-h does not bar the appellant from stocking the magazines and selling them to persons 17 years of age or older, and therefore the conviction is not invalid under our decision in *Butler* v. *Michigan,* 352 U.S. 380.

Obscenity is not within the area of protected speech or press. *Roth* v. *United States,* 354 U.S. 476, 485. The three-pronged test of subsection 1(f) for judging the obscenity of material sold to minors under 17 is a variable from the formulation for determining obscenity under *Roth* stated in the plurality opinion in *Memoirs* v. *Massachusetts,* 383 U.S. 413, 418. Appellant's primary attack upon Sec. 484-h is leveled at the power of the State to adapt this *Memoirs* formulation to define the material's obscenity on the basis of its appeal to minors, and thus exclude material so defined from the area of protected expression. He makes no argument that the magazines are not "harmful to minors" within the definition of subsection 1(f). Thus "[n]o issue is presented . . . concerning the obscenity of the material involved." *Roth,* 354 U.S., at 481, n. 8.

The New York Court of Appeals "upheld the Legislature's power to employ variable concepts of obscenity" in a case in which the same challenge

to state power to enact such a law was also addressed to Sec. 484-h. *The Bookcase, Inc.* v. *Broderick,* 18 N.Y. 2d 71. . . . In sustaining state power to enact the law, the Court of Appeals said, *Bookcase, Inc.,* p. 75:

. . . material which is protected for distribution to adults is not necessarily constitutionally protected from restriction upon its dissemination to children. In other words, the concept of obscenity or of unprotected matter may vary according to the group to whom the questionable material is directed or from whom it is quarantined. Because of the State's exigent interest in preventing distribution to children of objectionable material, it can exercise its power to protect the health, safety, welfare and morals of its community by barring the distribution to children of books recognized to be suitable for adults.

Appellant's attack is not that New York was without power to draw the line at age 17. Rather, his contention is the broad proposition that the scope of the constitutional freedom of expression secured to a citizen to read or see material concerned with sex cannot be made to depend upon whether the citizen is an adult or a minor. He accordingly insists that the denial to minors under 17 of access to material condemned by Sec. 484-h, insofar as that material is not obscene for persons 17 years of age or older, constitutes and unconstitutional deprivation of protected liberty.

We have no occasion in this case to consider the impact of the guarantees of freedom of expression upon the totality of the relationship of the minor and the State. . . . It is enough for the purposes of this case that we inquire whether it was constitutionally impermissible for New York, insofar as Sec. 484-h does so, to accord minors under 17 a more restricted right than that assured to adults to judge and determine for themselves what sex material they may read or see. We concluded that we cannot say that the statute invades the area of freedom of expression constitutionally secured to minors.

Appellant argues that there is an invasion of protected rights under Sec. 484-h constitutionally indistinguishable from the invasions under the Nebraska statute forbidding children to study German, which was struck down in *Meyer* v. *Nebraska,* 262 U.S. 390, the Oregon statute interfering with children's attendance at private and parochial schools, which was struck down in *Pierce* v. *Society of Sisters,* 268 U.S. 510, and the statute compelling children against their religious scruples to give the flag salute, which was struck down in *West Virginia State Board of Education* v. *Barnette,* 319 U.S. 624. We reject that argument. We do not regard New York's regulation in defining obscenity on the basis of its appeal to minors under 17 as involving an invasion of such minors' constitutionally protected freedoms. Rather Sec. 484-h simply adjusts the definition of obscenity ". . . to social realities by permitting the appeal of this type of material to be assessed in terms of the sexual interest . . ." of such minors. . . . That the State has power to make that adjustment seems clear, for we have recognized that even where there is an invasion of protected freedoms ". . . the power of the state to control the conduct of children reaches beyond the scope of its authority over adults. . . ." *Prince* v. *Massachusetts,* 321 U.S. 158, 170. In *Prince* we sustained the conviction of the guardian of a nine-year-old girl, both members of the sect of Jehovah's Witnesses, for violating the Massachusetts Child Labor Law by permitting the girl to sell the sect's tracts on the streets of Boston.

The well-being of its children is of course a subject within the State's constitutional power to regulate, and, in our view, two interests justify the limitations in Sec. 484-h upon the availability of sex material to minors under 17, at least if it was rational for the legislature to find that the minors' exposure to such material might be harmful. First of all, constitutional interpretation has consistently recognized that parents' claims to authority in their own households to direct the rearing of their children is basic in the structure of our society. "It is cardinal with us that the custody, care and nurture of the child reside first in the parents, whose primary function and freedom include preparation for obligations the state can neither supply nor hinder." *Prince* v. *Massachusetts, supra,* at 166. The legislature could properly conclude that parents and others, teachers for example, who have this primary responsibility for children's well-being are entitled to the support of laws designed to aid discharge of that responsibility. Indeed, subsection 1(f)(ii) of Sec. 484-h expressly recognizes the parental role in assessing sex-related material harmful to minors according "to prevailing standards in the adult community as a whole with respect to what is suitable material for minors." Moreover, the prohibition against sales to minors does not bar parents who so desire from purchasing the magazines for their children.

The State also has an independent interest in the well-being of its youth. The New York Court of Appeals squarely bottomed its decision on that interest in *Bookcase, Inc.* v. *Broderick, supra,* at 75. Judge Fuld, now Chief Judge Fuld, also emphasized its significance in the earlier case of *People* v. *Kahan,* 15 N.Y. 2d 311, which had struck down the first version of Sec. 484-h on grounds of vagueness. In his concurring opinion, 15 N.Y. 2d, at 312, he said:

While the supervision of children's reading may best be left to their parents, the knowledge that parental control or guidance cannot always be provided and society's transcendent interest in protecting the welfare of children justify reasonable regulation of the sale of material to them. It is, therefore, altogether fitting and proper for a state to include in a statute designed to regulate the sale of pornography to children special standards, broader than those embodied in legislation aimed at controlling dissemination of such material to adults.

In *Prince* v. *Massachusetts, supra,* at 165, this Court, too, recognized that the State has an interest "to protect the welfare of children" and to see that they are "safeguarded from abuses" which might prevent their "growth into free and independent well-developed men and citizens." The only question remaining, therefore, is whether the New York Legislature might rationally conclude, as it has, that exposure to the materials proscribed by Sec. 484-h constitutes such an "abuse."

. . . To sustain state power to exclude material defined as obscenity by Sec. 484-h requires only that we be able to say that it was not irrational for the legislature to find that exposure to material condemned by the statute is harmful to minors. In *Meyer* v. *Nebraska, supra,* at 400, we were able to say that children's knowledge of the German language "cannot reasonably be regarded as harmful." That cannot be said by us of minors' reading and seeing of sex material. To be sure, there is no lack of "studies" which purport to demonstrate that obscenity is or is not "a basic factor in impairing the ethical and moral development of . . . youth and a clear and present danger to the people of the state." But the growing consensus of commentators is that "[w]hile these studies all agree that a causal link has not been demonstrated, they are equally agreed that a causal link has not been disproved either." We do not demand of legislatures a "scientifically certain criteria of legislation." *Noble State Bank* v. *Haskell,* 219 U.S. 104, 110. We therefore cannot say that Sec. 484-h, in defining the obscenity of material on the basis of its appeal to minors under 17, has no rational relation to the objective of safeguarding such minors from harm.

Appellant challenges subsections (f) and (g) of Sec. 484-h as in any event void for vagueness. The attack on subsection (f) is that the definition of obscenity "harmful to minors" is so vague that an honest distributor of publications cannot know when he might be held to have violated Sec. 484-h. But the New York Court of Appeals construed this definition to be "virtually identical to the Supreme Court's most recent statement of the elements of obscenity. . . ." The definition therefore gives "men in acting adequate notice of what is prohibited" and does not offend the requirements of due process. . . .

As is required by *Smith* v. *California,* 361 U.S. 147, Sec. 484-h prohibits only those sales made "knowingly." The challenge to the *scienter* requirement of subsection (g) centers on the definition of "knowingly" insofar as it includes "reason to know" or "a belief or ground for belief which warrants further inspection or inquiry of both: (i) the character and content of any material described herein which is reasonably susceptible of examination by the defendant, and (ii) the age of the minor, provided however, that an honest mistake shall constitute an excuse from liability hereunder if the defendant made a reasonable bona fide attempt to ascertain the true age of such minor."

As to (i), Sec. 484-h was passed after the New York Court of Appeals decided *People* v. *Finkelstein,* 9 N.Y. 2d 342, which read the requirement of *scienter* into New York's general obscenity statute, Sec. 1141 of the Penal Law. The constitutional requirements of *scienter,* in the sense of knowledge of the contents of material, rests on the necessity "to avoid the hazard of self-censorship of constitutionally protected material and to compensate for the ambiguities inherent in the definition of obscenity." . . . The Court of Appeals in *Finkelstein* interpreted Sec. 1141 to require "the vital element of scienter" and defined that requirement in these terms: "A reading of the statute [Sec. 1141] as a whole clearly indicates that only those who are *in some manner aware of the character of the material* they attempt to distribute should be punished. It is not innocent but *calculated* purveyance of fifth which is exorcised. . . ." 9 N.Y. 2d, at 344–345. . . . When Sec. 484-h was before the New York Legislature its attention was directed to *People* v. *Finkelstein,* as defining the nature of *scienter* required to sustain the statute. . . . We may therefore infer that the reference in provision (i) to knowledge of "the *character* and content of any material described herein" incorporates the gloss given the term "character" in *People* v. *Finkelstein.* . . .

Appellant also attacks provision (ii) as impermissibly vague. This attack however is leveled only at the provision's proviso according the defendant a defense of "honest mistake" as to the age of the minor. Appellant argues that "the statute does not tell the bookseller what effort he must make before he can be excused." The argument is wholly without merit. The proviso states expressly that the defendant must be acquitted on the ground of "honest mistake" if the defendant proves that he made "a reasonable bona fide attempt to ascertain the true age of such minor."

MR. JUSTICE STEWART, *concurring in the result.*

A doctrinaire, knee-jerk application of the First Amendment would, of course, dictate the nullification of this New York statute. But that result is not required, I think, if we bear in mind what it is that the First Amendment protects.

The First Amendment guarantees liberty of human expression in order to preserve in our Nation what Mr. Justice Holmes called a "free trade in ideas." To that end, the Constitution protects more than just a man's freedom to say or write or publish what he wants. It secures as well the liberty of each man to decide for himself what he will read and to what he will listen. The Constitution guarantees, in short, a society of free choice. Such a society presupposes the capacity of its members to choose.

When expression occurs in a setting where the capacity to make a choice is absent, government regulation of that expression may co-exist with and even implement First Amendment guarantees. So it was that this Court sustained a city ordinance prohibiting people from imposing their opinions on others "by way of sound trucks with loud and raucous noises on city streets."* And so it was that my Brothers Black and Douglas thought that the First Amendment itself prohibits a person from foisting his uninvited views upon the members of a captive audience.†

I think a State may permissibly determine that, at least in some precisely delineated areas, a child—like someone in a captive audience—is not possessed of that full capacity for individual choice which is the presupposition of First Amendment guarantees. It is only upon such a premise, I should suppose, that a State may deprive children of other rights—the right to marry, for example, or the right to vote—deprivations that would be constitutionally intolerable for adults.

I cannot hold that this state law, on its face, violates the First and Fourteenth Amendments.

MR. JUSTICE DOUGLAS, *with whom* MR. JUSTICE BLACK *concurs, dissenting.*

While I would be willing to reverse the judgment on the basis of *Redrup* v. *New York* . . . for the reasons stated by my Brother Fortas, my objections strike deeper.

If we were in the field of substantive due process and seeking to measure the propriety of state law by the standards of the Fourteenth Amendment, I suppose there would be no difficulty under our decisions in sustaining this act. For there is a view held by many that the so-called "obscene" book or tract or magazine has a deleterious effect upon the young, although I seriously doubt the wisdom of trying by law to put the fresh, evanescent, natural blossoming of sex in the category of "sin."

That, however, was the view of our preceptor in this field, Anthony Comstock, who waged his war against "obscenity" from the year 1872 until his death in 1915. Some of his views are set forth in his book *Traps for the Young,* first published in 1883.

. . .

I would conclude from Comstock and his Traps for the Young and from other authorities that a legislature could not be said to be wholly irrational . . . if it decided that sale of "obscene" material to the young should be banned.

The problem under the First Amendment, however, has always seemed to me to be quite different. For its mandate . . . is directed to any law "abridging the freedom of speech, or of the press." I appreciate that there are those who think that "obscenity" is impliedly excluded; but I have indicated on prior occasions why I have been unable to reach that conclusion. See *Ginzburg* v. *United States,* 383 U.S. 463, 482 (dissenting opinion); *Jacobellis* v. *Ohio,* 378 U.S. 184, 196 (concurring opinion of MR. JUSTICE BLACK); *Roth* v. *United States,* 354 U.S. 476, 508 (dissenting opinion). And the corollary of that view, as I expressed it in *Public Utilities Comm'n* v. *Pollak,* 343 U.S. 451, 467, 468 (dissenting opinions), is that Big Brother can no more say what a person shall listen to or read than he can say what shall be published.

This is not to say that the Court and Anthony Comstock are wrong in concluding that the kind of literature New York condemns does harm. As a

---

* *Kovacs* v. *Cooper,* 336 U.S. 77, 86.

† *Public Utilities Comm'n* v. *Pollak,* 343 U.S. 451, 466 (dissenting opinion of Mr. Justice Black), 467 (dissenting opinion of Mr. Justice Douglas).

matter of fact, the notion of censorship is founded on the belief that speech and press sometimes do harm and therefore can be regulated. I once visited a foreign nation where the regime of censorship was so strict that all I could find in the bookstalls were tracts on religion and tracts on mathematics. Today the Court determines the constitutionality of New York's law regulating the sale of literature to children on the basis of the reasonablness of the law in the light of the welfare of the child. If the problem of state and federal regulaiton of "obscenity" is in the field of substantive due process, I see no reason to limit the legislatures to protecting children alone. The "juvenile delinquents" I have known are mostly over 50 years of age. If rationality is the measure of the validity of this law, then I can see how modern Anthony Comstocks could make out a case for "protecting" many groups in our society, not merely children.

While I find the literature and movies which come to us for clearance exceedingly dull and boring, I understand how some can and do become excited and alarmed and think that something should be done to stop the flow. It is one thing for parents and the religious organizations to be active and involved. It is quite a different matter for the State to become implicated as a censor. As I read the First Amendment, it was designed to keep the State and the hands of all state officials off the printing presses of America and off the distribution systems for all printed literature. Anthony Comstock wanted it the other way; he indeed put the police and prosecutor in the middle of this publishing business.

I think it would require a constitutional amendment to achieve that result. If there were a constitutional amendment, perhaps the people of the community would come up with some national board of censorship. Censors are of course propelled by their own neuroses. That is why a universally accepted definition of obscenity is impossible. Any definition is indeed highly subjective, turning on the neurosis of the censor. Those who have a deep-seated, subconscious conflict may well become either great crusaders against a particular kind of literature or avid customers of it. That, of course, is the danger of letting any group of citizens be the judges of what other people, young or old, should read. Those would be issues to be canvassed and debated in case of a constitutional amendment creating a regime of censorship in the country. And if the people, in their wisdom, launches us on that course, it would be a considered choice.

Today this Court sits as the Nation's board of censors. With all respect, I do not know of any group in the country less qualified, first, to know what obscenity is when they see it, and second, to have any considered judgment as to what the deleterious or beneficial impact of a particular publication may have on minds either young or old.

I would await a constitutional amendment that authorized the modern Anthony Comstocks to censor literature before publishers, authors, or distributors can be fined or jailed for what they print or sell.

Mr. Justice Fortas, *dissenting.*

. . .

The Court avoids facing the problem whether the magazines in the present case are "obscene" when viewed by a 16-year-old boy, although not "obscene" when viewed by someone 17 years of age or older. It says that Ginsberg's lawyer did not choose to challenge the conviction on the ground that the magazines are not "obscene." He chose only to attack the statute on its face. Therefore, the Court reasons, we need not look at the magazines and determine whether they may be excluded from the ambit of the First Amendment as "obsccne" for purposes of this case. But this Court has made strong and comprehensive statements about its duty in First Amendment cases—statements with which I agree. . . .

In my judgment, the Court cannot properly avoid its fundamental duty to define "obscenity" for purposes of censorship of material sold to youths, merely because of counsel's position. By so doing the Court avoids the essence of the problem; for if the State's power to censor freed from the prohibitions of the First Amendment depends upon obscenity, and if obscenity turns on the specific content of the publication, how can we sustain the conviction here without deciding whether the particular magazines in question are obscene?

The Court certainly cannot mean that the States and cities and counties and villages have unlimited power to withhold anything and everything that is written or pictorial from younger people. But it here justifies the conviction of Sam Ginsberg because the impact of the Constitution, it says, is variable, and what is not obscene for an adult may be obscene for a child. This it calls "variable obscenity." I do not disagree with this, but I insist that to assess the principle—certainly to apply it—the Court must define it. We must know the extent to which literature or pictures may be less offensive than *Roth* requires in order to be "obscene" for purposes of a statute confined to youth. . . .

I agree that the State in the exer-cise of its police power—even in the First Amendment domain—may make proper and careful differentiation between adults and children. But I do not agree that this power may be used on an arbitrary, free-wheeling basis. This is not a case where, on any standard enunciated by the Court, the magazines are obscene, nor one where the seller is at fault. Petitioner is being prosecuted for the sale of magazines which he had a right under the decisions of this Court to offer for sale, and he is being prosecuted without proof of "fault"—without even a claim that he deliberately, calculatedly sought to induce children to buy "obscene" material. Bookselling should not be a hazardous profession.

The conviction of Ginsberg on the present facts is a serious invasion of freedom. To sustain the conviction without inquiry as to whether the material is "obscene" and without any evidence of pushing or pandering, in face of this Court's asserted solicitude for First Amendment values, is to give the State a role in the rearing of children which is contrary to our traditions and to our conception of family responsibility. . . . It begs the question to present this undefined, unlimited censorship as an aid to parents in the rearing of hteir children. This decision does not merely protect children from activities which all sensible parents would condemn. Rather, its undefined and unlimited approval of state censorship in this area denies to children free access to books and works of art to which many parents may wish their children to have uninhibited access. For denial of access to these magazines, without any standard or definition of their allegedly distinguishing characteristics, is also denial of access to great works of art and literature.

If this statute were confined to the

punishment of pushers or panderers of vulgar literature I would not be so concerned by the Court's failure to circumscribe state power by defining its limits in terms of the meaning of "obscenity" in this field. The State's police power may, within very broad limits, protect the parents and their children from public aggression of panderers and pushers. This is de-fensible on the theory that they cannot protect themselves from such assaults. But it does not follow that the State may convict a passive luncheonette operator of a crime because a 16-year-old boy maliciously and designedly picks up and pays for two girlie magazines which are presumably *not* obscene. . . .

## FREEDMAN v. MARYLAND

### 380 U. S. 51; 13 L. Ed. 2d 649; 85 S. Ct. 734 (1965)

MR. JUSTICE BRENNAN *delivered the opinion of the Court.*

Appellant sought to challenge the constitutionality of the Maryland motion picture censorship statute, . . . and exhibited the film "Revenge at Daybreak" at his Baltimore theatre without first submitting the picture to the State Board of Censors as required by . . . the statute. The State concedes that the picture does not violate the statutory standards and would have received a license if properly submitted, but the appellant was convicted of a . . . violation despite his contention that the statute in its entirety unconstitutionally impaired freedom of expression. The Court of Appeals of Maryland affirmed. . . .

In *Times Film Corp.* v. *City of Chicago,* 365 U.S. 43, we considered and upheld a requirement of submission of motion pictures in advance of exhibition. The Court of Appeals held, on the authority of that decision, that "the Maryland censorship law must be held to be not void on its face as violative of the freedoms protected against State action by the First and Fourteenth Amendments."

This reliance on *Times Film* was misplaced. The only question tendered for decision in that case was "whether a prior restraint was necessarily unconstitutional *under all circumstances.*" *Bantam Books, Inc.* v. *Sullivan,* 372 U.S. 58, 70, n. 10. The exhibitor's argument that the requirement of submission without more amounted to a constitutionally prohibited prior restraint was interpreted by the Court in *Times Film* as a contention that the "constitutional protection includes complete and absolute freedom to exhibit, at least once, any and every kind of motion picture . . . even if this film contains the basest type of pornography, or incitement to riot, or forceful overthrow of orderly government. . . ." The Court held that on this "narrow" question, the argument stated the principle against prior restraints too broadly; citing a number of our decisions, the Court quoted the statement from *Near* v. *Minnesota,* 283 U.S. 697, 716, that "the protection even as to previous restraint is not absolutely unlimited." In rejecting the proffered proposition in *Times Film* the Court emphasized, however, that "[i]t is that question alone which we decide," 365 U.S., at 46, and it would therefore be inaccurate to say that *Times Film* upheld the specific features of the Chicago censorship ordinance.

Unlike the petitioner in *Times Film,* appellant does not argue that [the statute] is unconstitutional simply because it may prevent even the first showing of a film whose exhibition may legitimately be the subject of an obscenity prosecution. He presents a question quite distinct from that passed on in *Times Film*; accepting the rule in *Times Film,* he argues that [the statute] constitutes an invalid prior restraint because, in the context of the remainder of the statute, it presents a danger of unduly suppressing protected expression. He focuses particularly on the procedure for an initial decision by the censorship board, which, without any judicial participation, effectively bars exhibition of any disapproved film, unless and until the exhibitor undertakes a time-consuming appeal to the Maryland courts and succeeds in having the Board's decision reversed. Under the statute, the exhibitor is required to submit the film to the Board for examination, but no time limit is imposed for completion of Board action. If the film is disapproved, or any elimination ordered, [the statute] provides that:

the person submitting such film or view for examination will receive immediate notice of such elimination or disapproval, and if appealed from, such film or view will be promptly re-examined, in the presence of such person, by two or more members of the Board, and the same finally approved or disapproved promptly after such re-examination, with the right of appeal from the decision of the Board to the Baltimore City Court of Baltimore City. There shall be a further right of appeal from the decision of the Baltimore

City Court to the Court of Appeals of Maryland, subject generally to the time and manner provided for taking appeal to the Court of Appeals.

Thus there is no statutory provision for judicial participation in the procedure which bars a film, nor even assurance of prompt judicial review. Risk of delay is built into the Maryland procedure . . . ; in the only reported case indicating the length of time required to complete an appeal, the initial judicial determination has taken four months and final vindication of the film on appellate review, six months. . . .

In the area of freedom of expression it is well established that one has standing to challenge a statute on the ground that it delegates overly broad licensing discretion to an administrative office, whether or not his conduct could be proscribed by a properly drawn statute, and whether or not he applied for a license. "One who might have had a license for the asking may . . . call into question the whole scheme of licensing when he is prosecuted for failure to procure it." . . . Although we have no occasion to decide whether the vice of overbroadness infects the Maryland statute, we think that appellant's assertion of a similar danger in the Maryland apparatus of censorship—one always fraught with danger and viewed with suspicion—gives him standing to make that challenge. In substance his argument is that, because the apparatus operates in a statutory context in which judicial review may be too little and too late, the Maryland statute lacks sufficient safeguards for confining the censor's action to judicially determined constitutional limits, and therefore contains the same vice as a statute delegating excessive administrative discretion.

Although the Court has said that motion pictures are not "necessarily subject to the precise rules governing any other particular method of expression," *Joseph Burstyn, Inc.* v. *Wilson,* 343 U.S. 495, 503, it is as true here as of other forms of expression that "[a]ny system of prior restraints of expression comes to this Court bearing a heavy presumption against its constitutional validity." . . . The administration of a censorship system for motion pictures presents peculiar dangers to constitutionally protected speech. Unlike a prosecution for obscenity, a censorship proceeding puts the initial burden on the exhibitor or distributor. Because the censor's business is to censor, there inheres the danger that he may well be less responsive than a court—part of an independent branch of government—to the constitutionally protected interests in free expression. And if it is made unduly onerous, by reason of delay or otherwise, to seek judicial review, the censor's determination may in practice be final.

Applying the settled rule of our cases, we hold that a noncriminal process which requires the prior submission of a film to a censor avoids constitutional infirmity only if it takes place under procedural safeguards designed to obviate the dangers of a censorship system. First, the burden of proving that the film is unprotected expression must rest on the censor. As we said in *Speiser* v. *Randall,* 357 U.S. 513, 526, "Where the transcendent value of speech is involved, due process certainly requires . . . that the State bear the burden of persuasion to show that the appellants engaged in criminal speech." Second, while the State may require advance submission of all films, in order to proceed effectively to bar all showings of unprotected films, the requirement cannot be administered in a manner which would lend an effect of finality to the censor's determination whether a film constitutes protected expression. The teaching of our cases is that, because only a judicial determination in an adversary proceedings ensures the necessary sensivity to freedom of expression, only a procedure requiring a judicial determination suffices to impose a valid final restraint. . . . To this end, the exhibitor must be assured, by statute or authoritative judicial construction, that the censor will, within a specified brief period, either issue a license or go to court to restrain showing the film. Any restraint imposed in advance of a final judicial determination on the merits must similarly be limited to preservation of the status quo for the shortest fixed period compatible with sound judicial resolution. Moreover, we are well aware that, even after expiration of a temporary restraint, an administrative refusal to license, signifying the censor's view that the film is unprotected, may have a discouraging effect on the exhibitor. . . . Therefore, the procedure must also assure a prompt final judicial decision, to minimize the deterrent effect of an interim and possibly erroneous denial of a license.

Without these safeguards, it may prove too burdensome to seek review of the censor's determination. Particularly in the case of motion pictures, it may take very little to deter exhibition in a given locality. The exhibitor's stake in any one picture may be insufficient to warrant a protracted and onerous course of litigation. The distributor, on the other hand, may be equally unwilling to accept the burdens and delays of litigation in a particular area when, without such difficulties, he can freely exhibit his film in most of the rest of the country; for we are told that only four States and a handful of municipalities have active censorship laws.

It is readily apparent that the Maryland procedural scheme does not satisfy these criteria. First, once the censor disapproves the film, the exhibitor must assume the burden of instituting judicial proceedings and of persuading the courts that the film is protected expression. Second, once the Board has acted against a film, exhibition is prohibited pending judicial review, however protracted. Under the statute, appellant could have been convicted if he had shown the film after unsuccessfully seeking a license, even though no court had ever ruled on the obscenity of the film. Third, it is abundantly clear that the Maryland statute provides no assurance of prompt judicial determination. We hold, therefore, that appellant's conviction must be reversed. The Maryland scheme fails to provide adequate safeguards against undue inhibition of protected expression, and this renders the Sec. 2 requirement of prior submission of films to the Board an invalid previous restraint.

. . .

The requirement of prior submission to a censor in *Times Film* is consistent with our recognition that films differ from other forms of expression. Similarly, we think that the nature of the motion picture industry may suggest different time limits for a judicial determination. It is common knowledge that films are scheduled well before actual exhibition, and the requirement of advance submission in Sec. 2 recognizes this. One possible scheme would be to allow the exhibitor or distributor to submit his film early enough to ensure an orderly final disposition of the case before the scheduled exhibition date —far enough in advance so that the exhibitor could safely advertise the opening on a normal basis. Failing such a scheme or sufficiently early submission under such a scheme, the statute would have to require adjudication considerably more prompt than has been the case under the Maryland statute. Otherwise, litigation might be unduly expensive and protracted, or the victorious exhibitor might find the most propitious opportunity for exhibition past. We do not mean to lay down rigid time limits or procedures, but to suggest considerations in drafting legislation to accord with local exhibition practices, and in doing so to avoid the potentially chilling effect of the Maryland statute on protected expression.

*Reversed.*

MR. JUSTICE DOUGLAS, *whom* MR. JUSTICE BLACK *joins, concurring.*

On several occasions I have indicated my view that movies are entitled to the same degree and kind of protection under the First Amendment as other forms of expression. . . . For the reasons there stated, I do not believe any form of censorship—no matter how speedy or prolonged it may be—is permissible. As I see it, a pictorial presentation occupies as preferred a position as any other form of expression. If censors are banned from the publishing business, from the pulpit, from the public platform—as they are—they should be banned from the theatre. I would not admit the censor even for the limited role accorded him in *Kingsley Books, Inc.* v. *Brown.* . . . I adhere to my dissent in that case. Any authority to obtain a temporary injunction gives the States "the paralyzing power of a censor." The regime in *Kingsley Books* "substitutes punishment by contempt for punishment by jury trial." I would put an end to all forms and types of censorship and give full literal meaning to the command of the First Amendment.

## SELECTED REFERENCES

Harris, Paul, "Black Power Advocacy: Criminary Anarchy or Free Speech," 56 *Calif. L. Rev.* 702 (1968).

Kramer, D. C., "Right To Denounce Public Officials in England and the United States," 17 *J. Pub. Law* 78 (1968).

Krislov, Samuel, *The Supreme Court and Political Freedom* (New York: The Free Press, 1968).

Loewy, A. H., "Free Speech: The 'Missing Link' In The Law of Obscenity," 16 *J. Pub. Law* 81 (1967).

Note, "Developments in the Law—Academic Freedom," 81 *Harv. L. Rev.* 1045 (1968) esp. pp. 1128–1134 on constitutional protection of student speech and association.

Note, "Freedom of Expression under State Constituitons," 20 *Stanford L. Rev.* 318 (1968).

Note, "Privacy and Efficient Government: Proposals For A National Data Center," 82 *Harv. L. Rev.* 400 (1968).

Shapiro, Martin, *Freedom of Speech: The Supreme Court and Judicial Review* (Prentice-Hall, Inc., 1966).

Velvel, Lawrence R., "Freedom of Speech and the Draft Card Burning Cases," 16 *Kansas L. Rev.* 149 (1968).

# 4. Freedom of Expression and Association: Internal Security and Loyalty

*Dennis v. United States     Scales v. United States*

*Keyishian v. Board of Regents of State University of New York*

*Albertson v. Subversive Activities Control Board*

In the years following World War II, Americans found that the cessation of hostilities did not necessarily guarantee the security they desired. The stark reality was that the Soviet Union emerged from the conflict with a war machine and a military capability comparable to that of the United States. Even more disturbing to many was the political ideology advocated by this "ally." World communism was the goal, and the Soviet government was to engineer its realization. Thus, in the necessary rehabilitation of a war-ravaged world, the objectives and methods of the two "super powers" were often in conflict. Relations between Washington and the Kremlin deteriorated in the immediate postwar era to such an extent as to commence a prolonged period of "cold war."

The tensions thus resulting had a profound impact on American public opinion. Uncertainty and suspicion of Soviet motives, fear of internal subversion by Soviet agents and native Communists, and the unthinkable threat of nuclear war led to another "Red scare."[1] Under such conditions greater stress is usually placed on national security. Patriotism, loyalty, and conformity become expected norms of behavior; dissent, questioning, and nonconformity are denounced as unpatriotic and disloyal.

At one time or another national, state, and local governments in the United States have taken actions with the stated objective of protecting national security. Quite often, however, some of these actions have collided with individual rights and liberties protected by the Constitution. In our governmental system, the courts play a major role in reconciling these conflicting interests. Hence, we now focus our attention on how the courts have responded to this problem.

---

[1] The action directed at Communists by Attorney General A. Mitchell Palmer immediately following World War I has been characterized as the first "Red scare."

## SEDITION AND ESPIONAGE

The Bill of Rights was less than a decade old when war hysteria (activated by France) prompted the Federalist-dominated Congress to enact several measures in 1798 to protect the government from internal subversion. One of these—the Sedition Act—contained restrictions which cut deeply into the free speech and press guarantees of the First Amendment. Aimed at stifling criticism of the Administration's foreign policies, the most suppressive provision of the Act made it illegal for anyone to "write, print or publish . . . any false, scandalous and malicious writing . . . against the government of the United States, or either house of the Congress . . . , or the President . . . , with intent to defame . . . , or to bring them . . . into contempt or disrepute or to excite against them . . . the hatred of the good people of the United States. . . ." In short, the Act allowed legal punishment for nothing more than political criticism of governmental officials. Federalist-dominated courts, however, generally precluded constitutional challenges to the Act by those charged with violating it. Consequently, the Supreme Court was never presented with the issue since the Act, passed as a temporary measure, expired in 1801 after being in force a little less than three years.

Some of President Lincoln's actions during the Civil War produced severe tensions between the exercise of federal warpower and liberties guaranteed by the Bill of Rights. However, Congress did not enact policy again in this area until World War I, at which time it enacted two measures. The Espionage Act of 1917 made it a crime for any person to attempt to obstruct military recruiting, to attempt to cause acts of insubordination in the armed forces, and to make false statements and reports calculated to interfere with the successful prosecution of the war. The Act also authorized the Postmaster General to exclude from the mails treasonable and seditious matter.

In 1918, Congress passed the Sedition Act as a comprehensive amendment to the Espionage Act. This new law was much more suppressive than the 1917 Espionage Act, and its language was similar in tone to the 1798 Sedition Act. The most stringent provision of the 1918 law made it a crime to ". . . utter, print or publish disloyal, profane, scurrilous, or abusive language about the form of government, the Constitution, soldiers and sailors, [the] flag, or uniform of the armed forces . . ." with intent to bring scorn, contempt and disrepute upon them. The provision also made it illegal for one "by word or act [to] support or favor the cause of the . . . [enemy] in the present war, or by word or act [to] oppose the cause of the United States."

Unlike the first congressional enactments in this area, the constitutionality of these statutes was passed upon by the Supreme Court. The validity of the Espionage Act was considered in *Schenck* v. *United States* (249 U.S. 47, 1919). Schenck was convicted for printing and circulating leaflets allegedly calculated to obstruct recruiting and to cause insubordination in the military forces. One side of the leaflet in question proclaimed that the Conscription Act violated the Thirteenth Amendment in that "a conscript is little more than a convict." It also intimated that the war was a monstrous wrong against humanity perpetrated by Wall Street interests. On the other side of the leaflet, an article entitled "Assert Your Rights," reference was made to arguments in support of the draft as coming from "cunning politicians" and "a mercenary capitalist press." It further encouraged people to speak out in opposition to the draft for "silent consent [helps] to support an infamous conspiracy."

In appealing the conviction, Schenck argued that the statute infringed his freedom of speech and press guarantees of the First Amendment. However, Justice Oliver Wendell Holmes, speaking for a unanimous Court, rejected this contention. It was here that Holmes put forth the now familiar clear-and-present-danger test. Said Holmes: "The question in every case is whether the words used are used in such circumstances and are of such a nature as to create a clear and present danger that they will bring about the substantive evils that Congress has a right to prevent." Applying this test, Holmes rejected the notion that freedom of speech and freedom of the press were absolutes; rather, he contended that judges must consider the circumstances in which such expressions are made. "The most stringent protection of free speech," said Holmes, "would not protect a man in falsely shouting fire in a theater and causing a panic." He concluded by noting that "[w]hen a nation is at war, many things that might be said in time of peace are such a hindrance to its effort that their utterance will not be endured so long as men fight, and no Court could regard them as protected by any constitutional right."

The clear-and-present-danger test, although portending protection for all but the most dangerous views calculated to produce substantive evils immediately, did not achieve that purpose in subsequent prosecutions under both the Espionage and Sedition Acts. For example, in *Frohwerk* v. *United States* (249 U.S. 204, 1919)[2] the Court upheld an Espionage Act conviction where the accused had published, in a German-language newspaper, articles examining the constitutionality of the war and the draft. Obviously, the danger from such publication was not imminent, but Justice Holmes begged the question when he contended: ". . . it is impossible to say that it might not have been found that the circulation of the paper was in quarters where a little breath would be enough to kindle a flame and that the fact was known and relied upon by those who sent the paper out."

The constitutionality of the Sedition Act was sustained in *Abrams* v.

2 See also *Debs* v. *United States* (249 U.S. 211, 1919), and *Pierce* v. *United States* (252 U.S. 239, 1920).

*United States* (250 U.S. 616, 1919). The case was an appeal of a conviction for publishing two leaflets in which abusive language, the indictment charged, "intended to bring the form of government of the United States into contempt." In condemning the government's sending an expeditionary force to Russia, one leaflet referred to the "President's cowardly silence about the intervention in Russia, [as revealing] the hypocrisy of the plutocratic gang in Washington." The leaflet went on to charge "that German militarism combined with allied capitalism . . . to crush the Russian revolution" and that capitalism is the "only . . . enemy of the workers of the world." The other leaflet, entitled "Workers—Wake Up!," called for a general strike and reminded Russian-emigrant factory workers that they were producing ammunition that was being used not only to murder Germans but also to kill Russians fighting for freedom.

The Supreme Court virtually ignored the clear-and-present-danger test in affirming the conviction. In rejecting the appellant's contention that the leaflets were within the protection of the First Amendment, Justice John Clark's opinion for the Court emphasized that the purpose of the pamphlets was "not an attempt to bring about a change of administration by candid discussion." Rather, the justice contended, the pamphlets were designed to "excite, at the supreme crisis of the war, disaffection, sedition, riots, and . . . revolution" in an attempt to defeat the government's war plans. Consequently, the argument that the pamphlets had only the limited purpose of preventing injury to the Russian cause was not a sufficient defense. "Men," argued Clark, "must be held to have intended and to be accountable for the effects which their acts were likely to produce."

Justices Holmes and Brandeis dissented. Holmes's dissent has since become a classic statement in defense of freedom of speech. To him, the Court should have used the clear-and-present-danger test. "Nobody can suppose that the surreptitious publishing of a silly leaflet by an unknown man without more," said Holmes, "would present any immediate danger that its opinions would hinder the success of government arms or have any appreciable tendency to do so."

He concluded:

Persecution for the expression of opinions seems to me perfectly logical. If you have no doubt of your premises or your power and want a certain result with all your heart you naturally express your wishes in law and sweep away all opposition. To allow opposition by speech seems to indicate that you think the speech impotent, as when a man says that he has squared the circle, or that you do not care whole-heartedly for the result, or that you doubt either your power or your premises. But when men have realized that time has upset many fighting faiths, they may come to believe even more than they believe the very foundations of their own conduct that the ultimate good desired is better reached by free trade in ideas—that the best test of truth is the power of the thought to get itself accepted in the competition of the market, and that truth is the only ground upon which their wishes safely can be carried out. . . . [I] think that we should be eternally vigilant against attempts to check the expression of opinions that we loathe and believe to be fraught with death unless they so imminently threaten immediate interference with the lawful and pressing purposes of the law that an immediate check is required to save the country.

But Holmes's views were not to carry the day. The Court majority continued to ignore the clear-and-present-danger test and affirmed several convictions where nothing more than discussion of the merits of the war was involved.

In 1940, Congress enacted the Alien Registration Act, now popularly known as the Smith Act. Concerned with the increasing possibility of United States involvement in World War II, the act was viewed as an essential wartime measure designed to prevent espionage and sedition. One of the first prosecutions under the act involved a group of Trotskyites who were convicted of conspiring to advocate insubordination in the armed forces and the overthrow of the government by force and violence. The convictions were affirmed by the court of appeals and the Supreme Court refused to hear the appeals. (*Dunne* v. *United States,* 138 F2d 137; 320 U.S. 790, 1943). In another early prosecution under the act several pro-Nazis were indicted for conspiracy to violate Section 1 of the act by distributing leaflets that urged insubordination in the armed forces. The trial judge died during the trial and the indictment was later ordered dismissed when the government failed to undertake a new trial. (*United States* v. *McWilliams,* 163 F2d 695, 1947.)

The most significant and controversial litigation, however, was to come in the post-war era against native Communists under the advocacy, conspiracy, and membership clauses of Section 2. Specifically, these provisions made it illegal for any person to: (1) knowingly or willfully advocate . . . or teach the overthrow or destruction of any government in the United States by force and violence; (2) print, publish and disseminate written matter advocating such overthrow; (3) participate in the organization of any group dedicated to such purposes; and (4) acquire and hold membership in such a group with knowledge of its purposes.

In the years immediately following World War II relations between the United States and the Soviet Union deteriorated to the point of a "cold-war" impasse. Suspicion mounted that the international Communist conspiracy was being actively supported by native Communists and these suspicions were stirred into a kind of widespread public hysteria as some Republican politicians charged that Communists were occupying positions in government and had infiltrated the military-industrial complex. Stung by Republican charges of official insensitivity to and toleration of Communists in such vital places, the Democratic party realized that being tagged with a "soft on Communism" label could be very damaging in the forthcoming general elections. Hence, in 1948 the Justice Department moved to enforce the Smith Act against the American Communist party when eleven of its leaders were charged in an indictment with: (1) willfully and knowingly conspiring to organize the Communist party, a group of persons who teach and advocate the overthrow of the government by force and violence; and (2) willfully and knowingly advocating and teaching the duty and necessity of overthrowing the government by force and violence.

After a marathon trial lasting nine months, the Communist leaders were found guilty as charged. Subsequently, their convictions were affirmed by both the Court of Appeals for the Second Circuit and the Supreme Court in *Dennis* v. *United States.* Both courts found that the act, on its face and as applied, did not cut too deeply into constitutional guarantees. In fact, Chief Justice Fred Vinson, writing the leading opinion for the Supreme Court, adopted as correct and appropriate the test applied in the court of appeals by Judge Learned Hand. To Judge Hand, the crucial question was "whether the gravity of the evil, discounted by its improbability, justifies such invasion of free speech as is necessary to avoid the danger." The Chief Justice reasoned that since the government's very existence was at stake, the clear-and-present-danger test did not mean that the government could not act until the *putsch* was about to be executed. Knowledge of the existence of a group aiming at overthrow "as speedily as circumstances would permit" was deemed sufficient to justify restrictive governmental action. "The contention that success or probability of success," concluded Vinson, must be rejected as the criterion for governmental action.

Justices Frankfurter and Jackson wrote concurring opinions in which they focused on the application of the clear-and-present-danger test in such cases. Frankfurter, reiterating his position in earlier decisions, rejected the test as "a sonorous formula which is in fact only a euphemistic disguise for an unresolved conflict" incapable of resolving the conflicting interests in the case. For him, a "candid and informed weighing of competing interests within the confines of the judicial process" provides a more meaningful approach to the conflict resolution.

Unlike Frankfurter, Justice Jackson did not make an outright condemnation of the clear-and-present-danger test. It was certainly applicable to the kinds of cases for which it was originally devised—"hotheaded speech on a street corner, or circulation of a few incendiary pamphlets, or parading by some zealots behind a red flag, or refusal of a handful of school children to salute [the American] flag." But, he contended, the test was never intended to be applied to this kind of case. To adhere to the test, he concluded, would in effect "hold [the] Government captive in a judge-made verbal trap."

The dissents of Black and Douglas condemned the statute as unconstitutional on its face because it permitted previous restraint on freedom of speech and freedom of the press. In addition, they both complained that the clear-and-present-danger test had not been met by the majority. As Douglas observed: "How it can be said that there is a clear and present danger that this advocacy will succeed is . . . a mystery."

Having successfully enforced the act against the Communist party's highest leaders, the Government moved against many lower-level leaders. Public opinion in support of such action had been molded by the "exposés" of Senator Joseph McCarthy, the deadlocked Korean war, and continued uneasy relations with the Soviet Union. In the final years of the Truman Administration and the first years of the Eisenhower presidency almost one hundred convictions under sections 2 and 3 of the act were obtained and the Supreme Court refused to review them. In 1955, however, the Court granted certiorari in the cases of fourteen second-string Communists from California and, in its decision two years later (*Yates* v. *United States,* 354 U.S. 298, 1957), modified its *Dennis* holding. Contending that the government's reliance on *Dennis* was misplaced, Justce John Marshall Harlan emphasized in his opinion for the Court that *Dennis* had not obliterated the distinction between mere advocacy of the abstract doctrine of forcible overthrow of the government and action-inciting advocacy calculated to achieve forcible overthrow. Having failed to make such a distinction, he argued, the evidence presented in *Yates* (primarily the same upon which the *Dennis* convictions rested) was insufficient to prove "advocacy of action." Harlan also rejected the district court's conclusion that the act punished per se "mere doctrinal justification of forcible overthrow," engaged in with an intent to bring the overthrow about. On the contrary, he contended that although such advocacy may be "uttered with the hope that it may ultimately lead to violent revolution, [it] is too remote from concrete action to be regarded as the kind of indoctrination preparatory to action which was condemned in *Dennis*."

To be sure, the Court did not return to the pre-*Dennis* clear-and-present-danger rule. However, *Yates* laid down more stringent evidentiary requirements. Showing that defendants had advocated and taught the doctrines set forth in the various Communist classics was held to be insufficient. It was necessary to show that such advocacy was one of an incitement to action with a specific intent to bring about that action.

The more stringent evidentiary requirements made further convictions under the advocacy and conspiracy clauses of the act extremely difficult, if not impossible. As a matter of fact, the indictments against nine of the *Yates* defendants, whose cases were remanded by the Court for new trials, were dismissed after the government admitted that it was unable to satisfy those requirements. In addition, the *Yates* ruling served as a basis for reversal of a number of convictions by the courts of appeals and the government dropped other prosecutions.

The Court's retreat from *Dennis* must be considered in the context of swiftly changing foreign and domestic conditions. In the first place, aggression of the North Korean Communists had been successfully checked with the conclusion of peace negotiations in 1953. Furthermore, the public hysteria over internal subversion by native Communists had subsided with the McCarthy censure action in the United States Senate in 1954 and his subsequent death. In addition, Stalin's death in 1953 was followed by a slight thaw in the cold war and a move toward peaceful coexistence in American-Soviet relations. Add to these factors the changes in Supreme Court personnel after 1953, particularly the addition of Warren and Brennan, and the move away from *Dennis* to the more libertarian construction of the Smith Act in *Yates* is more readily understood.

Several prosecutions under the membership clause of the Smith Act had been initiated prior to the government's setback in *Yates*. After some seven years of litigation, the Supreme Court sustained the constitutionality of the clause in *Scales* v. *United States*. Justice John Marshall Harlan's opinion for the 5–4 majority rejected the petitioner's contention that the membership clause had been repealed by section 4(f) of the Internal Security Act of 1950 which stipulates that "neither the holding of office nor membership in any Communist organization . . . shall constitute per se a violation of . . . this section or of any other criminal statute." Harlan contended that there was a constitutional difference between the membership to which section 4(f) applied and the membership made illegal by the Smith Act. The latter was "knowing" and "active" membership—the "active" quality being correctly applied in the lower court's construction of the clause. This distinction not only saved the provision from the alleged repeal but it overcame the argument that the clause was unconstitutionally broad because of its condemnation of mere passive and nominal membership. Thus, Scales's conviction was valid because the trial court had appropriately construed the statute as condemning only "active" membership, applicable to those who had knowledge of or who personally harbored, a specific intent to bring about the forcible overthrow of the government.

In dissent, Justice Douglas complained that the majority's action legalized "guilt by association." He contended that there was no evidence of overt acts but only beliefs and ideas, and no matter how revolting they are, the First Amendment protects them. He also contended, as did the other dissenters, that the majority had "practically rewritten the statute" to save it.

In another membership clause decision announced with *Scales* (*Noto* v. *United States,* 367 U.S. 290, 1961), the Court reversed the conviction on the grounds of insufficient evidence. Justice Harlan held that the government's evidence did not satisfy the statutory requirement of proof of "present illegal party advocacy." The only fact the evidence showed, he concluded, was that the Communist party to which Noto belonged was merely engaged in "abstract teaching of Communist theory."

The increasing intensity in the opposition to United States involvement in the Vietnam war has once again raised questions pertaining to the limits of freedom of expression in challenging governmental war policies. To supplement existing laws against obstruction of the draft, Congress, in 1965, passed a statute making destruction of draft cards a federal crime. The statute's aim was to put an end to the well publicized "draft-card burning" ceremonies as an expression of opposition to the war. Several persons have been convicted under the statute and the Supreme Court affirmed the convictions and upheld the constitutionality of the statute in *United States* v. *O'Brien, supra.*

In a related action against Vietnam war protestors, several persons (including famed pediatrician Dr. Benjamin Spock and Yale University Chaplain William Sloan Coffin) were indicted and convicted for violating a provision of the Selective Service Act (50 U.S.C. 462a, 1958 ed.) by conspiring to counsel and aid persons in resisting the draft for service in the Vietnam war. The convictions were reversed by the Court of Appeals for the First Circuit. Dr. Spock and another defendant were ordered acquitted because of insufficient evidence of conspiracy on their part, while the cases of Chaplain Coffin and another defendant were remanded for possible new trials because of trial court error. The court made it clear, however, that while the kind of expression used by the defendants was intricately tied in with general anti-war advocacy which is protected by the First Amendment, conspiracy to counsel and aid young men to resist the draft does not have such protection. (*U.S.* v. *Spock*, 38 L. W. 1017, 1969).

Legislation against sedition and subversion has not been limited to congressional action; a number of states have enacted and enforced laws directed at expressions inimical to the general welfare and security of the government. Variously titled as "criminal anarchy" or "criminal syndicalism" statutes, such laws were originally enacted to deal with late 19th- and early 20th-century anarchists. But they served as convenient tools against various brands of revolutionaires during the "Red scare" period of the 1920s and the 1930s. The New York statute enacted in 1902 was typical of legislation on the subject. It defined criminal anarchy as the doctrine which held that organized government should be overthrown by force and violence—by assassination of governmental executives or by other unlawful means—and the statute made it a crime for any person to advocate the doctrine in writing or in speech.[3] The statute

[3] The California Criminal Syndicalism Act, which contained limitations on expression similar to those in the New York law discussed here, was upheld in *Whitney* v. *California* (274 U.S. 357, 1927). In that case, Justice Louis Brandeis' concurring opinion was devoted to a further clarification of the clear-and-present-danger test. In brief, he contended that "[t]o justify suppression of free speech there must be reasonable grounds to fear that serious evil will result if free speech is practiced. . . ." Moreover,

was upheld in *Gitlow* v. *New York* against the challenge that it abridged the constitutional guarantees of freedom of speech and freedom of the press.[4]

After World War II, when there was considerable federal activity directed at subversion generally and Communist activities specifically, the Court showed concern about possible conflicting state regulatory activity in this area. In *Pennsylvania* v. *Nelson* (350 U.S. 497, 1956) a majority of six Justices agreed that a state sedition law must be set aside because Congress had preempted the field in protecting the country from seditious conduct. Chief Justice Earl Warren contended that the "pervasiveness" of federal legislation was indicative of the congressional intention to have sole occupancy in the field. State laws have to be limited to sedition against the state. Justices Harold Burton, Sherman Minton, and Stanley Reed dissented, arguing that in the absence of an expressed exclusivity by Congress, states shared concurrent power in the area.

## INCULCATING LOYALTY

Following World War II, both the federal and the state governments instituted procedures designed to protect their operations from internal subversion. Generally, the procedures had two objectives: (1) securing loyal employees, and (2) detecting and dismissing disloyal employees.

The first postwar federal loyalty program was instituted in 1947 by an Executive Order issued by the Truman Administration. The order required the Civil Service Commission to conduct loyalty investigations of almost all employees before they were permitted to enter the competitive service of the Executive branch. A pre-entry loyalty check of a non-competitive appointee was to be conducted by the specific agency making the appointment. The order also created loyalty boards in the various agencies of the Executive branch and required them to conduct hearings on charges of disloyalty brought against any employee of the agency. Several levels of review were available for a person challenging the determination of his agency board, with the ultimate administrative review assigned to the Loyalty Review Board created by the executive order.

Many charged that the order and the procedures instituted to enforce it cut deeply into constitutional guarantees. For one thing, gossip and

---

he maintained, "no danger flowing from speech can be deemed clear and present, unless the incidence of the evil apprehended is so imminent that it may befall before there is opportunity for full discussion." On the other hand, he concluded, ,'[i]f there be time to explore through discussion the falsehood and fallacies, to avert evil by the processes of education, the remedy . . . is more speech, not enforced silence."

4 For a discussion of the Court's "legislative reasonableness" test applied in *Gitlow,* see Chapter 3.

rumor could be the basis for an investigation in which the employee often was not afforded confrontation and cross-examination privileges. Furthermore, the order collided with First Amendment associational guarantees by authorizing the Attorney General to compile a list of subversive organizations and by directing investigators to consider a person's membership in, or sympathy with, such groups in determining his loyalty. In a subsequent Executive Order issued by President Truman, it became possible to dismiss an employee when a hearing resulted in inconclusive findings but a reasonable doubt as to loyalty existed. This new standard led to the reopening of a number of earlier cases decided under the stricter standard and the ultimate dismissal of a number of persons who had previously been given clearance.

The standard for discharge on loyalty grounds became more sweeping under the program inaugurated by President Eisenhower in 1953. In fact, the standard of "disloyalty" was replaced by the standard of "security risk." Under it, discharge was possible after a hearing in which it was found merely that a person's employment "may not be consistent with the interests of national security." An employee could be labelled a "security risk" and dismissed for: (1) sexual immorality and perversion; (2) drug addiction; (3) excessive intoxication; (4) criminal, infamous, dishonest, or notoriously disgraceful conduct; (5) conspiring to commit, or committing, acts of treason, sabotage, sedition, or espionage; (6) membership in, or affiliation and sympathetic association with, subversive groups, etc. Furthermore, investigations were not restricted to current behavior; earlier cases in which clearance had been granted could be reopened and tested against the new standard.

The Court considered the constitutionality of the Truman program in two 1951 cases. In *Bailey* v. *Richardson* (182 F2d 46, 1950; 341 U.S. 918, 1951) the Court of Appeals for the District of Columbia sustained a removal for disloyalty, but it held that under the doctrine enunciated in *United States* v. *Lovett* (328 U.S. 303, 1946),[5] the loyalty board order barring an employee from the federal service for three years constituted a bill of attainder. The validity of the removal was based on the principle that since there is no constitutional right to federal employment, the due process and First Amendment claims are without merit. An equally divided Supreme Court (Justice Clark did not participate) affirmed the decision without opinion.

At issue in the second case—*Joint Anti-Fascist Refugee Committee* v. *McGrath* (341 U.S. 123, 1951)—was the Attorney General's procedure in compiling the list of subversive organizations. In a 5–3 decision (Justice Tom Clark did not participate), the Supreme Court reversed

---

[5] The Court held as an unconstitutional bill of attainder a rider appended to an appropriations act which prohibited payment of the salaries of three designated federal officials who had incurred the wrath of the House Committee on Un-American Activities.

a lower court ruling which had denied relief to several groups in attempts to remove their names from the Attorney General's list. That each of the majority justices (Burton, Frankfurter, Jackson, Douglas, and Black) wrote an opinion is indicative of the difficulty in reaching agreement in this area. Only Justice Douglas agreed with Justice Burton, who announced the judgment in this case. They took the position that the Attorney General's action in designating the complaining groups was arbitrary and without authority under the Executive Order. Other opinions by majority justices stressed the denial of due process because the Attorney General had blacklisted the groups without notice and hearing. For Justice Black, the Executive Order itself was unconstitutional because the First Amendment bars punishing organizations and their members merely because of beliefs. He also contended that "officially prepared and proclaimed blacklists" constitute a bill of attainder.

In the years following the *Bailey* and *Joint Anti-Fascist* rulings, the Warren Court ruled on a number of "loyalty dismissals" but carefully avoided constitutional issues. Instead, reversals were based on such procedural and statutory grounds as the lack of authorization for discharge under the terms of the loyalty order held in *Peters* v. *Hobby* (349 U.S. 331, 1955); the lack of statutory authority for dismissals in "nonsensitive" positions in *Cole* v. *Young* (351 U.S. 536, 1956); or the failure to follow established administrative procedures noted in *Service* v. *Dulles* (354 U.S. 363, 1957).

Several congressional enactments have included provisions designed to protect national security from disloyal individuals operating in the private sector. Aware of Communist infiltration into the labor movement, Congress included a provision in the Taft-Hartley Act of 1947 designed to stimulate a kind of "self-policing" by labor unions. Specifically, section 9(h) of the act denied any labor union access to the facilities of the National Labor Relations Board unless each of its officers had executed and filed with the board an affidavit swearing: (1) that he is not a member of, or affiliated with, the Communist party; and (2) that he does not believe in, is not a member of, or does not support any organization that believes in or teaches the doctrine of forcible overthrow of the government of the United States. The Court upheld the constitutionality of the provision in *American Communications Association* v. *Douds* (339 U.S. 94, 1950). Chief Justice Fred Vinson, announcing the Court's judgment and writing the principal opinion, accepted the statute as a valid exercise of the commerce power. He admitted that the statute imposed some restriction on political freedom but contended that the legislative action designed to prevent disruptive political strikes justified the relatively small restrictions placed on First Amendment freedoms. In dissent, Justice Hugo Black expressed his oft-proclaimed view that governments can impose penalties for personal conduct but not for beliefs or for the conduct of others with whom one associates. He felt it most unfortunate that the majority had, in effect, legalized "guilt by association."

In practice, Section 9(h) of the Taft-Hartley Act—the affidavit provision—upheld in *Douds* proved ineffective. Consequently, it was repealed by the Labor Management Reporting and Disclosure Act of 1959 and replaced by a provision (Section 504) which made it a crime for a member of the Communist party to serve as an officer or as an employee (excluding clerical and custodial positions) of any labor organization. This new statute, however, did not fare as well in the courts as did its predecessor. In *United States* v. *Brown* (381 U.S. 437, 1965) the Supreme Court held that it was an unconstitutional bill of attainder. Chief Justice Earl Warren, writing the opinion for the 5–4 majority, noted that the statute does not—as it should—set forth a general rule of conduct detailing "specified acts" and "specified characteristics," the commission or possession of which would make a person ineligible for union office and employment. Nor does it "leave to the courts and juries the job of deciding what persons have committed the specified acts or possess the specified characteristics." Instead, the Chief Justice contended, Congress was guilty of usurping the judicial function by "designating in no uncertain terms the persons who possess the feared characteristics" (members of the Communist party) who are thus prohibited from holding "union office without incurring criminal liability." In short, he concluded, Congress "cannot specify the people upon whom the sanction it prescribes is to be levied."

Justice Byron White disagreed, in an opinion supported by Justices Tom Clark, John Marshall Harlan, and Potter Stewart. He argued that tested against the traditional definition of a bill of attainder, the statute in no way imposes "legislative punishment of particular individuals." Criticizing the majority for its "too narrow view of the legislative process," White contended that Congress had done no more than adopt a fairer and more effective method of forestalling political strikes. Certainly, he noted, there were ample findings to support the conclusion of Congress "that members of the Communist party were likely to call political strikes." Hence, he concluded that the statute did not have a punitive purpose; rather, it was "reasonably related to a permissible legislative objective."

In another action designed to prevent disruption of industrial production for national defense purposes, Congress included a provision in the Subversive Activities Control Act of 1950 which made it illegal for a member of a Communist-action group which is under final order to register[6] "to engage in any employment in any defense facility." However, the Supreme Court declared the provision unconstitutional in *United States* v. *Robel* (389 U.S. 258, 1967). In his opinion for the 7–2

[6] See The Communist Party Registration Controversy discussed in the next section of this chapter.

majority, Chief Justice Earl Warren emphasized that while Congress has the power to enact legislation "to keep from sensitive positions in defense facilities those who would use their positions to disrupt production," it may not enact legislation (as involved here) which is so sweeping that it condemns not only association which may be constitutionally proscribed but also association which is protected by the First Amendment as well. Justice Byron White's dissent questioned the majority's balancing of the interests in favor of a right "not mentioned in the Constitution." Chiding the majority for concluding that the danger presented by Robel was insufficient to put him to the choice of membership in the Communist party or employment in a defense facility, he indicated a preference for the judgment of Congress and the Executive branch in weighing those competing interests.

Uncovering and removing disloyal employees has been a major concern of the several states also. The basic ingredients of these loyalty programs have been the oath-taking requirement and/or the filing of a non-Communist disclaimer affidavit. The courts until recently have generally found such requirements constitutionally acceptable on the grounds that one does not have a constitutional right to state employment and that states, exercising their authority to determine the fitness and competence of their employees, may require of employees some type of affirmation or disclaimer that they have not or do not advocate forcible overthrow of the government nor belong to organizations engaged in such advocacy. Justice Tom Clark emphasized this principle in *Garner* v. *Board of Public Works* (341 U.S. 716, 1951) in which the Court upheld the Los Angeles loyalty program covering municipal employees. Approving the disclaimer affidavit, upon which every employee was required to indicate his past (limited to the preceding five years) or present affiliation with the Communist party or the Communist Political Association, Justice Clark contended:

Past conduct may well relate to present fitness; past loyalty may have a reasonable relationship to present and future trust. Both are commonly inquired into in determining fitness for both high and low positions in private industry and are not less relevant in public employment.

The oath requirement in which an employee had to indicate that he had not advocated or taught the doctrine of forcible overthrow of the government during the preceding five-year period was sustained against ex post facto and bill of attainder claims. Justice Clark noted simply that the ordinance requiring the oath did not impose "punishment for past conduct lawful at the time it was engaged in." He further noted that the activity proscribed by the oath had been denied employees by a Charter provision enacted two years prior to the "preceding five-year period" covered by the oath. He also brushed aside the bill of attainder attack with the statement that "we are unable to conclude that punishment is imposed by a general regulation which merely provides standards or qualifications and eligibility for employment."

Supporters of loyalty oaths thought it essential to shield juvenile innocence and young adult idealism from the "cunning proselytizing" of Communists and subversives who had somehow managed to infiltrate the sensitive setting of the public schoolroom. The Court's early approach to oaths for public school teachers is illustrated in *Adler* v. *Board of Education* (342 U.S. 485, 1952). At issue was New York's Feinberg Law which required the State Board of Regents to publish, after notice and hearing, a list of subversive organizations which advocate the forcible overthrow of the government. Membership in an organization included on this list was *prima facie* evidence of disqualification. An earlier statutory provision denied employment in the civil service and public school system to any person who advocated the forcible overthrow of the government or who was affiliated with any organization engaged in such advocacy.

The Court upheld the law and, in an opinion by Justice Sherman Minton, reasserted the doctrines that one does not have a constitutional right to public employment and that disclosure of associational ties with subversive groups may be compelled of employees in determining their fitness and competence. Justice Minton underscored the justification for such an inquiry of those seeking employment in the public schools when he noted:

> A teacher works in a sensitive area in a schoolroom. There he shapes the attitude of young minds towards the society in which they live. In this the state has a vital concern. It must preserve the integrity of the schools.

In both the *Garner* and *Adler* cases, *supra,* the statutes were upheld because they carefully distinguished between "knowing membership" and "innocent membership," without knowledge of the organization's illegal purposes. By excluding the latter from punishment, the laws did not suffer the infirmity of "overbreadth." In striking down Oklahoma's loyalty-oath statute in *Wieman* v. *Updegraff* (344 U.S. 183, 1952) the Court made it clear that the Constitution requires such a distinction. As Justice Tom Clark noted in the opinion for the Court, the state courts had construed the statute so that "the fact of membership alone disqualifies," and as such the "indiscriminate classification of innocent with knowing activity must fall as an assertion of arbitrary power."

A practice employed in some states was to disqualify from public employment any person who, asserting the Fifth Amendment guarantee against compulsory self-incrimination, refused to answer questions put to him by investigating committees concerning Communist and subversive activities. In *Slochower* v. *Board of Higher Education of the City of New York* (350 U.S. 551, 1956) the Supreme Court condemned this practice as applied to a college professor because of the automatic assumption of one's guilt merely for asserting a valid constitutional privilege. The net effect was to punish a person for invoking a constitutional right. The Court extended this precedent to strike down actions denying lawyers admission to the bar for refusing to answer questions concerning their Communist affiliations and activities. (*Schware* v. *New Mexico Board of Bar Examiners,* 353 U.S. 232, 1957; *Konigsberg* v. *State Bar of California,* 353 U.S. 252, 1957.)

The Court undercut the impact of its *Slochower, Schware,* and *Konigsberg* rulings in *Belian* v. *Board of Education* (357 U.S. 399, 1958) and *Lerner* v. *Casey* (357 U.S. 468, 1958). In each case, the employee had been dismissed after invoking the Fifth Amendment in refusing to answer questions concerning Communist party affiliations and activities. In *Belian,* the Court felt that the Board's action in discharging a teacher for "incompetence"[7] rather than for disloyalty was not in conflict with the *Slochower* line of cases. Likewise, the Court held that Lerner's discharge as a New York subway employee on "reliability" ground was sufficiently distinguishable from *Slochower* so as not to offend due process.

The Court's current approach to state loyalty oaths for public employees is illustrated in *Elfbrandt* v. *Russell* (384 U.S. 11, 1966), *Keyishian* v. *Board of Regents of New York,* and *Whitehall* v. *Elkins* (389 U.S. 54, 1967). At issue in *Elfbrandt* was the constitutionality of the Arizona loyalty oath requiring an affirmation of allegiance and support of the federal and the Arizona constitutions and laws. The oath was supplemented by a statute which made criminal the knowing membership in the Communist party or in any other organization which has as one of its purposes the violent overthrow of the government. The Court held that the oath and the accompanying statute abridged the freedom of association protected by the First and the Fourteenth Amendments. Justice William O. Douglas' opinion for the majority found both the oath and the statute constitutionally defective for failure to exclude from penalty association by one who does not subscribe to an organization's unlawful ends. In *Keyishian,* the Court reversed *Adler* v. *Board of Education* and struck down New York's Feinberg law and other provisions of the education law implementing the loyalty program. Justice William J. Brennan's opinion emphasized the need for precision and specificity in regulations touching First Amendment freedoms. He contended that New York's scheme was interwoven in a maze of vagueness and "wholly lacking in terms susceptible of objective measurement." Likewise, in *Whitehall* v. *Elkins,* the Court found the statutory basis of the Maryland oath suffering from a similar infirmity of vagueness. Justice William O. Douglas, in delivering the opinion for the majority, called the case a "classic example of the need for 'narrowly drawn'

---

[7] Belian had refused to answer questions about her past Communist activities even before invoking the Fifth Amendment at a subsequent HUAC hearing.

legislation . . . in this sensitive and important First Amendment area."

Congress has not overlooked the possibility of stamping out subversion through use of the non-Communist disclaimer affidavit for participation in federally financed general welfare programs. For example, the execution of a disclaimer affidavit was initially required of all students seeking financial assistance under the National Defense Education Loan Act. Vigorous opposition to this "loyalty test" from many segments of the academic community and the refusal of a number of "prestige" institutions of higher learning to participate in the program under such terms led to a repeal of the provision in 1962. Similar disclaimers were required of those entering the Job Corps and various programs operating under the Economic Opportunity Act of 1964, but in 1965 the disclaimer requirement was repealed. Congress also included for a non-Communist disclaimer affidavit provision in the Medicare law, but after vigorous opposition, including the filing of several suits testing its constitutionality, the Department of Health, Education, and Welfare ruled that failure to answer the disclaimer question on the application form would not be used as a basis for disqualification.

## THE COMMUNIST PARTY REGISTRATION CONTROVERSY

Congress employed the "exposure" technique designed to bring Communist groups out into the open by setting forth an elaborate registration scheme in the Internal Security Act of 1950. Declaring that the Communist conspiracy represented a threat to national security, the act required "communist-action" and "communist-front" organizations to register with the Attorney General. A Subversive Activities Control Board was created and charged with the duty of conducting hearings to determine the status of organizations to which the Government sought to apply the act. Under the act, a finding against an organization results in an order to register in the category designated, which requires a disclosure of officers, finances, etc. The act of registration produces a number of disabilities for the organization and its members, e.g., restriction on organizational mailing privileges and denial of passports.

After a protracted hearing, the Board found the act applicable to the Communist party, U.S.A., and an order was entered in April, 1953, requiring the Party to register as a "communist-action" group. That order was set aside by the Supreme Court in 1956 because the Board's finding included some tainted evidence by several Government witnesses. A subsequent hearing produced a similar finding and an order to register. In *Communist Party* v. *Subversive Activities Control Board* (367 U.S. 1, 1961) the Supreme Court affirmed the order and sustained the constitutionality of the registration provisions. Justice Felix Frankfurter's voluminous opinion boiled down to a balancing of competing interests. The

Government's interest in protecting against the threat from such groups far outweighed the First Amendment claims. In this connection, the case was very distinguishable from the NAACP membership cases where the alleged public interest in disclosure was too insubstantial to warrant such an intrusion into First Amendment rights. Frankfurter was careful to avoid the Fifth Amendment self-incrimination issue, insisting that the claim was prematurely raised since it had not been invoked by party officers as individuals. The issue would be appropriately litigable in proceedings stemming from a failure to register under a final order.

When faced with a final order to register shortly thereafter, Party leaders refused to comply, asserting the self-incrimination claim. The Party was subsequently prosecuted, convicted, and fined $120,000 for failure to register. The Court of Appeals for the District of Columbia reversed the conviction in *Communist Party of the United States* v. *United States* (331 F2d 807, 1963), holding that the trial court had erred in refusing to consider the self-incrimination issue. In his opinion for the Court, Chief Judge David Bazelon emphasized that "the act of registering [under the act] is necessarily incriminating" although no other information except the registrant's name is given. He contended that a letter sent to the Attorney General (signed with the party seal) refusing to comply for fear of self-incrimination was a sufficient assertion of the claim. Hence, since no one was available to complete the forms by reason of a valid claim of the self-incrimination guarantee, the government had the burden of showing that a volunteer was available to provide the information. Judge Bazelon was careful to deny any organizational assertion of the privilege or assertion of it by an individual for the organization or its members. The Supreme Court refused to review the case, allowing the court of appeals holding to stand.

Having failed in its efforts to require the Communist party to register, the government proceeded to enforce the provisions of the act requiring individual members of a "communist-action" group to register upon default of the organization. In *Albertson* v. *Subversive Activities Control Board* the Supreme Court reversed a court of appeals decision which had affirmed Board orders for individual registration. Justice William J. Brennan contended, in his opinion for the Court, that the lower court had erred in holding that the self-incrimination claim was prematurely raised. The effect of the holding below, he continued, was to force the petitioners to a choice of registration without a decision on the merits of their self-incrimination claim or of refusing to register and risk "mounting penalties while awaiting the government's pleasure" of initiating prosecution for failure to register. He concluded that putting them to such a choice amounts to a denial of the Fifth Amendment protection against compulsory self-incrimination because the admission of membership in the Communist party could result in prosecution under the membership clause of the Smith Act, *supra*.

## OUTLAWING THE COMMUNIST PARTY

On March 4, 1954, Congressman Martin Dies,[8] speaking in the House of Representatives in support of a bill he had introduced to outlaw the American Communist party, declared:

We have been investigating communism for 18 years. The time has come now to do something very definite and conclusive about it. The present laws are inadequate, as shown by the fact that under these laws we have only prosecuted a handful of Communists. Under my measure, I promise you, if my experience of 7 years as head of [HUAC] means anything, that it will once and for all end the issue so far as the United States is concerned.

Over the next several months this bill was considered with a variety of other anti-Communist measures proposed by both major parties. After considerable debate and the intervention of the Republican Administration, the Communist Control Act eventually emerged and was passed on August 24, 1954.

The act set forth a finding of Congress that the Communist party of the United States is "in fact an instrumentality of a conspiracy" directed by a hostile foreign power and that because of its dedication to the forcible overthrow of the government, its existence presents "a clear, present and continuing danger" to national security. Consequently, the act declares that the Party "should be outlawed." The key provision of the act withholds from the Communist party all "of the rights, privileges, and immunities attendant upon legal bodies created under the jurisdiction of the laws of the United States or any political subdivisions thereof." However, a degree of legal existence is preserved for the Party under a provision that states that the Party and its members are still subject to the requirements of the Internal Security Act of 1950. In any event, the major consequence of the Communist Control Act is the elimination of Communist party candidates from election ballots for public office.

Several other provisions of the act are directed at Communists in the labor movement. The category of "Communist-infiltrated" organizations is established as an addition to the "Communist-action" and "Communist-front" organizations to which the registration and penalty provisions of the Internal Security Act of 1950 apply. Upon a finding by the Subversive Activities Control Board that a labor union is a "Communist-infiltrated" organization, it loses privileges accorded labor unions under federal labor legislation. In addition, those who remain members of the "tainted" unions are prohibited employment in facilities engaged in production for national defense.

The Supreme Court has never been asked to consider the constitutionality of the act's outlawry provision. However, its decisions in such matters as registration under the Internal Security Act, Communists as

[8] Dies was chairman of the Un-American Activities Committee from its creation in 1938 until 1945.

officials of labor unions and as employees in defense facilities, and the right of Communists to travel abroad[9] would seem to indicate a partial rejection of Congress' ultimate intent.

## LEGISLATIVE INVESTIGATIONS

The manner in which Congress has allowed some of its committees to use the investigatory power as a means of dealing with the Communist threat has been a subject of continuous controversy since the end of World War II. Undoubtedly convinced that exposure of Communist and fellow travelers served a useful purpose in protecting national security, investigators went virtually unchecked by Congress in their quest to uncover Communists and to expose their operations. By far the most celebrated and controversial uses of the investigative power for that purpose were by the House Un-American Activities Committee and the Senate Permanent Sub-Committee on Investigations under the domination of Senator Joseph McCarthy, of Wisconsin. While there were complaints that the various inquiries of these committees were not in pursuance of a valid legislative purpose but were instead undertaken for personal aggrandizement, the most critical charges were directed at the committees' operational methods. The general atmosphere created was that of a "trial," but a trial in which the witness did not enjoy the safeguards of a trial. Charges were made against witnesses by using hearsay evidence, allowing the witnesses no opportunity to confront their accusers. Probers badgered witnesses and treated them with rank discourtesy. Not infrequently there were one-member hearings, after which that member proceeded to formulate the committee's report on an issue.

Constitutional questions raised by the methods of the House Committee on Un-American Activities were first considered by the Supreme Court in *Watkins* v. *United States* (354 U.S. 178, 1957). The case involved a contempt conviction of a witness before the House Committee on Un-American Activities for refusal to answer questions about his associates in his past Communist party activities. The witness rested his refusal on First Amendment grounds stressing that the Committee had no authority to ask the questions since they were not relevant to its legislative concerns. He further contended that the Committee lacked power "to undertake the public exposure of persons because of their past activities." In a 6–1 decision (Justices Burton and Whittaker did not participate), the Court reversed the conviction on due process grounds. Chief Justice Earl Warren's opinion stressed the vagueness of the Committee's authorizing resolution and the failure of the sub-committee chairman to provide sufficient clarifying information relative to the subject of the investigation. Since the Committee must "limit its inquiries to sta-

9 These matters are discussed elsewhere in this chapter.

tutory pertinency," the witness was given no basis for determining that pertinency in trying to decide whether he should answer the questions. Although the decision was grounded in the "void for vagueness" principle, the Chief Justice further emphasized the applicability of limiting principles of the Bill of Rights to legislative investigations. He contended that not only are the guarantees against compulsory self-incrimination and unreasonable searches and seizures applicable, but congressional invesitgating committees are limited by the First Amendment freedoms as well. Justice Tom Clark's dissent was largely a plea for judicial restraint in dealing with powers of Congress. To him, the majority action represented a "mischievous curbing of the informing function of the Congress," and it erroneously sustained the witness' claim of a "right to silence" under conditions which the Constitution does not guarantee.

The Court applied similar restrictions to state legislative investigations in *Sweezy* v. *New Hampshire* (354 U.S. 234, 1957), a case decided on the same day as *Watkins*. Like Watkins, Sweezy was convicted of contempt for refusal to answer questions of a legislative committee (a one-man committee comprised of the state Attorney General) concerning his activities in the Wallace Progressive party on the ground of impertinency. Also like Watkins, Sweezy contended that the inquiry infringed First Amendment freedoms. While condemning the vagueness of the authorizing resolution and the unfettered discretion given to the Attorney General as the central vices in the case, Chief Justice Warren's opinion was even more emphatic regarding First Amendment restrictions on legislative investigations. He contended that political freedom of the individual is a fundamental principle of a democratic society and that the rights to engage in political expression and association are basic premises undergirding the American constitutional system that are enshrined in the First Amendment and are applicable to the states through the Fourteenth Amendment.

Two years later in *Barenblatt* v. *United States* (360 U.S. 109, 1959) the Court made a significant retreat from its *Watkins* and *Sweezy* position. In a 5–4 decision it sustained a contempt conviction of a witness who invoked the First Amendment in refusing to answer questions put to him by the House Committee on Un-American Activities. Undoubtedly reacting to congressional criticism of its rulings in Communist cases and to threats to curb the its jurisdiction, the Court majority now considered the HUAC authorizing resolution sufficiently clear and definitive when supplemented by the clarifying statements of the probers. Justice John Marshall Harlan contended for the majority that the vagueness condemned in *Watkins* had resulted from the failure of the Committee to make sufficient clarifying and illuminating statements regarding the purpose of the inquiry. Such was not the case in *Barenblatt*. The chairman had specified the subject of the inquiry with sufficient clarity. Over the vigorous dissent of Justice Hugo Black, Harlan dismissed Barenblatt's

First Amendment claims by asserting that the Government's national security interests override the competing interests of the individual.

In a companion case, *Uphaus* v. *Wyman* (360 U.S. 72, 1959), the Court applied the principles of *Barenblatt* to reject an attack on the legislative investigating procedures of New Hampshire that had been condemned two years earlier in *Sweezy*. After applying the *Barenblatt* principles to uphold contempt convictions in *Wilkinson* v. *United States* (365 U.S. 399) and *Braden* v. *United States* (365 U.S. 431) in 1961, the Court returned to the stricter standards laid down in *Watkins* and reversed a number of contempt convictions between 1961 and 1965 (cf. *Deutch* v. *United States*, 367 U.S. 456, 1961; *Russell* v. *United States*, 369 U.S. 749, 1962; and *Yellin* v. *United States*, 374 U.S. 109, 1963). As we move into the 1970's repeated challenges to the authority of HUAC (now the House Committee on Internal Security) could very well present the Supreme Court with hard constitutional questions.


## NATIONAL SECURITY AND TRAVEL ABROAD

Federal law requires that in order to travel abroad a person must be issued a valid passport by the Secretary of State. Few questions relative to the scope of the Secretary's passport power arose prior to the end of World War II. Curtailment of foreign travel during the two world wars was considered essential to national security. But when the Government adopted, as a Cold War strategem, the policy of refusing passports to native Communists and their sympathizers because their travel abroad would be detrimental to national interests, serious constitutional questions were raised. To be sure, when travel restrictions are applied to persons merely because of their associations and beliefs, basic First Amendment freedoms are placed under serious stress.

The Supreme Court first considered the passport problem in *Kent* v. *Dulles* (356 U.S. 116, 1957). In that case passports were denied because of a refusal to file an affidavit concerning Communist party membership. In a 5–4 decision the Court held that the Secretary of State did not have the statutory authority to deny the passports for failure to file the required affidavit. Justice Willam O. Douglas, in his opinion for the Court, contended that the right to travel was embraced in the liberty protected by the Fifth Amendment. Furthermore, Douglas contended that since the Secretary's action was not based on a grant of legislative authority, the important First Amendment belief and associational issues need not be considered. The four dissenters—Justices Clark, Harlan, Burton, and Whittaker—contended that the necessary statutory authority existed.

That the High Court did not look with favor upon the indiscriminate restrictions on travel, allowed under a provision of the Internal Security

Act of 1950, is illustrated in *Aptheker* v. *Secretary of State* (378 U.S. 500, 1964). The provision, which denied passports to members of "Communist-action" and "front" organizations, was considered too sweeping to be consistent with constitutionally protected freedoms. In declaring the provision unconstitutional, Justice Arthur Goldberg pointed out for the majority that the restrictions applied regardless of the purpose of the proposed travel and the "security-sensitivity of the areas in which [a member of such an organization] wishes to travel." The dissenters—Justices Clark, Harlan, and White—once again contended that in a proper balancing of competing interests, "the degree of restraint upon travel is outweighed by the dangers to our very existence."

The Court made good on its "security-sensitivity of areas" exception one year later in *Zemel* v. *Rusk* (381 U.S. 1, 1965). In affirming a State Department refusal to issue passports for travel to Cuba, Chief Justice Earl Warren contended for the Court that area restrictions are supported by legislative authority and that the "liberty" to travel established in *Kent* v. *Dulles, supra,* is not absolute but may be subject to reasonable restrictions in the interest of national security. The First Amendment claims were rejected also as the Chief Justice held that "[t]he right to speak and publish does not carry with it the unrestrained right to gather information." He concluded that the restrictions here were not based upon associations or beliefs but "upon foreign policy considerations affecting all citizens." Jusitce William O. Douglas' dissent stressed the view that the restriction had been made for the wrong reason. For example, he noted that "a theater of war may be too dangerous for travel," but the "so-called danger" involved here was Cuban communism. Since there are numbers of such regimes and considerable Communist thought in the world, he contended that Americans must mingle with them if those phenomena are to be known and understood.

The State Department has applied the *Zemel* rule to refuse travel to students, professors, chess players, and others to specified Communist countries. Some persons have insisted on traveling to the restricted areas despite the possibility of criminal sanctions. In 1963, a group of fifty-eight students defied the Cuban travel ban by initiating their trips from Prague and Paris. Having been advised that traveling to Cuba without a passport validated for that purpose was a violation of travel control law and regulations, several persons were indicted for conspiring to induce American citizens to travel to a restricted area without a valid passport. In affirming the federal district court dismissal of the charge in *United States* v. *Laub* (385 U.S. 475, 1967), the Supreme Court held that the statutory provision under which criminal charges were brought was not intended by Congress to enforce the State Department's area restrictions policy. The statute was merely directed at departure from, and entry into, the United States. In addition, the Court noted that great weight must be given to the State Department's consistent position over a long period of time that there was no statutory authority for criminal prosecution for travel to restricted areas.

In a decision on December 20, 1967, the Court of Appeals for the District of Columbia appeared to modify *Zemel* significantly by holding that the State Department could not enforce its restricted-area travel policy by denying passports to persons who might visit such places. The case developed from a denial of a passport to Professor Staughton Lynd for travel to England. His passport had been revoked earlier for defying the ban on travel to North Vietnam. The court maintained that the State Department did not possess the statutory authority to control a person's travel; it could only prescribe the areas where passports could be taken. Hence, the government's only weapon to prohibit travel to restricted areas is the extraction of a promise from the traveller that he will not take the passport into a restricted area. The court emphasized that the passport must be issued although the traveller indicates his intention to disregard the ban and enter the restricted area without his passport. In short, the Secretary of State can "control the lawful travel of the passport" but is without "authority to control the travel of the person." The State Department decided against an appeal of the decision, but it has endorsed a bill which would make it criminal to travel to countries declared "off limits" for national security reasons.

The cases that follow illustrate the variety of issues touching on internal security that have been considered by the Supreme Court.

## DENNIS *v.* UNITED STATES

341 U. S. 494; 95 L. Ed. 1137; 71 S. Ct .857 (1951)

MR. CHIEF JUSTICE VINSON *announced the judgment of the Court and an opinion in which* MR. JUSTICE REED, MR. JUSTICE BURTON, *and* MR. JUSTICE MINTON *join.*

Petitioners were indicted in July 1948, for violation of the conspiracy provisions of the Smith Act 54 Stat 670, 671, ch 439, 18 USC (1946 ed) section 11, during the period of April, 1945, to July, 1948. . . . [T]he case was set for trial on January 17, 1949 [and a] verdict of guilty as to all the petitioners was returned by the jury

on October 14, 1949. The Court of Appeals affirmed the convictions. . . . We granted certiorari . . . limited to the following two questions: (1) Whether either section 2 or section 3 of the Smith Act, inherently or as construed and applied in the instant case, violates the First Amendment and other provisions of the Bill of Rights; (2) whether either section 2 or section 3 of the Act, inherently or as construed and applied in the instant case, violates the First and Fifth Amendment because of indefiniteness.

Sections 2 and 3 of the Smith Act,

54 Stat 670, 671, ch 439, 18 USC (1946 ed) sections 10, 11 (see present 18 USC section 2385), provide as follows:

Sec. 2.

(a) It shall be unlawful for any person—

(1) to knowingly or willfully advocate, abet, advise, or teach the duty, necessity, desirability, or propriety of overthrowing or destroying any government in the United States by force or violence, or by the assassination of any officer of such government;

(2) with the intent to cause the overthrow or destruction of any government in the United States, to print, publish, edit, issue, circulate, sell, distribute, or publicly display any written or printed matter advocating, advising, or teaching the duty, necessity, desirability, or propriety of overthrowing or destroying any government in the United States by force or violence;

(3) to organize or help to organize any society, group, or assembly of persons who teach, advocate, or encourage the overthrow or destruction of any government in the United States by force or violence; or to be or become a member of, or affiliate with, any such society, group, or assembly of persons, knowing the purposes thereof.

(b) For the purposes of this section, the term "government in the United States" means the Government of the United States, the government of any State, Territory, or possession of the United States, the government of the District of Columbia, or the government of any political subdivision of any of them.

Sec. 3. It shall be unlawful for any person to attempt to commit, or to conspire to commit, any of the acts prohibited by the provisions of . . . this title.

The indictment charged the petitioners with willfully and knowingly conspiring (1) to organize as the Communist Party of the United States of America a society, group and assembly of persons who teach and advocate the overthrow and destruction of the Government of the United States by force and violence, and (2) knowingly and wilfully to advocate and teach the duty and necessity of overthrowing and destroying the Government of the United States by force and violence. The indictment further alleged that section 2 of the Smith Act proscribes these acts and that any conspiracy to take such action is a violation of section 3 of the Act.

. . . Our limited grant of the writ of certiorari has removed from our consideration any question as to the sufficiency of the evidence to support the jury's determination that petitioners are guilty of the offense charged. Whether on this record petitioners did in fact advocate the overthrow of the Government by force and violence is not before us, and we must base any discussion of this point upon the conclusions stated in the opinion of the Court of Appeals, which treated the issue in great detail. That court held that the record in this case amply supports the necessary finding of the jury that petitioners, the leaders of the Communist Party in this country, were unwilling to work within our framework of democracy, but intended to initiate a violent revolution whenever the propitious occasion appeared.

. . .

It will be helpful in clarifying the issues to treat next the contention that the trial judge improperly interpreted the statute by charging that the statute required an unlawful intent before the jury could convict. More specifically, he charged that the jury could not find the petitioners guilty under the indictment unless they found that petitioners had the intent "to overthrow the government by force and violence as speedily as circumstances permit."

. . . The structure and purpose of

the statute demand the inclusion of intent as an element of the crime. Congress was concerned with those who advocate and organize for the overthrow of the Government. Certainly those who recruit and combine for the purpose of advocating overthrow intend to bring about that overthrow. We hold that the statute requires as an essential element of the crime proof of the intent of those who are charged with its violation to overthrow the Government by force and violence.

. . .

The obvious purpose of the statute is to protect existing Government, not from change by peaceable, lawful and constitutional means, but from change by violence, revolution and terrorism. That it is within the *power* of the Congress to protect the Government of the United States from armed rebellion is a proposition which requires little discussion. Whatever theoretical merit there may be to the argument that there is a "right" to rebellion against dictatorial governments is without force where the existing structure of the government provides for peaceful and orderly change. We reject any principle of governmental helplessness in the face of preparation for revolution, which principle, carried to its logical conclusion, must lead to anarchy. No one could conceive that it is not within the power of Congress to prohibit acts intended to overthrow the Government by force and violence. The question with which we are concerned here is not whether Congress has such *power,* but whether the *means* which it has employed conflict with the First and Fifth Amendments to the Constitution.

One of the bases for the contention that the means which Congress has employed are invalid takes the form of an attack on the face of the statute on the grounds that by its terms it prohibits academic discussion of the merits of Marxism-Leninism, that it stifles ideas and is contrary to all concepts of a free speech and a free press. Although we do not agree that the language itself has that significance, we must bear in mind that it is the duty of the federal courts to interpret federal legislation in a manner not inconsistent with the demands of the Constitution. . . .

The very language of the Smith Act negates the interpretation which petitioners would have us impose on that Act. It is directed at advocacy, not discussion. Thus, the trial judge properly charged the jury that they could not convict if they found that petitioners did "no more than pursue peaceful studies and discussions or teaching and advocacy in the realm of ideas." He further charged that it was not unlawful "to conduct in an American college and university a course explaining the philosophical theories set forth in the books which have been placed in evidence." Such a charge is in strict accord with the statutory language, and illustrates the meaning to be placed on those words. Congress did not intend to eradicate the free discussion of political theories, to destroy the traditional rights of Americans to discuss and evaluate ideas without fear of governmental sanction. Rather Congress was concerned with the very kind of activity in which the evidence showed these petitioners engaged.

But although the statute is not directed at the hypothetical cases which petitioners have conjured, its application in this case has resulted in convictions for the teaching and advocacy of the overthrow of the Government by force and violence, which, even though coupled with the intent to accomplish that overthrow, contains an element of speech. For this reason, we must pay special heed to the demands of the First Amendment marking out the boundaries of speech.

We pointed out in *Douds* . . . that the basis of the First Amendment is the hypothesis that speech can rebut speech, propaganda will answer propaganda, free debate of ideas will result in the wisest governmental policies. It is for this reason that this Court has recognized the inherent value of free discourse. An analysis of the leading cases in this Court which have involved direct limitations on speech, however, will demonstrate that both the majority of the Court and the dissenters in particular cases have recognized that this is not an unlimited, unqualified right, but that the societal value of speech must, on occasion, be subordinated to other values and considerations.

No important case involving free speech was decided by this Court prior to *Schenck* v. *United States* . . . (1919). Indeed, the summary treatment accorded an argument based upon an individual's claim that the First Amendment protect certain utterances indicates that the Court at earlier dates placed no unique emphasis upon that right. It was not until the classic dictum of Justice Holmes in the Schenck case that speech per se received that emphasis in a majority opinion. . . . Writing for a unanimous Court, Justice Holmes stated that the "question in every case is whether the words used are used in such circumstances and are of such a nature as to create a clear and present danger that they will bring about the substantive evils that Congress has a right to prevent." . . .

[Here Vinson examines the appli-cation of clear and present danger between *Schenck* and *Gitlow*.]

. . .

The rule we deduce from these cases is that where an offense is specified by a statute in nonspeech or nonpress terms, a conviction relying upon speech or press as evidence of violation may be sustained only when the speech or publication created a "clear and present danger" of attempting or accomplishing the prohibited crime, e.g., interference with enlistment. The dissents, we repeat, in emphasizing the value of speech, were addressed to the argument of the sufficiency of the evidence.

The next important case before the Court in which free speech was the crux of the conflict was *Gitlow* v. *New York,* 268 U.S. 652. . . . There New York had made it a crime to "advocate . . . the necessity or propriety of overthrowing . . . the government by force. . . ." The evidence of violation of the statute was that the defendant had published a Manifesto attacking the Government and capitalism. The convictions were sustained, Justices Holmes and Brandeis dissenting. The majority refused to apply the "clear and present danger" test to the specific utterance. Its reasoning was as follows: The "clear and present danger" test was applied to the utterance itself in *Schenck* because the question was merely one of sufficiency of evidence under an admittedly constitutional statute. *Gitlow,* however, presented a different question. There a legislature had found that a certain kind of speech was, itself, harmful and unlawful. The constitutionality of such a state statute had to be adjudged by this Court just as it determined the constitutionality of any state statute, namely, whether the statute was "reasonable." Since it was entirely reasonable for a state to attempt to protect itself from violent overthrow, the statute was perforce reasonable. The only question remaining in the case became whether there was evidence to support the conviction, a question which gave the majority no difficulty. Justices Holmes and Brandeis refused to accept this approach, but insisted that wherever speech was the evidence of the violation, it was necessary to show that the speech created the "clear and present-danger" of the substantive evil which the legislature had the right to prevent. Justices Holmes and Brandeis, then, made no distinction between a federal statute which made certain acts unlawful, the evidence to support the conviction being speech, and a statute which made speech itself the crime. This approach was emphasized in *Whitney* v. *California,* 274 U.S. 357. . . .

Although no case subsequent to *Whitney* and *Gitlow* has expressly overruled the majority opinions in those cases, there is little doubt that subsequent opinions have inclined toward the Holmes-Brandeis rationale. . . .

In this case we are squarely presented with the application of the "clear and present danger" test, and must decide what that phrase imports. We first note that many of the cases in which this Court has reversed convictions by use of this or similar tests have been based on the fact that the interest which the State was attempting to protect was itself too insubstantial to warrant restriction of speech. . . . Overthrow of the Government by force and violence is certainly a substantial enough interest for the Government to limit speech. Indeed, this is the ultimate value of any society, for if a society cannot protect its very structure from armed internal attack, it must follow that no subordinate value can be protected. If, then, this interest may be protected, the literal problem which is presented is what has been meant by the use of the phrase "clear and present danger" of the utterances bringing about the evil within the power of Congress to punish.

Obviously, the words cannot mean that before the Government may act, it must wait until the *putsch* is about to be executed, the plans have been laid and the signal is awaited. If Government is aware that a group aiming at its overthrow is attempting to indoctrinate its members and to commit them to a course whereby they will strike when the leaders feel the circumstances permit, action by the Government is required. The argument that there is no need for Government to concern itself, for Government is strong, it possesses ample powers to put down a rebellion, it may defeat the revolution with ease needs no answer. For that is not the question. Certainly an attempt to overthrow the Government by force even though doomed from the outset because of inadequate numbers or power of the revolutionists, is a sufficient evil for Congress to prevent. The damage which such attempts create both physically and politically to a nation makes it impossible to measure the validity in terms of the probability of success, or the immediacy of a successful attempt. In the instant case the trial judge charged the jury that they could not convict unless they found that petitioners intended to overthrow the Government "as speedily as circumstances would permit." This does not mean, and could not properly mean, that they would not strike until there was certainty of success. What was meant was that the revolutionists would strike when they thought the time was ripe. We must therefore reject the contention that success or probability of success is the criterion.

The situation with which Justices Holmes and Brandeis were concerned in *Gitlow* was a comparatively isolated event, bearing little relation in their minds to any substantial threat to the safety of the community. . . . They were not confronted with any situation comparable to the instant one—the development of an apparatus designed and dedicated to the overthrow of the Government, in the context of world crisis after crisis.

Chief Judge Learned Hand, writing for the majority below, interpreted the phrase as follows: "In each case [courts] must ask whether the gravity of the 'evil,' discounted by its improbability, justifies such invasion of free speech as is necessary to avoid the danger." 183 F2d at 212. We adopt this statement of the rule. . . . [I]t is as succinct and inclusive as any other we might devise at this time. It takes into consideration those factors which we deem relevant, and relates their significances. More we cannot expect from words.

Likewise, we are in accord with the court below, which affirmed the trial court's finding that the requisite danger existed. The mere fact that from the period 1945 to 1948 petitioners' activities did not result in an attempt to overthrow the Government by force and violence is of course no answer to the fact that there was a group that was ready to make the attempt. The formation by petitioners of such a highly organized conspiracy, with rigidly disciplined members subject to call when the leaders, these petitioners, felt that the time had come for action, coupled with the inflammable nature of world conditions, similar uprisings in other

countries, and the touch-and-go nature of our relations with countries with whom petitioners were in the very least ideologically attuned, convince us that their convictions were justified on this score. And this analysis disposes of the contention that a conspiracy to advocate, as distinguished from the advocacy itself, cannot be constitutionally restrained, because it comprises only the preparation. It is the existence of the conspiracy which creates the danger. . . . If the ingredients of the reaction are present, we cannot bind the Government to wait until the catalyst is added.

Although we have concluded that the finding that there was a sufficient danger to warrant the application of the statute was justified on the merits, there remains the problem of whether the trial judge's treatment of the issue was correct. He charged the jury, in relevant part, as follows:

In further construction and interpretation of the statute I charge you that it is not the abstract doctrine of overthrowing or destroying organized government by unlawful means which is denounced by this law, but the teaching and advocacy of action for the accomplishment of that purpose, by language reasonably and ordinarily calculated to incite persons to such action. Accordingly, you cannot find the defendants or any of them guilty of the crime charged unless you are satisfied beyond a reasonable doubt that they conspired to organize a society, group and assembly of persons who teach and advocate the overthrow or destruction of the Government of the United States by force and violence and to advocate and teach the duty and necessity of overthrowing or destroying the government of the United States by force and violence, with the intent that such teaching and advocacy be of a rule or principle of action and by language reasonably and ordinarily calculated to incite persons to such action, all with the intent to cause the overthrow or destruction of the Government of the United States by force and violence as speedily as circumstances would permit.

. . .

If you are satisfied that the evidence establishes beyond a reasonable doubt that the defendants, or any of them, are guilty of a violation of the statute, as I have interpreted it to you, I find as a matter of law that there is sufficient danger of a substantive evil that the Congress has a right to prevent to justify the application of the statute under the First Amendment of the Constitution. . . .

It is thus clear that he reserved the question of the existence of the danger for his own determination, and the question becomes whether the issue is of such a nature that it should have been submitted to the jury.

. . . The argument that the action of the trial court is erroneous, in declaring as a matter of law that such violation shows sufficient danger to justify the punishment despite the First Amendment, rests on the theory that a jury must decide a question of the application of the First Amendment. We do not agree.

When facts are found that establish the violation of a statute, the protection against conviction afforded by the First Amendment is a matter of law. The doctrine that there must be a clear and present danger of a substantive evil that Congress has a right to prevent is a judicial rule to be applied as a matter of law by the courts. The guilt is established by proof of facts. Whether the First Amendment protects the activity which constitutes the violation of the statute must depend upon a judicial determination of the scope of the First Amendment applied to the circumstances of the case. . . .

The question in this case is whether the statute which the legislature has enacted may be constitutionally applied. In other words, the Court must examine judicially the application of the statute to the particular situation to ascertain if the Constitution prohibits the conviction. We hold that the statute may be applied where there is a "clear and present danger" of the substantive evil which the legislature had the right to prevent. Bearing, as it does, the marks of a "question of law," the issue is properly one for the judge to decide.

There remains to be discussed the question of vagueness—whether the statute as we have interpreted it is too vague, not sufficiently advising those who would speak of the limitations upon their activity. It is urged that such vagueness contravenes the First and Fifth Amendments. This argument is particularly nonpersuasive when presented by petitioners, who, the jury found, intended to overthrow the Government as speedily as circumstances would permit. . . .

We agree that the standard as defined is not a neat, mathematical formulary. Like all verbalizations it is subject to criticism on the score of indefiniteness. But petitioners themselves contend that the verbalization, "clear and present danger," is the proper standard. We see no difference from the standpoint of vagueness, whether the standard of "clear and present danger" is one contained in *haec verba* within the statute, or whether it is the judical measure of constitutional applicability. We have shown the indeterminate standard the phrase necessarily connotes. We do not think we have rendered that standard any more indefinite by our attempt to sum up the factors which are included within its scope. . . . Where there is doubt as to the intent of the defendants, the nature of their activities, or their power to bring about the evil, this Court will review the convictions with the scrupulous care demanded by our Constitution. But we are not convinced that because there may be borderline cases at some time in the future, these convictions should be reversed because of the argument that these petitioners could not know that their activities were constitutionally proscribed by the statute.

. . .

We hold that sections 2 (a) (1), (2) (a) (3) and 3 of the Smith Act, do not inherently, or as construed or applied in the instant case, violate the First Amendment and other provisions of the Bill of Rights, or the First and Fifth Amendments because of indefiniteness. Petitioners intended to overthrow the Government of the United States as speedily as the circumstances would permit. Their conspiracy to organize the Communist Party and to teach and advocate the overthrow of the Government of the United States by force and violence created a "clear and present danger" of an attempt to overthrow the Government by force and violence. They were properly and constitutionally convicted for violation of the Smith Act. The judgments of conviction are

*Affirmed.*

MR. JUSTICE CLARK *took no part in the consideration or decision of this case.*

MR. JUSTICE FRANKFURTER, *concurring in affirmance of the judgment.*

. . .

The demands of free speech in a democratic society as well as the interest in national security are better served by candid and informed weighing of the competing interests, within the confines of the judicial process, than by announcing dogmas too inflexible for the non-Euclidian problems to be solved.

But how are competing interests to be assessed? Since they are not subject to quantitative ascertainment, the issue necessarily resolves itself into asking, who is to make the adjustment?—who is to balance the relevant factors and ascertain which interest is in the circumstances to prevail? Full responsibility for the choice cannot be given to the courts. Courts are not representative bodies. They are not designed to be a good reflex of a democratic society. Their judgment is best informed, and therefore most dependable, within narrow limits. Their essential quality is detachment, founded on independence. History teaches that the independence of the judiciary is jeopardized when courts become embroiled in the passions of the day and assume primary responsibility in choosing between competing political, economic and social pressures.

Primary responsibility for adjusting the interests which compete in the situation before us of necessity belongs to the Congress. The nature of the power to be exercised by this Court has been delineated in decisions not charged with the emotional appeal of situations such as that now before us. We are to set aside the judgment of those whose duty it is to legislate only if there is no reasonable basis for it. . . . [W]e must scrupulously observe the narrow limits of judicial authority even though self-restraint is alone set over us. Above all we must remember that this Court's power of judicial review is not "an exercise of the powers of a super-legislature."

. . .

. . . Unless we are to compromise judicial impartiality and subject these defendants to the risk of an ad hoc judgment influenced by the impregnating atmosphere of the times, the constitutionality of their conviction must be determined by principles established in cases decided in more tranquil periods. If those decisions are to be used as a guide and not as an argument, it is important to view them as a whole and to distrust the easy generalizations to which some of them lend themselves.

[Frankfurter here reviews how the Court has recognized and resolved conflict between speech and competing interests in various types of cases.]

. . .

I must leave to others the ungrateful task of trying to reconcile all these decisions. In some instances we have too readily permitted juries to infer deception from error, or intention from argumentative or critical statements. . . . In other instances we weighted the interest in free speech so heavily that we permitted essential conflicting values to be destroyed. . . . Viewed as a whole, however, the decisions express an attitude toward the judicial function and a standard of values which for me are decisive of the case before us.

*First.*—Free-speech cases are not an exception to the principle that we are not legislators, that direct policy-making is not our province. How best to reconcile competing interests is the business of legislatures, and the balance they strike is a judgment not to be displaced by ours, but to be respected unless outside the pale of fair judgment.

On occasion we have strained to interpret legislation in order to limit its effect on interests protected by the First Amendment. . . . In some instances we have denied to States the deference to which I think they are entitled. . . .

But in no case has a majority of this Court held that a legislative judgment, even as to freedom of utterance, may be overturned merely because the Court would have made a different choice between the competing interests had the initial legislative judgment been for it to make.

. . .

*Second.*—A survey of the relevant decisions indicates that the results which we have reached are on the whole those that would ensure from careful weighing of conflicting interests. The complex issues presented by regulation of speech in public places, by picketing, and by legislation prohibiting advocacy of crime have been resolved by scrutiny of many factors besides the imminence and gravity of the evil threatened. The matter has been well summarized by a reflective student of the Court's work.

The truth is that the clear-and-present-danger test is an oversimplified judgment unless it takes account also of a number of other factors: the relative seriousness of the danger in comparison with the value of the occasion for speech or political activity; the availability of more moderate controls than those which the state has imposed; and perhaps the specific intent with which the speech or activity is launched. No matter how rapidly we utter the phrase "clear and present danger", or how closely we hyphenate the words, they are not a substitute for the weighing of values. They tend to convey a delusion of certitude when what is most certain is the complexity of the strands in the web of freedoms which the judge must disentangle. Freund, On Understanding the Supreme Court, 27, 28.

. . .

*Third.*—Not every type of speech

occupies the same position on the scale of values. There is no substantial public interest in permitting certain kinds of utterances: "the lewd and obscene, the profane, the libelous, and the insulting or 'fighting' words— those which by their very utterance inflict injury or tend to incite an immediate breach of the peace." *Chaplinsky* v. *New Hampshire,* 315 U.S. 568. . . . We have frequently indicated that the interest in protecting speech depends on the circumstances of the occasion. . . . It is pertinent to the decision before us to consider where on the scale of values we have in the past placed the type of speech now claiming constitutional immunity.

The defendants have been convicted of conspiring to organize a party of persons who advocate the overthrow of the Government by force and violence. . . .

. . . Even though advocacy of overthrow deserves little protection, we should hesitate to prohibit it if we thereby inhibit the interchange of rational ideas so essential to representative government and free society.

But there is underlying validity in the distinction between advocacy and the interchange of ideas, and we do not discard a useful tool because it may be misused. That such a distinction could be used unreasonably by those in power against hostile or unorthodox views does not negate the fact that it may be used reasonably against an organization wielding the power of the centrally controlled international Communist movement. The object of the conspiracy before us is clear enough that the chance of error in saying that the defendants conspired to advocate rather than to express ideas is slight. Mr. Justice Douglas quite properly points out

that the conspiracy before us is not a conspiracy to overthrow the Government. But it would be equally wrong to treat it as a seminar in political theory.

These general considerations underlie decision of the case before us.

On the one hand is the interest in security. The Communist Party was not designed by these defendants as an ordinary political party. For the circumstances of its organization, its aims and methods, and the relation of the defendants to its organization and aims we are concluded by the jury's verdict. The jury found that the Party rejects the basic premise of our political system. . . .

. . . But in determining whether application of the statute to the defendants is within the constitutional powers of Congress, we are not limited to the facts found by the jury. We must view such a question in the light of whatever is relevant to a legislative judgment. We may take judicial notice that the Communist doctrines which these defendants have conspired to advocate are in the ascendency in powerful nations who cannot be acquitted of unfriendliness to the institutions of this country. We may take account of evidence brought forward at this trial and elsewhere, much of which has long been common knowledge. In sum, it would amply justify a legislature in concluding that recruitment of additional members for the Party would create a substantial danger to national security.

. . .

On the other hand is the interest in free speech. The right to exert all governmental powers in aid of maintaining our institutions and resisting their physical overthrow does not include intolerance of opinions and speech that cannot do harm although opposed and perhaps alien to dominant, traditional opinion. The treatment of its minorities, especially their legal position, is among the most searching tests of the level of civilization attained by a society. It is better for those who have almost unlimited power of government in their hands to err on the side of freedom. We have enjoyed so much freedom for so long that we are perhaps in danger of forgetting how much blood it cost to establish the Bill of Rights.

. . . Suppressing advocates of overthrow inevitably will also silence critics who do not advocate overthrow but fear that their criticism may be so construed. No matter how clear we may be that the defendants now before us are preparing to overthrow our Government at the propitious moment, it is self-delusion to think that we can punish them for their advocacy without adding to the risks run by loyal citizens who honestly believe in some of the reforms these defendants advance. It is a sobering fact that in sustaining the conviction before us we can hardly escape restriction on the interchange of ideas.

. . .

It is not for us to decide how we would adjust the clash of interests which this case presents were the primary responsibility for reconciling it ours. Congress has determined that the danger created by advocacy of overthrow justifies the ensuing restriction on freedom of speech. The determination was made after due deliberation, and the seriousness of the congressional purpose is attested by the volume of legislation passed to effectuate the same ends.

Can we then say that the judgment Congress exercised was denied it by the Constitution? Can we establish a constitutional doctrine which forbids the elected representatives of the people to make this choice? Can we hold that the First Amendment deprives Congress of what it deemed necessary for the Government's protection?

To make validity of legislation depend on judicial reading of events still in the womb of time—a forecast, that is, of the outcome of forces at best appreciated only with knowledge of the topmost secrets of nations—is to charge the judiciary with duties beyond its equipment.

. . .

MR. JUSTICE JACKSON, *concurring.*

The Communist Party . . . does not seek its strength primarily in numbers. Its aim is a relatively small party whose strength is in selected, dedicated, indoctrinated, and rigidly disciplined members. From established policy it tolerates no deviation and no debate. It seeks members that are, or may be, secreted in strategic posts in transportation, communications, industry, government, and especially in labor unions where it can compel employers to accept and retain its members. It also seeks to infiltrate and control organizations of professional and other groups. Through these placements in positions of power it seeks a leverage over society that will make up in power of coercion what it lacks in power of persuasion.

The Communists have no scruples against sabotage, terrorism, assassination, or mob disorder; but violence is not with them, as with the anarchists, an end in itself. The Communist Party advocates force only when prudent and profitable. Their strategy of stealth precludes premature or uncoordinated outbursts of violence, except, of course, when the blame will be placed on shoulders other than their own. They resort to violence as to truth, not as a principle but as an expedient. Force or violence, as they would resort to it, may never be necessary, because infiltration and deception may be enough.

Force would be utilized by the Communist Party not to destroy government but for its capture.

. . .

The foregoing is enough to indicate that, either by accident or design, the Communist stratagem outwits the anti-anarchist pattern of statute aimed against "overthrow by force and violence" if qualified by the doctrine that only "clear and present danger" of accomplishing that result will sustain the prosecution.

The "clear-and-present-danger" test was an innovation by Mr. Justice Holmes in the Schenck Case, reiterated and refined by him and Mr. Justice Brandeis in later cases, all arising before the era of World War II revealed the subtlety and efficacy of modernized revolutionary techniques used by totalitarian parties. In those cases, they were faced with convictions under so-called criminal syndicalism statutes aimed at anarchists but which, loosely construed, had been applied to punish socialism, pacifism, and left-wing ideologies, the charges often resting on far-fetched inferences which, if true, would establish only technical or trivial violations. They proposed "clear and present danger" as a test for the sufficiency of evidence in particular cases.

I would save it, unmodified, for application as a "rule of reason" in the kind of case for which it was devised. When the issue is criminality of a hot-headed speech on a street corner, or circulation of a few incendiary pamphlets, or parading by some zealots behind a red flag, or refusal of a handful of school children to salute our flag, it is not beyond the capacity of the judicial process to gather, comprehend, and weigh the necessary materials for decision whether it is a clear and present danger of substantive evil or a harmless letting off of steam. It is not a prophecy, for the danger in such cases has matured by the time of trial or it was never present. The test applies and has meaning where a conviction is sought to be based on a speech or writing which does not directly or explicitly advocate a crime but to which such tendency is sought to be attributed by construction or by implication from external circumstances. The formula in such cases favors freedoms that are vital to our society, and, even if sometimes applied too generously, the consequences cannot be grave. But its recent expansion has extended, in particular to Communists, unprecedented immunities. Unless we are to hold our Government captive in a judge-made verbal trap, we must approach the problem of a well-organized nation-wide conspiracy, such as I have described, as realistically as our predecessors faced the trivialities that were being prosecuted until they were checked with a rule of reason.

I think reason is lacking for applying that test to this case.

If we must decide that this Act and its application are constitutional only if we are convinced that petitioners' conduct creates a "clear and present danger" of violent overthrow, we must appraise imponderables, including international and national phenomena which baffle the best informed foreign offices and our most experienced politicians. We would have to foresee and predict the effectiveness of Communist propaganda, opportunities for infiltration, whether, and when, a time will come that they consider propitious for action, and whether and how fast our existing government will deteriorate. And we would have to speculate as to whether an approaching Communist coup would not be anticipated by a nationalistic fascist movement. No doctrine can be sound whose application requires us to make a prophecy of that sort in the guise of a legal decision. The judicial process simply is not adequate to a trial of such far-flung issues. The answers given would reflect our own political predilections and nothing more.

The authors of the clear-and-present-danger test never applied it to a case like this, nor would I. If applied as it is proposed here, it means that the Communist plotting is protected during its period of incubation; its preliminary stages of organization and preparation are immune from the law; the Government can move only after imminent action is manifest, when it would, of course, be too late.

. . .

What really is under review here is a conviction of conspiracy, after a trial for conspiracy, on an indictment charging conspiracy, brought under a statute outlawing conspiracy. With due respect to my colleagues, they seem to me to discuss anything under the sun except the law of conspiracy. One of the dissenting opinions even appears to chide me for "invoking the law of conspiracy." As that is the case before us, it may be more amazing that its reversal can be proposed without even considering the law of conspiracy.

. . .

I do not suggest that Congress could punish conspiracy to advocate something, the doing of which it may not punish. Advocacy or exposition of the doctrine of communal property ownership, or any political philosophy unassociated with advocacy of its im-position by force or seizure of government by unlawful means would not be reached through conspiracy prosecution. But it is not forbidden to punish its teaching or advocacy, and the end being punishable, there is no doubt of the power to punish conspiracy for the purpose.

. . .

While I think there was power in Congress to enact this statute and that, as applied in this case, it cannot be held unconstitutional, I add that I have little faith in the long-range effectiveness of this conviction to stop the rise of the Communist movement. Communism will not go to jail with these Communists. No decision by this Court can forestall revolution whenever the existing government fails to command the respect and loyalty of the people and sufficient distress and discontent is allowed to grow up among the masses. Many failures by fallen governments attest that no government can long prevent revolution by outlawry. Corruption, ineptitude, inflation, oppressive taxation, militarization, injustice, and loss of leadership capable of intellectual initiative in domestic or foreign affairs are allies on which the Communists count to bring opportunity knocking to their door. Sometimes I think they may be mistaken. But the Communists are not building just for today—the rest of us might profit by their example.

MR. JUSTICE BLACK *dissenting*.

. . .

At the outset I want to emphasize what the crime involved in this case is, and what it is not. These petitioners were not charged with an attempt to overthrow the Government. They were not charged with overt acts of any kind designed to overthrow the Government. They were not even charged with saying anything or writing anything designed to overthrow the Government. The charge was that they agreed to assemble and to talk and publish certain ideas at a later date: The indictment is that they conspired to organize the Communist Party and to use speech or newspapers and other publications in the future to teach and advocate the forcible overthrow of the Government. No matter how it is worded, this is a virulent form of prior censorship of speech and press, which I believe the First Amendment forbids. I would hold section 3 of the Smith Act authorizing this prior restraint unconstitutional on its face and as applied.

. . .

So long as this Court exercises the power of judicial review of legislation, I cannot agree that the First Amendment permits us to sustain laws suppressing freedom of speech and press on the basis of Congress' or our own notions of mere "reasonableness." Such a doctrine waters down the First Amendment so that it amounts to little more than an admonition to Congress. The Amendment as so construed is not likely to protect any but those "safe" or orthodox views which rarely need its protection. . . .

Public opinion being what it now is, few will protest the conviction of these Communist petitioners. There is hope, however, that in calmer times, when present pressures, passions and fears subside, this or some later Court will restore the First Amendment liberties to the high preferred place where they belong in a free society.

MR. JUSTICE DOUGLAS, *dissenting.*

If this were a case where those who claimed protection under the First Amendment were teaching the techniques of sabotage, the assassination of the President, the filching of documents from public files, the planting of bombs, the art of street warfare, and the like, I would have no doubts. The freedom to speak is not absolute; the teaching of methods of terror and other seditious conduct should be beyond the pale along with obscenity and immorality. This case was argued as if those were the facts. The argument imported much seditious conduct into the record. That is easy and it has popular appeal, for the activities of Communists in plotting and scheming against the free world are common knowledge. But the fact is that no such evidence was introduced at the trial. There is a statute which makes a seditious conspiracy unlawful. Petitioners, however, were not charged with a "conspiracy to overthrow'" the Government. They were charged with a conspiracy to form a party and groups and assemblies of people who teach and advocate the overthrow of our Government by force or violence and with a conspiracy to advocate and teach its overthrow by force and violence. It may well be that indoctrination in the techniques of terror to destroy the Government would be indictable under either statute. But the teaching which is condemned here is of a different character.

So far as the present record is concerned, what petitioners did was to organize people to teach and themselves teach the Marxist-Leninist doctrine contained chiefly in four books: Foundations of Leninism by Stalin (1924), The Communist Manifesto by Marx and Engels (1848), State and Revolution by Lenin (1917), History of the Communist Party of the Soviet Union (B) (1939).

Those books are to Soviet Communism what Mein Kampf was to Nazism. If they are understood, the ugliness of Communism is revealed, its deceit and cunning are exposed, the nature of its activities becomes apparent, and the chances of its success less likely. That is not, of course, the reason why petitioners chose these books for their classrooms. They are fervent Communists to whom these volumes are gospel. They preached the creed with the hope that some day it would be acted upon.

The opinion of the Court does not outlaw these texts nor condemn them to the fire, as the Communists do literature offensive to their creed. But if the books themselves are not outlawed, if they can lawfully remain on library shelves, by what reasoning does their use in a classroom become a crime? It would not be a crime under the Act to introduce these books to a class, though that would be teaching what the creed of violent overthrow of the government is. The Act, as construed, requires the element of intent—that those who teach the creed believe in it. The crime then depends not on what is taught but on who the teacher is. That is to make freedom of speech turn not on *what is said,* but on the intent with which it is said. Once we start down that road we enter territory dangerous to the liberties of every citizen.

. . .

Free speech has occupied an exalted position because of the high service it has given our society. Its protection is essential to the very existence of a democracy. The airing of ideas releases pressures which otherwise might become destructive. When ideas compete in the market for acceptance, full and free discussion exposes the false and they gain few adherents. Full and free discussion even of ideas we hate encourages the testing of our own prejudices and preconceptions. Full and free discussion keeps a society from becoming stagnant and unprepared for the stresses and strains that work to tear all civilizations apart.

Full and free discussion has indeed been the first article of our faith. We have founded our political system on it. It has been the safeguard of every religious, political, philosophical, economic, and racial group amongst us. We have counted on it to keep us from embracing what is cheap and false; we have trusted the common sense of our people to choose the doctrine true to our genius and to reject the rest. This has been the one single outstanding tenet that has made our institutions the symbol of freedom and equality. We have deemed it more costly to liberty to suppress a despised minority than to let them vent their spleen. We have above all else feared the political censor. We have wanted a land where our people can be exposed to all the diverse creeds and cultures of the world.

There comes a time when even speech loses its constitutional immunity. Speech innocuous one year may at another time fan such destructive flames that it must be halted in the interests of the safety of the Republic. That is the meaning of the clear and present danger test. When conditions are so critical that there will be no time to avoid the evil that the speech threatens, it is time to call a halt. Otherwise, free speech which is the strength of the Nation will be the cause of its destruction.

Yet free speech is the rule, not the exception. The restraint to be constitutional must be based on more than fear, on more than passionate opposition against the speech, on more than a revolted dislike for its contents. There must be some immediate injury to society that is likely if speech is allowed.

. . .

The nature of Communism as a force on the world scene would, of course, be relevant to the issue of clear and present danger of petitioners' advocacy within the United States. But the primary consideration is the strength and tactical position of petitioners and their converts in this country. On that there is no evidence in the record. If we are to take judicial notice of the threat of Communists within the nation, it should not be difficult to conclude that *as a political party* they are of little consequence. Communists in this country have never made a respectable or serious showing in any election. I would doubt that there is a village, let alone a city or county or state, which the Communists could carry. Communism in the world scene is no bogey-man; but Communists as a political faction or party in this country plainly is. Communism has been so thoroughly exposed in this country that it has been crippled as a political force. Free speech has destroyed it as an effective political party. It is inconceivable that those who went up and down this country preaching the doctrine of revolution which petitioners espouse would have any success. In days of trouble and confusion when bread lines were long, when the unemployed walked the streets, when people were starving, the advocates of a shortcut by revolution might have a chance to gain adherents. But today there are no such conditions. The country is not in despair; the people know Soviet Communism; the doctrine of Soviet revolution is exposed in all of its ugliness and the American people want none of it.

How it can be said that there is a clear and present danger that this advocacy will succeed is, therefore, a mystery. Some nations less resilient than the United States, where illiteracy is high and where democratic traditions are only budding, might have to take drastic steps and jail these men for merely speaking their creed. But in America they are miserable merchants of unwanted ideas; their wares remain unsold. The fact that their ideas are abhorrent does not make them powerful.

The political impotence of the Communists in this country does not, of course, dispose of the problem. Their numbers; their positions in industry and government; the extent to which they have in fact infiltrated the police, the armed services, transportation, stevedoring, power plants, munitions works, and other critical places —these facts all bear on the likelihood that their advocacy of the Soviet theory of revolution will endanger the Republic. But the record is silent on these facts. If we are to proceed on the basis of judicial notice, it is impossible for me to say that the Communists in this country are so potent or so strategically deployed that they must be suppressed for their speech. I could not so hold unless I were willing to conclude that the activities in recent years of committees of Congress, of the Attorney General, of labor unions, of state legislatures, and of Loyalty Boards were so futile as to leave the country on the edge of grave peril. To believe that petitioners and their following are placed in such critical positions as to endanger the Nation is to believe the incredible. It is safe to say that the followers of the creed of Soviet Communism are known to the F.B.I.; that in case of war with Russia they will be picked up overnight as were all prospective saboteurs at the commencement of World War II; that the invisible army of petitioners is the best known, the most beset, and the least thriving of any fifth column in history. Only those held by fear and panic could think otherwise.

. . .

The First Amendment provides that "Congress shall make no law . . . abridging the freedom of speech." The Constitution provides no exception. This does not mean, however, that the Nation need hold its hand until it is in such weakened condition that there is not time to protect itself from incitement to revolution. Seditious conduct can always be punished. But the command of the First Amendment is so clear that we should not allow Congress to call a halt to free speech except in the extreme case of peril from the speech itself. The First Amendment makes confidence in the common sense of our people and in their maturity of judgment the great postulate of our democracy. Its philosophy is that violence is rarely, if ever, stopped by denying civil liberties to those advocating resort to force. The First Amendment reflects the philosophy of Jefferson "that it is time enough for the rightful purposes of civil government for its officers to interfere when principles break out into overt acts against peace and good order." The political censor has no place in our public debates. Unless and until extreme and necessitous circumstances are shown, our aim should be to keep speech unfettered and to allow the processes of law to be invoked only when the provocateurs among us move from speech to action.

Vishinsky wrote in 1948 in The Law of the Soviet State, "In our state, naturally there can be no place for freedom of speech, press, and so on for the foes of socialism."

Our concern should be that we accept no such standard for the United States. Our faith should be that our people will never give support to these advocates of revolution, so long as we remain loyal to the purposes for which our Nation was founded.

## SCALES v. UNITED STATES

367 U. S. 203; 6 L. Ed. 2d 782; 81 S. Ct. 1469 (1961)

MR. JUSTICE HARLAN *delivered the opinion of the Court.*

Our writ issued in this case . . . to review a judgment of the Court of Appeals affirming petitioner's conviction under the so-called membership clause of the Smith Act. . . . The Act, among other things, makes a felony the acquisition or holding of knowing membership in any organiation which advocates the overthrow of the Government of the United States by force or violence.[*] The indictment charged that from January 1946 to the date of its filing (November 18, 1954) the Communist Party of the United States was such an organization, and that petitioner throughout that period was a member thereof, with knowledge of the Party's

* Section 2385 . . . reads:
Whoever organizes or helps or attempts to organize any society, group, or assembly of persons who teach, advocate, or encourage the overthrow or destruction of any such government by force or violence; *or becomes or is a member of,* or affiliates with, *any such*

illegal purpose and a specific intent to accomplish overthrow "as speedily as circumstances would permit."

The validity of this conviction is challenged on statutory, constitutional, and evidentiary grounds, and further on the basis of certain alleged trial and procedural errors. . . .

### STATUTORY CHALLENGE

Petitioner contends that the indictment fails to state an offense against the United States. The claim is that Sec. 4(f) of the Internal Security Act of 1950 constitutes a *pro tanto* repeal of the membership clause of the Smith Act by excluding from the reach of that clause membership in any Communist organization. Section 4(f) provides:

Neither the holding of office nor membership in any Communist organization by any person shall constitute per se a violation of subsection (a) or subsection (c) of this section or of any other criminal statute. The fact of the registration of any person under section 7 or section 8 of this title as an officer or member of any Communist organization shall not be received in evidence against such person in any prosecution for any alleged violation of subsection (a) or subsection (c) of this section or for any alleged violation of any other criminal statute. . . .

To prevail in his contention petitioner must, of course, bring himself within the first sentence of this provision, since the second sentence manifestly refers only to exclusion from evidence of the fact of registra-

*society, group, or assembly of persons, knowing the purposes thereof—*

Shall be fined not more than $20,000 or imprisoned not more than twenty years, or both, and shall be ineligible for employment by the United States or any department or agency thereof, for the five years next following his conviction. . . .

tion, thus assuming that a prosecution may take place.

We turn . . . to the provision . . . and find that, as to petitioner's construction of it, the language is at best ambiguous if not suggestive of a contrary conclusion. Section 4(f) provides that membership or officeholding in a Communist organization shall not constitute "per se a violation of subsection (a) or subsection (c) of this section or of any other criminal statute." Petitioner would most plainly be correct if the statute under which he was indicted purported to proscribe membership in Communist organizations, as such, and to punish membership per se in an organization engaging in proscribed advocacy. But the membership clause of the Smith Act on its face, much less as we construe it in this case, does not do this, for it neither proscribes membership in Communist organizations, as such, but only in organizations engaging in advocacy of violent overthrow, nor punishes membership in that kind of organization except as to one "knowing the purposes thereof," and, as we have interpreted the clause, with a specific intent to further those purposes. . . . We have also held that the proscribed membership must be active, and not nominal, passive or theoretical. . . . Thus the words of the first sentence of Sec. 4(f) by no means unequivocally demand the result for which petitioner argues. When we turn from those words to their context, both in the section as a whole and in the scheme of the Act of which they are a part, whatever ambiguity there may be must be resolved, in our view, against the petitioner's contention.

In the context of Sec. 4 as a whole, the first sentence of subsection (f) does not appear to be a provision repealing in whole or in part any other provision of the Internal Security Act. Subsection (a) of Sec. 4 makes it a crime

for any person knowingly to combine, conspire, or agree with any other person to perform any act which would substantially contribute to the establishment within the United States of a totalitarian dictatorship . . . the direction and control of which is to be vested in or exercised by or under the domination or control of, any foreign government, foreign organization or foreign individual. . . .

Subsection (c) makes it a crime for any officer or member of a "Communist organization" to obtain classified information. We should hesitate long before holding that subsection (f) operates to repeal pro tanto either one of these provisions which are found in the same section of which subsection (f) is a part; and indeed the petitioner does not argue for any such quixotic result. The natural tendency of the first sentence of subsection (f) as to the criminal provisions specifically mentioned is to provide clarification of the meaning of those provisions, that is, that an offense is not made out on proof of mere membership in a Communist organization. As to these particularly mentioned criminal provisions, immunity, such as there is, is specifically granted in the second sentence only, where it is said that the fact of registration shall not be admitted in evidence. Yet petitioner argues that when we come to the last phrase of the first sentence, the tag "or . . . any other criminal statute," the operative part of the sentence, "membership . . . shall [not] constitute per se a violation," has an altogether different purport and effect. What operated as a clarification and guide to construction to the specifically identified provisions is, petitioner argues, a partial repealer as to

the statutes referred to in the omnibus clause at the end of the sentence.

It seems apparent from the foregoing that the language of Sec. 4(f) in its natural import and context should not be taken to immunize members of Communist organizations from the membership clause of the Smith Act, but rather as a mandate to the courts charged with the construction of subsections (a) and (c) "or . . . any other criminal statute" that neither those two named criminal provisions nor any other shall be construed so as to make "membership" in a Communist organization "per se a violation." Indeed, as we read the first sentence of Sec. 4(f), even if the membership clause of the Smith Act could be taken as punishing naked Communist Party membership, it would then be our duty under Sec. 4(f) to construe it in accordance with that mandate, certainly not to strike it down. Although we think that the membership clause on its face goes beyond making mere Party membership a violation, in that it requires a showing both of illegal Party purposes and of a member's knowledge of such purposes, we regard the first sentence of Sec. 4(f) as a clear warrant for construing the clause as requiring not only knowing membership, but active and purposive membership, purposive that is as to the organization's criminal ends. . . . By its terms, then, subsection (f) does not effect a pro tanto repeal of the membership clause; at most it modifies it.

. . .

Although this Court will often strain to construe legislation so as to save it against constitutional attack, it must not and will not carry this to the point of perverting the purpose of a statute. Certainly the section before us cannot be construed as petitioner argues. The fact of registration may provide a significant investigatory lead not only in prosecutions under the membership clause of the Smith Act, but equally probably to prosecutions under Sec. 4(a) of the Internal Security Act, let alone Sec. 4(c). Thus, if we accepted petitioner's argument that Sec. 4(f) must be read as a partial repealer of the membership clause, we would be led to the extraordinary conclusion that Congress also intended to immunize under Sec. 4(f) what it prohibited in these other subsections which it passed at the same time. Furthermore, the thrust of petitioner's argument cannot be limited to the membership clause, for it is equally applicable to any prosecution under any of a host of criminal provisions where Communist Party membership might provide an investigatory lead as to the elements of the crime. We cannot attribute any such sweeping purpose to Congress on the basis of the attenuated inference offered by petitioner.

. . .

#### CONSTITUTIONAL CHALLENGE TO THE MEMBERSHIP CLAUSE ON ITS FACE

Petitioner's constitutional attack goes both to the statute on its face and as applied. . . .

It will bring the constitutional issues into clearer focus to notice first the premises on which the case was submitted to the jury. The jury was instructed that in order to convict it must find that within the three-year limitations period (1) the Communist Party advocated the violent overthrow of the Government, in the sense of present "advocacy of action" to accomplish that end as soon as circumstances were propitious; and (2) petitioner was an "active" member of the Party, and not merely "a nominal, passive, inactive or purely technical" member, with knowledge of the

Party's illegal advocacy and a specific intent to bring about violent overthrow "as speedily as circumstances would permit."

The constitutional attack upon the membership clause, as thus construed, is that the statute offends (1) the Fifth Amendment, in that it impermissibly imputes guilt to an individual merely on the basis of his associations and sympathies, rather than because of some concrete personal involvement in criminal conduct; and (2) the First Amendment, in that it infringes on free political expression and association. Subsidiarily, it is argued that the statute cannot be interpreted as including a requirement of a specific intent to accomplish violent overthrow, or as requiring that membership in a proscribed organization must be "active" membership, in the absence of both or either of which it is said the statute becomes *a fortiori* unconstitutional. . . .

#### 1. Statutory Construction

Before reaching petitioner's constitutional claims, we should first ascertain whether the membership clause permissibly bears the construction put upon it below. We think it does.

The trial court's definition of the kind of organizational advocacy that is proscribed was fully in accord with what was held in *Yates* v. *United States*. . . .

Petitioner's particular constitutional objections to this construction are misconceived. The indictment was not defective in failing to charge that Scales was an "active" member of the Party, for that factor was not in itself a discrete element of the crime, but an inherent quality of the membership element. As such it was a matter not for the indictment, but for elucidating instructions to the jury on what the term "member" in the statute meant. Nor do we think that the objection on the score of vagueness is a tenable one. The distinction between "active" and "nominal" membership is well understood in common parlance . . . and the point at which one shades into the other is something that goes not to the sufficiency of the statute, but to the adequacy of the trial court's guidance to the jury by way of instructions in a particular case. . . . Moreover, whatever abstract doubts might exist on the matter, this case presents no such problem. For petitioner's actions on behalf of the Communist Party most certainly amounted to active membership by whatever standards one could reasonably anticipate, and he can therefore hardly be considered to have acted unadvisedly on this score.

We find no substance in the further suggestion that petitioner could not be expected to anticipate a construction of the statute that included within its elements activity and specific intent, and hence that he was not duly warned of what the statute made criminal. . . .

## 2. Fifth Amendment

In our jurisprudence guilt is personal, and when the imposition of punishment on a status or on conduct can only be justified by reference to the relationship of that status or conduct to other concededly criminal activity (here advocacy of violent overthrow), that relationship must be sufficiently substantial to satisfy the concept of personal guilt in order to withstand attack under the Due Process Clause of the Fifth Amendment. Membership, without more, in an organization engaged in illegal advocacy, it is now said, has not heretofore been recognized by the Court to be such

a relationship. This claim stands, and we shall examine it, independently of the claim made under the First Amendment.

Any thought that due process puts beyond the reach of the criminal law all individual associational relationships, unless accompanied by the commission of specific acts of criminality, is dispelled by familiar concepts of the law of conspiracy and complicity. While both are commonplace in the landscape of the criminal law, they are not natural features. Rather they are particular legal concepts manifesting the more general principle that society, having the power to punish dangerous behavior, cannot be powerless against those who work to bring about that behavior. . . .

What must be met, then, is the argument that membership, even when accompanied by the elements of knowledge and specific intent, affords an insufficient quantum of participation in the organization's alleged criminal activity, that is, an insufficiently significant form of aid and encouragement to permit the imposition of criminal sanctions on that basis. It must indeed be recognized that a person who merely becomes a member of an illegal organization, by that "act" alone need be doing nothing more than signifying his assent to its purposes and activities on one hand, and providing, on the other, only the sort of moral encouragement which comes from the knowledge that others believe in what the organization is doing. It may indeed be argued that such assent and encouragement do fall short of the concrete, practical impetus given to a criminal enterprise which is lent for instance by a commitment on the part of a conspirator to act in furtherance of that enterprise. A member, as distinguished from a conspirator, may indicate his approval of a criminal enterprise by the very fact of his membership without thereby necessarily committing himself to further it by any act or course of conduct whatever.

In an area of the criminal law which this Court has indicated more than once demands its watchful scrutiny . . . these factors have weight and must be found to be overborne in a total constitutional assessment of the statute. We think, however, they are duly met when the statute is found to reach only "active" members having also a guilty knowledge and intent, and which therefore prevents a conviction on what otherwise might be regarded as merely an expression of sympathy with the alleged criminal enterprise, unaccompanied by any significant action in its support of any commitment to undertake such action.

. . .

### 3. *First Amendment*

. . . It was settled in *Dennis* that the advocacy with which we are here concerned is not constitutionally protected speech, and it was further established that a combination to promote such advocacy, albeit under the aegis of what purports to be a political party, is not such association as is protected by the First Amendment. We can discern no reason why membership, when it constitutes a purposeful form of complicity in a group engaging in this same forbidden advocacy, should receive any greater degree of protection from the guarantees of that Amendment.

. . . It is . . . true that quasi-political parties or other groups that may embrace both legal and illegal aims differ from a technical conspiracy, which is defined by its criminal purpose, so that all knowing association with the conspiracy is a proper

subject for criminal proscription as far as First Amendment liberties are concerned. If there were a similar blanket prohibition of association with a group having both legal and illegal aims, there would indeed be a real danger that legitimate political expression or association would be impaired, but the membership clause, as here construed, does not cut deeper into the freedom of association than is necessary to deal with "the substantive evils that Congress has a right to prevent." *Schenck* v. *United States*. . . . The clause does not make criminal all association with an organization which has been shown to engage in illegal advocacy. There must be clear proof that a defendant "specifically intend[s] to accomplish [the aims of the organization] by resort to violence." *Noto* v. *United States, 367* U.S. 1. Thus the member for whom the organization is a vehicle for the advancement of legitimate aims and policies does not fall within the ban of the statute: he lacks the requisite specific intent "to bring about the overthrow of the government as speedily as circumstances would permit." Such a person may be foolish, deluded, or perhaps merely optimistic, but he is not by this statute made a criminal.

We conclude that petitioner's constitutional challenge must be overruled.

#### EVIDENTIARY CHALLENGE

Only in rare instances will this Court review the general sufficiency of the evidence to support a criminal conviction, for ordinarily that is a function which properly belongs to and ends with the Court of Appeals. We do so in this case . . . —our first review of convictions under the membership clause of the Smith Act—not only to make sure that substantive constitutional standards have not been thwarted, but also to provide guidance for the future to the lower courts in an area which borders so closely upon constitutionally protected rights.

. . .

We agree with petitioner that the evidentiary question here is controlled in large part by *Yates.* The decision in *Yates* rested on the view . . . that the Smith Act offenses, involving as they do subtler elements than are present in most other crimes, call for strict standards in assessing the adequacy of the proof needed to make out a case of illegal advocacy. This premise is as applicable to prosecutions under the membership clause of the Smith Act as it is to conspiracy prosecutions under the statute as we had in *Yates.*

. . .

We conclude that this evidence sufficed to make a case for the jury on the issue of illegal Party advocacy. *Dennis* and *Yates* have definitely laid at rest any doubt that present advocacy of future action for violent overthrow satisfies statutory and constitutional requirements equally with advocacy of immediate action to that end. . . . Hence this record cannot be considered deficient because it contains no evidence of advocacy for immediate overthrow.

. . .

*The judgment of the Court of Appeals must be affirmed.*

MR. JUSTICE DOUGLAS *dissenting.*

When we allow petitioner to be sentenced to prison for six years for being a "member" of the Communist Party, we make a sharp break with traditional concepts of First Amendment rights and make serious Mark Twain's light-hearted comment that "it is by the goodness of God that in our country we have those three unspeakably precious things: freedom of speech, freedom of conscience, and the prudence never to practice either of them."

. . . There is here no charge of conspiracy, no charge of any overt act to overthrow the Government by force and violence, no charge of any other criminal act. The charge is being a "member" of the Communist Party, "well knowing" that it advocated the overthrow of the Government by force and violence, "said defendant intending to bring about such overthrow by force and violence as speedily as circumstances would permit." That falls short of a charge of conspiracy. Conspiracy rests not in intention alone but in an agreement with one or more others to promote an unlawful project. . . . No charge of any kind or sort of agreement hitherto embraced in the concept of a conspiracy is made here.

We legalize today guilt by association, sending a man to prison when he committed no unlawful act. Today's break with tradition is a serious one. It borrows from the totalitarian philosophy.

. . .

Not one single illegal act is charged to petitioner. That is why the essence of the crime covered by the indictment is merely belief—belief in the proletarian revolution, belief in Communist creed.

. . .

Nothing but beliefs is on trial in this case. They are unpopular and to most of us revolting. But they are nonetheless ideas or dogmas or faiths within the broad famework of the First Amendment. . . . The creed truer to our faith was stated by the Bar Committee headed by Charles E.

Hughes which in 1920 protected the refusal of the New York Assembly to seat five members of the Socialist Party:

> . . . it is of the essence of the institutions of liberty that it recognized that guilt is personal and cannot be attributed to the holding of opinion or to mere intent in the absence of overt acts. . . .

Belief in the principle of revolution is deep in our traditions. The Declaration of Independence proclaims it:
> . . . whenever any Form of Government becomes destructive of these Ends, it is the Right of the People to alter or to abolish it, and to institute new Government, laying its Foundation on such Principles, and organizing its Powers in such Form, as to them shall seem most likely to effect their Safety and Happiness.

. . .

Of course, government can move against those who take up arms against it. Of course, the constituted authority has the right of self-preservation. But we deal in this prosecution of Scales only with the legality of ideas and beliefs, not with overt acts. The Court speaks of the prevention of "dangerous behavior" by punishing those "who work to bring about that behavior." That formula returns man to the dark days when government determined what behavior was "dangerous" and then policed the dissidents for tell-tale signs of advocacy.

. . .

In recent years we have been departing, I think, from the theory of government expressed in the First Amendment. We have too often been "balancing" the right of speech and association against other values in society to see if we, the judges, feel that a particular need is more important than those guaranteed by the Bill of Rights. *Dennis* v. *United States,* 341 U.S. 414, 5080509; *Communications Assn.* v. *Douds,* 339 U.S. 382, 399–400; *N.A.A.C.P.* v. *Alabama,* 357 U.S. 449, 463–466; *Uphaus* v. *Wyman,* 360 U.S. 126–134; *Bates* v. *Little Rock,* 361 U.S. 516, 524; *Shelton* v. *Tucker,* 364 U.S. 479; *Wilkinson* v. *United States,* 365 U.S. 399; *Braden* v. *United States,* 365 U.S. 431; *Konigsberg* v. *State Bar,* 366 U.S. 36; *In re Anastaplo,* 366 U.S. 82. This approach, which treats the command of the First Amendment as "no more than admonitions of moderation" (see Hand, The Spirit of Liberty (1960 ed.), p. 278) runs counter to our prior decisions.

. . .

What we lose by majority vote today may be reclaimed at a future date when the fear of advocacy, dissent, and nonconformity no longer casts a shadow over us.

MR. JUSTICE BLACK *and* MR. JUSTICE BRENNAN *also dissented in separate opinions which are omitted here.*

# KEYISHIAN v. BOARD OF REGENTS OF UNIVERSITY OF STATE OF NEW YORK

385 U. S. 589; 17 L. Ed. 2d 629; 87 S. Ct. 675 (1967)

MR. JUSTICE BRENNAN *delivered the opinion of the Court.*

Appellants were members of the faculty of the privately owned and operated University of Buffalo, and became state employees when the University was merged in 1962 into the State University of New York, an institution of higher education owned and operated by the State of New York. As faculty members of the State University their continued employment was conditioned upon their compliance with a New York plan, formulated partly in statutes and partly in administrative regulations, which the State utilizes to prevent the appointment or retention of "subversive" persons in state employment.

Appellants Hochfeld and Maud were Assistant Professors of English, appellant Keyishian an instructor in English, and appellant Garver, a lecturer in philosophy. Each of them refused to sign, as regulations then in effect required, a certificate that he was not a Communist, and that if he had ever been a Communist, he had communicated that fact to the President of the State University of New York. Each was notified that his failure to sign the certificate would require his dismissal. Keyishian's one-year-term contract was not renewed because of his failure to sign the certificate. Hochfeld and Garver, whose contracts still had time to run, continued to teach, but subject to proceedings for their dismissal if the constitutionality of the New York plan is sustained. Maud has voluntarily resigned and therefore no longer has standing in this suit.

. . .

Appellants brought this action for declaratory and injunctive relief alleging that the state program violated the Federal Constitution in various respects. A three-judge federal court held that the program was constitutional. . . .

We considered some aspects of the constitutionality of the New York plan 15 years ago in *Adler* v. *Board of Education.* . . . That litigation arose after New York passed the Feinberg Law which added Sec. 3022 to the Education Law, McKinney's Consol. Laws, c. 16. The Feinberg Law was enacted to implement and enforce two earlier statutes. The first was a 1917 law, now Sec. 3021 of the Education Law, under which "the utterance of any treasonable or seditious word or words or the doing of any treasonous or seditious act" is a ground for dismissal from the public school system. The second was a 1939 law which was Sec. 12-a of the Civil Service Law when *Adler* was decided and, as amended, is now Sec. 105 of that law. . . . This law disqualifies from the Civil Service and from employment in the educational system any person who advocates the overthrow of government by force, violence, or any unlawful means, or publishes material advocating such overthrow or organizes or joins any society or group of persons advocating such doctrine.

The Feinberg Law charged the State Board of Regents with the duty of promulgating rules and regulations providing procedures for the disqualification or removal of persons in the public school system who violate the 1917 law or who are ineligible for appointment to or retention in the public school system under the 1939 law. . . . [T]he Board was directed to provide in its rules and regulations that membership in any listed organization should constitute prima facie evidence of disqualification for appointment to or retention in any office or position in the public schools of the State.

The Board of Regents thereupon promulgated rules and regulations containing procedures to be followed by appointing authorities to discover persons ineligible for appointment or retention under the 1939 law, or because of violation of the 1917 law. The Board also announced its intention to list "subversive" organizations after requisite notice and hearing, and provided that membership in a listed organization after the date of its listing should be regarded as constituting prima facie evidence of disqualification, and that membership prior to listing should be presumptive evidence that membership has continued, in the absence of a showing that such membership was terminated in good faith. Under the regulations, an appointing official is forbidden from making an appointment until after he has first inquired of an applicant's former employers and other persons to ascertain whether the applicant is disqualified or ineligible for appointment. In addition, an annual inquiry must be made to determine whether an appointed employee has ceased to be qualified for retention, and a report of findings must be filed.

*Adler* was a declaratory judgment suit in which the Court held, in effect, that there was no constitutional infirmity in former Sec. 12-a or in the Feinberg Law on their faces and that they were capable of constitutional application. But the contention urged in this case that both Sec. 3021 and Sec. 105 are unconstitutionally vague was not heard or decided. . . . Appellants in this case timely asserted below the unconstitutionality of all these sections on grounds of vagueness and that question is now properly before us for decision. Moreover, to the extent that *Adler* sustained the provision of the Feinberg Law constituting membership in an organization advocating forceful overthrow of government, a ground for disqualification, pertinent constitutional doctrines have since rejected the premises upon which that conclusion rested. *Adler* is therefore not dispositive of the constitutional issues we must decide in this case.

A 1953 amendment extended the application of the Feinberg Law to personnel of any college or other institution of higher education owned and operated by the State or its subdivisions. In the same year, the Board of Regents, after notice and hearing, listed the Communist Party of the United States and of the State of New York as "subversive oranizations." In 1956 the Board required that each applicant for an appointment or the renewal of an appointment sign the so-called "Feinberg Certificate" declaring the he had read the Regents Rules and understood that the Rules and the statutes constituted terms of employment, and declaring further that he was not a member of the Communist Party, and that if he had ever been a member he had communicated that fact to the President of the State University. This was the certificate that appellants . . . refused to sign.

In June 1965, shortly before the trial of this case, the Feinberg Certificate was rescinded and it was announced that no person then employed would be deemed ineligible for continued employment "solely" because he refused to sign the certificate. In lieu of the certificate, it was provided that each applicant be informed before assuming his duties that the statutes, Sections 3021 and 3022 of the Education Law and Sec. 105 of the Civil Service Law, constituted part of his contract. He was particularly to be informed of the disqualification which flowed from membership in a listed "subversive" organization. The 1965 announcement further provides: "Should any question arise in the course of such inquiry such candidate may request . . . a personal interview. Refusal of a candidate to answer any question relevant to such inquiry by such officer shall be sufficient ground to refuse to make or recommend appointment." . . .

The change in procedure in no wise moots appellants' constitutional questions raised in the context of their refusal to sign the now abandoned Feinberg Certificate. The substance of the statutory and regulatory complex remains and from the outset appellants' basic claim has been that they are aggrieved by its application.

Section 3021 requires removal for "treasonable or seditious" utterances or acts. The 1958 amendment to Sec. 105 of the Civil Service Law, now subsection 3 of that section, added such utterances or acts as a ground for removal under that law also. The same wording is used in both statutes —that "the utterance of any treasonable or seditious word or words or the doing of any treasonable or seditious act or acts" shall be ground for removal. But there is a vital difference between the two laws. Section 3021 does not define the terms "treasonable or seditious" as used in that section; in contrast, subsection 3 of Sec. 105 of the Civil Service Law provides that the terms "treasonable word or act" shall mean "treason" as defined in the Penal Law and the terms "seditious word or act" shall mean "criminal anarchy" as defined in the Penal Law.

. . .

. . . [A]ssuming that "treasonable" and "seditious" in Sec. 3021 and Sec. 105(3) have the same meaning, the uncertainty is hardly removed. The definition of "treasonable" in the Penal Law presents no particular problem. The difficulty centers upon the meaning of "seditious." Subsection 3 equates the term "seditious" with "criminal anarchy" as defined in the Penal Law. Is the reference only to [the] Penal Law [provision] . . . , defining criminal anarchy as 'the doctrine that organized government should be overthrown by force or violence, or by assassination of the executive head or of any of the executive officials of government, or by any unlawful means?" But that section ends with the sentence "The advocacy of such doctrine either by word of mouth or writing is a felony." If so, the possible scope of "seditious" utterance or acts has virtually no limit. For under Penal Law, Sec. 161, one commits the felony of advocating criminal anarchy if he ". . . publicly displays any book . . . containing or advocating, advising or teaching the doctrine that organized government should be overthrown by force, violence or any unlawful means." Does the teacher who carries a copy of the *Communist Manifesto* on a public street thereby advocate criminal anarchy? It is no answer to say that the statute would not be applied in such a case. We cannot gainsay the potential effect of this obscure wording on "those with a conscientous and scrupulous regard for such undertakings." *Baggett* v. *Bullitt,* 377 U.S. 360. . . . The teacher cannot know the extent, if any, to which a "seditious" utterance must transcend mere statement about abstract doctrine, the extent to which it must be intended to and tend to indoctrinate or incite to action in furtherance of the defined doctrine. The crucial consideration is that no teacher can know just where the line is drawn between "seditious" and nonseditious utterances and acts.

Other provisions of Sec. 105 also have the same defect of vagueness. Subsection (1)(a) of Sec. 105 bars employment of any person who "by word of mouth or writing wilfully and deliberately advocates, advises or teaches the doctrine" of forceful overthrow of government. This provision is plainly susceptible to sweeping and improper application. It may well prohibit the employment of one who merely advocates the doctrine in the abstract without any attempt to indoctrinate others, or to incite others to action in furtherance of unlawful aims. . . . And in prohibiting "advising" the "doctrine" of unlawful overthrow does the statute prohibit mere "advising" of the existence of the doctrine, or advising another to support the doctrine? Since "advocacy" of the doctrine of forceful overthrow is separately prohibited, need the person "teaching" or "advising" this doctrine himself "advocate" it? Does the teacher who informs his class about the precepts of Marxism or the Declaration of Independence violate this prohibition?

Similar uncertainty arises as to the application of subsection (1)(b) of Sec. 105. That subsection requires the qualification of an employee involved with the distribution of written material "containing or advocating, advising or teaching the doctrine" of forceful overthrow, and who himself "advocates, advises, teaches, or embraces the duty, necessity or propriety of adopting the doctrine contained therein." Here again, mere advocacy of abstract doctrine is apparently included. And does the prohibition of distribution of matter "containing" the doctrine bar histories of Marxist doctrine or tracing the background of the French, American, and Russian revolutions? The additional requirement, that the person participating in distribution of the material be the one who "advocates, advises, teaches, or embraces the duty, necessity or propriety of adopting the doctrine" of

forceful overthrow, does not alleviate the uncertainty in the scope of the section, but exacerbates it. . . .

We do not have the benefit of a judicial gloss by the New York courts enlightening us as to the scope of this complicated plan. In light of the intricate administrative machinery for its enforcement, this is not surprising. The very intricacy of the plan and the uncertainty as to the scope of its proscriptions make it a highly efficient *in terrorem mechanism*. It would be a bold teacher who would not stay as far as possible from utterance or acts which might jeopardize his living by enmeshing him in this intricate machinery. The uncertainty as to the utterances and acts proscribed increases that caution in "those who believe the written law means what it says." *Baggett* v. *Bullitt, supra,* 377 U.S., at 374. . . . The result must be to stifle "that free play of the spirit which all teachers ought especially to cultivate and practice. . . ." That probability is enhanced by the provisions requiring an annual review of every teacher to determine whether any utterance or act of his, inside the classroom or out, came within the sanctions of the laws. For a memorandum warns employees that under the statutes "subversive" activities may take the form of "writing of articles, the distribution of pamphlets, the endorsement of speeches made or articles written or acts performed by others," and reminds them "that it is the primary duty of the school authorities in each school district to take positive action to eliminate from the school system any teacher in whose case there is evidence that he is guilty of subversive activity. . . ."

There can be no doubt of the legitimacy of New York's interest in protecting its education system from subversion. But "even though the governmental purpose be legitimate and substantial, that purpose cannot be pursued by means that broadly stifle fundamental personal liberties when the end can be more narrowly achieved." *Shelton* v. *Tucker,* 364 U.S. 479. . . . The principle is not inapplicable because the legislation is aimed at keeping subversives out of the teaching ranks. . . .

Our Nation is deeply committed to safeguarding academic freedom, which is of transcendent value to all of us and not merely to the teachers concerned. That freedom is therefore a special concern of the First Amendment, which does not tolerate laws that cast a pall of orthodoxy over the classroom. "The vigilant protection of constitutional freedoms is nowhere more vital than in the community of American schools." *Shelton* v. *Tucker, supra,* 365 U.S., at 487. The classroom is peculiarly the "marketplace of ideas." The Nation's future depends upon leaders trained through wide exposure to that robust exchange of ideas which discovers truth "out of a multitude of tongues, [rather] than through any kind of authoritative selection." *United States* v. *Associated Press,* D.C., 52 F. Supp. 362, 372. . . .

We emphasize once again that "[p]recision of regulation must be the touchstone in an area so closely touching our most precious freedoms." *N.A.A.C.P.* v. *Button,* 371 U.S. 415; "For standards of permissible statutory vagueness are strict in the area of free expression. . . . Because First Amendment freedoms need breathing space to survive, government may regulate in the area only with narrow specificity." *Id.,* at 432–433. New York's complicated and intricate scheme plainly violates that standard. . . .

The regulatory maze created by New York is wholly lacking in "terms susceptible of objective measurement." *Cramp* v. *Board of Public Instruction.* . . . Vagueness of wording is aggravated by prolixity and profusion of statutes, regulations, and administrative machinery, and by manifold cross-references to interrelated enactments and rules.

We therefore hold that Sec. 3021 of the Education Law and subsections (1)(a), (1)(b) and (3) of the Civil Service Law as implemented by the machinery created pursuant to Sec. 3022 of the Education Law are unconstitutional.

Appellants have also challenged the constitutionality of the discrete provisions of subsection (1)(c) of Sec. 105 and subsection (2) of the Feinberg Law, which make Communist Party membership, as such, prima facie evidence of disqualification. . . . Subsection (2) of the Feinberg Law was, however, before the Court in *Adler* and its constitutionality was sustained. But constitutional doctrine which has emerged since that decision has rejected its major premise. That premise was that public employment, including academic employment, may be conditioned upon the surrender of constitutional rights which could not be abridged by direct government action. Teachers, the Court said in *Adler,* "may work for the school system upon the reasonable terms laid down by the proper authorities of New York. If they do not choose to work on such terms, they are at liberty to retain their beliefs and associations and go elsewhere." . . .

However, the Court of Appeals for the Second Circuit correctly said in an earlier stage of this case, ". . . the theory that public employment which may be denied altogether may be subjected to any conditions, regardless of how unreasonable, has been uniformly rejected." . . . Indeed, that theory was expressly rejected in a series of decisions following *Adler.* See *Wieman* v. *Updegraff,* 344 U.S. 183; *Slochower* v. *Board of Higher Education,* 350 U.S. 551; *Cramp* v. *Board of Public Instruction, supra; Baggett* v. *Bullitt, supra; Shelton* v. *Tucker, supra.* . . .

We proceed then to the question of the validity of the provisions of subsection (c) of Sec. 105 and subsection (2) of Sec. 3022, barring employment to members of listed organizations. Here again constitutional doctrine has developed since *Adler.* Mere knowing membership without a specific intent to further the unlawful aims of an organization is not a constitutionally adequate basis for exclusion from such positions as those held by appellants.

In *Elfbrandt* v. *Russell,* 384 U.S. 11 . . . [w]e . . . struck down a statutorily required oath binding the state employee not to become a member of the Communist Party with knowledge of its unlawful purpose, on threat of discharge and perjury prosecution if the oath were violated. We found that "[a]ny lingering doubt that proscription of mere knowing membership, without any showing of 'specific intent,' would run afoul of the Constitution was set at rest by our decision in *Aptheker* v. *Secretary of State,* 378 U.S. 500. . . . In *Aptheker* we held that Party membership, without knowledge of the Party's unlawful purposes *and* specific intent to further its unlawful aims, could not constitutionally warrant deprivation of the right to travel abroad.

. . .

. . . *Elfbrandt* and *Aptheker* state the governing standard: legislation which sanctions membership unaccompanied by specific intent to further the unlawful goals of the organization or which is not active membership violates constitutional limitations.

Measured against this standard, both Civil Service Law Sec. 105(1)(c) and Education Law Sec. 3022(2) sweep overbroadly into association which may not be sanctioned. The presumption of disqualification arising from proof of mere membership may be rebutted, but only by (a) a denial of membership, (b) a denial that the organization advocates the overthrow of government by force, or (c) a denial that the teacher has knowledge of such advocacy. . . . Thus proof of nonactive membership or a showing of the absence of intent to further unlawful aims will not rebut the presumption and defeat dismissal. This is emphasized in official administrative interpretations. . . . This official administrative interpretation is supported by the legislative preamble to the Feinberg Law, Sec. 1, in which that legislature concludes as a result of its findings that "it is essential that the laws prohibiting persons who are *members* of subversive groups, such as the communist party and its affiliated organizations, from obtaining or retaining employment in the public schools, be vigorously enforced."

Thus Sec. 105(1)(c) and Sec. 3022(2) suffer from impermissible "overbreadth." . . . They seek to bar employment both for association which legitimately may be sanctioned and for association which may not be sanctioned consistently with First Amendment rights. . . .

We therefore hold that Civil Service Law Sec. 105(1)(c) and Education Law Sec. 3022(2) are invalid insofar as they sanction mere knowing membership without any showing of specific intent to further the unlawful aims of the Communist Party of the United States or of the State of New York.

*The judgment of the District Court is reversed and the case is remanded for further proceedings consistent with this opinion.*

. . .

MR. JUSTICE CLARK, *with whom* MR. JUSTICE HARLAN, MR. JUSTICE STEWART *and* MR. JUSTICE WHITE *join, dissenting.*

. . .

This is a declaratory judgment action testing the *application* of the Feinberg Law to appellants. The certificate and statement once required by the Board and upon which appellants base their attack were, before the case was tried, abandoned by the Board and are no longer required to be made. Despite this fact the majority proceeds to its decision striking down New York's Feinberg Law and other of its statutes as applied to appellants on the basis of the old certificate and statement. It does not explain how the statute can be applied to appellants under procedures which have been for over two years a dead letter. The issues posed are, therefore, purely abstract and entirely speculative in character. The Court under such circumstances has in the past refused to pass upon constitutional questions. In addition, the appellants have neither exhausted their administrative remedies, nor pursued the remedy of judicial review of agency action as provided earlier by subdivision(d) of Sec. 12-a of the Civil Service Law. Finally, one of the sections stricken, Sec. 105(3), has been amended and under its terms will not become effective until September 1, 1967. (L. 1965, Ch. 1030.).

. . .

It is clear that the Feinberg Law, in which this Court found "no constitutional infirmity" in 1952, has been given its death blow today. Just as the majority here finds that there "can be no doubt of the legitimacy of New York's interest in protecting its education system from subversion" there can also be no doubt that "the be-all and end-all" of New York's effort is here. And regardless of its correctness neither New York nor the several States that have followed the teaching of *Adler* for some 15 years, can ever put the pieces together again. No court has ever reached out so far to destroy so much with so little.

The section (Sec. 3021 of the Education Law) which authorizes the removal of superintendents, teachers, or employees in the public school in any city or school district of New York for the utterance of any treasonable or seditious word or words is also struck down, even though it does not apply to appellants, as we shall discuss below.

Also declared unconstitutional are the subsections [(1)(a), (1)(b) and (1)(c) of Sec. 105 of the Civil Service Act].

. . .

[Here Justice Clark examined *Garner* v. *Board of Works of Los Angeles, Adler* v. *Board of Education, Beilan* v. *Board of Education, Lerner* v. *Casey* and other *Adler* line cases.]

Lastly stricken is the subsection [(3) of Sec. 105] which authorizes the discharge of any person in the civil service of the State or any civil division thereof who utters any treasonable or seditious word or does any treasonable or seditious act, although this subsection is not and never has been a part of the Feinberg Law and New York specifically disclaims its applicability to the appellants. In addition, how can the Court pass upon this law *as applied* when the State has never attempted to and now renounces its application to appellants?

This Court has again and again, since at least 1951, approved procedures either identical or at the least similar to the ones the Court condemns today.

. . .

In view of this long list of decisions covering over 15 years of this Court's history, in which no opinion of this Court even questioned the validity of the *Adler* line of cases, it is strange to me that the Court now finds that the "constitutional doctrine which has emerged since . . . has rejected (*Adler's*) major premise." With due respect, as I read them, our cases have done no such thing.

The majority also finds that *Adler* did not pass upon Sec. 3021 of the Education Law, nor subsection (1)(3) of Sec. 105 of the Civil Service Law nor upon the vagueness questions of subsections (1)(a), (1)(b), and (1)(c) of Sec. 105. We will now discuss them.

1. Section 3021 is not applicable to these appellants. . . . [T]his section by its own terms only applies to superintendents, teachers and employees in the "public schools, in any city or school district of the state. . . ." It does not apply to teachers in the State University at all.

2. Likewise subsection (1)(3) of Sec. 105 is also inapplicable. . . . [T]he law before us has to do with the qualifications of college level personnel not covered by Civil Service. . . . [N]o superintendent, teacher, or employee of the educational system has ever been charged with violating Sec. 105(3). The Court seems to me to be building straw men.

3. The majority also says that no challenge of vagueness points were passed upon in *Adler*. A careful examination of the briefs in that case casts considerable doubt on this conclusion. In the appellant's brief, point 3, in *Adler,* the question is stated in this language: "The statutes and the regulations issued thereunder violate the due process clause of the Fourteenth Amendment because of their vagueness." Certainly the word "subversive" is attacked as vague and the Court finds that it "has a very definite meaning, namely, an organization that teaches and advocates the overthrow of government by force or violence." . . . Also significant is the fact that the *Adler* opinion's last sentence is "We find no constitutional infirmity in Sec. 12-a [(now (1)(a), (1) (b) and (1)(c) of Sec. 105] of the Civil Service Law of New York or in the Feinberg Law which implemented it. . . ."

. . . The majority makes much over the horribles that might arise from subsection (1)(b) of Sec. 105 which condemns the printing, publishing, selling, etc., of matter containing such doctrine. But the majority fails to state that this action is condemned only *when and if* the teacher also personally advocates, advises, teaches, etc., the necessity or propriety of adopting such doctrine. This places this subsection on the same footing as (1)(a). And the same is true of subsection (1)(c) where a teacher organizes, helps to organize or becomes a member of an organization which teaches or advocates such doctrine, for scienter would also be a necessary ingredient under our opinion in *Garner,* supra. Moreover, membership is only prima facie evidence of disqualification and could be rebutted, leaving the burden of proof on the State. Furthermore, all of these procedures are protected by an adversary hearing with full judicial review.

In the light of these considerations the strained and unbelievable suppositions that the majority poses could hardly occur. As was said in *Dennis,* "we are not convinced that because there may be borderline cases" the State should be prohibited the protections it seeks. . . . Where there is doubt as to one's intent or the nature of his activities we cannot assume that the administrative boards will not give those offended full protection. Furthermore the courts always sit to make certain that this is done.

The majority says that the Feinberg Law is bad because it has an 'overboard sweep." I regret to say—and I do so with deference—that the majority has by its broadside swept away one of our most precious rights, namely, the right of self-preservation. Our public educational system is the genius of our democracy. The minds of our youth are developed there and the character of that development will determine the future of our land. Indeed, our very existence depends upon it. The issue here is a very narrow one. It is not freedom of speech, freedom of thought, freedom of press, freedom of assembly, or of association, even in the Communist Party. It is simply this: May the State provide that one who, after a hearing with full judicial review, is found to wilfully and deliberately advocate, advise, or teach that our Government should be overthrown by force or violence or other unlawful means; or who wilfully and deliberately prints, publishes, etc., any book or paper that so advocates *and who personally* advocates such doctrine himself; or who wilfully and deliberately becomes a member of an organization that advocates such doctrine, is prima facie disqualified from teaching in its university? My answer, in keeping with all of our cases up until today, is "Yes"!

I dissent.

## ALBERTSON v. SUBVERSIVE ACTIVITIES CONTROL BOARD

382 U. S. 70; 15 L. Ed. 2d 165; 86 S. Ct. 194 (1965)

MR. JUSTICE BRENNAN *delivered the opinion of the Court.*

The Communist Party of the United States of America failed to register with the Attorney General as required by the order of the Subversive Activities Control Board sustained in *Communist Party of the United States* v. *SACB.* . . . Accordingly no list of Party members was filed as required by Section 7(d) of the Subversive Activities Control Act of 1950. . . . Sections 8(a) and (c) of the Act provide that, in that circumstance, each member of the organization must register and file a registration statement; in default thereof, Section 13(a) authorizes the Attorney General to petition the Board for an order requiring the member to register. The Attorney General invoked Section 13(a) against petitioners, and the Board, after evidentiary hearings, determined that petitioners were Party members and ordered each of them to register pursuant to section 8(a) and (c). . . . The Court of Appeals affirmed the orders. . . . We granted certiorari. . . . We reverse.

Petitioners address several constitutional challenges to the validity of the orders, but we consider only the contention that the orders violate their Fifth Amendment privilege against self-incrimination.

The Court of Appeals affirmed the orders without deciding the privilege issue, expressing the view that under our decision in *Communist Party,* 367 U.S., at 105–110 . . . the issue was not ripe for adjudication and would be ripe only in a prosecution for failure to register if the petitioners did not register. . . . We disagree. . . . Here . . . the contingencies upon which the members' duty to register arises have already matured; the Party did not register within 30 days after the order to register became final and the requisite 60 days since the order became final have elapsed. . . . [T]he considerations which led the Court in *Communist Party* to hold that the claims on behalf of unnamed officers were premature are not present in this case.

There are other reasons for holding that petitioners' self-incrimination claims are ripe for decision. Specific orders requiring petitioners to register have been issued. The Attorney General has promulgated regulations requiring that registration shall be accomplished . . . and petitioners risk very heavy penalties if they fail to register by completing and filing [specific] forms. . . . [F]or example, each day of failure to register constitutes a separate offense punishable by a fine up to $10,000 or imprisonment up to five years, or both. Petitioners must either register without a decision on the merits of their privilege claims, or fail to register and risk onerous and rapidly mounting penalties while awaiting the Government's pleasure whether to initiate a prosecution against them. To ask, in these circumstances, that petitioners await such a prosecution for an adjudication of

their self-incrimination claims is, in effect, to contend that they should be denied the protection of the Fifth Amendment privilege intended to relieve claimants of the necessity of making a choice between incriminating themselves and risking serious punishments for refusing to do so.

. . .

The risks of incrimination which the petitioners take in registering are obvious. Form 1S-52a requires an admission of membership in the Communist Party. Such an admission of membership may be used to prosecute registrant under the membership clause of the Smith Act . . . or under section 4(a) of the Subversive Activities Control Act . . . to mention only two federal criminal statutes. . . . Accordingly, we have held that mere association with the Communist Party presents sufficient threat of prosecution to support a claim of privilege. . . .

The statutory scheme, in providing that registration "shall be accompanied'" by a registration statement, clearly implies that there is a duty to file Form 1S-52, the registration statement, only if there is an enforceable obligation to accomplish registration by completing and filing Form 1S-52a. Yet, even if the statute and regulations required petitioners to complete and file Form IS-52 without regard to the validity of the order to register on Form IS-52a, the requirement to complete and file Form IS-52 would also invade the privilege. Like the admission of Party membership demanded by Form IS-52a, the information called for by Form IS-52—the organization of which the registrant is a member, his aliases, place and date of birth, a list of offices held in the organization and duties thereof— might be used as evidence in or at least supply investigatory leads to a criminal prosecuiton. The Government, relying on *United States* v. *Sullivan,* 274 U.S. 259, . . . argues that petitioners might answer some questions and appropriately claim the privilege on the form as to others, but cannot fail to submit a registration statement altogether. Apart from our conclusion that nothing in the Act or regulations permits less than literal and full compliance with the requirements of the form, the reliance on *Sullivan* is misplaced. Sullivan upheld a conviction for failure to file an income tax return on the theory that "[i]f the form of return provided called for answers that the defendant was privileged from making, he could have raised the objection in the return, but could not on that account refuse to make any return at all." 274 U.S., at 263. . . . In *Sullivan* the questions in the income tax return were neutral on their face and directed at the public at large, but here they are directed at a highly selective group inherently suspect of criminal activities. Petitioners' claims are not asserted in an essentially non-criminal and regulatory area of inquiry, but against an inquiry in an area permeated with criminal statutes, where response to any of the form's questions in context might involve the petitioners in the admission of a crucial element of a crime.

Section 4(f) of the Act,* the purported immunity provision, does not save the registraiton orders from petitioners' Fifth Amendment challenge. In *Counselman* v. *Hitchcock,* 142 U.S. 547, . . . decided in 1892, the Court

* Section 4 (f) . . . provides:
'Neither the holding of office nor membership in any Communist organization by any person shall constitute *per se* a violation of subsection (a) or subsection (c) of this section

held "that no [immunity] statute which leaves the party or witness subject to prosecution after he answers the criminating question put to him, can have the effect of supplanting the privilege . . . ," and that such a statute is valid only if it supplies "a complete protection from all the perils against which the constitutional prohibition was designed to guard . . ." by affording "absolute immunity against future prosecution for the offence to which the question relates." . . . Measured by these standards, the immunity granted by section 4(f) is not complete. . . . It does not preclude any use of the information called for by Form IS-52, either as evidence or as an investigatory lead. With regard to the act of registering on Form IS-52a, section 4(f) provides only that the admission of Party membership thus required shall not *per se* constitute a violation of sections 4(a) and (c) or any other criminal statute, or "be received in evidence" against a registrant in any criminal prosecution; it does not preclude the use of the admission as an investigatory lead, a use which is barred by the privilege.

*The judgment of the Court of Appeals is reversed and the Board's orders are set aside.*
*It is so ordered.*

MR. JUSTICE BLACK *concurs in the reversal for all the reasons set out in*

or of any other criminal statute. The fact of the registration of any person under section 787 or section 788 of this title as an officer or member of any Communist organization shall not be received in evidence against any person in any prosecution for any alleged violation of subsection (a) or subsection (c) of this section or for any alleged violation of any other criminal statute."

the Court's opinion as well as those set out in his dissent in Communist Party of the United States *v.* SACB, *367 U.S. 1,* . . .

MR. JUSTICE WHITE *took no part in the consideration or decision of this case.*

## SELECTED REFERENCES

Barber, Kathleen, "Legal Status of the American Communist Party," 15 *Journal of Public Law* 94 (1966).

Chafee, Zechariah, *Free Speech in the United States* (Cambridge: Harvard University Press, 1948).

Chase, Harold W., "The Libertarian Case for Making it a Crime to be a Communist," 29 *Temple Law Quarterly* 121 (1956).

Cook, Thomas I., *Democratic Rights versus Communist Activity* (Garden City: Doubleday & Co., Inc., 1954).

Goodman, Walter, *The Committee: The Extraordinary Career of the House Committee on Un-American Activities* (New York: Farrar, Straus & Giroux, Inc., 1968).

Guttmann, Allen and Benjamin Zielger, editors, *Communism, the Courts and the Constitution* (Boston: D. C. Heath, 1964).

Israel, Jerold, "Elfbrandt v. Russell: The Demise of the Oath?" 1966 *Supreme Court Review* 193 (1966).

Latham, Earl, *The Communist Controversy in Washington From the New Deal to McCarthy* (Cambridge: Harvard University Press, 1966).

McCloskey, Robert G., "Free Speech, Sedition and the Constitution," 45 *American Political Science Review* 662 (1951).

Mansfield, John H., "The Albertson Case: Conflict Between the Privilege Against Self-Incrimination and the Government's Need for Information," 1966 *Supreme Court Review* 103 (1966).

# 5. The Rights of the Accused

*Mapp v. Ohio     Camara v. City and County of San Francisco*

*Terry v. Ohio     Katz v. United States     Malloy v. Hogan*

*Griffin v. California     Gideon v. Wainwright     Escobedo v. Illinois*

*Miranda v. Arizona     In re Gault     Duncan v. Louisiana*

*Pointer v. Texas     Klopfer v. North Carolina*

*Sheppard v. Maxwell     Robinson v. California*

*Scoggin v. Lincoln University*

The Warren Court wrought radical changes in the constitutional rules applying to "cops and robbers." Prior to these revolutionary changes, state criminal procedures were based largely on state constitutional and statutory provisions. Specific guarantees of the federal Bill of Rights were not applicable; Chief Justice Marshall's early decision in *Barron* v. *Baltimore* supported this position. Although eroded after 1925, *Barron* still was considered good law, particularly where the rights of the accused were concerned. Time and again the Court brushed aside arguments that the Fourteenth Amendment was intended to reverse *Barron* and to incorporate the Bill of Rights. Even the Court's acceptance of the "selective incorporation" theory announced in *Palko* v. *Connecticut, supra,* did not result in any immediate change in the application of Bill of Rights guarantees to state criminal procedures. For more than two decades after *Palko,* the Court held to the position that the states were not restricted by specific procedures of the Bill of Rights in their criminal procedures. But beginning in 1961 the Court made a dramatic change in its position —so dramatic in fact that it may be characterized as revolutionary. A brief survey of the various criminal law areas demonstrates these changes brought about by the Warren Court.

## THE SEARCH AND SEIZURE PROBLEM

Despite the noble profession of justice expressed in the Fourth Amendment that "the right of the people to be secure in their persons, houses, papers, and effects, against unreasonable searches and seizures, shall not be violated . . . ," most persons whose liberty was in conflict with state governmental authority were not the beneficiaries of this guarantee. For the states, as primary enforcers of criminal law under our federal system, were not bound by the Fourth Amendment. State actions were governed by similar provisions in state bills of rights, and the enforcement of those guarantees were at best wavering, uncertain, and uneven. By contrast, for those whose liberty was in conflict with federal authority, the Fourth Amendment had real meaning. As far back as 1886, in *Boyd* v. *United States* (116 U.S. 616), the Court tied the Fourth Amendment to the Fifth Amendment's self-incrimination provision holding that an unreasonable search and seizure is the same as a compulsion of a person to be a witness against himself. Subsequently, the Court ruled in *Weeks* v. *United States* (232 U.S. 383, 1914) that evidence obtained in violation of the Amendment is inadmissible in criminal prosecutions.

Some states voluntarily adopted the *Weeks* rule, but most did not, and when in *Wolf* v. *Colorado* (338 U.S. 25, 1949) the Court was urged to make the rule obligatory on the states, it refused to do so. Though the Court agreed that the Fourth Amendment guarantee against unreasonable searches and seizures was enforceable against the states through the Fourteenth Amendment, the Court nevertheless concluded that the exclusionary rule announced in *Weeks* was not an "essential ingredient" of that guarantee. The Court emphasized that the exclusionary rule was merely a rule of evidence imposed on federal courts, and state courts were free to admit or exclude illegally seized evidence as their laws might require.

Subsequent cases involving the Fourth Amendment revealed the impracticality of the *Wolf* rule. In *Rochin* v. *California* (342 U.S. 165, 1952), for example, the Court bypassed the rule in reversing a state narcotics conviction. The evidence admitted in the case had been obtained after forcible entry without a warrant and the subsequent pumping of the stomach of the accused. Clearly here was a case where the evidence was tainted, but the *Wolf* precedent would allow its admission. However, Justice Felix Frankfurter solved the dilemma by simply holding that due process was offended because the conduct used by the police to obtain the evidence "shocks the conscience."

But in *Irvine* v. *California* (347 U.S. 128, 1954) the Court still clung to *Wolf*. Here, evidence used in supporting a conviction for illegal bookmaking was obtained by taking advantage of Irvine's periodic absences from his residence. A key made by a locksmith enabled the police to enter Irvine's house and plant a concealed microphone that allowed them to monitor his conversations from a neighboring garage. On two subsequent occasions the police reentered the residence to relocate the microphone for better results. Testimony as to what the officers heard was admitted at the trial. Justice Robert H. Jackson delivered the opinion for the five-man majority affirming the conviction. Though Justice Jackson recognized the unsavory methods employed in obtaining the evidence and suggested that there was evidence of trespassing and probably burglary, he nevertheless held that under the *Wolf* rule the evidence was admissible. His defense of the rule was essentially this: to exclude the evidence would result in the guilty person escaping punishment and his subsequent release would further endanger society, while the exclusion does nothing to punish the wrong-doing official. Justice Frankfurter dissented and said he would have followed the *Rochin* rule because of the "additional aggravating conduct" of the police. Justice William O. Douglas' dissent echoed his familiar theme that the Court should never have departed from the exclusionary rule when it decided *Wolf,* while Justice Hugo Black thought the action infringed the self-incrimination guarantee. Justice Tom Clark, although concurring, expressed serious doubts about the admissibility of evidence allowed under *Wolf* and stated that had he been on the Court in 1949 he would have supported the application of the *Weeks* rule to the states.

Two subsequent actions portended the demise of the *Wolf* rule. First, Chief Justice Earl Warren's strong dissent in *Briethaupt* v. *Abram* (352 U.S. 432, 1957) indicated that at least four justices were ready to overrule *Wolf.* The Court majority in *Briethaupt* upheld a conviction based on evidence obtained by taking a blood sample from the accused (while he was unconscious in a hospital) to prove intoxication. In a second action in 1960, the Court struck down the "silver platter" doctrine in *Elkins* v. *United States* (364 U.S. 206). That doctrine had permitted evidence illegally obtained by state officers to be admitted in federal prosecutions so long as there was no complicity.

In 1961 the *Wolf* rule was finally laid to rest in *Mapp* v. *Ohio. Mapp* commenced a period of revolutionary holdings in criminal due process by the Warren Court. Here the Court reversed a conviction for possession of obscene literature in which the evidence against the accused was obtained by forcible police entry without a search warrant. In his opinion for the five-man majority, Justice Tom Clark stressed the need to observe the command of the Fourth Amendment. He noted that the Court had held in *Wolf* that the right to privacy embodied in that Amendment was enforceable against the states and that it should no longer be permitted "to remain an empty promise." He concluded that "nothing can destroy a government more quickly than its failure to observe its laws, or worse, its disregard of the charter of its own existence."

Justice John Marshall Harlan's dissent was essentially a plea for judicial restraint and observance of precedents. He cautioned the majority that "the preservation of a proper balance between state and federal responsibility in the administration of criminal justice demands patience on the part of those who might like to see things move faster among the states [in this area]."

In its first application of the *Mapp* rule, the Court appeared to make a mild retreat. In *Ker* v. *California* (374 U.S. 23, 1963) the Court affirmed a conviction where the evidence was obtained without a search warrant and entry was gained by using the building manager's passkey. Justice Clark's opinion for the majority distinguished between evidence held inadmissible because it is prohibited by the Constitution and that which is inadmissible because it violates a federal statute. Noting that the evidence would have been inadmissible in a federal prosecution because a federal statute would bar it, he emphasized that such a prohibition had no application to a state prosecution "where admissibility is governed by constitutional standards." He concluded that the "demands of our federal system" compel such a distinction and that the states should not be "precluded from developing workable rules governing arrests, searches, and seizures to meet the practical demands of effective criminal investigation and law enforcement" so long as such rules do not offend federal constitutional standards.

But if *Ker* implied any "soft" application of *Mapp,* it was quickly dispelled one year later in *Aguillar* v. *Texas* (378 U.S. 108, 1964). Here the Court reversed a narcotics conviction and in doing so made it clear that the *Mapp* rule must be obeyed and that no shabby subterfuges would be tolerated. In speaking for the Court, Justice Arthur Goldberg said that an inquiry as to the constitutionality of a search warrant should begin with the rule that "the informed and deliberate determinations of magistrates empowered to issue warrants . . . are to be preferred over the hurried action of officers . . . who may happen to make the arrests." The "informant's 'suspicion', 'belief', or 'mere conclusion' " are not enough, insisted Goldberg. Probable cause to support issuance of a warrant must "be found from facts or circumstances presented under oath or affirmation."

One of the most expansive applications of the *Mapp* rule was made in *Camara* v. *City and County of San Francisco.* There, the Court held that administrative searches by municipal health and safety inspectors are limited by the safeguards of the Fourth Amendment. Justice Byron White's opinion for the majority emphasized the basic purpose of the Amendment—to safeguard the privacy and the security of individuals against arbitrary invasions by governmental officials. He made it clear, however, that the ruling was not intended to foreclose a prompt inspection, even without a warrant, when an emergency dictates it.

Should *Mapp* be applied prospectively to cases arising after that decision or retrospectively to cases decided under the *Wolf* rule where such persons had long since exhausted judicial remedies and were serving sentences? This question was answered almost four years after *Mapp* in *Linkletter* v. *Walker* (381 U.S. 618, 1965). Speaking for the majority, Justice Tom Clark noted that the Constitution is silent on the question and thus the Court was free to make its own determination based on the purpose of the decision. In making that determination, Clark examined several factors, including the purpose of the new rule, reliance placed on the old *Wolf* rule, and the impact and effect on the administration of justice resulting from a retrospective application. This examination led him and the Court to conclude that *Mapp* should be applied prospectively.

Near the end of the 1967 term, the Court upheld the controversial "stop and frisk" laws in *Terry* v. *Ohio* and in *Sibron* v. *New York* (392 U.S. 40, 1968).[1] Generally these laws permit policemen to stop and frisk suspicious persons without meeting the "probable cause" standard of the Fourth Amendment. Speaking for the 8–1 majority in *Terry*, Chief Justice Earl Warren made it clear that the Court was not retreating from the warrant requirement of the Fourth Amendment but was merely applying a more practical standard, which exempts from the probable cause requirement a limited search for weapons if the search is otherwise reasonable. He emphasized that the sole justification of a search of this nature "is the protection of the police officer and others nearby and it must therefore be confined in scope to an intrusion reasonably designed to discover [hidden weapons]" which may be used in assaulting the officer. The Chief Justice concluded that the reasonableness of each search will have to be decided according to its circumstances.

Justice Douglas was the lone dissenter. He said it was illogical to let police search without probable cause when they acted without a warrant, while they had to show probable cause if they applied to a magistrate for a warrant. "To give the police greater power than a magistrate is to take a long step down the totalitarian path. Perhaps such a step is desirable to cope with modern forms of lawlessness. But if it is taken, it should be the deliberate choice of the people through a constitutional amendment."

The "stop and frisk" decision somewhat reversed the trend of the Warren Court decisions which tended to protect those suspected of crime from the hands of overzealous police. Consequently, the outspoken "law and order" critics of the Court were pleased by the decision. But by the same token the decision aroused the apprehension and disapproval of minority groups and other civil liberties spokesmen.

Technological advances of the 20th century have added another dimension to the problem of protecting privacy. Major difficulties center around wiretapping and recording conversations through concealed electronic devices. Privacy can easily be invaded by employing such methods and the consequences are often as damaging as those resulting from forced entry and seizure. Nevertheless, the Supreme Court recognized a constitutional difference in *Olmstead* v. *United States* (227 U.S. 438, 1928). In that case, it affirmed a conviction for conspiracy to violate the National Prohibition Act where evidence was obtained by wiretapping. Chief Justice William H. Taft's opinion for the five-man majority

---

[1] In *Sibron,* the police action was authorized by a state statute. In *Terry* no statutory authorization was involved; the police merely followed customary practice.

emphasized the historical purpose of the Fourth Amendment as being the protection of one's house, person, papers, and effects from forced governmental search and seizure. He maintained that "the language of the Amendment cannot be extended and expanded to include telephone wires, reaching the whole world from the defendant's house or office." Taft concluded that "[t]he intervening wires are not part of his house or office, any more than are the highways along which they are stretched."

The dissenters were greatly disturbed at the possibilities for dilution of the privacy guarantee that the decision portended. Justice Oliver Wendell Holmes found this method of obtaining evidence "dirty business" and warned that "the government ought not use evidence obtainable, and only obtainable by a criminal act," for it is "a less evil that some criminals should escape than that the Government should play an ignoble part." Justice Louis Brandeis' more comprehensive dissent condemned the majority's narrow application of the Fourth Amendment. He expressed considerable concern about government intrusion into privacy in the future when he noted:

The progress of science in furnishing the Government with means of espionage is not likely to stop with wiretapping. Ways may some day be developed by which the Government, without removing papers from secret drawers, can reproduce them in court, and by which it will be enabled to expose to a jury the most intimate occurences at home. Advances in the psychic and related sciences may bring means of exploring unexpressed beliefs, thoughts and emotions. . . . Can it be that the Constitution affords no protection against such invasions of individual security?

Six years later Congress acted to plug the privacy gap left by *Olmstead*. The Federal Communications Act of 1934 included a provision (Section 605) prohibiting the intercepting and divulging of tele-communications. The provision's effectiveness in federal prosecutions was assured in *Nardonne* v. *United States* (302 U.S. 397, 1937) where the Court held inadmissible evidence obtained by federal officials through wiretapping. But an attempt to extend this prohibition to state criminal prosecutions was rejected in *Schwartz* v. *Texas* (344 U.S. 199, 1952). Undoubtedly, the Court's distinction was based on the *Wolf* rule governing the admissibility of evidence in state courts. However, an attempt to use *Schwartz* as a means of evading *Nardonne* was rejected in *Benanti* v. *United States* (355, U.S. 96, 1957) when the Court held inadmissible in federal prosecutions evidence obtained by state officers under state-approved wiretapping systems.

When the *Wolf* rule was struck down in *Mapp* the major support for *Schwartz* was undermined, and in *Lee* v. *Florida* (392 U.S. 378, 1968) the Court announced that "*Schwartz* . . . cannot survive the demise of *Wolf*. . . ." Justice Potter Stewart's opinion for the Court stressed that the wiretapping law is applicable to the states by its unequivocal prohibition of the interception and divulging of telephone messages. Stewart concluded that the statutory prohibition supported by the *Mapp* exclusionary rule renders inadmissible, in state prosecutions, evidence obtained by wiretapping. Justices Black and Harlan wrote separate dissenting opinions in which they contended that the statute should not be interpreted as prescribing a rule of evidence. Black charged that the majority, impatient with Congress "in this day of rapid creation of new judicial rules," was rewriting the statute through judicial decree. He warned that the inevitable result of such new rules was "to make conviction of criminals more difficult."

Congress' failure to heed Justice Brandeis' warning in his *Olmstead* dissent when it passed the Federal Communications Act, left law enforcement officers free to employ a variety of electronic eavesdropping devices to invade the privacy of the unsuspecting. Thus the Court, following the narrow *Olmstead* construction of the Fourth Amendment, affirmed a number of convictions in which evidence obtained by various eavesdropping devices was admitted. In *Goldman* v. *United States* (316 U.S. 129, 1942) use of a detectaphone to monitor conversations in an adjoining office was not considered an unreasonable search and seizure. Likewise, the Court held that the Fourth Amendment was not breached in *On Lee* v. *United States* (343 U.S. 747, 1952). Here *On Lee* made incriminating statements to a former employee who just "happened" to drop by for a "friendly chat" but who had concealed on his person a radio transmitter that enabled a narcotics agent to monitor the "friendly chat." The agent's testimony as to what he heard was admitted as evidence in the successful prosecution. In addition, the Court allowed convictions to stand where evidence was obtained by electronic devices devoid of unlawful physical invasion of privacy or where "undercover agents" were privy to conversations with the consent of the "suspect." (*Lopez* v. *United States*, 373 U.S. 427, 1963; *Hoffa* v. *United States*, 385 U.S. 293, 1966; and *Osborn* v. *United States*, 385 U.S. 323, 1966.)

The Court has made it clear, however, that overzealous methods to invade privacy are inconsistent with the Fourth Amendment. In *Silverman* v. *United States* (363 U.S. 505, 1961) the Court condemned as an unreasonable invasion of privacy the transformation of the entire heating system into a conductor of sound.[2] Likewise, New York's permissive eavesdrop statute[3] was invalidated in *Berger* v. *New York* (388 U.S. 41, 1967) because of its failure to conform with the essential safeguards for

[2] See also *Wong Sun* v. *United States* (371 U.S. 471, 1963) where the Court for the first time specifically held that the Fourth Amendment excludes verbal evidence which "derives . . . immediately from an unlawful entry and unauthorized arrest."

[3] The New York statute authorizes the issuance of a general warrant for eavesdropping upon affirmation by a law enforcement official who merely states his belief that evidence of a crime may thereby be obtained; describes the person whose communications are to be intercepted and the purpose of the interception; and identifies the telephone number or telegraph line involved.

searches and seizures required by the Fourth and Fourteenth Amendments. Justice Tom Clark's opinion for the majority emphasized that the use of electronic devices to capture conversations was a " 'search' within the meaning of the [Fourth] Amendment." Consequently, he argued, the statute cannot stand because it lacks that particularity required by the Fourth Amendment as to the specific crime committed or being committed, the conversations sought, or the place to be searched. He concluded that the statute was a "broadside authorization . . . resulting in trespassory intrusion" of privacy rather than one "carefully circumscribed" so as to prevent unauthorized invasions thereof.

Justice William O. Douglas wrote a brief concurring opinion setting forth the view that "at long last" the Court had overruled *"sub silentio, Olmstead . . .* and its offspring. . . ."

Justice Hugo Black complained in dissent that the Court had forged requirements that make the enactment of an acceptable eavesdropping statute "completely impossible . . . because of [its] hostility to eavesdropping as 'ignoble' and 'dirty business.' " He reemphasized his view expressed in *Wolf* and *Mapp* that the Fourth Amendment does not, in and of itself, contain an exclusionary requirement and, hence, does not forbid the use of the evidence obtained under the New York statute. His basic disagreement with the majority, therefore, was one of interpretation. To him, the framers of the Bill of Rights did not include "words" in enumerating the things secured against unreasonable searches and seizures by the Fourth Amendment. But the Court's decision, he argued, is one of "judicial substitution"—adding the term "words" to the Fourth Amendment.

The Fourth Amendment is also a barrier to the electronic eavesdropping activities of federal officials such as those involved in *Katz* v. *United States. Katz* involved a conviction for the interstate transmission of betting information by telephone where evidence against the accused was obtained by electronic listening and recording devices affixed to a public telephone booth from which he placed his calls. The Court reversed the conviction and held that the methods employed by the government constituted a search and seizure within the meaning of the Fourth Amendment. In his opinion for the Court, Justice Potter Stewart made it clear that one does not shed his right to privacy because he makes his calls from a public telephone booth. When a person enters such a booth, said Stewart, closes the door behind him and pays his toll to make a call, he is "entitled to assume that the words he utters into the mouthpiece will not be broadcast to the world." Justice Stewart concluded that "[t]o read the Constitution more narrowly is to ignore the vital role that the public telephone has come to play in private communication."

Justice Hugo Black, the lone dissenter, objected because he did not believe that electronic eavesdropping constitutes a search or seizure within the meaning of the Fourth Amendment. Reiterating his strict constructionist view of Bill of Rights guarantees, Black contended that the Court did not possess the power to "update" the Amendment to achieve a result which many now consider desirable.

Many members of Congress felt even more strongly than Justice Black about *Katz* and the other Court decisions which limit the use of wiretapping and bugging in criminal investigations. This congressional attitude reflected a growing public concern about "crime in the streets" and the need for greater police authority to combat it. Hence, Congress included in the Omnibus Crime Control and Safe Streets Act of 1968 a provision permitting limited use of wiretapping and bugging in the investigation of a variety of federal crimes.[4] A warrant must be obtained from a federal judge granting permission for such surveillance, but in cases of "emergency" investigations of organized crime and national security matters, a law enforcement officer may proceed to employ his listening devices for 48 hours without a warrant. In addition, the statute authorizes the use of wiretaps and oral intercepts by state officials under warrants issued by state courts in the investigation of "any crime dangerous to life, limb, or property and punishable by imprisonment for more than one year." Just as the Court tested the police action in *Katz* and other cases under the standards prescribed by the Fourth Amendment, so will the Omnibus Crime Control Act have to be weighed in the inevitable challenges to its constitutionality.

In *Alderman* v. *United States* (394 U.S. 165, 1969) the Supreme Court dealt a crushing blow to the federal government's electronic surveillance activities by holding that the accused must be allowed to examine the records of any illegal eavesdropping of his private conversations and other conversations that took place on his premises. This was necessary, the Court explained, in order for the accused to ascertain if the evidence against him was derived from the illegal bugging. Furthermore, by rejecting the argument that the accused should only have access to such records after a camera examination by the trial judge as to relevancy, the Court presented the government a choice: either risk some disclosures that may have an adverse effect on its national security and other investigations, or drop some prosecutions. Undoubtedly, the government will have to make that choice.

## SELF-INCRIMINATION

The Fifth Amendment provides in part that "no person . . . shall

4 Included are: violations of the Atomic Energy Act, sabotage, treason, rioting, unlawful payments or loans to labor organizations, murder, kidnapping, robbery, sports bribes, wagering offenses, presidential assassination, extortion, embezzlement from pension and welfare funds, racketeering offenses, theft from interstate shipment, and interstate transportation of stolen property.

be compelled in any criminal case to be a witness against himself. . . ."
Over the years the Supreme Court has given an expansive interpretation
to this guarantee as applied to federal action. For example, it has
permitted persons to invoke the claim in grand jury proceedings and
congressional committee hearings. (*Counselman* v. *Hitchcock,* 142 U.S.
546; *Emspak* v. *United States,* 349 U.S. 190, 1955.)

The most revolutionary change in the judicial attitude relative to this
federal constitutional guarantee has been in its application to state
proceedings. Beginning with *Twining* v. *New Jersey* (211 U.S. 78, 1908),
the Supreme Court held for more than half a century that state proceedings were not governed by its provisions. At issue in that case
was a state procedure that permitted the trial jury to consider the
failure of the defendant to take the witness stand and deny evidence
presented against him. In rejecting the appellant's self-incrimination
claim, the Court held that the protection against compulsory self-
incrimination was not one of the privileges and immunities protected
by the Fourteenth Amendment from state infringement. Rather, the
crucial question was whether the self-incrimination privilege was "an
immutable principle of justice which is the inalienable possession of
every citizen of a free government."

While the Court held steadfastly to this position in the decades following *Twining* and reaffirmed it in *Adamson* v. *California, supra* (where
a similar criminal procedure raised the same issue), it did reverse a
number of state convictions on due process grounds in which the
alleged compulsory self-incrimination took the form of coerced confessions. (*Brown* v. *Mississippi,* 297 U.S. 278, 1936; *Chambers* v. *Florida,*
309 U.S. 227, 1940; *Spano* v. *New York,* 360 U.S. 315, 1959). The early
coerced confession cases generally involved some physical abuse on the
part of the law enforcement official to break down the will of the
accused, but the general pattern since *Brown* v. *Mississippi* and *Chambers* v. *Florida* has been to induce the confession by employing mental
and psychological ploys and trickery. Thus in *Spano* v. *New York,* the
Court reversed a state conviction for murder, which was based upon a
confession obtained after eight hours of continuous questioning by a
team of officers, followed by a plea from a rookie policeman—a childhood
friend of the suspect—who used this relationship to get the suspect's
sympathy by falsely stating that his job would be lost (at a time when
his wife was expecting their fourth child) if the defendant did not
cooperate and confess. The interrogators persisted in their quest for a
confession despite the suspect's repeated refusals to answer questions on
the advice of his lawyer who had personally surrendered his client to
the police. Chief Justice Earl Warren's opinion emphasized the need
for the police to "obey the law while enforcing the law." He concluded
that the confession lacked the "voluntariness" required by due process

because the "petitioner's will was overborne by official pressure, fatigue and sympathy falsely aroused."

The Court has continued to reject confessions extracted by coercive methods, but a growing minority of Justices expressed dissatisfaction with the majority's test for determining the "involuntariness" of confessions in *Haynes* v. *Washington* (373 U.S. 503, 1963). A bare majority of the Court reversed Haynes' conviction for robbery because the confession upon which it was based was obtained after 16 hours of incommunicado interrogation (during which the accused was not allowed to call his family) in a general "atmosphere of substantial coercion and inducement created by statements and actions of state authorities." Justice Tom Clark, speaking for the four dissenters, contended that the majority had departed from earlier precedents in confession cases and had enlarged the requirements under which state courts had previously determined the voluntariness of confessions.

The long line of coerced confession cases gradually eroded the *Twining-Adamson* doctrine. The Court's action in *Mapp* made the *Weeks* rule applicable to the states; its 1963 decision in *Gideon* made the Sixth Amendment's guarantee of assistance of counsel obligatory on the states. It was a logical development to the application of the self-incrimination provision of the Fifth Amendment to the states which was announced in *Malloy* v. *Hogan*. It is not surprising, then, that Justice Harlan, in dissent, characterized the majority's approach as amounting to "nothing more or less than 'incorporation' [of the guarantees of the first eight amendments into the Fourteenth] in snatches." In delivering the majority opinion in *Malloy*, Justice William J. Brennan took note of the shift to the federal standard in many post-*Twining* and *Adamson* state cases and contended that such a "shift reflects recognition that the American system of criminal prosecution is accusatorial, not inquisitorial, and that the Fifth Amendment privilege is its essential mainstay." He concluded that "the Fourteenth Amendment secures against state invasion the same privilege [to remain silent] that the Fifth Amendment guarantees against federal infringement. . . ."

On the same day the Court announced the *Malloy* ruling, it decided the related issue of whether one jurisdiction in our federal system (a state) may compel a witness to answer questions after a grant of immunity from prosecution under its laws, while simultaneously leaving him open to prosecution in another jurisdiction (the federal government) on the basis of testimony thus diclosed. In *Murphy* v. *Waterfront Commission of New York Harbor* (378 U.S. 52, 1964) the Court foreclosed this possibility and declared that "in light of the history, policies and purposes of the privilege against self-incrimination . . . , [the privilege] protects a state witness against incrimination under federal as well as state law and a federal witness against incrimination under state law as well as federal law."

In *Griffin* v. *California* the Court cited *Malloy* as authority to strike down the "comment" rule (on failure of defendant to testify at his trial) which had been approved almost 60 years earlier in *Twining* and reaffirmed in *Adamson*. In his opinion for the majority, Justice William O. Douglas made it clear that whether authorized by statute or not, the comment rule is a relic of the "inquisitorial system of criminal justice" which, in effect, is a court-imposed penalty for exercising a constitutional right. As such, he concluded, the procedure violates the Fifth and Fourteenth amendments.

The Court was not so generous when asked to discard another precedent on the authority of *Malloy* and its earlier decision in *Mapp* v. *Ohio*. In *Schmerber* v. *California* (384 U.S. 755, 1966) the Court was asked to reverse a conviction where evidence of intoxication was obtained from a blood sample taken from the injured petitioner (at the direction of the police and over his objection) while in the emergency room of a hospital. In rejecting the petitioner's claim that the action abridged the privilege against self-incrimination, Justice William J. Brennan's opinion for the majority stressed the testimonial and communicative nature of evidence to which the privilege extended. He concluded that the withdrawal of blood under the circumstances did not involve the type of compulsion condemned by the Constitution.

Aside from eliminating the comment rule in criminal trials, *Malloy's* most significant impact has been in the area of investigations by various state bodies. In *Spevack* v. *Klein* (385 U.S. 11, 1967), for example, the Court held that an attorney may not be disbarred for invoking the self-incrimination privilege in refusing to produce demanded records and to testify in a judicial inquiry. In an opinion joined by three other members of the Court, Justice William O. Douglas contended that there is "no room in the privilege against self-incrimination for classifications of people" and that the protection extends to lawyers just as to other individuals. He concluded that the guarantee "should not be watered down by imposing the dishonor of disbarment and the deprivation of livelihood as a price for asserting it." Similarly, in *Garrity* v. *New Jersey* (385 U.S. 493, 1967), decided the same day, the Court extended the guarantee to protect police officers who had refused to answer questions during an investigation by the state attorney general on alleged traffic ticket-fixing. The officers were advised that they could assert their self-incrimination protection, but in doing so they would be subject to removal from office. Put to such a choice, they chose to answer questions, some of which formed the basis for a subsequent prosecution for conspiracy to obstruct the enforcement of traffic laws.

In the opinion supporting the Court's reversal of these convictions, Justice Goldberg maintained that the crucial question presented was not whether a governmental employee had a constitutional right to his job, but whether the government can obtain incriminating evidence from him by threatening to discharge him. In rejecting the exercise of such authority, Goldberg concluded that the choice given the officers between self-incrimination or loss of employment was a form of compulsion prohibited by the Fourteenth Amendment.

## THE RIGHT TO COUNSEL

One of the basic tenets of American jurisprudence is that a person charged with a criminal offense should have his "day" in court. Hence, the framers of the Bill of Rights included in the Sixth Amendment a provision that guarantees to the accused "in all criminal prosecutions," the right to assistance of counsel for his defense. Pursuant to that provision congressional action and judicial decisions secured the right in federal prosecutions. But as a result of the doctrine enunciated in *Barron* v. *Baltimore, supra,* the states were left free to determine their own rules on counsel.

Almost a century after *Barron* was decided, the Due Process Clause of the Fourteenth Amendment began to be invoked as a limitation on the states with respect to the counsel guarantee. In 1932, the Court decided *Powell* v. *Alabama* (287 U.S. 45), the first of the celebrated *Scottsboro* cases. Seven ignorant and illiterate Negro boys had been charged for the rape of two white girls, a capital crime in Alabama. During the arraignment, at which they pleaded not guilty, the presiding judge did not inquire as to whether they wished or were able to employ counsel, or if they had relatives or friends with whom they might wish to communicate for purposes of obtaining assistance. Instead, he appointed all members of the local bar to serve as counsel for "the purpose of arraignment." When the trial of the first case began six days later, no counsel appeared for the defendants, nor was there any indication that any member of the local bar had made any preparation for the trial of the case. At this time, however, an attorney from Tennessee (the home of the defendants) appeared "at the request of persons interested in the case" to lend what assistance he could to local counsel appointed by the court. After an attempt to place the full responsibility for representation on the "volunteer" from Tennessee failed, one member of the local bar accepted the assignment reluctantly and the case proceeded to trial.

The subsequent convictions were affirmed by the state supreme court, but the United States Supreme Court reversed on the grounds that the rather casual and callous manner in which counsel was provided offended the due process clause of the Fourteenth Amendment. Justice George Sutherland's opinion for the seven-man majority emphasized assistance of counsel as a fundamental ingredient of a fair trial. He contended that the right to be heard would be of little consequence, even for the educated and intelligent, "if it did not comprehend the right to be heard by counsel." In reaching its decision, the Court took judicial notice of the youthfulness of the defendants, their illiteracy, the public hostility, the incommunicado imprisonment while awaiting trial and, above all, the capital nature of the crime with which they were charged. Subsequently, Justice Sutherland's opinion was construed to be limited to the circumstances of the case.

Nevertheless, much of Sutherland's discussion of counsel tended to support the position advanced by some that assistance of counsel in any criminal trial was an essential requirement of due process. Ten years later in *Betts* v. *Brady* (316 U.S. 455, 1942) the issue was before the Court again. In affirming a conviction in a non-capital case in which the defendant was denied court-appointed counsel, the Court made it clear that "[t]he due process clause of the Fourteenth Amendment does not [automatically] incorporate . . . the specific guarantees found in the Sixth Amendment." It did recognize, however, that "the denial by a state of rights or privileges embodied in that and other . . . amendments may, in certain circumstances," constitute in a given case a deprivation of "due process of law in violation of the Fourteenth Amendment." Reduced to its simplest terms, what the Court said was that assistance of counsel was not essential to a fair trial in some cases, but that it was in others if "special circumstances" existed. Hence, this rule became the standard for a case-by-case determination of the essentiality of the counsel guarantee.

Twenty-one years later, however, the Court abandoned the "special circumstances" rule in *Gideon* v. *Wainwright.* Justice Black's opinion for the Court made it clear that in its current view of the due process clause of the Fourteenth Amendment the counsel guarantee of the Sixth Amendment is obligatory on the states. Black indicated that the Court, in reality, was merely returning to the principles enunciated in *Powell* v. *Alabama.*

The decision had an immediate impact on the administration of criminal justice. On the same day it decided *Gideon,* the Court held in *Douglas* v. *California* (372 U.S. 353, 1963) that the right to counsel extends to the first appeal from a criminal conviction where appeal is granted as a matter of right under state law. Justice Douglas contended for the six-man majority that "where the merits of the one and only appeal which an indigent has of right are decided without benefit of counsel, . . . an unconstitutional line has been drawn between rich and poor." He concluded that if counsel is denied at this stage, "[t]he indigent, where the record is unclear or the errors are hidden, has only the right to a meaningless ritual, while the rich man has a meaningful appeal."

During its next term the Court approved, without opinion, the retrospective application of the *Gideon* rule in *Pickelsimer* v. *Wainwright* (375 U.S. 2, 1963).

## THE COUNSEL AND SELF-INCRIMINATION RULES IN PRE-TRIAL INTERROGATION

One of the questions left unanswered in *Gideon* was whether or not a suspect is entitled to counsel during police interrogation. The answer came one year later in *Escobedo* v. *Illinois*. There, the Court reversed a murder conviction based upon statements made during interrogation because police denied the repeated requests of the suspect's counsel to consult with his client. Justice Arthur Goldberg's opinion for the majority stressed the need for counsel when the police action shifts from the investigatory to the accusatory stage, i.e., when the focus is directed on the accused and the purpose of interrogation is to elicit a confession. Goldberg pointed out that at that stage legal aid and advice are most critical and the accused is entitled to consult with counsel. The case also points up an inextricable relationship between the protection against compulsory self-incrimination and the right to assistance of counsel.

Much of the criticism directed at the Court for its *Escobedo* ruling was misplaced since the limited question decided was merely the right of a suspect to consult with retained counsel. Left unanswered, however, were several crucial questions which go to the heart of police operations in solving crimes. The two with the greatest potential impact pertained to: (1) police responsibility for informing the suspect of his constitutional rights; and (2) whether or not a suspect can make an intelligent waiver of those rights without the advice of counsel. The Court answered both questions two years later in *Miranda* v. *Arizona* and in doing so reversed four convictions. Condemning the custodial interrogation methods used in each case, Chief Justice Earl Warren's majority opinion made it clear that the prosecution may not use statements against the accused elicited during custodial interrogation "unless it demonstrates the use of effective safeguards to secure" his constitutional rights. Hence, prior to any questioning, the accused must be: (1) warned of his right to remain silent and that any statement he makes may be used as evidence against him; and (2) informed of his right to the presence of counsel. If he desires counsel and is indigent, the government must make provision for it. Warren recognized that there may be cases where the accused may wish to proceed without counsel, but he cautioned that such waiver must be "made voluntarily, knowingly, and intelligently," and that proof of such waiver is the burden of the prosecution.

Undoubtedly, the Court was not oblivious to the sweeping impact such rulings could have upon the administration of state criminal law.[5] Consequently, it held in *Johnson* v. *New Jersey* (384 U.S. 719, 1966), decided one week later, that both *Escobedo* and *Miranda* would be limited to a prospective application. In fact, the Court ruled that the new standards announced in *Escobedo* and *Miranda* would apply only to cases *begun after* the announcement of these two cases. Thus, the Court was even more restrictive here than in its earlier prospective application of *Mapp* and *Griffin* where the new standards applied to cases *still pending* on direct appeal.

In *United States* v. *Wade* (388 U.S. 218, 1967) the Court considered another pre-trial matter by examining the traditional "lineup" procedure used in identifying suspects. The Court denied a self-incrimination challenge to this method of identification but held that the accused *is entitled* to the presence of counsel at this "critical stage" in criminal investigation and that counsel for the accused *must be notified* of the impending "lineup."[6]

In *In re Gault* the Court was faced with yet another crucial question: whether the constitutional safeguards available to adults accused of crime apply also to juveniles. Here the Court reversed a decision committing the defendant to an industrial school for the remainder of his minority (six years). It held that the Due Process Clause of the Fourteenth Amendment requires that in juvenile proceedings: (1) adequate notice of the hearing must be given; (2) the child must be informed of his right to counsel (including assigned counsel); and (3) the privileges against self-incrimination and confrontation must be extended to him. Justice Abe Fortas' opinion for the five-man majority was careful to limit the holding to the actual "proceedings" process. He concluded that the unique values of the juvenile system would be in no way impaired by this "constitutional domestication."

[5] A provision of the Omnibus Crime Control and Safe Streets Act of 1968 makes the *Miranda* rules inapplicable to federal cases, thus allowing admission in evidence of voluntary confessions, even if the suspect was not warned of his constitutional rights. The Act also set aside the *Mallory* rule (*Mallory* v. *United States*, 352 U.S. 449, 1957) under which delayed arraignment could render a voluntary confession inadmissible in a federal trial. The new procedure permits police to hold a suspect up to six hours before arraignment without rendering defective a confession obtained during that pre-arraignment period.

[6] The Omnibus Crime Control Act of 1968 negates the counsel guarantee announced in *Wade* by permitting the admission of testimony in federal prosecutions of those identifying a suspect even if the suspect had no lawyer when identified in a police lineup.

## OTHER FAIR TRIAL ISSUES

During the "criminal law explosion" of the 1960s, the Supreme Court handed down a number of decisions on the scope of the fair trial guarantees proclaimed in the Sixth Amendment. In several trials, guarantees which had previously been construed as limiting only the federal government, were made binding on the states. The historic right to a trial by jury in criminal cases was made obligatory on the states in *Duncan* v. *Louisiana*. To be sure, all states guarantee jury trials in cases involving *serious* offenses, but there are wide variations among them as to what constitutes a *serious* offense. The *Duncan* case involved a conviction for simple battery which, under Louisiana law, carries a maximum penalty of a two-year jail term and/or a fine of not more than $300. The defendant was sentenced to only 60 days in jail and was fined $150. However, because the trial court had denied his request for a jury trial, the Supreme Court held that the statutory penalty was heavy enough to classify the offense as "serious." Under such circumstances, the Court concluded, the Fourteenth Amendment entitles the accused to the jury trial guarantee proclaimed in the Sixth Amendment.

A new dimension to the impartial jury issue was considered by the Court in *Witherspoon* v. *Illinois* (391 U.S. 510, 1968). In earlier cases the Court had held: (1) that persons may not be systematically excluded from juries because of race (*Norris* v. *Alabama*, 294 U.S. 587, 1935); (2) that states may fix different and higher qualification for jurors for special types of criminal cases (*Fay* v. *New York*, 332 U.S. 261, 1947); and (3) that states may exempt women from jury duty (*Hoyt* v. *Florida*, 368 U.S. 57, 1961). The *Witherspoon* case involved an appeal of a convicted murderer who was awaiting execution. He challenged the long established practice of excusing all prospective jurors who indicate that they have conscientious scruples against capital punishment. The Supreme Court held that such a procedure results in the selection of a "prosecution prone" jury that is more likely than the average jury to make a finding of guilt and to impose the death penalty. In an opinion for the 6–3 majority, Justice Potter Stewart contended that "a state may not entrust the determination of whether a man should live or die to a tribunal organized to return a verdict of death." But Stewart carefully limited the holding to the imposition of the death penalty and not to the actual determination of guilt.

Justice Hugo Black wrote a vigorous dissent in which he charged that the decision would result in the selection of juries with a bias against capital punishment. On the larger issue of the role of the Court in reviewing state criminal procedures, Black accused the majority of "making law" and of weakening law enforcement "at a time of serious crime in our nation."

The Court considered the right to a speedy trial in *Klopfer* v. *North Carolina*. In reversing a state court action approving a statutory *nolle prosequi* procedure (which permits the prosecutor to reopen the case at his pleasure), the Supreme Court held that the Fourteenth Amendment makes obligatory on the states the Sixth Amendment's guarantee of a speedy trial. Chief Justice Warren's opinion noted that the state procedure condoned a form of oppression by making it impossible for the accused to exonerate himself until the prosecutor chooses to restore his case to the court calendar.

The Sixth Amendment right of confrontation and cross-examination was made applicable to state criminal proceedings in *Pointer* v. *Texas*. The Court reversed a conviction because the testimony of a witness in a preliminary hearing—where the defendant was without counsel and no cross-examination was allowed—was admitted as evidence at the trial. The Court cited both *Malloy* and *Gideon* and held that the right of the accused to confront the witnesses against him is a fundamental right essential to a fair trial. Justice Hugo Black's opinion for the Court emphasized that the right of cross-examination is, without doubt, included in the confrontation guarantee.

In another Sixth Amendment action, the Court held in *Washington* v. *Texas* (388 U.S. 14, 1967) that the right of the accused "to have the compulsory process for obtaining witnesses in his favor" is binding on the states through the due process clause of the Fourteenth Amendment. At issue was a statutory procedure which prohibited persons charged or convicted as co-participants in the same crime from testifying for one another, but which allowed the prosecution to use them to testify against one another. Chief Justice Warren, who spoke for the majority, emphasized the right of the accused not only to confront and challenge the testimony of prosecution witnesses but also to present his own witnesses to establish his defense. Contending that the defendant has just as much right as the prosecution to present his version of the facts to the jury, Warren concluded:

The right of an accused to have compulsory process for obtaining witnesses in his favor stands on no lesser footing than the other Sixth Amendment rights that we have previously held applicable to the states. . . .

One of the most controversial issues to reach the Court during the 1960s involved the conflicting constitutional claims of the accused to a fair trial free from prejudicial publicity and of a "free press" to gather and report news about a criminal case. In balancing these interests, the Court emphasized that the maintenance of an atmosphere free from inflamed public opinion is essential to the selection of an unbiased jury. Thus in *Irwin* v. *Dowd* (366 U.S. 717, 1961) the Court, for the first time, reversed a state conviction solely on the ground of prejudicial pre-trial publicity. Justice Tom Clark's opinion for the Court cited the "pattern of deep and bitter prejudice" permeating the community which was reflected in the "voir dire examination of the majority of the jurors finally" selected to hear the case. He further noted that eight of the 12 jurors had expressed the belief that the petitioner was guilty. Consequently, he concluded that the sincere assurances of fairness and impartiality proclaimed by jurors could be given little weight in meeting the constitutional requirement of impartiality, particularly where one's life was at stake.

Five years later, in *Sheppard* v. *Maxwell* the Court reversed a state murder conviction because of prejudicial publicity both before and during the trial. Referring to the "Roman holiday" atmosphere created by "circulation conscious editors catering to the insatiable interest of the American public in the bizarre," Justice Tom Clark contended that the public had been so inflamed and prejudiced as to make impossible a fair trial before an impartial jury. He condemned the trial court for permitting the trial to take place in a "carnival atmosphere" and for its failure to take necessary precautions for insulation of the jury.[7]

The use of television has presented the Court with another dimension of the free press–fair trial issue. In *Rideau* v. *Louisiana* (373 U.S. 723, 1963) the Court reversed a murder conviction where the defendant's confession was presented on "live" television and then rerun by video-tape on two other occasions. Noting that the station's viewing range covered the entire area from which jurors were drawn, the Court held that refusal of the defendant's request for a change of venue was a denial of due process.

Televising of the actual trial was at issue in *Estes* v. *Texas* (381 U.S. 532, 1965). The case presented an appeal of the conviction of Texas financier Billie Sol Estes for swindling. Under Texas law, the question of televising court proceedings was left to the discretion of the trial

---

[7] In 1968, the American Bar Association made significant modifications in its Cannons of Professional Ethics. Recommended by a committee headed by Massachusetts Supreme Court Judge Paul C. Reardon, the major thrust of the new rules is directed at the conduct and responsibilities of prosecutors, defense attorneys, judges, court employees, and law enforcement officials in the discharge of their duties in criminal proceedings. Attorneys, for example, are forbidden to release or authorize release of information in connection with pending or imminent criminal litigation with which they are associated if there is a reasonable likelihood that such dissemination will interfere with a fair trial. This restriction applies to such matters as comment on prior criminal record, the existence or contents of a confession or statement of the accused, results of any tests or the refusal to submit to tests, the identity of prospective witnesses, and the possible nature of the plea. The restrictions recommended to govern the conduct of court employees and law enforcement officers are similar in nature and the new rules simply recommend that "judges should refrain from any conduct or the making of any statements that may tend to interfere with the right of the people or of the defendant to a fair trial." Appropriate judicial and law enforcement officials are urged to adopt regulations with appropriate sanctions to make the standards applicable to their employees. A limited use of the contempt power is recommended to enforce compliance in addition to the professional sanctions which the Bar may apply to its members.

judge. A motion to prohibit televising the trial was rejected (the hearing on the motion was itself televised) and it proceeded under limited video coverage. In a 5–4 decision, the Court reversed the conviction and emphasized the right of the accused to have his day in court free from the distractions inherent in telecasting. Justice Tom Clark, speaking for the majority, said that "the chief function of our judicial machinery is to ascertain the truth" and that the use of television injects an irrelevant factor toward that end. Furthermore, he noted that television has an infectious impact on the participants in a trial. The jury, "nerve center of the fact-finding process," is subjected to considerable distraction. The testimony of witnesses will often be impaired. If the trial is being conducted before an elective judge, the political capital to be gained from such exposure may impair his effectiveness. And finally, the defendant may suffer from "a form of mental harrassment resembling a police lineup or the third degree."

In the major dissent, Justice Potter Stewart thought the introduction of television into the courtroom an unwise policy but that on the specific record of the "limited use of the medium," the defendant's constitutional rights were not impaired. Stewart expressed great concern about the "intimation" in the majority and concurring opinions that "there are limits upon the public's right to know what goes on in the courts" and the implicit limitations upon First Amendment guarantees.

## THE PROTECTION AGAINST CRUEL AND UNUSUAL PUNISHMENT

In the celebrated "electric chair" case (*Louisiana ex rel. Francis* v. *Resweber*, 329 U.S. 459, 1947) the Court assumed that the Eighth Amendment's prohibition against cruel and unusual punishment was applicable to the states under the Fourteenth Amendment. Nevertheless, it rejected the petitioner's claim that to subject him to the electric chair for a second time, after mechanical failure had prevented his execution the first time, constituted cruel and unusual punishment. Justice Stanley Reed's opinion emphasized that the cruelty against which the constitutional prohibition is directed is "cruelty inherent in the method of punishment, not the necessary suffering involved in any method employed to extinguish life humanely."

A decade later in *Trop* v. *Dulles* (356 U.S. 86, 1958) the Court invoked the cruel and unusual punishment provision to invalidate a section of the Immigration and Nationality Act of 1940 which permitted the taking away of citizenship as punishment for wartime desertion from the military. In the prevailing opinion, Chief Justice Earl Warren stressed the serious consequences of denationalization. He contended that such punishment is the "total destruction of the individual's status in organized society" and "[h]is very existence is at the sufferance of the country in which he happens to find himself."

In a subsequent action, the Warren Court extended the cruel and unusual punishment prohibition to invalidate a state statute making drug addiction a crime. In *Robinson* v. *California* the Court held that the statute allowed the infliction of a cruel and unusual punishment because it "makes the 'status' of narcotics addiction a criminal offense, for which the offender may be prosecuted 'at any time before he reforms'." Several lower courts have construed this decision and its assumptions and have invalidated convictions for public drunkenness of chronic alcoholics. In *Driver* v. *Hinnant* (356 F2d 761, 1966), for example, the Court of Appeals for the Fourth Circuit reversed such a conviction and concluded that "the chronic alcoholic has not drunk voluntarily," rather, "his . . . excess now derives from disease."

The Supreme Court refused to accept this logic in *Powell* v. *Texas* (392 U.S. 514, 1968). In a 5–4 decision, the Court held that jailing a chronic alcoholic for public drunkenness did not constitute cruel and unusual punishment. While no opinion gained majority support, Justice Thurgood Marshall's plurality opinion warned of the danger of undermining the common law doctrine of criminal responsibility with an extension of the *Robinson* holding to cases like *Powell*. Carefully distinguishing the two cases, Marshall noted that in *Robinson,* the Court condemned the state action because it inflicted punishment for mere status of addiction, whereas in *Powell* the state had properly "imposed upon the appellant a criminal sanction for public behavior which may create substantial health and safety hazards both for the appellant and for members of the general public, and which offends the moral and esthetic sensibilities of a large segment of the population."

Marshall was further troubled by the argument that the chronic alcoholic suffers from a compulsion to drink over which he has no control. He noted that if the appellant could not be convicted for public drunkenness, then it would be difficult to see how a person could be convicted for murder, "if that [person], while exhibiting normal behavior in all other respects, suffers from a compulsion to kill. . . ." He concluded that existing medical knowledge is inconclusive as to whether chronic alcoholics "suffer from such an irresistible compulsion to drink and to get drunk in public that they are utterly unable to control their performance of either or both of these acts. . . ." In the end, he argued that in the almost complete absence of rehabilitation and treatment facilities, it would be difficult to contend that "the criminal process [as applied here] is utterly lacking in social value." What Marshall really seems to be suggesting is that in most instances a derelict might be better off in jail for a fixed term.

Justice Abe Fortas' dissent accepted the contention that alcoholism is

a disease that removes a person's will to stay sober. He argued that the
*Robinson* drug addiction holding is controlling, since to jail a person for
being drunk in public is to punish him for a condition that he cannot
change. Hence, the state action constitutes cruel and unusual punishment.

## DUE PROCESS AND STUDENT DISCIPLINARY PROCEDURES[8]

The social and political ferment in America has permeated the once
tranquil college and university campus. Students are demanding that
academy, like other institutions, become "relevant." University policies,
rules, and regulations are seen as irrelevant and outmoded, and are openly broken and flouted. The student prescription for change on campus
is no different from that used outside the "halls of ivy." Demands, followed by disruptive demonstrations and even violence, have created
serious dilemmas in American academic life and in education generally.
While such campus conflict raises a number of issues, our major concern
here is with the procedural rights of students who are accused of violating
university rules and regulations. For example, is a student in his relation
with the university entitled to the same constitutional guarantees as he
would be in relation to the state? Or to what extent does the "special
mission or function" of the university create a "special relationship"
between the university and the student in regulating his behavior? Can
a student get a fair hearing before a university disciplinary committee
without having benefit of the same constitutional guarantees—assistance
of counsel, confrontation and cross-examination of witnesses—as he would
in civil court? Cases involving these and other questions are increasingly
being brought to court. In *Dixon* v. *Alabama State Board of Education*
(294 F2d 150, 1961) the Court of Appeals for the Fifth Circuit held that
due process requires notice and some opportunity for a hearing before
a student attending a public college may be expelled for misconduct.
However, Circuit Judge Richard T. Rives made it clear that the court's
holding did not imply the right to "a full-dress judicial hearing."

One of the most definitive statements on the issue was made by the
Federal District Court for the Western District of Missouri. Sitting en
banc, the court heard *Scoggin* v. *Lincoln University* and *Esteban* v. *Central Missouri State College* for the purpose of formulating standards of
student disciplinary cases arising in public institutions of higher learning. Public colleges and universities, the court held, have a "special mission" and may therefore, in their regulation of student behavior, impose
higher standards than those imposed on other citizens by criminal and

---

[8] Though technically civil actions, these student disciplinary cases raise significant
issues of criminal due process. Hence, we include a discussion of the problem in this
chapter.

civil law. Consequently, the court concluded that in student disciplinary cases procedural due process does not require such guarantees as assistance of counsel, confrontation and cross-examination of witnesses, warnings about privileges, and immunity from self-incrimination.

A federal district court in Alabama used similar reasoning in *Moore* v. *Student Affairs Committee of Troy State University* (284 F. Supp. 725, 1968). Here the court had before it an action in which a student challenged a university proceeding which resulted in his indefinite suspension. The crucial argument urged on the court was that the evidence of possession of marijuana was not admissible because it was obtained in violation of the search and seizure requirements of the Fourth Amendment. The search of the student's room was conducted by two state narcotics agents accompanied by the dean of men without a search warrant or the consent of the student. At the time, the University had in force a regulation in which it reserved the right to enter residence hall rooms for inspection and, if necessary, conduct a search including the opening of baggage. In rejecting the Fourth Amendment claim, Judge Frank M. Johnson emphasized the "special relationship" between students who reside in dormitories and the university. Hence, he contended, the university "has an 'affirmative obligation' to promulgate and to enforce reasonable regulations designed to protect campus order and discipline and to promote an environment consistent with the educational process." Judge Johnson concluded that "[a] reasonable right of inspection is necessary to the institution's performance of [its educational mission] even though it may infringe on the outer boundaries of a dormitory student's Fourth Amendment rights. . . ."

The cases that follow focus on some of the significant constitutional issues reviewed in this commentary.

## *MAPP* v. *OHIO*

### 367 U. S. 643; 6 L. Ed. 2d 1081; 81 S. Ct. 1684 (1961)

MR. JUSTICE CLARK *delivered the opinion of the Court.*

Appellant stands convicted of knowingly having had in her possession and under her control certain lewd and lascivious books, pictures, and photographs in violation of . . . Ohio's Revised Code. . . .

On May 23, 1957, three Cleveland police officers arrived at appellant's residence in that city pursuant to information that "a person [was] hiding out in the home, who was wanted for questioning in connection with a recent bombing, and that there was a large amount of policy paraphernalia being hidden in the home." Miss Mapp and her daughter by a former marriage lived on the top floor of the two-family dwelling. Upon their arrival at that house, the officers knocked on the door and demanded entrance but appellant, after telephoning her attorney, refused to admit them without a search warrant. They advised their headquarters of the situation and undertook a surveillance of the house.

The officers again sought entrance some three hours later when four or more additional officers arrived on the scene. When Miss Mapp did not come to the door immediately, at least one of the several doors to the house was forcibly opened and the policemen gained admittance. Meanwhile Miss Mapp's attorney arrived, but the officers, having secured their own entry, and continuing in their defiance of the law, would permit him neither to see Miss Mapp nor to enter the house. It appears that Miss Mapp was halfway down the stairs from the upper floor to the front door when the officers, in this highhanded manner, broke into the hall. A paper, claimed to be a warrant, was held up by one of the officers. She grabbed the "warrant" and placed it in her bosom. A struggle ensued in which the officers recovered the piece of paper and as a result of which they handcuffed appellant because she had been "belligerent" in resisting their official rescue of the "warrant" from her person. Running roughshod over appellant, a policeman "grabbed" her, "twisted [her] hand," and she "yelled [and] pleaded with him" because "it was hurting." Appellant, in handcuffs, was then forcibly taken upstairs to her bedroom where the officers searched a dresser, a chest of drawers, a closet and some suitcases. They also looked into a photo album and through personal papers belonging to the appellant. The search spread to the rest of the second floor including

the child's bedroom, the living room, the kitchen and a dinette. The basement of the building and a trunk found therein were also searched. The obscene materials for possession of which she was ultimately convicted were discovered in the course of that widespread search.

At the trial no search warrant was produced by the prosecution, nor was the failure to produce one explained or accounted for. At best, [said the State Supreme Court] "There is, in the record, considerable doubt as to whether there ever was any warrant for the search of defendant's home." . . . The Ohio Supreme Court believed a "reasonable argument" could be made that the conviction should be reversed "because the 'methods' employed to obtain the [evidence] . . . were such as to 'offend "a sense of justice," ' " but the court found determinative the fact that the evidence had not been taken "from defendant's person by the use of brutal or offensive physical force against defendant." . . . [Hence, it found that the conviction was valid.]

The State says that even if the search were made without authority, or otherwise unreasonably, it is not prevented from using the unconstitutionally seized evidence at trial, citing *Wolf* v. *Colorado* . . . in which this Court did indeed hold "that in a prosecution in a State court for a State crime the Fourteenth Amendment does not forbid the admission of evidence obtained by an unreasonable search and seizure." . . .

Seventy-five years ago in *Boyd* v. *United States,* 116 U.S. 616 (1886) . . . , considering the Fourth and Fifth Amendments as running "almost into each other" on the facts before it, this Court held that the doctrines of those Amendments "apply to all invasions on the part of the government and its employees of the sanctity of a man's home and the privacies of life. It is not the breaking of his doors, and the rummaging of his drawers, that constitutes the essence of the offense; but it is the invasion of his indefeasible right of personal security, personal liberty and private liberty. . . . Breaking into a house and opening boxes and drawers are circumstances of aggravation; but any forcible and compulsory extortion of a man's own testimony or of his private papers to be used as evidence to convict him of crime or to forfeit his goods, is within the condemnation . . . [of those Amendments]".

. . . The Court in the *Weeks* case clearly stated that use of the seized evidence involved "a denial of the constitutional rights of the accused." . . . Thus, in the year 1914, in the *Weeks* case, this Court "for the first time" held that "in a federal prosecution the Fourth Amendment barred the use of evidence secured through an illegal search and seizure." (*Wolf* v. *Colorado.* . . .) This Court has ever since required of federal law officers a strict adherence to that command which this Court has held to be a clear, specific, and constitutionally required—even if judicially implied— deterrent safeguard without insistence upon which the Fourth Amendment would have been reduced to "a form of words." . . . It meant, quite simply, that conviction by means of unlawful seizures and enforced confessions . . . should find no sanction in the judgments of the courts. . . ."

There are in the cases of this Court some passing references to the *Weeks* rule as being one of evidence. But the plain and unequivocal language of *Weeks*—and its later paraphrase in *Wolf*—to the effect that the *Weeks* rule is of constitutional origin, re-

mains entirely undisturbed. . . .

In 1949, thirty-five years after *Weeks* was announced, this Court, in *Wolf* v. *Colorado* . . . , again for the first time, discussed the effect of the Fourth Amendment upon the States through the operation of the Due Process Clause of the Fourteenth Amendment. It said:

[W]e have no hesitation in saying that were a State affirmatively to sanction such police incursion into privacy it would run counter to the guaranty of the Fourteenth Amendment.

Nevertheless, after declaring that the "security of one's privacy against arbitrary intrusion by the police" is "implicit in the 'concept of ordered liberty' and as such enforceable against the States through the Due Process Clause," cf. *Palko* v. *Connecticut, 302 U.S. 319* (1937) . . . , and announcing that it "stoutly adhere[d]" to the *Weeks* decision, the Court decided that the *Weeks* exclusionary rule would not then be imposed upon the States as "an essential ingredient of the right." . . . The Court's reasons for not considering essential to the right of privacy, as a curb imposed upon the States by the Due Process Clause, that which decades before had been posited as part and parcel of the Fourth Amendment's limitation upon federal encroachment of individual privacy, were bottomed on factual considerations.

While they are not basically relevant to a decision that the exclusionary rule is an essential ingredient of the Fourth Amendment as the right it embodies is vouchsafed against the States by the Due Process Clause, we will consider the current validity of the factual grounds upon which *Wolf* was based.

The Court in *Wolf* first stated that "[t]he contrariety of views of the

States" on the adoption of the exclusionary rule of *Weeks* was "particularly impressive" . . . ; and, in this connection, that it could not "brush aside the experience of States which deem the incidence of such conduct by the police too slight to call for a deterrent remedy . . . by overriding the [States'] relevant rules of evidence." . . . While in 1949, prior to the *Wolf* case, almost two-thirds of the States were opposed to the use of the exclusionary rule, now, despite the *Wolf* case, more than half of those since passing upon it, by their own legislative or judicial decision, have wholly or partly adopted or adhered to the *Weeks* rule. See *Elkins* v. *United States,* 364 U.S. 206 (1960). . . . Significantly, among those now following the rule is California which, according to its highest court, was "compelled to reach that conclusion because other remedies have completely failed to secure compliance with the constitutional provisions. . . ." The experience of California that such other remedies have been worthless and futile is buttressed by the experience of other States. The obvious futility of relegating the Fourth Amendment to the protection of other remedies has, moreover, been recognized by this Court since *Wolf*. . . .

Likewise, time has set its face against what *Wolf* called the "weighty testimony" of *People* v. *Defore,* 242 N.Y. 13, 150 N.E. 585 (1926). There Justice (then Judge) Cardozo, rejecting adoption of the *Weeks* exclusionary rule in New York, had said that "'the Federal rule as it stands is either to strict or too lax." . . . However, the force of that reasoning has been largely vitiated by later decisions of this Court. These include the recent discarding of the "silver plater" doctrine which allowed federal judicial use of evidence seized in violation of the Constitution by state agents, *Elkins* v. *United States,* 364 U.S. 206, 111; the relaxation of the formerly strict requirements as to standing to challenge the use of evidence thus seized, so that now the procedure of exclusion, "ultimately referable to constitutional safeguards," is available to anyone even "legitimately on [the] premises" unlawfully searched, *Jones* v. *United States,* 362 U.S. 257, 111 (1960); and, finally, the formulation of a method to prevent state use of evidence unconstitutionally seized by federal agents, *Rea* v. *United States,* 350 U.S. 214, 111 (1956). Because there can be no fixed formula, we are admittedly met with "recurring questions of the reasonableness of searches." But less is not to be expected when dealing with a Constitution, and, at any rate, "reasonableness is in the first instance for the [trial court] . . . to determine." *United States* v. *Rabinowitz,* 339 U.S. 56, . . . (1950).

It, therefore, plainly appears that the factual considerations supporting the failure of the *Wolf* Court to include the *Weeks* exclusionary rule when it recognized the enforceability of the right to privacy against the States in 1949, while not basically relevant to the constitutional consideration, could not, in any analysis, now be deemed controlling.

. . . Only last Term, after again carefully re-examining the *Wolf* doctrine in *Elkins* v. *United States* . . . , the Court pointed out that "the controlling principles" as to search and seizure and the problem of admissibility "seemed clear" . . . until the announcement in *Wolf* "that the Due Process Clause of the Fourteenth Amendment does not itself require state courts to adopt the exclusionary rule" of the *Weeks* case. . . . At the same time the Court pointed out, "the underlying constitutional doctrine which *Wolf* established . . . that the Federal Constitution . . . prohibits unreasonable searches and seizures by state officers" had undermined the "foundation upon which the admissibility of state-seized evidence in a federal trial originally rested. . . ." *Ibid.* The Court concluded that it was therefore obliged to hold, although it chose the narrower ground on which to do so, that all evidence obtained by an unconstitutional search and seizure was inadmissible in a federal court regardless of its source. Today we once again examine *Wolf*'s constitutional documentation of the right to privacy free from unreasonable state intrusion, and, after its dozen years on our books, are led by it to close the only courtroom door remaining open to evidence secured by official lawlessness in flagrant abuse of that basic right, reserved to all persons as a specific guarantee against that very same unlawful conduct. We hold that all evidence obtained by searches and seizures in violation of the Constitution is, by the same authority, inadmissible in a state court.

Since the Fourth Amendment's right of privacy has been declared enforceable against the States through the Due Process Clause of the Fourteenth, it is enforceable against them by the same sanction of exclusion as is used against the Federal Government. . . .

Indeed, we are aware of no restraint, similar to that rejected today, conditioning the enforcement of any other basic constitutional right. The right to privacy, no less important than any other right carefully and particularly reserved to the people, would stand in marked contrast to all other rights declared as "basic to a free society." *Wolf* v. *Colorado*, . . . (338 U.S., at 27). This Court has not hesitated to enforce as strictly against the States as it does against the Federal Government the rights of free speech and of a free press, the rights to notice and to a fair public trial, including, as it does, the right not to be convicted by use of a coerced confession, however logically relevant it be, . . . and without regard to its reliability. *Rogers* v. *Richmond*, 365 U.S. 534, . . . (1961). And nothing could be more certain than that when a coerced confession is involved, "the relevant rules of evidence" are overridden without regard to "the incidence of such conduct by the police," slight or frequent. Why should not the same rule apply to what is tantamount to coerced testimony by way of unconstitutional seizure of goods, papers, effects, documents, etc.? . . .

Moreover, our holding that the exclusionary rule is an essential part of both the Fourth and Fourteenth Amendments is not only the logical dictate of prior cases, but it also makes very good sense. There is no war between the Constitution and common sense. Presently, a federal prosecutor may make no use of evidence illegally seized, but a State's attorney across the street may, although he supposedly is operating under the enforceable prohibitions of the same Amendment. Thus the State, by admitting evidence unlawfully seized, serves to encourage disobedience to the Federal Constitution which it is bound to uphold. . . .

There are those who say, as did Justice (then Judge) Cardozo, that under our constitutional exclusionary doctrine "the criminal is to go free because the constable has blundered." *People* v. *Defore*, 242 N.Y. at 21. . . . In some cases this will undoubtedly be the result. But, as was said in *Elkins,* "there is another consideration—the imperative of judicial integrity." . . . The criminal goes free, if he must, but it is the law that sets him free. Nothing can destroy a government more quickly than its failure to observe its laws, or worse, its disregard of the charter of its own existence. . . .

The ignoble shortcut to conviction left open to the State tends to destroy the entire system of constitutional restraints on which the liberties of the people rest. Having once recognized that the right to privacy embodied in the Fourth Amendment is enforceable against the States, and that the right to be secure against rude invasions of privacy by state officers is, therefore, constitutional in origin, we can no longer permit that right to remain an empty promise. Because it is enforceable in the same manner and to like effect as other basic rights secured by the Due Process Clause, we can no longer permit it to be revocable at the whim of any police officer who, in the name of law enforcement itself, chooses to suspend its enjoyment. Our decision, founded on reason and truth, gives to the individual no more than that which the Constitution guarantees him, to the police officer no less than that to which honest law enforcement is entitled, and, to the courts, that judicial integrity so necessary in the true administration of justice.

The judgment of the Supreme Court of Ohio is reversed and the cause remanded for further proceedings not inconsistent with this opinion.

*Reversed and remanded.*

MR. JUSTICE BLACK, *concurring.*

I am still not persuaded that the Fourth Amendment, standing alone, would be enough to bar the introduction into evidence against an accused of papers and effects seized from him in violation of its commands. For the Fourth Amendment does not itself contain any provision expressly precluding the use of such evidence, and I am extremely doubtful that such a provision could properly be inferred from nothing more than the basic command against unreasonable searches and seizures. Reflection on the problem, however, in the light of cases coming before the Court since *Wolf,* has led me to conclude that when the Fourth Amendment's ban against unreasonable searches and seizures is considered together with the Fifth Amendment's ban against compelled self-incrimination, a constitutional basis emerges which not only justifies but actually requires the exclusionary rule.

The close interrelationship between the Fourth and Fifth Amendments, as they apply to this problem, has long been recognized and, indeed, was expressly made the ground for this Court's holding in *Boyd* v. *United States.* There the Court fully discussed this relationship and declared itself "unable to perceive that the seizure of a man's private books and papers to be used in evidence against him is substantially different from compelling him to be a witness against himself." It was upon this ground that Mr. Justice Rutledge largely relied in his dissenting opinion in the *Wolf* case. And, although I rejected the argument at that time, its force has, for me at least, become compelling with the more thorough understanding of the problem brought on by recent cases. In the final analysis, it seems to me that the *Boyd* doctrine, though perhaps not required by the express language of the Constitution strictly construed, is amply justified from an historical standpoint, soundly based in reason, and entirely consistent with what I regard to be the proper approach to interpretation of our Bill of Rights. . . .

. . . As I understand the Court's opinion in this case, we again reject the confusing "shock-the-conscience" standard of the *Wolf* and *Rochin* cases and, instead, set aside this state conviction in reliance upon the precise, intelligible and more predictable constitutional doctrine enunciated in the *Boyd* case. I fully agree with Mr. Justice Bradley's opinion that the two Amendments upon which the *Boyd* doctrine rests are of vital importance in our constitutional scheme of liberty and that both are entitled to a liberal rather than a niggardly interpretation. The courts of the country are entitled to know with as much certainty as possible what scope they cover. The Court's opinion, in my judgment, dissipates the doubt and uncertainty in this field of constitutional law and I am persuaded, for this and other reasons stated, to depart from my prior views, to accept the *Boyd* doctrine as controlling in this state case and to join the Court's judgment and opinion which are in accordance with that constitutional doctrine.

MR. JUSTICE DOUGLAS, *concurring.*

When we allow States to give constitutional sanction to the "shabby business" of unlawful entry into a home (to use an expression of Mr. Justice Murphy, *Wolf* v. *People of State of Colorado*), . . . we did indeed rob the Fourth Amendment of much meaningful force. . . .

Without judicial action making the exclusionary rule applicable to the States, *Wolf* v. *People of State of Colorado* in practical effect reduced the guarantee against unreasonable searches and seizures to "a dead letter," as Mr. Justice Rutledge said in his dissent. . . .

. . . Once evidence, inadmissible in a federal court, is admissible in a state court a "double standard" exists which, as the Court points out, leads to "working arrangements" that undercut federal policy and reduce some aspects of law enforcement to shabby business. The rule that supports that practice does not have the force of reason behind it.

MR. JUSTICE HARLAN, *whom* MR. JUSTICE FRANKFURTER *and* MR. JUSTICE WHITTAKER *join, dissenting.*

In overruling the *Wolf* case the Court, in my opinion, has forgotten the sense of judicial restraint which, with due regard for *stare decisis,* is one element that should enter into deciding whether a past decision on this Court should be overruled. Apart from that I also believe that the *Wolf* rule represents sounder Constitutional doctrine than the new rule which now replaces it.

From the Court's statement of the case one would gather that the central, if not controlling, issue on this appeal is whether illegally state-seized evidence is Constitutionally admissible in a state prosecution, an issue which would of course face us with the need for re-examining *Wolf.* However, such is not the situation. For, although that question was indeed raised here and below among appellant's subordinate points, the new and pivotal issue brought to the Court by this appeal is whether Sec. 2905.34 of the Ohio Revised Code making criminal the *mere* knowing possession or control of obscene material, and under which appellant has been convicted, is consistent with the rights of free thought and expression assured against state action by the Fourteenth Amendment. That was the principal issue which was decided by the Ohio Supreme Court, which was tendered by appellant's Jurisdictional Statement, and which was briefed and argued in this Court.

In this posture of things, I think it fair to say that five members of this Court have simply "reached out" to overrule *Wolf*. With all respect for the views of the majority, and recognizing that *stare decisis* carries different weight in Constitutional adjudication than it does in nonconstitutional decision, I can perceive no justification for regarding this case as an appropriate occasion for re-examining *Wolf*.

The action of the Court finds no support in the rule that decision of Constitutional issues should be avoided wherever possible. For in overruling *Wolf*, the Court, instead of passing upon the validity of Ohio's Sec. 2905.34, has simply chosen between two Constitutional questions. Moreover, I submit that it has chosen the more difficult and less appropriate of the two questions. The Ohio statute which, as construed by the State Supreme Court, punishes knowing possession or control of obscene material, irrespective of the purposes of such possession or control (with exceptions not here applicable) and irrespective of whether the accused had any reasonable opportunity to rid himself of the material after discovering that it was obscene, surely presents a constitutional question which is both simpler and less far-reaching than the question which the Court decides today. It seems to me that justice might well have been done in this case without overturning a decision on which the administration of

criminal law in many of the States has long justifiably relied. . . .

I am bound to say that what has been done is not likely to promote respect either for the Court's adjudicatory process or for the stability of its decisions. . . .

I would not impose upon the States this federal exclusionary remedy. The reasons given by the majority for now suddenly turning its back on *Wolf* seem to me notably unconvincing.

First, it is said that "the factual grounds upon which *Wolf* was based" have since changed, in that more States now follow the *Weeks* exclusionary rule than was so at the time *Wolf* was decided. While that is true, a recent survey indicated that at present one half of the States still adhere to the common-law nonexclusionary rule, and one, Maryland, retains the rule as to felonies. . . . But in any case surely all this is beside the point, as the majority itself indeed seems to recognize. Our concern here, as it was in *Wolf*, is not with the desirability of that rule but only with the question whether the States are Constitutionally free to follow it or not as they may themselves determine, and the relevance of the disparity of views among the States on this point lies simply in the fact that the judgment involved is a debatable one. Moreover, the very fact on which the majority relies, instead of lending support to what is now being done, points away from the need of replacing voluntary state action with federal compulsion.

The preservation of a proper balance between state and federal responsibility in the administration of criminal justice demands patience on the part of those who might like to see things move faster among the States in this respect. Problems of criminal law enforcement vary widely from State to State. One State, in considering the totality of its legal picture, may conclude that the need for embracing the *Weeks* rule is pressing because other remedies are unavailable or inadequate to secure compliance with the substantive Constitutional principle involved. Another, though equally solicitous of Constitutional rights, may choose to pursue one purpose at a time, allowing all evidence relevant to guilt to be brought into a criminal trial, and dealing with Constitutional infractions by other means. Still another may consider the exclusionary rule too rough and ready a remedy, in that it reaches only unconstitutional intrusions which eventuate in criminal prosecution of the victims. Further, a State after experimenting with the *Weeks* rule for a time may, because of unsatisfactory experience with it, decide to revert to a nonexclusionary rule. And so one. . . . For us the question remains, as it has always been, one of state power, not one of passing judgment on the wisdom of one state course or another. In my view this Court should continue to forbear from fettering the States with an adamant rule which may embarrass them in coping with their own peculiar problems in criminal law enforcement.

Further, we are told that imposition of the *Weeks* rule on the States makes "very good sense," in that it will promote recognition by state and federal officials of their "mutual obligation to respect the same fundamental criteria" in their approach to law enforcement, and will avoid "needless conflict between state and federal courts." Indeed the majority now finds an incongruity in *Wolf's* discriminating perception between the demands of "ordered liberty" as respects the basic right of "privacy" and

the means of securing it among the States. That perception, resting both on a sensitive regard for our federal system and a sound recognition of this Court's remoteness from particular state problems, is for me the strength of that decision.

An approach which regards the issue as one of achieving procedural symmetry or of serving administrative convenience surely disfigures the boundaries of this Court's functions in relation to the state and federal courts. Our role in promulgating the *Weeks* rule and its extensions . . . was quite a different one than it is here. There, in implementing the Fourth Amendment, we occupied the position of a tribunal having the ultimate responsibility for developing the standards and procedures of judicial administration within the judicial system over which it presides. Here we review State procedures whose measure is to be taken not against the specific substantive commands of the Fourth Amendment but under the flexible contours of the Due Process Clause. I do not believe that the Fourteenth Amendment empowers this Court to mould state remedies effectuating the right to freedom from "arbitrary intrusion by the police" to suit its own notions of how things should be done. . . .

In conclusion, it should be noted that the majority opinion in this is in fact an opinon only for the *judgment* overruling *Wolf,* and not for the basic rationale by which four members of the majority have reached that result. For my Brother Black is unwilling to subscribe to their view that the *Weeks* exclusionary rule derives from the Fourth Amendment itself, . . . but joins the majority opinion on the premise that its end result can be achieved by bringing the Fifth Amendment to the aid of the Fourth. . . . On that score I need only say that whatever the validity of the "Fourth-Fifth Amendment" correlation which the *Boyd* case . . . found, . . . we have only very recently again reiterated the long-established doctrine of this Court that the Fifth Amendment privilege against self-incrimination is not applicable to the States. . . .

I regret that I find so unwise in principle and so inexpedient in policy a decision motivated by the high purpose of increasing respect for Constitutional rights. But in the last analysis I think this Court can increase respect for the Constitution only if it rigidly respects the limitations which the Constitution places upon it, and respects as well the principles inherent in its own processes. In the present case I think we exceed both, and that our voice becomes only a voice of power, not of reason.

# CAMARA v. MUNICIPAL COURT OF CITY AND COUNTY OF SAN FRANCISCO

### 387 U. S. 523; 18 L. Ed. 2d 930; 87 S. Ct. 1727 (1967)

MR. JUSTICE WHITE *delivered the opinion of the Court.*

In *Frank* v. *State of Maryland,* 359 U.S. 360, 79 S. Ct. 804, 3 L. Ed. 2d 877, this Court upheld, by a five-to-four vote, a state court conviction of a homeowner who refused to permit a municipal health inspector to enter and inspect her premises without a search warrant. In *Ohio ex rel. Eaton* v. *Price,* 364 U.S. 263, 80 S. Ct. 1463, 4 L. Ed. 2d 1708, a similar conviction was affirmed by an equally divided Court. Since those closely divided decisions, more intensive efforts at all levels of government to contain and eliminate urban blight have led to increasing use of such inspection techniques, while numerous decisions of this Court have more fully defined the Fourth Amendment's effect on state and municipal action. . . . In view of the growing nationwide importance of the problem, we noted probable jurisdiction in this case . . . to re-examine whether administration inspection programs, as presently authorized and conducted, violate Fourth Amendment rights as those rights are enforced against the States through the Fourteenth Amendment. . . .

Appellant brought this action . . . alleging that he was awaiting trial on a criminal charge of violating the San Francisco Housing Code by refusing to permit a warrantless inspection of his residence, and that a writ of prohibition should issue to the criminal court because the ordinance authorizing such inspections is unconstitutional on its face. The Superior Court denied the writ, the District Court of Appeal affirmed, and the Supreme Court of California denied a petition for hearing. . . .

. . . On November 6, 1963, an inspector of the Division of Housing Inspection of the San Francisco Department of Public Health entered an apartment building to make a routine annual inspection for possible violations of the city's Housing Code. The building's manager informed the inspector that appellant, lessee of the ground floor, was using the rear of his leasehold as a personal residence. Claiming that the building's occupancy did not allow residential use of the ground floor, the inspector confronted appellant and demanded that he permit an inspection of the premises. Appellant refused to allow the inspection because the inspector lacked a search warrant.

The inspector returned on November 8, again without a warrant, and appellant again refused to allow an inspection. A citation was then mailed ordering appellant to appear at the district attorney's office. When appellant failed to appear, two inspectors returned to his apartment on November 22. They informed appellant that he was required by law to permit an inspection, under Sec. 503 of the Housing Code:

"Sec. 503 RIGHT TO ENTER BUILDING. Authorized employees of the City departments or City agencies, so far as may be necessary for the performance of their duties, shall, upon presentation of credentials, have the right to enter, at reasonable times, any building, structure, or premises in the City to perform any duty imposed upon them by the Municipal Code."

Appellant nevertheless refused the inspectors access to his apartment without a search warrant. Thereafter, a complaint was filed charging him with refusing to permit a lawful inspection in violation of Sec. 507 of the Code. Appellant was arrested on December 2 and released on bail. When his demurrer to the criminal complaint was denied, appellant filed this petition for a writ of prohibition.

Appellant has argued throughout this litigation that Sec. 503 is contrary to the Fourth and Fourteenth Amendments in that it authorizes municipal officials to enter a private dwelling without a search warrant and without probable cause to believe that a violation of the Housing Code exists therein. Consequently, appellant contends, he may not be prosecuted . . . for refusing to permit an inspection unconstitutionally authorized by Sec. 503. Relying on *Frank* v. *State of Maryland, Eaton* v. *Price,* and decisions in other States, the District Court of Appeal held that Sec. 503 does not violate Fourth Amendment rights because it "is part of a regulatory scheme which is essentially civil rather than criminal in nature, inasmuch as that section creates a right of inspection which is limited in scope and may not be exercised under unreasonable conditions." Having concluded that *Frank* v. *State of Maryland,* to the extent that it sanctioned such warrantless inspections, must be overruled, we reverse.

. . .

To the *Frank* majority, municipal fire, health, and housing inspection programs "touch at most upon the periphery of the important interests safeguarded by the Fourteenth Amendment's protection against official intrusions," . . . because the inspections are merely to determine whether physical conditions exist which do not comply with minimum standards prescribed in local regulatory ordinances. Since the inspector does not ask that the property owner open his doors to a search for "evidence of criminal action" which may be used to secure the owner's criminal conviction, historic interests of "self-protection" jointly protected by the Fourth and Fifth Amendments are said not to be involved, but only the less intense "right to be secure from intrusion into personal privacy." . . .

We may agree that a routine inspection of the physical condition of private property is a less hostile intrusion than the typical policeman's search for the fruits and instrumentalities of crime. For this reason alone, *Frank* differed from the great bulk of Fourth Amendment cases which have been considered by this Court. But we cannot agree that the Fourth Amendment interests at stake in these inspection cases are merely "peripheral." It is surely anomalous to say that the individual and his private property are fully protected by the Fourth Amendment only when the individual is suspected of criminal behavior. For instance, even the most law-abiding citizen has a very tangible interest in limiting the circumstances under which the sanctity of his home may be broken by official authority, for the possibility of criminal entry under the guise of official sanction is a serious threat to personal and family security. And even accepting *Frank's* rather remarkable premise, inspections of the kind we are here considering do in fact jeopardize "self protection" interests of the property owner. Like most regulatory laws, fire, health, and housing codes are enforced by criminal processes. In some cities, discovery of a violation by the inspector leads to a criminal complaint. Even in cities where discovery of a violation produces only an administrative compliance order, refusal to comply is a criminal offense, and the fact of compliance is verified by a second inspection, again without a warrant. Finally, as this case demonstrates, refusal to permit an inspection is itself a crime, punishable by fine or even by jail sentence.

The *Frank* majority suggested, and appellee reasserts, two other justifications for permitting administrative health and safety inspections without a warrant. First, it is argued that these inspections are "designed to make the least possible demand on the individual occupant." . . . The ordinances authorizing inspections are hedged with safeguards and at any rate the inspector's particular decision to enter must comply with the constitutional standard of reasonableness even if he may enter without a warrant. In addition, the argument proceeds, the warrant process could not function effectively in this field. The decision to inspect an entire municipal area is based upon legislative or administrative assessment of broad factors such as the area's age and condition. Unless the magistrate is to review such policy matters, he must issue a "rubber stamp" warrant which provides no protection at all to the property owner.

In our opinion, these arguments unduly discount the purposes behind the warrant machinery contemplated by the Fourth Amendment. Under the present system, when the inspector demands entry, the occupant has no way of knowing whether enforcement of the municipal code involved requires inspection of his premises, no way of knowing the lawful limits of the inspector's power to search, and no way of knowing whether the inspector himself is acting under proper authorization. These are questions which may be reviewed by a neutral magistrate without any reassessment of the basic agency decision to canvas an area. Yet, only by refusing entry and risking a criminal conviction can the occupant at present challenge the inspector's decision to search. And even if the occupant possesses sufficient fortitude to take this risk, as appellant did here, he may never learn any more about the reason for the inspection than that the law generally allows housing inspectors to gain entry. The practical effect of this system is to leave the occupant subject to the discretion of the official in the field. This is precisely the discretion to invade private property which we have consistently circumscribed by a requirement that a disinterested party warrant the need to search. . . .

The final justification suggested for warrantless administrative searches is that the public interest demands such a rule: it is vigorously argued that the health and safety of entire urban populations is dependent upon enforcement of minimum fire, housing, and sanitation standards, and that the only executive means of enforcing such codes is by routine systematized inspection of all physical structures. . . . But we think this argument misses the mark. The question is not, at this stage at least, whether these inspections may be made, but whether they may be made without a warrant. . . . In assessing whether the public interest demands creation of a general exception to the Fourth Amendment's warrant requirement, the question is not whether the public interest justifies the type of search in question, but whether the authority to search should be evidenced by a warrant, which in turn depends in part upon whether the burden of obtaining a warrant is likely to frustrate the governmental purpose behind the search. . . . It has nowhere been urged that fire, health, and housing code inspection programs could not achieve their goals within the confines of a reasonable search warrant requirement. Thus, we do not find the public need

argument dispositive.

In summary, we hold that administrative searches of the kind at issue here are significant intrusions upon the interests protected by the Fourth Amendment, that such searches when authorized and conducted without a warrant procedure lack the traditional safeguards which the Fourth Amendment guarantees to the individual, and that the reasons put forth in *Frank* v. *State of Maryland* and in other cases for upholding these warrantless searches are insufficient to justify so substantial a weakening of the Fourth Amendment's protections. Because of the nature of the municipal programs under consideration, however, these conclusions must be the beginning, not the end of our inquiry. . .

. . . [A]ppellant argues not only that code enforcement inspection programs must be circumscribed by a warrant procedure, but also that warrants should issue only when the inspector possesses probable cause to believe that a particular dwelling contains violations of the minimum standards prescribed by the code being enforced. We disagree.

In cases in which the Fourth Amendment requires that a warrant to search be obtained, "probable cause" is the standard by which a particular decision to search is tested against the constitutional mandate of reasonableness. To apply this standard, it is obviously necessary first to focus upon the governmental interest which allegedly justifies official intrusion upon the constitutionally protected interests of the private citizen. . . .

Unlike the search pursuant to a criminal investigation, the inspection programs at issue here are aimed at securing city-wide compliance with minimum physical standards for private property. The primary governmental interest at stake is to prevent even the unintentional development of conditions which are hazardous to public health and safety. Because fires and epidemics may ravage large urban areas, because unsightly conditions adversely affect the economic values of neighboring structures, numerous courts have upheld the police power of municipalities to impose and enforce such minimum standards even upon existing structures. In determining whether a particular inspection is reasonable—and thus in determining whether there is probable cause to issue a warrant for that inspection—the need for the inspection must be weighed in terms of these reasonable goals of code enforcement.

There is unanimous agreement among those most familiar with this field that the only effective way to seek universal compliance with the minimum standards required by municipal codes is through routine periodic inspections of all structures. It is here that the probable cause debate is focused, for the agency's decision to conduct an area inspection is unavoidably based on its appraisal of conditions in the area as a whole, no on its knowledge of conditions in each particular building. Appellee contends that, if the probable cause standard urged by appellant is adopted, the area inspection will be eliminated as a means of seeking compliance with code standards and the reasonable goals of code enforcement will be dealt a crushing blow.

In meeting this contention, appellant argues first, that his probable cause standard would not jeopardize area inspection programs because only a minute portion of the population will refuse to consent to such inspections, and second, that individual privacy in any event should be given preference to the public interest in conducting such inspections. The first argument, even if true, is irrelevant to the question whether the area inspection is reasonable within the meaning of the Fourth Amendment. The second argument is in effect an assertion that the area inspection is an unreasonable search. Unfortunately, there can be no ready test for determining reasonableness other than by balancing the need to search against the invasion which the search entails. But we think that a number of persuasive factors combine to support the reasonableness of code enforcement area inspections. First, such programs have a long history of judicial and public acceptance. . . . Second, the public interest demands that all dangerous conditions be prevented or abated, yet it is doubtful that any other canvassing technique would achieve acceptable results. Many such conditions—faulty wiring is an obvious example—are not observable from outside the building and indeed may not be apparent to the inexpert occupant himself. Finally, because the inspections are neither personal in nature nor aimed at the discovery of evidence of crime, they involve a relatively limited invasion of the urban citizen's privacy. Both the majority and the dissent in *Frank* emphatically supported this conclusion.

. . .

Having concluded that the area inspection is a "reasonable" search of private property within the meaning of the Fourth Amendment, it is obvious that "probable cause" to issue a warrant to inspect must exist if reasonable legislative or administrative standards for conducting an area inspection are satisfied with respect to a particular dwelling. Such standards, which will vary with the municipal program being enforced, may be based upon the passage of time, the nature of the building (*e.g.,* a multi-family apartment house), or the condition of the entire area, but they will not necessarily depend upon specific knowledge of the condition of the particular dwelling. It has been suggested that so to vary the probable cause test from the standard applied in criminal cases would be to authorize a "synthetic search warrant" and thereby to lessen the overall protections of the Fourth Amendment. . . . But we do not agree. The warrant procedure is designed to guarantee that a decision to search private property is justified by a reasonable governmental interest. But reasonableness is still the ultimate standard. If a valid public interest justifies the intrusion contemplated, then there is probable cause to issue a suitably restricted search warrant. . . . Such an approach neither endangers time-honored doctrines applicable to criminal investigations nor makes a nullity of the probable cause requirement in this area. It merely gives full recognition to the competing public and private interests here at stake and, in so doing, best fulfills the historic purpose behind the constitutional right to be free from unreasonable government invasions of privacy. . . .

Since our holding emphasizes the controlling standard of reasonableness, nothing we say today is intended to foreclose prompt inspections, even without a warrant, that the law has

traditionally upheld in emergency situations. See *North American Cold Storage Co.* v. *City of Chicago,* 211 U.S. 306, 29 S.Ct. 101, 53 L.Ed. 195 (seizure of unwholesome food); *Jacobson* v. *Commonwealth of Massachusetts,* 197 U.S. 11, 25 S.Ct. 358, 49 L.Ed. 643 (compulsory smallpox vaccination) . . . On the other hand, in the case of most routine area inspections, there is no compelling urgency to inspect at a particular time or on a particular day. Moreover, most citizens allow inspections of their property without a warrant. Thus, as a practical matter and in light of the Fourth Amendment's requirement that a warrant specify the property to be searched, it seems likely that warrants should normally be sought only after entry is refused unless there has been a citizen complaint or there is other satisfactory reason for securing immediate entry. Similarly, the requirement of a warrant procedure does not suggest any change in what seems to be the prevailing local policy, in most situations, of authorizing entry, but not entry by force, to inspect.

In this case, appellant has been charged with a crime for his refusal to permit housing inspectors to enter his leasehold without a warrant. There was no emergency demanding immediate access; in fact, the inspectors made three trips to the building in an attempt to obtain appellant's consent to search. Yet no warrant was obtained and thus appellant was unable to verify either the need for or the appropriate limits of the inspection. No doubt, the inspectors entered the public portion of the building with the consent of the landlord, through the building's manager, but appellee does not contend that such consent to authorize inspection of appellant's premises. . . . Assuming the facts to be as the parties have alleged, we therefore conclude that appellant had a constitutional right to insist that the inspectors obtain a warrant to search and that appellant may not constitutionally be convicted for refusing to consent to the inspection. . . .

The judgment is vacated and the case is remanded for further proceedings not inconsistent with this opinion. It is so ordered.

## TERRY v. OHIO

392 U. S. 1; 20 L. Ed. 2d 889; 88 S. Ct. 1868 (1968)

MR. CHIEF JUSTICE WARREN *delivered the opinion of the Court.*

This case presents serious questions concerning the role of the Fourth Amendment in the confrontation on the street between the citizen and the policeman investigating suspicious circumstances.

Petitioner Terry was convicted of carrying a concealed weapon and sentenced to the statutorily prescribed term of one to three years in the penitentiary. Following the denial of a pretrial motion to suppress, the prosecution introduced in evidence two revolvers and a number of bullets seized from Terry and a codefendant, Richard Chilton, by Cleveland Police Detective Martin McFadden. At the hearing on the motion to suppress this evidence, Officer McFadden testified that while he was patrolling in plain clothes in downtown Cleveland at approximately 2:30 in the afternoon of October 31, 1963, his attention was attracted by two men . . . standing on the corner of Huron Road and Euclid Avenue. He had never seen the two men before, and he was unable to say precisely what first drew his eye to them. However, he testified that he had been a policeman for 39 years and a detective for 35

and that he had been assigned to patrol this vicinity of downtown Cleveland for shoplifters and pickpockets for 30 years. He explained that he had developed routine habits of observation over the years and that he would "stand and watch people or walk and watch people at many intervals of the day." He added: "Now, in this case when I looked over they didn't look right to me at the time."

His interest aroused, Officer McFadden took up a post of observation in the entrance to a store 300 to 400 feet away from the two men. "I get more purpose to watch them when I seen their movements," he testified. He saw one of the men leave the other one and walk southwest on Huron Road, past some stores. The man paused for a moment and looked in a store window, then walked a short distance, turned around and walked back toward the corner, pausing once again to look in the same store window. He rejoined his companion at the corner, and the two conferred briefly. Then the second man went through the same series of motions, strolling down Huron Road, looking in the same window, walking on a short distance, looking back, peering in the store window again, and returning to confer with the first man at the corner. The two men repeated this ritual alternately between five and six times apiece—in all, roughly a dozen trips. At one point, while the two were standing together on the corner, a third man approached them and engaged them briefly in conversation. This man then left the two others and walked west on Euclid Avenue. Chilton and Terry resumed their measured pacing, peering, and conferring. After this had gone on for 10 to 12 minutes, the two men walked off together, heading west on Euclid Avenue, following the path taken earlier by the third man.

By this time Officer McFadden had become thoroughly suspicious. He testified that . . . he suspected the two men of "casing a job, a stick-up," and that he considered it his duty as a police officer to investigate further. He added that he feared "they may have a gun." Thus, Officer McFadden followed Chilton and Terry and saw them stop in front of Zucker's store to talk to the same man who had conferred with them earlier on the street corner. Deciding that the situation was ripe for direct action, Officer McFadden approach[ed] the three men, identified himself as a police officer and asked for their names. At this point his knowledge was confined to what he had observed. He was not acquainted with any of the three men by name or by sight, and he had received no information concerning them from any other source. When the men "mumbled something" in response to his inquiries, Officer McFadden grabbed petitioner Terry, spun him around so that they were facing the other two, with Terry between McFadden and the others, and patted down the outside of his clothing. In the left breast pocket of Terry's overcoat Officer McFadden

felt a pistol. He reached inside the overcoat pocket, but was unable to remove the gun. At this point, keeping Terry between himself and the others, the officer ordered all three men to enter Zucker's store. As they went in, he removed Terry's overcoat completely, retrieved a .38 caliber revolver from the pocket and ordered all three men to face the wall with their hands raised. Officer McFadden proceeded to pat down the outer clothing of Chilton and the third man, Katz. He discovered another revolver in the outer pocket of Chilton's overcoat, but no weapons were found on Katz. The officer testified that he only patted the men down to see whether they had weapons, and that he did not put his hands beneath the outer garments of either Terry or Chilton until he felt their guns. So far as appears from the record, he never placed his hands beneath Katz's outer garments. Officer McFadden seized Chilton's gun, asked the proprietor of the store to call a police wagon, and took all three men to the station, where Chilton and Terry were formally charged with carrying concealed weapons.

On the motion to suppress the guns the prosecution took the position that they had been seized following a search incident to a lawful arrest. The trial court rejected this theory, stating that it "would be stretching the facts beyond reasonable comprehension" to find that Officer McFadden had had probable cause to arrest the men before he patted them down for weapons. However, the court denied the defendant's motion on the ground that Officer McFadden, on the basis of his experience, "had reasonable cause to believe . . . that the defendants were conducting themselves suspiciously, and some interrogation should be made of their action."

Purely for his own protection, the court held, the officer had the right to pat down the outer clothing of these men, whom he had reasonable cause to believe might be armed. The court distinguished between an investigatory "stop" and an arrest, and between a "frisk" of the outer clothing for weapons and a full-blown search for evidence of crime. The frisk, it held, was essential to the proper performance of the officer's investigatory duties, for without it "the answer to the police officer may be a bullet, and a loaded pistol discovered during the frisk is admissible."

After the court denied their motion to suppress, Chilton and Terry waived jury trial and pleaded not guilty. The court adjudged them guilty, and the Court of Appeals for the Eighth Judicial District, Cuyahoga County, affirmed. . . . The Supreme Court of Ohio dismissed petitioner's appeal on the ground that no "substantial constitutional question" was involved. . . .

. . . Unquestionably petitioner was entitled to the protection of the Fourth Amendment as he walked down the street in Cleveland. . . . The question is whether in all the circumstances of this on-the-street encounter, his right to personal security was violated by an unreasonable search and seizure.

We would be less than candid if we did not acknowledge that this question thrusts to the fore difficult and troublesome issues regarding a sensitive area of police activity—issues which have never before been squarely presented to this Court. Reflective of the tensions involved are the practical and constitutional arguments pressed with great vigor on both sides of the public debate over the power of the police to "stop and frisk"—as it is sometimes euphemistically termed—suspicious persons.

On the one hand, it is frequently argued that in dealing with the rapidly unfolding and often dangerous situations on city streets the police are in need of an escalating set of flexible responses, graduated in relation to the amount of information they possess. For this purpose it is urged that distinctions should be made between a "stop" and an "arrest" (or a "seizure" of a person), and between a "frisk" and a "search." Thus, it is argued, the police should be allowed to "stop" a person and detain him briefly for questioning upon suspicion that he may be connected with criminal activity. Upon suspicion that the person may be armed, the police should have the power to "frisk" him for weapons. If the "stop" and the "frisk" give rise to probable cause to believe that the suspect has committed a crime, then the police should be empowered to make a formal "arrest," and a full incident "search" of the person. This scheme is justified in part upon the notion that a "stop" and a "frisk" amount to a mere "minor inconvenience and petty indignity," which can properly be imposed upon the citizen in the interest of effective law enforcement on the basis of a police officer's suspicion.

On the other side the argument is made that the authority of the police must be strictly circumscribed by the law of arrest and search as it has developed to date in the traditional jurisprudence of the Fourth Amendment. It is contended with some force that there is not—and cannot be—a variety of police activity which does not depend solely upon the voluntary cooperation of the citizen and yet which stops short of an arrest based upon probable cause to make such an arrest. The heart of the Fourth Amendment, the argument runs, is a severe requirement of specific justification for any intrusion upon protected personal security, coupled with a highly developed system of judicial controls to enforce upon the agents of the State the commands of the Constitution. Acquiescence by the courts in the compulsion inherent in the field interrogation practices at issue here, it is urged, would constitute an abdication of judicial control over, and indeed an encouragement of, substantial interference with liberty and personal security by police officers whose judgment is necessarily colored by their primary involvement in "the often competitive enterprise of ferreting out crime." *Johnson* v. *United States, 333* U.S. 10, 14 (1948). This, it is argued, can only serve to exacerbate police–community tensions in the crowded centers of our Nation's cities.

In this context we approach the issues in this case mindful of the limitations of the judicial function in controlling the myriad daily situations in which policemen and citizens confront each other on the street. The State has characterized the issue here as "the right of a police officer . . . to make an on-the-street stop, interrogate and pat down for weapons (known in the street vernacular as 'stop and frisk')." But this is only partly accurate. For the issue is not the abstract propriety of the police conduct, but the admissibility against petitioner of the evidence uncovered by the search and seizure.

. . .

Our first task is to establish at what point in this encounter the Fourth Amendment becomes relevant. That is, we must decide whether and when Officer McFadden "seized" Terry and whether and when he conducted a "search." There is some suggestion in the use of such terms as "stop" and "frisk" that such police conduct is outside the purview of the Fourth Amendment because neither action rises to the level of a "search" or "seizure" within the meaning of the Constitution. We emphatically reject this notion. It is quite plain that the Fourth Amendment governs "seizures" of the person which do not eventuate in a trip to the station house and prosecution for crime— "arrests" in traditional terminology. It must be recognized that whenever a police officer accosts an individual and restrains his freedom to walk away, he has "seized" that person. And it is nothing less than sheer torture of the English language to suggest that a careful exploration of the outer surfaces of a person's clothing all over his or her body in an attempt to find weapons is not a "search." Moreover, it is simply fantastic to urge that such a procedure performed in public by a policeman while the citizen stands helpless, perhaps facing a wall with his hands raised, is a "petty indignity." It is a serious intrusion upon the sanctity of the person, which may inflict great indignity and arouse strong resentment, and it is not to be undertaken lightly.

The danger in the logic which proceeds upon distinctions between a "stop" and an "arrest," or "seizure" of the person, and between a "frisk" and a "search" is two-fold. It seeks to isolate from constitutional scrutiny the initial stages of the contact between the policeman and the citizen. And by suggesting a rigid all-or-nothing model of justification and regulation under the Amendment, it obscures the utility of limitations upon the scope, as well as the initiation, of police action as a means of constitutional regulation. This Court has held in the past that a search which is reasonable at its inception may violate the Fourth Amendment by virtue of its intolerable intensity and scope. . . . The scope of the search must be "strictly tied to and justified by" the circumstances which rendered its initiation permissible. . . .

The distinctions of classical "stop-and-frisk" theory thus serve to divert attention from the central inquiry under the Fourth Amendment—the reasonableness in all the circumstances of the particular governmental invasion of a citizen's personal security. "Search" and "seizure" are not talismans. We therefore reject the notions that the Fourth Amendment does not come into play at all as a limitation upon police conduct if the officers stop short of something called a "technical arrest" or a "full-blown search".

In this case there can be no question, then, that Officer McFadden "seized" petitioner and subjected him to a "search" when he took hold of him and patted down the outer surfaces of his clothing. We must decide whether at that point it was reasonable for Office McFadden to have interfered with petitioner's personal security as he did. And in determining whether the seizure and search were "unreasonable" our inquiry is a dual one—whether the officer's action was justified at its inception, and whether it was reasonably related in scope to circumstances which justified the interference in the first place.

If this case involved police conduct subject to the Warrant Clause of the Fourth Amendment, we would have to ascertain whether "probable cause" existed to justify the search and seizure which took place. However, that is not the case. We do not retreat from our holdings that the police must, whenever practicable, obtain advance judicial approval of searches and seizures through the warrant procedure . . . or that in most instances failure to comply with the warrant requirement can only be excused by exigent circumstances. . . . But we deal here with an entire rubric of police conduct—necessarily swift action predicated upon the on-the-spot observations of the officer on the beat—which historically has not been, and as a practical matter could not be, subjected to the warrant procedure. Instead, the conduct involved in this case must be tested by the Fourth Amendment's general proscription against unreasonable searches and seizures.

Nonetheless, the notions which underlie both the warrant procedure and the requirement of probable cause remain fully relevant in this context. In order to assess the reasonableness of Officer McFadden's conduct as a general proposition, it is necessary "first to focus upon the governmental interest which allegedly justifies official intrusion upon the constitutionally protected interests of the private citizen." . . . And in justifying the particular intrusion the police officer must be able to point to specific and articulable facts which, taken together with rational inferences from those facts, reasonably warrant that intrusion. The scheme of the Fourth Amendment becomes meaningful only when it is assured that at some point the conduct of those charged with enforcing the laws can be subjected to the more detached, neutral scrutiny of a judge who must evaluate the reasonableness of a particular search or seizure in light of the particular circumstances. And in making that assessment it is imperative that the facts be judged against an objective standard: would the facts available to the officer at the moment of the seizure or the search "warrant a man of reasonable caution in the belief" that the action taken was appropriate? . . . Anything less would invite intrusions upon constitutionally guaranteed rights based on nothing more substantial than inarticulate hunches, a result this Court has consistently refused to sanction. . . .

Applying these principles to this case, we consider first the nature and extent of the governmental interests involved. One general interest is of course that of effective crime prevention and detection; it is this interest which underlies the recognition that a police officer may in appropriate circumstances and in an appropriate manner approach a person for purposes of investigating possible criminal behavior even though there is no probable cause to make an arrest. It was this legitimate investigative function Officer McFadden was discharging when he decided to approach petitioner and his companions. He had observed Terry, Chilton, and Katz go through a series of acts, each of them perhaps innocent in itself, but which taken together warranted further investigation. There is nothing unusual in two men standing together on a street corner, perhaps waiting for someone. Nor is there anything suspicious about people in such circumstances strolling up and down the street, singly or in pairs. Store windows, moreover, are made to be looked in. But the story is quite different where, as here, two men hover about a street corner for an extended period of time, at the end of which it becomes apparent that they are not waiting for anyone or anything; where these men pace alternately along an identical route, pausing to stare in the same store window roughly 24 times; where each completion of this route is followed immediately by a conference between the two men on the corner; where they are joined in one of these conferences by a third man who leaves swiftly; and where the two men finally follow the third and rejoin him a couple of blocks away. It would have been poor police work indeed for an officer of 30 years' experience in the detection of thievery from stores in this same neighborhood to have failed to investigate this behavior further.

The crux of this case, however, is not the propriety of Officer McFadden's taking steps to investigate petitioner's suspicious behavior, but rather, whether there was justification for McFadden's invasion of Terry's personal security by searching him for weapons in the course of that investigation. We are now concerned with more than the governmental interest in investigating crime; in addition, there is the more immediate interest of the police officer in taking steps to assure himself that the person with whom he is dealing is not armed with a weapon that could unexpectedly and fatally be used against him. Certainly it would be unreasonable to require that police officers take unnecessary risks in the performance of their duties. American criminals have a long tradition of armed violence, and every year in this country many law enforcement officers are killed in the line of duty, and thousands more are wounded. Virtually all of these deaths and a substantial portion of the injuries are inflicted with guns and knives.

In view of these facts, we cannot

blind ourselves to the need for law enforcement officers to protect themselves and other prospective victims of violence in situations where they may lack probable cause for an arrest. When an officer is justified in believing that the individual whose suspicious behavior he is investigating at close range is armed and presently dangerous to the officer or to others, it would appear to be clearly unreasonable to deny the officer the power to take necessary measures to determine whether the person is in fact carrying a weapon and to neutralize the threat of physical harm.

We must still consider, however, the nature and quality of the intrusion on individual rights which must be accepted if police officers are to be conceded the right to search for weapons in situations where probable cause to arrest for crime is lacking. Even a limited search of the outer clothing for weapons constitutes a severe, though brief, intrusion upon cherished personal security, and it must surely be an annoying, frightening, and perhaps humiliating experience. Petitioner contends that such an intrusion is permissible only incident to a lawful arrest, either for a crime involving the possession of weapons or for a crime the commission of which led the officer to investigate in the first place. However, this argument must be closely examined.

Petitioner does not argue that a police officer should refrain from making any investigation of suspicious circumstances until such time as he has probable cause to make an arrest; nor does he deny that police officers in properly discharging their investigative function may find themselves confronting persons who might well be armed and dangerous. Moreover, he does not say that an officer is always unjustified in searching a suspect to discover weapons. Rather, he says it is unreasonable for the policeman to take that step until such time as the situation evolves to a point where there is probable cause to make an arrest. When that point has been reached, petitioner would concede the officer's right to conduct a search of the suspect for weapons, fruits or instrumentalities of the crime, or "mere" evidence, incident to the arrest.

There are two weaknesses in this line of reasoning, however. First, it fails to take account of traditional limitations upon the scope of searches, and thus recognizes no distinction in purpose, character, and extent between a search incident to an arrest and a limited search for weapons. The former, although justified in part by the acknowledged necessity to protect the arresting officer from assault with a concealed weapon, . . . is also justified on other grounds . . . and can therefore involve a relatively extensive exploration of the person. A search for weapons in the absence of probable cause to arrest, however, must, like any other search, be strictly circumscribed by the exigencies which justify its initiation. . . . Thus it must be limited to that which is necessary for the discovery of weapons which might be used to harm the officer or others nearby, and may realistically be characterized as something less than a "full" search, even though it remains a serious intrusion.

A second, and related, objection to petitioner's argument is that it assumes that the law of arrest has already worked out the balance between the particular interests involved here—the neutralization of danger to the policeman in the investigative circumstance and the sanctity of the individual. But this is not so. An arrest is a wholly different kind of intrusion upon individual freedom from a limited search for weapons, and the interests each is designed to serve are likewise quite different. An arrest is the initial stage of a criminal prosecution. It is intended to vindicate society's interest in having its laws obeyed, and it is inevitably accompanied by future interference with the individual's freedom of movement, whether or not trial or conviction ultimately follows. The protective search for weapons, on the other hand, constitutes a brief, though far from inconsiderable, intrusion upon the sanctity of the person. It does not follow that because an officer may lawfully arrest a person only when he is apprised of facts sufficient to warrant a belief that the person has committed or is committing a crime, the officer is equally unjustified, absent that kind of evidence, in making any intrusions short of an arrest. Moreover, a perfectly reasonable apprehension of danger may arise long before the officer is possessed of adequate information to justify taking a person into custody for the purpose of prosecuting him for a crime. Petitioner's reliance on cases which have worked out standards of reasonableness with regard to "seizures" constituting arrests and searches incident thereto is thus misplaced. It assumes that the interests sought to be vindicated and the invasions of personal security may be equated in the two cases, and thereby ignores a vital aspect of the analysis of the reasonableness of particular types of conduct under the Fourth Amendment. . . .

Our evaluation of the proper balance that has to be struck in this type of case leads us to conclude that there must be a narrowly drawn authority to permit a reasonable search for weapons for the protection of the police officer, where he has reason to believe that he is dealing with an armed and dangerous individual, regardless of whether he has probable cause to arrest the individual for a crime. The officer need not be absolutely certain that the individual is armed; the issue is whether a reasonably prudent man in the circumstances would be warranted in the belief that his safety or that of others was in danger. . . . And in determining whether the officer acted reasonably in such circumstances, due weight must be given, not to his inchoate and unparticularized suspicion or "hunch," but to the specific reasonable inferences which he is entitled to draw from the facts in light of his experience. . . .

We must now examine the conduct of Officer McFadden in this case to determine whether his search and seizure of petitioner were reasonable, both at their inception and as conducted. He had observed Terry, together with Chilton and another man, acting in a manner he took to be preface to a "stick-up." We think on the facts and circumstances Officer McFadden detailed before the trial judge a reasonably prudent man would have been warranted in believing petitioner was armed and thus presented a threat to the officer's safety while he was investigating his suspicious behavior. The actions of Terry and Chilton were consistent with McFadden's hypothesis that these men were contemplating a daylight robbery—which, it is reasonable to assume, would be likely to involve the use of weapons—and nothing in their conduct from the time he first noticed them until the time he confronted them and identified himself as a police officer gave him sufficient reason to negate that hypothesis. Although the trio had departed the original scene, there was nothing to indicate abandonment of an intent to commit a robbery at some point. Thus, when Officer McFadden approached the three men gathered before the display window at Zucker's store he had observed enough to make it quite reasonable to fear that they were armed; and nothing in their response to his hailing them, identifying himself as a police officer, and asking their names served to dispel that reasonable belief. We cannot say his decision at that point to seize Terry and pat his clothing for weapons was the product of a volatile or inventive imagination, or was undertaken simply as an act of harassment; the record evidences the tempered act of a policeman who in the course of an investigation had to make a quick decision as to how to protect himself and others from possible danger, and took limited steps to do so.

The manner in which the seizure and search were conducted is, of course, as vital a part of the inquiry as whether they were warranted at all. The Fourth Amendment proceeds as much by limitations upon the scope of governmental action as by imposing preconditions upon its initiation. . . . The entire deterrent purpose of the rule excluding evidence seized in violation of the Fourth Amendment rests on the assumption that "limitations upon the fruit to be gathered tend to limit the quest itself." . . . Thus, evidence may not be introduced if it was discovered by means of a seizure and search which were not reasonably related in scope to the justification for their initiation. . . .

We need not develop at length in this case, however, the limitations which the Fourth Amendment places upon a protective seizure and search for weapons. These limitations will have to be developed in the concrete factual circumstances of individual cases. . . . Suffice it to note that such a search, unlike a search without a warrant incident to a lawful arrest, is not justified by any need to prevent the disappearance or destruction of evidence of crime. . . . The sole justification of the search in the present situation is the protection of the police officer and others nearby, and it must therefore be confined in scope to an intrusion reasonably designed to discover guns, knives, clubs, or other hidden instruments for the assault of the police officer.

The scope of the search in this case presents no serious problem in light of these standards. . . . Officer McFadden confined his search strictly to what was minimally necessary to learn whether the men were armed and to disarm them once he discovered the weapons. He did not conduct a general exploratory search for whatever evidence of criminal activity he might find.

We conclude that the revolver seized from Terry was properly admitted in evidence against him. . . . We merely hold today that where a police officer observes unusual conduct which leads him reasonably to conclude in light of his experience that criminal activity may be afoot and that the persons with whom he is dealing may be armed and presently dangerous; where in the course of investigating this behavior he identifies himself as a policeman and makes reasonable inquiries; and where nothing in the initial stages of the encounter serves to dispel his reasonable fear for his own or others' safety, he is entitled for the protection of himself and others in the area to conduct a carefully limited search of the outer clothing of such persons in an attempt to discover weapons which might be used to assault him. Such a search is a reasonable search under the Fourth Amendment, and any weapons seized may properly be introduced in evidence against the person from whom they were taken.

*Affirmed.*

MR. JUSTICE BLACK *concurs in the judgment and the opinion except where the opinion quotes from and relies upon this Court's opinion in* Katz *v.* United States *and the concurring opinion in* Warden *v.* Hayden.

MR. JUSTICE HARLAN, *concurring.*

While I unreservedly agree with the Court's ultimate holding in this case, I am constrained to fill in a few gaps, as I see them, in its opinion. I do this because what is said by this Court today will serve as initial guidelines for law enforcement authorities and courts throughout the land as this important new field of law develops.

. . . Since the question in this and most cases is whether evidence produced by a frisk is admissible, the problem is to determine what makes a frisk reasonable.

If the State of Ohio were to provide that police officers could, on articulable suspicion less than probable cause, forcibly frisk and disarm persons thought to be carrying concealed weapons, I would have little doubt that action taken pursuant to such authority could be constitutionally reasonable. Concealed weapons create an immediate and severe danger to the public, and though that danger might not warrant routine general weapons checks, it could well warrant action on less than a "probability." I mention this line of analysis because I think it vital to point out that it cannot be applied in this case. On the record before us Ohio has

not clothed its policemen with routine authority to frisk and disarm on suspicion; in the absence of state authority, policemen have no more right to "pat down" the outer clothing of passers-by, or of persons to whom they address casual questions, than does any other citizen. Consequently, the Ohio courts did not rest the constitutionality of this frisk upon any general authority in Officer McFadden to take reasonable steps to protect the citizenry, including himself, from dangerous weapons.

The state courts held, instead, that when an officer is lawfully confronting a possible hostile person in the line of duty he has a right, springing only from the necessity of the situation and not from any broader right to disarm, to frisk for his own protection. This holding, with which I agree and with which I think the Court agrees, offers the only satisfactory basis I can think of for affirming this conviction. The holding has, however, two logical corollaries that I do not think the Court has fully expressed.

In the first place, if the frisk is justified in order to protect the officer during an encounter with a citizen, the officer must first have constitutional grounds to insist on an encounter, to make a *forcible* stop. Any person, including a policeman, is at liberty to avoid a person he considers dangerous. If and when a policeman has a right instead to disarm such a person for his own protection, he must first have a right not to avoid him but to be in his presence. That right must be more than the liberty (again, possessed by every citizen) to address questions to other persons, for ordinarily the person addressed has an equal right to ignore his interrogator and walk away; he certainly need not submit to a frisk for the questioner's protection. I would make it perfectly clear that the right to frisk in this case depends upon the reasonableness of a forcible stop to investigate a suspected crime.

Where such a stop is reasonable, however, the right to frisk must be immediate and automatic if the reason for the stop is, as here, an articulable suspicion of a crime of violence. Just as a full search incident to a lawful arrest requires no additional justification, a limited frisk incident to a lawful stop must often be rapid and routine. There is no reason why an officer, rightfully but forcibly confronting a person suspected of a serious crime, should have to ask one question and take the risk that the answer might be a bullet.

. . .

I would affirm this conviction for what I believe to be the same reasons the Court relies on. I would, however, make explicit what I think is implicit in affirmance on the present facts. Officer McFadden's right to interrupt Terry's freedom of movement and invade his privacy arose only because circumstances warranted forcing an encounter with Terry in an effort to prevent or investigate a crime. Once that forced encounter was justified, however, the officer's right to take suitable measures for his own safety followed automatically.

Upon the foregoing premises, I join the opinion of the Court.

MR. JUSTICE WHITE's *brief concurring opinion is not reprinted here.*

MR. JUSTICE DOUGLAS, *dissenting.*

I agree that petitioner was "seized" within the meaning of the Fourth Amendment. I also agree that frisking petitioner and his companions for guns was a "search." But it is a mystery how that "search" and that "seizure" can be constitutional by Fourth Amendment standards, unless there was "probable cause" to believe that (1) a crime had been committed or (2) a crime was in the process of being committed or (3) a crime was about to be committed.

The opinion of the Court disclaims the existence of "probable cause." If loitering were an issue and that was the offense charged, there would be "probable cause" shown. But the crime here is carrying concealed weapons; and there is no basis for concluding that the officer had "probable cause" for believing that a crime was being committed. Had a warrant been sought, a magistrate would, therefore, have been unauthorized to issue one, for he can act only if there is a showing of "probable cause." We hold today that the police have greater authority to make a "seizure" and conduct a "search" than a judge has to authorize such action. We have said precisely the opposite over and over again.

In other words, police officers, up to today have been permitted to effect arrests or searches without warrants only when the facts within their personal knowledge would satisfy the constitutional standard of *probable cause.* At the time of their "seizure" without a warrant they must possess facts concerning the person arrested that would have satisfied a magistrate that "probable cause" was indeed present. The term "probable cause" rings a bell of certainty that is not sounded by phrases such as "reasonable suspicion." Moreover, the meaning of "probable cause" is deeply imbedded in our constitutional history. . . .

The infringement on personal liberty of any "seizure" of a person can only be "reasonable" under the Fourth Amendment if we require the police to possess "probable cause" before they seize him. Only that line draws a meaningful distinction between an officer's mere inkling and the presence of facts within the officer's personal knowledge which would convince a reasonable man that the person seized has committed, is committing, or is about to commit a particular crime. "In dealing with probable cause . . . as the very name implies, we deal with probabilities. These are not technical; they are the factual and practical considerations of everyday life on which reasonable and prudent men, not legal technicians, act." *Brinegar* v. *United States,* 338 U.S. 160, 175.

To give the police greater power than a magistrate is to take a long step down the totalitarian path. Perhaps such a step is desirable to cope with modern forms of lawlessness. But if it is taken, it should be the deliberate choice of the people through a constitutional amendment. Until the Fourth Amendment, which is closely allied with the Fifth, is rewritten, the person and the effects of the individual are beyond the reach of all government agencies until there are reasonable grounds to believe (probable cause) that a criminal venture has been launched or is about to be launched.

There have been powerful hydraulic pressures throughout our history that bear heavily on the Court to water down constitutional guarantees and give the police the upper hand. That hydraulic pressure has probably never been greater than it is today.

Yet if the individual is no longer to be sovereign, if the police can pick him up whenever they do not like the cut of his gib, if they can "seize" and "search" him in their discretion, we enter a new regime. The decision to enter it should be made only after a full debate by the people of this country.

## KATZ v. UNITED STATES

389 U. S. 347; 19 L. Ed. 2d 576; 88 S. Ct. 507 (1967)

MR. JUSTICE STEWART *delivered the opinion of the Court.*

The petitioner was convicted . . . under an eight-count indictment charging him with transmitting wagering information by telephone from Los Angeles to Miami and Boston in violation of a federal statute. At trial the Government was permitted, over the petitioner's objection, to introduce evidence of the petitioner's end of telephone conversations, overheard by FBI agents who had attached an electronic listening and recording device to the outside of the public telephone booth from which he had placed his calls. In affirming his conviction, the Court of Appeals rejected the contention that the recordings had been obtained in violation of the Fourth Amendment, because "[t]here was no physical entrance into the area occupied by [the petitioner]." We granted certiorari in order to consider the constitutional questions thus presented.

The petitioner has phrased those questions as follows:

A. Whether a public telephone booth is a constitutionally protected area so that evidence obtained by attaching an electronic listening device to the top of such a booth is obtained in violation of the right to privacy of the user of the booth. B. Whether physical penetration of a constitutionally protected area is necessary before a search and seizure can be said to be violative of the Fourth Amendment to the United States Constitution.

We decline to adopt this formulation of the issues. In the first place the correct solution of Fourth Amendment problems is not necessarily promoted by incantation of the phrase "constitutionally protected area." Secondly, the Fourth Amendment cannot be translated into a general constitutional "right to privacy." That Amendment protects individual privacy against certain kinds of government intrusion, but its protections go further, and often have nothing to do with privacy at all. Other provisions of the Constitution protect personal privacy from other forms of government invasion. But the protection of a person's right to privacy—his right to be let alone by other people—is, like the protection of his property and of his very life, left largely to the law of the individual States.

Because of the misleading way the issues have been formulated, the parties have attached great significance to the characterization of the telephone booth from which the petitioner placed his calls. The petitioner has strenuously argued that the booth was a "constitutionally protected area." The Government has maintained with equal vigor that it was not. But this effort to decide whether or not a given "area," viewed in the abstract, is "constitutionally protected" deflects attention from the problem presented by this case. For the Fourth Amendment protects people, not places. What a person knowingly exposes to the public, even in his own home or office, is not a subject of Fourth Amendment protection. . . . But what he seeks to preserve as private, even in an area accessible to the public, may be constitutionally protected. . . .

The Government stresses the fact that the telephone booth from which the petitioner made his calls was constructed partly of glass, so that he was as visible after he entered it as he would have been if he had remained outside. But what he sought to exclude when he entered the booth was not the intruding eye—it was the uninvited ear. He did not shed his right to do so simply because he made his calls from a place where he might be seen. No less than an individual in a business office, in a friend's apartment, or in a taxicab, a person in a telephone booth may rely upon the protection of the Fourth Amendment. One who occupies it, shuts the door behind him, and pays the toll that permits him to place a call, is surely entitled to assume that the words he utters into the mouthpiece will not be broadcast to the world. To read the Constitution more narrowly is to ignore the vital role that the public telephone has come to play in private communication.

The Government contends, however, that the activities of its agents in this case should not be tested by the Fourth Amendment requirements, for the surveillance technique they employed involved no physical penetration of the telephone booth from which the petitioner placed his calls. It is true that the absence of such penetration was at one time thought to foreclose further Fourth Amendment inquiry. *Olmstead* v. *United States,* 277 U.S. 438, 48 S. Ct. 564, 72

L. Ed. 944; *Goldman* v. *United States,* 316 U.S. 129, 62 S. Ct. 993, 86 L. Ed. 1322, for that Amendment was thought to limit only searches and seizures of tangible property. But "[t]he premise that property interests control the right of the Government to search and seize has been discredited." . . . Thus, although a closely divided Court supposed in *Olmstead* that surveillance without any trespass and without the seizure of any material object fell outside the ambit of the Constitution, we have since departed from the narrow view on which that decision rested. Indeed, we have expressly held that the Fourth Amendment governs not only the seizure of tangible items, but extends as well to the recording of oral statements overheard without any "technical trespass under . . . local property law." *Silverman* v. *United States,* 365 U.S. 505, 511, 81 S. Ct. 679, 682, 5 L. Ed. 2d 734. Once this much is acknowledged, and once it is recognized that the Fourth Amendment protects people—and not simply "areas"—against unreasonable searches and seizures it becomes clear that the reach of that Amendment cannot turn upon the presence or absence of a physical intrusion into any given enclosure.

We conclude that the underpinnings of *Olmstead* and *Goldman* have been so eroded by our subsequent decisions that the "trespass" doctrine there enunciated can no longer be regarded as controlling. The Government's activities in electronically listening to and recording the petitioner's words violated the privacy upon which he justifiably relied while using the telephone booth and thus constituted a "search and seizure" within the meaning of the Fourth Amendment. The fact that the electronic device employed to achieve that end did not happen to penetrate the wall of the booth can have no constitutional significance.

The question remaining for decision, then, is whether the search and seizure conducted in this case complied with constitutional standards. In that regard, the Government's position is that its agents acted in an entirely defensible manner: They did not begin their electronic surveillance until investigation of the petitioner's activities had established a strong probability that he was using the telephone in question to transmit gambling information to persons in other States, in violation of federal law. Moreover, the surveillance was limited, both in scope and in duration, to the specific purpose of establishing the contents of the petitioner's unlawful telephonic communications. The agents confined their surveillance to the brief periods during which he used the telephone booth, and they took great care to overhear only the conversations of the petitioner himself.

Accepting this account of the Government's actions as accurate, it is clear that this surveillance was so narrowly circumscribed that a duly authorized magistrate, properly notified of the need for such investigation, specifically informed of the basis on which it was to proceed, and clearly apprised of the precise intrusion it would entail, could constitutionally have authorized, with appropriate safeguards, the very limited search and seizure that the Government asserts in fact took place. Only last Term we sustained the validity of such an authorization, holding that under sufficiently "precise and discriminate circumstances," a federal court may empower government agents to employ a concealed electronic device "for the narrow and particularized purpose of ascertaining the truth of the . . . allegations" of a "detailed factual affidavit alleging the commission of a specific criminal offense." *Osborn* v. *United States,* 385 U.S. 323, 329–330, 87 S. Ct. 429, 433, 17 L. Ed. 2d 394. Discussing that holding, the Court in *Berger* v. *New York,* 388 U.S. 41, 87 S. Ct. 1873, 18 L. Ed. 2d 1040, said that "the order authorizing the use of the electronic device" in *Osborn* "afforded similar protections to those . . . of conventional warrants authorizing the seizure of tangible evidence." Through those protections, "no greater invasion of privacy was permitted than was necessary under the circumstances."

. . .

The Government . . . urges the creation of a new exception to cover this case. It argues that surveillance of a telephone booth should be exempted from the usual requirement of advance authorization by a magistrate upon a showing of probable cause. We cannot agree. Omission of such authorization

bypasses the safeguards provided by an objective predetermination of probable cause, and substitutes instead the far less reliable procedure of an after-the-event justification for the . . . search, too likely to be subtly influenced by the familiar shortcomings of hindsight judgment. *Beck* v. *State of Ohio,* 379 U. S. 89, 85 S. Ct. 223, 228, 13 L. Ed. 2d 142.

And bypassing a neutral predetermination of the *scope* of a search leaves individuals secure from Fourth Amendment violations "only in the discretion of the police." Id., at 97, 85 S. Ct. at 229.

These considerations do not vanish when the search in question is transferred from the setting of a home, an office, or a hotel room, to that of a telephone booth. Wherever a man may be, he is entitled to know that he will remain free from unreasonable searches and seizures. The government agents here ignored "the procedure of antecedent justification . . . that is central to the Fourth Amendment," a procedure that we hold to be a constitutional precondition of the kind of electronic surveillance involved in this case. Because the surveillance here failed to meet that condition, and because it led to the petitioner's conviction, the judgment must be reversed.

*It is so ordered.*
*Judgment reversed.*

MR. JUSTICE MARSHALL *took no part in the consideration or decision of this case.*

JUSTICES HARLAN, WHITE, *and* DOUGLAS, *with whom* MR. JUSTICE BRENNAN *joined, wrote separate concurring opinions.*

MR. JUSTICE BLACK, *dissenting.*

If I could agree with the Court that eavesdropping carried on by electronic means (equivalent to wiretapping) constitutes a "search" or "seizure," I would be happy to join the Court's opinion. For on that premise my Brother Stewart sets out methods in accord with the Fourth Amendment to guide States in the enactment and enforcement of laws passed to regulate wiretapping by government. In this respect today's opinion differs sharply from *Berger* v. *State of New York,* 388 U.S. 41, 87 S. Ct. 1873, 18 L. Ed. 2d 1040, decided last Term, which held void on its face a New York statute authorizing wiretapping on warrants issued by magistrates on showings of probable causes. The *Berger* case also set up what appeared to be insuperable obstacles to the valid passage of such wiretapping laws by States. The Court's opinion in this case, however, removes the doubts about state power in this field and abates to a large extent the confusion and near paralyzing effect of the *Berger* holding. Notwithstanding these good efforts of the Court, I am still unable to agree with its interpretation of the Fourth Amendment.

My basic objection is twofold: (1) I do not believe that the words of the Amendment will bear the meaning given them by today's decision, and (2) I do not believe that it is the proper role of this Court to rewrite the Amendment in order "to bring it into harmony with the times" and thus reach a result that many people believe to be desirable.

. . . The first clause protects "persons, houses, papers, and effects, against unreasonable searches and seizures. . . ." These words connote the idea of tangible things with size, form, and weight, things capable of being searched, seized, or both. The second clause of the Amendment still further establishes its Framers' purpose to limit its protection to tangible things by providing that no warrants shall issue but those "particularly describing the place to be searched and the person or things to be seized." A conservation overheard by eavesdropping whether by plain snooping or wiretapping, is not tangible and, under the normally accepted meanings of these words, can neither be searched nor seized. In addition the language of the second clause indicates that the Amendment refers to something not only tangible so it can be seized but to something already in existence so it can be described. Yet the Court's interpretation would have the Amendment apply to overhearing future conversations which by their very nature are nonexistent until they take place. How can one "describe" a future conversation, and if not, how can a magistrate issue a warrant to eavesdrop one in the future? It is argued that information showing what is expected to be said is sufficient to limit the boundaries of what later can be admitted into evidence; but does such general information really meet the specific language of the Amendment which says "particularly describing?" Rather than using language in a completely artificial way, I must conclude that the Fourth Amendment simply does not apply to eavesdropping.

Tapping telephone wires, of course, was an unknown possibility at the time the Fourth Amendment was adopted. But eavesdropping (and wiretapping is nothing more than eavesdropping by telephone) was, as even the majority opinion in *Berger, supra,* recognized, "an ancient practice which at common law was condemned as a nuisance. IV Blackstone, Commentaries Sec. 168. In those days the eavesdropper listened by naked ear under the eaves of houses or their windows, or beyond their walls seeking out private discourse." 388 U.S. at 45, 87 S. Ct. at 1876. There can be no doubt that the Framers were aware of this practice, and if they had desired to outlaw or restrict the use of evidence obtained by eavesdropping, I believe that they would have used the appropriate language to do so in the Fourth Amendment. They certainly would not have left such a task to the ingenuity of language-stretching judges. No one, it seems to me, can read the debates on the Bill of Rights without reaching the conclusion that its Framers and critics well knew the meaning of the words they used, what they would be understood to mean by others, their scope and their limitations.

Under these circumstances it strikes me as a charge against their scholarship, their commonsense and their candor to give to the Fourth Amendment's language the eavesdropping meaning the Court imputes to it today.

I do not deny that common sense requires and that this Court often has said that the Bill of Rights' safeguards should be given a liberal construction. This principle, however, does not justify construing the search and seizure amendment as applying to eavesdropping or the "seizure" of conversations. The Fourth Amendment was aimed directly at the abhorred practice of breaking in, ransacking and searching homes and other buildings and seizing peoples' personal belongings without warrants issued by magistrates. The Amendment deserves, and this Court has given it, a liberal construction in order to protect against warrantless searches of buildings and seizures of tangible personal effects. But until today this Court has refused to say that eavesdropping comes within the ambit of Fourth Amendment restrictions.

. . .

With this decision the Court has completed, I hope, its rewriting of the Fourth Amendment, which started only recently when the Court began referring incessantly to the Fourth Amendment not so much as a law against *unreasonable* searches and seizures as one to protect an individual's privacy. By clever word juggling the Court finds it plausible to argue that language aimed specifically at searches and seizures of things that can be searched and seized may, to protect privacy, be applied to eavesdropped evidence of conversations that can neither be searched nor seized. Few things happen to an individual that do not affect his privacy in one way or another. Thus, by arbitrarily substituting the Court's language, designed to protect privacy, for the Constitution's language, designed to protect against unreasonable searches and seizures, the Court has made the Fourth Amendment its vehicle for holding all laws violative of the Constitution which offend the Court's broadest concept of privacy. As I said in *Griswold* v. *State of Connecticut*, 381 U.S. 479, 85 S. Ct. 1678, 14 L. Ed. 2d 510, "The Court talks about a constitutional 'right of privacy' as though there is some constitutional provision or provisions forbidding any law ever passed which might abridge the 'privacy' of individuals. But there is not." (Dissenting opinion, p. 508, 85 S. Ct. p. 1695.) I made clear in that dissent my fear of the dangers involved when this Court uses the "broad, abstract and ambiguous concept" of "privacy" as a "comprehensive substitute for the Fourth Amendment's guarantee against 'unreasonable searches and seizures.' " (See generally dissenting opinion, pp. 507–527, 85 S. Ct. pp. 1694–1705.)

The Fourth Amendment protects privacy only to the extent that it prohibits unreasonable searches and seizures of "persons, houses, papers and effects." No general right is created by the Amendment so as to give this Court the unlimited power to hold unconstitutional everything which affects privacy. Certainly the Framers, well acquainted as they were with the excesses of governmental power, did not intend to grant this Court such omnipotent lawmaking authority as that. The history of governments proves that it is dangerous to freedom to repose such powers in courts.

For these reasons I respectfully dissent.

# MALLOY v. HOGAN

378 U. S. 1; 12 L. Ed. 2d 653; 84 S. Ct. 1489 (1964)

MR. JUSTICE BRENNAN *delivered the opinion of the Court.*

In this case we are asked to reconsider prior decisions holding that the privilege against self-incrimination is not safeguarded against state action by the Fourteenth Amendment. . . .

The petitioner was arrested during a gambling raid in 1959 by Hartford, Connecticut, police. He pleaded guilty to the crime of pool-selling, a misdemeanor, and was sentenced to one year in jail and fined $500. The sentence was ordered to be suspended after 90 days, at which time he was to be placed on probation for two years. About 16 months after his guilty plea, petitioner was ordered to testify before a referee appointed by the Superior Court of Hartford County to conduct an inquiry into alleged gambling and other criminal activities in the county. The petitioner was asked a number of questions related to events surrounding his arrest and conviction. He refused to answer any question "on the grounds it may tend to incriminate me." The Superior Court adjudged him in contempt, and committed him to prison until he was willing to answer the questions. Petitioner's application for a writ of habeas corpus was denied by the Superior Court, and the Connecticut Supreme Court of Errors affirmed. . . . The latter court held that the Fifth Amendment's privilege against self-incrimination was not available to a witness in a state proceeding, that the Fourteenth Amendment extended no privilege to him, and that

the petitioner had not properly invoked the privilege available under the Connecticut Constitution. We granted certiorari. . . . We reverse. We hold that the Fourteenth Amendment guaranteed the petitioner the protection of the Fifth Amendment's privilege against self-incrimination, and that under the applicable federal standard, the Connecticut Supreme Court of Errors erred in holding that the privilege was not properly invoked.

. . .

We hold today that the Fifth Amendment's exception from compulsory self-incrimination is also protected by the Fourteenth Amendment against abridgment by the States. Decisions of the Court since *Twining* and *Adamson* have departed from the contrary view expressed in those cases. We discuss first the decisions which forbid the use of coerced confessions in state criminal prosecutions.

*Brown* v. *Mississippi*, 297 U.S. 278, . . . was the first case in which the Court held that the Due Process Clause prohibited the States from using the accused's coerced confessions against him. The Court in *Brown* felt impelled, in light of *Twining*, to say that its conclusion did not involve the privilege against self-incrimination. "Compulsion by torture to extort a confession is a different matter." 297 U.S. 285. . . . But this distinction was soon abandoned, and today the admissibility of a confession in a state criminal prosecution is tested by the same standard applied in federal prosecutions since 1897, when, in *Bram* v. *United States,*

168 U.S. 532, . . . the Court held that "In criminal trials, in the courts of the United States, wherever a question arises whether a confession is incompetent because not voluntary, the issue is controlled by that portion of the Fifth Amendment to the Constitution of the United States commanding that no person 'shall be compelled in any criminal case to be a witness against himself.' " . . . Under this test, the constitutional inquiry is not whether the conduct of state officers in obtaining the confession was shocking, but whether the confession is "free and voluntary. . . ." In other words the person must not have been compelled to incriminate himself. We have held inadmissible even a confession secured by so mild a whip as the refusal under certain circumstances, to allow a suspect to call his wife until he confessed. *Haynes* v. *Washington,* 373 U.S. 503.

The marked shift to the federal standard in state cases began with *Lisenba* v. *California,* 314 U.S. 219, . . . where the Court spoke of accused's "free choice to admit, to deny, or to refuse to answer." . . . The shift reflects recognition that the American system of criminal prosecution is accusatorial, not inquisitorial, and that the Fifth Amendment privilege is its essential mainstay. . . . Governments, state and federal, are thus constitutionally compelled to establish guilt by evidence independently and freely secured, and may not by coercion prove a charge against an accused out of his own mouth. Since the Fourteenth Amendment prohibits the States from inducing a person to confess through "sympathy falsely aroused," . . . or other like inducement far short of "compulsion by torture," . . . it follows *a fortiori* that it also forbids the States to resort

to imprisonment, as here, to compel him to answer questions that might incriminate him. The Fourteenth Amendment secures against state invasion the same privilege that the Fifth Amendment guarantees against federal infringement—the right of a person to remain silent unless he chooses to speak in the unfettered exercise of his will, and to suffer no penalty, as held in *Twining,* for such silence.

. . .

The respondent Sheriff concedes in his brief that under our decisions, particularly those involving coerced confessions, "the accusatorial system has become a fundamental part of the fabric of our society and, hence, is enforceable against the States." The State urges, however, that the availability of the federal privilege to a witness in a state inquiry is to be determined according to a less stringent standard than is applicable in a federal proceeding. We disagree. We have held that the guarantees of the First Amendment, . . . the prohibition of unreasonable searches and seizures of the Fourth Amendment, . . . and the right to counsel guaranteed by the Sixth Amendment, . . . are all to be enforced against the States under the Fourteenth Amendment according to the same standards that protect those personal rights against federal encroachment. In the coerced confession cases, involving the policies of the privilege itself, there has been no suggestion that a confession might be considered coerced if used in a federal but not a state tribunal. The Court thus has rejected the notion that the Fourteenth Amendment applies to the states only a "watered-down, subjective version of the individual guarantees of the Bill of Rights." . . . What is accorded is a privilege of refusing to incriminate one's self, and the feared prosecution may be by either federal or state authorities. . . . It would be incongruous to have different standards determine the validity of a claim of privilege based on the same feared prosecution, depending on whether the claim was asserted in a state or federal court. Therefore, the same standards must determine whether an accused's silence in either a federal or state proceeding is justified.

We turn to the petitioner's claim that the State of Connecticut denied him the protection of his federal privilege. It must be considered irrelevant that the petitioner was a witness in a statutory inquiry and not a defendant in a criminal prosecution, for it has long been settled that the privilege protects witnesses in similar federal inquiries. . . . We recently elaborated the content of the federal standard in *Hoffman* v. *United States*, 341 U.S. 479:

The privilege afforded not only extends to answers that would in themselves support a conviction . . . but likewise embraces those which would furnish a link in the chain of evidence needed to prosecute . . . if the witness, upon interposing his claim, were required to prove the hazard . . . he would be compelled to surrender the very protection which the privilege is designed to guarantee. To sustain the privilege, it need only be evident from the implications of the question, in the setting in which it is asked, that a responsive answer to the question or an explanation of why it cannot be answered might be dangerous because injurious disclosure could result. 341 U. S. at 486-487, 71 S. Ct. at 818.

We also said that, in applying that test, the judge must be

"*perfectly clear*, from a careful consideration of all the circumstances in the case, that the witness is mistaken, and that the answer[s] *cannot possibly* have such tendency" to incriminate. 341 U.S. at 488. . . .

The State of Connecticut argues that the Connecticut courts properly applied the federal standards to the facts of this case. We disagree.

The investigation in the course of which petitioner was questioned began when the Superior Court of Hartford County appointed the Honorable Ernest A. Inglis, formerly Chief Justice of Connecticut, to conduct an inquiry into whether there was reasonable cause to believe the crimes, including gambling, were being committed in Hartford County. Petitioner appeared on January 16 and 25, 1961, and in both instances he was asked substantially the same questions about the circumstances surrounding his arrest and conviction for pool-selling in late 1959. The questions which petitioner refused to answer may be summarized as follows: (1) for whom did he work on September 11, 1959; (2) who selected and paid his counsel in connection with his arrest on that date and subsequent conviction; (3) who selected and paid his bondsman; (4) who paid his fine; (5) what was the name of the tenant in the apartment in which he was arrested; and (6) did he know John Bergoti. The Connecticut Supreme Court of Errors ruled that the answers to these questions could not tend to incriminate him because the defenses of double jeopardy and the running of the one-year statute of limitations on misdemeanors would defeat any prosecution growing out of his answers to the first five questions. As for the sixth question, the court held that petitioner's failure to explain how a revelation of his relationship with Bergoti would incriminate him vitiated his claim to the protection of the privilege afforded by state law.

The conclusions of the Court of Errors, tested by the federal standard, fails to take sufficient account of the setting in which the questions were asked. The interrogation was part of a wide-ranging inquiry into crime, including gambling, in Hartford. It was admitted on behalf of the State at oral argument—and indeed it is obvious from the questions themselves —that the State desired to elicit from the petitioner the identity of the person who ran the pool-selling operation in connection with which he had been arrested in 1959. It was apparent that petitioner might apprehend that if this person were still engaged in unlawful activity, disclosure of his name might furnish a link in a chain of evidence sufficient to connect the petitioner with a more recent crime for which he might still be prosecuted.

. . .

*Reversed.*

While MR. JUSTICE DOUGLAS *joins the opinion of the Court, he also adheres to his concurrence in* Gideon v. Wainwright, *372 U.S. 335, 345.*

MR. JUSTICE HARLAN, *whom* MR. JUSTICE CLARK *joins, dissenting.*

Connecticut has adjudged this petitioner in contempt for refusing to answer questions in a state inquiry. The courts of the State, whose laws embody a privilege against self-incrimination, refused to recognize the petitioner's claim of privilege, finding that the questions asked him were not incriminatory. This Court now holds the contempt adjudication unconstitutional because, it is decided: (1) the Fourteenth Amendment makes the Fifth Amendment privilege against self-incrimination applicable to the States; (2) the federal standard justifying a claim of this privilege likewise applies to the States; and (3) judged by that standard the petitioner's claim of privilege should have been upheld.

Believing that the reasoning behind the Court's decision carries extremely mischievous, if not dangerous consequences for our federal system in the realm of criminal law enforcement, I must dissent. . . .

I can only read the Court's opinion as accepting in fact what it rejects in theory: the application to the States, via the Fourteenth Amendment, of the forms of federal criminal procedure embodied within the first eight Amendments to the Constitution. While it is true that the Court deals today with only one aspect of state criminal procedure, and rejects the wholesale "incorporation" of such federal constitutional requirements, the logical gap between the Court's premises and its novel constitutional conclusion can, I submit, be bridged only by the additional premise that the Due Process Clause of the Fourteenth Amendment is a shorthand directive to this Court to pick and choose among the provisions of the first eight amendments and apply those chosen, freighted with their entire accompanying body of federal doctrine, to law enforcement in the States.

I accept and agree with the proposition that continuing reexamination of the constitutional conception of the Fourteenth Amendment "due process" of law is required, and that development of the community's sense of justice may in time lead to expansion of the protection which due process affords. In particular in this case, I agree that principles of justice to which due process gives expression, as reflected in decisions of this Court, prohibit a State, as the Fifth Amendment prohibits the Federal Government, from imprisoning a person *solely* because he refuses to give evidence which may incriminate him under the laws of the State. I do not understand, however, how this process of re-examination, which must refer always to the guiding standard of due process of law, including, of course, reference to the particular guarantees of the Bill of Rights, can be short-circuited by the simple device of incorporating into due process, without critical examination, the whole body of law which surrounds a specific prohibition directed against the Federal Government. The consequence of such an approach to due process as it pertains to the States is inevitably disregard of all relevant differences which may exist between state and federal criminal law and its enforcement. The ultimate result is compelled uniformity, which is inconsistent with the purpose of our federal system and which is achieved either by encroachment on the States' sovereign powers or by dilution in federal law enforcement of the specific protections found in the Bill of Rights.

. . .

The Court's approach in the present case is in fact nothing more or less than "incorporation" in snatches. If, however, the Due Process Clause *is* something more than a reference to the Bill of Rights and protects only those rights which derive from fundamental principles, as the majority purports to believe, it is just as contrary to precedent and just as illogical to incorporate the provision of the Bill of Rights one at a time as it is to incorporate them all at once.

The Court's undiscriminating approach to the Due Process Clause carries serious implications for the sound working of our federal system in the field of criminal law.

The Court concludes, almost without discussion, that "the same standards must determine whether an accused's silence in either a federal or state proceeding is justified." . . . About all that the Court offers in explanation of this conclusion is the observation that it would be "incongruous" if different standards governed the assertion of a privilege to remain silent in state and federal tribunals. Such "incongruity," however, is at the heart of our federal system. The powers and responsibilities of the state and federal governments are not congruent; under our Constitution, they are not intended to be. Why should it be thought, as an *a priori* matter, that limitations on the investigative power of the States are in all respects identical with limitations on the investigative power of the Federal Government? This certainly does not follow from the fact that we deal here with constitutional requirements; for the provisions of the Constitution which are construed are different.

As the Court pointed out in *Abbate* v. *United States,* 359 U.S. 187, . . . "the States under our federal system have the principal responsibility for defining and prosecuting crimes." The Court endangers this allocation of responsibility for the prevention of crime when it applies to the States doctrines developed in the context of federal law enforcement, without any attention to the special problems which the State as a group or particular States may face. If the power of the States to deal with local crime is unduly restricted, the likely consequence is a shift of responsibility in this area to the Federal Government, with its vastly greater resources. Such a shift, if it occurs, may in the end serve to weaken the very liberties which the Fourteenth Amendment safeguards by bringing us close to the monolithic society which our federalism rejects. Equally dangerous to our liberties is the alternative of watering down protections against the Federal Government embodied in the Bill of Rights so as not unduly to restrict the powers of the States. . . .

Rather than insisting, almost by rote, that the Connecticut court, in considering the petitioner's claim of privilege, was required to apply the "federal standard," the Court should have fulfilled its responsibility under the Due Process Clause by inquiring whether the proceedings below met the demands of fundamental fairness which due process embodies. Such an approach may not satisfy those who see in the Fourteenth Amendment a set of easily applied "absolutes" which can afford a haven from unsettling doubt. It is, however, truer to the spirit which requires this Court constantly to re-examine fundamental principles and at the same time enjoins it from reading its own preferences into the Constitution.

. . .

MR. JUSTICE WHITE *wrote a brief dissent in which* MR. JUSTICE STEWART *concurred.*


# GRIFFIN v. CALIFORNIA

380 U. S. 609; 14 L. Ed. 2d 106; 85 S. Ct. 1229 (1965)


MR. JUSTICE DOUGLAS *delivered the opinion of the Court.*

Petitioner was convicted of murder in the first degree after a jury trial in the California court. He did not testify at the trial on the issue of guilt, though he did testify at the separate trial on the issue of penalty. The trial court instructed the jury on the issue of guilt stating that a defendant has a constitutional right not to testify. But it told the jury:[*]

As to any evidence or facts against him which the defendant can reasonably be expected to deny or explain because of

* Article I, Sec. 13, of the California Constitution provides in part: . . . in any criminal case, whether the defendant testifies or not, his failure to explain or to deny by his testimony and evidence or facts in the case against him may be commented upon by the court and by counsel, and may be considered by the court or the jury.

facts within his knowledge, if he does not testify or if, though he does testify, he fails to deny or explain such evidence, the jury may take that failure into consideration as tending to indicate the truth of such evidence and as indicating that among the inferences that may be reasonably drawn therefrom those unfavorable to the defendant are the more probable.

It added, however, that no such inference could be drawn as to evidence respecting which he had no knowledge. It stated that failure of a defendant to deny or explain the evidence of which he had knowledge does not create a presumption of guilt nor by itself warrant an inference of guilt nor relieve the prosecution of any of its burden of proof.

Petitioner had been seen with the deceased the evening of her death, the evidence placing him with her in the alley where her body was found. The prosecutor made much of the failure of petitioner to testify:

The defendant certainly knows whether Essie Mae had this beat up appearance at the time he left her apartment and went down the alley with her.

What kind of a man is it that would want to have sex with a woman that beat up if she was beat up at the time he left?

He would know that. He would know how she got down the alley. He would know how the blood got on the bottom of the concrete steps. He would know how long he was with her in that box. He would know whether he beat her or mistreat her. He would know whether he walked away from that place cool as a cucumber when he saw Mr. Villasenor because he was conscious of his own guilt and wanted to get away from that damaged or injured woman.

These things he has not seen fit to take the stand and deny or explain.

And in the whole world, if anybody would know, this defendant would know.

Essie Mae is dead, she can't tell you her side of the story. The defendant won't.

The death penalty was imposed and the California Supreme Court affirmed. . . . The case is here on a petition for a writ of certiorari which we granted . . . to consider the single question whether comment on the failure to testify violated the Self-Incrimination Clause of the Fifth Amendment which we made applicable to the States by the Fourteenth in *Malloy* v. *Hogan* . . . decided after the Supreme Court of California had affirmed the present conviction.

If this were a federal trial, reversible error would have been committed. *Wilson* v. *United States,* 149 U.S. 60, 13 S. Ct. 765, 37 L. Ed. 650, so holds. It is said, however, that the Wilson decision rested not on the Fifth Amendment, but on an Act of Congress. 18 U.S.C. Sec. 3481.[†] That indeed is the fact, as the opinion of the Court in the Wilson case states. . . . But that is the beginning, not the end of our inquiry. The question remains whether, statute or not, the comment rule, approved by California, violates the Fifth Amendment.

We think it does. It is in substance a rule of evidence that allows the State the privilege of tendering to the jury for its consideration the failure of the accused to testify. No formal offer of proof is made as in other situations; but the prosecutor's comment and the court's acquiescence are the equivalent of an offer of evidence and its acceptance. The Court in the Wilson case stated:

. . . the Act was framed with a due regard also to those who might prefer to rely upon the presumption of innocence which the law gives to every one, and not wish to be witnesses. It is not every one who can safely venture on the witness stand, though entirely innocent of the charge against him. Excessive timidity, nervousness when facing others and attempting to explain transactions of a suspicious character, and offenses charged against him, will often confuse and embarrass him to such a degree as to increase rather than remove prejudices against him. It is not everyone, however honest, who would therefore willingly be

† Section 3481 reads as follows:

In trial of all persons charged with the commission of offenses against the United States and in all proceedings in courts martial and courts of inquiry in any State, District, Possession or Territory, the person charged shall, at his own request, be a competent witness. His failure to make such request shall not create any presumption against him. June 25, 1948, c. 645, 62 Stat. 833.

The legislative history shows that 18 U.S.C. Sec. 3481 was designed, *inter alia,* to bar counsel for the prosecution from commenting on the defendant's refusal to testify. . . .

placed on the witness stand. The statute, in tenderness to the weakness of those who from the causes mentioned might refuse to ask to be witnesses, particularly when they may have been in some degree compromised by their association with others, declares that the failure of a defendant in a criminal action to request to be a witness shall not create any presumption against him. . . .

If the words "Fifth Amendment" are substituted for "Act" and for "statute" the spirit of the Self-Incrimination Clause is reflected. For comment on the refusal to testify is a remnant of the "inquisitorial system of criminal justice," . . . which the Fifth Amendment outlaws. It is a penalty imposed by courts for exercising a constitutional privilege. It cuts down on the privilege by making its assertion costly. It is said, however, that the inference of guilt for failure to testify as to facts particularly within the accused's knowledge is in any event natural and irresistible, and that comment on the failure does not magnify that inference into a penalty for asserting a constitutional privilege. . . . What the jury may infer given no help from the court is one thing. What they may infer when the court solemnizes the silence of the accused into evidence against him is quite another. . . .

We said in *Malloy* v. *Hogan*. . . . that "the same standards must determine whether an accused's silence in either a federal or state proceeding is justified." We take that in its literal sense and hold that the Fifth Amendment, in its direct application to the federal government and its bearing on the States by reason of the Fourteenth Amendment, forbids either comment by the prosecution on the accused's silence or instructions by the court that such silence is evidence of guilt.

*Reversed.*

The CHIEF JUSTICE *took no part in the decision of this case.*

MR. JUSTICE HARLAN, *concurring.*

. . . [G]iven last Term's decision in *Malloy* v. *Hogan,* that the Fifth Amendment applies to the States in all its refinements, I see no legitimate escape from today's decision and therefore concur in it. I do so, however, with great reluctance, since for me the decision exemplifies the creeping paralysis with which this Court's recent adoption of the "incorporation" doctrine is infecting the operation of the federal system. . . .

While I would agree that the accusatorial rather than inquisitorial process is a fundamental part of the "liberty" guaranteed by the Fourteenth Amendment, my Brother Stewart in dissent . . . fully demonstrates that the no-comment rule "might be lost, and justice still be done." . . . As a "non-fundamental" part of the Fifth Amendment . . . I would not, but for *Malloy,* apply the no-comment rule to the States. . . .

It has also recently been suggested that measuring state procedures against standards of fundamental fairness . . . "would require this Court to intervene in the state judicial process with considerable lack of predictability and with a consequent likelihood of considerable friction," *Pointer* v. *State of Texas,* 380 U.S. 400 . . . (concurring opinion of Goldberg, J.). This approach to the requirements of federalism . . . apparently leads, in cases like this, to the conclusion that the way to eliminate friction with state judicial systems is not to attempt a working harmony, but to override them altogether.

Although compelled to concur in this decision, I am free to express the hope that the Court will eventually return to constitutional paths which, until recently, it has followed throughout its history.

MR. JUSTICE STEWART, *with whom* MR. JUSTICE WHITE *joins, dissenting.*

No claim is made that the prosecutor's argument or the trial judge's instructions to the jury in this case deprived the petitioner of due process of law as such. This Court long ago decided that the Due Process Clause of the Fourteenth Amendment does not of its own force forbid this kind of comment on a defendant's failure to testify. *Twining* v. *State of New Jersey,* 211 U.S. 78 . . . ; *Adamson* v. *People of State of California,* 332 U.S. 46. . . . The Court holds, however, that the California constitutional provision violates the Fifth Amendment's injunction that no person "shall be compelled in any criminal case to be a witness against himself," an injunction which the Court less than a year ago for the first time found was applicable to trials in the courts of the several States.

With both candor and accuracy, the Court concedes that the question before us is one of first impression here. It is a question which has not arisen before, because until last year the self-incrimination provision of the Fifth Amendment had been held to apply only to federal proceedings, and in the federal judicial system the matter has been covered by a specific Act of Congress which has been in effect ever since defendants have been permitted to testify at all in federal

criminal trials. . . .

We must determine whether the petitioner has been "compelled to be a witness against himself." Compulsion is the focus of the inquiry. Certainly, if any compulsion be detected in the California procedure, it is of a dramatically different and less palpable nature than that involved in the procedures which historically gave rise to the Fifth Amendment guarantee. When a suspect was brought before the Court of the High Commission or the Star Chamber, he was commanded to answer whatever was asked of him, and subjected to a far-reaching and deeply probing inquiry in an effort to ferret out some unknown and frequently unsuspected crime. He declined to answer on pain of incarceration, banishment, or mutilation. And if he spoke falsely, he was subject to further punishment. Faced with this formidable array of alternatives, his decision to speak was unquestionably coerced.

Those were the lurid realities which lay behind enactment of the Fifth Amendment, a far cry from the subject matter of the case before us. I think that the Court in this case stretches the concept of compulsion beyond all reasonable bounds, and that whatever compulsion may exist derives from the defendant's choice not to testify, not from any comment by court or counsel. In support of its conclusion that the California procedure does compel the accused to testify, the Court has only this to say: "It is a penalty imposed by courts for exercising a constitutional privilege. It cuts down on the privilege by making its assertion costly." Exactly what the penalty imposed consists of is not clear. It is not, as I understand the problem, that the jury becomes aware that the defendant has chosen not to testify in his own defense, for the jury will, of course, realize this quite evident fact, even though the choice goes unmentioned. Since comment by counsel and the court does not compel testimony by creating such an awareness, the Court must be saying that the California constitutional provision places some other compulsion upon the defendant to incriminate himself, some compulsion which the Court does not describe and which I cannot readily perceive.

It is not at all apparent to me, on any realistic view of the trial process, that a defendant will be at more of a disadvantage under the California practice than he would be in a court which permitted no comment at all on his failure to take the witness stand. How can it be said that the inferences drawn by a jury will be more detrimental to a defendant under the limiting and carefully controlling language of the instruction here involved than would result if the jury were left to roam at large with only their untutored instincts to guide them, to draw from the defendant's silence broad inferences of guilt? The instructions in this case expressly cautioned the jury that the defendant's failure to testify "does not create a presumption of guilt or by itself warrant an inference of guilt"; they were further admonished that such failure does not "relieve the prosecution of its burden of proving every essential element of the crime," and finally the trial judge warned that the prosecution's burden remained that of proof "beyond a reasonable doubt." Whether the same limitations would be observed by a jury without the benefit of protective instructions shielding the defendant is certainly open to real doubt.

Moreover, no one can say where the balance of advantage might lie as a result of counsels' discussion of the matter. No doubt the prosecution's argument will seek to encourage the drawing of inferences unfavorable to the defendant. However, the defendant's counsel equally has an opportunity to explain the various other reasons why a defendant may not wish to take the stand, and thus rebut the natural if uneducated assumption that it is because the defendant cannot truthfully deny the accusations made.

I think the California comment rule is not a coercive device which impairs the right against self-incrimination, but rather a means of articulating and bringing into the light of rational discussion a fact inescapably impressed on the jury's consciousness. The California procedure is not only designed to protect the defendant against unwarranted inferences which might be drawn by an uninformed jury; it is also an attempt by the State to recognize and articulate what it believes to be the natural probative force of certain facts. Surely no one would deny that the State has an important interest in throwing the light of rational discussion on that which transpires in the course of a trial, both to protect the defendant from the very real dangers of silence and to shape a legal process designed to ascertain the truth.

The California rule allowing comment by counsel and instruction by the judge on the defendant's failure to take the stand is hardly an idiosyncratic aberration. The Model Code of Evidence, and the Uniform Rules of Evidence both sanction the use of such procedures. The practice had been endorsed by resolution of the American Bar Association, and has the support of the weight of scholarly opinion.

The formulation of procedural rules to govern the administration of criminal justice in the various States is properly a matter of local concern. . . . California has honored the constitutional command that no person "shall be compelled in any criminal case to be a witness against himself." The petitioner was not compelled to testify, and he did not do so. But whenever in a jury trial a defendant exercises this constitutional right, the members of the jury are bound to draw inferences from his silence. No constitution can prevent the operation of the human mind. . . . Some might differ, as a matter of policy, with the way California has chosen to deal with the problem, or even disapprove of the judge's specific instructions in this case. But, so long as the constitutional command is obeyed, such matters of state policy are not for this Court to decide.

I would affirm the judgment.

## GIDEON v. WAINWRIGHT

### 372 U. S. 335; 9 L. Ed. 2d 799; 83 S. Ct. 792 (1963)

MR. JUSTICE BLACK *delivered the opinion of the Court.*

Petitioner was charged in a Florida state court with having broken and entered a poolroom with intent to commit a misdemeanor. This offense is a felony under Florida law. Appearing in court without funds and without a lawyer, petitioner asked the court to appoint counsel for him, whereupon the following colloquy took place:

"The Court: Mr. Gideon, I am sorry, but I cannot appoint Counsel to represent you in this case. Under the laws of the State of Florida, the only time the Court can appoint Counsel to represent a Defendant is when that person is charged with a capital offense. I am sorry, but I will have to deny your request to appoint Counsel to defend you in this case."

"The Defendant: The United States Supreme Court says I am entitled to be represented by Counsel."

Put to trial before a jury, Gideon conducted his defense about as well as could be expected from a layman. He made an opening statement to the jury, cross-examined the State's witnesses, presented witnesses in his own defense, declined to testify himself, and made a short argument "emphasizing his innocence to the charge contained in the Information filed in this case." The jury returned a verdict of guilty, and petitioner was sentenced to serve five years in the state prison. Later, petitioner filed in the Florida Supreme Court this habeas corpus petition attacking his conviction and sentence on the ground that the trial court's refusal to appoint counsel for him denied him rights "guaranteed by the Constitution and the Bill of Rights by the United States Government." . . . [T]he State Supreme Court, "upon consideration thereof" but without an opinion, denied all relief. . . .

The facts upon which Betts claimed that he had been unconstitutionally denied the right to have counsel appointed to assist him are strikingly like the facts upon which Gideon here bases his federal constitutional claim. Betts was indicted for robbery in a Maryland state court. In arraignment, he told the trial judge of his lack of funds to hire a lawyer and asked the court to appoint one for him. Betts was advised that it was not the practice in that county to appoint counsel for indigent defendants except in murder and rape cases. He then pleaded not guilty, had witnesses summoned, cross-examined the State's witnesses, examined his own, and chose not to testify himself. He was found guilty by the judge, sitting without a jury, and sentenced to eight years in prison. Like Gideon, Betts sought release by habeas corpus, alleging that he had been denied the right to assistance of counsel in violation of the Fourteenth Amendment. Betts was denied any relief, and on review this Court affirmed. It was held that a refusal to appoint counsel for an indigent defendant charged with a felony did not necessarily violate the "due process" clause of the Fourteenth Amendment, which for reasons given the Court deemed to be the only applicable federal constitutional provision. The Court said:

Asserting denial [of due process] is to be tested by an appraisal of the totality of facts in a given case. That which may, in one setting, constitute a denial of fundamental fairness, shocking to the universal sense of justice, may, in other circumstances, and in the light of other considerations, fall short of such denial. (316 U. S., at 462).

Treating due process as "a concept less rigid and more fluid than those envisaged in other specific and particular provisions of the Bill of Rights," the Court held that refusal to appoint counsel under the particular facts and circumstances in the *Betts* case was not so "offensive to the common and fundamental ideas of fairness" as to amount to a denial of due process.

Since the facts and circumstances of the two cases are so nearly indistinguishable, we think the *Betts* v. *Brady* holding if left standing would require us to reject Gideon's claim that the Constitution guarantees him the assistance of counsel. Upon full reconsideration we conclude that *Betts* v. *Brady* should be overruled.

The Sixth Amendment provides, "In all criminal prosecutions, the accused shall enjoy the right . . . to have the Assistance of Counsel for his defense." We have construed this to mean that in federal courts counsel must be provided for defendants unable to employ counsel unless the right is competently and intelligently waived. (*Johnson* v. *Zerbst,* 304 U.S. 458, 1958.) Betts argued that this right is extended to indigent defendants in state courts by the Fourteenth Amendment. In response the Court stated that, while the Sixth Amendment laid down "no rule for the conduct of the states, the question recurs whether the constraint laid by the amendment upon the national courts expresses a rule so fundamental and essential to a fair trial, and so, to due process of law, that it is made obligatory upon the states by the Fourteenth Amendment." (316 U.S., at 465.) In order to decide whether the Sixth Amendment's guarantee of counsel is of this fundamental nature, the Court in *Betts* set out and considered "relevant data on the subject . . . afforded by constitutional and statutory provisions subsisting in the colonies and the states prior to the inclusion of the Bill of Rights in the national Constitution, and in the constitutional, legislative, and judicial history of the states to the present." (316 U.S., 471.) It was for this reason the *Betts* Court refused to accept the contention that the Sixth

Amendment's guarantee of counsel for indigent federal defendants was extended to, or, in the words of that court, "made obligatory upon the states by the Fourteenth Amendment." Plainly, had the Court concluded that appointment of counsel for an indigent criminal defendant was "a fundamental right, essential to a fair trial," it would have held that the Fourteenth Amendment requires appointment of counsel in a state court, just as the Sixth Amendment requires a federal court.

We think the Court in *Betts* had ample precedent for acknowledging that those guarantees of the Bill of Rights which are fundamental safeguards of liberty immune from federal abridgment are equally protected against state invasion by the "due process" clause of the Fourteenth Amendment. This same principle was recognized, explained, and applied in *Powell* v. *Alabama,* 287 U.S. 45 (1932), a case upholding the right of counsel, where the Court held that despite sweeping language to the contrary in *Hurtado* v. *California,* 110 U.S. 516 (1884), the Fourteenth Amendment "embraced" those "fundamental principles of liberty and justice which lie at the base of all our civil and political institutions," even though they had been "specifically dealt with in another part of the federal Constitution." (287 U.S., at 67.) In many cases other than *Powell* and *Betts,* this Court has looked to the fundamental nature of the original Bill of Rights guarantees to decide whether the Fourteenth Amendment makes them obligatory on the states. Explicitly recognized to be of this "fundamental nature" and therefore made immune from state invasion by the Fourteenth, or some part of it, are the First Amendment's freedoms of speech, press, religion,

assembly, association, and petition for redress of grievances. For the same reason, though not always in precisely the same terminology, the Court has made obligatory on the states the Fifth Amendment's command that private property shall not be taken for public use without just compensation, the Fourth Amendment's prohibition of unreasonable searches and seizures, and the Eighth's ban on cruel and unusual punishment. On the other hand, this Court in *Palko* v. *Connecticut,* 302 U.S. 319 (1937), refused to hold that the Fourteenth Amendment made the double jeopardy provision of the Fifth Amendment obligatory on the states. In so far as refusing, however, the court, speaking through Mr. Justice Cardozo, was careful to emphasize that "immunities that are valid against the federal government by force of the specific pledges of particular amendments have been found to be implicit in the concept of ordered liberty, and thus, through the Fourteenth Amendment, become valid as against the states" and that guarantees "in their origin . . . effective against the federal government alone" had by prior cases "been taken over from the earlier articles of the Federal Bill of Rights and brought within the Fourteenth Amendment by a process of absorption." (302 U.S., at 324–325, 326.)

We accept *Betts* v. *Brady's* assumption, based as it was on our prior cases, that a provision of the Bill of Rights which is "fundamental and essential to a fair trial" is made obligatory upon the states by the Fourteenth Amendment. We think the Court in *Betts* was wrong, however, in concluding that the Sixth Amendment's guarantee of counsel is not one of these fundamental rights. Ten years before *Betts* v. *Brady,* this

Court, after full consideration of all historical data examined in *Betts,* had unequivocally declared that "the right to the aid of counsel is of this fundamental character." *Powell* v. *Alabama,* 287 U.S. 45, 68 (1932). While the Court at the close of its *Powell* opinion did by its language, as it frequently does, limit its holding to the particular facts and circumstances of that case, its conclusions about the fundamental nature of the right to counsel are unmistakable. Several years later, in 1936, the Court re-emphasized what it had said about the fundamental nature of the right to counsel in this language:

We concluded that certain fundamental rights, safeguarded by the first eight amendments against federal action, were also safeguarded against state action by the due process clause of the Fourteenth Amendment, and among them the fundamental right of the accused to the aid of counsel in a criminal prosecution. *Grossjean* v. *American Press Co.,* 297 U. S. 233, 243-244 (1936).

And again in 1938 this Court said:

[The assistance of counsel] is one of the safeguards of the Sixth Amendment deemed necessary to insure fundamental human rights of life and liberty. . . . The Sixth Amendment stands as a constant admonition that if the constitutional safeguards it provides be lost, justice will not "still be done." *Johnson* v. *Zerbst,* 304 U. S. 458, 462 (1938). . . .

In the light of these and many other prior decisions of this Court, it is not surprising that the *Betts* Court, when faced with the contention that "one charged with crime, who is unable to obtain counsel, must be furnished counsel by the state," conceded that "expressions in the opinions of this court lend color to the argument . . ." 316 U.S., at 462–463. The fact is that in deciding as it did—that "appointment of counsel

is not a fundamental right, essential to a fair trial"—the Court in *Betts* v. *Brady* made an abrupt break with its own well-considered precedents. In returning to these old precedents, sounder we believe than the new, we but restore constitutional principles established to achieve a fair system of justice. Not only these precedents but also reason and reflection require us to recognize that in our adversary system of criminal justice, any person haled into court, who is too poor to hire a lawyer, cannot be assured a fair trial unless counsel is provided for him. This seems to us to be an obvious truth. Governments, both state and federal, quite properly spend vast sums of money to establish machinery to try defendants accused of crime. Lawyers to prosecute are everywhere deemed essential to protect the public's interest in an orderly society. Similarly, there are few defendants charged with crime, few, indeed, who fail to hire the best lawyers they can get to prepare and present their defenses. That government hires lawyers to prosecute and defendants who have the money to hire lawyers to defend are the strongest indications of a widespread belief that lawyers in criminal courts are necessities, not luxuries. The right of one charged with crime to counsel may not be deemed fundamental and essential to fair trials in some countries, but it is in ours. From the very beginning, our state and national constitutions and laws have laid great emphasis on procedural and substantive safeguards designed to assure fair trials before impartial tribunals in which every defendant stands equal before the law. This noble ideal cannot be realized if the poor man charged with crime has to face his accusers without a lawyer to assist him. A defendant's need for a lawyer is nowhere better stated than in the moving words of Mr. Justice Sutherland in *Powell* v. *Alabama*:

The right to be heard would be, in many cases, of little avail if it did not comprehend the right to be heard by counsel. Even the intelligent and educated layman has small and sometimes no skill in the science of law. If charged with crime, he is incapable, generally, of determining for himself whether the indictment is good or bad. He is unfamiliar with the rules of evidence. Left without the aid of counsel he may be put on trial without a proper charge, and convicted upon incompetent evidence, or evidence irrelevant to the issue or otherwise inadmissible. He lacks both the skill and knowledge adequately to prepare his defense, even though he have a perfect one. He requires the guiding hand of counsel at every step in the proceedings against him. Without it, though he be not guilty, he faces the danger of conviction because he does not know how to establish his innocence. 287 U.S., at 68–69.

The Court in *Betts* v. *Brady* departed from the sound wisdom upon which the Court's holding in *Powell* v. *Alabama* rested. Florida, supported by two other states, asked that *Betts* v. *Brady* be left intact. Twenty-two states, as friends of the Court, argue that *Betts* was "an anachronism when handed down" and that it should now be overruled. We agree.

> *The Judgment is reversed and the cause is remanded to the Supreme Court of Florida for further action not inconsistent with this opinion.*

MR. JUSTICE CLARK, *concurring.*

I must conclude . . . that the Constitution makes no distinction between capital and noncapital cases. The Fourteenth Amendment requires due process of law for the deprivation of "liberty" just as for deprivation of "life,"

and there cannot constitutionally be a difference in the sanction involved. How can the Fourteenth Amendment tolerate a procedure which it condemns in capital cases on the ground that deprivation of liberty may be less onerous than deprivation of life—a value judgment not universally accepted—or that only the latter deprivation is irrevocable? I can find no acceptable rationalization for such a result, and I therefore concur in the judgment of the Court.

MR. JUSTICE HARLAN, *concurring.*

I agree that *Betts* v. *Brady* should be overruled, but consider it entitled to a more respectful burial than has been accorded, at least on the part of those of us who were not on the Court when that case was decided.

I cannot subscribe to the view that *Betts* v. *Brady* represented "an abrupt break with its own well-considered precedents." . . . The principles declared in *Powell* and *Betts* . . . had a troubled journey throughout the years that have followed first the one case and then the other. Even by the time of the *Betts* decision, dictum in at least one of the Court's opinions had indicated that there was an absolute right to the services of counsel in the trial of state capital cases. "Such dicta continued to appear in subsequent decisions" and any lingering doubts were finally eliminated by the holding of *Hamilton* v. *Alabama*, 368 U.S. 52.

In noncapital cases, the "special circumstances" rule has continued to exist in form while its substance has been substantially and steadily eroded. . . . The Court has come to recognize, in other words, that the mere existence of a serious criminal charge constituted in itself special circumstances requiring the services of counsel at trial. In truth the *Betts v. Brady* rule is no longer a reality.

This evolution, however, appears not to have been fully recognized by many state courts, in this instance charged with the front-line responsibility for the enforcement of constitutional rights. . . . To continue a rule which is honored by this Court only with lip service is not a healthy thing and in the long rule will do disservice to the federal system.

The special circumstances rule has been formally abandoned in capital cases, and the time has now come when it should be abandoned in noncapital cases, at least as to offenses which, as the one involved here, carry the possibility of a substantial prison sentence. (Whether the rule should extend to all criminal cases need not be decided.) This indeed does no more than to make explicit something that has long since been foreshadowed in our decisions.

In agreeing with the Court that the right to counsel in a case such as this should now be expressly recognized as a fundamental right embraced in the Fourteenth Amendment, I wish to make a further observation. When we hold a right or immunity, valid against the Federal Government, to be "implicit in the concept of ordered liberty" and thus valid against the States, I do not read our past decisions to suggest that by so holding, we automatically carry over an entire body of federal law and apply it in full sweep to the States. Any such concept would disregard the frequently wide disparity between the legitimate interests of the States and of the Federal Government, the divergent problems that they face, and the significantly different consequences of their actions. . . . In what is done today I do not understand the Court to depart from the principles laid down in *Palko* v. *Connecticut* . . . or to embrace the concept that the Fourteenth Amendment "incorporates" the Sixth Amendment as such.

On these premises I join in the judgment of the Court.

## *ESCOBEDO v. STATE OF ILLINOIS*

378 U. S. 478; 12 L. Ed. 2d 974; 84 S. Ct. 1758 (1964)

MR. JUSTICE GOLDBERG *delivered the opinion of the Court.*

The critical question in this case is whether, under the circumstances, the refusal by the police to honor petitioner's request to consult with his lawyer during the course of an interrogation constitutes a denial of "the Assistance of Counsel" in violation of the Sixth Amendment to the Constitution as "made obligatory upon the States by the Fourteenth Amendment," *Gideon* v. *Wainwright*, 372 U.S. 335, 342, 83 S.Ct. 792, 795, 9 L. Ed. 2d 799, and thereby renders inadmissible in a state criminal trial any incriminating statement elicited by the police during the interrogation.

On the night of January 19, 1960, petitioner's brother-in-law was fatally shot. At 2:30 A.M. that morning, petitioner was arrested without a warrant and interrogated. Petitioner made no statement to the police and was released at 5 P.M. that afternoon pursuant to a state court writ of habeas corpus obtained by . . . a lawyer who had been retained by petitioner.

On January 30, Benedict DiGerlando, who was then in police custody and who was later indicted for the murder along with petitioner, told the police that petitioner had fired the fatal shots. Between 8 and 9 P.M. that evening, petitioner and his sister, the widow of the deceased, were arrested and taken to police headquarters. En route to the police station, the police "had handcuffed the defendant behind his back," and "one of the arresting officers, told defendant that DiGerlando had named him as the one who shot" the deceased. Petitioner testified, without contradiction, that the "detectives said they had us pretty well, up pretty tight, and we might as well admit to this crime," and that he replied, "I am sorry but I would like to have advice from my lawyer." A police officer testified that although petitioner was not formally charged "he was in custody" and "couldn't walk out the door."

Shortly after petitioner reached police headquarters, his retained lawyer arrived. The lawyer described the ensuing events in the following terms:

"On that day I received a phone call [from "the mother of another defendant"] and pursuant to that phone call I went to the Detective Bureau at 11th and State. The first person I talked to was the Sergeant on duty at the Bureau Desk, Sergeant Pidgeon. I asked Sergeant Pidgeon for permission to speak to my client, Danny Escobedo. . . . Sergeant Pidgeon made a call to the Bureau lockup and informed me that the boy had been taken from the lockup to the Homicide Bureau. This was between 9:30 and 10:00 in the evening. Before I went anywhere, he called the Homicide Bureau and told them there was an attorney waiting to see Escobedo. He told me that I could not

see him. Then I went upstairs to the Homicide Bureau. There were several Homicide Detectives around and I talked to them. I identified myself as Escobedo's attorney and asked permission to see him. They said I could not. . . . The police officers told me to see Chief Flynn who was on duty. I identified myself to Chief Flynn and asked permission to see my client. He said I could not. . . . I think it was approximately 11:00 o'clock. He said I couldn't see him because they hadn't completed questioning. . . . [F]or a second or two I spotted him in an office in the Homicide Bureau. The door was open and I could see through the office. . . . I waved to him and he waved back and then the door was closed by one of the officers at Homicide.* There were four or five officers milling around the Homicide Detail that night. As to whether I talked to Captain Flynn any later that day, I waited around for another hour or two and went back again and renewed by (sic) request to see my client. He again told me I could not. . . . I filed an official complaint with Commissioner Phelan of the Chicago Police Department. I had a conversation with every officer I could find. I was told at Homicide that I couldn't see him and I would have to get a writ of habeas corpus. I left the Homicide Bureau and from the Detective Bureau at 11th and State at approximately 1:00 A.M. [Sunday morning] I had no opportunity to talk to my client that night. I quoted to Captain Flynn the Section of the Criminal Code which allows an attorney the right to see his client."†

* Petitioner testified that this ambiguous gesture "could have meant most anything," but that he "took it upon [his] own to think that [the lawyer was telling him] not to say anything," and that the lawyer "wanted to talk" to him.

† The statute then in effect provided in pertinent part that: All public officers . . . having the custody of any person . . . restrained of his liberty for any alleged cause whatever, shall, except in cases of imminent danger of escape, admit any practicing attorney . . . whom such person . . . may desire to see or consult. . . ." Ill. Rev. Stat. (1959), c. 38, par. 477. . . .

Petitioner testified that during the course of the interrogation he repeatedly asked to speak to his lawyer and that the police said that his lawyer "didn't want to see" him. The testimony of the police officers confirmed these accounts in substantial detail.

Notwithstanding repeated requests by each, petitioner and his retained lawyer were afforded no opportunity to consult during the course of the entire interrogation. . . . Petitioner testified "that he heard a detective telling the attorney that the latter would not be allowed to talk to [him], 'until they were done'" and that he heard the attorney being refused permission to remain in the adjoining room. A police officer testified that he had told the lawyer that he could not see petitioner until "we were through interrogating" him.

There is testimony by the police that during the interrogation, petitioner, a 22-year-old of Mexican extraction with no record of previous experience with the police, "was handcuffed" in a standing position and that he "was nervous, he had circles under his eyes and he was upset" and was "agitated" because "he had not slept well in over a week."

It is undisputed that during the course of the interrogation Officer Montejano, who "grew up" in petitioner's neighborhood, who knew his family, and who uses "Spanish language in [his] police work," conferred alone with petitioner "for about a quarter of an hour. . . ." Petitioner testified that the officer said to him "in Spanish that my sister and I could go home if I pinned it on Benedict DiGerlando," that "he would see to it that we would go home and be held only as witnesses, if anything, if we had made a statement against

DiGerlando . . . , that we would be able to go home that night." Petitioner testified that he made the statement in issue because of this assurance. Officer Montejano denied offering any such assurance.

A police officer testified that during the interrogation the following occurred:

I informed him of what DiGerlando told me and when I did, he told me that DiGerlando was [lying] and I said, "Would you care to tell DiGerlando that?" And he said, "Yes, I will." So I brought . . . Escobedo in and he confronted DiGerlando and he told him that he was lying and said, "I didn't shoot Manuel, you did it."

In this way, petitioner, for the first time admitted to some knowledge of the crime. After that he made additional statements further implicating himself in the murder plot. At this point an Assistant State's Attorney . . . was summoned "to take" a statement. . . . [He] "took" petitioner's statement by asking carefully framed questions apparently designed to assure the admissibility into evidence of the resulting answers. [The Assistant State's Attorney] testified that he did not advise petitioner of his constitutional rights, and it is undisputed that no one during the course of the interrogation so advised him.

Petitioner moved both before and during trial to suppress the incriminating statement, but the motions were denied. Petitioner was convicted of murder and he appealed the conviction.

The Supreme Court of Illinois, in its original opinion . . . held the statement inadmissible and reversed the conviction. . . . The State petitioned for, and the court granted, rehearing. The court then affirmed the conviction. It said: "[T]he officer denied making the promise and the trier of fact believed him. We find no reason for disturbing the trial court's finding that the confession was voluntary." . . .

In *Massiah* v. *United States,* 377 U.S. 201, . . . this Court observed that "a Constitution which guarantees a defendant the aid of counsel at . . . trial could surely vouchsafe no less to an indicted defendant under interrogation by the police in a completely extra-judicial proceeding. Anything less . . . might deny a defendant 'effective representation by counsel at the only stage when legal aid and advice would help him.' " . . .

The interrogation here was conducted before petitioner was formally indicted. But in the context of this case, that fact should make no difference. When petitioner requested, and was denied, an opportunity to consult with his lawyer, the investigation had ceased to be a general investigation of "an unsolved crime." . . . Petitioner had become the accused, and the purpose of the interrogation was to "get him" to confess his guilt despite his constitutional right not to do so. At the time of his arrest and throughout the course of the interrogation, the police told petitioner that they had convincing evidence that he had fired the fatal shots. Without informing him of his absolute right to remain silent in the face of this accusation, the police urged him to make a statement. . . . Petitioner, a layman, was undoubtedly unaware that under Illinois law an admission of "mere" complicity in the murder plot was legally as damaging as an admission of firing of the fatal shots. . . . The "guiding hand of counsel" was essential to advise petitioner of his rights in this delicate situation. . . . This was the "stage when legal aid and advice" were most critical to petitioner. . . . What happened at this interrogation could certainly "affect the whole trial," . . . since rights "may be as irretrievably lost, if not then and there asserted, as they are when an accused represented by counsel waives a right for strategic purposes." It would exalt form over substance to make the right to counsel, under these circumstances, depend on whether at the time of the interrogation, the authorities had secured a formal indictment. Petitioner had, for all practical purposes, already been charged with murder.

. . .

In *Gideon* v. *Wainwright,* . . . we held that every person accused of a crime, whether state or federal, is entitled to a lawyer at trial. The rule sought by the State here, however, would make the trial no more than an appeal from the interrogation; and the "right to use counsel at the formal trial [would be] a very hollow thing [if], for all practical purposes, the conviction is already assured by pretrial examination." In re Groban, 352 U.S. 330, 334, . . . (Black, J., dissenting),‡ "one can imagine a cynical prosecutor saying: 'Let them have the most illustrious counsel, now. They can't escape the noose. There is nothing that counsel can do for them at trial.' " Ex parte Sullivan, D.C., 107 F. Supp. 514, 517–518.

It is argued that if the right to

‡ The Soviet criminal code does not permit a lawyer to be present during the investigation. The Soviet trial has thus been aptly described as "an appeal from the pretrial investigation." Feifer, *Justice in Moscow* (1964), 86.

counsel is afforded prior to indictment, the number of confessions obtained by the police will diminish significantly, because most confessions are obtained during the period between arrest and indictment, and "any lawyer worth his salt will tell the suspect in no uncertain terms to make no statement to police under any circumstances." *Watts* v. *Indiana,* 338 U.S. 49, 50. . . . This argument, of course, cuts two ways. The fact that many confessions are obtained during this period points up its critical nature as a "stage when legal aid and advice" are surely needed. . . . The right to counsel would indeed be hollow if it began at a period when few confessions were obtained. There is necessarily a direct relationship between the importance of a stage to the police in their quest for a confession and the criticalness of that stage to the accused in his need for legal advice. Our Constitution, unlike some others, strikes the balance in favor of the right of the accused to be advised by his lawyer of his privilege against self-incrimination. . . .

We have learned the lesson of history, ancient and modern, that a system of criminal law enforcement which comes to depend on the "confession" will, in the long run, be less reliable and more subject to abuses than a system which depends on extrinsic evidence independently secured through skillful investigation. . . . This Court also has recognized that "history amply shows that confessions have often been extorted to save law enforcement officials the trouble and effort of obtaining valid and independent evidence. . . ." *Haynes* v. *Washington,* 373 U.S. 503, 519. . . .

We have also learned the companion lesson of history that no system of criminal justice can, or should, survive if it comes to depend for its continued effectiveness on the citizens' abdication through unawareness of their constitutional rights. No system worth preserving should have to *fear* that if an accused is permitted to consult with a lawyer, he will become aware of, and exercise, these rights. If the exercise of constitutional rights will thwart the effectiveness of a system of law enforcement, then there is something very wrong with that system.

We hold, therefore, that where, as here, the investigation is no longer a general inquiry into an unsolved crime but has begun to focus on a particular suspect, the suspect has been taken into police custody, the police carry out a process of interrogations that lends itself to eliciting incriminating statements, the suspect has requested and been denied an opportunity to consult with his lawyer, and the police have not effectively warned him of his absolute constitutional right to remain silent, the accused has been denied "the Assistance of Counsel" in violation of the Sixth Amendment to the Constitution as "made obligatory upon the States by the Fourteenth Amendment," *Gideon* v. *Wainwright, 372* U.S., at 342, . . . and that no statement elicited by the police during the interrogation may be used against him at a criminal trial.

. . .

Nothing we have said today affects the powers of the police to investigate "an unsolved crime," . . . by gathering information from witnesses and by other "proper investigative efforts." . . . We hold only that when the process shifts from investigatory to accusatory—when its focus is on the accused and its purpose is to elicit a confession—our adversary system begins to operate, and, under the circumstances here, the accused must be permitted to consult with his lawyer.

The judgment of the Illinois Supreme Court is reversed and the case remanded for proceedings not inconsistent with this opinion.

*Reversed and remanded.*

MR. JUSTICE HARLAN, *dissenting.*

I would affirm the judgment of the Supreme Court of Illinois on the basis of *Cicenia* v. *La Gay,* 357 U.S. 504. . . . Like my Brother White, . . . I think the rule announced today is most ill-conceived and that it seriously and unjustifiably fetters perfectly legitimate methods of criminal law enforcement.

MR. JUSTICE STEWART, *dissenting.*
. . .
*Massiah* v. *United States* . . . is not in point here. In that case a federal grand jury had indicted Massiah. He had retained a lawyer and entered a formal plea of not guilty. Under our system of federal justice an indictment and arraignment are followed by a trial, at which the Sixth Amendment guarantees the defendant the assistance of counsel. But Massiah was released on bail, and thereafter agents of the Federal Government deliberately elicited incriminating statements from him in the absence of his lawyer. We held that the use of these statements against him at his trial denied him the basic protections of the Sixth Amendment guarantee. Putting to one side the fact that the case now before us is not a federal case, the vital fact remains that this case does not involve the deliberate interrogation of a defendant after the initiation of judicial proceedings against him. The

Court disregards this basic difference between the present case and Massiah's, with the bland assertion that "that fact should make no difference." . . .

It is "that factor," I submit, which makes all the difference. Under our system of criminal justice the institution of formal, meaningful judicial proceedings, by way of indictment, information, or arraignment, marks the point at which a criminal investigation has ended and adversary litigative proceedings have commenced. It is at this point that the constitutional guarantees attach which pertain to a criminal trial. . . .

The confession which the Court today holds inadmissible was a voluntary one. It was given during the course of a perfectly legitimate police investigation of an unsolved murder. The Court says that what happened during this investigation "affected" the trial. I had always supposed that the whole purpose of a police investigation of a murder was to "affect" the trial of the murderer, and that it would be only an incompetent, unsuccessful, or corrupt investigation which would not do so. The Court further says that the Illinois police officers did not advise the petitioner of his "constitutional rights" before he confessed to the murder. This Court has never held that the Constitution requires the police to give any "advice" under circumstances such as these. . . .

. . . [T]he Court today converts a routine police investigation of an unsolved murder into a distorted analogue of a judicial trial. It imports into this investigation constitutional concepts historically applicable only after the onset of formal prosecutorial proceedings. By doing so, I think the Court perverts those precious constitutional guarantees, and frustrates the vital interests of society in preserving the legitimate and proper function of honest and purposeful police investigation.

Like my Brother Clark, I cannot escape the logic of my Brother White's conclusions as to the extraordinary implications which emanate from the Court's opinion in this case, and I share their views as to the untold and highly unfortunate impact today's decision may have upon the fair administration of criminal justice. I can only hope we have completely misunderstood what the Court has said.

MR. JUSTICE WHITE, *with whom* MR. JUSTICE CLARK *and* MR. JUSTICE STEWART *join, dissenting.*

In *Massiah* v. *United States* . . . the Court held that as of the date of the indictment the prosecution is disentitled to secure admissions from the accused. The Court now moves that date back to the time when the prosecution begins to "focus" on the accused. Although the opinion purports to be limited to the facts of this case, it would be naive to think that the new constitutional right announced will depend upon whether the accused has retained his own counsel . . . or has asked to consult with counsel in the course of interrogation. . . . At the very least the Court holds that once the accused becomes a suspect and, presumably, is arrested, any admission made to the police thereafter is inadmissible in evidence unless the accused has waived his right to counsel. The decision is thus another major step in the direction of the goal which the Court seemingly has in mind—to bar from evidence all admissions obtained from an individual suspected of crime, whether involuntarily made or not. It

does of course put us one step "ahead" of the English judges who have had the good sense to leave the matter a discretionary one with the trial court. I reject this step and the invitation to go farther which the Court has now issued.

By abandoning the voluntary-involuntary test for admissibility of confessions, the Court seems driven by the notion that it is uncivilized law enforcement to use an accused's own admissions against him at his trial. It attempts to find a home for this new and nebulous rule of due process by attaching it to the right to counsel guaranteed in the federal system by the Sixth Amendment and binding upon the States by virtue of the due process guarantee of the Fourteenth Amendment. . . . The right to counsel now not only entitles the accused to counsel's advice and aid in preparing for trial but stands as an impenetrable barrier to any interrogation once the accused has become a suspect. From that very moment apparently his right to counsel attaches, a rule wholly unworkable and impossible to administer unless police cars are equipped with public defenders and undercover agents and police informants have defense counsel at their side. . . . Under this new approach one might just as well argue that a potential defendant is constitutionally entitled to a lawyer before, not after, he commits a crime, since it is then that crucial incriminating evidence is put within the reach of the government by the would be accused. Until now there simply has been no right guaranteed by the Federal Constitution to be free from the use at trial of a voluntary admission made prior to indictment.

It is incongruous to assume that the provision for counsel in the Sixth

Amendment was meant to amend or supersede the self-incrimination provision of the Fifth Amendment, which is now applicable to the States. . . . That amendment addresses itself to the very issues of incriminating admissions of an accused and resolves it by proscribing only compelled statements. Neither the Framers, the constitutional language, [nor] a century of decisions of this Court . . . provide an iota of support for the idea that an accused has an absolute constitutional right not to answer even in the absence of compulsion—the constitutional right not to incriminate himself by making voluntary disclosures.

. . .

. . . It might be appropriate for a legislature to provide that a suspect should not be consulted during a criminal investigation; that an accused never be called before a grand jury to answer, even if he wants to, what may well be incriminating questions; and that no person, whether he be a suspect, guilty criminal or innocent bystander should be put to the ordeal of responding to orderly non-compulsory inquiry by the State. But this is not the system our Constitution requires. The only "inquisitions" the Constitution forbids are those which compel incrimination. Escobedo's statements were not compelled and the Court does not hold that they were.

This new American judge's rule, which is to be applied in both federal and state courts, is perhaps thought to be a necessary safeguard against the possibility of extorted confessions.

To this extent it reflects a deep seated distrust of law enforcement officers everywhere, unsupported by relevant data or current material based upon our own experience. Obviously law enforcement officers can make mistakes and exceed their authority, as today's decision shows that even judges can do, but I have somewhat more faith than the Court evidently has in the ability and desire of prosecutors and of the power of the appellate courts to discern and correct such violations of the law.

The Court may be concerned with a narrower matter; the unknowing defendant who responds to police questioning because he mistakenly believes that he must and that his admissions will not be used against him. But this worry hardly calls for the broadside the Court has now fired. The failure to inform an accused that he need not answer and that his answers may be used against him is very relevant indeed to whether the disclosures are compelled. . . . But, in this case Danny Escobedo knew full well that he need not answer and knew full well that his lawyer had advised him not to answer.

I do not suggest for a moment that law enforcement will be destroyed by the rule announced today. The need for peace and order is too insistent for that. But it will be crippled and its task made a great deal more difficult, all in my opinion, for unsound, unstated reasons, which can find no home in any of the provisions of the Constitution.

# MIRANDA v. ARIZONA

384 U. S. 436; 16 L. Ed. 2d 694; 86 S. Ct. 1602 (1966)*

MR. CHIEF JUSTICE WARREN *delivered the opinion of the Court.*

The cases before us raise questions which go to the roots of our concepts of American criminal jurisprudence: the restraints society must observe consistent with the Federal Constitution in prosecuting individuals for crime. More specifically, we deal with the admissibility of statements obtained from an individual who is subjected to custodial police interrogation and the necessity for procedures which assure that the individual is accorded his privilege under the Fifth Amendment to the Constitution not to be compelled to incriminate himself.

We dealt with certain phases of this problem recently in *Escobedo* v. *State of Illinois.* . . .

. . . We granted certiorari in these cases . . . in order further to explore some facets of the problems, thus exposed, of applying the privilege against self-incrimination to in-custody interrogation, and to give concrete constitutional guidelines for law enforcement agencies and courts to follow.

We start here, as we did in *Escobedo,* with the premise that our holding is not an innovation in our jurisprudence, but is an application of principles long recognized and applied in other settings. We have undertaken a thorough re-examination of the *Escobedo* decision and the

* This opinion applies to the companion cases of *Vignera* v. *New York, Westover* v. *United States,* and *California* v. *Stewart* (EDS.).

principles it announced, and we re-affirm it.

. . .

Our holding will be spelled out with some specificity in the pages which follow but briefly stated it is this: the prosecution may not use statements, whether exculpatory or inculpatory, stemming from custodial interrogation of the defendant unless it demonstrates the use of procedural safeguards effective to secure the privilege against self-incrimination. By custodial interrogation, we mean questioning initiated by law enforcement officers after a person has been taken into custody or otherwise deprived of his freedom of action in any significant way. As for the procedural safeguards to be employed, unless other fully effective means are devised to inform accused persons of their right of silence and to assure a continuous opportunity to exercise it, the following measures are required. Prior to any questioning, the person must be warned that he has a right to remain silent, that any statement he does make may be used as evidence against him, and that he has a right to the presence of any attorney, either retained or appointed. The defendant may waive effectuation of these rights, provided the waiver is made voluntarily, knowingly and intelligently. If, however, he indicates in any manner and at any stage of the process that he wishes to consult with an attorney before speaking there can be no questioning. Likewise, if the individual is alone and indicates in any manner that he does not wish to be interrogated, the police may not question him. The mere fact that he may have answered some questions or volunteered some statements on his own does not deprive him of the right to refrain from answering any further inquiries until he has consulted with an attorney and thereafter consents to be questioned.

The constitutional issue we decided in each of these cases is the admissibility of statements obtained from a defendant questioned while in custody and deprived of his freedom of action. In each, the defendant was questioned by police officers, detectives, or a prosecuting attorney in a room in which he was cut off from the outside world. In none of these cases was the defendant given a full and effective warning of his rights at the outset of the interrogation process. In all the cases, the questioning elicited oral admissions, and in three of them, signed statements as well which were admitted at their trials. They all thus share salient features—incommunicado interrogation of individuals in a police-dominated atmosphere, resulting in self-incriminating statements without full warning of constitutional rights.

An understanding of the nature and setting of this in-custody interrogation is essential to our decisions today. The difficulty in depicting what transpires at such interrogations stems from the fact that in this country they have largely taken place incommunicado. From extensive factual studies undertaken in the early 1930's, including the famous Wickersham Report to Congress by a Presidential Commission, it is clear that police violence and the "third degree" flourished at that time. In a series of cases decided by this Court long after these studies, the police resorted to physical brutality—beating, hanging,

whipping—and to sustained and protracted questioning incommunicado in order to extort confessions. The 1961 Commission on Civil Rights found much evidence to indicate that "some policemen still resort to physical force to obtain confessions." . . . The use of physical brutality and violence is not, unfortunately, relegated to the past or to any part of the country. . . .

The examples given above are undoubtedly the exception now, but they are sufficiently widespread to be the object of concern. Unless a proper limitation upon custodial interrogation is achieved—there can be no assurance that practices of this nature will be eradicated in the foreseeable future. . . .

Again we stress that the modern practice of in-custody interrogation is psychologically rather than physically oriented. . . . Interrogation still takes place in privacy. Privacy results in secrecy and this in turn results in a gap in our knowledge as to what in fact goes on in the interrogation rooms. A valuable source of information about present police practices, however, may be found in various police manuals and texts which document procedures employed with success in the past, and which recommend various other effective tactics. These texts are used by law enforcement agencies themselves as guides.* It

* The methods described by Inbau and Reid, Criminal Interrogation and Confessions (1962) are a revision and enlargement of material presented in three prior editions of a predecessor text, Lie Detection and Criminal Interrogation (3rd ed. 1953). The authors and their associates are officers of the Chicago Police Scientific Crime Detection Laboratory and have had extensive experience in writing, lecturing and speaking to law enforcement authorities over a 20-year period. They say that the techniques portrayed in their manuals reflect their experiences and are the most effective psychological

should be noted that these texts professedly present the most enlightened and effective means presently used to obtain statements through custodial interrogation. By considering these texts and other data, it is possible to describe procedures observed and noted around the country.

The officers are told by the manuals that the "principal psychological factor contributing to a successful interrogation is privacy—being alone with the person under interrogation."†

. . .

The texts . . . stress that the major qualities an interrogator should possess are patience and perseverance.
. . .

The manuals [also] suggest that the suspect be offered legal excuses for his actions in order to obtain initial admission of guilt. Where there is a suspected revenge-killing, for example, the interrogator may say:

Joe, you probably didn't go out looking for this fellow with the purpose of shooting him. My guess is, however, that you expected something from him and that's why you carried a gun—for your own protection. You knew him for what he was, no good. Then when you met him he probably started using foul, abusive language and he gave some indication that he was about to pull a gun on you, and that's when you had to act to save your own life. That's about it, isn't it, Joe?

Having then obtained the admission of shooting, the interrogator is advised

to refer to circumstantial evidence which negates the self-defense explanation. This should enable him to secure the entire story. One text notes that "Even if he fails to do so, the inconsistency between the subject's original denial of the shooting and his present admission of at least doing the shooting will serve to deprive him of a self-defense 'out' at the time of trial.

When the techniques described above prove unavailing the texts recommend they be alternated with a show of some hostility. One ploy often used has been termed the "friendly-unfriendly" or the "Mutt and Jeff" act:

. . . In this technique, two agents are employed. Mutt, the relentless investigator who knows the subject is guilty and is not going to waste any time. He's sent a dozen men away for this crime and he's going to send the subject away for the full term. Jeff, on the other hand, is obviously a kindhearted man. He has a family himself. He has a brother who was involved in a little scrape like this. He disapproves of Mutt and his tactics and will arrange to get him off the case if the subject will cooperate. He can't hold Mutt off for very long. The subject would be wise to make a quick decision. The technique is applied by having both investigators present while Mutt acts out his role. Jeff may stand by quietly and demur at some of Mutt's tactics. When Jeff makes his pleas for cooperation, Mutt is not present in the room.

The interrogators sometimes are instructed to induce a confession out of trickery. The technique here is quite effective in crimes which require identification or which run in series. In the identification situation, the interrogator may take a break in his questioning to place the subject among a group of men in a line-up. "The witness or complainant (previously coached, if necessary) studies

stratagems to employ during interrogations. Similarly, the techniques described in O'Hara, *Fundamentals of Criminal Investigation* (1959), were gleaned from long service as observer, lecturer in police science, and work as a federal criminal investigator. All these texts have had rather extensive use among law enforcement agencies and among students of police science, with total sales and circulation of over 44,000.

† Inbau and Reid, *supra*, at 1.

the line-up and confidently points out the subject as the guilty party." Then the questioning resumes "as though there were now no doubt about the guilt of the subject." A variation on this technique is called the "reverse line-up":

The accused is placed in a line-up, but this time he is identified by several fictitious witnesses or victims who associated him with different offenses. It is expected that the subject will become desperate and confess to the offense under investigation in order to escape from the false accusations.

The manuals also contain instructions for police on how to handle the individual who refuses to discuss the matter entirely, or who asks for an attorney or relatives. The examiner is to concede him the right to remain silent. "This usually has a very undermining effect. First of all, he is disappointed in his expectation of an unfavorable reaction on the part of the interrogator. Secondly, a concession of this right to remain silent impresses the subject with the apparent fairness of his interrogator." After this psychological conditioning, however, the officer is told to point out the incriminating significance of the suspect's refusal to talk:

Joe, you have a right to remain silent. That's your privilege and I'm the last person in the world who'll try to take it from you. If that's the way you want to leave this, O.K. But let me ask you this. Suppose you were in my shoes and I were in yours and you called me in to ask me about this and I told you, "I don't want to answer any of your questions." You'd think I had something to hide, and you'd probably be right in thinking that. That's exactly what I'll have to think about you, and so will everybody else. So let's sit here and talk this whole thing over.

Few will persist in their initial re-

fusals to talk, it is said, if this monologue is employed correctly.

. . .

From these representative samples of interrogation technique, the setting prescribed by the manuals and observed in practice becomes clear. In essence, it is this: To be alone with the subject is essential to prevent distraction and to deprive him of any outside support. The aura of his confidence in his guilt undermines his will to resist. He merely confirms the preconceived story the police seek to have him describe. Patience and persistence, at times relentless questioning are employed. To obtain a confession, the interrogator must "patiently maneuver himself or his quarry into a position from which the desired object may be obtained." When normal procedures fail to produce the needed result, the police may resort to deceptive stratagems such as giving false legal advice. It is important to keep the subject off balance, for example, by trading on his insecurity about himself or his surroundings. The police then persuade, trick, or cajole him out of exercising his constitutional rights.

Even without employing brutality, the "third-degree" or the specific stratagems described above, the very fact of custodial interrogation exacts a heavy toll on individual liberty and trades on the weakness of individuals. . . .

In the cases before us today, given this background, we concern ourselves primarily with this interrogation atmosphere and the evils it can bring. In No. 759, *Miranda* v. *Arizona,* the police arrested the defendant and took him to a special interrogation room where they secured a confession. In No. 760, *Vignera* v. *New York,* the defendant made oral admissions to the police after interrogation in the afternoon, and then signed an inculpatory statement upon being questioned by an assistant district attorney later the same evening. In No. 761, *Westover* v. *United States,* the defendant was handed over to the Federal Bureau of Investigation by local authorities after they had detained and interrogated him for a lengthy period, both at night and the following morning. After some two hours of questioning, the federal officers had obtained signed statements from the defendant. Lastly, in No. 584, *California* v. *Stewart,* the local police held the defendant five days in the station and interrogated him on nine separate occasions before they secured his inculpatory statement.

In these cases, we might not find the defendants' statements to have been involuntary in traditional terms. Our concern for adequate safeguards to protect precious Fifth Amendment rights is, of course, not lessened in the slightest. In each of the cases, the defendant was thrust into an unfamiliar atmosphere and run through menacing police interrogation procedures. The potentiality for compulsion is forcefully apparent, for example, in *Miranda,* where the indigent Mexican defendant was a seriously disturbed individual with pronounced sexual fantasies, and in *Stewart,* in which the defendant was an indigent Los Angeles Negro who had dropped out of school in the sixth grade. To be sure, the records do not evince overt physical coercion or patented psychological ploys. The fact remains that in none of these cases did the officers undertake to afford appropriate safeguards at the outset of the interrogation to insure that the statements were truly the product of free choice.

. . .

The question in these cases is whether the privilege is fully applicable during a period of custodial interrogation. . . . We are satisfied that all the principles embodied in the privilege apply to informal compulsion exerted by law-enforcement officers during in-custody questioning. An individual swept from familiar surroundings into police custody, surrounded by antagonistic forces, and subjected to the techniques of persuasion described above cannot be otherwise than under compulsion to speak. As a practical matter, the compulsion to speak in the isolated setting of the police station may well be greater than in courts or other official investigations, where there are often impartial observers to guard against intimidation or trickery.

. . .

Today, then, there can be no doubt that the Fifth Amendment privilege is available outside of criminal court proceedings and serves to protect persons in all settings in which their freedom of action is curtailed from being compelled to incriminate themselves. . . . In order to combat [inherently compelling] pressures and to permit a full opportunity to exercise the privilege against self-incrimination, the accused must be adequately and effectively apprised of his rights and the exercise of those rights must be fully honored.

It is impossible for us to foresee the potential alternatives for protecting the privilege which might be devised by Congress or the States in the exercise of their creative rule-making capacities. Therefore we cannot say that the Constitution necessarily requires adherence to any particular solution for the inherent compulsions of the interrogation process as it is presently conducted. Our decision in no way creates a constitutional straitjacket which will handicap sound efforts at reform, nor is it intended to have this effect. We encourage Congress and the States to continue their laudable search for increasingly effective ways of protecting the rights of the individual while promoting efficient enforcement of our criminal laws. However, unless we are shown other procedures which are at least as effective in apprising accused persons of their right of silence and in assuring a continuous opportunity to exercise it, the following safeguards must be observed.

At the outset, if a person in custody is to be subjected to interrogation he must first be informed in clear and unequivocal terms that he has the right to remain silent. For those unaware of the privilege the warning is needed simply to make them aware of it—the threshold requirement for an intelligent decision as to its exercise. More important, such a warning is an absolute prerequisite in overcoming the inherent pressures of the interrogation atmosphere. It is not just the subnormal or woefully ignorant who succumb to an interrogator's imprecations, whether implied or expressly stated, that the interrogation will continue until a confession is obtained or that silence in the face of accusation is itself damning and will bode ill when presented to a jury. Further, the warning will show the individual that his interrogators are prepared to recognize his privilege should he choose to exercise it.

The Fifth Amendment privilege is so fundamental to our system of constitutional rule and the expedient of giving an adequate warning as to the availability of the privilege so simple, we will not pause to inquire in individual cases whether the defendant was aware of his rights without a warning being given. Assessments of the knowledge the defendant possessed, based on information as to his age, education, intelligence, or prior contact with authorities, can never be more than speculation; a warning is a clearcut fact. More important, whatever the background of the person interrogated, a warning at the time of the interrogation is indispensable to overcome its pressure and to insure that the individual knows he is free to exercise the privilege at that point in time.

The warning of the right to remain silent must be accompanied by the explanation that anything said can and will be used against the individual in court. This warning is needed in order to make him aware not only of the privilege, but also of the consequences of foregoing it. It is only through an awareness of these consequences that there can be any assurance of real understanding and intelligent exercise of the privilege. Moreover, this warning may serve to make the individual more acutely aware that he is faced with a phase of the adversary system—that he is not in the presence of persons acting solely in his interest.

The circumstances surrounding incustody interrogation can operate very quickly to overbear the will of one merely made aware of his privilege by his interrogators. Therefore, the right to have counsel present at the interrogation is indispensable to the protection of the Fifth Amendment privilege under the system we delineate today. Our aim is to assure that the individual's right to choose between silence and speech remains unfettered throughout the interrogation process. A once-stated warning, delivered by those who will conduct the interrogation cannot itself suffice to that end among those who most require knowledge of their rights. A mere warning given by the interrogators is not alone sufficient to accomplish that end. Prosecutors themselves claim that the admonishment of the right to remain silent without more "will benefit only the recidivist and the professional." Brief for the National District Attorneys Association as *amicus curiae,* p. 14. Even preliminary advice given to the accused by his own attorney can be swiftly overcome by the secret interrogation process. . . . Thus, the need for counsel to protect the Fifth Amendment privilege comprehends not merely a right to consult prior to questioning, but also to have counsel present during any questioning if the defendant so desires.

The presence of counsel at the interrogation may serve several significant subsidiary functions as well. If the accused decides to talk to his interrogators, the assistance of counsel can mitigate the dangers of untrustworthiness. With a lawyer present the likelihood that the police will practice coercion is reduced, and if coercion is nevertheless exercised the lawyer can testify to it in court. The presence of a lawyer can also help to guarantee that the accused gives a fully accurate statement to the police and that the statement is rightly reported by the prosecution at trial. . . .

An individual need not make a pre-interrogation request for a lawyer. While such request affirmatively secures his right to have one, his failure to ask for a lawyer does not constitute a waiver. No effective waiver of the right to counsel during interrogation can be recognized unless specifically made after the warnings we here delineate have been given. The accused who does not know his rights and therefore does not make a request may be the person who most needs counsel. . . .

Accordingly we hold that an individual held for interrogation must be clearly informed that he has the right to consult with a lawyer and to have the lawyer with him during interrogation under the system for protecting the privilege we delineate today. As with the warnings of the right to remain silent and that anything stated can be used in evidence against him, this warning is an absolute prerequisite to interrogation. No amount of circumstantial evidence that the person may have been aware of this right will suffice to stand in its stead. Only through such a warning is there ascertainable assurance that the accused was aware of this right.

If an individual indicates that he wishes the assistance of counsel before any interrogation occurs, the authorities cannot rationally ignore or deny his request on the basis that the individual does not have or cannot afford a retained attorney. The financial ability of the individual has no relationship to the scope of the rights involved here. The privilege against self-incrimination secured by the Constitution applies to all individuals. The need for counsel in order to protect the privilege exists for the indigent as well as the affluent. In fact, were we to limit these constitutional rights to those who can retain an attorney, our decision today would be of little significance. . . . While authorities are not required to relieve the accused of his poverty, they have the obligation not to take advantage of indigence in the administration of justice. . . .

In order fully to apprise a person interrogated of the extent of his rights under this system then, it is necessary to warn him not only that he has the right to consult with an attorney, but also that if he is indigent a lawyer will be appointed to represent him. . . .

Once warnings have been given, the subsequent procedure is clear. If the individual indicates in any manner, at any time prior to or during questioning, that he wishes to remain silent, the interrogation must cease. At this point he has shown that he intends to exercise his Fifth Amendment privileges; any statement taken after the person invokes his privilege cannot be other than the product of compulsion, subtle or otherwise. Without the right to cut off questioning, the setting of in-custody interrogation operates on the individual to overcome free choice in producing a statement after the privilege has been once invoked. If the individual states that he wants an attorney, the interrogation must cease until an attorney is present. At that time, the individual must have an opportunity to confer with the attorney and to have him present during any subsequent questioning. If the individual cannot obtain an attorney and he indicates that he wants one before speaking to police, they must respect his decision to remain silent.

This does not mean, as some have suggested, that each police station must have a "station house lawyer" present at all times to advise prisoners. It does mean, however, that if police propose to interrogate a person they must make known to him that he is entitled to a lawyer and that if he cannot afford one, a lawyer will be provided for him prior to any interrogation. . . .

If the interrogation continues without the presence of an attorney and a statement is taken, a heavy burden rests on the Government to demonstrate that the defendant knowingly and intelligently waived his privilege against self-incrimination and his right to retained or appointed counsel. . . .

An express statement that the individual is willing to make a statement and does not want an attorney followed closely by a statement could constitute a waiver. But a valid waiver will not be presumed simply from the silence of the accused after warnings are given or simply from the fact that a confession was in fact eventually obtained. . . . Moreover, where in-custody interrogation is involved, there is no room for the contention that the privilege is waived if the individual answers some questions or gives some information on his own prior to invoking his right to remain silent when interrogated.

Whatever the testimony of the authorities as to waiver of rights by an accused, the fact of lengthy interrogation or incommunicado incarceration before a statement is made is strong evidence that the accused did not validly waive his rights. In these circumstances the fact that the individual eventually made a statement is consistent with the conclusion that the compelling influence of the interrogation finally forced him to do so. It is inconsistent with any notion of a voluntary relinquishment of the privilege. Moreover, any evidence that the accused was threatened, tricked, or cajoled into a waiver will, of course, show that the defendant did not voluntarily waive his privilege. The requirement of warnings and waiver of rights is a fundamental with respect to the Fifth Amendment privilege and not simply a preliminary ritual to existing methods of interrogation. . . .

. . . No distinction can be drawn

between statements which are direct confessions and statements which amount to "admissions" of part or all of an offense. The privilege against self-incrimination protects the individual from being compelled to incriminate himself in any manner; it does not distinguish degrees of incrimination. Similarly, for precisely the same reason, no distinction may be drawn between inculpatory statements and statements alleged to be merely intended to be exculpatory by the defendant are often used to impeach his testimony at trial or to demonstrate untruths in the statement given under interrogation and thus to prove guilt by implication. These statements are incriminating in any meaningful sense of the word and may not be used without the full warnings and effective waiver required for any other statement. In *Escobedo* itself, the defendant fully intended his accusation of another as the slayer to be exculpatory as to himself.

. . .

Our decision is not intended to hamper the traditional function of police officers in investigating crime. . . . When an individual is in custody on probable cause, the police may, of course, seek out evidence in the field to be used at trial against him. Such investigation may include inquiry of persons not under restraint. General on-the-scene-questioning as to facts surrounding a crime or other general questioning of citizens in the fact-finding process is not affected by our holding. It is an act of responsible citizenship for individuals to give whatever information they may have to aid in law enforcement. In such situations the compelling atmosphere inherent in the process of in-custody interrogation is not necessarily present.

In dealing with statements obtained through interrogation, we do not purport of find all confessions inadmissible. Confessions remain a proper element in law enforcement. Any statement given freely and voluntarily without any compelling influences is, of course, admissible in evidence. The fundamental import of the privilege while an individual is in custody is not whether he is allowed to talk to the police without the benefit of warnings and counsel, but whether he can be interrogated. There is no requirement that police stop a person who enters a police station and states that he wishes to confess to a crime, or a person who calls the police to offer a confession or any other statement he desires to make. Volunteered statements of any kind are not barred by the Fifth Amendment and their admissibility is not affected by our holding today.

To summarize, we hold that when an individual is taken into custody or otherwise deprived of his freedom by the authorities and is subjected to questioning, the privilege against self-incrimination is jeopardized. Procedural safeguards must be employed to protect the privilege, and unless other fully effective means are adopted to notify the person of his right of silence and to assure that the exercise of the right will be scrupulously honored, the following measures are required. He must be warned prior to any questioning that he has the right to remain silent, that anything he says can be used against him in a court of law, that he has the right to the presence of an attorney, and that if he cannot afford an attorney one will be appointed for him prior to any questioning if he so desires. Opportunity to exercise these rights must be afforded to him throughout the interrogation. After such warnings have been given, and such opportunity afforded him, the individual may knowingly and intelligently waive these rights and agree to answer questions or make a statement. But unless and until such warnings and waiver are demonstrated by the prosecution at trial, no evidence obtained as a result of interrogation can be used against him.

[Here Chief Justice Warren examines the argument that society's need for interrogation outweighs the privileges.]

. . .

Because of the nature of the problem and because of its recurrent significance in numerous cases, we have to this point discussed the relationship of the Fifth Amendment privilege to police interrogation without specific concentration on the facts of the cases before us. We turn now to these facts to consider the application to these cases of the constitutional principles discussed above. In each instance, we have concluded that statements were obtained from the defendant under circumstances that did not meet constitutional standards for protection of the privilege.

*No. 759.* Miranda *v.* Arizona.

On March 13, 1963, petitioner, Ernesto Miranda, was arrested at his home and taken in custody to a Phoenix police station. He was there identified by the complaining witness. The police then took him to "Interrogation Room No. 2" of the detective bureau. There he was questioned by two police officers. The officers admitted at trial that Miranda was not advised that he had a right to have an attorney present. Two hours later, the officers emerged from the interrogation room with a written confession signed by Miranda. At the top of the statement was a typed paragraph stat-

ing that the confession was made voluntarily, without threats or promise of immunity and "with full knowledge of my legal rights, understanding any statement I make may be used against me."‡

At his trial before a jury, the written confession was admitted into evidence over the objection of defense counsel. . . . Miranda was found guilty of kidnapping and rape. . . . On appeal, the Supreme Court of Arizona held that Miranda's constitutional rights were not violated in obtaining the confession and affirmed the conviction. In reaching its decision, the court emphasized heavily the fact that Miranda did not specifically request counsel.

We reverse. From the testimony of the officers and by the admission of respondent, it is clear that Miranda was not in any way apprised of his right to consult with an attorney and to have one present during the interrogation, nor was his right not to be compelled to incriminate himself effectively protected in any other manner. Without these warnings the statements were inadmissible. The mere fact that he signed a statement which contained a typed-in clause stating that he had "full knowledge" of his "legal rights" does not approach the knowing and intelligent waiver required to relinquish constitutional rights. . . .

*No. 760.* Vignera *v.* New York.

Petitioner, Michael Vignera was picked up by New York police on October 14, 1960, in connection with the robbery three days earlier of a Brooklyn dress shop. They took him to the 17th Detective Squad head-

‡ One of the officers testified that he read this paragraph to Miranda. Apparently, however, he did not do so until after Miranda had confessed orally.

quarters in Manhattan. Sometime thereafter he was taken to the 66th Detective Squad. There a detective questioned Vignera with respect to the robbery. Vignera orally admitted the robbery to the detective. The detective was asked on crossexamination at trial by defense counsel whether Vignera was warned of his right to counsel before being interrogated. The prosecution objected to the question and the trial judge sustained the objection. Thus, the defense was precluded from making any showing that warnings had not been given. While at the 66th Detective Squad, Vignera was identified by the store owner and a saleslady as the man who robbed the dress shop. At about 3:00 P.M. he was formally arrested. The police then transported him to still another station, the 70th Precinct in Brooklyn, "for detention." At 11:00 P.M. Vignera was questioned by an assistant district attorney in the presence of a hearing reporter who transcribed the questions and Vignera's answers. This verbatim account of these proceedings contains no statement of any warnings given by the assistant district attorney. At Vignera's trial on a charge of first degree robbery, the detective testified as to the oral confession. The transcription of the statement taken was also introduced in evidence. At the conclusion of the testimony, the trial judge charged the jury in part as follows:

The law doesn't say that the confession is void or invalidated because the police officer didn't advise the defendant as to his rights. Did you hear what I said? I am telling you what the law of the State of New York is.

Vignera was found guilty of first degree robbery. . . . The conviction was affirmed without opinion by the Appellate Division, Second Depart-

ment . . . and by the Court of Appeals, also without opinion. . . . In argument to the Court of Appeals, the State contended that Vignera had no constitutional right to be advised of his right to counsel or his privilege against self-incrimination.

We reverse. The foregoing indicates that Vignera was not warned of any of his rights before the questioning by the detective and by the assistant district attorney. No other steps were taken to protect these rights. Thus he was not effectively apprised of his Fifth Amendment privilege or of his right to have counsel present and his statements are inadmissible.

*No. 761.* Westover *v.* United States.

At approximately 9:45 P.M. on March 20, 1963, petitioner, Carl Calvin Westover, was arrested by local police in Kansas City as a suspect in two Kansas City robberies. A report was also received from the FBI that he was wanted on a felony charge in California. The local authorities took him to a police station and placed him in a line-up on the local charges, and at about 11:45 P.M. he was booked. Kansas City police interrogated Westover on the night of his arrest. He denied any knowledge of criminal activities. The next day local officers interrogated him again throughout the morning. Shortly before noon they informed the FBI that they were through interrogating Westover and that the FBI could proceed to interrogate him. There is nothing in the record to indicate that Westover was ever given any warning as to his rights by local police. . . . After two or two and one-half hours, Westover signed separate confessions to each of these two robberies which had been prepared by one of the agents during this interrogation. At trial one of the agents testified, and a paragraph on each of the statements states, that the agents advised Westover that he did not have to make a statement, that any statement he made could be used against him, and that he had the right to see an attorney.

Westover was tried by a jury in federal court and convicted of the California robberies. His statements were introduced at trial. . . . On appeal, the conviction was affirmed by the Court of Appeals for the Ninth Circuit. . . .

We reverse. On the facts of this case we cannot find that Westover knowingly and intelligently waived his right to remain silent and his right to consult with counsel prior to the time he made the statement. At the time the FBI agents began questioning Westover, he had been in custody for over 14 hours and had been interrogated at length during that period. The FBI interrogation began immediately upon the conclusion of the interrogation by Kansas City police and was conducted in local police headquarters. Although the two law enforcement authorities are legally distinct and the crimes for which they interrogated Westover were different, the impact on him was that of a continuous period of questioning. There is no evidence of any warning given prior to the FBI interrogation nor is there any evidence of an articulated waiver of rights after the FBI commenced their interrogation. . . . Despite the fact that the FBI agents gave warnings at the outset of their interview, from Westover's point of view the warnings came at the end of the interrogation process. In these circumstances an intelligent waiver of constitutional rights cannot be assumed.

We do not suggest that law enforcement authorities are precluded from questioning any individual who has been held for a period of time by other authorities and interrogated by them without appropriate warnings. A different case would be presented if an accused were taken into custody by the second authority, removed both in time and place from his original surroundings, and then adequately advised of his rights and given an opportunity to exercise them. But here the FBI interrogation was conducted immediately following the state interrogation in the same police station—in the same compelling surroundings. Thus, in obtaining a confession from Westover, the federal authorities were the beneficiaries of the pressure applied by the local in-custody interrogation. . . .

## No. 584. California *v.* Stewart.

In the course of investigating a series of purse-snatch robberies in which one of the victims had died of injuries inflicted by her assailant, Roy Allen Stewart, was pointed out to Los Angeles police as the endorser of dividend checks taken in one of the robberies. . . . At the time of Stewart's arrest, police also arrested Stewart's wife and three other persons who were visiting him. These four were jailed along with Stewart and were interrogated. Stewart was taken to the University Station of the Los Angeles Police Department where he was placed in a cell. During the next five days, police interrogated Stewart on nine different occasions. Except during the first interrogation session, when he was confronted with an accusing witness, Stewart was isolated with his interrogators.

During the ninth interrogation session, Stewart admitted that he had robbed the deceased and stated that he had not meant to hurt her. Police then brought Stewart before a magistrate for the first time. Since there was no evidence to connect them with any crime, the police then released the other four persons arrested with him.

Nothing in the record specifically indicates whether Stewart was or was not advised of his right to remain silent or his right to counsel. . . .

. . . At his trial, transcripts of the first interrogation and the confession at the last interrogation were introduced in evidence. The jury found Stewart guilty of robbery and first degree murder and fixed the penalty as death. On appeal, the Supreme Court of California reversed. . . . It held that under this Court's decision in *Escobedo,* Stewart should have been advised of his right to remain silent and of his right to counsel and that it would not presume in the face of a silent record that the police advised Stewart of his rights.

We affirm. In dealing with custodial interrogation, we will not presume that a defendant has been effectively apprised of his rights and that his privilege against self-incrimination has been adequately safeguarded on a record that does not show that any warnings have been given or that any effective alternative has been employed. Nor can a knowing and intelligent waiver of these rights be assumed on a silent record. Furthermore, Stewart's steadfast denial of the alleged offenses through eight of the nine interrogations over a period of five days is subject to no other construction than that he was compelled by persistent interrogation to forgo his Fifth Amendment privilege.

> *Therefore, in accordance with the foregoing, the judgments [below] . . . are reversed. It is so ordered.*

MR. JUSTICE CLARK'S *opinion dis-*

*senting in Nos. 759, 760, and 761, and concurring in the result in No. 584 is not reprinted here.*

MR. JUSTICE HARLAN, *whom* MR. JUSTICE STEWART *and* MR. JUSTICE WHITE *join, dissenting.*

I believe the decision of the Court represents poor constitutional law and entails harmful consequences for the country at large. How serious these consequences may prove to be only time can tell. But the basic flaws in the Court's justification seem to me readily apparent now once all sides of the problem are considered.

. . .

While the fine points of this scheme [the majority's requirement of warnings in interrogation] are far less clear than the Court admits, the tenor is quite apparent. The new rules are not designed to guard against police brutality or other unmistakably banned forms of coercion. Those who use third-degree tactics and deny them in court are equally able and destined to lie as skillfully about warnings and waivers. Rather, the thrust of the new rules is to negate all pressures, to reinforce the nervous or ignorant suspect, and ultimately to discourage any confession at all. The aim in short is toward "voluntariness" in a utopian sense, or to view it from a different angle, voluntariness with a vengeance.

To incorporate this notion into the Constitution requires a strained reading of history and precedent and a disregard of the very pragmatic concerns that alone may on occasion justify such strains. I believe that reasoned examination will show that the Due Process Clauses provide an adequate tool for coping with confessions and that, even if the Fifth Amendment privilege against self-incrimination be invoked, its precedents taken as a whole do not sustain the present rules. Viewed as a choice based on pure policy, these new rules prove to be a highly debatable if not one-sided appraisal of the competing interests imposed over widespread objection, at the very time when judicial restraint is most called for by the circumstances.

It is most fitting to begin an inquiry into the constitutional precedents by surveying the limits on confessions the Court has evolved under the Due Process Clause of the Fourteenth Amendment. This is so because these cases show that there exists a workable and effective means of dealing with confessions in a judicial manner; because the cases are the baseline from which the Court now departs and so serve to measure the actual as opposed to the professed distance it travels; and because examination of them helps reveal how the Court has coasted into its present position.

The earliest confession cases in this Court emerged from federal prosecutions and were settled on a nonconstitutonal basis, the Court adopting the common-law rule that the absence of inducements, promises, and threats made a confession voluntary and admissible. *Hopt* v. *People of Territory of Utah*, 110 U.S. 574, 4 S.Ct. 202, 28 L.Ed. 262; *Pierce* v. *United States*, 160 U.S. 355, 16 S.Ct. 321, 40 L.Ed. 454. While a later case said the Fifth Amendment privilege controlled admissibility, this proposition was not itself developed in subsequent decisions. . . .

[A] new line of decisions, testing admissibility by the Due Process Clause, began in 1936 with *Brown* v. *State of Mississippi* and must now embrace somewhat more than 30 full opinions of the Court. While the voluntariness rubric was repeated in many instances, . . . the Court never pinned it down to a single meaning but on the contrary infused it with a number of different values. To travel quickly over the main theme, there was an initial emphasis on reliability, e.g., *Ward* v. *State of Texas*, 316 U.S. 547, . . . supplemented by concern over the legality and fairness of the police practices, e.g., *Ashcraft* v. *State of Tennessee*, 322 U.S. 143, . . . in an "accusatorial" system of law enforcement, *Watts* v. *State of Indiana*, 388 U.S. 49, . . . and eventually by close attention to the individual's state of mind and capacity for effective choice, e.g., *Callegos* v. *State of Colorado*, 370 U.S. 49, . . . The outcome was a continuing reevaluation on the facts of each case of *how much* pressure on the suspect was admissible. . . .

There are several relevant lessons to be drawn from this constitutional history. The first is that with over 25 years of precedent the Court has developed an elaborate, sophisticated, and sensitive approach to admissibility of confessions. It is "judicial" in its treatment of one case at a time, . . . flexible in its ability to respond to the endless mutations of fact presented, and ever more familiar to the lower courts. Of course, strict certainty is not obtained in this developing process but this is often so with constitutional principles and disagreement is usually confined to that borderland of close cases where it matters least.

The second point is that in practice and from time to time in principle, the Court has given ample recognition to society's interest in suspect questioning as an instrument of law enforcement. Cases countenancing quite significant pressures can be cited without difficulty and the lower courts may often have been yet more tolerant. Of course the limitations imposed today were rejected by necessary implication in case after case, the right to warnings having been explicitly rebuffed in this Court many years ago. . . . As recently as *Haynes* v. *State of Washington* . . . the Court openly acknowledged that questioning of witnesses and suspects "is undoubtedly an essential tool in effective law enforcement." . . .

Finally, the cases disclose that the language in many opinions overstates the actual course of decision. It has been said, for example, that an admissible confession must be made by the suspect "in the unfettered exercise of his own will," . . . and that "a prisoner is not 'to be made the deluded instrument of his own conviction.' " . . . Though often repeated such principles are rarely observed in full measure. Even the word "voluntary" may be deemed somewhat misleading, especially when one considers many of the confessions that have been brought under its umbrella. . . .

I turn now to the Court's asserted reliance on the Fifth Amendment, an approach which I frankly regard as a *trompe l'oeil*. The Court's opinion in any view reveals no adequate basis for extending the Fifth Amendment's privilege against self-incrimination to the police station. Far more important, it fails to show that the Court's new rules are well supported, let alone compelled, by Fifth Amendment precedents. Instead, the new rules actually derive from quotation and analogy drawn from precedents under the Sixth Amendment, which should properly have no bearing on police interrogation.

The Court's opening contention, that the Fifth Amendment governs police station confessions, is perhaps not an impermissible extension of the law but it has little to commend itself in the present circumstances. Historically, the privilege against self-incrimination did not bear at all on the use of extra-legal confessions, for which distinct standards evolved; indeed, "the *history* of the two principles is wide apart, differing by one hundred years in origin, and derived through separate lines of precedents. . . ." 8 Wigmore, Evidence Sec. 2266, at 401 (McNaughton rev. 1951). Practice under the two doctrines has also differed in a number of important respects. Even those who would enlarge the privilege must concede some linguistic difficulties since the Fifth Amendment in terms proscribes only compelling any person "in any criminal case to be a witness against himself." . . .

Though weighty, I do not say these points and similar ones are conclusive, for as the Court reiterates the privilege embodies basic principles always capable of expansion. Certainly the privilege does represent a protective concern for the accused and an emphasis upon accusatorial rather than inquisitorial values in law enforcement, although this is similarly true of their other limitations such as the grand jury requirement and the reasonable doubt standard. Accusatorial values, however, have openly been absorbed into the due process standard governing confessions; this indeed is why at present "the kinship of the two rules [governing confessions and self-incrimination] is too apparent for denial." McCormick, Evidence 155 (1954). Since extension of the general principle has already occurred, to insist that the privilege applies as such serves only to carry over inapposite historical details and engaging rhetoric and to obscure the policy choices to be made in regulating confessions.

Having decided that the Fifth Amendment privilege does apply in the police station, the Court reveals that the privilege imposes more exacting restrictions than does the Fourteenth Amendment's voluntariness test. It then emerges from a discussion of *Escobedo* that the Fifth Amendment requires for an admissible confession that it be given by one distinctly aware of his right not to speak and shielded from "the compelling atmosphere" of interrogation. . . . From these key premises, the Court finally develops the safeguards of warning, counsel and so forth. I do not believe these premises are sustained by precedents under the Fifth Amendment.

. . .

The Court appears similarly wrong in thinking that precise knowledge of one's rights is a settled prerequisite under the Fifth Amendment to the loss of its protection. A number of lower federal court cases have held that grand jury witnesses need not always be warned of their privilege, . . . and Wigmore states this to be the better rule for trial witnesses. See 8 Wigmore, Evidence Sec. 2269 (McNaughton rev. 1961). . . . No Fifth Amendment precedent is cited for the Court's contrary view. . . .

A closing word must be said about the Assistance of Counsel Clause of the Sixth Amendment, which is never expressly relied on by the Court but whose judicial precedents turn out to be linchpins of the confession rules announced today. . . .

The only attempt in this Court to carry the right to counsel into the station occurred in *Escobedo*, the Court repeating several times that that stage was no less "critical" than trial itself. . . . This is hardly persuasive when we consider that a grand jury inquiry, the filing of a certiorari petition, and certainly the purchase of narcotics by an undercover agent from a prospective defendant may all be equally "critical" yet provision of counsel and advice on the score have never been thought compelled by the Constitution in such cases. The sound reason why this right is so freely extended for a criminal trial is the severe injustice risked by confronting an untrained defendant with a range of technical points of law, evidence, and tactics familiar to the prosecutor but not to himself. This danger shrinks markedly in the police station where indeed the lawyer in fulfilling his professional responsibilities of necessity may become an obstacle to truthfinding. . . .

Examined as an expression of public policy, the Court's new regime proves so dubious that there can be no due compensation for its weakness in constitutional law.

. . .

The Court's new rules aim to offset . . . minor pressures and disadvantages intrinsic to any kind of police interrogation. . . . The rules work for reliability in confessions almost only in the Pickwickian sense that they can prevent some from being given at all. . . .

What the Court largely ignores is that its rules impair, if they will not eventually serve wholly to frustrate, an instrument of law enforcement that has long and quite reasonably been thought worth the price paid for it. There can be little doubt that the Court's new code would markedly decrease the number of confessions. To warn the suspect that he may remain silent and remind him that his confession may be used in court are minor obstructions. To require also an express waiver by the suspect and an end to questioning whenever he demurs must heavily handicap questioning. And to suggest or provide counsel for the suspect simply invites the end of the interrogation. . . .

How much harm this decision will inflict on law enforcement cannot fairly be predicted with accuracy. Evidence on the role of confessions is notoriously incomplete. . . . We do know that some crimes cannot be solved without confessions, that ample expert testimony attests to their importance in crime control, and that the Court is taking a real risk with society's welfare in imposing its new regime on the country. The social costs of crime are too great to call the new rules anything but a hazardous experimentation.

While passing over the costs and risks of its experiment, the Court portrayed the evils of normal police questioning in terms which I think are exaggerated. Albeit stringently confined by the due process standards interrogation is no doubt often inconvenient and unpleasant for the suspect. However, it is no less so for a man to be arrested and jailed, to have his house searched, or to stand trial in court, yet all this may properly happen to the most innocent given probable cause, a warrant, or an indictment. Society has always paid a stiff price for law and order, and peaceful interrogation is not one of the dark moments of the law.

. . .

In closing this necessarily truncated discussion of policy considerations attending the new confession rules, some reference must be made to their ironic untimeliness. There is now in progress in this country a massive reexamination of criminal law enforcement procedures on a scale never before witnessed. . . .

It is no secret that concern has been expressed lest long-range and lasting reforms be frustrated by this Court's too rapid departure from existing constitutional standards. Despite the Court's disclaimer, the practical effect of the decision made today must inevitably be to handicap seriously sound efforts at reform. . . . Of course legislative reform is rarely speedy or unanimous, though this Court has been more patient in the past. But the legislative reforms when they came would have the vast advantage of empirical data and comprehensive study, they would allow experimentation and use of solutions not open to the courts, and they would restore the initiative in criminal law reform to those forums where it truly belongs.

. . . I would adhere to the due process test and reject the new requirements inaugurated by the Court. On this premise my disposition of each of these cases can be stated briefly.

In two of the three cases coming from state courts, *Miranda* v. *Arizona* (No. 759) and *Vignera* v. *New York* (No. 760), the confessions were held admissible and no other errors worth comment are alleged by petitioners. I would affirm in these two cases. The other state case is *California* v. *Stewart* (No. 584) where the state supreme court held the confession inadmissible and reversed the conviction. In that case I would dismiss the writ of certiorari on the ground that no final judgment is before us. . . . If the merits of the decision in *Stewart* be reached, then I believe it should be reversed and the case remanded so the state supreme court may pass on the other claims available to respondent.

In the federal case, *Westover* v. *United States* (No. 761) . . . [i]t is urged that the confession was . . . inadmissible because not voluntary even measured by due process standards and because federal-state cooperation brought the *McNabb-Mallory* rule into play under *Anderson* v.

*United States,* 318 U.S. 350. . . . However, the facts alleged fall well short of coercion in my view, and I believe the involvement of federal agents in petitioner's arrest and detention by the State too slight to invoke *Anderson.* . . . I would therefore affirm Westover's conviction.

In conclusion: Nothing in the letter or the spirit of the Constitution or in the precedents squares with the heavy handed and one-sided action that is so precipitously taken by the Court in the name of fulfilling its constitutional responsibilities. The foray which the Court takes today brings to mind the wise and far-sighted words of Mr. Justice Jackson in *Douglas* v. *City of Jeanette,* 319 U.S. 157 . . . (separate opinon): "This Court is forever adding new stories to the temples of constitutional law, and the temples have a way of collapsing when one story too many is added." . . .

Mr. Justice White, *with whom* Mr. Justice Harlan *and* Mr. Justice Stewart *join, dissenting.*

. . .

. . . [I]nstead of confining itself to protection of the right against compelled self-incrimination the Court has created a limited Fifth Amendment right to counsel—or, as the Court expresses it, a right to "counsel to protect the Fifth Amendment privilege. . . ." The focus then is not on the will of the accused but on the will of counsel and how much influence he can have on the accused. Obviously there is no warrant in the Fifth Amendment for thus installing counsel as the arbiter of the privilege. . . .

. . . Equally relevant [in criticism of the Court's opinion] is an assessment of the rule's consequences measured against community values. The Court's duty to assess the consequences of its action is not satisfied by the utterance of the truth that a value of our system of criminal justice is "to respect the inviolability of the human personality" and to require government to produce the evidence against the accused by its own independent labors. More than the human dignity of the accused is involved; the human personality of others in the society must also be preserved. Thus the values reflected by the privilege are not the sole desideratum; society's interest in the general security is of equal weight.

The obvious underpinning of the Court's decision is a deep-seated distrust of all confessions. . . . [T]he not so subtle overtone of the opinion [is] that it is inherently wrong for the police to gather evidence from the accused himself. And this is precisely the nub of this dissent. I see nothing wrong or immoral, and certainly nothing unconstitutional, with the police asking a suspect whom they have reasonable cause to arrest whether or not he killed his wife or with confronting him with the evidence on which the arrest is based, at least where he has been plainly advised that he may remain completely silent. . . . Until today, "the admissions or confessions of the prisoner, when voluntarily and freely made, have always ranked high in the scale of incriminating evidence." . . . Moreover, it is by no means certain that the process of confessing is injurious to the accused. To the contrary it may provide psychological relief and enhance the prospects for rehabilitation.

This is not to say that the value of respect for the inviolability of the accused's individual personality should be accorded no weight or that all confessions should be indiscriminately admitted. . . . But I see no sound basis, factual or otherwise, and the Court gives none, for concluding that the present rule against the receipt of coerced confessions is inadequate for the task of sorting out inadmissible evidence and must be replaced by the *per se* rule which is now imposed. . . .

The most basic function of any government is to provide for the security of the individual and of his property. . . . These ends of society are served by the criminal laws which for the most part are aimed at the prevention of crime. Without the reasonably effective performance of the task of preventing private violence and rehabilitation, it is idle to talk about human dignity and civilized values. . . .

The rule announced today will measurably weaken the ability of the criminal law to perform in these tasks. It is a deliberate calculus to prevent interrogations, to reduce the incidence of confessions and pleas of guilty and to increase the number of trials. Criminal trials, no matter how efficient the police are, are not sure bets for the prosecution, nor should they be if the evidence is not forthcoming. Under the present law, the prosecution fails to prove its case in about 30% of the criminal cases actually tried in the federal courts. . . . But it is something else again to remove from the ordinary criminal case all those confessions which heretofore have been held to be free and voluntary acts of the accused and to thus establish a new constitutional barrier to the ascertainment of truth by the judicial process. There is, in my view, every reason to believe that a good many criminal defendants, who otherwise would have been convicted on what this Court has previously thought to be the most satis-

factory kind of evidence, will now under this new version of the Fifth Amendment, either not be tried at all or acquitted if the State's evidence, minus the confession, is put to the test of litigation.

I have no desire whatsoever to share the responsibility for any such impact on the present criminal process.

In some unknown number of cases the Court's rule will return a killer, a rapist or other criminal to the streets and to the environment which produced him, to repeat his crime whenever it pleases him. As a consequence, there will not be a gain, but a loss in human dignity. The real concern is not the unfortunate consequences of this new decision on the criminal law as an abstract, disembodied series of authoritative proscriptions, but the impact on those who rely on the public authority for protection and who without it can only engage in violent self-help with guns, knives and the help of their neighbors similarly inclined. There is, of course, a saving factor: the next victims are uncertain, unnamed and unrepresented in this case.

. . .

There is another aspect of the effect of the Court's rule on the persons whom the police have arrested on probable cause. The fact is that he may not be guilty at all and may be able to extricate himself quickly and simply if he were told the circumstances of his arrest and were asked to explain. This effort, and his release, must now await the hiring of a lawyer or his appointment by the court, consultation with counsel and then a session with the police or the prosecutor. Similarly, where probable cause exists to arrest several suspects, as where the body of the victim is discovered in a house having several residents . . . it will often be true that a suspect may be cleared only through the results of interrogation of other suspects. Here too the release of the innocent may be delayed by the Court's rule. . . .

Applying the traditional standards to the cases before the Court, I would hold these confessions voluntary. I would therefore affirm in Nos. 759, 760, and 761 and reverse in No. 584.

# IN RE GAULT

387 U. S. 1; 18 L. Ed. 2d 527; 87 S. Ct. 1428 (1967)

MR. JUSTICE FORTAS *delivered the opinion of the Court.*

This is an appeal under 28 U.S.C. Sec. 1257(2) from a judgment of the Supreme Court of Arizona affirming the dismissal of a petition for a writ of habeas corpus. . . . The petition sought the release of Gerald Francis Gault, petitioners' 15-year-old son, who had been committed as a juvenile delinquent to the State Industrial School by the Juvenile Court of Gila County, Arizona. The Supreme Court of Arizona affirmed dismissal of the writ. . . . The court agreed that the constitutional guarantee of due process of law is applicable in such proceedings. It held that Arizona's Juvenile Code is to be read as "impliedly" implementing the "due process concept." . . . It concluded that the proceedings ending in commitment of Gerald Gault did not offend those requirements. We do not agree, and we reverse. We begin with a statement of the facts.

On Monday, June 8, 1964, at about 10 A.M., Gerald Francis Gault and a friend, Ronald Lewis, were taken into custody by the Sheriff of Gila County. Gerald was then still subject to a six months' probation order. . . . The police action on June 8 was taken as the result of a verbal com-

plaint by a neighbor of the boys, Mrs. Cook, about a telephone call made to her in which the caller or callers made lewd or indecent remarks. It will suffice for the purposes of this opinion to say that the remarks or questions put to her were of the irritatingly offensive, adolescent, sex variety.

At the time Gerald was picked up, his mother and father were both at work. No notice that Gerald was being taken into custody was left at the home. No other steps were taken to advise them that their son had, in effect, been arrested. Gerald was taken to the Children's Detention Home. . . . The deputy probation officer, Flagg, who was also superintendent of the Detention Home told Mrs. Gault "why Jerry was there" and said that a hearing would be held in Juvenile Court at 3 o'clock the following day, June 9.

Officer Flagg filed a petition with the Court on the hearing day, June 9, 1964. It was not served on the Gaults. Indeed, none of them saw this petition until the habeas corpus hearing on August 17, 1964. The petition was certainly formal. It made no reference to any factual basis for the judicial action which it initiated. It recited only that "said minor is under the age of 18 years and in need of the protection of this Honorable Court [and that] said minor is a delinquent minor." It prayed for a hearing and an order regarding "the care and custody of said minor." . . .

On June 9, Gerald, his mother, his older brother, and Probation Officers Flagg and Henderson appeared before the Juvenile Judge in chambers. Gerald's father was not there. He was at work out of the city. Mrs. Cook, the complainant, was not there. No one was sworn at this hearing. No transcript or recording was made. No memorandum or record of the substance of the proceedings was prepared. Our information about the proceedings and the subsequent hearing on June 15, derives entirely from the testimony of the Juvenile Court Judge, Mr. and Mrs. Gault, and Officer Flagg at the habeas corpus proceedings conducted two months later. From this, it appears that at the July 9 hearing Gerald was questioned by the judge about the telephone call. There was conflict as to what he said. His mother recalled that Gerald said he only dialed Mrs. Cook's number and then handed the telephone to his friend, Ronald. Officer Flagg recalled that Gerald had admitted making the lewd remarks. Judge McGhee testified that Gerald "admitted making one of these [lewd] statements." At the conclusion of the hearing, the judge said he would "think about it." Gerald was taken back to the Detention Home. . . . On June 11 or 12, after having been detained since June 8, Gerald was released and driven home.* There is

---

* There is a conflict between the recollection of Mrs. Gault and that of Officer Flagg. Mrs. Gault testified that Gerald was released on Friday, June 12, Officer Flagg that it had been on Thursday, June 11. This was from memory; he had no record, and the note was undated.

no explanation in the record as to why he was kept in the Detention Home or why he was released. At 5 P.M. on the day of Gerald's release, Mrs. Gault received a note signed by Officer Flagg. It was on plain paper, not letterhead. Its entire text is as follows:

"Mr. Gault:

Judge McGHEE has set Monday June 15, 1964 at 11:00 A.M. as the date and time for further Hearings on Gerald's delinquency

/s/Flagg"

At the appointed time on Monday, June 15, Gerald, his father and mother, Ronald Lewis and his father, and Officers Flagg and Henderson were present before Judge McGhee. Witnesses at the habeas corpus proceedings differed in their recollections of Gerald's testimony at the June 15 hearing. Mr. and Mrs. Gault recalled that Gerald again testified that he had only dialed the number and that the other boy had made the remarks. Officer Flagg agreed that at this hearing Gerald did not admit making the lewd remarks. But Judge McGhee recalled that "there was some admission again of some of the lewd statements. He—he didn't admit any of the more serious lewd statements." Again, the complainant, Mrs. Cook, was not present. Mrs. Gault asked that Mrs. Cook be present "so she could see which boy had done the talking, the dirty talking over the phone." The Juvenile Judge said "she didn't have to be present at that hearing." The judge did not speak to Mrs. Cook or communicate with her at any time. Probation Officer Flagg had talked to her once—over the telephone on June 9.

At this June 14 hearing a "referral report" made by the probation officers was filed with the court, although not disclosed to Gerald or his parents.

This listed the charge as "Lewd Phone Calls." At the conclusion of the hearing, the judge committed Gerald as a juvenile delinquent to the State Industrial School "for the period of his minority (that is, until 21), unless sooner discharged by the process of law." . . .

No appeal is permitted by Arizona law in juvenile cases. On August 3, 1964, a petition for a writ of habeas corpus was filed with the Supreme Court of Arizona and referred by it to the Superior Court for hearing.

At the habeas corpus hearing on August 17, Judge McGhee was vigorously cross-examined as to the basis for his actions. He testified that he had taken into account the fact that Gerald was on probation. He was asked "under what section of . . . the code you found the boy delinquent?" . . .

. . . In substance, he concluded that Gerald came within [the state statute] which specifies that a "delinquent child" includes one "who has violated a law of the state or an ordinance or regulation of a political subdivision thereof." . . . The judge also testified that he acted under [the statutory provision] which includes in the definition of a "delinquent child" one who, as the judge phrased it, is "habitually involved in immoral matters." . . .

The Superior Court dismissed the writ, and appellants sought review in the Arizona Supreme Court. . . .

The Supreme Court handed down an elaborate and wide-ranging opinion affirming dismissal of the writ. . . . [Appellants] urge that we hold the Juvenile Code of Arizona invalid on its face or as applied in this case because, contrary to the Due Process Clause of the Fourteenth Amendment, the juvenile is taken from the custody of his parents and committed to a state institution pursuant to proceedings in which the Juvenile Court has virtually unlimited discretion, and in which the following basic rights are denied:

1. Notice of the charges;
2. Right to counsel;
3. Right to confrontation and cross-examination;
4. Privilege against self-incrimination;
5. Right to a transcript of the proceedings; and
6. Right to appellate review.

. . .

This Court has not heretofore decided the precise question. In *Kent* v. *United States,* 383 U.S. 541, 86 S.Ct. 1045, 16 L.Ed. 2d 84 (1966), we considered the requirements for a valid waiver of the "exclusive" jurisdiction of the Juvenile Court of the District of Columbia so that a juvenile could be tried in the adult criminal court of the District. . . . [We] emphasized the necessity that "the basic requirements of due process and fairness" be satisfied in such proceedings. *Hale* v. *State of Ohio,* 332 U.S. 596, 68 S.Ct. 302, 92 L.Ed. 224 (1948), involved the admissibility, in a state criminal court of general jurisdiction, of a confession of a 15-year-old boy. The Court held that the Fourteenth Amendment applied to prohibit the use of the coerced confession. Mr. Justice Douglas said, "Neither man nor child can be allowed to stand condemned by methods which flout constitutional requirements of due process of law." . . . Accordingly, while these cases relate only to restricted aspects of the subject, they unmistakably indicate that, whatever may be their precise impact, neither the Fourteenth Amendment nor the Bill of Rights is for adults alone.

. . .

From the inception of the juvenile court system, wide differences have been tolerated—indeed insisted upon —between the procedural rights accorded to adults and those of juveniles. In practically all jurisdictions, there are rights granted to adults which are withheld from juveniles. In addition to the specific problems involved in the present case, for example, it has been held that the juvenile is not entitled to bail, to indictment by grand jury, to a public trial or to trial by jury. It is frequent practice that rules governing the arrest and interrogation of adults by the police are not observed in the case of juveniles.

. . .

The right of the State, as *parens patriae,* to deny to the child procedural rights available to his elders was elaborated by the assertion that a child, unlike an adult, has a right "not to liberty but to custody." He can be made to attorn to his parents, to go to school, etc. If his parents default in effectively performing their custodial functions—that is, if the child is "delinquent"—the state may intervene. In doing so, it does not deprive the child of any rights, because he has none. It merely provides the "custody" to which the child is entitled. On this basis, proceedings involving juveniles were described as "civil" not "criminal" and therefore not subject to the requirements which restrict the state when it seeks to deprive a person of his liberty.

. . . Juvenile court history has . . . demonstrated that unbridled discretion, however benevolently motivated, is frequently a poor substitute for principle and procedure. . . . The absence of substantive standards has not necessarily meant that children receive careful, compassionate, individualized treatment. The absence of procedural rules based upon constitutional principle has not always produced fair, efficient, and effective procedures. Departures from established principles of due process have frequently resulted not in enlightened procedure, but in arbitrariness.

. . .

. . . [I]t is urged that the juvenile benefits from informal proceedings in the court. The early conception of the juvenile court proceeding was one in which a fatherly judge touched the heart and conscience of the erring youth by talking over his problems, by paternal advice and admonition, and in which, in extreme situations, benevolent and wise institutions of the State provided guidance and help "to save him from a downward career." Then, as now, goodwill and compassion were admirably prevalent. But recent studies have, with surprising unanimity, entered sharp dissent as to the validity of this gentle conception. They suggest that the appearance as well as the actuality of fairness, the partiality and orderliness —in short, the essentials of due process may be a more impressive and more therapeutic attitude so far as the juvenile is concerned. . . . While due process requirements will, in some instances, introduce a degree of order and regularity to juvenile court proceedings to determine delinquency, and in contested cases will introduce some elements of the adversary system, nothing will require that the conception of the kindly juvenile judge be replaced by its opposite, nor do we here rule upon the question whether ordinary due process requirements must be observed with respect to hearings to determine the disposition of the delinquent child.

Ultimately, however, we confront the reality of that portion of the juvenile court process with which we deal in this case. A boy is charged with misconduct. The boy is committed to an institution where he may be restrained of liberty for years. It is of no constitutional consequence—and of limited practical meaning—that the institution to which he is committed is called an Industrial School. The fact of the matter is that, however euphemistic the title, a "receiving home" or an "industrial school" for juveniles is an institution of confinement in which the child is incarcerated for a greater or lesser time. His world becomes "a building with white-washed walls, regimented routine and institutional laws. . . ." Instead of mother and father and sisters and brothers and friends and classmates, his world is peopled by guards, custodians, state employees, and "delinquents" confined with him for anything from waywardness to rape and homicide.

In view of this, it would be extraordinary if our Constitution did not require the procedural regularity and the exercise of care implied in the phrase "due process." Under our Constitution, the condition of a boy does not justify a kangaroo court. The traditional ideas of juvenile court procedure, indeed, contemplated that time would be available and care would be used to establish precisely what the juvenile did and why he did it—was it a prank of adolescence or a brutal act threatening serious consequences to himself or society unless corrected? Under traditional notions, one would assume that in a case like that of Gerald Gault, where the juvenile appears to have a home, a working mother and father, and an older brother, the Juvenile Judge would have made a careful inquiry and judgment as to the possibility that the boy could be disciplined and dealt with at home, despite his previous trans-

gressions. Indeed, so far as appears in the record before us, except for some conversation with Gerald about his school work and his "wanting to go to . . . Grand Canyon with his father," the points to which the judge directed his attention were little different from those that would be involved in determining any charge of violation of a penal statute. The essential difference between Gerald's case and a normal criminal case is that safeguards available to adults were discarded in Gerald's case. The summary procedure as well as the long commitment were possible because Gerald was 15 years of age instead of over 18.

If Gerald had been over 18, he would not have been subject to Juvenile Court proceedings. For the particular offense immediately involved, the maximum punishment would have been a fine of $5 to $50, or imprisonment in jail for not more than two months. Instead, he was committed to custody for a maximum of six years. If he had been over 18 and had committed an offense to which such a sentence might apply, he would have been entitled to substantial rights under the Constitution of the United States as well as under Arizona's laws and constitution. The United States Constitution would guarantee him rights and protections with respect to arrest, search, [*sic*] and seizure, and pretrial interrogation. It would assure him of specific notice of the charges and adequate time to decide his course of action and to prepare his defense. He would be entitled to clear advice that he could be represented by counsel, and, at least if a felony were involved, the State would be required to provide counsel if his parents were unable to afford it. If the court acted on the basis of his confession, careful procedures would be required to assure it voluntariness. If the case went to trial, confrontation and opportunity for cross-examination would be guaranteed. So wide a gulf between the State's treatment of the adult and of the child requires a bridge sturdier than mere verbiage, and reasons more persuasive than cliché can provide. . . .

We now turn to the specific issues which are presented to us in the present case.

### NOTICE OF CHARGES
. . .
We cannot agree with the court's conclusion that adequate notice was given in this case. Notice, to comply with due process requirements, must be given sufficiently in advance of scheduled court proceedings so that reasonable opportunity to prepare will be afforded, and it must "set forth the alleged misconduct with particularity." . . . The "initial hearing" in the present case was a hearing on the merits. Notice at that time is not timely; and even if there were a conceivable purpose served by the deferral proposed by the court below, it would have to yield to the requirements that the child and his parents or guardian be notified, in writing, of the specific charge or factual allegations to be considered at the hearing, and that such written notice be given at the earliest practicable time, and in any event sufficiently in advance of the hearing to permit preparation. Due process of law requires notice of the sort we have described—that is, notice which would be deemed constitutionally adequate in a civil or criminal proceedings. . . .

### RIGHT TO COUNSEL

Appellants charge that the Juvenile Court proceedings were fatally defective because the court did not advise Gerald or his parents of their right to counsel, and proceeded with the hearing, the adjudication of delinquency and the order of commitment in the absence of counsel. . . . The Supreme Court of Arizona pointed out that "[t]here is disagreement [among the various jurisdictions] as to whether the court must advise the infant that he has a right to counsel."
. . . It referred to a provision of the Juvenile Code which it characterized as requiring "that the probation officer shall look after the interests of neglected, delinquent and dependent children," including representing their interests in court. The court argued that "The parent and the probation officer may be relied upon to protect the infant's interests." . . . It said that juvenile courts have the discretion, but not the duty, to allow such representation. . . . We do not agree. Probation officers, in the Arizona scheme, are also arresting officers. They initiate proceedings and file petitions which they verify . . . alleging the delinquency of the child; and they testify . . . against the child. And here the probation officer was also superintendent of the Detention Home. The probation officer cannot act as counsel for the child. His role in the adjudicatory hearing, by statute and in fact, is as arresting officer and witness against the child. Nor can the judge represent the child. . . . A proceeding where the issue is whether the child will be found to be "delinquent" and subjected to the loss of his liberty for years is comparable in seriousness to a felony prosecution. The juvenile needs the assistance of counsel to cope with problems of law, to make skilled inquiry into the facts, to insist upon regularity of the proceedings, and to ascertain whether he has a defense and to prepare and submit it. The child

"requires the guiding hand of counsel at every step in the proceedings against him."

. . .

## CONFRONTATION, SELF-INCRIMINATION, CROSS-EXAMINATION

Appellants urge that the writ of habeas corpus should have been granted because of the denial of the rights of confrontation and cross-examination in the Juvenile Court hearings, and because the privilege against self-incrimination was not observed. . . .

Our first question, then, is whether Gerald's admission was improperly obtained and relied on as the basis of decision, in conflict with the Federal Constitution. For this purpose, it is necessary briefly to recall the relevant facts.

Mrs. Cook, the complainant, and the recipient of the alleged telephone call, was not called as a witness. Gerald's mother asked the Juvenile Court Judge why Mrs. Cook was not present and the judge replied that "she didn't have to be present." So far as appears, Mrs. Cook was spoken to only once, by Officer Flagg, and this was by telephone. . . . Gerald had been questioned by the probation officer after having been taken into custody. The exact circumstances of this questioning do not appear in the record. Gerald was also questioned by the Juvenile Court Judge at each of the two hearings. The judge testified in the habeas corpus proceeding that Gerald admitted making "some of the lewd statements . . . [but not] any of the more serious lewd statements."

. . .

We shall assume that Gerald made admissions of the sort described by the Juvenile Court Judge. . . . Neither Gerald nor his parents was ad-vised that he did not have to testify or make a statement, or that an incriminating statement might result in his commitment as a "delinquent."

. . .

. . . Specifically, the question is whether, in such a proceeding, an admission by the juvenile may be used against him in the absence of clear and unequivocal evidence that the admission was made with knowledge that he was not obligated to speak and would not be penalized for remaining silent. In light of *Miranda* v. *Arizona*, . . . we must also consider whether, if the privilege against self-incrimination is available, it can effectively be waived unless counsel is present or the right to counsel has been waived.

. . .

It would indeed be surprising if the privilege against self-incrimination were available to hardened criminals but not to children. The language of the Fifth Amendment . . . is unequivocal and without exception. And the scope of the privilege is comprehensive.

. . .

Against the application to juveniles of the right to silence, it is argued that juvenile proceedings are "civil" and not "criminal," and therefore the privilege should not apply. It is true that the statement of the privilege in the Fifth Amendment . . . is that no person "shall be compelled in any *criminal* case to be a witness against himself." However, it is also clear that the availability of the privilege does not turn upon the type of proceeding in which its protection is invoked, but upon the nature of the statement or admission and the exposure which it invites. . . .

It would be entirely unrealistic to carve out of the Fifth Amendment all statements by juveniles on the ground that these cannot lead to "criminal" involvement. . . . [J]uvenile proceedings to determine "delinquency," which may lead to commitment to a state institution, must be regarded as "criminal" for purposes of the privilege against self-incrimination. To hold otherwise would be to disregard substance because of the feeble enticement of the "civil" label-of-convenience which has been attached to juvenile proceedings. Instead, in over half of the States, there is not even assurance that the juvenile will be kept in separate institutions, apart from adult "criminals." . . . For this purpose, at least, commitment is a deprivation of liberty. It is incarceration against one's will, whether it is called "criminal" or "civil."

. . .

We conclude that the constitutional privilege against self-incrimination is applicable in the case of juveniles as it is with respect to adults. We appreciate that special problems may arise with respect to waiver of the privilege by or on behalf of children, and that there may well be some differences in techniques—but not in principle—depending upon the age of the child and the presence and competence of parents. The participation of counsel will, of course, assist the police, juvenile courts and appellate courts in administering the privilege. If counsel is not present for some permissible reason when an admission is obtained, the greatest care must be taken to assure that the admission was voluntary, in the sense not only that it has not been coerced or suggested, but also that it is not the product of ignorance of rights or of adolescent fantasy, fright or despair.

. . .

. . . We now hold that, absent a valid confession, a determination of delinquency and an order of commitment to a state institution cannot be sustained in the absence of sworn testimony subjected to the opportunity for cross-examination in accordance with our law and constitutional requirements.

. . .

*Judgment reversed and cause remanded with directions.*

Mr. Justice Black *and* Mr. Justice White *wrote separate concurring opinions which are not reprinted here.*

Mr. Justice Stewart, *dissenting.*

The Court today uses an obscure Arizona case as a vehicle to impose upon thousands of juvenile courts throughout the Nation restrictions that the Constitution made applicable to adversary criminal trials. I believe the Court's decision is wholly unsound as a matter of constitutional law, and sadly unwise as a matter of judicial policy. Whether treating with a delinquent child, a neglected child, a defective child, or a dependent child, a juvenile proceeding's whole purpose and mission is the very opposite of the mission and purpose of a prosecution in a criminal court. The object of the one is the correction of a condition. The object of the other is conviction and punishment for a criminal act.

. . .

The inflexible restrictions that the Constitution so wisely made applicable to adversary criminal trials have no inevitable place in the proceedings of those public social agencies known as juvenile or family courts. And to impose the Court's long catalog of requirements upon the country is to invite a long step backwards into the Nineteenth Century. In that era there were no juvenile proceedings, and a child was tried in a conventional criminal court with all the trappings of a conventional trial. So it was that a 12-year-old boy named James Guild was tried in New Jersey for killing Catherine Beakes. A jury found him guilty of murder, and he was sentenced to death by hanging. The sentence was executed. It was all very constitutional.

A state in all its dealings must, of course, accord every person due process of law. And due process may require that some of the restrictions which the Constitution has placed upon criminal trials must be imposed upon juvenile proceedings. For example, I suppose that all would agree that a brutally coerced confession could not constitutionally be considered in a juvenile court hearing. But it surely does not follow that the testimonial privilege against self-incrimination is applicable in all juvenile proceedings. Similarly, due process clearly requires timely notice of the purpose and scope of any proceedings affecting the relationship of parent and child. . . . But it certainly does not follow that notice of a juvenile hearing must be framed with all the technical niceties of a criminal indictment. . . .

In any event, there is no reason to deal with issues such as these in the present case. The Supreme Court of Arizona found that the parents of Gerald Gault "knew of their right to counsel, to subpoena and cross examine witnesses against Gerald and the possible consequences of a finding of delinquency." . . . It further found that "Mrs. Gault knew the exact nature of the charge against Gerald from the day he was taken to the detention home." . . . And . . . no issue of compulsory self-incrimination is presented by this case.

I would dismiss the appeal.

## DUNCAN v. LOUISIANA
### 391 U. S. 145; 20 L. Ed. 2d 491; 88 S. Ct. 1444 (1968)

MR. JUSTICE WHITE *delivered the opinion of the Court.*

Appellant, Gary Duncan, was convicted of simple battery in the Twenty-fifth Judicial District Court of Louisiana. Under Louisiana law simple battery is a misdemeanor, punishable by two years' imprisonment and a $300 fine. Appellant sought trial by jury, but because the Louisiana Constitution grants jury trials only in cases in which capital punishment or imprisonment at hard labor may be imposed, the trial judge denied the request. Appellant was convicted and sentenced to serve 60 days in the parish prison and pay a fine of $150. Appellant sought review in the Supreme Court of Louisiana, asserting that the denial of jury trial violated rights guaranteed to him by the United States Constitution. The Supreme Court . . . denied appellant a writ of certiorari. Pursuant to 28 U.S.C. Sec. 1257 (2) appellant sought review in this Court, alleging that the Sixth and Fourteenth Amendments to the United States Constitution secure the right to jury trial in state criminal prosecutions where a sentence as long as two years may be imposed. . . .

Appellant was 19 years of age when tried. While driving on Highway 23 in Plaquemines Parish on October 18, 1966, he saw two younger cousins engaged in a conversation by the side of the road with four white boys. Knowing his cousins, Negroes who had recently been transferred to a formerly all-white high school, had reported the occurrence of racial incidents at the school, Duncan stopped the car, got out, and approached the six boys. At trial the white boys and a white onlooker testified, as did appellant and his cousins. The testimony was in dispute on many points, but the witnesses agreed that appellant and the white boys spoke to each other, that appellant encouraged his cousins to break off the encounter and enter his car, and that appellant was about to enter the car himself for the purpose of driving away with his cousins. The whites testified that just before getting in the car appellant slapped Herman Landry, one of the white boys, on the elbow. The Negroes testified that appellant had not slapped Landry, but had merely touched him. The trial judge concluded that the State had proved beyond a reasonable doubt that Duncan had committed simple battery, and found him guilty.

. . . [M]any of the rights guaranteed by the first eight Amendments to the Constitution have been held to be protected against state action by the Due Process Clause of the Fourteenth Amendment. That clause now protects the right to compensation for property taken by the State; the rights of speech, press, and religion covered by the First Amendment; the Fourth Amendment rights to be free from unreasonable searches and seizures and to have excluded from criminal trials any evidence illegally seized; the right guaranteed by the Fifth Amendment to be free of compelled self-incrimination; and the Sixth Amendment rights to counsel, to a speedy and public trial, to confrontation of opposing witnesses, and to compulsory process for obtaining witnesses.

The test for determining whether a right extended by the Fifth and Sixth Amendments with respect to federal criminal proceedings is also protected against state action by the Fourteenth Amendment has been phrased in a variety of ways in the opinions of this Court. The question has been asked whether a right is among those " 'fundamental principles of liberty and justice which lie at the base of all our civil and political institutions,' " *Powell* v. *Alabama,* 287 U.S. 45, 67 (1932); whether it is "basic in our system of jurisprudence," *In re Oliver,* 333 U.S. 257, 273 (1948); and whether it is "a fundamental right, essential to a fair trial," *Gideon* v. *Wainwright,* 372 U.S. 1, 335, 343-344 (1963); *Malloy* v. *Hogan,* 378 U.S. 1, 6 (1964); *Pointer* v. *Texas,* 380 U.S. 400, 403 (1965). The claim before us is that the right to trial by jury guaranteed by the Sixth Amendment meets these tests. The position of Louisiana, on the other hand, is that the Constitution imposes upon the States no duty to give a jury trial in any criminal case, regardless of the seriousness of the crime, or the size of the punishment which may be imposed. Because we believe that trial by jury in criminal cases is fundamental to the American scheme of justice, we hold that the Fourteenth Amendment guarantees a right of jury trial in all criminal cases which—were they to be tried in a federal court—would come within the Sixth Amendment's guarantee. . . .

[Here followed a brief summary of the history of trial by jury in criminal cases in the United States.]

. . .

Jury trial continues to receive strong support. The laws of every State guarantee right to jury trial in serious criminal cases; no State has dispensed with it; nor are there significant movements underway to do so. Indeed, the three most recent state constitutional revisions, in Maryland, Michigan, and New York, carefully preserved the right of the accused to have the judgment of a jury when tried for a serious crime.

We are aware of prior cases in this Court in which the prevailing opinion contains statements contrary to our holding today that the right to trial by jury in serious criminal cases is a fundamental right and hence must be recognized by the States as part of their obligation to extend due process of law to all persons within their jurisdiction. Louisiana relies especially on *Maxwell* v. *Dow,* 176 U.S. 581 (1900); *Palko* v. *Connecticut,* 302 U.S. 319 (1937) and *Snyder* v. *Massachusetts,* 291 U.S. 97 (1934). None of these cases, however, dealt with a State which had purported to dispense entirely with a jury trial in serious criminal cases. *Maxwell* held that no provision of the Bill of Rights applied to the States—a position long since repudiated—and that the Due Process Clause of the Fourteenth Amendment did not prevent a State from trying a defendant for a noncapital offense with fewer than 12 men on the jury. It did not deal with a case in which no jury at all had been provided. In neither *Palko* nor *Snyder* was jury trial actually at issue, although both cases contain important dicta asserting that the right to jury trial is not essential to ordered liberty and may be dispensed with by the States re-

gardless of the Sixth and Fourteenth Amendments. These observations, though weighty and respectable, are nevertheless dicta, unsupported by holdings in this Court that a State may refuse a defendant's demand for a jury trial when he is charged with a serious crime. . . . In *Malloy* v. *Hogan,* . . . the Court rejected *Palko*'s discussion of the self-incrimination clause. Respectfully, we reject the prior dicta regarding jury trial in criminal cases.

The guarantees of jury trial in the Federal and State Constitutions reflect a profound judgment about the way in which law should be enforced and justice administered. A right to jury trial is granted to criminal defendants in order to prevent oppression by the Government. Those who wrote our constitutions knew from history and experience that it was necessary to protect against unfounded criminal charges brought to eliminate enemies and against judges too responsive to the voice of higher authority. The framers of the constitutions strove to create an independent judiciary but insisted upon further protection against arbitrary action. Providing an accused with the right to be tried by a jury of his peers gave him an inestimable safeguard against the corrupt or overzealous prosecutor and against the compliant, biased, or eccentric judge. If the defendant preferred the common-sense judgment of a jury to the more tutored but perhaps less sympathetic reaction of the single judge, he was to have it. Beyond this, the jury trial provisions in the Federal and State Constitutions reflect a fundamental decision about the exercise of official power—a reluctance to entrust plenary powers over the life and liberty of the citizen to one judge or to a group of judges. Fear of the unchecked power, so typical of our State and Federal Governments in other respects, found expression in the criminal law in this insistence upon community participation in the determination of guilt or innocence. The deep commitment of the Nation to the right of jury trial in serious criminal cases as a defense against arbitrary law enforcement qualifies for protection under the Due Process Clause of the Fourteenth Amendment, and must therefore be respected by the States.

Of course jury trial has "its weaknesses and the potential for misuse." . . . We are aware of the long debate, especially in this century, among those who write about the administration of justice, as to the wisdom of permitting untrained laymen to determine the facts in civil and criminal proceedings. Although the debate has been intense, with powerful voices on either side, most of the controversy has centered on the jury in civil cases. Indeed, some of the severest critics of civil juries acknowledge that the arguments for criminal juries are much stronger. In addition, at the heart of the dispute have been express or implicit assertions that juries are incapable of adequately understanding evidence or determining issues of fact, and that they are unpredictable, quixotic, and little better than a roll of dice. Yet, the most recent and exhaustive study of the jury in criminal cases concluded that juries do understand the evidence and come to sound conclusions in most of the cases presented to them and that when juries differ with the result at which the judge would have arrived, it is usually because they are serving some of the very purposes for which they were created and for which they are now employed.*

* [H.] Kalven & [H.] Zeisel, . . . [The American Jury].

The State of Louisiana urges that holding that the Fourteenth Amendment assures a right to jury trial will cast doubt on the integrity of every trial conducted without a jury. Plainly, this is not the import of our holding. Our conclusion is that in the American States, as in the federal judicial system, a general grant of jury trial for serious offenses is a fundamental right, essential for preventing miscarriages of justice and for assuring that fair trials are provided for all defendants. We would not assert, however, that every criminal trial—or any particular trial—held before a judge alone is unfair or that a defendant may never be as fairly treated by a judge as he would be by a jury. Thus we hold no constitutional doubts about the practices, common in both federal and state courts, of accepting waivers of jury trial and prosecuting petty crimes without extending a right to jury trial. . . .

Louisiana's final contention is that even if it must grant jury trials in serious criminal cases, the conviction before us is valid and constitutional because here the petitioner was tried for simple battery and was sentenced to only 60 days in the parish prison. We are not persuaded. It is doubtless true that there is a category of petty crimes or offenses which is not subject to the Sixth Amendment jury trial provision and should not be subject to the Fourteenth Amendment jury trial requirement here applied to the States. . . . But the *penalty authorized* [emphasis added] for a particular crime is of major relevance in determining whether it is serious or not and may in itself, if severe enough, subject the trial to the mandates of the Sixth Amendment. . . . The penalty authorized by the law of the locality may be taken "as a gauge of its social and ethical judgments," . . . of the crime in question. . . . In the case before us the Legislature of Louisiana has made simple battery a criminal offense punishable by imprisonment for two years and a fine. The question, then, is whether a crime carrying such a penalty is an offense which Louisiana may insist on trying without a jury.

We think not. So-called petty offenses were tried without juries both in England and in the Colonies and have always been held to be exempt from the otherwise comprehensive language of the Sixth Amendment's jury trial provisions. There is no substantial evidence that the Framers intended to depart from this established common-law practice, and the possible consequences to defendants from convictions for petty offenses have been thought insufficient to outweigh the benefits to efficient law enforcement and simplified judicial administration resulting from the availability of speedy and inexpensive nonjury adjudications. These same considerations compel the same result under the Fourteenth Amendment. Of course the boundaries of the petty offense category have always been ill defined, if not ambulatory. In the absence of an explicit constitutional provision, the definitional task necessarily falls on the courts, which must either pass upon the validity of legislative attempts to identify those petty offenses which are exempt from jury trial or, where the legislature has not addressed itself to the problem, themselves face the question in the first instance. In either case it is necessary to draw a line in the spectrum of crime, separating petty from serious infractions. This process, although essential, cannot be wholly satisfactory, for it requires attaching

different consequences to events which, when they lie near the line, actually differ very little.

In determining whether the length of the authorized prison term or the seriousness of other punishment is enough in itself to require a jury trial, we . . . [must] refer to objective criteria, chiefly the existing laws and practices in the Nation. In the federal system, petty offenses are defined as those punishable by no more than six months in prison and a $500 fine. In 49 of the 50 States crimes subject to trial without a jury were for the most part punishable by no more than a six-month prison term, although there appear to have been exceptions to this rule. We need not, however, settle in this case the exact location of the line between petty offenses and serious crimes. It is sufficient for our purposes to hold that a crime punishable by two years in prison is, based on past and contemporary standards in this country, a serious crime and not a petty offense. Consequently, appellant was entitled to a jury trial and it was error to deny it.

The judgment below is reversed and the case is remanded for proceedings not inconsistent with this opinion.

MR. JUSTICE BLACK, *with whom* MR. JUSTICE DOUGLAS *joins, concurring.*

The Court today holds that the right to trial by jury guaranteed defendants in criminal cases in federal courts by Art. III of the United States Constitution and by the Sixth Amendment is also guaranteed by the Fourteenth Amendment to defendants tried in state courts. With this holding I agree for reasons given by the Court. I also agree because of reasons given in my dissent in *Adamson* v. *California,* 332 U.S. 46, 68. In that dissent . . . I took the position, contrary to the holding in *Twining* v. *New Jersey,* 211 U.S. 78, that the Fourteenth Amendment made all of the provisions of the Bill of Rights applicable to the States. This Court in *Palko* v. *Connecticut,* 302 U.S. 319 . . . [said] "there is no such general rule," . . . [and was of the opinion] that certain Bill of Rights' provisions were made applicable to the States by bringing them "within the Fourteenth Amendment by a process of absorption." Thus *Twining* v. *New Jersey* . . . refused to hold that any one of the Bill of Rights' provisions was made applicable to the States by the Fourteenth Amendment, but *Palko,* which must be read as overruling *Twining* on this point, concluded that the Bill of Rights' Amendments that are "implicit in the concept of ordered liberty" are "absorbed" by the Fourteenth as protections against state invasion. In this situation I said in *Adamson* v. *California,* 332 U.S., at 89, that while "I would extend to all the people of the nation the complete protection of the Bill of Rights," that "[i]f the choice must be between the selective process of the *Palko* decision applying some of the Bill of Rights to the States, or the *Twining* rule applying none of them, I would choose the *Palko* selective process." And I am very happy to support this selective process through which our Court has since the *Adamson* case held most of the specific Bill of Rights' protections applicable to the States to the same extent they are applicable to the Federal Government. . . .

. . . The dissent in this case . . . makes a spirited and forceful defense of that now discredited doctrine. I do not believe that it is necessary for me to repeat the historical and logical reasons for my challenge to the *Twining* holding contained in my *Adamson* dissent and Appendix to it. What I wrote there in 1947 was the product of years of study and research. My appraisal of the legislative history followed 10 years of legislative experience as a Senator of the United States, not a bad way, I suspect, to learn the value of what is said in legislative debates, committee discussions, committee reports, and various other steps taken in the course of passage of bills, resolutions, and proposed constitutional amendments. My Brother Harlan's objections to my *Adamson* dissent history, like that of most of the objections, relies most heavily on a criticism written by Professor Charles Fairman and published in the Stanford Law Review, 2 Stan. L. Rev. 5 (1949). I have read and studied this article extensively, including the historical references, but am compelled to add that in my view it has completely failed to refute the inferences and arguments that I suggested in my *Adamson* dissent. Professor Fairman's "history" relies very heavily on what was *not* said in the state legislatures that passed on the Fourteenth Amendment. Instead of relying on this kind of negative pregnant, my legislative experience has convinced me that it is far wiser to rely on what *was* said, and most importantly, said by the men who actually sponsored the Amendment in the Congress. I know from my years in the United States Senate that it is to men like Congressman Bingham, who steered the Amendment through the House, and Senator Howard, who introduced it in the Senate, that members of Congress look when they seek the real meaning of what is being offered. And they vote for or against a bill based on what the sponsors of that bill and those who oppose it tell them it means. The historical appendix to my *Adamson* dissent leaves no doubt in my mind that both its sponsors and those who opposed it believed the Fourteenth Amendment made the first eight Amendments of the Constitution (The Bill of Rights) applicable to the States.

In addition to the adoption of Professor Fairman's "history," the dissent states that "the great words of the four clauses of the first section of the Fourteenth Amendment would have been an exceedingly peculiar way to say that 'The rights heretofore guaranteed against federal intrusion by the first eight amendments are henceforth guaranteed against State intrusion as well.' " . . . In response to this I can say only that the words "No State shall make or enforce any law which shall abridge the privileges or immunities of citizens of the United States" seems to me an eminently reasonable way of expressing the idea that henceforth the Bill of Rights shall apply to the States.† What more precious "privilege" of American citizenship could there be than that privilege to claim the protection of our great Bill of Rights? I suggest that any reading of "privileges and immunities of citizens of the United States" which excludes the Bill of Rights' safeguards renders the words of this section of the Fourteenth Amendment meaningless. . . .

While I do not wish at this time to discuss at length my disagreement

with Brother Harlan's forthright and frank restatement of the now discredited *Twining* doctrine, I do want to point out what appears to me to be the basic difference between us. His view, as was indeed the view of *Twining,* is that "due process is an evolving concept" and therefore that it entails a "gradual process of judicial inclusion and exclusion" to ascertain those "immutable principles of free government which no member of the Union may disregard." Thus the Due Process Clause is treated as prescribing no specific and clearly ascertainable constitutional command that judges must obey in interpreting the Constitution, but rather as leaving judges free to decide at any particular time whether a particular rule or judicial formulation embodies an "immutable principle of free government" or "is implicit in the concept of ordered liberty," or whether certain conduct "shocks the judge's conscience" or runs counter to some other similar, undefined and undefinable standard. Thus due process, according to my Brother Harlan, is to be a word with no permanent meaning, but one which is found to shift from time to time in accordance with judges' predilections and understandings of what is best for the country. If due process means this, the Fourteenth Amendment, in my opinion, might as well have been written that "no person shall be deprived of life, liberty or property except by laws that the judges of the United States Supreme Court shall find to be consistent with the immutable principles of free government." It is impossible for me to believe that such unconfined power is given to judges in our Constitution that is a written one in order to limit governmental power.

Another tenet of the *Twining* doctrine as restated by my Brother

† My view has been and is that the Fourteenth Amendment, *as a whole,* makes the Bill of Rights applicable to the States. This would certainly include the language of the Privileges and Immunities Clause, as well as the Due Process Clause.

Harlan is that "due process of law requires only fundamental fairness." But the "fundamental fairness" test is one on a par with that of shocking the conscience of the Court. Each of such tests depends entirely on the particular judge's idea of ethics and morals instead of requiring him to depend on the boundaries fixed by the written words of the Constitution. Nothing in the history of the phrase "due process of law" suggests that constitutional controls are to depend on any particular judge's sense of values. . . . [T]he Due Process Clause gives all Americans, whoever they are and wherever they happen to be, the right to be tried by independent and unprejudiced Courts using established procedures and applying valid pre-existing laws. There is not one word of legal history that justifies making the term "due process of law" mean a guarantee of a trial free from laws and conduct which the courts deem at the time to be "arbitrary," "unreasonable," "unfair," or "contrary to civilized standards." The due process of law standard for a trial is one tried in accordance with the Bill of Rights and laws passed pursuant to constitional power, guaranteeing to all alike a trial under the general law of the land.

Finally I want to add that I am not bothered by the argument that applying the Bill of Rights to the States, "according to the same standards that protect those rights against federal encroachment," interferes with our concept of federalism in that it may prevent States from trying novel social and economic experiments. I have never believed that under the guise of federalism the States should be able to experiment with the protections afforded our citizens through the Bill of Rights. . . .

In closing I want to emphasize that I believe as strongly as ever that the Fourteenth Amendment was intended to make the Bill of Rights applicable to the States. I have been willing to support the selective incorporation doctrine, however, as an alternative, although perhaps less historically supportable than complete incorporation. The selective incorporation process, if used properly, does limit the Supreme Court in the Fourteenth Amendment field to specific Bill of Rights' protection only and keeps judges from roaming at will in their own notions of what policies outside the Bill of Rights are desirable and what are not. And, most importantly for me, the selective incorporation process has the virtue of having already worked to make most of the Bill of Rights' protections applicable to the States.

MR. JUSTICE HARLAN, *whom* MR. JUSTICE STEWART *joins, dissenting.*

Every American jurisdiction provides for trial by jury in criminal cases. The question before us is not whether jury trial is an ancient institution, which it is; nor whether it plays a significant role in the administration of criminal justice, which it does; nor whether it will endure, which it shall. The question in this case is whether the State of Louisiana, which provides trial by jury for all felonies, is prohibited by the Constitution from trying charges of simple battery to the court alone. In my view, the answer to that question, mandated alike by our constitutional history and by the longer history of trial by jury, is clearly "no."

The States have always borne primary responsibility for operating the machinery of criminal justice within their borders, and adapting it to their particular circumstances. In exercising this responsibility, each State is compelled to conform its procedures to the requirements of the Federal Constitution. The Due Process Clause of the Fourteenth Amendment requires that those procedures be fundamentally fair in all respects. It does not, in my view, impose or encourage nationwide uniformity for its own sake; it does not command adherence to forms that happen to be old; and it does not impose on the States the rules that may be in force in the federal courts except where such rules are also found to be essential to basic fairness.

The Court's approach to this case is an uneasy and illogical compromise among the views of various Justices on how the Due Process Clause should be interpreted. The Court does not say that those who framed the Fourteenth Amendment intended to make the Sixth Amendment applicable to the States. And the Court concedes that it finds nothing unfair about the procedure by which the present appellant was tried. Nevertheless, the Court reverses his conviction: it holds, for some reason not apparent to me, that the Due Process Clause incorporates the particular clause of the Sixth Amendment that requires trial by jury in federal criminal cases—including, as I read its opinion, the sometimes trivial accompanying baggage of judicial interpretation in federal contexts. I have raised my voice many times before against the Court's continuing undiscriminating insistence upon fastening on the States federal notions of criminal justice, and I must do so again in this instance. With all respect, the Court's approach and its reading of history are altogether topsy-turvy.

I believe I am correct in saying that every member of the Court for at least the last 135 years has agreed that our Founders did not consider the requirements of the Bill of Rights so fundamental that they should operate directly against the States. They were wont to believe rather that the security of liberty in America rested primarily upon the dispersion of governmental power across a federal system. The Bill of Rights was considered unnecessary by some but insisted upon by others in order to curb the possibility of abuse of power by the strong central government they were creating.

The Civil War Amendments dramatically altered the relation of the Federal Government to the States. The first section of the Fourteenth Amendment imposes highly significant restrictions of state action. But the restrictions are couched in very broad and general terms: citizenship, privileges and immunities; due process of law; equal protection of the laws. Consequently, for 100 years this Court has engaged in the difficult process Professor Jaffe has well called "the search for intermediate premises." . . .

A few members of the Court have taken the position that the intention of those who drafted the first section of the Fourteenth Amendment was simply, and exclusively, to make the provisions of the first eight amendments applicable to state action. This view has never been accepted by this Court. In my view, often expressed elsewhere, the first section of the Fourteenth Amendment was meant neither to incorporate, nor to be limited to, the specific guarantees of the first eight amendments. The overwhelming historical evidence marshalled by Professor Fairman demonstrates, to me conclusively, that the Congressmen and state legislators who wrote, debated, and ratified the Fourteenth Amendment did not think they were "incorporating" the Bill of Rights and the very breadth and generality of the Amendment's provisions suggests that its authors did not suppose that the Nation would always be limited to mid-19th century conceptions of "liberty" and "due process of law" but that the increasing experience and evolving conscience of the American people would add new "intermediate premises." In short, neither history, nor sense, supports using the Fourteenth Amendment to put the States in a constitutional straitjacket with respect to their own development in the administration of criminal or civil law.

Although I therefore fundamentally disagree with the total incorporation view of the Fourteenth Amendment, it seems to me that such a position does at least have the virtue lacking in the Court's selective incorporation approach, of internal consistency; we look to the Bill of Rights, word for word, clause for clause, precedent for precedent because, it is said, the men who wrote the Amendment wanted it that way. For those who do not accept this "history," a different source of "intermediate premises" must be found. The Bill of Rights is not necessarily irrelevant to the search for guidance in interpreting the Fourteenth Amendment, but the reason for and the nature of its relevance must be articulated.

Apart from the approach taken by the absolute incorporationists, I can see only one method of analysis that has any internal logic. This is to start with the words "liberty" and "due process of law" and attempt to define them in a way that accords with American traditions and our system of government. This approach, involving a much more discriminating process of adjudication than does "incorporation," is, albeit difficult, the

one that was followed throughout the Nineteenth and most of the present century. It entails a "gradual process of judicial inclusion and exclusion," seeking, with due recognition of constitutional tolerance for state experimentation and disparity, to ascertain those "immutable principles of free government which no member of the Union may disregard." Due process was not restricted to rules fixed in the past, for that "would be to deny every quality of the law but its age, and to render it incapable of progress or improvement." . . .

Through this gradual process, this Court sought to define "liberty" by isolating freedoms that Americans of the past and of the present considered more important than any suggested countervailing public objective. The Court also, by interpretation of the phrase "due process of law," enforced the Constitution's guarantee that no State may imprison an individual except by fair and impartial procedures.

The relationship of the Bill of Rights to this "gradual process" seems to me to be twofold. In the first place it has long been clear that the Due Process Clause imposes some restrictions on state action that parallel Bill of Rights restrictions on federal action. Second, and more important than this accidental overlap, is the fact that the Bill of Rights is evidence, at various points, of the content Americans find in the term "liberty" and of American standards of fundamental fairness.

An example, both of the phenomenon of parallelism and the use of the first eight amendments as evidence of a historic commitment, is found in the partial definition of "liberty" offered by Mr. Justice Holmes, dissenting in *Gitlow* v. *New York,* 268 U.S. 652:

The general principle of free speech . . . must be taken to be included in the Fourteenth Amendment, in view of the scope that has been given to the word "liberty" as there used, although perhaps it may be accepted with a somewhat larger latitude of interpretation than is allowed to Congress by the sweeping language that governs or ought to govern the laws of the United States. *Id.,* at 672. . . .

The Court has also found among the procedural requirements of "due process of law" certain rules paralleling requirements of the first eight amendments. For example, in *Powell* v. *Alabama,* 287 U.S. 45, the Court ruled that a State could not deny counsel to an accused in a capital case. . . . Later, the right to counsel was extended to all felony cases. The Court has also ruled, for example, that "due process" means a speedy process, so that liberty will not be long restricted prior to an adjudication, and evidence of fact will not become stale; that in a system committed to the resolution of issues of fact by adversary proceedings the right to confront opposing witnesses must be guaranteed; and that if issues of fact are tried to a jury, fairness demands a jury impartially selected. . . .

In all these instances, the right guaranteed against the States by the Fourteenth Amendment was one that had also been guaranteed against the Federal Government by one of the first eight amendments. The logically critical thing, however, was not that the rights had been found in the Bill of Rights, but that they were deemed, in the context of American legal history, to be fundamental. . . .

Today's Court still remains unwilling to accept the total incorporationists' view of the history of the Fourteenth Amendment. This, if accepted, would afford a cogent reason for applying the Sixth Amendment to the States. The Court is also, apparently, unwilling to face the task of determining whether denial of trial by jury in the situation before us, or in other situations, is fundamentally unfair. Consequently, the Court has compromised on the ease of the incorporationist position, without its internal logic. It has simply assumed that the question before us is whether the Jury Trial Clause of the Sixth Amendment should be incorporated into the Fourteenth, jot-for-jot and case-for-case, or ignored. Then the Court merely declares that the clause in question is "in" rather than "out."

The Court has justified neither its starting place nor its conclusion. If the problem is to discover and articulate the rules of fundamental fairness in criminal proceedings, there is no reason to assume that the whole body of rules developed in this Court constituting Sixth Amendment jury trial must be regarded as a unit. The requirement of trial by jury in federal criminal cases has given rise to numerous subsidiary questions respecting the exact scope and content of the right. It surely cannot be that every answer the Court has given, or will give, to such a question is attributable to the Founders; or even that every rule announced carries equal conviction of this Court; still less can it be that every such subprinciple is equally fundamental to ordered liberty.

. . .

Even if I could agree that the question before us is whether Sixth Amendment jury trial is totally "in" or totally "out," I can find in the Court's opinion no real reasons for concluding that it should be "in." The basis for differentiating among clauses in the Bill of Rights cannot be that only some clauses are in the

Bill of Rights, or that only some are old and much praised, or that only some have played an important role in the development of federal law. These things are true of all. The Court says that some clauses are more "fundamental" than others, but it turns out to be using this word in a sense that would have astonished Mr. Justice Cardozo and which, in addition, is of no help. The word does not mean "analytically critical to procedural fairness" for no real analysis of the role of the jury in making procedures fair is even attempted. Instead, the word turns out to mean "old," "much praised," and "found in the Bill of Rights." The definition of "fundamental" thus turns out to be circular.

. . .

This Court, other courts, and the political process are available to correct any experiments in criminal procedure that prove fundamentally unfair to defendants. That is not what is being done today: instead, and quite without reason, the Court has chosen to impose upon every State one means of trying criminal cases; it is a good means, but it is not the only fair means, and it is not demonstrably better than the alternatives States might devise.

I would affirm the judgment of the Supreme Court of Louisiana.

## POINTER *v. TEXAS*

380 U. S. 400; 13 L. Ed. 2d 923; 85 S. Ct. 1065 (1965)

MR. JUSTICE BLACK *delivered the opinion of the Court.*

The Sixth Amendment provides in part:

In all criminal prosecutions, the accused shall enjoy the right . . . to be confronted with the witnesses against him . . . and to have the Assistance of Counsel for his defense. . . .

. . . The question we find necessary to decide in this case is whether the Amendment's guarantee of a defendant's right "to be confronted with the witnesses against him," which has been held to include the right to cross-examine those witnesses, is also made applicable to the States by the Fourteenth Amendment.

The petitioner Pointer and one Dillard were arrested in Texas and taken before a state judge for a preliminary hearing (in Texas called the "examining trial") on a charge of having robbed Kenneth W. Phillips of $375 "by assault, or violence, or by putting in fear of life or bodily injury, in violation of Texas Penal Code Art. 1408. At this hearing an Assistant District Attorney conducted the prosecution and examined witnesses, but neither of the defendants, both of whom were laymen, had a lawyer. Phillips as chief witness for the State gave his version of the alleged robbery in detail, identifying petitioner as the man who had robbed him at gunpoint. Apparently Dillard tried to cross-examine Phillips, but Pointer did not, although Pointer was said to have tried to cross-examine some other witnesses at the hearing. Petitioner was subsequently indicted on a charge of having committed the robbery. Some time before the trial was held, Phillips moved to California. After putting in evidence to show that Phillips had moved and did not intend to return to Texas, the State at the trial offered the transcript of Phillips' testimony given at the preliminary hearing as evidence against petitioner. Petitioner's counsel immediately objected to introduction of the transcript, stating, "Your Honor, we will object to that, as it is a denial of the confrontation of the witnesses against the Defendant." Similar objections were repeatedly made by petitioner's counsel but were overruled by the trial judge, apparently in part because, as the judge viewed it, petitioner had been present at the preliminary hearing and therefore had been "accorded the opportunity of cross examining the witnesses there against him." The Texas Court of Criminal Appeals, the highest state court to which the case could be taken, affirmed petitioner's conviction, rejecting his contention that use of the transcript to convict him denied him rights guaranteed by the Sixth and Fourteenth Amendment. . . . We granted certiorari to consider the important constitutional question the case involves. . . .

. . . In this case the objections and arguments in the trial court as well as the arguments in the Court of Criminal Appeals and before us make it clear that petitioner's objection is based not so much on the fact that he had no lawyer when Phillips made his statement at the preliminary hearing, as on the fact that use of the transcript of that statement at the trial denied petitioner any opportunity to have the benefit of counsel's cross-examination of the principal witness against him. It is that latter question which we decide here.

. . . We hold today that the Sixth Amendment's right of an accused to confront the witnesses against him is likewise a fundamental right and is made obligatory on the States by the Fourteenth Amendment.

It cannot seriously be doubted at this late date that the right of cross-examination is included in the right of an accused in a criminal case to confront the witnesses against him. And probably no one, certainly no one experienced in the trial of lawsuits, would deny the value of cross-examination in exposing falsehood and bringing out the truth in the trial of a criminal case. . . . The fact that this right appears in the Sixth Amendment of our Bill of Rights reflects the belief of the Framers of those liberties and safeguards that confrontation was a fundamental right essential to a fair trial in a criminal prosecution. Moreover, the decision of this Court and other courts throughout the years have constantly emphasized the necessity for cross-examination as a protection for defendants in criminal cases. . . . There are few subjects, perhaps, upon which this Court and other courts have been more nearly unanimous than in their expressions of belief that the right of confrontation and cross-examination is an essential and fundamental requirement for the kind of fair trial which is this country's constitutional goal. Indeed, we have expressly declared that to deprive an accused of the right to cross-examine the witnesses against him is a denial of the Fourteenth Amendment's guarantees of due process of law. In *In re Oliver,* 333 U.S. 257 . . . this Court said:

A person's right to reasonable notice of a charge against him, and an opportunity to be heard in his defense—a right to his day in court—are basic in our system of jurisprudence; and these rights include, as a minimum, a right to examine the witnesses against him, to offer testimony, and to be represented by counsel. . . .

We are aware that some cases, particularly *West* v. *State of Louisiana,* 194 U.S. 258, 264, have stated that the Sixth Amendment's right of confrontation does not apply to trials in state courts, on the ground that the entire Sixth Amendment does not so apply. . . . But of course since *Gideon* v. *Wainwright,* . . . it no longer can broadly be said that the Sixth Amendment does not apply to state courts. And as this Court said in *Malloy* v. *Hogan,* . . . "The Court has not hesitated to re-examine past decisions according the Fourteenth Amendment a less central role in the preservation of basic liberties than that which was contemplated by its Framers when they added the Amendment to our constitutional scheme." . . . In the light of *Gideon, Malloy,* and other cases cited in those opinions holding various provisions of the Bill of Rights applicable to the States by virtue of the Fourteenth Amendment, the statements made in *West* and similar cases generally declaring that the Sixth Amendment does not apply to the States can no longer be regarded as the law. We hold that petitioner was entitled to be tried in accordance with the protection of the confrontation guarantee of the Sixth Amendment, and that that guarantee, like the right against compelled self-incrimination, is "to be enforced against the States under the Fourteenth Amendment according to the same standards that protect those personal rights against federal encroachment." . . .

. . . Because the transcript of Phillips' statement offered against petitioner at his trial had not been taken at a time and under circumstances affording petitioner through counsel an adequate opportunity to cross-examine Phillips, its introduction in a federal court in a criminal case against Pointer would have amounted to denial of the privilege of confrontation guaranteed by the Sixth Amendment. Since we hold that the right of an accused to be confronted with the witnesses against him must be determined by the same standards whether the right is denied in a federal or state proceeding, it follows that use of the transcript to convict petitioner denied him a constitutional right, and that his conviction must be reversed.

*Reversed and remanded.*

MR. JUSTICE HARLAN, *concurring in the result.*

I agree that in the circumstances the admission of the statement in question deprived the petitioner of a right of "confrontation" assured by the Fourteenth Amendment. I cannot subscribe, however, to the constitutional reasoning of the Court.

The Court holds that the right of confrontation guaranteed by the Sixth Amendment in federal criminal trials is carried into state criminal cases by the Fourteenth Amendment. This is another step in the onward march of the long-since discredited "incorporation" doctrine . . . which for some reason that I have not yet been able to fathom has come into the sunlight in recent years. . . .

For me this state judgment must be reversed because a right of confrontation is "implicit in the concept of ordered liberty," . . . reflected in the Due Process Clause of the Fourteenth Amendment independently of the Sixth.

While either of these constitutional approaches brings one to the same end result in this particular case, there is a basic difference between the two in the kind of future constitutional development they portend. The concept of Fourteenth Amendment due process embodied in *Palko* and a host of other thoughtful past decisions now rapidly falling into discard, recognizes that our Constitution tolerates, indeed encourages, differences between the methods used to effectuate legitimate federal and state concerns, subject to the requirements of fundamental fairness "implicit in the concept of ordered liberty." The philosophy of "incorporation," on the other hand, subordinates all such state differences to the particular requirements of the Federal Bill of Rights . . . and increasingly subjects state legal processes to enveloping federal judicial authority. "Selective" incorporation or "absorption" amounts to little more than a diluted form of the full incorporation theory. Whereas it rejects full incorporation because of recognition that not all of the guarantees of the Bill of Rights should be deemed "fundamental," it at the same time ignores the possibility that not all phases of any given guaranty described in the Bill of Rights are necessarily fundamental.

It is too often forgotten in these times that the American federal system is itself constitutionally ordained, that it embodies values profoundly making for lasting liberties in this country, and that its legitimate requirements demand continuing solid recognition in all phases of the work of this Court. The "incorporation" doctrines, whether full blown or selective, are both historically and constitutionally unsound and incompatible with the maintenance of our federal system on even course.

MR. JUSTICE STEWART'S *brief concurring opinion is not printed here.*

MR. JUSTICE GOLDBERG, *concurring.*

. . . My Brother Harlan, while agreeing with the result reached by the Court, deplores the Court's reasoning as "another step in the onward march of the long-since discredited 'incorporation' doctrine," . . . Since I was not on the Court when the incorporation issue was joined, . . . I deem it appropriate to set forth briefly my view on this subject. . . .

With all deference to my Brother Harlan, I cannot agree that this process has "come into the sunlight in recent years." . . . Rather, I believe that it has its origins at least as far back as *Twining* v. *State of New Jersey* . . . where the Court stated that "it is possible that some of the personal rights safeguarded by the first eight Amendments against national action may also be safeguarded against state action, because a denial of them would be a denial of due process of law. . . . This passage . . . make[s] clear that what is protected by the Fourteenth Amendment are "rights," which apply in every case, not solely in those cases where it seems "fair" to a majority of the Court to afford the protection. Later cases reaffirm that the process of "absorption" is one of extending "rights." . . . I agree with these decisions, as is apparent from my votes in *Gideon* v. *Wainwright* . . . ; *Malloy* v. *Hogan* . . . and *Murphy* v. *Waterfront Comm'n* . . . and my concurring opinion in *New York Times Co.* v. *Sullivan,* . . . and I subscribe to the process by which fundamental guarantees of the Bill of Rights are absorbed by the Fourteenth Amendment and thereby applied to the States.

Furthermore, I do not agree with my Brother Harlan that once a provision of the Bill of Rights has been held applicable to the States by the

Fourteenth Amendment, it does not apply to the States in full strength. Such a view would have the Fourteenth Amendment apply to the States "only a 'watered-down, subjective version of the individual guarantees of the Bill of Rights.' " . . . It would allow the States greater latitude than the Federal Government to abridge concededly fundamental liberties protected by the Constitution. While I quite agree with Mr. Justice Brandeis that "[i]t is one of the happy incidents of the federal system that a . . . state may . . . serve as a laboratory; and try novel social and economic experiments," *New State Ice Co.* v. *Liebmann*, 285 U.S. 262, 280, 311 . . . I do not believe that this includes the power to experiment with the fundamental liberties of citizens safeguarded by the Bill of Rights. . . .

Finally, I do not see that my Brother Harlan's view would further any legitimate interests of federalism. It would require this Court to intervene in the state judicial process with considerable lack of predictability and with a consequent likelihood of considerable friction. This is well illustrated by the difficulties which were faced and were articulated by the state courts attempting to apply this Court's now discarded rule of *Betts* v. *Brady*. . . . And, to deny to the States the power to impair a fundamental constitutional right is not to increase federal power, but, rather, to limit the power of both federal and state governments in favor of safeguarding the fundamental rights and liberties of the individual. In my view this promotes rather than undermines the basic policy of avoiding excess concentration of power in government, federal or state, which underlies our concepts of federalism. . . .

## KLOPFER v. STATE OF NORTH CAROLINA

386 U. S. 213; 18 L. Ed. 2d 1; 87 S. Ct. 988 (1967)

Mr. Chief Justice Warren *delivered the opinion of the Court.*

The question involved in this case is whether a State may indefinitely postpone prosecution on an indictment without stated jurisdiction over the objection of an accused who has been discharged from custody. It is presented in the context of an application of an unusual North Carolina criminal procedural device known as the *"nolle prosequi* with leave."*

* N. C. Gen. Stat. par. 15–175 (1965):
A *nolle prosequi* 'with leave' shall be entered in all criminal actions in which the indictment has been pending for two terms of the court and the defendant has not been apprehended and in which a *nolle prosequi* has not been entered, unless the judge for good cause shall order otherwise. The clerk of the superior court shall issue a capias for the arrest of any defendant named in any criminal action in which a *nolle prosequi* has been entered when he has reasonable ground for believing that such defendant may be arrested or upon the application of the solicitor of the district. When any defendant shall be arrested it shall be the duty of the clerk to issue a subpoena for the witnesses for the State indorsed on the indictment.

The provision was originally enacted in 1905.

Under North Carolina criminal procedure, when the prosecuting attorney of a county, denominated the solicitor, determines that he does not desire to proceed further with a prosecution, he may take a *nolle prosequi,* thereby declaring "that he will not, at this time, prosecute the suit further. Its effect is to put the defendant without day, that is, he is discharged and permitted to go whithersoever he will, without entering into a recognizance to appear at any other time." But the taking of the *nolle prosequi* does not permanently terminate proceedings on the indictment. On the contrary, "When a *nolle prosequi* is entered, the case may be restored to the trial docket when ordered by the judge upon the solicitor's application." . . . And if the solicitor petitions the court to *nolle prosequi* the case "with leave," the consent required to reinstate the prosecution at a future date is implied in the order "and the solicitor (without further order) may have the case restored for trial." Since the indictment is not discharged by either a *nolle prosequi* or a *nolle prosequi* with leave, the statute of limitations remains tolled. . . .

. . . In the present case, neither the court below nor the solicitor offer any reason why the case of petitioner should have been *nolle prosequi* except for the suggestion of the Supreme Court that the solicitor, having tried the defendant once and having obtained a disagreement, "may have concluded that another go at it would not be worth the time and expense of another effort." In his brief in this Court, the Attorney General quotes this language from the opinion below in support of the judgment.

Whether this procedure is presently sustained by the North Carolina courts under a statute or under their conception of the common-law procedure is not indicated by the opinion of the court, the transcript or the briefs of the parties in the present case. The only statutory reference to a *nolle prosequi* is in paragraph 15-175, General Statutes of North Carolina, which on its face does not apply to the facts of this case. . . .

The consequence of this extraordinary criminal procedure is made apparent by the case before the Court. A defendant indicted for a misdemeanor may be denied an opportunity to exonerate himself in the discretion of the solicitor and held subject to trial, over his objection, throughout the unlimited period in which the solicitor may restore the case to the calendar. During that period, there is no means by which he can obtain a dismissal or have the case restored to the calendar for trial. In spite of this result, both the Supreme Court and the Attorney General state as a fact, and rely upon it for affirmance in this case, that this procedure as applied to the petitioner placed no limitations upon him, and was in no way violative of his rights. With this we cannot agree.

This procedure was applied to the petitioner in the following circumstances:

On February 24, 1964, petitioner was indicted by the grand jury of Orange County for the crime of criminal trespass, a misdemeanor punishable by fine and imprisonment in an amount and duration determined by the court in the exercise of its discretion. The bill charged that he entered a restaurant on January 3, 1964, and, "after being ordered . . . to leave the said premises, willfully and unlawfully refused to do so, knowing or having reason to know that he . . . had no license therefor. . . ." Prosecution on the indictment began with admirable promptness during the March 1964 Special Criminal Session of the Superior Court of Orange County; but, when the jury failed to reach a verdict, the trial judge declared a mistrial and ordered the case continued for the term.

Several weeks prior to the April 1965 Criminal Session of the Superior Court, the State's solicitor informed petitioner of his intention to have a *nolle prosequi* with leave entered in the case. During the session, petitioner, through his attorney, opposed the entry of such an order in open court. The trespass charge, he contended, was abated by the Civil Rights Act of 1964 as construed in *Hamm* v. *City of Rock Hill,* 379 U.S. 306; 85 S. Ct. 384; 13 L. Ed. 2d 300 (1964). In spite of petitioner's opposition, the court indicated that it would approve entry of a *nolle prosequi* with leave if requested to do so by the solicitor. But the solicitor declined to make a motion for a *nolle prosequi* with leave. Instead, he moved the court to continue the case for yet another term; which motion was granted.

The calendar for the August 1965 Criminal Session of the court did not list Klopfer's case for trial. To ascertain the status of his case, petitioner filed a motion expressing his desire to have the charge pending against him "permanently concluded in accordance with the applicable laws of the State of North Carolina and of the United States as soon as is reasonably possible." Noting that some 18 months had elapsed since the presentment, petitioner, a professor of zoology at Duke University, contended that the pendency of the indictment greatly interfered with his professional activities and with his travel here and abroad. "Wherefore," the motion concluded, "the defendant . . . petitions the Court that the

Court in the exercise of its general supervisory jurisdiction inquire into the trial status of the charge pending against the defendant and to ascertain the intention of the State in regard to the trial of said charge and as to when the defendant will be brought to trial."

In response to the motion, the trial judge considered the status of petitioner's case in open court on Monday, August 9, 1965, at which time the solicitor moved the court that the State be permitted to take a *nolle prosequi* with leave. Even though no jurisdiction for the proposed entry was offered by the State, and, in spite of petitioner's objection to the order, the court granted the State's motion.

On appeal to the Supreme Court of North Carolina, petitioner contended that the entry of the *nolle prosequi* with leave deprived him of his right to a speedy trial as required by the Fourteenth Amendment to the United States Constitution. Although the Supreme Court acknowledged that entry of the *nolle prosequi* with leave did not permanently discharge the indictment, it nevertheless affirmed.

. . .

The North Carolina Supreme Court's conclusion—that the right to a speedy trial does not afford affirmative protection against an unjustified postponement of trial for an accused discharged from custody—has been explicitly rejected by every other state court which has considered the question. . . .

We, too, believe that the position taken by the court below was erroneous. The petitioner is not relieved of the limitations placed upon his life and liberty by this prosecution merely because its suspension permits him to go "whithersoever he will." The pendency of the indictment may subject him to public scorn and deprive him of employment, and almost certainly will force curtailment of his speech, associations and participation in unpopular causes. By indefinitely prolonging this oppression, as well as the "anxiety and concern accompanying public accusation," the criminal procedure condoned in this case by the Supreme Court of North Carolina clearly denies the petitioner the right to a speedy trial which we hold is guaranteed to him by the Sixth Amendment of the Constitution of the United States.

While there has been a difference of opinion as to what provisions of this Amendment to the Constitution apply to the States through the Fourteenth Amendment, that question has been settled as to some of them in the recent cases of *Gideon* v. *Wainwright,* 372 U.S. 335, 83 S. Ct. 792, 9 L. Ed. 2d 799 (1963), and *Pointer* v. *State of Texas,* 380 U.S. 400, 85 S. Ct. 1065, 13 L. Ed. 2d 923 (1965). . . .

We hold here that the right to a speedy trial is as fundamental as any of the rights secured by the Sixth Amendment. That right has its roots at the very foundation of our English law heritage. . . .

The history of the right to a speedy trial and its reception in this country clearly establishes that it is one of the most basic rights preserved by our Constitution.

For the reasons stated above, the judgment must be reversed and remanded for proceedings not incon-sistent with the opinion of the Court. It is so ordered.

*Judgment reversed
and case remanded.*

MR. JUSTICE STEWART *concurs in the result.*

MR. JUSTICE HARLAN, *concurring in the result.*

While I entirely agree with the result reached by the Court, I am unable to subscribe to the constitutional premises upon which that result is based—quite evidently the viewpoint that the Fourteenth Amendment "incorporates" or "absorbs" *as such* all or some of the specific provisions of the Bill of Rights. I do not believe that this is sound constitutional doctrine. See my concurring opinion in *Pointer* v. *State of Texas,* 380 U.S. 400, 85 S. Ct. 1065, 13 L. Ed. 2d 923.

I would rest decision of this case not on the "speedy trial" provision of the Sixth Amendment, but on the ground that this unusual North Carolina procedure, which in effect allows state prosecuting officials to put a person under the cloud of an unliquidated criminal charge for an indeterminate period, violates the requirement of fundamental fairness assured by the Due Process Clause of the Fourteenth Amendment. To support that conclusion I need only refer to the traditional concepts of due process set forth in the opinion of The Chief Justice.

# SHEPPARD v. MAXWELL

384 U. S. 333; 16 L. Ed. 2d 600; 86 S. Ct. 1507 (1966)

MR. JUSTICE CLARK *delivered the opinion of the Court.*

This federal habeas corpus application involves the question whether Sheppard was deprived of a fair trial in his state conviction for the second-degree murder of his wife because of the trial judge's failure to protect Sheppard sufficiently from the massive, pervasive and prejudicial publicity that attended his prosecution. The United States District Court held that he was not afforded a fair trial and granted the writ subject to the State's right to put Sheppard to trial again. . . . The Court of Appeals for the Sixth Circuit reversed. . . . We granted certiorari . . . [and] . . . have concluded that Sheppard did not receive a fair trial consistent with the Due Process Clause of the Fourteenth Amendment and, therefore, reverse the judgment.

Marilyn Sheppard, petitioner's pregnant wife, was bludgeoned to death in the upstairs bedroom of their lakeshore home in Bay Village, Ohio, a suburb of Cleveland.

. . .

From the outset officials focused suspicion on Sheppard. After a search of the house and premises on the morning of the tragedy, Dr. Gerber, the Coroner, is reported—and it is undenied—to have told his men, "Well, it is evident the doctor did this, so let's go get the confession out of him." He proceeded to interrogate and examine Sheppard while the latter was under sedation in his hospital room. . . . At the end of the interrogation Shotke (an interrogator) told Sheppard: "I think you killed your wife." Still later in the same afternoon a physician sent by the Coroner was permitted to make a detailed examination of Sheppard. Until the Coroner's inquest on July 22, at which time he was subpoenaed, Sheppard made himself available for frequent and extended questioning without the presence of an attorney.

On July 7, the day of Marilyn Sheppard's funeral, a newspaper story appeared in which Assistant County Attorney Mahon—later the chief prosecutor of Sheppard—sharply criticized the refusal of the Sheppard family to permit his immediate questioning. From there on headline stories repeatedly stressed Sheppard's lack of cooperation with the police and other officials. Under the headline "Testify Now In Death, Bay Doctor Is Ordered," one story described a visit by Coroner Gerber and four police officers to the hospital on July 8. When Sheppard insisted that his lawyer be present, the Coroner wrote out a subpoena and served it on him. Sheppard then agreed to submit to questioning without counsel and the subpoena was torn up. . . . The newspapers also played up Sheppard's refusal to take a lie detector test and "the protective ring" thrown up by his family. Front-page newspaper headlines announced on the same day that "Doctor Balks At Lie Test; Retells Story." . . . The next day, another headline story disclosed that Sheppard had "again late yesterday refused to take a lie detector test'" and quoted an Assistant County Attorney as saying that "at the end of a nine-hour questioning of Dr. Sheppard, I felt he was now ruling [a test] out completely." But subsequent newspaper articles reported that the Coroner was still pushing Sheppard for a lie detector test. More stories appeared when Sheppard would not allow authorities to inject him with "truth serum."*

On the 20th, the "editorial artillery" opened fire with a front-page charge that somebody is "getting away with murder." The editorial attributed the ineptness of the investigation to "friendships, relationships, hired lawyers, a husband who ought to have been subjected instantly to the same third-degree to which any other person under similar circumstances is subjected. . . ." The following day, July 21, another page-one editorial was headed: "Why No Inquest? Do It Now, Dr. Gerber." The Coroner called an inquest the same day and subpoenaed Sheppard. It was staged the next day in a school gymnasium; the Coroner presided with the County Prosecutor as his advisor and two detectives as bailiffs. In the front of the room was a long table occupied by reporters, television and radio personnel, and broadcasting equipment. The hearing was broadcast with live microphones placed at the Coroner's seat and the witness stand. A swarm of reporters and photographers attended. Sheppard was brought into the room by police who searched him in full view of several hundred spectators. Sheppard's counsel were present during the three-day inquest but were not permitted to participate. When Sheppard's chief

counsel attempted to place some documents in the record, he was forcibly ejected from the room by the Coroner, who received cheers, hugs, and kisses from ladies in the audience. Sheppard was questioned for five and one-half hours about his actions on the night of the murder, his married life, and a love affair with Susan Hayes.† At the end of the hearing the Coroner announced that he "could" order Sheppard held for the grand jury, but did not do so.

Throughout this period the newspapers emphasized evidence that tended to incriminate Sheppard and pointed out discrepancies in his statements to authorities. At the same time, Sheppard made many public statements to the press and wrote feature articles asserting his innocence. . . .‡ The newspapers also delved into Sheppard's personal life. Articles stressed his extramarital love affairs as a motive for the crime. The newspapers portrayed Sheppard as a Lothario, fully explored his relationship with Susan Hayes, and named a number of other women who were allegedly involved with him. The testimony at trial never showed that Sheppard had any illicit relationships besides the one with Susan Hayes.

. . . A front-page editorial on July 30 asked: "Why Isn't Sam Sheppard in Jail?" It was later titled "Quit Stalling—Bring Him In." After calling Sheppard "the most unusual murder suspect ever seen around these parts" the article said that

---

* At the same time, the newspapers reported that other possible suspects had been "cleared" by lie detector tests. One of these persons was quoted as saying that he could not understand why an innocent man would refuse to take such a test.

† The newspapers had heavily emphasized Sheppard's illicit affair with Susan Hayes, and the fact that he had initially lied about it.

‡ A number of articles calculated to evoke sympathy for Sheppard were printed, such as the letters Sheppard wrote to his son while in jail. These stories often appeared together with news coverage which was unfavorable to him.

"[e]xcept for some superficial questioning during Coroner Sam Gerber's inquest he has been scot-free of any official grilling. . . ." It asserted that he was "surrounded by an iron curtain of protection [and] concealment."

That night at 10 o'clock Sheppard was arrested at his father's home on a charge of murder. He was taken to the Bay Village City Hall where hundreds of people, newscasters, photographers and reporters were awaiting his arrival. He was immediately arraigned—having been denied a temporary delay to secure the presence of counsel—and bound over to the grand jury.

The publicity then grew in intensity until his indictment on August 17. Typical of the coverage during this period is a front-page interview entitled: "DR. SAM: 'I Wish There Was Something I Could Get Off My Chest—but There Isn't.'" Unfavorable publicity included items such as a cartoon of the body of a sphinx with Sheppard's head and the legend below: "'I Will Do Everything In My Power to Help Solve This Terrible Murder.'—Dr. Sam Sheppard." Headlines announced, *inter alia,* that: "Doctor Evidence is Ready for Jury," "Corrigan Tactics Stall Quizzing," "Sheppard 'Gay Set' Is Revealed By Houk," "Blood Is Found In Garage," "New Murder Evidence Is Found, Police Claim," "Dr. Sam Faces Quiz At Jail On Marilyn's Fear Of Him." On August 18, an article appeared under the headline, "Dr. Sam Writes His Own Story." And reproduced across the entire front page was a portion of the typed statement signed by Sheppard: "I am not guilty of the murder of my wife, Marilyn. How could I, who have been trained to help people and devoted my life to saving life, commit such a terrible and revolting crime?" We do not de-

tail the coverage further. There are five volumes filled with similar clippings from each of the three Cleveland newspapers covering the period from the murder until Sheppard's conviction in December 1954. The record includes no excerpts from newscasts on radio and television but since space was reserved in the courtroom for these media we assume that their coverage was equally large.

With this background the case came on for trial two weeks before the November general election at which the chief prosecutor was a candidate for common pleas judge and the trial judge, Judge Blythin, was a candidate to succeed himself. Twenty-five days before the case was set, 75 veniremen were called as prospective jurors. All three Cleveland newspapers published the names and addresses of the veniremen. As a consequence, anonymous letters and telephone calls, as well as calls from friends, regarding the impending prosecution were received by all of the prospective jurors. . . .

The courtroom in which the trial was held measured 26 by 48 feet. A long temporary table was set up inside the bar, in back of the single counsel table. It ran the width of the courtroom, parallel to the bar railing, with one end less than three feet from the jury box. Approximately 20 representatives of newspapers and wire services were assigned seats at this table by the court. Behind the bar railing there were four rows of benches. These seats were likewise assigned by the court for the entire trial. The first row was occupied by representatives of television and radio stations, and the second and third rows by reporters from out-of-town newspapers and magazines. One side of the last row, which accommodated 14 people, was assigned to Sheppard's family and the other to Marilyn's. The public was permitted to fill vacancies in this row on special passes only. Representatives of the news media also used all the rooms on the courtroom floor, including the room where cases were ordinarily called and assigned for trial. Private telephone lines and telegraphic equipment were installed in these rooms so that reports from the trial could be speeded to the papers. Station WSRS was permitted to set up broadcasting facilities on the third floor of the courthouse next door to the jury room, where the jury rested during recesses in the trial and deliberated. Newscasts were made from this room throughout the trial, and while the jury reached its verdict.

. . .

All of these arrangements with the news media and their massive coverage of the trial continued during the entire nine weeks of the trial. The courtroom remained crowded to capacity with representatives of news media. . . . Furthermore, the reporters clustered within the bar of the small courtroom made confidential talk among Sheppard and his counsel almost impossible during the proceedings. They frequently had to leave the courtroom to obtain privacy. And many times when counsel wished to raise a point with the judge out of the hearing of the jury it was necessary to move to the judge's chambers. Even then, news media representatives so packed the judge's anteroom that counsel could hardly return from the chambers to the courtroom. The reporters vied with each other to find out what counsel and the judge had discussed, and often these matters later appeared in newspapers accessible to the jury.

. . .

The jurors themselves were con-

stantly exposed to the news media. Every juror, except one, testified at *voir dire* to reading about the case in the Cleveland papers or to having heard broadcasts about it. Seven of the 12 jurors who rendered the verdict had one or more Cleveland papers delivered in their home; the remaining jurors were not interrogated on the point. Nor were there questions as to radios or television sets in the jurors' homes, but we must assume most of them owned such conveniences. As the selection of the jury progressed, individual pictures of prospective jurors appeared daily. During the trial, pictures of the jury appeared over 40 times in the Cleveland papers alone. The court permitted photographers to take pictures of the jury in the box, and individual pictures of the members in the jury room. . . .

. . .

We now reach the conduct of the trial. While the intense publicity continued unabated, it is sufficient to relate only the more flagrant episodes:

1. On October 9, 1954, nine days before the case went to trial, an editorial in one of the newspapers criticized defense counsel's random poll of people on the streets as to their opinion of Sheppard's guilt or innocence in an effort to use the resulting statistics to show the necessity for change of venue. The article said the survey "smacks of mass jury tampering," called on defense counsel to drop it, and stated that the bar association should do something about it. . . .

2. On the second day of *voir dire* examination a debate was staged and broadcast live over WHK radio. The participants, newspaper reporters, accused Sheppard's counsel of throwing roadblocks in the way of the prosecution and asserted that Sheppard conceded his guilt by hiring a prominent

criminal lawyer. Sheppard's counsel objected to this broadcast and requested a continuance, but the judge denied the motion. When counsel asked the court to give some protection from such events, the judge replied that "WHK doesn't have much coverage," and that "[a]fter all, we are not trying this case by radio or in newspapers or any other means. We confine ourselves seriously to it in this courtroom and do the very best we can."

3. While the jury was being selected, a two-inch headline asked: "But Who Will Speak for Marilyn?" The front-page story spoke of the "perfect face" of the accused. "Study that face as long as you want. Never will you get from it a hint of what might be the answer. . . ." The two brothers of the accused were described as "Prosperous, poised. His two sisters-in-law. Smart, chic, well-groomed. His elderly father. Courtly, reserved. A perfect type for the patriarch of a staunch clan." The author then noted Marilyn Sheppard was "still off stage," and that she was an only child whose mother died when she was very young and whose father had no interest in the case. But the author—through quotes from Detective Chief James McArthur—assured readers that the prosecution's exhibits would speak for Marilyn. . . .

4. . . . [T]he jury viewed the scene of the murder on the first day of the trial. Hundreds of reporters, cameramen and onlookers were there, and one representative of the news media was permitted to accompany the jury while it inspected the Sheppard home. The time of the jury's visit was revealed so far in advance that one of the newspapers was able to rent a helicopter and fly over the house taking pictures of the jurors on their tour.

5. On November 19, a Cleveland police officer gave testimony that tended to contradict details in the written statement Sheppard made to the Cleveland police. Two days later, in a broadcast heard over Station WHK in Cleveland, Robert Considine likened Sheppard to a perjuror and compared the episode to Alger Hiss' confrontation with Whittaker Chambers. Though defense counsel asked the judge to question the jury to ascertain how many heard the broadcast, the court refused to do so. . . .

6. On November 24, a story appeared under an eight-column headline: "Sam Called A 'Jekyll-Hyde' By Marilyn, Cousin To Testify." It related that Marilyn had recently told friends that Sheppard was a "Dr. Jekyll and Mr. Hyde" character. No such testimony was ever presented at the trial. The story went on to announce: "The prosecution has a 'bombshell witness' on tap who will testify to Dr. Sam's display of fiery temper—countering the defense claim that the defendant is a gentle physician with an even disposition." Defense counsel made motions for change of venue, continuance and mistrial, but they were denied. . . .

7. When the trial was in its seventh week, Walter Winchell broadcast over WXEL television and WJW radio that Carole Beasley, who was under arrest in New York City for robbery, had stated that, as Sheppard's mistress, she had borne him a child. The defense asked that the jury be queried on the broadcast. Two jurors admitted in open court that they had heard it. The judge asked each: "Would that have any effect upon your judgment?" Both replied, "No." This was accepted by the judge as sufficient; he merely asked the jury to "pay no attention whatever to that type of scavenging. . . ."

8. On December 9, while Sheppard was on the witness stand he testified that he had been mistreated by Cleveland detectives after his arrest. Although he was not at the trial, Captain Kerr of the Homicide Bureau issued a press statement denying Sheppard's allegations which appeared under the headline: " 'Barefaced Liar,' Kerr Says of Sam" Captain Kerr never appeared as a witness at the trial.

9. After the case was submitted to the jury, it was sequestered for its deliberations, which took five days and four nights. After the verdict, defense counsel ascertained that the jurors had been allowed to make telephone calls to their homes every day while they were sequestered at the hotel. . . . [T]he jurors were permitted to use the phones in the bailiffs' rooms. . . . The court had not instructed the bailiffs to prevent such calls. By a subsequent motion, defense counsel urged that this ground alone warranted a new trial, but the motion was overruled and no evidence was taken on the question.

The principle that justice cannot survive behind walls of silence has long been reflected in the "Anglo-American distrust for secret trials." *In re Oliver,* 333 U.S. 257, 268 (1948). A responsible press has always been regarded as the handmaiden of effective judicial administration, especially in the criminal field. Its function in this regard is documented by an impressive record of service over several centuries. The press does not simply publish information about trials but guards against the miscarriage of justice by subjecting the police, prosecutors, and judicial processes to extensive public scrutiny and criticism. This Court has, therefore, been unwilling to place any direct limitations on the freedom traditionally exercised by the news media for "[w]hat transpires in the court room is public property." *Craig* v. *Harney,* 331 U.S. 367, 374 (1947). . . . And where there was "no threat or menace to the integrity of the trial," *Craig* v. *Harney, supra,* at 377, we have consistently required that the press have a free hand, even though we sometimes deplored its sensationalism.

But the Court has also pointed out that "[l]egal trials are not like elections, to be won through the use of the meeting-hall, the radio, and the newspaper." *Bridges* v. *California,* . . . (314 U.S. 252, 271). And the Court has insisted that no one be punished for a crime without "a charge fairly made and fairly tried in a public tribunal free of prejudice, passion, excitement, and tyrannical power." *Chambers* v. *Florida,* 309 U.S. 227, 236–237 (1940). "Freedom of discussion should be given the widest range compatible with the essential requirement of the fair and orderly administration of justice." *Pennekamp* v. *Florida,* 328 U.S. 331, 347 (1946). But it must not be allowed to divert the trial from the "very purpose of a court system . . . to adjudicate controversies, both criminal and civil, in the calmness and solemnity of the courtroom according to legal procedures." *Cox* v. *Louisiana,* 379 U.S. 559, 583 (1965) (Black, J., dissenting). . . .

The undeviating rule of this Court was expressed by Mr. Justice Holmes over half a century ago in *Patterson* v. *Colorado,* 205 U.S. 454, 462 (1907): "The theory of our system is that the conclusion to be reached in a case will be induced only by evidence and argument in open court, and not by any outside influence, whether of private talk or public print." . . .

Only last Term in *Estes* v. *Texas,* 381 U.S. 532 (1965), we set aside a conviction despite the absence of any showing of prejudice. We said there:

It is true that in most cases involving claims of due process deprivations we require a showing of identifiable prejudice to the accused. Nevertheless, at times a procedure employed by the State involves such a probability that prejudice will result that it is deemed inherently lacking in due process. . . .

It is clear that the totality of circumstances in this case also warrants such an approach. Unlike Estes, Sheppard was not granted a change of venue to a locale away from where the publicity originated; nor was his jury sequestered. The Estes jury saw none of the television broadcasts from the courtroom. On the contrary, the Sheppard jurors were subjected to newspaper, radio and television coverage of the trial while not taking part in the proceedings. They were allowed to go their separate ways outside of the courtroom, without adequate directions not to read or listen to anything concerning the case.

. . .

The press coverage of the Estes trial was not nearly as massive and pervasive as the attention given by the Cleveland newspapers and broadcasting stations to Sheppard's prosecution. . . . For months the virulent publicity about Sheppard and the murder had made the case notorious. . . .

While we cannot say that Sheppard was denied due process by the judge's refusal to take precautions against the influence of pretrial publicity alone, the court's later rulings must be considered against the setting in which the trial was held. In light of this background, we believe that the arrangements made by the judge with the news media caused Sheppard to be deprived of that "judicial serenity and calm to which [he] was entitled." . . . The fact is that bedlam reigned

at the courthouse during the trial and newsmen took over practically the entire courtroom, hounding most of the participants in the trial, especially Sheppard. . . . The erection of a press table for reporters inside the bar is unprecedented. The bar of the court is reserved for counsel, providing them a safe place in which to keep papers and exhibits, and to confer privately with client and co-counsel. It is designed to protect the witness and the jury from any distractions, intrusions or influences, and to permit bench discussions of the judge's rulings away from the hearing of the public and the jury. Having assigned almost all of the available seats in the courtroom to the news media the judge lost his ability to supervise that environment. . . .

There can be no question about the nature of the publicity which surrounded Sheppard's trial. We agree, as did the Court of Appeals, with the findings in Judge Bell's opinion for the Ohio Supreme Court:

Murder and mystery, society, sex and suspense were combined in this case in such a manner as to intrigue and captivate the public fancy to a degree perhaps unparalleled in recent annals. Throughout the preindictment investigation, the subsequent legal skirmishes and the nine-week trial, circulation-conscious editors catered to the insatiable interest of the American public in the bizarre. . . . In this atmosphere of a "Roman holiday" for the news media, Sam Sheppard stood trial for his life. . . .

Indeed, every court that has considered this case, save the court that tried it, has deplored the manner in which the news media inflamed and prejudiced the public.

Much of the material printed or broadcast during the trial was never heard from the witness stand. . . . As the trial progressed, the newspapers summarized and interpreted the evidence, devoting particular attention to the material that incriminated Sheppard, and often drew unwarranted inferences from testimony. At one point, a front-page picture of Mrs. Sheppard's blood-stained pillow was published after being "doctored" to show more clearly an alleged imprint of a surgical instrument.

Nor is there doubt that this deluge of publicity reached at least some of the jury. On the only occasion that the jury was queried, two jurors admitted in open court to hearing the highly inflammatory charge that a prison inmate claimed Sheppard as the father of her illegitimate child. Despite the extent and nature of the publicity to which the jury was exposed during the trial, the judge refused defense counsel's other requests that the jurors be asked whether they had read or heard specific prejudicial comment about the case, including the incidents we have previously summarized. In these circumstances, we can assume that some of this material reached members of the jury. . . .

The court's fundamental error is compounded by the holding that it lacked power to control the publicity about the trial. From the very inception of the proceedings the judge announced that neither he nor anyone else could restrict prejudicial news accounts. And he reiterated this view on numerous occasions. Since he viewed the news media as his target, the judge never considered other means that are often utilized to reduce the jury from outside influence. We conclude that these procedures would have been sufficient to guarantee Sheppard a fair trial and so do not consider what sanctions might be available against a recalcitrant press nor the charges of bias now made against the state trial judge.

The carnival atmosphere at trial could easily have been avoided since the courtroom and courthouse premises are subject to the control of the court. As we stressed in *Estes,* the presence of the press at judicial proceedings must be limited when it is apparent that the accused might otherwise be prejudiced or disadvantaged. Bearing in mind the massive pretrial publicity, the judge should have adopted stricter rules governing the use of the courtroom by newsmen, as Sheppard's counsel requested. . . .

Secondly, the court should have insulated the witnesses. All of the newspapers and radio stations apparently interviewed prospective witnesses at will, and in many instances disclosed their testimony. A typical example was the publication of numerous statements by Susan Hayes, before her appearance in court, regarding her love affair with Sheppard. Although the witnesses were barred from the courthouse during the trial the full verbatim testimony was available to them in the press. This completely nullified the judge's imposition of the rule. . . .

Thirdly, the court should have made some effort to control the release of leads, information, and gossip to the press by police officers, witnesses, and the counsel for both sides. Much of the information thus disclosed was inaccurate, leading to groundless rumors and confusion. . . . Defense counsel immediately brought to the court's attention the tremendous amount of publicity in the Cleveland press that "misrepresented entirely the testimony" in the case. Under such circumstances, the judge should have at least warned the newspapers to check the accuracy of their accounts. And it is obvious that the judge should have further sought to alleviate this problem by imposing control over the statements made to the news media by counsel, witnesses, and especially the Coroner and police officers. The prosecution repeatedly made evidence available to the news media which was never offered in the trial. Much of the "evidence" disseminated in this fashion was clearly inadmissible. The exclusion of such evidence in court is rendered meaningless when news media make it available to the public. . . .

The fact that many of the prejudicial news items can be traced to the prosecution, as well as the defense, aggravates the judge's failure to take any action. . . . Effective control of these sources—concededly within the court's power—might well have prevented the divulgence of inaccurate information, rumors, and accusations that made up much of the inflammatory publicity, at least after Sheppard's indictment.

More specifically, the trial court might well have proscribed extrajudicial statements by any lawyer, party, witness, or court official which divulged prejudicial matters, such as the refusal of Sheppard to submit to interrogation or take any lie detector tests; any statement made by Sheppard to officials; the identity of prospective witnesses or their probable testimony; any belief in guilt or innocence; or like statements concerning the merits of the case. . . . Being advised of the great public interest in the case, the mass coverage of the press, and the potential prejudicial impact of the publicity, the court could also have requested the appropriate city and county officials to promulgate a regulation with respect to dissemination of information about the case by their employees. In addition, reporters who wrote or broadcast prejudicial stories, could have been warned as to the im-

propriety of publishing material not introduced in the proceedings. . . . In this manner, Sheppard's right to a trial free from outside interference would have been given added protection without corresponding curtailment of the news media. Had the judge, the other officers of the court, and the police placed the interest of justice first, the news media would have soon learned to be content with the task of reporting the case as it unfolded in the courtroom—not pieced together from extrajudicial statements.

From the cases coming here we note that unfair and prejudicial news comment on pending trials has become increasingly prevalent. Due process requires that the accused receive a trial by an impartial jury free from outside influences. Given the pervasiveness of modern communications and the difficulty of effacing prejudicial publicity from the minds of the jurors, the trial courts must take strong measures to ensure that the balance is never weighed against the accused. And appellate tribunals have the duty to make an independent evaluation of the circumstances. Of course, there is nothing that proscribes the press from reporting events that transpire in the courtroom. But where there is a reasonable likelihood that prejudicial news prior to trial will prevent a fair trial, the judge should continue the case until the threat abates, or transfer it to another county not so permeated with publicity. . . . If publicity during the proceedings threatens the fairness of the trial, a new trial should be ordered. But we must remember that reversals are but palliatives; the cure lies in those remedial measures that will prevent their processes from prejudicial outside interference. Neither prosecutors, counsel for defense, the accused, witnesses, court staff nor enforcement officers coming under the jurisdiction of the court should be permitted to frustrate its function. Collaboration between counsel and the press as to information affecting the fairness of a criminal trial is not only subject to regulation, but is highly censurable and worthy of disciplinary measures.

Since the state trial judge did not fulfill his duty to protect Sheppard from the inherently prejudicial publicity which saturated the community and to control disruptive influences in the courtroom, we must reverse the denial of the habeas petition. The case is remanded to the District Court with instructions to issue the writ and order that Sheppard be released from custody unless the State puts him to its charges again within a reasonable time.

*It is so ordered.*

MR. JUSTICE BLACK *dissents.*

## ROBINSON v. CALIFORNIA
370 U. S. 660; 8 L. Ed. 2d 758; 82 S. Ct. 1417 (1962)

MR. JUSTICE STEWART *delivered the opinion of the Court.*

A California statute makes it a criminal offense for a person to "be addicted to the use of narcotics." This appeal draws into question the constitutionality of that provision of the state law, as construed by the California courts in the present case.

The appellant was convicted after a jury trial in the Municipal Court of Los Angeles. The evidence against him was given by two Los Angeles police officers. Officer Brown testified that he had had occasion to examine the appellant's arms one evening on a street in Los Angeles some four months before the trial. The officer testified that at the time he had observed "scar tissue and discoloration on the inside" of the appellant's left arm, and "what appeared to be numerous needle marks and a scab which was approximately three inches below the crook of the elbow" on the appellant's left arm. The officer also testified that the appellant under questioning had admitted to the occasional use of narcotics.

Officer Lindquist testified that he had examined the appellant the following morning in the Central Jail in Los Angeles. The officer stated that at that time he had observed discolorations and scabs on the appellant's arms, and he identified photographs which had been taken of the appellant's arms shortly after his arrest the night before. Based upon more than ten years of experience as a member of the Narcotic Division of the Los Angeles Police Department, the witness gave his opinion that "these marks and the discolorations were the result of the injection of hypodermic needles into the tissue into the vein that was not sterile." He stated that the scabs were several days old at the time of his examination, and that appellant was neither under the influence of narcotics nor suffering withdrawal symptoms at the time he saw him. This witness also testified that appellant had admitted using narcotics in the past.

The appellant testified in his own behalf, denying the alleged conversations with the police officers and denying that he had ever used narcotics or been addicted to their use. He explained the marks on his arms as resulting from an allergic condition contracted during his military service. His testimony was corroborated by two witnesses.

The trial judge instructed the jury that the statute made it a misdemeanor for a person "either to use narcotics, or to be addicted to the use of narcotics. . . .* That portion of the statute referring to the 'use' of narcotics is based upon the 'act' of using. That portion of the statute referring to 'addicted to the use' of narcotics is based upon a condition or status. They are not identical. . . . To be addicted to the use of narcotics is said to be a status or condition and not an act. It is a continuing offense and differs from most other offenses in the fact that [it] is chronic rather than acute; that it continues after it is complete and subjects the offender to arrest at any time before he reforms. The existence of such a chronic condition may be ascertained from a single examination, if the characteristic reactions of that condition be found present."

The judge further instructed the jury that the appellant could be convicted under a general verdict if the jury agreed *either* that he was of the "status" *or* had committed the "act" denounced by the statute. "All that the People must show is either

that the defendant did use a narcotic in Los Angeles County, or that while in the City of Los Angeles he was addicted to the use of narcotics. . . ."†

Under these instructions the jury returned a verdict finding the appellant "guilty of the offense charged." An appeal was taken to the Appellate Department of the Los Angeles County Superior Court, "the highest court of a State in which a decision could be had" in this case. . . . Although expressing some doubt as to the constitutionality of "the crime of being a narcotic addict," the reviewing court in an unreported opinion affirmed the judgment of conviction, citing two of its own previous unreported decisions which had upheld the constitutionality of the statute. We noted probable jurisdiction of this appeal . . . because it squarely presents the issue whether the statute as construed by the California courts in this case is repugnant to the Fourteenth Amendment of the Constitution.

. . .

. . . [T]he range of valid choice which a State might make in this area is undoubtedly a wide one, and the wisdom of any particular choice within the allowable spectrum is not for us to decide. Upon that premise we turn to the California law in issue here.

It would be possible to construe the

---

† The instructions continued "and it is then up to the defendant to prove that the use, or of being addicted to the use of narcotics was administered by or under the direction of a person licensed by the State of California to prescribe and administer narcotics or at least to raise a reasonable doubt concerning the matter." No evidence, of course, had been offered in support of this affirmative defense, since the appellant had denied that he had used narcotics or been addicted to their use.

---

* The judge did not instruct the jury as to the meaning of the term "under the influence of" narcotics, having previously ruled that there was no evidence of a violation of that provision of the statute. . . .

statute under which the appellant was convicted as one which is operative only upon proof of the actual use of narcotics within the State's jurisdiction. But the California courts have not so construed this law. Although there was evidence in the present case that the appellant had used narcotics in Los Angeles, the jury were instructed that they could convict him even if they disbelieved that evidence. The appellant could be convicted, they were told, if they found simply that the appellant's "status" or "chronic condition" was that of being "addicted to the use of narcotics." And it is impossible to know from the jury's verdict that the defendant was not convicted upon precisely such a finding.

The instructions of the trial court, implicitly approved on appeal, amounted to "a ruling on a question of state law that is as binding on us as though the precise words had been written" into the statute. . . . "We can only take the statute as the state courts read it." . . .

This statute, therefore, is not one which punishes a person for the use of narcotics, for their purchase, sale or possession, or for antisocial or disorderly behavior resulting from their administration. It is not a law which even purports to provide or require medical treatment. Rather, we deal with a statute which makes the "status" of narcotic addiction a criminal offense, for which the offender may be prosecuted "at any time before he reforms." California had said that a person can be continuously guilty of this offense, whether or not he has ever used or possessed any narcotics within the State, and whether or not he has been guilty of any antisocial behavior there.

It is unlikely that any State at this moment in history would attempt to make it a criminal offense for a person to be mentally ill, or a leper, or to be afflicted with a venereal disease. A State might determine that the general health and welfare require that the victims of these and other human afflictions be dealt with by compulsory treatment, involving quarantine, confinement, or sequestration. But, in the light of contemporary human knowledge, a law which made a criminal offense of such a disease would doubtless be universally thought to be an infliction of cruel and unusual punishment in violation of the Eighth and Fourteenth Amendments. See *Francis* v. *Resweber,* 329 U.S. 459.

We cannot but consider the statute before us as of the same category. In this Court counsel for the State recognized that narcotic addiction is an illness. Indeed, it is apparently an illness which may be contracted innocently or involuntarily. We hold that a state law which imprisons a person thus afflicted as a criminal, even though he has never touched any narcotic drug within the State or been guilty of any irregular behavior there, inflicts a cruel and unusual punishment in violation of the Fourteenth Amendment. To be sure, imprisonment for ninety days is not, in the abstract, a punishment which is either cruel or unusual. But the question cannot be considered in the abstract. Even one day in prison would be a cruel and unusual punishment for the "crime" of having a common cold.

We are not unmindful that the vicious evils of the narcotics traffic have occasioned the grave concern of government. There are, as we have said, countless fronts on which those evils may be legitimately attacked. We deal in this case only with an individual provision of a particularized local law as it has so far been interpreted by the California courts.

*Reversed.*

MR. JUSTICE FRANKFURTER *took no part in the consideration or decision of this case.*

MR. JUSTICE DOUGLAS, *concurring.*

While I join the Court's opinion, I wish to make more explicit the reasons why I think it is "cruel and unusual" punishment in the sense of the Eighth Amendment to treat as a criminal a person who is a drug addict.

. . .

Today we have our differences over the legal definition of insanity. But however insanity is defined, it is in [*sic*] end effect treated as a disease. While afflicted people may be confined either for treatment or for the protection of society, they are not branded as criminals.

Yet terror and punishment linger on as means of dealing with some diseases. As recently stated:

. . . the idea of basing treatment for disease on purgatorial acts and ordeals is an ancient one in medicine. It may trace back to the Old Testament belief that disease of any kind, whether mental or physical, represented punishment for sin; and thus relief could take the form of a final heroic act of atonement. This superstition appears to have given support to fallacious medical rationales for such procedures as purging, bleeding, induced vomiting, and blistering, as well as an entire chamber of horrors constituting the early treatment of mental illness. The latter included a wide assortment of shock techniques, such as the 'water cures' (dousing, ducking, and near-drowning), spinning in a chair, centrifugal swinging, and an early form of electric shock. All, it would appear, were planned as means of driving from the body some evil spirit or toxic vapor. Action for

Mental Health (1961), pp. 27–28.

That approach continues as respects drug addicts. Drug addiction is more prevalent in this country than in any other nation of the western world. . . . It is sometimes referred to as "a contagious disease." . . . But those living in a world of black and white put the addict in the category of those who could, if they would, forsake their evil ways.

. . .

Some States punish addiction, though most do not. See S. Doc. No. 120, 84th Cong., 2d Sess., pp. 41, 42. Nor does the Uniform Narcotic Drug Act, first approved in 1932 and now in effect in most of the States. Great Britain, beginning in 1920 placed "addiction and the treatment of addicts squarely into the hands of the medical profession." Lindesmith, The British System of Narcotics Control, 22 Law & Contemp. Proh. 138 (1957). In England the doctor "has almost complete professional autonomy in reaching decisions about the treatment of addicts." Schurm British Narcotics Policies, 51 J. Crim. L. & Criminology 619, 621 (1961). Under British law "addicts are patients, not criminals." *Ibid.* . . .

The fact that England treats the addict as a sick person, while a few of our States, including California, treat him as a criminal, does not, of course, establish the unconstitutionality of California's penal law. But we do know that there is "a hard core" of "chronic and incurable drug addicts who, in reality, have lost their power of self-control." S. Rep. No. 2033, 84th Cong., 2d Sess., p. 8. . . .

The impact that an addict has on a community causes alarm and often leads to punitive measures. Those measures are justified when they relate to acts of transgression. But I do not see how under our system *being an addict* can be punished as a crime. If addicts can be punished for their addiction, then the insane can also be punished for their insanity. Each has a disease and each must be treated as a sick person.

. . .

The command of the Eighth Amendment, banning "cruel and unusual punishments," stems from the Bill of Rights of 1688. . . . And it is applicable to the States by reason of the Due Process Clause of the Fourteenth Amendment. . . .

The historic punishments that were cruel and unusual included "burning at the stake, crucifixion, breaking on the wheel" (*In re Kemmler,* 136 U.S. 436, 446), quartering, the rack and thumbscrew (see *Chambers* v. *Florida,* 309 U.S. 227, 237), and in some circumstances even solitary confinement (see *Medley,* 134 U.S. 160, 167–168).

The question presented in the earlier cases concerned the degree of severity with which a particular offense was punished or the element of cruelty present. A punishment out of all proportion to the offense may bring it within the ban against "cruel and unusual punishments." See *O'Neil* v. *Vermont,* 144 U.S. 323, 331. So may the cruelty of the method of punishment, as, for example, disemboweling a person alive. See *Wilkerson* v. *Utah,* 99 U.S. 130, 135. But the principle that would deny power to exact capital punishment for a petty crime would also deny power to punish a person by fine or imprisonment for being sick.

. . .

By the time of Coke, enlightenment was coming as respects the insane. Coke said that the execution of a madman "should be a miserable spectacle, both against law, and of extreme inhumanity and cruelty, and can be no example to others." 6 Coke's Third Inst. (4th ed. 1797), p. 6. Blackstone endorsed this view of Coke. 4 Commentaries (Lewis ed. 1897), p. 25.

We should show the same discernment respecting drug addiction. The addict is a sick person. He may, of course, be confined for treatment or for the protection of society. Cruel and unusual punishment results not from confinement, but from convicting the addict of a crime. The purpose of Sec. 11721 is not to cure, but to penalize. Were the purpose to cure, there would be no need for a mandatory jail term of not less than 90 days. Contrary to my Brother Clark, I think the means must stand constitutional scrutiny, as well as the end to be achieved. A prosecution for addiction, with its resulting stigma and irreparable damage to the good name of the accused, cannot be justified as a means of protecting society, where a civil commitment would do as well. . . . This prosecution has no relationship to the curing of an illness. Indeed, it cannot, for the prosecution is aimed at penalizing an illness, rather than at providing medical care for it. We would forget the teachings of the Eighth Amendment if we allowed sickness to be made a crime and permitted sick people to be punished for being sick. This age of enlightenment cannot tolerate such barbarous action.

MR. JUSTICE HARLAN *wrote a brief concurring opinion not printed here.*

MR. JUSTICE CLARK, *dissenting.*

The Court finds Sec. 11721 of California's Health and Safety Code, making it an offense to "be addicted to the use of narcotics," violative of due process as "a cruel and unusual punishment." I cannot agree.

The statute must first be placed in perspective. California has a comprehensive and enlightened program for the control of narcotism based on the overriding policy of prevention and cure. It is the product of an extensive investigation made in the mid-Fifties by a committee of distinguished scientists, doctors, law enforcement officers and laymen. . . . The committee filed a detailed study entitled "Report on Narcotic Addiction" which was given considerable attention. No recommendation was made therein for the repeal of Sec. 11721, and the State Legislature in its discretion continued the policy of that section.

Apart from prohibiting specific acts such as the purchase, possession and sale of narcotics, California has taken certain legislative steps in regard to the status of being a narcotic addict—a condition commonly recognized as a threat to the State and to the individual. The Code deals with this problem in realistic stages. . . . It provides that a person found to be addicted to the use of narcotics shall serve a term in the county jail of not less than 90 days nor more than one year, with the minimum 90-day confinement applying in all cases without exception. Provision is made for parole with periodic tests to detect readdiction.

The trial court defined "addicted to narcotics" as used in Sec. 11721 in the following charge to the jury:

The word 'addicted' means, strongly disposed to some taste or practice or habituated, especially to drugs. In order to inquire as to whether a person is addicted to the use of narcotics is in effect an inquiry as to his habit in that regard. Does he use them habitually? To use them often or daily is, according to the ordinary acceptance of those words, to use them habitually.

There was no suggestion that the term "narcotic addict" as here used included a person who acted without volition or who had lost the power of self-control. Although the section is penal in appearance—perhaps a carry-over from a less sophisticated approach—its present provisions are quite similar to those for civil commitment and treatment of addicts who have lost the power of self-control, and its present purpose is reflected in a statement which closely follows Sec. 11721: "The rehabilitation of narcotic addicts and the prevention of continued addiction to narcotics is a matter of statewide concern." California Health and Safety Code Sec. 11721.

Where narcotic addiction has progressed beyond the incipient volitional stage, California provides for commitment of three months to two years in a state hospital. . . . This proceeding is clearly civil in nature with a purpose of rehabilitation and cure. Significantly, if it is found that a person committed under Sec. 5355 will not receive substantial benefit from further hospital treatment and is not dangerous to society, he may be discharged—but only after a minimum confinement of three months. . . .

Thus, the "criminal" provision applies to the incipient narcotic addict who retains self-control, requiring confinement of three months to one year and parole with frequent tests to detect renewed use of drugs. Its overriding purpose is to cure the less seriously addicted persons by preventing further use. On the other hand, the "civil" commitment provision deals with addicts who have lost the power of self-control, requiring hospitalization up to two years. Each deals with a different type of addict but with a common purpose. This is most apparent when the sections overlap: if after civil commitment of an addict it is found that hospital treatment will not be helpful, the addict is confined for a minimum period of three months in the same manner as is the volitional addict under the "criminal" provision.

In the instant case the proceedings against the petitioner were brought under the volitional-addict section. There was testimony that he had been using drugs only four months with three to four relatively mild doses a week. At arrest and trial he appeared normal. His testimony was clear and concise, being simply that he had never used drugs. The scabs and pocks on his arms and body were caused, he said, by "overseas shots" administered during army service preparatory to foreign assignment. He was very articulate in his testimony but the jury did not believe him, apparently because he had told the clinical expert while being examined after arrest that he had been using drugs. . . . There was no evidence in the record of withdrawal symptoms. Obviously he could not have been committed under Sec. 5355 as one who had completely "lost the power of self-control." . . . A general verdict was returned against petitioner, and he was ordered confined for 90 days to be followed by a two-year parole during which he was required to take periodic Nalline tests.

The majority strikes down the conviction primarily on the grounds that petitioner was denied due process by the imposition of criminal penalties for nothing more than being in a status. This viewpoint is premised upon the theme that Sec. 11721 is a "criminal" provision authorizing a punishment, for the majority admits that "a State might establish a program of compulsory treatment for those addicted to narcotics" which "might require periods of involuntary confinement." I submit that California has done exactly that. The majority's error is in instructing the California Legislature that hospitalization is the *only treatment* for narcotics addiction—that anything less is a punishment denying due process. California has found otherwise after a study which I suggest was more extensive than that conducted by the Court. . . .

However, the case in support of the judgment below need not rest solely on this reading of California law. For even if the overall statutory scheme is ignored and a purpose and effect of punishment is attached to Sec. 11721, that provision still does not violate the Fourteenth Amendment. The majority acknowledges, as it must, that a State can punish persons who purchase, possess, or use narcotics. Although none of these acts are harmful to society *in themselves,* the State constitutionally may attempt to deter and prevent them through punishment because of the grave threat of future harmful conduct which they pose. Narcotics addiction—including the incipient, volitional addiction to which this provision speaks—is no different. California courts have taken judicial notice that "the inordinate use of a narcotic drug tends to create an irresistible craving and forms a habit for its continued use until one becomes an addict, and he respects no convention or obligation and will lie, steal, or use any other base means to gratify his passion for the drug, being lost to all considerations of duty or social position." *People* v. *Jaurequi,* 142 Cal. App. 2d 555, 561, 298 P. 2d 896, 900 (1956). Can this Court deny the legislative and judicial judgment of California that incipient, volitional narcotic addiction poses a threat of serious crime similar to the threat inherent in the purchase or possession of narcotics? And if such a threat is inherent in addiction, can this Court say that California is powerless to deter it by punishment?

It is no answer to suggest that we are dealing with an involuntary status and thus penal sanctions will be ineffective and unfair. The section at issue applies only to persons who use narcotics often or even daily but not to the point of losing self-control. When dealing with involuntary addicts California moves only through Sec. 5355 of its Welfare Institutions Code which clearly is not penal. Even

if it could be argued that Sec. 11721 may not be limited to volitional addicts, the petitioner in the instant case undeniably retained the power of self-control and thus to him the statute would be constitutional. Moreover, "status" offenses have long been known and recognized in the criminal law. 4 Blackstone, Commentaries (Jones ed. 1916), 170. A ready example is drunkenness, which plainly is as involuntary after addiction to alcohol as is the taking of drugs.

. . .

I would affirm the judgment.

Mr. Justice White *wrote a dissenting opinion which is not printed here.*

---

## SCOGGIN v. LINCOLN UNIVERSITY
## ESTEBAN v. CENTRAL MISSOURI STATE COLLEGE
### 45 F.R.D.133 (1968)
### (U.S.D.C., W.D. Mo., En Banc)

*General Order on Judicial Standards of Procedure and Substance in Review of Student Discipline in Tax Supported Institutions of Higher Education*

The recent filing in this Court of three major cases for review of student discipline in tax supported educational institutions of higher learning has made desirable hearings by this Court en banc in two such cases, namely Civil Actions No. 16852–4 (Western Division) and No. 1259 (Central Division). These hearings were desirable to develop uniform standards to be applied in the two civil actions and to ensure, as far as practicable, that in the future decisions in similar cases in the four decisions of this Court would be

consistent.

. . . After consideration of the briefs and arguments this Court en banc does hereby.

ORDER that hereafter, until further Order of the Court en banc, in the absence of exceptional circumstances, the judicial standards of procedure and substance, enunciated in the attached Memorandum, be treated as applicable to cases in this Court wherein questions involving disciplinary action of students in tax supported institutions of higher learning are presented; provided, however, that in any civil action, the jurisdiction and powers of the individual judge to whom the case is assigned are not affected hereby; and provided further, that no party to an action be precluded from submitting and requesting therein a decision *de novo* inconsistent with these standards. . . .

## Memorandum on Judicial Standards of Procedure and Substance in Review of Student Discipline in Tax Supported Institutions of Higher Learning

### INTRODUCTION

The number of actions for review of student disciplinary action has been increasing in this and other courts as shown by the cases in this Court and the reported cases.*

These cases reflect rapid development and much controversy concerning appropriate procedural and substantive standards of judicial review in such cases. Because of the importance in this district of clearly enunciated reliable standards, this Court scheduled hearings in the second

---

* *Esteban, et al.* v. *Central Missouri State College, et al.,* (W.D. Mo., 1967) 277 F. Supp. 649; *Esteban, et al.* v. *Central Missouri State College,* (W.D. Mo.) Civil Action No. 16852-4 (pending herein); *Scoggin, et al.* v. *Lincoln University, et al.,* (W.D. Mo.) Civil Action No. 1259 (pending herein); *Barker* v. *Hardway* (C.A. 4, 1968) 399 F. 2d 638, No. 12,600 (not yet reported), affirming (S.D. W. Va., 1968) 283 F. Supp. 228; *Madera* v. *Board of Education of City of New York,* (C.A. 2, 1967) 386 F. 2d 778, reversing (S.D.N.Y., 1967) 267 F. Supp. 356; *Dixon* v. *Alabama State Board of Education,* (C.A. 5, 1961) 294 F. 2d 150, reversing (M.D. Ala., 1960) 186 F. Supp. 945; *Moore* v. *Student Affairs Committee of Troy State University,* (M.D. Ala., 1968) 284 F. Supp. 725; *Zanders* v. *Louisiana State Board of Education* (W.D. La., 1968) 281 F. Supp. 747; *Buttny* v. *Smiley* (D. Colo., 1968) 281 F. Supp. 280; *Dickson* v. *Sitterson* (M.D.N.C., 1968) 280 F. Supp. 486; *Jones* v. *State Board of Education of and for the State of Tennessee* (M.D. Tenn., 1968) 279 F. Supp. 190; *Dickey* v. *Alabama State Board of Education* (M.D. Ala., 1967) 273 F. Supp. 613; *Hammond* v. *South Carolina State College* (D. S.C., 1967) 272 F. Supp. 947; *Due* v. *Florida A. and M. University* (N.D. Fla., 1963) 233 F. Supp. 396.

*Esteban* case and in the *Scoggin* case for the purpose of hearing arguments and suggestions of the parties and of interested *amici curiae* on the standards which would be applied regardless of the judge to whom the cases are assigned by lot. This was done for the purpose of uniformity of decision in this district.

The following memorandum represents a statement of judicial standards of procedure and substance applicable, in the absence of exceptional circumstances, to actions concerning discipline of students in tax supported educational institutions of higher learning.

### RELATIONS OF COURTS AND EDUCATION

. . . The modern courts are, and will continue to be, greatly indebted to higher education for their personnel, their innovations, their processes, their political support, and their future in the political and social order. Higher education is the primary source of study and support of improvement in the courts. For this reason, among others, the courts should exercise caution when importuned to intervene in the important processes and functions of education. A court should never intervene in the processes of education without understanding the nature of education.

Before undertaking to intervene in the educational processes, and to impose judicial restraints and mandates on the educational community, the courts should acquire a general knowledge of the lawful missions and the continually changing processes, functions, and problems of education. Judicial action without such knowledge would endanger the public interest and be likely to lead to gross injustice.

Education is the living and growing source of our progressive civilization, of our open repository of increasing knowledge, culture and our salutary democratic traditions. As such, education deserves the highest respect and the fullest protection of the courts in the performance of its lawful missions.

There have been, and no doubt in the future there will be, instances of erroneous and unwise misuse of power by those invested with powers of management and teaching in the academic community, as in the case of all human fallible institutions. When such misuse of power is threatened or occurs, our political and social order has made available a wide variety of lawful, non-violent, political, economic, and social means to prevent or end the misuse of power. These same lawful, non-violent, political, economic, and social means are available to correct an unwise, but lawful choice of educational policy or action by those charged with the powers of management and teaching in the academic community. Only where the erroneous and unwise actions in the field of education deprive students of federally protected rights or privileges does a federal court have power to intervene in the educational process.

### LAWFUL MISSIONS OF TAX SUPPORTED HIGHER EDUCATION

. . .

The tax supported educational institution is an agency of the national and state governments. Its missions include, by teaching, research and action, assisting in the declared purposes of government in this nation.
. . .

The nihilist and the anarchist, determined to destroy the existing political and social order, who directs his primary attack on the educational institutions, understands fully the mission of education in the United States.

Federal law recognizes the powers of the tax supported institutions to accomplish these missions and has frequently furnished economic assistance for these purposes.

. . .

If it is true, as it well may be, that man is in a race between education and catastrophe, it is imperative that educational institutions not be limited in the performance of their lawful missions by unwarranted judicial interference.

### OBLIGATIONS OF A STUDENT

Attendance at a tax supported educational institution of higher learning is not compulsory. The federal constitution protects the equality of opportunity of all qualified persons to attend. Whether this protected opportunity be called a qualified "right" or "privilege" is unimportant. It is optional and voluntary.

The voluntary attendance of a student in such institutions is a voluntary entrance into the academic community. By such voluntary entrance, the student voluntarily assumes obligations of performance and behavior reasonably imposed by the institution of choice relevant to its lawful missions, processes, and functions. These obligations are generally much higher than those imposed on all citizens by the civil and criminal law. So long as there is no invidious discrimination, no deprival of due process, no abridgement of a right protected in the circumstances, and no capricious, clearly unreasonable or unlawful action employed, the institution may discipline students to secure compliance with these higher obligations as a teaching method or to sever the student from the academic community.

No student may, without liability to lawful discipline, intentionally act to impair or prevent the accomplishment of any lawful mission, process, or function of an educational institution.

### THE NATURE OF STUDENT DISCIPLINE COMPARED TO CRIMINAL LAW

The discipline of students in the educational community is, in all but the case of irrevocable expulsion, a part of the teaching process. In the case of irrevocable expulsion for misconduct, the process is not punitive or deterrent in the criminal law sense, but the process is rather the determination that the student is unqualified to continue as a member of the educational community. Even then, the disciplinary process is not equivalent to the criminal law processes of federal and state criminal law. For, while the expelled student may suffer damaging effects, sometimes irreparable, to his educational, social, and economic future, he or she may not be imprisoned, fined, disenfranchised, or subjected to probationary supervision. The attempted analogy of student discipline to criminal proceedings against adults and juveniles is not sound.

In the lesser disciplinary procedures, including but not limited to guidance counseling, reprimand, suspension of social or academic privileges, probation, restriction to campus and dismissal with leave to apply for readmission, the lawful aim of discipline may be teaching in performance of a lawful mission of the institution. The nature and proce-dures of the disciplinary process in such cases should not be required to conform to federal processes of criminal law, which are far from perfect, and designed for circumstances and ends unrelated to the academic community. By judicial mandate to impose upon the academic community in student discipline the intricate, time consuming, sophisticated procedures, rules and safeguards of criminal law would frustrate the teaching process and render the institutional control impotent.

A federal court should not intervene to reverse or enjoin disciplinary actions relevant to a lawful mission of an educational institution unless there appears one of the following:

(1) a deprival of due process, that is, fundamental concepts of fair play;
(2) invidious discrimination, for example, on account of race or religion;
(3) denial of federal rights, constitutional or statutory, protected in the academic community; or
(4) clearly unreasonable, arbitrary or capricious action.

[Here follows a technical discussion of Provisional Procedural and Jurisdictional Standards.]

. . .

*Provisional Substantive Standards in Student Discipline Cases Under Section 1983, Title 42*
Equal opportunity for admission and attendance by qualified persons at tax supported state educational institutions of higher learning is protected by the equal privileges and immunities, equal protection of laws, and due process clauses of the Fourteenth Amendment to the United States Constitution. . . . It is unimportant whether this protected

opportunity is defined as a right or a privilege. The protection of the opportunity is the important thing.

. . .

In the field of discipline, scholastic and behavioral, an institution may establish any standards reasonably relevant to the lawful missions, processes, and functions of the institution. It is not a lawful mission, process, or function of an institution to prohibit the exercise of a right guaranteed by the Constitution or a law of the United States to a member of the academic community under the circumstances. Therefore, such prohibitions are not reasonably relevant to any lawful mission, process or function of an institution.

Standards so established may apply to student behavior on and off campus when relevant to any lawful mission, process, or function of the institution. By such standards of student conduct the institution may prohibit any action or ommission which impairs, interferes with, or obstructs the missions, processes and functions of the institution.

Standards so established may require scholastic attainments higher than the average of the population and may require superior ethical and moral behavior. In establishing standards of behavior, the institution is not limited to the standards or the forms of criminal law.

An institution may establish appropriate standards of conduct (scholastic and behavioral) in any form and manner reasonably calculated to give adequate notice of the scholastic attainments and behavior expected of the student.

The notice of the scholastic and behavioral standards to the students may be written or oral, or partly written and partly oral, but preferably written. The standards may be positive or negative in form.

. . .

Outstanding educational authorities in the field of higher education believe, on the basis of experience, that detailed codes of prohibited student conduct are provocative and should not be employed in higher education.

For this reason, general affirmative statements of what is expected of a student may in some areas be preferable in higher education. Such affirmative standards may be employed, and discipline of students based thereon.

The legal doctrine that a prohibitory statute is void if it is overly broad or unconstitutionally broad does not, in the absence of exceptional circumstances, apply to standards of student conduct. The validity of the form of standards of student conduct, relevant to the lawful missions of higher education, ordinarily should be determined by recognized educational standards.

In severe cases of student discipline for alleged misconduct, such as final expulsion, indefinite or longterm suspension, dismissal with deferred leave to reapply, the institution is obligated to give to the student minimal procedural requirements of due process of law. The requirements of due process do not demand an inflexible procedure for all such cases. . . . Three minimal requirements apply in cases of severe discipline, growing out of fundamental conceptions of fairness implicit in procedural due process. First, the student should be given adequate notice in writing of the specific ground or grounds and the nature of the evidence on which the disciplinary proceedings are based. Second, the student should be given an opportunity for a hearing in which the disciplinary authority provides a fair opportunity for hearing of the student's position, explanations and evidence. The third requirement is that no disciplinary action be taken on grounds which are not supported by any substantial evidence. Within limits of due process, institutions must be free to devise various types of disciplinary procedures relevant to their lawful missions, consistent with their varying processes and functions, and not an unreasonable strain on their resources and personnel.

There is no general requirement that procedural due process in student disciplinary cases provide for legal representation, a public hearing, confrontation and cross-examination of witnesses, warnings about privileges, self-incrimination, application of principles of former or double jeopardy, compulsory production of witnesses, or any of the remaining features of federal criminal jurisprudence. Rare and exceptional circumstances, however, may require provision of one or more of these features in a particular case to guarantee the fundamental concepts of fair play.

It is encouraging to note the current unusual efforts of the institutions and the interested organizations which are devising and recommending procedures and policies in student discipline which are based on standards, in many features, far higher than the requirements of due process.

. . .

## SELECTED REFERENCES

Center for the Study of Democratic Institutions, *Fair Trial vs. A Free Press* (New York: The Fund for the Republic Inc., 1965).

Fellman, David, *The Defendant's Rights* (New York: Holt, Rinehart & Winston, Inc., 1958).

Friendly, Henry J., "The Bill of Rights as a Code of Criminal Procedure," 53 *California Law Review* 929 (1965).

Green, Wayne E., "Sociology in Court: 'Socio-Legal' Research Plays an Expanding Role in Shaping Criminal Law," 169 *Wall Street Journal* 1 (April 10, 1967).

Judicial Conference of the United States, *Report of the Committee to Implement the Criminal Justice Act of 1964*, House of Re. Doc. 62, 89th Cong., 1st Sess.

Kamisar, Yale, Inbau, Fred and Thurman Arnold, *Criminal Justice in Our Time* (Charlottesville: University of Virginia Press, 1965).

Landynski, Jacob W., *Search and Seizure and the Supreme Court* (Baltimore: The Johns Hopkins Press, 1966).

Lewis, Anthony, *Gideon's Trumpet* (New York: Random House, Inc., 1964).

Medalie, Richard J., *From Escobedo to Miranda; the Anatomy of a Supreme Court Decision* (Washington: Lerner Law Book Inc., 1966).

Murphy, Walter F., *Wiretapping on Trial: A Case Study in the Judicial Process* (New York: Random House, Inc., 1965).

Note, "Developments in the Law—Academic Freedom," 81 *Harvard Law Review* 1045 (1968) especially pp. 1134–1157 on procedural due process and judicial review and student rights.

Pye, A. Kenneth, "The Role of Legal Services in the Antipoverty Program," 31 *Law and Contemporary Problems* 211 (1966).

"Should Law Enforcement Agencies be Given More Freedom in Crime Investigation and Prosecution? Pro and Con," 44 *Congressional Digest* 225 (1965).

Silverman, Lee, "The Continuing Impact of *Gideon* v. *Wainwright* on the States," 51 *American Bar Association Journal* 1023 (1965).

"Symposium on the Supreme Court and the Police" (see especially, Packer, Herbert, "The Courts, the Police and the Rest of Us"; Kuh, Richard, " 'The Rest of Us' in the 'Policing the Police' Controversy"; Souris, Theodore, "Stop and Frisk or Arrest and Search—The Use and Misuse of Euphemisms"; Broderick, Vincent, "The Supreme Court and the Police: A Police Viewpoint"; and English, Robert, "Lawyers in the Station House") 57 *The Journal of Criminal Law, Criminology and Police Science* 238 (1966).

"Symposium: Student Rights and Campus Rules" (see especially, Sherry, Arthur H., "Governance of the University: Rules, Rights and Responsibilities" and Heyman, Ira M., "Some Thoughts on University Disciplinary Proceedings") 54 *California Law Review* 1 (1966).

# 6. Black Americans and Constitutional Standards of Equality

*Plessy v. Ferguson*     *Brown v. Board of Education*

*Griffin v. School Board of Prince Edward County*

*Bell v. School City of Gary*

*Green v. School Board of New Kent County*

*Heart of Atlanta Motel v. United States*     *Watson v. Memphis*

*Reitman v. Mulkey*     *Jones v. Mayer*     *Gomillion v. Lightfoot*

*South Carolina v. Katzenbach*     *Loving v. Virginia*

After the Civil War and for almost a half century, the judicial role in promoting racial justice was anything but positive. The Civil War and Reconstruction, to be sure, brought about enactments of the 13th, 14th, and 15th Amendments. However, decisions of the Supreme Court, such as that in the *Civil Rights Cases* (109 U.S. 3, 1883) effectively thwarted, or at the least put into mothballs, the efforts to make the provisions of the Civil War Amendments more than empty guarantees. This, along with other decisions by the Court, created a climate conducive to fostering rather than eliminating racial segregation. Consequently, and as the situation in the South returned to "normalcy"—white southerners again fully in control—state legislatures were able to design fairly comprehensive systems of racial segregation in both the public and private sectors of society.

The Court gave approval and impetus to segregation practices when in *Plessy* v. *Ferguson* it upheld as a valid exercise of state police power a Louisiana statute requiring racial segregation of passengers on trains. The Court construed the statute's racial separation provisions as non-discriminatory. Segregation of the races was not the discrimination proscribed by the equal protection clause. However, the first Justice John Marshall Harlan, the lone dissenter, took issue with his fellow justices. Harlan maintained that "the Constitution is color-blind" and does not permit authorities to consider race in their actions.

Nevertheless by its decision in *Plessy,* the Court gave support to those who fostered racial segregation and injustice, not only in the area of transportation but in other areas such as education and places of public accommodation. But just as *Plessy* supported and legitimated widespread racial injustice, the famous School Desegregation Cases of 1954 (*Brown v. Board of Education of Topeka*) reversed that trend and spurred the drive for racial justice in American life. Let us trace judicial activity in various problem areas.

## PUBLIC EDUCATION

The field of public education probably affords the best illustration of the separate-but-equal doctrine in practice and the evolution of the present judicial attitude on the equal protection clause of the Fourteenth Amendment. Just three years after the *Plessy* decision, the Court had before it *Cumming* v. *Board of Education,* (175 U.S. 528, 1899), a case which illustrates the practical economic problems of operating a bi-racial school system. Challenged was the action of a county school board in Georgia discontinuing the Negro high school because of financial difficulties while maintaining the high school for whites. Black taxpayers had sought unsuccessfully to restrain the expenditure of public funds for support of the white high school so long as a high school was not available for their children. The Supreme Court sustained the state court's denial of this relief and Justice Harlan, the dissenter in *Plessy,* contended that the relief sought was not a proper remedy. He argued that the record showed that the school was suspended temporarily for economic reasons and did not reveal any desire on the part of the school board to act in a racially discriminatory manner. Thus, the Court avoided the constitutional issue of segregation.

The issue was again avoided nine years later in *Berea College* v. *Kentucky,* (211 U.S. 45, 1908), where the Court upheld as a valid regulation of corporate charters a Kentucky law requiring both public and private educational institutions to keep blacks and whites separate in their operations. Similarly, the constitutional issue was avoided in *Gong Lum* v. *Rice* (275 U.S. 78, 1927), when the Court upheld Mississippi's power to exclude Orientals from white public schools. Thus, in avoiding the school segregation issue the Court, in effect, sanctioned its constitutional foundation.

A change in judicial attitude on segregated education first appeared in a decision of the Maryland Court of Appeals. In *Pearson* v. *Murray,* (182 Atl. 590, 1936), a qualified black applicant was denied admission to the University of Maryland School of Law solely on account of race. Instead, the applicant was offered an out-of-state scholarship which covered expenses for his legal education elsewhere. While refusing to rule on the issue of segregated education, the state court did examine the standard of equality afforded and found the policy deficient. Adhering to the doctrine of the "present" nature of constitutional rights, the court

held that establishment of a separate school for blacks to begin operations at some future date was not an adequate remedy; rather, immediate
equality could only be furnished by admission to the white law school.

This was essentially the position adopted by the United States Supreme
Court two years later in *Missouri ex rel. Gaines* v. *Canada,* (305 U.S.
337, 1938). Like Maryland, Missouri provided blacks an opportunity
to obtain legal education via the "out-of-state scholarship arrangement."
However, the Supreme Court held that admission to the white law school
was the only appropriate remedy consistent with the constitutional
standard of equality. The Court also gave notice that it would no
longer ignore the "equal" part of the separate-but-equal formula. Chief
Justice Charles Evans Hughes, who delivered the Court's opinion,
stressed equality of treatment in rejecting the "scholarship arrangement."
He contended:

The basic consideraiton is not as to what sort of opportunities other states provide, but as to what opportunities Missouri itself furnishes to white students and
denies to [N]egroes wholly upon the ground of color. The admissibility of laws
separating the races in the enjoyment of privileges afforded by the State rests
wholly upon the equality of the privileges which the laws give to the separated
groups within the State. The question here is not of a duty of the state to supply legal training, or of the equality of the training which it does supply, but of
its duty when it provides such training to furnish it to the residents of the
State upon the basis of an equality of right. . . .

The Court reaffirmed the *Gaines* doctrine ten years later in *Sipuel* v.
*Board of Regents of the University of Oklahoma,* (332 U.S. 631, 1948).

Missouri and five southern states responded to the *Gaines* ruling by
establishing separate law schools for blacks.[1] This action inevitably
led to litigation focusing on comparable facilities of separate schools in
determining the standard of equality required by the equal protection
clause. The first case in which the Supreme Court was presented the
"comparable facilities" issue was *Sweatt* v. *Painter,* (339 U.S. 629, 1950).
Involved were the law schools for whites and blacks in Texas. The
Court found that the educational opportunities at the Negro law school
were not equal to those afforded white students at the University of
Texas. Though the Court stopped short of overturning the separate-but-
equal doctrine, per se, as urged by petitioner, it was apparent that the
doctrine was being eroded. In fact the language of Chief Justice Fred
Vinson's opinion appeared to forecast its doom when he noted that
there were "qualities which are incapable of objective measurement"
and that the law school "cannot be effective in isolation from the
individuals and institutions with which the law interacts."

Further evidence of this erosion came in *McLaurin* v. *Oklahoma,*
(339 U.S. 637, 1950), announced on the same day with *Sweatt.* In

[1] Texas, Louisiana, Florida, North Carolina, and South Carolina.

McLaurin, a black graduate student was admitted to the University of Oklahoma but was segregated from white students through special seating arrangements in the classroom, library, and cafeteria. The Court held that these practices conflicted with the equal protection clause since that clause requires that black students be accorded the same treatment as other students. The Court said that the segregated practices to which McLaurin was subjected impaired his "ability to study, to engage in discussion and exchange views with other students, and, in general, to learn his profession."

Immediately following the *Sweatt* and *McLaurin* decisions, the legal attack on segregated education shifted from the graduate and professional schools to the elementary and secondary school level. The first action brought in December, 1950 challenged the constitutionality of South Carolina's school segregation laws. Similar challenges were made in Kansas, Virginia, Delaware and the District of Columbia during the following year. The constitutional issue of racially segregated educational facilities was argued in each case, but the lower courts held steadfastly to the separate-but-equal doctrine.

In the Supreme Court the four actions against state laws were consolidated for purposes of argument and decision in *Brown* v. *Board of Education of Topeka, Kansas,* infra; they raised the same issue under the equal protection clause of the Fourteenth Amendment. The District of Columbia case, *Bolling* v. *Sharpe,* (347 U.S. 497, 1954), raised the same question, but was decided under the due process clause of the Fifth Amendment because the equal protection clause of the Fourteenth Amendment is not applicable to the District's policies. Speaking for a unanimous Court on May 17, 1954, Chief Justice Earl Warren declared the separate-but-equal doctrine unconstitutional in public education, thus overruling the fifty-eight year old *Plessy* precedent. The Court went to the core of the problem and considered not only tangible inequalities, but also the nature and consequences of segregation. Warren found sufficient evidence that segregation inculcates a sense of inferiority in black children and impairs their ability to learn. Consequently, such segregation with the sanction of law denies the black children the equal protection of the laws.

The Court, probably anticipating the impact of its decision, announced its judgment but delayed its decree. After examination of additional briefs and further argument on the question of the appropriate remedy during the 1954 Fall Term, the implementation decree was announced on May 31, 1955. (*Brown* v. *Board of Education,* 349 U.S. 294, 1955). The Court rejected the "immediacy" argument of the victorious appellants and leaned more toward the "gradualism" urged by the appellees. The cases were remanded to the federal district courts with instructions to order local school districts to proceed with desegregation of public schools "with all deliberate speed."

In practice, district courts showed considerable leniency in passing on local desegregation plans. They tolerated procedural maneuvers and often granted delays which were hardly consistent with the intent of the Court's "deliberate speed" formula. At times delays resulted from actions by state legislatures and state officials that made it difficult if not impossible for local school boards to follow court mandates. These boards were also under heavy local pressures to resist, evade, or at least delay final desegregation orders. In addition, there were threats of violence. But in *Cooper* v. *Aaron* (358 U.S. 1, 1958) the Supreme Court made it clear that it would not tolerate postponement of court orders (and hence enjoyment of constitutional rights) in the face of threatened or actual violence. Meeting in a rare special session (necessitated by the need to resolve the issue of postponing a desegregation order before the beginning of the school term), the Court rejected the rationale supporting the postponement of the Little Rock desegregation plan and condemned the actions of state officials designed to scuttle enforcement of the district court order. Holding that "the constitutional rights of the [black children] are not to be sacrificed or yielded to the violence and disorder which have followed upon the actions of the Governor and Legislature . . . ," the Court concluded that "the constitutional rights of children not to be discriminated against in school admission on grounds of race or color can neither be nullified openly and directly by state [officials] nor nullified indirectly by them through evasive schemes for segregation whether attempted 'ingeniously or ingenuously.' "

While the Court had used strong language in *Cooper* to condemn the obstruction to desegregation attempted by state officials, it showed considerable leniency and deference to lower courts when presented with plans designed to keep the number of blacks attending schools with whites at a minimum. For example, shortly after its decision in *Cooper* the Court upheld the Alabama pupil-placement laws in *Shuttlesworth* v. *Birmingham Board of Education* (358 U.S. 101, 1958). Essentially, this was an arrangement adopted by several states to delay and/or minimize the impact of the *Brown* decision. Under the guise of using such non-racial factors as scholastic aptitude and achievement, health, moral character, and residence in assignment of pupils to schools, local school authorities could control the number of blacks attending white schools. A three-judge federal district court upheld the Alabama law, noting that its purpose was to admit pupils to schools on the basis of individual merit irrespective of race. The court presumed that the law would be administered to accomplish that purpose only. The Supreme Court's affirmance was on "these limited grounds" and without opinion.

An extreme state response to the *Brown* decision was the provision for closing public schools when faced with a final desegregation decree. This was part of Virginia's "massive resistance" program fashioned by Governor J. Lindsay Almond. This "weapon" was used by Prince

Edward County, when authorities (Prince Edward County was one of the school districts involved in the *Brown* case), faced with a final desegregation order, closed schools in 1959. During the ensuing five-year period, while the issue was kicked up and down the judicial ladder, white children attended private segregated schools largely supported by a state financed grant-in-aid tuition program. Black children, however, had no formal schooling at all, having rejected a segregated program similar to that provided for whites. The Supreme Court finally resolved the issue and rejected this evasive approach in *Griffin* v. *School Board of Prince Edward County*. Not only did the Court find the Virginia law defective because of its discriminatory purpose and effect, but it took the unusual step of empowering the federal district court to order the taxing authority to exercise its power in providing funds "to reopen, operate and maintain" the public school system on a nondiscriminatory basis.

Toward the end of the first decade of controversy over school desegregation in the South, the problem of de facto school segregation in the North emerged. It rapidly developed into an emotion-packed issue, focusing attention on the traditional neighborhood school policy, housing patterns, and the myriad problems of urban ghettoes.

Those attacking de facto segregation argued that *Brown* imposed a duty on school authorities to eliminate such conditions, though the segregation had developed spontaneously and without any positive official action. In effect, they contended that there was a constitutional duty to take positive action to "integrate" segregated schools and bring about a better racial balance.

Proponents of the neighborhood school policy countered with the argument that the command of *Brown* was essentially a negative obligation, i.e., school authorities could not operate public schools in a racially discriminatory manner. Essentially, they argued that *Brown* was directed at segregation resulting from positive action of public authorities, but it did not condemn school segregation resulting from changing residential patterns where only private action is involved.

These conflicting interpretations of the *Brown* decision were argued in state courts (principally in New York) and in lower federal courts. As frequently happens, judges of state and federal courts differ in their interpretation of decisions of the Supreme Court. Here, they differ on whether *Brown* places a constitutional duty on school authorities to take positive action to eliminate de facto segregation not of their own making. In this regard, the New York Court of Appeals has applied the "positive action" theory more liberally than most courts by holding in *Balaban* v. *Rubin,* (250 N.Y.S. 2d 281, 1964), that school boards may consider race among other relevant factors in achieving a particular balance of population groups within an attendance zone.

A leading federal case on the issue is *Bell* v. *School City of Gary,*

*Indiana* (cf. *Barksdale* v. *Springfield School Committee,* 237 F. Supp. 543, 348 F. 2d 261, 1965). There, the Court of Appeals for the Seventh Circuit affirmed a district court judgment dismissing a complaint against the Gary school board alleging the operation of segregated schools contrary to the *Brown* rule. In his opinion of a unanimous court, Circuit Judge F. Ryan Duffy upheld the neighborhood school policy, accepting the school board's contention that "there is no affirmative U.S. Constitutional duty to change innocently arrived at school attendance districts by the mere fact that shifts in population either increase or decrease the percentage of either Negro or white pupils." Judge Duffy's opinion did not curtail the board's authority to take action on its own to eliminate de facto segregation. But his acceptance of the district court's holding (that a school system developed on the neighborhood policy without any intention or purpose of racial segregation does not have to be abandoned because the resulting effect is to have a racial imbalance) certainly strengthens the position of school board members advocating the status quo.

However, in *Hobson* v. *Hansen* (269 F. Supp. 401, 1967) Circuit Judge J. Skelly Wright (sitting in the District Court for the District of Columbia pursuant to 23 U.S.C. sec. 291 [c]) delivered a most scathing attack on de facto segregation. In his opinion, Judge Wright made an expansive and bold application of *Brown.* Upon a finding of racial and economic discrimination in the operation of the District of Columbia school system, he issued an injunction prohibiting the use of the ability-grouping "track system" and optional attendance zones. He further ordered the bussing of black children from overcrowded schools to the under-populated schools in white neighborhoods and a substantial integration of the faculty of each school. The district school board (controlled by blacks) would not authorize Superintendent Hansen to appeal whereupon he resigned, threatening to make the appeal as a private citizen.

The Supreme Court refused to review the *Balaban* and *Bell* cases, thereby leaving the law on de facto segregation essentially this: the *Brown* rule *does not require* school authorities to take action to eliminate de facto segregation, *nor does it prohibit* official action that uses *race* among other factors to achieve a desired balance among racial groups in a school district.

Overall slow pace of school desegregation has been very disappointing to those who viewed *Brown* as a major step toward full equality for blacks. Not only was a start toward desegregation in some districts delayed for years by legal maneuvering, but the grade-a-year plan allowed up to a dozen years to effect complete desegregation. The Supreme Court indicated its growing impatience with the manner in which the "deliberate speed" formula was being abused when, in rejecting a plan for gradual desegregation of recreational facilities in *Watson* v. *Memphis* Justice Arthur Goldberg asserted:

It is far from clear that the mandate of the second Brown decision requiring that desegregation proceed with "all deliberate speed" would today be fully satisfied by types of plans or programs for desegregation of public educational facilities which eight years ago might have been deemed sufficient.

The Court showed further disgust with the pace of desegregation in *Rogers* v. *Paul* (382 U.S. 198, 1965). Here, it ordered immediate admission of blacks to a Fort Smith, Arkansas high school where the grade-a-year plan adopted in 1957 was three years short of complete implementation.

Growing discontent with the progress of school desegregation moved the issue into the political arena as Congress was considering an omnibus civil rights bill in 1963. When Congress eventually enacted the measure (Civil Rights Act of 1964) it contained a title on public school desegregation. That title denies federal financial aid to any program administered in a racially discriminatory manner. Pursuant to this provision, the U.S. Office of Education late in 1964 made eligibility for federal aid contingent on compliance with a court-ordered desegregation plan or in the absence thereof, compliance with guidelines for school desegregation issued by the Department of Health, Education and Welfare, popularly known as the *H.E.W. Guidelines.*

The new policy had an immediate impact since the withholding of federal financial aid would have serious fiscal consequences for many school districts where no effort at all or at most a token effort had been made to desegregate their schools. Faced with the possibility of a loss of substantial funds, especially in view of the passage of the Elementary and Secondary Education Act of 1965, most districts grudgingly moved to comply with the *Guidelines.*[2]

Indeed, the most authoritative statement on the constitutionality of the *H.E.W. Guidelines* was given by Circuit Judge John Minor Wisdom of the Court of Appeals for the Fifth Circuit in *United States* v. *Jefferson County Board of Education* (372 F2d 836, 1966). In reversing district court holdings involving seven school districts in Alabama and Louisiana, Judge Wisdom held that the standards for desegregation prescribed by the *Guidelines* are within the rationale of the *Brown* ruling and the congressional objectives of the Civil Rights Act of 1964. In what must be considered the most far-reaching statement on the

[2] These first *Guidelines,* issued in April 1965, set the fall of 1967 as the target date for desegregation of all public school systems. A revision of the *Guidelines* in March 1968 moved the target date to the opening of the 1968–1969 school year, or, at the latest, the opening of the 1969–1970 year.

Without rejecting the policy of "compliance now" or abandoning the 1969–1970 target, the Nixon Administration adopted a flexible policy under which delays in implementing desegregation plans would be granted if warranted by "bona fide educational and administrative problems." On such grounds, the Court of Appeals for the Fifth Circuit granted the Administration's request for a three-month delay in implementing the plans of 33 recalcitrant districts in Mississippi as the 1969–1970 school year began. But the Supreme Court overturned these actions (see p. 390).

obligation of school boards, Judge Wisdom asserted that "the law imposes an absolute duty to integrate, in the sense that a disproportionate concentration of Negroes in certain schools cannot be ignored [for] racial mixing of students is a high priority goal." Upon petition for a rehearing, the Court of Appeals (en banc) adopted Judge Wisdom's opinion, attaching some clarifying statements and alterations to the decree. (*United States* v. *Jefferson County Board of Education,* 380 F2d 385, 1967). The Supreme Court refused to review this judgment in *Caddo Parish School Board* v. *United States* (386 U.S. 1001, 1967).

After avoiding for 13 years the issue of whether *Brown* required school boards to take affirmative action to integrate schools,[3] on May 27, 1968 the Supreme Court decided three cases in which it intimated that in order to meet the command of *Brown,* school officials may have to take positive action to integrate. In *Green* v. *County School Board of New Kent County, Virginia* the Court examined the "freedom-of-choice" desegregation plan (which allows a pupil to choose his own school) and found its operational results unacceptable in meeting the *Brown* requirement "of a racially nondiscriminatory school system." Justice Brennan's opinion for the Court emphasized that the burden on a school board today is to come forth with realistically workable plans for a speedier and more effective conversion to a unitary, nonracial school system. Brennan noted that not a single white student had chosen to attend the black school and that 85 per cent of black school children still attended the all-black school. He said that an acceptable system must not have "a 'white' school and a 'Negro' school, but just schools." The other two cases—*Monroe* v. *Board of Commissioners* (391 U.S. 450) and *Raney* v. *Board of Education* (391 U.S. 443)—raised the same issue, although the plan under attack in *Monroe* was a variation of the "freedom-of-choice" plan known as "free transfer."

The Court was careful to limit its ruling to the specific plans involved in *Green* and did not declare such plans unconstitutional on their face. Nonetheless, in *Alexander* v. *Holmes County Board of Education* (90 S. Ct. 29, 1969), the Court dashed any hope that "freedom-of-choice" or any other plan could be used constitutionally to delay further the implementation of *Brown.* In a unanimous per curiam opinion, the "new" Burger Court blunted actions of the Nixon administration by overturning a decision of the Court of Appeals for the Fifth Circuit that had sanctioned a delay in desegregation of 33 Mississippi school dis-

---

[3] The Court had refused to hear lower court actions which held that *Brown* only prohibits segregation and does not require integration, Cf. *Bell* v. *School City of Gary, Indiana,* infra and *Downs* v. *Board of Education,* (336 F 2d 988, 10th Cir., 1964). However, it did uphold a ruling in the Court of Appeals for the Fifth Circuit sustaining the constitutionality of the *H.E.W. Guidelines* where Circuit Judge John Minor Wisdom, declared that *Brown* imposes an absolute duty to integrate where there is a disproportionate concentration of blacks in certain schools. See *United States* v. *Jefferson County Board of Education, supra.*

tricts. The Court declared the standard of "all deliberate speed [no] longer constitutionally permissible" and ordered desegregation "at once."[4]

## PUBLIC TRANSPORTATION

The separate-but-equal doctrine was proclaimed in the transportation field in *Plessy* v. *Ferguson*. This applied to purely intrastate transportation but, in practice, interstate carriers respected local segregation laws despite the anti-discrimination provision of the Interstate Commerce Act which provides in part:

It shall be unlawful for any common carrier by motor vehicle engaged in interstate or foreign commerce to make, give, or cause any undue and unreasonable preference or advantage to any particular person . . . ; or to subject any particular person to any unjust discrimination or any unjust or unreasonable prejudice or disadvantage in any respect whatsoever. . . . (Sec. 216 [d], Part II, Interstate Commerce Act, 49 U.S.C. sec. 3 [1]).

In *Morgan* v. *Virginia* (328 U.S. 623, 1946), the Supreme Court cited this provision in declaring unconstitutional the application of a Virginia segregation statute to passenger busses in interstate commerce. The law was held to place an unreasonable burden on interstate commerce because in practice it compelled a black passenger on an interstate journey to change his seat repeatedly to conform with the state policy.

Four years later in *Henderson* v. *United States* (339 U.S. 816, 1950), the Court used the commerce clause to strike down segregated dining car practices in interstate commerce. In reversing a federal district court ruling that sustained the Interstate Commerce Commission's approval of the practices, the Court held that the segregation in question subjected black passengers "to unreasonable prejudice or disadvantage" in violation of the Interstate Commerce Act. It concluded that "where a dining car is available to passengers holding tickets entitling them to use it," all passengers are entitled to use the facilities on an equal basis.

The *Henderson* decision had a limited impact since it did not directly touch the issue of segregated passenger cars on interstate trains. Hence, the Commission continued to permit carriers to follow the *Plessy* doctrine. With the rejection of that doctrine in the *Brown* case in 1954, the Commission was under considerable pressure to change its construction of the Act's discriminatory provisions to conform with the new

---

[4] These recent decisions of the Court could hold important implications for de facto segregation in the North. In the first suit brought by the Government against a northern school district under the 1964 Civil Rights Act, the South Holland school district (operating in three Chicago suburbs) was found to have been deliberately discriminating against its black pupils and teachers and accordingly was ordered to end such practices. (See *United States* v. *School District 151 of Cook County, Illinois,* 286 F. Supp. 786, 1968, and 404 F. 2d, 1125, 1969.)

standard of equality. Hence, in November, 1955, the Commission issued a comprehensive order banning racial segregation as of January 10, 1956, on all carriers (and their terminal facilities) under its jurisdiction.

The Court's decisions and the I.C.C. orders did not touch intrastate travel, most of which involved city transit systems that transported large numbers of black passengers daily. In the meantime, however, public protests and pressures to eliminate this last stronghold of segregated transportation mounted. The most celebrated movement in this protest was the Montgomery, Alabama bus boycott, spearheaded by the late Reverend Martin Luther King Jr., which began in December, 1955 and lasted for 382 days. While this economic pressure and moral persuasion were being applied, the issue was also being fought in the courts. In *Gayle* v. *Browder* (142 F. Supp. 707, 1956), a federal district court struck down the Alabama and Montgomery statutes requiring segregated bus travel as unconstitutional infringements of the equal protection and due process clauses of the Fourteenth Amendment. The Supreme Court affirmed the decision in a per curiam opinion on November 13, 1956.

## PUBLIC ACCOMMODATIONS AND HOUSING

While school desegregation was proceeding with obviously more "deliberation" than "speed," a vigorous campaign began against segregation practices of eating places, hotels, theaters, and other places providing accommodations for the public. The tactics employed were markedly different from those used in the school segregation controversy—sit-ins and massive demonstrations were substituted for court challenges. Of course, these tactics themselves became the subject of litigation as discussed in Chapter 3. The objective was to prod the conscience of the various communities and the nation generally into a reexamination of racial segregation as a moral proposition. Beginning in 1960, demonstrations spread throughout the South and thousands of demonstrators, mostly college and high school students, were arrested and jailed. Though numerous appeals were taken to the Supreme Court, the Court was able to dispose of the cases without tackling the tough constitutional issue of segregated accommodations. Cf. *Garner* v. *Louisiana* (368 U.S. 157, 1961). Apparently, most of the justices were not yet ready to reexamine the *Civil Rights Cases* (109 U.S. 3, 1883), where the Court limited the command of the equal protection clause to state action only, excluding the discriminatory actions of private individuals who provide various accommodations for the public.

In a few scattered instances segregation practices were abandoned as a result of demonstrations, but in the end it took the public accommodations title of the 1964 Civil Rights Act to ban this form of private discrimination. This legislation was challenged immediately after it was signed by President Johnson. But a federal district court in Georgia sustained the constitutionality of the Act and denied attempts to enjoin its enforcement as applied to a restaurant and a motel. In Alabama, however, a federal district court held the public accommodations title unconstitutional as applied to a local eating establishment. Upon appeal of both rulings, the Supreme Court held the legislation to be a valid exercise of the commerce power (*Heart of Atlanta Motel* v. *United States,* and *Katzenbach* v. *McClung,* 379 U.S. 294, 1964).

Having waged a successful campaign against segregated public accommodations, civil rights groups marshalled forces for a concerted effort against discrimination in the housing market. State action promoting racially segregated housing had long ago been declared an infringement of the equal protection clause of the Fourteenth Amendment. In 1917, the Supreme Court invalidated an ordinance of Louisville, Kentucky which established separate residential districts for blacks and whites (*Buchanan* v. *Warley,* 245 U.S. 60), and in 1948, the Court dealt restrictive covenant arrangements a crushing blow by holding them unenforceable in state courts. (*Shelley* v. *Kraemer,* 324 U.S. 1; see also *Barrows* v. *Jackson,* 346 U.S. 249, 1952). However, segregated housing patterns continued to develop primarily as a result of private action initiated and sustained by policies of the real estate industry.

The technique employed by groups challenging housing discrimination was essentially that of massive demonstrations and pressure on state and local legislative bodies for "open occupancy" legislation. Where these efforts were successful, the courts have upheld such legislation as a valid exercise of state power to achieve a non-discriminatory housing market. However, a challenge to the California fair housing law went beyond the courts to the people in the 1964 general election. Using the popular initiative and referendum, opponents of open housing pushed through an amendment to the state constitution nullifying the state fair housing law and rendering the legislature powerless to enact such legislation in the future. In the referendum, the people of California overwhelmingly approved as state policy "private" discrimination in the housing market. But after examining the amendment in terms of its "immediate objective," the state supreme court declared adoption of the amendment to be an unconstitutional state involvement in promoting private discrimination contrary to the equal protection of the laws. The U.S. Supreme Court affirmed this judgment in *Reitman* v. *Mulkey* on the same equal protection grounds and in doing so rejected the proposition that constitutional rights may be submitted to a popular referendum. In 1969 the Supreme Court in *Hunter* v. *Erickson* (393 U.S. 385) held unconstitutional as a denial of equal protection an amendment to the City Charter of Akron, Ohio. Even though adopted in a popular referendum by majority vote, the amendment, in effect, placed "special burdens" on racial minorities by preventing the City

Council from enacting fair housing ordinances unless approved in a referendum by a majority of the city's voters. "The sovereignty of the people," said the Court, "is itself subject to those constitutional limitations which have been duly adopted and remain unrepealed."

Despite the spread of fair housing laws at the state and local level, the Johnson administration pushed for a national law to ban discrimination in the sale and rental of housing. For three successive years (1966–1968) President Lyndon Johnson included such a proposal in civil rights bills submitted to Congress. The proposal got nowhere in 1966 and 1967; in 1968 it was floundering with only a remote possibility of passage. However, the assassination of the Reverend Martin Luther King, Jr., on April 4, 1968 and the widespread urban violence that followed, spurred immediate congressional approval of a fair housing law. And in signing the measure President Johnson hailed "fair housing for all human beings who live in this country as now a part of the American way of life."

When fully effective in 1970, the law bans discrimination in the sale and rental of 80 per cent of the nation's housing. Excluded from its provisions are owner-occupied dwellings of four units or less and privately-owned single family homes where sale and rental transactions do not involve the services of a real estate broker. The nondiscriminatory provisions also extend to financing and brokerage services. The Department of Housing and Urban Development is charged with seeking voluntary compliance, but enforcement is possible through individual civil actions and, where the Attorney General finds a pattern or general practice of discrimination, he is authorized to file suits against the offender(s).

Just two months after the enactment of the 1968 law, the Supreme Court resurrected an amorphous federal statute that had been passed to enforce the Thirteenth Amendment and construed it to apply to private discrimination in the housing market. In *Jones* v. *Mayer* the Court held that the provision of the Civil Rights Act of 1866 which guarantees to black citizens the same right "enjoyed by white[s] . . . to inherit, purchase, lease, sell, hold, and convey real and personal property" prohibits racial discrimination in the sale of housing by a private developer. Justice Potter Stewart, who wrote the Court's opinion, said that the statute's language was "plain and unambigious" in its declaration of property rights available to *all* citizens and "on its face . . . appears to prohibit *all* discrimination against Negroes in sale or rental of property." Furthermore, Justice Stewart had no doubt about the authority of Congress to act. He noted that the act was grounded in the Thirteenth Amendment which proclaims in absolute terms that "neither slavery nor involuntary servitude . . . shall exist within the United States. . . ." Stewart concluded that while this amendment "by its own unaided force and effect abolished slavery and established universal freedom," the enabling section empowered Congress to enact "all laws necessary and proper to abolish all badges and incidents of slavery."

The Court emphasized that its action in no way "diminished the significance of the [1968 fair housing law]" since there were vast differences between the two measures. Justice Stewart noted, for example, that the 1866 Act was "a general statute applicable only to racial discrimination in the rental and sale of property" with remedial relief available only through private action while, on the other hand, the 1968 statute was a comprehensive housing measure (applicable to a number of discriminatory practices and exempting specific types of units) "enforceable by a complete arsenal of federal authority."

Justices John Harlan and Byron White dissented and, in an opinion written by Harlan, felt that the decision was "most ill-considered and ill-advised." Harlan thought that since the political branches had recently produced fair housing legislation geared to the current dynamics of society there was no need to grant the relief sought under the old statute. However, the heart of Harlan's dissent was that neither the language of the 1866 Act nor its legislative history can support the conclusion reached by the majority that the statute was intended to extend to private action.

In a related development, the Supreme Court interpreted the public accommodations section of the Civil Rights Act of 1964 to cover a privately owned recreational facility that catered to interstate travelers. (*Daniel* v. *Paul,* 395 U.S. 298, 1969). Justice William J. Brennan, who spoke for the Court, brushed aside attempts of defendant Paul, owner of the Lake Nixon Club (located about 12 miles from Little Rock, Arkansas) to evade the strictures of the act by selling membership cards and advertising his establishment as a "private club." Brennan found that the operations of the club generally, and its snack bar in particular, were so affected by interstate commerce that the entire facility was a place of public accommodation within the meaning of the 1964 act. This ruling could very well have a significant impact on one of the remaining symbols (and strongholds) of white racism in America, the so-called private club.

## VOTING RIGHTS

Despite the voting rights guarantee of the Fifteenth Amendment, systematic exclusion of black Americans from the political process was commonplace. This condition was in large measure a consequence of our federal system. States not only exercise the power to determine who can vote in state and local contests, but in practice, one's participation in federal elections is essentially in the hands of state officials as well.

Putting aside earlier practices of threats and physical intimidation, states devised several legal schemes to circumvent the Fifteenth Amendment and thwart its objective. While such legal barriers were successful in generally disfranchising Southern blacks, they were gradually eliminated as the Supreme Court found them constitutionally deficient.

One of the early schemes was the so-called "grandfather-clause" literacy provision. Its basic design was to employ a literacy test for voting and exclude from its application all persons whose ancestors had voted on or before January 1, 1866. Obviously few, if any, blacks could inherit this permanent enfranchisement, while most whites could. In *Guinn* v. *United States* (238 U.S. 347, 1915), the Supreme Court struck down this Oklahoma scheme as an infringement of the Fifteenth Amendment.

The traditional one-party system in the South facilitated one of the most effective legal barriers to Negro suffrage. With the Republican party largely dormant, the real contests for public office were in the Democratic party primary elections. Hence, the black man's vote could be rendered ineffective by denying his participation in Democratic party primaries. A decision of the Supreme Court in *Newberry* v. *United States* (256 U.S. 232, 1921), in which the majority held that as far as federal elections were concerned the primary was "in no real sense" a part thereof, undoubtedly influenced the Texas legislature as it took action to perfect the white primary. After two unsuccessful attempts to exclude blacks from Democratic primaries by state law, (*Nixon* v. *Herndon,* 273 U.S. 536, 1927 and *Nixon* v. *Condon,* 286 U.S. 73, 1932), the action of the state Democratic party convention to exclude blacks from its primaries avoided constitutional infirmity. In *Grovey* v. *Townsend* (295 U.S. 45, 1935), the Court ruled that this party action did not infringe the Fourteenth Amendment since no state action was involved. The Court concluded that the Democratic party was simply acting as a private voluntary group.

By 1941, a change in judicial attitude on the status of primary elections was indicated in *United States* v. *Classic* (313 U.S. 299). Involved was a federal prosecution of a Louisiana election official for ballot fraud in a Congressional primary election. The district court had rejected federal regulation of such contests largely on the authority of the *Newberry* decision. But in reversing this holding, the Supreme Court held that the right to vote in such primary elections is secured by the federal Constitution and that Congress has the authority to regulate primaries "when they are a step in the exercise by the people of their choice of representatives in Congress."

The *Classic* decision clearly forecast the downfall of the white primary by rejecting the "private" status theory of primary elections. In fact that downfall came only three years later in *Smith* v. *Allwright* (321 U.S. 649, 1944), when the Court had before it another challenge to the Texas white primary system. The Court thus eliminated this impediment to Negro suffrage by directly reversing *Grovey* v. *Townsend*. Political parties and party primaries were regulated by massive state legislation and party action was for all practical purposes "state action." Hence, party action, which discriminated against blacks, was really state action contrary to the command of the Fifteenth Amendment.

Several schemes designed to resurrect the white primary proved to be little more than delaying nuisances. The South Carolina effort to make the party a truly private club by repealing some 150 statutory provisions governing primary elections was rejected by the lower federal courts and the Supreme Court denied certiorari (*Rice* v. *Elmore,* 33 U.S. 875, 1948). A Texas county's evasive scheme took the form of a pre-primary election from which black voters were excluded. The winner filed in the regular Democratic primary and was usually elected without opposition. In *Terry* v. *Adams* (345 U.S. 461, 1953), the Supreme Court rejected the "private" status claim of the "Jaybird" group and held that its primary was an intergral part of the election process that must conform with the command of the Fifteenth Amendment.

Despite the death of the white primary, blacks attempting to vote in many southern areas continued to meet stiff resistance from both official and nonofficial sources. Cumbersome registration procedures and "understanding" tests administered by hostile registration officials in an atmosphere of fear, threatened economic intimidation, and deeply-rooted apathy succeeded in keeping all but a few blacks off voter registration rolls. The larger the potential black vote, the more determined was the resistance. For example, when the large black registration in Tuskegee, Alabama (county seat of Macon County) presaged a possible take over of city government by black officials, the state legislature enacted a statute gerrymandering nearly all resident Negroes out of the city. In declaring the act unconstitutional in *Gomillion* v. *Lightfoot* the Supreme Court rejected Alabama's "political-question" argument. It held that while in form the act was merely a redefinition of municipal boundaries, "the inescapable human effect of [that] essay in geometry and geography" was to deprive blacks of their voting rights secured by the Fifteenth Amendment.

Black leaders and civil rights activists correctly recognized that judicial declarations alone would not secure the ballot for blacks. Hence, they marshaled forces in a concerted effort to break the remaining resistance to Negro suffrage by concentrating on presidential and congressional action to implement the Fifteenth Amendment. Their efforts resulted in the civil rights acts of 1957, 1960, 1964, and 1965.

Although the acts of 1957 and 1960[5] were generally viewed by blacks

---

[5] The 1957 Act created a Civil Rights Commission and charged it (among other duties) to gather evidence of denials of the right to vote. More significantly, blacks were relieved of the burden of filing their own lawsuits as the Attorney General was empowered to seek injunctions against those conspiring to deny the right to vote. The

and civil rights groups as rather mild palliatives for a serious defect in our democratic political system, the fact that Congress had finally taken some action to enforce the Fifteenth Amendment was considered a significant step in the southern blacks' quest for political equality. The chief defect of these acts was the continued reliance on the courts. Litigation could be dragged on for a long period of time in the courtrooms of local federal judges who might reasonably be expected to be sympathetic to maintenance of the status quo.

The 1964 Civil Rights Act, while primarily directed at discrimination in public accommodations and other areas, dealt a crippling blow to the literacy and "understanding" tests which had been effective in thwarting black voter registration. In *Lassiter* v. *Northampton County Board of Elections* (360 U.S. 45, 1959), the Supreme Court had warned that although literacy tests were constitutional, they could not be employed as instruments of racial discrimination. But evidence gathered by the Civil Rights Commission indicated that this warning has been largely ignored by southern registrars. Consequently, the Act provided that registration officials had to apply their standards equally and administer their tests in writing, keeping the test papers for possible review.

After the 1964 elections, there was considerable evidence that the black man's right to vote had still not been secured in many areas of the South. The registration machinery was still in the hands of state and local officials, most of whom were opposed to black voting rights. Consequently, at President Johnson's urging and following massive demonstrations in the South, Congress passed a comprehensive voting rights act in 1965. The major improvement over the earlier laws was the provision for federal machinery for voter registration. In addition, the act suspended the use of literacy, understanding, and other tests in states and voting districts where less than 50 per cent of the voting-age residents were registered in 1964 or actually voted in the 1964 presidential election. Criminal sanctions could be applied also to anyone attempting to harm, threaten, or prevent persons from voting or civil rights workers from assisting potential voters. Finally, the Act directed the Justice Department to institute injunctive action against the enforcement of the poll tax requirement in the five states retaining it.

One of the discrimination devices suspended by the Act—the "understanding" test—had been struck down in the case of *Louisiana* v. *United States* (380 U.S. 145, 1965) by the time the President signed the measure. In that case the Supreme Court upheld a district court ruling invalidating the Louisiana constitutional and statutory provisions which required

---

1960 Act continued to place reliance on the courts. Upon application of the Attorney General and after a finding of a persistent pattern of discrimination, federal district judges were empowered to appoint referees to register qualified persons to vote in both federal and state elections.

every applicant for voting to "be able to understand" and "give a reasonable interpretation" of any provision of the state or federal constitution. Justice Hugo Black's opinion for the Court emphasized the discriminatory manner in which the test had been applied:

> The applicant facing a registrar in Louisiana . . . [is] compelled to leave his voting fate to that official's uncontrolled power to determine whether the applicant's understanding of the Federal or State Constitution is satisfactory. As the evidence showed, colored people, even some with the most advanced education and scholarship, were declared by voting registrars with less education to have an unsatisfactory understanding of . . . [those constitutions]. This is not a test but a trap, sufficient to stop even the most brilliant man on his way to the voting booth.

As expected, officials in Louisiana, Alabama, and Mississippi immediately challenged the Act's constitutionality. The challenges came in the form of state court injunctions forbidding local election officials to enter on voting rolls the names of persons registered by federal examiners. Instead of instituting actions under section 12(d) of the Act to dissolve these injunctions, the Attorney General filed a motion to bring action in the original jurisdiction of the Supreme Court against the three states. In the meantime, South Carolina brought an injunctive action in the original jurisdiction of the Court against enforcement of the Act by the Attorney General. After a consideration of the complex jurisdictional questions posed by these simultaneous actions, the Supreme Court accepted the South Carolina suit—*South Carolina* v. *Katzenbach* —as an appropriate vehicle for testing the constitutionality of the Act's basic provisions. The Court upheld the act primarily on the authority of Congress to enact legislation pursuant to the Fifteenth Amendment. Chief Justice Earl Warren's opinion for the Court emphasized the massive findings of state defiance of the command of the Amendment, and the Congressional conclusion that sterner and more elaborate measures were needed to protect the right to vote. Quoting from Chief Justice John Marshall in *Gibbons* v. *Ogden* (9 Wheat. 1, 1824), Warren concluded that the power of Congress to enforce the Fifteenth Amendment, "like all others vested in [it], is complete in itself, may be exercised to its utmost extent, and acknowledges no limitations, other than are prescribed in the Constitution."

Soon after the *South Carolina* decision, the Court struck down the poll tax in *Harper* v. *Virginia Board of Elections* (383 U.S. 663, 1966). The Court based the holding entirely on the Equal Protection Clause of the Fourteenth Amendment. Justice William O. Douglas, speaking for the Court, maintained that "voter qualifications have no relation to wealth nor to paying or not paying" a tax. He concluded that "wealth, like race, creed, or color, is not germane to one's ability to participate intelligently in the electoral process."

The 1965 Voting Rights Act also contains a provision designed to aid Spanish-speaking voters. It provides that no person, who has obtained at least a sixth grade education from an accredited school in the United States or its territories, in which the predominant classroom language was other than English, shall be denied the right to vote because of his inability to read or write English. The provision had particular relevance for New York (with its large Puerto Rican population in East Harlem) where literacy in English is required as a condition for voting. In *Katzenbach* v. *Morgan* (384 U.S. 641, 1966), the Supreme Court reversed a ruling of the District Court for the District of Columbia and upheld the provision's constitutionality as a valid exercise of Congressional power to enforce the Equal Protection Clause of the Fourteenth Amendment. Justice William J. Brennan's opinion for the Court emphasized that the New York literacy test was not in question under the Fourteenth Amendment. The crucial question, however, was the power of Congress under the Amendment to suspend operation of the test. Referring to the "necessary and proper" clause, he concluded that the provision was appropriate legislation to enforce the Equal Protection Clause.

## THE MISCEGENATION ISSUE

In our federal system the regulation of domestic relations is reserved to the states. Laws in this area commonly prescribe such matters as the age of marital consent, the issuance of licenses, the marriage ceremony, grounds for divorce, and custody of children. Under this authority some states, in bolstering their segregation policies, enacted antimiscegenation statutes—laws prohibiting marriages between blacks and whites. But over the years the Supreme Court steadfastly declined to review state court decisions that upheld the validity of these antimiscegenation laws. However, the Court indicated a change in its attitude on the subject in its disposition of *McLaughlin* v. *Florida* (379 U.S. 184, 1964). At issue was the validity of a conviction under a Florida statute which provided:

Any [N]egro man and white woman, or any white man and [N]egro woman, who are not married to each other, who shall habitually live in and occupy in the nighttime the same room shall be punished by imprisonment not exceeding twelve months, or by fine not exceeding five hundred dollars.

A unanimous Court found that the statute unconstitutionally infringed the Equal Protection Clause of the Fourteenth Amendment. Justice Byron White pointed to the statute's discriminatory treatment of the interracial couple since "no other couple other than a Negro and white person [could] be convicted under the statute." Such a racial classification embodied in a criminal statute, White contended, is " 'constitutionally suspect' " and " 'in most circumstances irrelevant' to any constitutionally acceptable legislative purpose." But he made it clear that the Court was not reaching the interracial marriage issue.

Three years later, however, that issue was squarely before the Court in *Loving* v. *Virginia*. In that case the Virginia law prohibiting inter-racial marriages was struck down as an unconstitutional infringement of the Equal Protection and Due Process clauses of the Fourteenth Amendment. Chief Justice Earl Warren's opinion for a unanimous Court condemned the white supremacy basis of the statute and noted that the Court has consistently repudiated legislation with ancestral distinctions "as being 'odious to a free people whose institutions are founded upon the doctrine of equality.'"

### AS WE MOVE INTO THE 70's

This survey of judicial activity indicates the important role of the Supreme Court and other courts in coping with the general problems of racial justice. But as important as that role has been in the past, the future role of the judiciary can prove equally or even more important. It is clearly evident that in order for black Americans and others to benefit from the many favorable court decisions—as well as from recent civil rights legislation—we must come to grips with the many social and economic problems that face these groups. The findings of the *National Advisory Commission on Civil Disorders* (commonly referred to as the Kerner Commission) and its recommendations demonstrate the necessity for solving these problems to prevent our nation from moving toward "two societies, one black, one white—separate and unequal."[6] However, the slow response of Congress and the states to these and other recommen-dations relating to problems of social and economic justice indicates that if these emerging issues—the "new civil rights"—are to be attained without resort to violence it might be necessary once again to resort to the courts.[7] This is not to say that the judiciary can cure all ills; such would be an inaccurate analysis of the political system. But the role of the judiciary can prove important in dealing with such problems employ-ment, housing, and welfare. Of course, whether it chooses to play this role is another question.

In any event it seems quite likely that the judiciary will be called upon to provide the impetus for the political institutions to act on these "new problems" just as it has acted in the past on more traditional

[6] *Report of the National Advisory Commission on Civil Disorders* (U.S. Government Printing Office, 1968). Governor Otto Kerner of Illinois, now a federal court of appeals judge, served as chairman of the Commission.

[7] See the follow-up study of the Kerner Commission Report, *One Year Later*, made by two private groups, Urban America and the Urban Coalition. *New York Times*, February 23, 1969, pp. 1 ff.

legal problems relating to racial segregation, and legislative reapportionment. In fact, using the judicial route to stimulate the political institutions to act upon these emerging issues has already begun. For example, in a 1969 decision (*Shapiro* v. *Thompson*, 394 U.S. 618) that could have a significant impact in many areas, the Supreme Court held unconstitutional, as a violation of the Equal Protection Clause of the Fourteenth Amendment, the one-year state residency requirement for public welfare assistance. The Court found that such statutory requirements constituted an "invidious discrimination" between poor people who had lived in a state for at least one year and those who had not. And in Chicago, a federal district court (*Gautreaux et al.* v. *Chicago Housing Authority,* 296 F. Supp. 907, 1969) found the Chicago Housing Authority guilty of racial segregation in the procedures by which it selected building sites and assigned tenants. In addition, the vitality given by the Court to the post-Civil War statute involved in *Jones* v. *Mayer* supports those who hope to resort to the judiciary to secure the "new civil rights" by the use of old statutes.

Moreover, "the fourth estate of the law"—law reviews—has joined the battle for increased judicial action. One writer, for example, in addressing himself to decent housing, contends that "low-income and no-income tenants have a constitutional right to be free from the debilitating facts of slum existence.[8] Essentially he argues that "the failure of a governmental unit to act (such as those charged with enforcing housing codes) when under a duty to act" is as much a denial of the Equal Protection Clause of the Fourteenth Amendment as are specific governmental actions which are contrary to that clause. Moreover, the writer deplores the "highly artificial distinction" that courts have made in the past between the state action and the state inaction and holds that "whatever vitality remains in the unfortunate concept of 'state action'" does not appear to present "an insurmountable barrier to litigation involving failure to enforce housing regulations."

The emerging issues in the "new civil rights"—those relating to social and economic justice—hold significant implications for the political system. For one thing, the variety of actions required to meet these problems by all levels of government, especially the national government, is destined to forge new dimensions in our federal relationships. Moreover, as we move toward social and economic justice for black Americans and the poor, we can expect increased political participation from these groups. How this increased political participation will affect patterns in American politics is unclear, but affect them it will.

Achieving these "new civil rights" also forces us to face the basic question of whether and how representative government can resolve these problems within the framework of constitutional democracy, of

[8] Phillip Scott Ryan, "Decent Housing as a Constitutional Right—42 U.S.C. Sec. 1983 —Poor People's Remedy for Deprivation," 14 *Howard Law Journal* 338 (1968).

law and order. It certainly calls for imaginative and new perspectives in our legal system. The drafting and enforcement of laws to protect the rights of the poor, the scope and availability of legal services, and the type of legal education afforded in our law schools, could all have a definite bearing on and be affected by these "new civil rights" issues.

The cases that follow focus on some of the most crucial constitutional issues in the quest for equality of black Americans.

## PLESSY v. FERGUSON

163 U. S. 537; 41 L. Ed. 256; 16 S. Ct. 1138 (1896)

MR. JUSTICE BROWN *delivered the opinion of the Court.*

This case turns upon the constitutionality of an act of the general assembly of the state of Louisiana, passed in 1890, providing for separate railway carriages for the white and colored races. . . .

The 1st section of the statute enacts "that all railway companies carrying passengers in their coaches in this state shall provide equal but separate accommodations for the white and colored races, by providing two or more passenger coaches for each passenger train, or by dividing the passenger coaches by a partition so as to secure separate accommodations: *Provided,* That this section shall not be construed to apply to street railroads. No person or persons shall be permitted to occupy any coaches other than the ones assigned to them, on account of the race they belong to."

By the 2d section it was enacted "that the officers of such passenger trains shall have power and are hereby required to assign each passenger to the coach or compartment used for the race to which such passenger belongs; any passenger insisting on going into a coach or compartment to which by race he does not belong,

shall be liable to a fine of $25 or in lieu thereof to imprisonment for a period of not more than twenty days in the parish prison."

. . .

The information filed in the criminal district court charged in substance that Plessy, being a passenger between two stations within the state of Louisiana, was assigned by officers of the company to the coach used for the race to which he belonged, but he insisted upon going into a coach used by the race to which he did not belong. Neither in the information nor plea was his particular race or color averred.

The petition for the writ of prohibition averred that petitioner was seven eighths Caucasian and one eighth African blood; that the mixture of colored blood was not discernible in him, and that he was entitled to every right, privilege, and immunity secured to citizens of the United States of the white race; and that, upon such theory, he took possession of a vacant seat in a coach where passengers of the white race were accommodated, and was ordered by the conductor to vacate said coach and take a seat in another assigned to persons of the colored race, and having refused to comply with such demand he was forcibly ejected with the aid of a police officer, and imprisoned in the parish jail to answer a charge of having violated the above act.

The constitutionality of this act is attacked upon the ground that it conflicts both with the Thirteenth Amendment of the Constitution, abolishing slavery, and the Fourteenth Amendment, which prohibits certain restrictive legislation on the part of the states.

1. That it does not conflict with the Thirteenth Amendment, which abolished slavery and involuntary servitude, except as a punishment for crime, is too clear for argument.

. . .

A statute which implies merely a legal distinction between the white and colored races—a distinction which is founded in the color of the two races, and which must always exist so long as white men are distinguished from the other race by color—has no tendency to destroy the legal equality of the two races, or re-establish a state of involuntary servitude. Indeed, we do not understand that the Thirteenth Amendment is strenuously relied upon by the plaintiff in error in this connection.

2. By the Fourteenth Amendment, all persons born or naturalized in the United States, and subject to the jurisdiction thereof, are made citizens of the United States and of the state wherein they reside; and the states are forbidden from making or enforcing any law which shall abridge the privileges or immunities of citizens of the United States, or shall deprive any person of life, liberty, or property without due process of law, or deny to any person within their jurisdiction the equal protection of the laws.

. . .

The object of the amendment was undoubtedly to enforce the absolute equality of the two races before the law, but in the nature of things it could not have been intended to abolish distinctions based upon color, or to enforce social, as distinguished from political, equality, or a commingling of the two races upons terms unsatisfactory to either. Laws permitting and even requiring their separation in places where they are liable to be brought into contact do not necessarily imply the inferiority of either race to the other, and have been generally, if not universally, recognized as within the competency of the state legislatures in the exercise of their police power. The most common instance of this is connected with the establishment of separate schools for white and colored children, which have been held to be a valid exercise of the legislative power even by courts of states where the political rights of the colored race have been longest and most earnestly enforced.

One of the earliest of these cases is that of *Roberts* v. *Boston,* 5 Cush. 198, in which the supreme judicial court of Massachusetts held that the general school committee of Boston had power to make provision for the instruction of colored children in separate schools established exclusively for them, and to prohibit their attendance upon the other schools. . . . It was held that the powers of the committee extended to the "establishment of separate schools for children of different ages, sexes, and colors. . . . Similar laws have been enacted by Congress under its general power of legislation over the District of Columbia . . . as well as by the legislatures of many of the states, and have been generally, if not uniformly, sustained by the courts. . . .

Laws forbidding the intermarriage of the two races may be said in a technical sense to interfere with the freedom of contract, and yet have been universally recognized as within the police power of the state, *State* v. *Gibson*, 36 Ind. 389 (10 Am. Rep. 42).

The distinction between laws interfering with the political equality of the negro and those requiring the separation of the two races in schools, theaters, and railway carriages, has been frequently drawn by this court. Thus, in *Strauder* v. *West Virginia*, 100 U.S. 303: it was held that a law of West Virginia limiting to white male persons, twenty-one years of age and citizens of the state, the right to sit upon juries, was a discrimination which implied a legal inferiority in civil society, which lessened the security of the right of the colored race, and was a step towards reducing them to a condition of servility. . . .

Much nearer, and, indeed almost directly in point, is the case of the *Louisville, N.O. & T.R.Co.* v. *Mississippi*, 133 U.S. 587 wherein the railway company was indicted for a violation of a statute of Mississippi, enacting that all railroads carrying passengers should provide equal, but separate, accommodations for the white and colored races, by providing two or more passenger cars for each passenger train, or by dividing the passenger cars by a partition, so as to secure separate accommodations. The case was presented in a different aspect from the one under consideration, inasmuch as it was an indictment against the railway company for failing to provide the separate accommodations, but the question considered was the constitutionality of the law. In that case, the supreme court of Mississippi, 66 Miss. 662, had held that the statute applied solely to

commerce within the state, and, that being the construction of the state statute by its highest court, was accepted as conclusive. "If it be a matter," said the court, "respecting commerce wholly within a state, and not interfering with commerce between the states, then, obviously, there is no violation of the commerce clause of the Federal Constitution. . . . No question arises under this section as to the power of the state to separate in different compartments interstate passengers, or to affect in any manner, the privileges and rights of such passengers. All that we can consider is, whether the state has the power to require that railroad trains within her limits shall have separate accommodations for the two · races; that affecting only commerce within the state is no invasion of the powers given to Congress by the commerce clause."

. . .

. . . [I]t is . . . suggested by the learned counsel for the plaintiff in error that the same argument that will justify the state legislature in requiring railways to provide separate accommodations for the two races will also authorize them to require separate cars to be provided for people whose hair is of a certain color, or who are aliens, or who belong to certain nationalities, or to enact laws requiring colored people to walk upon one side of the street, and white people upon the other, or requiring white men's houses to be painted white, and colored men's black, or their vehicles or business signs to be of different colors, upon the theory that one side of the street is as good as the other, or that a house or vehicle of one color is as good as one of another color. The reply to all this is that every exercise of the police power must be reasonable, and extend only to such laws as are enacted in good faith for the promotion of the public good, and not for the annoyance or oppression of a particular class. . . .

So far, then, as a conflict with the Fourteenth Amendment is concerned, the case reduces itself to the question whether the statute of Louisiana is a reasonable regulation, and with respect to this there must necessarily be a large discretion on the part of the legislature. In determining the question of reasonableness it is at liberty to act with reference to the established usages, customs, and traditions of the people, and with a view to the promotion of their comfort, and the preservation of the public peace and good order. Gauged by this standard, we cannot say that a law which authorizes or even requires the separation of the two races in public conveyances is unreasonable or more obnoxious to the Fourteenth Amendment than the acts of Congress requiring separate schools for colored children in the District of Columbia, the constitutionality of which does not seem to have been questioned, or the corresponding acts of state legislatures.

We consider the underlying fallacy of the plaintiff's argument to consist in the assumption that the enforced separation of the two races stamps the colored race with a badge of inferiority. If this be so, it is not by reason of anything found in the act, but solely because the colored race chooses to put that construction upon it. The argument necessarily assumes that if, as has been more than once the case, and is not unlikely to be so again, the colored race should become the dominant power in the state legislature, and should enact a law in precisely similar terms, it would thereby relegate the white race to an inferior position. We imagine that the white race, at least, would not acquiesce in this assumption. The argument also assumes that social prejudices may be overcome by legislation, and that equal rights cannot be secured to the negro except by an enforced commingling of the two races. We cannot accept this proposition. If the two races are to meet on terms of social equality, it must be the result of natural affinities, a mutual appreciation of each other's merits and a voluntary consent of individuals. . . . Legislation is powerless to eradicate racial instincts or to abolish distinctions based upon physical differences, and the attempt to do so can only result in accentuating the difficulties of the present situation. If the civil and political rights of both races be equal, one cannot be inferior to the other civilly or politically. If one race be inferior to the other socially, the Constitution of the United States cannot put them upon the same plane.

It is true that the question of the proportion of colored blood necessary to constitute a colored person, as distinguished from a white person, is one upon which there is a difference of opinion in the different states, some holding that any visible admixture of black stamps the person as belonging to the colored race (*State* v. *Chavers,* 5 Jones, L. 11); others that it depends upon the predominance of blood (*Gray* v. *State,* 4 Ohio 354; *Monroe* v. *Collins,* 17 Ohio St. 665); and still others that the predominance of white blood must only be in the proportion of three fourths. *People* v. *Dean,* 14 Mich. 406; *Jones* v. *Com.* 80 Va. 544. But these are questions to be determined under the laws of each state and are not properly put in issue in this case. Under the allegation of his petition it may undoubtedly become a question of importance whether, under the laws of Louisiana, the petitioner belongs to the white or colored race.

*The judgment of the court below is therefore affirmed.*

MR. JUSTICE BREWER *did not hear the argument or participate in the decision of this case.*

MR. JUSTICE HARLAN *dissenting.*

. . .

. . . [W]e have before us a state enactment that compels, under penalties, the separation of the two races in railroad passenger coaches, and makes it a crime for a citizen of either race to enter a coach that has been assigned to citizens of the other race.

Thus the state regulates the use of a public highway by citizens of the United States solely upon the basis of race.

However apparent the injustice of such legislation may be, we have only to consider whether it is consistent with the Constitution of the United States.

. . .

In respect of civil rights, common to all citizens, the Constitution of the United States does not, I think, permit any public authority to know the race of those entitled to be protected in the enjoyment of such rights. Every true man has pride of race, and under appropriate circumstances, when the rights of others, his equals before the law, are not to be affected, it is his privilege to express such pride and to take such action based upon it as to him seems proper. But I deny that any legislative body or judicial tribunal may have regard to the race of citizens when the civil rights of those citizens are involved. Indeed such legislation as that here in question is inconsistent, not only with that equality of rights which pertains to

citizenship, national and state, but with the personal liberty enjoyed by every one within the United States.

. . .

. . . [The Thirteenth, Fourteenth and Fifteenth Amendments] removed the race line from our governmental systems. They had, as this court has said, a common purpose, namely, to secure "to a race recently emancipated, a race that through many generations have been held in slavery, all the civil rights that the superior race enjoys." They declared, in legal effect, this court has further said, "that the law in the states shall be the same for the black as for the white: that all persons, whether colored or white, shall stand equal before the laws of the states, and, in regard to the colored race, for whose protection the amendment was primarily designed, that no discrimination shall be made against them by law because of their color." We also said: "The words of the amendment, it is true, are prohibitory, but they contain a necessary implication of a positive immunity, or right, most valuable to the colored race—the right to exemption from unfriendly legislation against them distinctively as colored—exemption from legal discriminations, implying inferiority in civil society, lessening the security of their enjoyment of the rights which others enjoy, and discriminations which are steps towards reducing them to the condition of a subject race." . . .

It was said in argument that the statute of Louisiana does not discriminate against either race, but prescribes a rule applicable alike to white and colored citizens. But this argument does not meet the difficulty. Everyone knows that the statute in question had its origin in the purpose, not so much to exclude white persons from railroad cars occupied by blacks, as to exclude colored people from coaches occupied or assigned to white persons. Railroad corporations of Louisiana did not make discrimination among whites in the matter of accommodation for travelers. The thing to accomplish was, under the guise of giving equal accommodation for whites and blacks to compel the latter to keep to themselves while traveling in railroad passenger coaches. No one would be so wanting in candor to assert the contrary. The fundamental objection, therefore, to the statute is that it interferes with the personal freedom of citizens. "Personal liberty," it has been well said, "consists in the power of locomotion, of changing situation, or removing one's person to whatsoever place one's own inclination may direct, without imprisonment or restraint, unless by due course of law." 1 Bl. Com. 134. If a white man and a black man choose to occupy the same public conveyance on a public highway, it is their right to do so, and no government, proceeding alone on grounds of race, can prevent it without infringing the personal liberty of each.

It is one thing for railroad carriers to furnish, or to be required by law to furnish, equal accommodations for all whom they are under a legal duty to carry. It is quite another thing for government to forbid citizens of the white and black races from traveling in the same public conveyance, and to punish officers of railroad companies for permitting persons of the two races to occupy the same passenger coach. If a state can prescribe as a rule of civil conduct, that whites and blacks shall not travel as passengers in the same railroad coach, why may it not so regulate the use of the streets of its cities and towns as to

compel white citizens to keep on one side of the street and black citizens to keep on the other? Why may it not, upon like grounds, punish whites and blacks who ride together in street cars or in open vehicles on a public road or street? Why may it not require sheriffs to assign whites to one side of a court-room and blacks to the other? And why may it not also prohibit the commingling of the two races in the galleries of legislative halls or in public assemblages convened for the political questions of the day? Further, if this statute of Louisiana is consistent with the personal liberty of citizens, why may not the state require the separation in railroad coaches of native and naturalized citizens of the United States, or of Protestants and Roman Catholics?

The answer given at the argument to these questions was that regulations of the kind they suggest would be unreasonable, and could not, therefore, stand before the law. Is it meant that the determination of questions of legislative power depends upon the inquiry whether the statute whose validity is questioned is, in the judgment of the courts, a reasonable one, taking all the circumstances into consideration? A statute may be unreasonable merely because a sound public policy forbade its enactment. But I do not understand that the courts have anything to do with the policy or expediency of legislation. A statute may be valid, and yet upon grounds of public policy may well be characterized as unreasonable. Mr. Sedgwick correctly states the rule when he says that the legislative intention being clearly ascertained, "the courts have no other duty to perform than to execute the legislative will, without any regard to their views as to the wisdom or justice of the particular enactment." Sedgw. Stat. & Const. L. 324. . . .

The white race deems itself to be the dominant race in this country. And so it is, in prestige, in achievements, in education, in wealth, and in power. So, I doubt not that it will continue to be for all time, if it remains true to its great heritage and holds fast to the principles of constitutional liberty. But in view of the Constitution, in the eye of the law, there is in this country no superior, dominant, ruling class of citizens. There is no caste here. Our Constitution is color-blind, and neither knows nor tolerates classes among citizens. In respect of civil rights, all citizens are equal before the law. The humblest is the peer of the most powerful. The law regards man as man, and takes no account of his surroundings or of his color when his civil rights as guaranteed by the supreme law of the land are involved. It is therefore to be regretted that this high tribunal, the final expositor of the fundamental law of the land, has reached the conclusion that it is competent for a state to regulate the enjoyment by citizens of their civil rights solely upon the basis of race.

In my opinion, the judgment this day rendered will, in time, prove to be quite as pernicious as the decision made by this tribunal in the *Dred Scott Case*. . . . The recent amendments of the Constitution, it was supposed, had eradicated these principles (announced in that decision) from our institutions. But it seems that we have yet, in some of the states, a dominant race, a superior class of citizens, which assumes to regulate the enjoyment of civil rights, common to all citizens, upon the basis of race. The present decision, it may well be apprehended, will not stimulate aggressions, more or less brutal and irritating, upon the admitted rights of colored citizens, but will encourage the belief that it is possible, by means of state enactments, to defeat the beneficent purposes which the people of the United States had in view when they adopted the recent amendments of the Constitution. . . . Sixty millions of whites are in no danger from the presence here of eight millions of blacks. The destinies of the two races in this country are indissolubly linked together, and the interests of both require that the common government of all shall not permit the seeds of race hate to be planted under the sanction of law. What can more certainly arouse race hate, what more certainly create and perpetuate a feeling of distrust between these races, than state enactments which in fact proceed on the ground that colored citizens are so inferior and degraded that they cannot be allowed to sit in public coaches occupied by white citizens? That, as all will admit, is the real meaning of such legislation as was enacted in Louisiana.

The sure guaranty of the peace and security of each race is the clear, distinct, unconditional recognition by our governments, national and state, of every right that inheres in civil freedom, and of the equality before the law of all citizens of the United States without regard to race. State enactments, regulating the enjoyment of civil rights, upon the basis of race, are cunningly devised to defeat legitimate results of the war, under the pretense of recognizing equality of rights, can have no other result than to render permanent peace impossible and to keep alive a conflict of races, the continuance of which must do harm to all concerned.

. . .

The arbitrary separation of citizens, on the basis of race, while they are on a public highway, is a badge of servitude wholly inconsistent with the civil freedom and the equality before the law established by the Constitution. It cannot be justified upon any legal grounds.

If evils will result from the commingling of the two races upon public highways established for the benefit of all, they will be infinitely less than those that will surely come from state legislation regulating the enjoyment of civil rights upon the basis of race. We boast of the freedom enjoyed by our people above all other peoples. But it is difficult to reconcile that boast with a state of the law which, practically, puts the brand of servitude and degradation upon a large class of our fellow citizens, our equals before the law. The thin disguise of "equal" accommodations for passengers in railroad coaches will not mislead anyone, or atone for the wrong this day done.

. . .

I am of opinion that the statute of Louisiana is inconsistent with the personal liberty of citizens, white and black, in that state, and hostile to both the spirit and letter of the Constitution of the United States. If laws of like character should be enacted in the several states of the Union, the effect would be in the highest degree mischievous. Slavery as an institution tolerated by law would, it is true, have disappeared from our country, but there would remain a power in the states, by sinister legislation, to interfere with the full enjoyment of the blessings of freedom; to regulate civil rights, common to all citizens, upon the basis of race; and to place in a condition of legal inferiority a large body of American citizens, now constituting a part of the political community, called the people of the United States, for whom and by whom, through representatives, our government is administered. Such a system is inconsistent with the guarantee given by the Constitution to each state of a republican form of government, and may be stricken down by congressional action, or by the courts in the discharge of their solemn duty to maintain the supreme law of the land anything in the Constitution or laws of any state to the contrary notwithstanding.

For the reasons stated, I am constrained to withhold my assent from the opinion and judgment of the majority.

## BROWN v. BOARD OF EDUCATION OF TOPEKA, KANSAS

### 347 U. S. 483; 98 L. Ed. 873; 74 S. Ct. 686 (1954)

CHIEF JUSTICE WARREN *delivered the opinion of the Court.*

These cases came to us from the States of Kansas, South Carolina, Virginia, and Delaware. They are premised on different facts and different local conditions, but a common legal question justifies their consideration together in this consolidated opinion.

In each of the cases, minors of the Negro race, through their legal representatives, seek aid of the courts in obtaining admission to the public schools of their community on a non-segregated basis. . . . In each of the cases other than the Delaware case, a three-judge federal district court denied relief to the plaintiffs on the so-called "separate but equal" doctrine, announced by the Court in *Plessy* v. *Ferguson*. . . . In the Delaware case, the Supreme Court of Delaware adhered to that doctrine, but ordered that the plaintiffs be admitted to the white schools because of their superiority to the Negro schools.

The plaintiffs contend that segregated public schools are not "equal" and cannot be made "equal," and that hence they are deprived of the equal protection of the laws. Because of the obvious importance of the question presented, the Court took jurisdiction. Argument was heard in the 1952 Term, and reargument was heard this Term on certain questions propounded by the Court.

Reargument was largely devoted to the circumstances surrounding the adoption of the Fourteenth Amendment in 1868. It covered exhaustively consideration of the Amendment in Congress, ratification by the states, then existing practices in racial segregation, and the views of proponents and opponents of the Amendment. This discussion and our own investigation convince us that, although these sources cast some light, it is not enough to resolve the problem with which we are faced. At best, they are inconclusive. The most avid proponents of the post-War Amendments undoubtedly intended them to remove all legal distinctions among "all

persons born or naturalized in the United States." Their opponents, just as certainly, were antagonistic to both the letter and spirit of the Amendments and wished them to have the most limited effect. What others in Congress and the state legislatures had in mind cannot be determined with any degree of certainty.

An additional reason for the inconclusive nature of the Amendment's history, with respect to segregated schools, is the status of public education at that time. In the South, the movement toward free common schools, supported by general taxation, had not yet taken hold. Education for white children was largely in the hands of private groups. Education for Negroes was almost nonexistent, and practically all of the race was illiterate. In fact, any education of Negroes was forbidden by law in some states. Today, in contrast, many Negroes have achieved outstanding success in the arts and sciences as well as in the business and professional world. It is true that public education had already advanced further in the North, but the effect of the Amendment on Northern States was generally ignored in the Congressional debates. Even in the North, the conditions of public education did not approximate those existing today. The curriculum was usually rudimentary; ungraded schools were common in rural areas; the school term was but three months a year in many states; and compulsory school attendance was virtually unknown. As a consequence, it is not surprising that there should be so little in the history of the Fourteenth Amendment relating to its intended effect on public education.

In the first cases in this Court construing the Fourteenth Amendment, decided shortly after its adoption, the

Court interpreted it as proscribing all state-imposed discriminations against the Negro race. The doctrine of "separate but equal" did not make its appearance in the Court until 1896 in the case of *Plessy* v. *Ferguson,* . . . involving not education but transportation. American courts have since labored with the doctrine for over half a century. In this Court, there have been six cases involving the "separate but equal" doctrine in the field of public education. In *Cumming* v. *Board of Education of Richmond County* and *Gong Lum* v. *Rice,* the validity of the doctrine itself was not challenged. In more recent cases, all on the graduate school level, inequality was found in that specific benefits enjoyed by white students were denied to Negro students of the same educational qualifications (*State of Missouri ex. rel. Gaines* v. *Canada, Sipuel* v. *Board of Regents of University of Oklahoma, Sweatt* v. *Painter,* and *McLaurin* v. *Oklahoma State Regents*). In none of these cases was it necessary to re-examine the doctrine to grant relief to the Negro plaintiff. And in *Sweatt* v. *Painter,* . . . the Court expressly reserved decision on the question whether *Plessy* v. *Ferguson* should be held inapplicable to public education.

. . .

In approaching this problem, we cannot turn the clock back to 1868 when the Amendment was adopted, or even to 1896 when *Plessy* v. *Ferguson* was written. We must consider public education in the light of its full development and its present place in American life throughout the Nation. Only in this way can it be determined if segregation in public schools deprives these plaintiffs of the equal protection of the laws.

Today, education is perhaps the most important function of state and local governments. Compulsory school attendance laws and the great expenditures for education both demonstrate our recognition of the importance of education to our democratic society. It is required in the performance of our most basic public responsibilities, even service in the armed forces. It is the very foundation of good citizenship. Today it is a principal instrument in awakening the child to cultural values, in preparing him for later professional training, and in helping him to adjust normally to his environment. In these days, it is doubtful that any child may reasonably be expected to succeed in life if he is denied the opportunity of an education. Such an opportunity, where the state has undertaken to provide it, is a right which must be made available to all on equal terms.

We come then to the question presented: Does segregation of children in public schools solely on the basis of race, even though the physical facilities and other "tangible" factors may be equal, deprive the children of the minority group of equal educational opportunities? We believe that it does.

In *Sweatt* v. *Painter* . . . in finding that a segregated law school for Negroes could not provide them equal educational opportunities, this Court relied in large part on "those qualities which are incapable of objective measurement but which make for greatness in a law school." In *McLaurin* v. *Oklahoma State Regents,* . . . the Court, in requiring that a Negro admitted to a white graduate school to be treated like all other students, again resorted to intangible considerations: ". . . his ability to study, to engage in discussion and exchange views with other students, and, in general, to learn his profession." Such considerations apply with added force to children in grade and high schools. To separate them from others of similar age and qualifications solely because of their race generates a feeling of inferiority as to their status in the community that may affect their hearts and minds in a way unlikely ever to be undone. The effect of this separation on their educational opportunities was well stated by a finding in the Kansas case by a court which nevertheless felt compelled to rule against the Negro plaintiffs:

Segregation of white and colored children in public schools has a detrimental effect upon the colored children. The impact is greater when it has the sanction of the law; for the policy of separating the races is usually interpreted as denoting the inferiority of the negro group. A sense of inferiority affects the motivation of a child to learn. Segregation with the sanction of law, therefore, has a tendency to retard the educational and mental development of negro children and to deprive them of the benefits they would receive in a racial[ly] integrated school system.

Whatever may have been the extent of psychological knowledge at the time of *Plessy* v. *Ferguson,* this finding is amply supported by modern authority. Any language in *Plessy* v. *Ferguson* contrary to this finding is rejected. We conclude that in a field of public education the doctrine of "separate but equal" has no place. Separate educational facilities are inherently unequal. Therefore, we hold that the plaintiffs and others similarly situated for whom the actions have been brought are, by the reason of the segregation complained of, deprived of the equal protection of the laws guaranteed by the Fourteenth Amendment. This disposition makes unnecessary any discussion whether such segregation also violates the Due Process Clause of the Fourteenth Amendment.

Because these are class actions because of the wide applicability of the decision, and because of the great variety of local conditions, the formulation of decrees in these cases presents problems of considerable complexity. . . . In order that we may have the full assistance of the parties in formulating decrees, the cases will be restored to the docket, and the parties are requested to present further argument on [the appropriate decree]. The Attorney General of the United States is again invited to participate. The Attorneys General of the states requiring or permitting segregation in public education will also be permitted to appear as *amici curiae* upon request to do so by September 15, 1954, and submission of briefs by October 1, 1954.

*It is so ordered.*

Cases ordered restored to docket for further argument on question of appropriate decrees.

# BROWN v. BOARD OF EDUCATION OF TOPEKA, KANSAS

### 349 U. S. 294; 99 L. Ed. 1083; 75 S. Ct. 753 (1955)

CHIEF JUSTICE WARREN *delivered the opinion of the Court.*

These cases were decided on May 17, 1954. The opinions of that date, declaring the fundamental principle that racial discrimination in public education is unconstitutional, are incorporated herein by reference. All provisions of federal, state, or local law requiring or permitting such discrimination must yield to this principle. There remains for consideration the manner in which relief is to be accorded.

Because these cases arose under different local conditions and their disposition will involve a variety of local problems, we requested further argument on the question of relief. In view of the nationwide importance of the decision, we invited the Attorney General of the United States and the Attorneys General of all states requiring or permitting racial discrimination in public education to present their views on that question. The parties, the United States, and the States of Florida, North Carolina, Arkansas, Oklahoma, Maryland, and Texas filed briefs and participated in the oral argument.

These presentations were informative and helpful to the Court in its consideration of the complexities arising from the transition to a system of public education freed of racial discrimination. The presentations also demonstrated that substantial steps to eliminate racial discrimination in public schools have already been taken, not only in some of the communities in which these cases arose, but in some of the states appearing as *amici curiae,* and in other states as well. Substantial progress has been made in the District of Columbia and in the communities in Kansas and Delaware involved in this litigation. The defendants in the cases coming to us from South Carolina and Virginia are awaiting the decision of this Court concerning relief.

Full implementation of these constitutional principles may require solution of varied local school problems. School authorities have the primary responsibility for elucidating, assessing, and solving these problems; courts will have to consider whether the action of school authorities constitutes good faith implementation of the governing constitutional principles. Because of their proximity to local conditions and the possible need for further hearings, the courts which originally heard these cases can best perform this judicial appraisal. Accordingly, we believe it appropriate to remand the cases to those courts.

In fashioning and effectuating the decrees, the courts will be guided by equitable principles. Traditionally, equity has been characterized by a practical flexibility in shaping its remedies and by a facility for adjusting and reconciling public and private needs. These cases call for the exercise of these traditional attributes of equity power. At stake is the personal interest of the plaintiffs in admission to public schools as soon as practicable on a nondiscriminatory basis. To effectuate this interest may call for elimination of a variety of obstacles in making the transition to school systems operated in accordance with the constitutional principles set forth in our May 17, 1954, decision. Courts of equity may properly take into account the public interest in the elimination of such obstacles in a systematic and effective manner. But it would go without saying that the vitality of these constitutional principles cannot be allowed to yield simply because of disagreement with them.

While giving weight to these public and private considerations, the courts will require that the defendants make a prompt and reasonable start toward full compliance with our May 17, 1954, ruling. Once such a start has been made, the courts may find that additional time is necessary to carry out the ruling in an effective manner. The burden rests upon the defendants to establish that such time is necessary in the public interest and is consistent with good faith compliance at the earliest practicable date. To that end, the courts may consider problems related to administration, arising from the physical condition of the school plant, the school transportation system, personnel, revision of school districts and attendance areas into compact units to achieve a system of determining admission to the public schools on a nonracial basis, and a revision of local laws and regulations which may be necessary in solving the foregoing problems. They will also consider the adequacy of any plans the defendants may propose to meet these problems and to effectuate a transition to a racially nondiscriminatory school system. During this period of transition, the courts will retain jurisdiction of these cases.

The judgments below, except that in the Delaware case, are accordingly reversed and remanded to the District Courts to take such proceedings and enter such orders and degrees consistent with this opinion as are necessary and proper to admit to public schools on a racially non-discriminatory basis with all deliberate speed the parties to these cases. The judgment in Delaware case—ordering the immediate admission of the plaintiffs to schools previously attended only by white children—is affirmed on the basis of the principle stated on our May 17, 1954, opinion, but the case is remanded to the Supreme Court of Delaware for such further proceedings as that court may deem necessary in light of this opinion.

## GRIFFIN v. SCHOOL BOARD OF PRINCE EDWARD COUNTY

### 377 U. S. 218; 12 L. Ed. 2d 256; 84 S. Ct. 1226 (1964)

MR. JUSTICE BLACK delivered the opinion of the Court.

In *County School Board of Prince Edward County* v. *Griffin*, 204 Va. 650, 133 S.E. 2d 565 (1963), the Supreme Court of Appeals of Virginia upheld as valid under state law the closing of the Prince Edward County public schools, the state and county tuition grants for children who attend private schools, and the county's tax concessions for those who make contributions to private schools. The same opinion also held that each county had "an option to operate or not to operate public schools." 204 Va., at 671, 122 S.E. 2d, at 580. We accept this case as a definitive and authoritative holding of Virginia law, binding on us, but we cannot accept the Virginia court's further holding, based largely on the Court of Appeals' opinion in this case, 322 F. 2d 332, that closing the county's public schools under the circumstances of the case did not deny the colored school children of Prince Edward County equal protection of the laws guaranteed by the Federal Constitution.

Since 1959, all Virginia counties have had the benefits of public schools but one: Prince Edward. However, there is no rule that counties, as counties, must be treated alike; the Equal Protection Clause relates to equal protection of the laws "between persons as such rather than between areas." . . . Indeed, showing that different persons are treated differently is not enough, without more, to show a denial of equal protection. . . . It is the circumstances of each case which govern. . . .

Virginia law, as here applied, unquestionably treats the school children of Prince Edward differently from the way it treats the school children of all other Virginia counties. Prince Edward children must go to a private school or none at all; all other Virginia children can go to public schools. Closing Prince Edward's schools bears more heavily on Negro children in Prince Edward County since white children there have accredited private schools which they can attend, while colored children until very recently have had no available private schools, and even

the school they now attend is a temporary expedient. Apart from this expedient, the result is that Prince Edward County school children, if they go to school in their own county, must go to racially segregated schools, which, although designated as private, are beneficiaries of county and state support.

A State, of course, has a wide discretion in deciding whether laws shall operate statewide or shall operate only in certain counties, the legislature "having in mind the needs and desires of each." . . . A State may wish to suggest, as Maryland did in Salsburg, that there are reasons why one county ought not to be treated like another. . . . But the record in the present case could not be clearer that Prince Edward's public schools were closed and private schools operated in their place with state and county assistance, for one reason, and one reason only; to ensure, through measures taken by the county and the State, that white and colored children in Prince Edward County would not, under any circumstances, go to the same school. Whatever nonracial grounds might support a state's allowing a county to abandon public schools, the object must be a constitutional one, and grounds of race and opposition to desegregation do not qualify as constitutional.*

In *Hall* v. *St. Helena Parish School Board,* 197 F. Supp. 649 (D.C.E.D. La. 1961), a three-judge District Court invalidated a Louisiana statute which provided "a means by which public schools under desegregation orders may be changed to 'private' schools operated in the same way, in the

---

* "But it should go without saying that the validity of these constitutional principles cannot be allowed to yield simply because of disagreement with them." *Brown* v. *Board of Education,* 349 U.S. 294, 300 (1955).

same buildings, with the same furnishings, with the same money, and under the same supervision as the public schools." Id., at 561. In addition, that statute also provided that where the public schools were "closed," the school board was "charged with responsibility for furnishing free lunches, transportation, and grants-in-aid to the children attending the 'private' schools." Ibid. We affirmed the District Court's judgment invalidating the Louisiana statute as a denial of equal protection. 368 U.S. 515 (1962). While the Louisiana plan and the Virginia plan worked in different ways, it is plain that both were created to accomplish the same thing: the perpetuation of racial segregation by closing public schools and operating only segregated schools supported directly or indirectly by state or county funds. See *Cooper* v. *Aaron,* 358 U.S. 1 (1958). Either plan works to deny colored students equal protection of the laws. Accordingly, we agree with the District Court that closing the Prince Edward schools and meanwhile contributing to the support of the private segregated white schools that took their place denied petitioners the equal protection of the laws.

We come now to the question of the kind of decree necessary and appropriate to put an end to the racial discrimination practiced against these petitioners under authority of the Viriginia laws. That relief needs to be quick and effective. The party defendants are the Board of Supervisors, School Board, Treasurer, and Division Superintendent of Schools of Prince Edward County, and the State Board of Education and the State Superintendent of Education. All of these have duties which relate directly or indirectly to the financing, supervision, or operation of the

schools in Prince Edward County. The Board of Supervisors has the special responsibility to levy local taxes to operate public schools or to aid children attending the private schools now functioning there for white children. The District Court enjoined the county officials from paying county tuition grants or giving tax exemptions and from processing applications for state tuition grants so long as the county's public schools remained closed. We have no doubt of the power of the court to give this relief to enforce the discontinuance of the county's racially discriminatory practices. It has long been established that actions against a county can be maintained in United States courts in order to vindicate federally guaranteed rights. . . . The injunction against paying tuition grants and giving tax credits while public schools remain closed is appropriate and necessary since those grants and tax credits have been essential parts of the county's program, successful thus far, to deprive petitioners of the same advantages of a public school education enjoyed by children in every other part of Virginia. For the same reasons the District Court may, if necessary to prevent further racial discrimination, require the Supervisors to exercise the power that is theirs to levy taxes to raise funds adequate to reopen, operate, and maintain without racial discrimination a public school system in Prince Edward County like that operated in other counties in Virginia. . . .

The judgment of the Court of Appeals is reversed, the judgment of the District Court is affirmed, and the cause is remanded to the District Court with directions to enter a decree which will guarantee that these petitioners will get the kind of education that is given in the State's public schools. And, if it becomes necessary to add new parties to accomplish this end, the District Court is free to do so. It is so ordered.

*Judgment of Court of Appeals reversed, judgment of the District Court affirmed and cause remanded with directions.*

MR. JUSTICE CLARK *and* MR. JUSTICE HARLAN *disagree with the holding that the federal courts are empowered to order the reopening of the public schools in Prince Edward County, but otherwise join in the Court's opinion.*

# BELL v. SCHOOL CITY OF GARY, INDIANA

324 F. 2d 209 (7th Cir., 1963)

CIRCUIT JUDGE F. RYAN DUFFY *delivered the opinion of the Court.*

Approximately one hundred minor school children enrolled in the public schools of Gary, Indiana, brought this action for a declaratory judgment upon their own behalf and also upon behalf of all others similarly situated. The principal relief asked was that defendants be enjoined from operating and providing racially segregated public schools in Gary, Indiana.

Gary is a rapidly growing industrial city in northwest Indiana. . . . "Geographically it is shaped much like the capital letter 'T.' Its north boundary line is the southern shore of Lake Michigan. The stem of the 'T' extends approximately . . . two miles wide. The cross-bar of the 'T' is approximately four miles wide and extends east and west a distance of approximately ten and one-half miles. . . ."

In 1950, the population of Gary was 133,911, which included 39,326 Negroes. In 1960, the population was 178,320, of which 69,340 were Negroes.

The student population in the public schools of Gary for the 1951–1952 school year was 22,770 of which

8,406 or approximately 37 per cent were Negroes. In the 1961–1962 school year there were 43,090 students in the public school system, and 23,055 or approximately 53 per cent were Negroes.

In 1951, The School City of Gary maintained and used twenty school buildings. In 1961, the number of school buildings had increased to forty. Additional schools were in the process of completion at the time of the trial of this case.

In the school year 1961–1962, 16,242 students attended twelve schools which were populated from 99 to 100 per cent by Negroes; 6,981 students attended five schools which were 77 to 95 per cent Negroes; 4,066 attended four schools which had a range from 13 to 37 per cent Negroes; 5,465 attended five schools which had a Negro population of from 1 to 5 per cent.

The Negro population in Gary is concentrated in the "Central District" which occupies roughly the south half of the cross-bar of the "T" from east to west and is bounded on the north by the Wabash Railroad and on the south by the city limits and the Little Calumet River. Approximately 70,000 Negroes including 23,000 Negro school children live in this District which comprises about one third of the area of the city.

The City of Gary was organized in 1906. Originally, eight school districts were laid out, and as the school population required, one large school was built in each of the eight districts. As the school population expanded, elementary schools were built. At the same time, attendance zones were drawn for such elementary schools and as the students completed the course in the elementary school to which they were assigned, they then went to the high school in the district in which they resided for the completion of the public school education.

The Board of School Trustees is a bipartisan Board of five members appointed by the Mayor. The Board elects it own officers. Dr. LeRoy Bingham, a Negro, was the President of the Board when this suit was commenced. At the trial, he testified there was no policy of segregation of races in the Gary school system. He also testified the Board adopted a policy of transferring students from several congested areas to less congested areas in order to try to balance the load in the various buildings; that it was the policy of the Board to make complete use of the facilities available for the benefit of all the children in the school system without regard to race.

Those in charge of the administration of the Gary schools have had a difficult problem for more than a decade in maintaining facilities for the rapidly expanding school population. Twenty-two new schools or additions have been built in the last ten years and classrooms have been more than doubled. A school corporation in Indiana is limited in its bonding power to 2 per cent of the assessed valuation of the property in the District. The Gary School City has been bonded to its limits for the past several years. . . .

In addition to building new school buildings, the Board of Trustees and the School Administration have rented churches, storerooms, and utilized such buildings as armories and park buildings for the purpose of providing classrooms for children. Some schools have been operated on a two-shift basis. Roosevelt is predominantly a Negro school. It operates as a senior high school in the morning and as a junior high school in the afternoon. It should be noted that Wallace, an all white school, is operated in precisely the same manner. . . .

The transfer of students from one school to another is handled on an individual basis. There is no transfer as a matter of right from one school to the other. However, no racial characteristics are considered in allowing or disallowing a transfer.

The School Board has consistently followed the policy requiring students to attend the school designated to serve the district in which they live regardless of race. This was in accord with the Indiana statute which provides that all students in the public schools are to be admitted ". . . in the public or common school in their districts in which they reside without regard to race, creed or color, class or national origin. . . ." Sec. 28-5159 Burns Indiana Statutes.

Plaintiffs' position is grounded on the fundamental theory that their right to be integrated in school is such an over-riding purpose that little, if any, consideration needs to be given to the safety of the children, convenience of pupils and their parents, and costs of the operation of the school system. There was testimony that under plaintiffs' plan, at least six thousand pupils would have to be transported on each school day, presumably by bus, and that the cost of operating one bus was $20 per day. . . .

Let us consider Tolleston School in Gary. In the school year 1951–1952, this school was in a predominantly white neighborhood, only 4.3 per cent of its school-age children were colored. But, in the following ten years, colored people, on their own volition, moved in large numbers into this school district area. There was no change in the schol district boundary lines. At the end of this period, the percentage of colored pupils was 76.65 per cent. The plaintiffs claim that the voluntary Negro influx into this area has caused imbalance which defendants have the affirmative duty to change. In effect, plaintiffs say that defendants must somehow transplant from Tolleston enough Negro pupils to reduce their number to 50 per cent of capacity, or some other arbitrary figure, and then, by some means, go out into the forty-two square miles of the City of Gary into the so-called white districts, and bring into the Tolleston School a sufficient number of white students to correct the imbalance.

Plaintiffs are unable to point to any court decision which has laid down the principle which justifies their claim that there is an affirmative duty on the Gary School System to recast or realign school districts or areas for the purpose of mixing or blending Negroes and whites in a particular school.

Plaintiffs argue that *Brown* v. *Board of Education,* 347 U.S. 483, 74 S. Ct. 686, 98 L. Ed. 873, proclaims that segregated public education is incompatible with the requirements of the Fourteenth Amendment in a school system maintained pursuant to state law. However, the holding in *Brown* was that the forced segregation of children in public schools solely on the basis of race denied the children of the minority group the equal protection of the laws granted by the Fourteenth Amendment.

The situation in Brown is a far cry from the situation existing in Gary, Indiana. The School District boundaries in Gary were determined without any consideration of race or color. We agree with the argument of the defendants stated as "there is no affirmative U.S. Constitutional duty to change innocently arrived at school attendance districts by the mere fact that shifts in population either increase or decrease the percentage of either Negro or white pupils."

After the original opinion in *Brown* v. *Board of Education, supra,* the Court set the case for further argument on the question of how its decision should be implemented. Thereafter, a three-judge district court was designated in Kansas to consider the Kansas aspects of the instructions in the *Brown* case. That Court stated, *Brown* v. *Board of Education,* D.C., 139 F. Supp. 468, 470, "desegregation does not mean that there must be intermingling of the races in all school districts. It means only that they may not be prevented from intermingling or going to school together because of race or color."

In *Briggs* v. *Elliott,* (EDSC), 132 F. Supp. 776, 777, the Court said: "The Constitution, in other words, does not require integration. It merely forbids discrimination."

We agree with and the record fully sustains the District Court's finding: "An examination of the school boundary lines in the light of the various factors involved such as density of population, distances that the students have to travel and the safety of the children, particularly in the lower grades, indicates that the areas have been reasonably arrived at and that the lines have not been drawn for the purpose of including or excluding children of certain races."

We approve also of the statement in the District Court's opinion: "Nevertheless, I have seen nothing in the many cases dealing with the segregation problem which leads me to believe that the law requires that a school system developed on the neighborhood school plan, honestly and conscientiously constructed with no intention or purpose to segregate the races, must be destroyed or abandoned because the resulting effect is to have a racial imbalance in certain schools where the district is populated almost entirely by Negroes or whites. . . ."

We hold that the constitutional rights of the plaintiffs and others similarly situated were not violated by the manner in which the defendant School District of Gary, Indiana, maintained and operated its schools, and that the District Court was correct in dismissing the complaint herein.

*Affirmed.*

# GREEN v. SCHOOL BOARD OF NEW KENT COUNTY, VIRGINIA

391 U. S. 430; 20 L. Ed. 2d 883; 88 S. Ct. 1689 (1968)

MR. JUSTICE BRENNAN *delivered the opinion of the Court.*

The question for decision is whether, under all the circumstances here, respondent School Board's adoption of a "freedom-of-choice" plan which allows a pupil to choose his own public school constitutes adequate compliance with the Board's responsibility "to achieve a system of determining admission to the public schools on a non-racial basis. . . ." *Brown* v. *Board of Education,* 349 U.S. 294, 300–301 (*Brown II*).

Petitioners brought this action in March 1965 seeking injunctive relief against respondent's continued maintenance of an alleged racially segregated school system. New Kent County is a rural county in Eastern Virginia. About one-half of its population of some 4,500 are Negroes. There is no residential segregation in the county; persons of both races reside throughout. The school system has only two schools, the New Kent school on the east side of the county and the George W. Watkins school on the west side. In a memorandum filed May 17, 1966, the District Court found that the "school system serves approximately 1,300 pupils, of which 740 are Negro and 550 are white. The School Board operates one white combined elementary and high school [New Kent], and one Negro combined elementary and high school [George W. Watkins]. There are no attendance zones. Each school serves the entire county." The record indicates that 21 school buses—11 serving the Watkins school and 10 serving the New Kent school—travel overlapping routes throughout the county to transport pupils to and from the two schools.

. . . The respondent School Board continued the segregated operation of the system after the *Brown* decisions, presumably on the authority of several statutes enacted by Virginia in resistance to those decisions. Some of these statutes were held to be unconstitutional on their face or as applied. One statute, the Pupil Placement Act . . . not repealed until 1966, divested local boards of authority to assign children to particular schools and placed that authority in a State Pupil Placement Board. Under that Act children were each year automatically reassigned to the school previously attended unless upon their application the State Board assigned them to another school; students seeking enrollment for the first time were also assigned at the discretion of the State Board. To September 1964, no Negro pupil had applied for admission to the New Kent school under this statute and no white pupil had applied for admission to the Watkins school.

The School Board initially sought dismissal of this suit on the ground that petitioners had failed to apply to the State Board for assignment to New Kent school. However on August 2, 1965, five months after the suit was brought, respondent School Board, in order to remain eligible for federal financial aid, adopted a "freedom-of-choice" plan for desegregating the schools. Under that plan, each pupil may annually choose between the New Kent and Watkins schools and, except for the first and eighth grades, pupils not making a choice are assigned to the school previously attended; first and eighth grade pupils must affirmatively choose a school. After the plan was filed the District Court denied petitioner's plan for an injunction and granted respondent leave to submit an

amendment to the plan with respect to employment and assignment of teachers and staff on a racially non-discriminatory basis. The amendment was duly filed and on June 28, 1966, the District Court approved the "freedom-of-choice" plan as so amended. The Court of Appeals for the Fourth Circuit, *en banc,* 382 F. 2d 326, 338, affirmed the District Court's approval of the "freedom-of-choice" provisions of the plan but remanded the case to the District Court for entry of an order regarding faculty "which is much more specific and more comprehensive" and which would incorporate in addition to a "minimal, objective time table" some of the faculty provisions of the decree entered by the Court of Appeals for the Fifth Circuit in *United States* v. *Jefferson County Board of Education.* . . .

The pattern of separate "white" and "Negro" schools in the New Kent County school system established under compulsion of state laws is precisely the pattern of segregation to which *Brown I* and *Brown II* were particularly addressed, and which *Brown I* declared unconstitutionally denied Negro school children equal protection of the laws. Racial identification of the system's schools was complete, extending not just to the composition of student bodies at the two schools but to every facet of school operations—faculty, staff, transportation, extracurricular activities. . . .

It was such dual systems that 14 years ago *Brown I* held unconstitutional and a year later *Brown II* held must be abolished; school boards operating such school systems were *required* by *Brown II* "to effectuate a transition to a racially nondiscriminatory school system." . . . It is of course true that for the time immediately after *Brown II* the concern was with making an initial break in a long-established pattern of excluding Negro children from schools attended by white children. The principal focus was on obtaining for those Negro children courageous enough to break with tradition a place in the "white" schools. . . . Under *Brown II* that immediate goal was only the first step, however. The transition to a unitary, nonracial system of public education was and is the ultimate end to be brought about; it was because of the "complexities arising from the transition to a system of public education freed of racial discrimination" that we provided for "all deliberate speed" in the implementation of the principles of *Brown I*. . . . Yet we emphasized that the constitutional rights of Negro children required school officials to bear the burden of establishing that additional time to carry out the ruling in an effective manner "is necessary in the public interest and is consistent with good faith compliance at the earliest practicable date." . . .

It is against this background that 13 years after *Brown II* commanded the abolition of dual systems we must measure the effectiveness of respondent School Board's "freedom-of-choice" plan to achieve that end. The School Board contends that it has fully discharged its obligation by adopting a plan by which every student, regardless of race, may "freely" choose the school he will attend. The Board attempts to case the issue in its broadest form by arguing that its "freedom-of-choice" plan may be faulted only by reading the Fourteenth Amendment as universally requiring "compulsory integration," a reading it insists the wordings of the Amendment will not support. But

that argument ignores the thrust of *Brown II*. In the light of the command of that case, what is involved here is the question whether the Board has achieved the "racially nondiscriminatory school system" *Brown II* held must be effectuated in order to remedy the established unconstitutional deficiencies of its segregated system. In the context of the state-imposed segregated pattern of long standing, the fact that in 1965 the Board opened the doors of the former "white" school to Negro children and of the "Negro" schools to white children merely begins, not ends, our inquiry whether the Board has taken steps adequate to abolish its dual, segregated system. . . . *Brown II* was a call for the dismantling of well-entrenched dual systems. . . .

In determining whether respondent School Board met that command by adopting its "freedom-of-choice" plan, it is relevant that this first step did not come until some 11 years after *Brown I* was decided and 10 years after *Brown II* directed the making of a "prompt and reasonable start." This deliberate perpetuation of the unconstitutional dual system can only have compounded the harm of such a system. Such delays are no longer tolerable. . . . Moreover, a plan that at this late date fails to provide meaningful assurance of prompt and effective disestablishment of a dual system is also intolerable. "The time for mere 'deliberate speed' has run out," *Griffin* v. *County School Board* . . . ; "the context in which we must interpret and apply this language [of *Brown II*] to plans for desegregation has been significantly altered." *Goss* v. *Board of Education*, 373 U.S. 683, 689. . . . The burden on a school board today is to come forward with a plan that promises realistically to work, and promises realistically to work *now*.

The obligation of the district courts, as it always has been, is to assess the effectiveness of a proposed plan in achieving desegregation. There is no universal answer to complex problems of desegregation; there is obviously no one plan that will do the job in every case. The matter must be assessed in light of the circumstances present and the options available in every instance. It is incumbent upon the school board to establish that its proposed plan promises meaningful and immediate progress toward disestablishing state-imposed segregation. It is incumbent upon the district court to weigh that claim in light of the facts at hand and in light of any alternatives which may be shown as feasible and more promising in their effectiveness. Where the court finds the board to be acting in good faith and the proposed plan to have real prospects for dismantling the state-imposed dual system "at the earliest practicable date," then the plan may be said to provide effective relief. Of course, the availability to the board of other more promising courses of action may indicate a lack of good faith; and at the least it places a heavy burden upon the board to explain its preference for an apparently less effective method. Moreover, whatever plan is adopted will require evaluation in practice, and the court should retain jurisdiction until it is clear that state-imposed segregation has been completely removed. . . .

We do not hold that "freedom-of-choice" can have no place in such a plan. We do not hold that a "freedom-of-choice" plan might of itself be unconstitutional, although that argument has been urged upon us. Rather, all we decided today is that in desegregating a dual system a plan utilizing "freedom-of-choice" is not an end in itself. . . . Although the general experience under "freedom-of-choice" to date has been such as to indicate its ineffectiveness as a tool of desegregation,* there may well be instances in which it can serve as an effective device. Where it offers real promise of aiding a desegregation program to effectuate conversion of a state-imposed dual system to a unitary, nonracial system there might be no objection to allow-

* The views of the United States Commission on Civil Rights, which we neither adopt nor refuse to adopt, are as follows:

Freedom of choice plans, which have tended to perpetuate racially identifiable schools in the Southern and border States, require affirmative action by both Negro and white parents and pupils before such disestablishment can be achieved. There are a number of factors which have prevented such affirmative actions by substantial numbers of parents and pupils of both races:

(a) Fear of retaliation and hostility from the white community continue to deter many Negro families from choosing formerly all-white schools;

(b) . . . [I]n some areas of the South, Negro families with children attending previously all-white schools under free choice plans were targets of violence, threats of violence and economic reprisals by white persons and Negro children were subjected to harassment by white classmates notwithstanding conscientious efforts by many teachers and principals to prevent such misconduct;

(c) . . . [I]n some areas of the South public officials improperly influenced Negro families to keep their children in Negro schools and excluded Negro children attending formerly all-white schools from official functions;

(d) Poverty deters many Negro families in the South from choosing formerly all-white schools. Some Negro parents are embarrassed to permit their children to attend such schools without suitable clothing. In some districts special fees are assessed for courses which are available only in the white schools;

(e) Improvements in facilities and equipment . . . have been instituted in all-Negro schools in some school districts in a manner that tends to discourage Negroes from selecting white schools. . . .

ing such a device to prove itself in operation. On the other hand, if there are reasonably available other ways, such for illustration as zoning, promising speedier and more effective conversion to a unitary, nonracial school system, "freedom-of-choice" must be held unacceptable.

The New Kent School Board's "freedom-of-choice" plan cannot be accepted as a sufficient step to "effectuate a transition" to a unitary system. In three years of operation not a single white child has chosen to attend Watkins school and although 115 Negro children enrolled in New Kent school in 1967 (up from 35 in 1965 and 111 in 1966) 85% of the Negro children in the system still attend the all-Negro Watkins school. In other words, the school system remains a dual system. Rather than further the dismantling of the dual system, the plan has operated simply to burden children and their parents with a responsibility which *Brown II* placed squarely on the School Board. The Board must be required to formulate a new plan and, in light of other courses which appear open to the Board, such as zoning,† fashion

steps which promise realistically to convert promptly to a system without a "white" school and a "Negro" school, but just schools.

The judgment of the Court of Appeals is vacated insofar as it affirmed the District Court and the case is remanded to the District Court for further proceedings consistent with this opinion.

*It is so ordered.*

---

† In view of the situation found in New Kent County, where there is no residential segregation, the elimination of the dual school system and the establishment of a "unitary, non-racial system" could be readily achieved with a minimum of administrative difficulty by means of geographic zoning— simply by assigning students living in the eastern half of the county to the New Kent School and those living in the western half of the county to the Watkins School. Although a geographical formula is not universally appropriate, it is evident that here the Board, by separately busing Negro children across the entire county to the "Negro" school, and the white children to the "white" school, is deliberately maintaining a segregated system which would vanish with nonracial geographic zoning. The conditions in this county present a classical case for this expedient. *Bowman* v. *County School Board, supra*, n. 3, at 332 (concurring opinion). Petitioners have also suggested that the Board could consolidate the two schools, one site (e.g., Watkins) serving grades 1–7 and the other (e.g., New Kent) serving grades 8–12, this being the grade division respondent makes between elementary and secondary levels. Petitioners contend this would result in a more efficient system by eliminating costly duplication in this relatively small district while at the same time achieving immediate dismantling of the dual system.

These are two suggestions the District Court should take into account upon remand, along with any other proposed alternatives and in light of considerations respecting other aspects of the school system such as the matter of faculty and staff desegregation remanded to the court by the Court of Appeals.

# HEART OF ATLANTA MOTEL, INC.
## v. UNITED STATES

379 U. S. 241; 13 L. Ed. 2d 258; 85 S. Ct. 348 (1964)

MR. JUSTICE CLARK *delivered the opinion of the Court.*

This is a declaratory judgment action, 28 U.S.C. Sec. 2201 and Sec. 2202, attacking the constitutionality of Title II of the Civil Rights Act of 1964, 78 Stat. 241. In addition to declaratory relief the complaint sought an injunction restraining the enforcement of the Act and damages against respondents based on allegedly resulting injury in the event compliance was required. Appellees counterclaimed for enforcement under Sec. 206 (a) of the Act and asked for a three-judge district court under Sec. 206 (b). A three-judge court, empaneled under Sec. 206 (b) as well as 28 U.S.C. Sec. 2282, sustained the validity of the Act and issued a permanent injunction on appellee's counterclaim restraining appellants from continuing to violate the Act which remains in effect on order of Mr. Justice Black, 379 U.S.—, 85 S. Ct. 1. We affirm the judgment.

The case comes here on admissions and stipulated facts. Appellant owns and operates the Heart of Atlanta Motel which has 216 rooms available to transient guests. The motel is located on Courtland Street, two blocks from downtown Peachtree Street. It is readily accessible to interstate highways 75 and 85 and state highways 23 and 41. Appellant solicits patronage from outside the State of Georgia through various national advertising media, including magazines of national circulation; it maintains over 50 billboards and highway signs within the State, soliciting patronage for the motel; it accepts convention trade from outside Georgia and approximately 75 [per cent] of its registered guests are from out of State. Prior to passage of the Act the motel had followed a practice of refusing to rent rooms to Negroes, and it alleged that it intended to continue to do so. In an effort to perpetuate that policy this suit was filed.

The appellant contends that Congress in passing this Act exceeded its power to regulate commerce under Art. I, Sec. 8, cl. 3, of the Constitution of the United States; that the Act violates the Fifth Amendment because appellant is deprived of the right to choose its customers and operate its business as it wishes, resulting in a taking of its liberty and property without due process of law and a taking of its property without just compensation; and, finally, that by requiring appellant to rent available rooms to Negroes against its will, Congress is subjecting it to involuntary servitude in contravention of the Thirteenth Amendment.

The appellees counter that the unavailability to Negroes of adequate accommodations interferes significantly with interstate travel, and that Congress, under the Commerce Clause, has power to remove such obstructions and restraints; that the Fifth Amendment does not forbid reasonable regulation and that consequential damage does not constitute a "taking" within the meaning of that amendment; that the Thirteenth

Amendment claim fails because it is entirely frivolous to say that an amendment directed to the abolition of human bondage and the removal of wide-spread disabilities associated with slavery places discrimination in public accommodations, beyond the reach of both federal and state law. . . .

. . . Title (II of the Act) is divided into seven sections beginning with Sec. 201 (a) which provides that:

All persons shall be entitled to the full and equal enjoyment of the goods, services, facilities, privileges, advantages, and accommodations of any place of public accommodation, as defined in this section, without discrimination or segregation on the ground of race, color, religion, or national origin.

There are listed in Sec. 201 (b) four classes of business establishments, each of which "serves the public" and "is a place of public accommodation" within the meaning of Sec. 201 (a) "if its operations affect commerce, or if discrimination or segregation by it is supported by State action." . . . (Here Justice Clark enumerates the covered establishments.)

Section 201 (c) defines the phrase "affect commerce" as applied to the above establishments. It first declares that "any inn, hotel, motel, or other establishment which provides lodging to transient guests" affects commerce per se. Restaurants, cafeterias (and similar establishments) . . . affect commerce only if they serve or offer to serve interstate travelers or if a substantial portion of the food which they serve or products which they sell have "moved in commerce." Motion picture houses and other places listed in class three affect commerce if they customarily present films, performances, etc., "which move in commerce." And the establishments . . . (physically located within the

premises of others covered) affect commerce if they are within, or include within their own premises, an establishment "the operations of which affect commerce." Private clubs are excepted under certain conditions. . . .

Section 201 (d) declares that "discrimination or segregation" is supported by state action when carried on under color of any law, statute, ordinance, regulation or any custom or usage required or enforced by officials of the State or any of its subdivisions.

In addition, Sec. 202 affirmatively declares that all persons "shall be entitled to be free, at any establishment or place, from discrimination or segregation of any kind on the ground of race, color, religion, or national origin, if such discrimination or segregation is or purports to be required by any law, statute, ordinance, regulation, rule, or order of a State or any agency or political subdivision thereof."

Finally Sec. 203 prohibits the withholding or denial . . . of any right or privilege secured by Sec. 201 and Sec. 202 or the intimidation, threatening or coercion of any person with the purpose of interfering with any such right or the punishing . . . of any person for exercising or attempting to exercise any such right. . . .

(Here follows an analysis of remedies that may be invoked against violations of the Title.)

It is admitted that the operation of the motel brings it within the provisions of Sec. 201 (a) of the Act and that appellant refused to provide lodging for transient Negroes because of their race or color and that it intends to continue that policy unless restrained.

The sole question posed is, therefore, the constitutionality of the Civil

Rights Act of 1964 as applied to these facts. The legislative history of the Act indicates that Congress based the Act on Sec. 5 and the Equal Protection Clause of the Fourteenth Amendment as well as its power to regulate interstate commerce under Art. I, Sec. 8, cl. 3 of the Constitution.

The Senate Commerce Committee made it quite clear that the fundamental object of Title II was to vindicate "the deprivation of personal dignity that surely accompanies denials of equal access to public establishments." At the same time, however, it noted that such an objective has been and could be readily achieved "by congressional action based on the commerce power of the Constitution." S. Rep. No. 872, at 16–17. Our study of the legislative record, made in the light of prior cases, has brought us to the conclusion that Congress possessed ample power in this regard, and we have therefore not considered the other grounds relied upon. This is not to say that the remaining authority upon which it acted was not adequate, a question upon which we do not pass, but merely that since the commerce power is sufficient for our decision here we have considered it alone. Nor is Sec. 201 (d) or Sec. 202, having to do with state action, involved here and we do not pass upon those sections. . . .

The power of Congress to deal with these obstructions depends on the meaning of the Commerce Clause. Its meaning was first enunciated 140 years ago by the great Chief Justice John Marshall in *Gibbons* v. *Ogden*, 9 Wheat. 1, 6 L. Ed. 23 (1824), . . . [when he said that it is] "that commerce which concerns more states than one." . . . [He analyzed the power] in these words:

. . .

It is the power to regulate; it is, to prescribe the rule by which commerce is to be governed. This power, like all others vested in Congress is complete in itself, may be exercised to its utmost extent, and acknowledges no limitations, other than are prescribed in the constitution . . . If, as has always been understood, the sovereignty of Congress . . . is plenary as to those objects (specified in the Constitution), the power over commerce . . . is vested in Congress as absolutely as it would be in a single government, having in its constitution the same restrictions on the exercise of the power as are found in the constitution of the United States. The wisdom and the discretion of Congress, their identity with the people, and the influence which their constituents possess at elections, are, in this, as in many other instances, as that, for example, of declaring war, the sole restraints on which they have relied, to secure them from its abuse. They are the restraints on which the people must often rely solely, in all representative governments. (At 196-197.)

In short, the determinative test of the exercise of power by the Congress under the Commerce Clause is simply whether the activity sought to be regulated is "commerce which concerns more than one state" and has a real and substantial relation to the national interest. . . .

. . . In framing Title II of this Act Congress was also dealing with what is considered a moral problem. But that fact does not detract from the overwhelming evidence of the disruptive effect that racial discrimination has had on commercial intercourse. It was this burden which empowered Congress to enact appropriate legislation, and, given this basis for the exercise of its power, Congress was not restricted by the fact that the particular obstruction to interstate commerce with which it was dealing was also deemed a moral and social wrong.

It is said that the operation of the motel here is of a purely local character. But, assuming this to be true, "[i]f it is interstate commerce that feels the pinch, it does not matter how local the operation which applies the squeeze." *United States* v. *Women's Sportswear Mfg. Ass'n,* 336 U.S. 460, 464, 69 S. Ct. 714, 716, 93 L. Ed. 805 (1949). See *National Labor Relations Board* v. *Jones & Laughlin Steel Corp. . . .* As Chief Justice Stone put it in *United States* v. *Darby, . . . :*

The power of Congress over interstate commerce is not confined to the regulation of commerce among the states. It extends to those activities intrastate which so affect interstate commerce or the exercise of the power of Congress over it as to make regulation of them appropriate means to the attainment of a legitimate end, the exercise of the granted power of Congress to regulate interstate commerce. See *McCulloch* v. *Maryland,* 4 Wheat. 316, 421, 4 L. Ed. 579. (312 U. S. at 118, 61 S. Ct. at 459.)

Thus the power of Congress to promote interstate commerce also includes the power to regulate the local incidents thereof, including local activities in both the States of origin and destination, which might have a substantial and harmful effect upon that commerce. One need only examine the evidence which we have discussed above to see that Congress may—as it has—prohibit racial discrimination by motels serving travelers, however "local" their operations may appear.

Nor does the Act deprive appellant of liberty or property under the Fifth Amendment. The commerce power invoked here by the Congress is a specific and plenary one authorized by the Constitution itself. The only questions are: (1) whether Congress had a rational basis for finding that racial discrimination by motels affected commerce, and (2) if it had such a basis, whether the means it selected to eliminate that evil are reasonable and appropriate. If they are, appellant has no "right" to select its guests as it sees fit, free from governmental regulation.

There is nothing novel about such legislation. Thirty-two States now have it on their books either by statute or executive order and many cities provide such regulation. Some of these acts go back four-score years. It has been repeatedly held by this Court that such laws do not violate the Due Process Clause of the Fourteenth Amendment. Perhaps the first such holding was in the *Civil Rights Cases,* themselves, where Mr. Justice Bradley for the Court inferentially found that innkeepers, "by the laws of all the States, so far as we are aware, are bound, to the extent of their facilities, to furnish proper accommodation to all unobjectionable persons who in good faith apply for them." (109 U.S. at 25, 3 S. Ct. at 31.)

As we have pointed out, thirty-two States now have such statutes and no case has been cited to us where the attack on a state statute has been successful, either in federal or state courts. Indeed, in some cases the Due Process and Equal Protection Clause objections have been specifically discarded in this Court. *Bob-Lo Excursion Co.* v. *Michigan,* 333 U.S. 28, 34, 68 S. Ct. 358, 361, 92 L. Ed. 455, n. 12 (1948). As a result the constitutionality of such state statutes stands unquestioned. . . .

It is doubtful if in the long run appellant will suffer economic loss as a result of the Act. Experience is to the contrary where discrimination is completely obliterated as to all public accommodations. But whether this be true or not is of no consequence since this Court has specifically held that the fact that a "member of the class which is regulated may suffer economic losses not shared by others . . . has never been a barrier" to such legislation. *Bowles* v. *Willingham* . . . 64 S. Ct. at 649. Likewise in a long line of cases this Court has rejected the claim that the prohibition of racial discrimination in public accommodations interferes with personal liberty. See *District of Columbia* v. *John R. Thompson Co.*, 346 U.S. 100, 73 S. Ct. 1007, 97 L. Ed. 1480 (1953), and cases there cited, where we concluded that Congress had delegated law-making power to the District of Columbia "as broad as the police power of a state" which included the power to adopt a "law prohibiting discriminations against Negroes by the owners and managers of restaurants in the District of Columbia." At 110, 73 S. Ct. at 1013. Neither do we find any merit in the claim that the Act is a taking of property without just compensation. The cases are to the contrary. . . .

We find no merit in the remainder of appellant's contentions, including that of "involuntary servitude." As we have seen, 32 States prohibit racial discrimination in public accommodations. These laws but codify the common-law innkeeper rule which long predated the Thirteenth Amendment. It is difficult to believe that the Amendment was intended to abrogate this principle. Indeed, the opinion of the Court in the *Civil Rights Cases* is to the contrary as we have seen, it having noted with approval the laws of "all of the states" prohibiting discrimination. We could not say that the requirements of the Act in this regard are in any way "akin to African slavery." *Butler* v. *Perry*, 240 U.S. 328, 332, 36 S. Ct. 258, 259, 60 L. Ed. 672 (1916).

We, therefore, conclude that the action of the Congress in the adoption of the Act as applied here to a motel which concededly serves interstate travelers is within the power granted it by the Commerce Clause of the Constitution, as interpreted by this Court for 140 years. It may be argued that Congress could have pursued other methods to eliminate the obstructions it found in interstate commerce caused by racial discrimination. But this is a matter of policy that rests entirely with the Congress not with the courts. How obstructions in commerce may be removed—what means are to be employed—is within the sound and exclusive discretion of the Congress. It is subject only to one caveat—that the means chosen by it must be reasonably adapted to the end permitted by the Constitution. We cannot say that its choice here was not so adapted. The Constitution requires no more.

*Affirmed.*

# WATSON v. MEMPHIS

373 U. S. 526; 10 L. Ed. 2d 529; 83 S. Ct. 1314 (1963)

MR. JUSTICE GOLDBERG *delivered the opinion of the Court.*

The issue in this case, simply stated, is whether the City of Memphis may further delay in meeting fully its constitutional obligations under the Fourteenth Amendment to desegregate its public parks and other municipal recreational facilities.

The petitioners, adult Negro residents of Memphis, commenced this action . . . seeking declaratory and injunctive relief directing immediate desegregation of municipal parks and other city owned or operated recreational facilities. . . . The city denied neither the fact that the majority of the relevant facilities were operated on a segregated basis nor its duty under the Fourteenth Amendment to terminate its policy of conditioning use of such facilities on race. Instead, it pointed to the partial desegregation already effected and attempted to justify its further delay . . . by urging the need and wisdom of proceeding slowly and gradually in its desegregation efforts.

The District Court denied the relief sought by the petitioners and ordered the city to submit, within six months, a plan providing additional time for desegregation of the relevant facilities.* The Court of Appeals for the Sixth Circuit affirmed. . . . We granted certiorari . . . to consider the important question presented and the applicability here of the

principles enunciated by this Court in the second *Brown* decision.

. . .

It is important at the outset to note the chronological context in which the city makes its claim to entitlement to additional time within which to work out complete elimination of racial barriers to use of the public facilities here involved. . . . [I]t was almost eight years ago—in 1955, . . . that the constitutional proscription of state enforced racial segregation was found to apply to public recreational facilities. See *Dawson* v. *Mayor and City Council of Baltimore*, 220 F. 2d 386, aff'r, 350 U.S. 877; see also *Muir* v. *Louisville Park Theatrical Assn.*, 347 U.S. 971.

. . . In considering the appropriateness of the equitable decree entered below inviting a plan calling for an even longer delay in effecting desegregation, we cannot ignore the passage of a substantial period of time since the original declaration of the manifest unconstitutionality of racial practices such as are here challenged, the repeated and numerous decisions giving notice of such illegality, and the many intervening opportunities heretofore available to attain the equality of treatment which the Fourteenth Amendment commands the States to achieve. These factors must inevitably and substantially temper the present import of such broad policy considerations as may have underlain, even in part, the form of decree ultimately framed in the *Brown* case. Given the extended time which has elapsed, it is far from clear that the mandate of the second *Brown*

* The plan ultimately formulated, though not part of the record here, was described in oral argument before the Court of Appeals. It does not provide for complete desegregation of all facilities until 1971.

decision requiring that desegregation proceed with "all deliberate speed" would today be fully satisfied by types of plans or programs for desegregation of public educational facilities which eight years ago might have been deemed sufficient. *Brown* never contemplated that the concept of "deliberate speed" would countenance indefinite delay in elimination of racial barriers in schools, let alone other public facilities not involving the same physical problems or comparable conditions.

. . .

The nature of the ultimate resolution effected in the second *Brown* decision largely reflected no more than a recognition of the unusual and particular problems inhering in desegregating large numbers of schools throughout the country. The careful specification of factors relevant to a determination whether any delay in complying fully and completely with the constitutional mandate would be warranted demonstrated a concern that delay not be conditioned upon insufficient reasons or, in any event, tolerated unless it imperatively and compellingly appeared unavoidable.

This case presents no obvious occasion for the application of *Brown*. We are not here confronted with attempted desegregation of a local school system with any or all of the perhaps uniquely attendant problems, administrative and other, specified in the second *Brown* decision as proper considerations in weighing the need for further delay in vindicating the Fourteenth Amendment rights of petitioners. Desegregaton of parks and other recreational facilities does not present the same kinds of cognizable difficulties inhering in elimination of racial classification in schools, at which attendance is compulsory,

the adequacy of teachers and facilities crucial, and questions of geographic assignment often of major significance.

Most importantly, of course, it must be recognized that even the delay countenanced by *Brown* was a necessary, albeit significant, adaptation of the usual principle that any deprivation of constitutional rights calls for prompt rectification. The rights here asserted are, like all such rights, *present* rights; they are not merely hopes to some *future* enjoyment of some formalistic constitutional promise. The basic guarantees of our Constitution are warrants for the here and now and unless there is an overwhelmingly compelling reason, they are to be promptly fulfilled. The second *Brown* decision is but a narrowly drawn, and carefully limited, qualification upon usual precepts of constitutional adjudication and is not to be unnecessarily expanded in application.

. . . The city has effected, continues to effect, and claims the right or need to prolong patently unconstitutional racial discriminations violative of now long-declared and well-established individual rights. The claims of the city to further delay in affording the petitioners that to which they are clearly and unquestionably entitled cannot be upheld except upon the most convincing and impressive demonstration by the city that such delay is manifestly compelled by constitutionally cognizable circumstances warranting the exercise of an appropriate equitable discretion by a court. . . .

Examination of the facts of this case in light of the foregoing discussion discloses with singular clarity that this burden has not been sustained; indeed, it is patent from the record that the principles enunciated in the second *Brown* decision have absolutely no application here.

. . .

The city asserted . . . that its good faith in attempting to comply with the requirements of the Constitution is not in issue, and contends that gradual desegregation on a facility-by-facility basis is necessary to prevent interracial disturbances, violence, riots, and community confusion and turmoil. The compelling answer to this contention is that constitutional rights may not be denied simply because of hostility to their assertion or exercise. . . . As declared in *Cooper v. Aaron*, 358 U.S. 1, 16, "law and order are not . . . to be preserved by depriving the Negro children of their constitutional rights." . . .

Beyond this, however, neither the asserted fears of violence and tumult nor the asserted inability to preserve the peace was demonstrated at trial to be anything more than personal speculations or vague disquietudes of city officials. There is no indication that there had been any violence or meaningful disturbances when other recreational facilities had been desegregated. In fact, the only evidence in the record was that such prior transitions had been peaceful. . . . Moreover, there was no factual evidence to support the bare testimonial speculations that authorities would be unable to cope successfully with any problems which in fact might arise or to meet the need for additional protection should the occasion demand.

. . .

The other justifications for delay urged by the city or relied upon by the courts below are no more substantial, either legally or practically. It was, for example, asserted that immediate desegregation of playgrounds and parks would deprive a number of children—both Negro and white—of recreational facilities; this contention was apparently based on the premise that a number of such facilities would have to be closed because of the inadequacy of the "present" park budget to provide additional "supervision" assumed to be necessary to operate unsegregated playgrounds. As already noted, however, there is no warrant in this record for assuming that such added supervision would, in fact, be required, much less that police and recreation personnel would be unavailable to meet such needs if they should arise. More significantly, however, it is obvious that vindication of conceded constitutional rights cannot be made dependent upon any theory that it is less expensive to deny than to afford them. We will not assume that the citizens of Memphis accept the questionable premise implicit in this argument or that either the resources of the city are inadequate, or its government unresponsive, to the needs of all of its citizens.

. . .

Since the city has completely failed to demonstrate any compelling or convincing reason requiring further delay in implementing the constitutional proscription of segregation of publicly owned or operated recreational facilities, there is no cause whatsoever to depart from the generally operative and here clearly controlling principle that constitutional rights are to be promptly vindicated.

. . .

The judgment below must be and is reversed and the cause is remanded for further proceedings consistent herewith.

*Reversed.*

# REITMAN v. MULKEY

## 387 U. S. 369; 18 L. Ed. 2d 830; 87 S. Ct. 1627 (1967)

MR. JUSTICE WHITE *delivered the opinion of the Court.*

The question here is whether Art. I, Section 26 of the California Constitution denied "to any person . . . the equal protection of the laws" within the meaning of the Fourteenth Amendment of the Constitution of the United States. Section 26 of Art. I, an initiated measure submitted to the people as Proposition 14 in a statewide ballot in 1964, provides in part as follows:

Neither the State nor any subdivision or agency thereof shall deny, limit or abridge, directly or indirectly, the right of any person, who is willing or desires to sell, lease or rent any part or all of his real property, to decline to sell, lease or rent such property to such person or persons as he, in his absolute discretion, chooses.

The real property covered by Section 26 is limited to residential property and contains an exception for state-owned real estate.*

\* The following is the full text of Section 26: "Neither the State nor any subdivision or agency thereof shall deny, limit or abridge, directly or indirectly, the right of any person, who is willing or desires to sell, lease or rent any part or all of his real property, to decline to sell, lease or rent such property to such person or persons as he, in his absolute discretion, chooses.

" 'Person' includes individuals, partnerships, corporations and other legal entities and their agents or representatives but does not include the State or any subdivision thereof with respect to the sale, lease or rental of property owned by it.

" 'Real property' consists of any interest in real property of any kind or quality, present or future, irrespective of how obtained or financed, which is used, designed, constructed, zoned or otherwise devoted to or

The issue arose in two separate actions in the California Courts, *Reitman* v. *Mulkey* and *Prendergast* v. *Snyder.* In *Reitman,* the Mulkeys, who are husband and wife and respondents here, sued under Section 51 and Section 52 of the California Civil Code alleging that petitioners had refused to rent them an apartment solely on account of their race. An injunction and damages were demanded. Petitioners moved for summary judgment on the ground that Sections 51 and 52, insofar as they were the basis for the Mulkeys' action, had been rendered null and void by the adoption of Proposition 14 after the filing of the complaint. The trial court granted the motion and respondents took the case to the California Supreme Court.

In the *Prendergast* case, respondents, husband and wife, filed suit in December 1964 seeking to enjoin eviction from their apartment; respondents alleged that the eviction

limited for residential purposes whether as a single family dwelling or as a dwelling for two or more persons or families living together or independently of each other.

"This Article shall not apply to obtaining of property by eminent domain pursuant to Article I, Sections 14 and 14½ of this Constitution, nor to the renting or providing of any accommodations for lodging purposes by a hotel, motel or other similar public place engaged in furnishing lodging to transient guests.

"If any part or provision of this Article, or the application thereof to any person or circumstance, is held invalid, the remainder of the Article, including the application of such part or provision to other persons or circumstances, shall not be affected thereby and shall continue in full force and effect. To this end the provisions of this Article are severable." (Cal. Const., Art. I, Section 26.)

was motivated by racial prejudice and therefore would violate Section 51 and Section 52 of the Civil Code. Petitioner Snyder cross-complained for a judicial declaration that he was entitled to terminate the month-to-month tenancy even if his action was based on racial considerations. In denying petitioner's motion for summary judgment, the trial court found it unnecessary to consider the validity of Proposition 14 because it concluded that judicial enforcement of an eviction based on racial grounds would in any event violate the Equal Protection Clause of the United States Constitution. The cross-complaint was dismissed with prejudice and petitioner Snyder appealed to the California Supreme Court which considered the case along with *Reitman* v. *Mulkey*. That court, in reversing the *Reitman* case, held that Art. I, Section 26, was invalid as denying the equal protection of the laws guaranteed by the Fourteenth Amendment. . . . For similar reasons, the court affirmed the judgment in the *Prendergast* case. . . .

We affirm the judgment of the California Supreme Court. We first turn to the opinion of that court, which quite properly undertook to examine the constitutionality of Section 26 in terms of its "immediate objective," its "ultimate impact" and its "historical context and the conditions existing prior to its enactment." Judgments such as these we have frequently undertaken ourselves. . . . But here the California Supreme Court has addressed itself to these matters and we should give careful consideration to its views because they concern the purpose, scope, and operative effect of a provision of the California Constitution.

First, the court considered whether Section 26 was concerned at all with private discriminations in residential housing. This involved a review of past efforts by the California Legislature to regulate such discriminations. The Unruh Act, Civ. Code Sections 51–52, on which respondents based their cases, was passed in 1959. The Hawkins Act, formerly Health & Saf. Code Section 35700–35741, followed and prohibited discriminations in publicly assisted housing. In 1961, the legislature enacted proscriptions against restrictive covenants. Finally, in 1963, came the Rumford Fair Housing Act, Health & Saf. Code Section 35700–35744, superseding the Hawkins Act and prohibiting racial discriminations in the sale or rental of any private dwelling containing more than four units. That act was enforceable by the State Fair Employment Practice Commission.

It was against this background that Proposition 14 was enacted. Its immediate design and intent, the California court said, was "to overturn state laws that bore on the right of private sellers and lessors to discriminate," the Unruh and Rumford Acts, and "to forestall future state action that might circumscribe this right." This aim was successfully achieved: the adoption of Proposition 14 "generally nullifies both the Rumford and Unruh Acts as they apply to the housing market," and establishes "a purported constitutional right to privately discriminate on grounds which admittedly would be unavailable under the Fourteenth Amendment should state action be involved."

Second, the court conceded that the State was permitted a neutral position with respect to private racial discriminations and that the State was not bound by the Federal Constitution to forbid them. But, because a significant state involvement in private discriminations could amount to unconstitutional state action, *Burton* v. *Wilmington Parking Authority*, 365 U.S. 715, 81 S. Ct. 856, 6 L. Ed. 2d 45, the court deemed it necessary to determine whether Proposition 14 invalidly involved the State in racial discriminations in the housing market. Its conclusion was that it did.

To reach this result, the state court examined certain prior decisions in this Court in which discriminatory state action was identified. Based on these cases . . . it concluded that a prohibited state involvement could be found "even where the state can be charged with only encouraging." . . . Section 26 was said to have changed the situation from one in which discriminatory practices were restricted "to one wherein it is encouraged; . . ." Section 26 was legislative action "which authorized private discrimination" and made the State "at least a partner in the instant act of discrimination. . . ." The court could "conceive of no other purpose for an application of section 26 aside from authorizing the perpetration of a purported private discrimination. . . ." The judgment of the California court was that Section 26 unconstitutionally involves the State in racial discriminations and is therefore invalid under the Fourteenth Amendment.

There is no sound reason for rejecting this judgment. Petitioners contend that the California court has misconstrued the Fourteenth Amendment since the repeal of any statute prohibiting racial discrimination, which is constitutionally permissible, may be said to "authorize" and "encourage" discrimination because it makes legally permissible that which was formerly proscribed. But as we understand the California court, it did not posit a constitutional violation on the mere repeal of the Unruh and Rumford Acts. It did not read either our cases or the Fourteenth Amendment as establishing an automatic constitutional barrier to the repeal of an existing law prohibiting racial discrimination in housing; nor did the court rule that a State may never put in statutory form an existing policy of neutrality with respect to private discriminations. What the court below did was first to reject the notion that the State was required to have a statute prohibiting racial discriminations in housing. Second, it held the purpose and intent of Section 26 was to authorize private racial discriminations on the housing market, to repeal the Unruh and Rumford Acts and to create a constitutional right to discriminate on racial grounds in the sale and leasing of real property. Hence, the court dealt with Section 26 as though it expressly authorized and constitutionalized the private right to discriminate. Third, the court assessed the ultimate impact of Section 26 in the California environment and concluded that the section would encourage and significantly involve the State in private racial discrimination contrary to the Fourteenth Amendment.

The California court could very reasonably conclude that Section 26 would and did have wider impact than a mere repeal of existing statutes. Section 26 mentioned neither the Unruh nor Rumford Acts in so many words. Instead, it announced the constitutional right of any person to decline to sell or lease his real property to anyone to whom he did not desire to sell or lease. Unruh and Rumford were thereby *pro tanto* repealed. But the section struck more deeply and more widely. Private discriminations in housing were now not only free from Rumford and Unruh but they also enjoyed a far different status than was true before the passage of those statutes. The right to discriminate, including the right to discriminate on racial grounds, was now embodied in the State's basic charter, immune from legislative, executive, or judicial regulation at any level of the state government. Those practicing racial discriminations need no longer rely solely on their personal choice. They could now invoke express constitutional authority, free from censure or interference of any kind from official sources. All individuals, partnerships, corporations and other legal entities, as well as their agents and representatives, could now discriminate with respect to their residential real property, which is defined as any interest in real property of any kind or quality, "irrespective of how obtained or financed," and seemingly irrespective of the relationship of the State to such interests in real property. Only the State is excluded with respect to property owned by it. . . .

The assessment of Section 26 by the California court is similar to what this Court has done in appraising state statutes or other official actions in other contexts. In *McCabe* v. *Atchison, Topeka & Santa Fe Railway,* 235 U.S. 151, 35 S. Ct. 69, 59 L. Ed. 169, the Court dealt with a statute which, as construed by the Court, authorized carriers to provide cars for white persons but not for Negroes. Though dismissal of the complaint on a procedural ground was affirmed, the Court made it clear that such a statute was invalid under the Four-

teenth Amendment because a carrier refusing equal service to Negroes would be "acting in the matter under the authority of a state law." This was nothing less than considering a permissive state statute as an authorization to discriminate and as sufficient state action to violate the Fourteenth Amendment in the context of that case. Similarly, in *Nixon* v. *Condon,* 286 U.S. 73, 52 S. Ct. 484, 76 L. Ed. 984, the Court was faced with a statute empowering the executive committee of a political party to prescribe the qualifications of its members for voting or for other participation, but containing no directions with respect to the exercise of that power. This was authority which the committee otherwise might not have had and which was used by the committee to bar Negroes from voting in primary elections. Reposing this power in the executive committee was said to insinuate the State into the self-regulatory, decision-making scheme of the voluntary association; the exercise of the power was viewed as an expression of state authority contrary to the Fourteenth Amendment.

In *Burton* v. *Wilmington Parking Authority,* 365 U.S. 715, 81 S. Ct. 856, the operator-lessee of a restaurant located in a building owned by the State and otherwise operated for public purposes, refused service to Negroes. Although the State neither commanded nor expressly authorized or encouraged the discriminations, the State had "elected to place its power, property and prestige behind the admitted discrimination" and by "its inaction . . . has . . . made itself a party to the refusal of service . . ." which therefore could not be considered the purely private choice of the restaurant operator.

In *Peterson* v. *City of Greenville,* 373 U.S. 244, and in *Robinson* v. *Florida,* 378 U.S. 153, the Court dealt with state statutes or regulations requiring, at least in some respects, segregation in facilities and services in restaurants. These official provisions, although obviously unconstitutional and unenforceable, were deemed in themselves sufficient to disentitle the State to punish, as trespassers, Negroes who had been refused service in the restaurants. In neither case was any proof required that the restaurant owner had actually been influenced by the state statute or regulation. . . .

. . . Here we are dealing with a provision which does not just repeal an existing law forbidding private racial discriminations. Section 26 was intended to authorize, and does authorize, racial discrimination in the housing market. The right to discriminate is now one of the basic policies of the State. The California Supreme Court believes that the section will significantly encourage and involve the State in private discriminations. We have been presented with no persuasive considerations indicating that this judgment should be overturned.

*Affirmed.*

MR. JUSTICE DOUGLAS, *concurring.*

While I join the opinion of the Court, I add a word to indicate the dimensions of our problem.

This is not a case as simple as the one where a man with a bicycle or a car or a stock certificate or even a log cabin asserts the right to sell it to whomsoever he pleases, excluding all others whether they be Negro, Chinese, Japanese, Russians, Catholics, Baptists, or those with blue eyes. We

deal here with a problem in the realm of zoning, similar to the one we had in *Shelley* v. *Kramer,* . . . where we struck down restrictive covenants.

Those covenants are one device whereby a neighborhood is kept "white" or "Caucasian" as the dominant interests desire. Proposition 14 in the setting of our modern housing problem is only another device of the same character.

Real estate brokers and mortgage lenders are largely dedicated to the maintenance of segregated communities. Realtors commonly believe it is unethical to sell or rent to a Negro in a predominantly or all-white neighborhood, and mortgage lenders throw their weight alongside segregated communities, rejecting applications by a member of a minority group who tries to break the white phalanx save and unless the neighborhood is in process of conversion into a mixed or a Negro community. . . .

Proposition 14 is a form of sophisticated discrimination whereby the people of California harness the energies of private groups to do indirectly what they cannot under our decisions allow their government to do.

George A. McGanse, chairman of the legislative committee of the Texas Real Estate Association, while giving his views on Title IV of the proposed Civil Rights Act of 1966 (H.R. 14765), which would prohibit discrimination in housing by property owners, real estate brokers, and others engaged in the sale, rental or financing of housing, stated that he warned groups to which he spoke of "the grave dangers inherent in any type of legislation that would erode away the rights that go with the ownership of property." He pointed out that

[E]ach time we citizens of this country lose any of the rights that go with the ownership of property, we are moving that much closer to a centralized government in which ultimately the right to own property would be denied.

That apparently is a common view. It overlooks several things. First, the right to own or lease property is already denied to many solely because of the pigment of their skin; they are, indeed, under the control of a few who determine where and how the colored people shall live and what the nature of our cities will be. Second, the agencies that are zoning the cities along racial lines are state licensees.

Zoning is a state and municipal function. . . . When the State leaves that function to private agencies or institutions who are licensees and who practice racial discrimination and zone our cities into white and black belts or white and black ghettoes, it suffers a governmental function to be performed under private auspices in a way the State itself may not act. . . .

Leaving the zoning function to groups who practice racial discrimination and are licensed by the States constitutes state action in the narrowest sense in which *Shelley* v. *Kraemer, supra,* can be construed. . . .

Under California law no person may "engage in the business, act in the capacity of, advertise or assume to act as a real estate broker or a real estate salesman within this State without first obtaining a real estate license." West's Ann. Cal. Bus. & Prof. Code, Sec. 10130. These licensees are designated to serve the public. Their licenses are not restricted, and could not be restricted, to effectuate a policy of segregation. That would be state action that is barred by the Four-

teenth Amendment. There is no difference, as I see it, between a State authorizing a licensee to practice racial discrimination, and a State, without any express authorization of that kind nevertheless launching and countenancing the operation of a licensing system in an environment where the whole weight of the system is on the side of discrimination. In the latter situation the State is impliedly sanctioning what it may not do specifically.

If we were in a domain exclusively private, we would have different problems. But urban housing is in the public domain as evidenced not only by the zoning problems presented but by the vast schemes of public financing with which the States and the Nation have been extensively involved in recent years. Urban housing is clearly marked with the public interest. . . .

Since the real estate brokerage business is one that can be and is state regulated and since it is state licensed, it must be dedicated, like the telephone companies and the carriers and the hotels and motels to the requirements of service to all without discrimination—a standard that in its modern setting is conditoned by the demands of the Equal Protection Clause of the Fourteenth Amendment.

And to those who say that Proposition 14 represents the will of the people of California, one can only reply:

Wherever the real power in a Government lies, there is the danger of oppression. In our Governments the real power lies in the majority of the Community, and the invasion of private rights is *chiefly* to be apprehended, not from acts of Government contrary to the sense of its constituents, but from acts in which the Government is the mere instrument of the major number of the Constituents. This is a truth of great importance, but not yet sufficiently attended to. . . . Writings of James Madison (Hunt ed. 1904), p. 272.

MR. JUSTICE HARLAN, *whom* MR. JUSTICE BLACK, MR. JUSTICE CLARK, *and* MR. JUSTICE STEWART *join, dissenting.*

I consider that this decision, which cuts deeply into state political processes, is supported neither by anything "found" by the Supreme Court of California nor by any of our past cases decided under the Fourteenth Amendment. In my view today's holding, salutary as its result may appear at first blush, may in the long run actually serve to handicap progress in the extremely difficult field of racial concerns. I must respectfully dissent.

. . .

In the case at hand California, acting through the initiative and referendum, has decided to remain "neutral" in the realm of private discrimination affecting the sale or rental of private residential property; in such transactions private owners are now free to act in a discriminatory manner previously forbidden to them. In short, all that has happened is that California has effected a *pro tanto* repeal of its prior statutes forbidding private discrimination. This runs no more afoul of the Fourteenth Amendment than would have California's failure to pass any such antidiscrimination statutes in the first instance. The fact that such repeal was also accompanied by a constitutional prohibition against future enactment of such laws by the California Legislature cannot well be thought to affect, from a federal constitutional standpoint, the validity of what California has done. The Fourteenth Amendment does not reach such state constitutional action any more than it does a simple legislative repeal of legislation forbidding private discrimination.

I do not think the Court's opinion really denies any of these fundamental constitutional propositions. Rather it attempts to escape them by resorting to arguments which appear to me to be entirely ill-founded.

The Court attempts to fit Sec. 26 within the coverage of the Equal Protection Clause by characterizing it as in effect an affirmative call to residents of California to discriminate. The main difficulty with this viewpoint is that it depends upon a characterization of Sec. 26 that cannot fairly be made. The provision is neutral on its face, and it is only by in effect asserting that this requirement of passive official neutrality is camouflage that the Court is able to reach its conclusion. In depicting the provision as tantamount to active state encouragement of discrimination the Court essentially relies on the fact that the California Supreme Court so concluded. It is said that the findings of the highest court of California as to the meaning and impact of the enactment are entitled to great weight. I agree, of course, that *findings of fact* by a state court should be given great weight, but this familiar proposition hardly aids the Court's holding in this case.

There is no disagreement whatever but that Sec. 26 was meant to nullify California's fair-housing legislation and thus to remove from private residential property transactions the state-created impediment upon freedom of choice. There were no disputed issues of fact at all and indeed the California Supreme Court noted at the outset of its opinion that "[i]n the trial court proceedings allegations of the complaint were not factually challenged, no evidence was introduced, and the only matter placed in issue was the legal sufficiency of the allegations." . . . Moreover, the grounds which prompt legislators or state voters to repeal a law do not determine its constitutional validity. That question is decided by what the law does, not by what those who voted for it wanted it to do, and it must not be forgotten that the Fourteenth Amendment does not compel a State to put or keep any particular law about race on its books. The Amendment forbids only a State to pass or keep in effect laws discriminating on account of race. California has not done this.

A state enactment, particularly one that is simply permissive of private decision-making rather than coercive and one that has been adopted in this most democratic of processes, should not be struck down by the judiciary under the Equal Protection Clause without persuasive evidence of an invidious purpose or effect. The only "factual" matter relied on by the majority of the California Supreme Court was the context in which Proposition 14 was adopted, namely, that several strong antidiscrimination acts had been passed by the legislature and opposed by many of those who successfully led the movement for adoption of Proposition 14 by popular referendum. These circumstances, and these alone, the California court held, made Sec. 26 unlawful under this Court's cases interpreting the Equal Protection Clause. This, of course, is nothing but a legal conclusion as to federal constitutional law, the California Supreme Court not having relied in any way upon the State Constitution. Accepting all the suppositions under which the state court acted, I cannot see that its con-

clusion is entitled to any special weight in the discharge of our own responsibilities. Put in another way, I cannot transform the California court's conclusion of law into a finding of fact that the State through the adoption of Sec. 26 is actively promoting racial discrimination. It seems to me manifest that the state court rested entirely on what that court conceived to be the compulsion of the Fourteenth Amendment, not on any fact-finding by the state courts.

There is no question that the adoption of Sec. 26, repealing the former state antidiscrimination laws and prohibiting the enactment of such state laws in the future, constituted "state action" within the meaning of the Fourteenth Amendment. The only issue is whether this provision impermissibly deprives any person of equal protection of the laws. As a starting point, it is clear that any statute requiring unjustified discriminatory treatment is unconstitutional. . . . And it is no less clear that the Equal Protection Clause bars as well discriminatory governmental administration of a statute fair on its face. . . . This case fits within neither of these two categories: Section 26 is by its terms inoffensive, and its provisions require no affirmative governmental enforcement of any sort. A third category of equal protection cases, concededly more difficult to characterize, stands for the proposition that when governmental involvement in private discrimination reaches a level at which the State can be held responsible for the specific act of private discrimination, the strictures of the Fourteenth Amendment come into play. In dealing with this class of cases, the inquiry has been framed as whether the State has become "a joint participant in the challenged activity, which, on that account, cannot be considered to have been so 'purely private' as to fall without the scope of the Fourteenth Amendment." . . .

Given these latter contours of the equal protection doctrine, the assessment of particular cases is often troublesome, as the Court itself acknowledges. . . . However, the present case does not seems to me even to approach those peripheral situations in which the question of state involvement gives rise to difficulties. . . . The core of the Court's opinion is that Sec. 26 is offensive to the Fourteenth Amendment because it effectively *encourages* private discrimination. By focusing on "encouragement" the Court, I fear, is forging a slippery and unfortunate criterion by which to measure the constitutionality of a statute simply permissive in purpose and effect, and inoffensive on its face.

It is true that standards in this area have not been definitely formulated, and that acts of discrimination have been included within the compass of the Equal Protection Clause not merely when they were compelled by a state statute or other governmental pressures, but also when they were said to be "induced" or "authorized" by the State. Most of these cases, however, can be approached in terms of the impact and extent of affirmative state governmental activities. . . . In situations such as these the focus has been on positive state cooperation or partnership in affirmatively promoted activities, an involvement that could have been avoided. Here, . . . we have only the straight-forward adoption of a neutral provision restoring to the sphere of free choice, left untouched by the Fourteenth Amendment, private behavior within a limited area of the racial problem. The denial of equal protection emerges only from the conclusion reached by

the Court that the implementation of a new policy of governmental neutrality, embodied in a constitutional provision and replacing a former policy of antidiscrimination, has the effect of lending encouragement to those who wish to discriminate. In the context of the actual facts of the case, this conclusion appears to me to state only a truism: people who want to discriminate but were previously forbidden to do so by state law are now left free because the State has chosen to have no law on the subject at all. Obviously whenever there is a change in the law it will have resulted from the concerted activity of those who desire the change, and its enactment will allow those supporting the legislation to pursue their private goals.

A moment of thought will reveal the far-reaching possibilities of the Court's new doctrine, which I am sure the Court does not intend. Every act of private discrimination is either forbidden by state law or permitted by it. There can be little doubt that such permissiveness—whether by express constitutional or statutory provision, or implicit in the common law —to some extent "encourages" those who wish to discriminate to do so. Under this theory "state action" in the form of laws that do nothing more than passively permit private discrimination could be said to tinge *all* private discrimination with the taint of unconstitutional state encouragement. . . . I believe the state action required to bring the Fourteenth Amendment into operation must be affirmative and purposeful, actively fostering discrimination. Only in such a case is ostensibly "private" action more properly labeled "official." I do not believe that the mere enactment of Sec. 26, on the showing made here, falls within this class of cases.

I think that this decision is not only constitutionally unsound, but in its practical potentialities short-sighted. Opponents of state antidiscrimination statutes are now in a position to argue that such legislation should be defeated because, if enacted, it may be unrepealable. More fundamentally, the doctrine underlying this decision may hamper, if not preclude, attempts to deal with the delicate and troublesome problems of race relations through the legislative process. The lines that have been and must be drawn in this area, fraught as it is with human sensibilities and frailties of whatever race or creed, are difficult ones. The drawing of them requires understanding, patience, and compromise, and is best done by legislatures rather than by courts. When legislation in this field is unsuccessful

there should be wide opportunities for legislative amendment, as well as for change through such processes as the popular initiative and referendum. This decision, I fear, may inhibit such flexibility. Here the electorate itself overwhelmingly wished to overrule and check its own legislature on a matter left open by the Federal Constitution. By refusing to accept the decision of the people of California, and by contriving a new and ill-defined constitutional concept to allow federal judicial interference, I think the Court has taken to itself powers and responsibilities left elsewhere by the Constitution.

I believe the Supreme Court of California misapplied the Fourteenth Amendment, and would reverse its judgment, and remand the case for further appropriate proceedings.

# JONES v. MAYER

392 U. S. 409; 20 L. Ed. 2d 1189; 88 S. Ct. 2186 (1968)

MR. JUSTICE STEWART *delivered the opinion of the Court.*

In this case we are called upon to determine the scope and the constitutionality of an Act of Congress, 42 U.S.C. Sec. 1982, which provides that:

All citizens of the United States shall have the same rights, in every State and Territory, as is enjoyed by white citizens thereof to inherit, purchase, lease, sell, hold, and convey real and personal property.

On September 2, 1965, the petitioners filed a complaint in the District Court for the Eastern District of Missouri, alleging that the respondents had refused to sell them a home in the Paddock Woods community of

St. Louis County for the sole reason that petitioner . . . is a Negro. Relying in part upon Sec. 1982, the petitioners sought injunctive and other relief. The District Court sustained the respondents' motion to dismiss the complaint, and the Court of Appeals for the Eighth Circuit affirmed, concluding that Sec. 1982 applies only to state action and does not reach private refusals to sell. . . . [W]e reverse the judgment of the Court of Appeals [and] hold that Sec. 1982 bars *all* racial discrimination, private as well as public, in the sale or rental of property, and that the statute, thus construed, is a valid exercise of the power of Congress to enforce the Thirteenth Amendment.

At the outset, it is important to make clear precisely what this case does *not* involve. Whatever else it may be, 42 U.S.C. Sec. 1982 is not a comprehensive open housing law. In sharp contrast to the Fair Housing Title (Title VIII) of the Civil Rights Act of 1968 . . . the statute in this case deals only with racial discrimination and does not address itself to discrimination on grounds of religion or national origin. It does not deal specifically with discrimination in the provision of services or facilities in connection with the sale or rental of a dwelling. It does not prohibit advertising or other representations that indicate discriminatory preferences. It does not refer explicitly to discrimination in financing arrangements or in the provision of brokerage services. It does not empower a federal administrative agency to assist aggrieved parties. It makes no provision for intervention by the Attorney General. And, although it can be enforced by injunction, it contains no provision expressly authorizing a federal court to order the payment of damages.

Thus, although Sec. 1982 contains none of the exemptions that Congress included in the Civil Rights Act of 1968, it would be a serious mistake to suppose that Sec. 1982 in any way diminishes the significance of the law recently enacted by Congress. . . .

. . . [T]he Civil Rights Act of 1968 . . . underscored the vast differences between, on the one hand, a general statute applicable only to racial discrimination in the rental and sale of property and enforceable only by private parties acting on their own initiative, and, on the other hand, a detailed housing law, applicable to a broad range of discriminatory practices and enforceable by a complete arsenal of federal authority. Having noted these differences, we turn to a consideration of Sec. 1982 itself.

This Court has had occasion to consider the scope of 42 U.S.C. Sec. 1982 in 1948, in *Hurd* v. *Hodge, 334 U.S. 24.* That case arose when property owners in the District of Columbia sought to enforce racially restrictive convenants against the Negro purchasers of several homes in their block. A federal district court enforced the restrictive agreements by declaring void the deeds of the Negro purchasers. It enjoined further attempts to sell or lease them the properties in question and directed them to "remove themselves and all of their personal belongings" from the premises within 60 days. The Court of Appeals for the District of Columbia affirmed, and this Court granted certiorari to decide whether Sec. 1982, . . . barred enforcement of the racially restrictive agreements in that case.

The agreements in *Hurd* covered only two-thirds of the lots of a single city block, and preventing Negroes from buying or renting homes in that specific area would not have rendered them ineligible to do so elsewhere in the city. Thus, if Sec. 1982 had been thought to do no more than grant Negro citizens the legal capacity to buy and rent property free of prohibitions that wholly disabled them because of their race, judicial enforcement of the restrictive covenants at issue would not have violated Sec. 1982. But this Court took a broader view of the statute. Although the covenants could have been enforced without denying the general right of Negroes to purchase or lease real estate, the enforcement of those covenants would nonetheless have denied the Negro purchasers "the same right 'as is enjoyed by white citizens . . . to inherit, purchase, lease, sell, hold, and convey real and personal property.' " 334 U.S., at 34. That result, this Court concluded, was prohibited by Sec. 1982. To suggest otherwise, the Court said, "is to reject the plain meaning of language." *Ibid.*

*Hurd* v. *Hodge* . . . squarely held, therefore, that a Negro citizen who is denied the opportunity to purchase the home he wants "[s]olely because of [his] race and color," 334 U.S., at 34, has suffered the kind of injury that Sec. 1982 was designed to prevent. . . . The basic source of the injury in *Hurd* was, of course, the action of private individuals—white citizens who had agreed to exclude Negroes from a residential area. But an arm of the Government—in that case, a federal court—had assisted in the enforcement of that agreement. Thus *Hurd* v. *Hodge,* . . . did not present the question whether *purely* private discrimination, unaided by any action on the part of government, would violate Sec. 1982 if its effects were to deny a citizen the right to rent or buy property solely because of his race or color.

The only federal court (other than the Court of Appeals in this case) that has ever squarely confronted that question held that a wholly private conspiracy among white citizens to prevent a Negro from leasing a farm violated Sec. 1982. *United States* v. *Morris,* 125 F. 322. It is true that a dictum in *Hurd* said that Sec. 1982 was directed only toward "governmental action," 334 U.S., at 31, but neither *Hurd* nor any other case before or since has presented that precise too much issue for adjudication in this Court. Today we face that issue for the first time.

We begin with the language of the statute itself. In plain and unambiguous terms, Sec. 1982 grants to all citizens, without regard to race or color, "the same right" to purchase and lease property "as is enjoyed by white citizens." As the Court of Appeals in this case evidently recognized, that right can be impaired as effectively by "those who place property on the market" as by the State itself. For, even if the State and its agents lend no support to those who wish to exclude persons from their communities on racial grounds, the fact remains that, whenever property "is placed on the market for whites only, whites have a right denied to Negroes." So long as a Negro citizen who wants to buy or rent a home can be turned away simply because he is not white, he cannot be said to enjoy "the *same* right . . . as is enjoyed by white citizens . . . to . . . purchase [and] lease . . . real and personal property." 42 U.S.C. Sec. 1982 (Emphasis added.)

On its face, therefore, Sec. 1982 appears to prohibit *all* discrimination against Negroes in the sale or rental of property—discrimination by private owners as well as discrimination by public authorities. Indeed, even the respondents seem to concede that, if Sec. 1982 "means what it says"—to use the words of the respondents' brief—then it must encompass every racially motivated refusal to sell or rent and cannot be confined to officially sanctioned segregation in housing. Stressing what they consider to be the revolutionary implications of so literal a reading of Sec. 1982, the respondents argue that Congress cannot possibly have intended any such result. Our examination of the relevant history, however, persuades us that Congress meant exactly what it said. [Here follows a review of the legislative history of the statute.]

. . .

As we said in a somewhat different setting two Terms ago, "We think that history leaves no doubt that, if we are to give [the law] the scope that its origins dictate, we must accord it a sweep as broad as its language." *United States* v. *Price*, 383 U.S. 787, 801. "We are not at liberty to seek ingenious analytical instruments," *ibid.*, to carve from Sec. 1982 an exception for private conduct—even though its application to such conduct in the present context is without established precedent. And, as the Attorney General of the United States said at the oral argument of this case, "The fact that the statute lay partially dormant for many years cannot be held to diminish its force today."

The remaining question is whether Congress has power under the Constitution to do what Sec. 1982 purports to do: to prohibit all racial discrimination, private and public, in the sale and rental of property. Our starting point is the Thirteenth Amendment, for it was pursuant to that constitutional provision that Congress originally enacted what is now Sec. 1982. The Amendment consists of two parts. Section 1 states:

Neither slavery nor involuntary servitude, except as a punishment for a crime whereof the party shall have been duly convicted, shall exist within the United States, or any place subject to their jurisdiction.

Section 2 provides:

Congress shall have power to enforce this article by appropriate legislation.

As its text reveals, the Thirteenth Amendment "is not a mere prohibition of State laws establishing or upholding slavery, but an absolute declaration that slavery or involuntary servitude shall not exist in any part of the United States." *Civil Rights Cases*, 109 U.S. 3, 20. It has never been doubted, therefore, "that the power vested in Congress to enforce the article by appropriate legislation,"

*ibid.*, includes the power to enact laws "direct and primary, operating upon the acts of individuals, whether sanctioned by State legislation or not." *Id.*, at 23.

Thus, the fact that Sec. 1982 operates upon the unofficial acts of private individuals, whether or not sanctioned by state law, presents no constitutional problems. If Congress has power under the Thirteenth Amendment to eradicate conditions that prevent Negroes from buying and renting property because of their race or color, then no federal statute calculated to achieve that objective can be thought to exceed the constitutional power of Congress simply because it reaches beyond state action to regulate the conduct to private individuals. The constitutional question in this case, therefore, comes to this: Does the authority of Congress to enforce the Thirteenth Amendment "by appropriate legislation" include the power to eliminate all racial barriers to the acquisition of real and personal property? We think the answer to that question is plainly yes.

"By its own unaided force and effect," the Thirteenth Amendment "abolished slavery, and established universal freedom." *Civil Rights Cases*, 109 U.S. 3, 20. Whether or not the Amendment *itself* did any more than that—a question not involved in this case—it is at least clear that the Enabling Clause of that Amendment empowered Congress to do much more. For that clause clothed "Congress with power to pass *all laws necessary and proper for abolishing all badges and incidents of slavery in the United States.*" *Ibid.* [Emphasis added by Justice Stewart.]

. . .

. . . Surely Congress has the power under the Thirteenth Amendment rationally to determine what are the badges and the incidents of slavery, and the authority to translate that determination into effective legislation. Nor can we say that the determination Congress has made is an irrational one. For this Court recognized long ago that, whatever else they may have encompassed, the badges and incidents of slavery—its "burdens and disabilities"—included restraints upon "those fundamental rights which are the essence of civil freedom, namely, the same right . . . to inherit, purchase, lease, sell and convey property, as is enjoyed by white citizens." *Civil Rights Cases,* 109 U.S. 3, 22. Just as the Black Codes, enacted after the Civil War to restrict the free exercise of those rights, were substitutes for the slave system, so the exclusion of Negroes from white communities became a substitute for the Black Codes. And when racial discrimination herds men into ghettos and makes their ability to buy property turn on the color of their skin, then it too is a relic of slavery.

Negro citizens North and South, who saw in the Thirteenth Amendment a promise of freedom—freedom to "go and come at pleasure" and to "buy and sell when they please"—would be left with "a mere paper guarantee" if Congress were powerless to assure that a dollar in the hands of a Negro will purchase the same thing as a dollar in the hands of a white man. At the very least, the freedom that Congress is empowered to secure under the Thirteenth Amendment includes the freedom to buy whatever a white man can buy, the right to live wherever a white man can live. If Congress cannot say that being a free man means at least this much, then the Thirteenth Amendment made a promise the Na-

tion cannot keep.

. . .

*The judgment is Reversed.*

MR. JUSTICE DOUGLAS, *concurring.*

. . .

Enabling a Negro to buy and sell real and personal property is a removal of one of many badges of slavery. . . .

The true curse of slavery is not what it did to the black man, but what it has done to the white man. For the existence of the institution produced the notion that the white man was a superior character, intelligence, and morality. The blacks were little more than livestock—to be fed and fattened for the economic benefits they could bestow through their labors, and to be subjected to authority, often with cruelty, to make clear who was master and who slave.

Some badges of slavery remain today. While the institution has been outlawed, it has remained in the minds and hearts of many white men. Cases which have come to this Court depict a spectacle of slavery unwilling to die. We have seen contrivances by States designed to thwart Negro voting, *e.g., Lane* v. *Wilson,* 307 U.S. 268. Negroes have been excluded over and again from juries solely on account of their race, *e.g., Strauder* v. *West Virginia,* 100 U.S. 303, or have been forced to sit in segregated seats in court rooms, *Johnson* v. *Virginia,* 373 U.S. 61. They have been made to attend segregated and inferior schools, *e.g., Brown* v. *Board of Education,* 347 U.S. 483, or been denied entrance to colleges or graduate schools because of their color, *e.g., Pennsylvania* v. *Board of Trusts,* 353 U.S. 230; *Sweatt* v. *Painter,* 339 U.S. 629. Negroes have been prosecuted for marrying whites, *e.g., Loving* v. *Virginia,* 388 U.S. 1. They have been forced to live in segregated residential districts, *Buchanan* v. *Warley,* 245 U.S. 60, and residents of white neighborhoods have denied them entrance, *e.g., Shelley* v. *Kraemer,* 334 U.S. 1. Negroes have been forced to use segregated facilities in going about their daily lives, being excluded from railway coaches, *Plessy* v. *Ferguson,* 163 U.S. 537; public parks, *New Orleans* v. *Detiege,* 358 U.S. 54; restaurants, *Lombard* v. *Louisiana,* 373 U.S. 267; public beaches, *Mayor of Baltimore* v. *Dawson,* 350 U.S. 877; municipal golf courses, *Holmes* v. *City of Atlanta,* 350 U.S. 879; amusement parks, *Griffin* v. *Maryland,* 378 U.S. 130; busses, *Gayle* v. *Browder,* 352 U.S. 903; public libraries, *Brown* v. *Louisiana,* 383 U.S. 131. A state court judge in Alabama convicted a Negro woman of contempt of court because she refused to answer him when he addressed her as "Mary," although she had made the simple request to be called "Miss Hamilton." *Hamilton* v. *Alabama,* 376 U.S. 650.

That brief sampling of discriminatory practices, many of which continue today, stands almost as an annotation to what Frederick Douglass (1817–1895) wrote a century earlier:

Of all the races and varieties of men which have suffered from this feeling, the colored people of this country have endured most. They can resort to no disguises which will enable them to escape its deadly aim. They carry in front the evidence which marks them for persecution. They stand at the extreme point of difference from the Caucasian race, and their African origin can be instantly recognized, though they may be several removes from the typical African race. They may remonstrate like Shylock—"Hath not a Jew eyes? hath not a Jew hands, organs, dimensions, senses, affections, passions? fed with the same food, hurt with the same weapons, subject to the same dis-

eases, healed by the same means, warmed and cooled by the same summer and winter, as a Christian is?"—but such eloquence is unavailing. They are Negroes —and that is enough, in the eye of this unreasoning prejudice, to justify indignity and violence. In nearly every department of American life they are confronted by this insidious influence. It fills the air. It meets them at the workshop and factory, when they apply for work. It meets them at the church, at the hotel, at the ballot-box, and worst of all, it meets them in the jury-box. Without crime or offense against law or gospel, the colored man is the Jean Valjean of American society. He has escaped from the galleys, and hence all presumptions are against him. The workshop denies him work, and the inn denies him shelter; the ballot-box a fair vote, and the jury-box a fair trial. He has ceased to be the slave of an individual, but has in some sense become the slave of society. He may not now be bought and sold like a beast in the market, but he is the trammeled victim of a prejudice, well calculated to repress his manly ambition, paralyze his energies, and make him a dejected and spiritless man, if not a sullen enemy to society, fit to prey upon life and property and to make trouble generally.*

Today the black is protected by a host of civil rights laws. But the forces of discrimination are still strong.

A member of his race, duly elected by the people to a state legislature, is barred from that assembly because of his views on the Vietnam war. *Bond* v. *Floyd,* 385 U.S. 116.

Real estate agents use artifice to avoid selling "white property" to the blacks. The blacks who travel the country, though entitled by law to the facilities for sleeping and dining that are offered all tourists, *Heart of*

* Excerpt from Frederick Douglass, The Color Line, The North American Review, June 1881, IV The Life and Writings of Frederick Douglass, 343–344 (1955).

*Atlanta Motel* v. *United States,* 379 U.S. 241, may well learn that the "vacancy" sign does not mean what it says, especially if the motel has a swimming pool.

On entering a half-empty restaurant they may find "reserved" signs on all unoccupied tables.

The black is often barred from a labor union because of his race.

He learns that the order directing admission of his children into white schools has not been obeyed "with all deliberate speed," *Brown* v. *Board of Education,* 349 U.S. 294, 301, but has been delayed by numerous strategies and devices." State laws, at times, have even encouraged discrimination in housing. *Reitman* v. *Mulkey,* 387 U.S. 369.

This recital is enough to show how prejudices, once part and parcel of slavery, still persist. The men who sat in Congress in 1866 were trying to remove some of the badges or "customs" of slavery when they enacted Sec. 1982. And, as my Brother STEWART shows, the Congress that passed the so-called Open Housing Act of 1968 did not undercut any of the grounds on which Sec. 1982 rests.

MR. JUSTICE HARLAN, *whom* MR. JUSTICE WHITE *joins, dissenting.*

The decision in this case appears to me to be the most ill-considered and ill-advised.

. . .

. . . I believe that the Court's construction of Sec. 1982 as applying to purely private action is almost surely wrong, and at the least is open to serious doubt. The issue of constitutionality of Sec. 1982, as construed by the Court, and of liability under the Fourteenth Amendment alone, also present formidable difficulties. Moreover, the political processes of our own era have, since the date of oral argument in this case, given birth to a civil rights statute embodying "fair housing" provisions which would at the end of this year make available to others, though apparently not to the petitioners themselves, the type of relief which the petitioners now seek. It seems to me that this latter factor so diminishes the public importance of this case that by far the wisest course would be for this Court to refrain from decision and to dismiss the writ as improvidently granted.

I shall deal first with the Court's construction of Sec. 1982, which lies at the heart of its opinion. . . .

The Court's opinion focuses upon the statute's legislative history, but it is worthy of note that the precedents in this Court are distinctly opposed to the Court's view of the statute.

In the *Civil Rights Cases,* 109 U.S. 3, decided less than two decades after the enactment of the Civil Rights Act of 1866, from which Sec. 1982 is derived, the Court said in dictum of the 1866 Act:

This law is clearly corrective in its character, intended to counteract and furnish redress against State laws and proceedings, and customs having the force of law, which sanction the wrongful acts specified. . . . The Civil Rights Bill here referred to is analogous in its character to what a law would have been under the original Constitution, declaring that the validity of contracts should not be impaired, and that if any person bound by a contract should refuse to comply with it, under color or pretence that it had been rendered void or invalid by a State law, he should be liable in an action upon it in the courts of the United States, with the addition of a penalty for setting up such an unjust and unconstitutional defence. *Id.,* at 16-17.

In *Corrigan* v. *Buckley,* 271 U.S. 323, the question was whether the courts of the District of Columbia might enjoin prospective breaches of racially restrictive covenants. The Court held that it was without jurisdiction to consider the petitioners' argument that the covenant was void because it contravened the Fifth, Thirteenth, and Fourteenth Amendments and their implementing statutes. . . . In *Hurd* v. *Hodge*, 334 U.S. 24, the issue was again whether the courts of the District might enforce racially restrictive covenants. At the outset of the process of reasoning by which it held that judicial enforcement of such a covenant would violate the predecessor to Sec. 1982, the Court said:

We may start with the proposition that the statute does not invalidate private restrictive agreements so long as the purpose of those agreements are achieved by the parties through voluntary adherence to the terms. The action toward which the provisions of the statute under consideration is [*sic*] directed is governmental action. . . .

Like the Court, I begin analysis of Sec. 1982 by examining its language. In its present form, the section provides:

All citizens of the United States shall have the same right, in every State and Territory, as is enjoyed by white citizens thereof to inherit, purchase, lease, sell, hold and convey real and personal property.

The Court finds it "plain and unambiguous," . . . that this language forbids purely private as well as state-authorized discrimination. With all respect, I do not find it so. For me, there is an inherent ambiguity in the term "right," as used in Sec. 1982. The "right" referred to may either be a right to equal status under law, in which case the statute operates only against state-sanctioned discrimination, or it may be an "absolute" right

enforceable against private individuals. To me, the words of the statute, taken alone, suggest the former interpretation, not the latter.

Further, since intervening revisions have not been meant to alter substance, the intended meaning of Sec. 1982 must be drawn from the words in which it was originally enacted. Section 1982 originally was a part of Section 1 of the Civil Rights Act of 1866. . . . Sections 1 and 2 of that Act provided in relevant part:

That all persons born in the United States and not subject to any foreign power . . . are hereby declared to be citizens of the United States; and such citizens, of every race and color . . . , shall have the same right, in every State and Territory in the United States, . . . to inherit, purchase, lease, sell, hold and convey real and personal property . . . as is enjoyed by white citizens, and shall be subject to like punishments, pains, and penalties, and to none other, any law, statute, ordinance, regulation, or custom, to the contrary notwithstanding.

Sec. 2. . . . That any person who, under color of any law, statute, ordinance, regulation, or custom, shall subject, or cause to be subjected, any inhabitant of any State or Territory to the deprivation of any right secured or protected by this act . . . shall be deemed guilty of a misdemeanor. . . .

It seems to me that this original wording indicates even more strongly than the present language that Sec. 1 of the Act (as well as Sec. 2, which is explicitly so limited) was intended to apply only to action taken pursuant to state or community authority, in the form of a "law, statute, ordinance, regulation, or custom." . . .

[Here follows an examination of the legislative history of the statute to show that the debates do not overwhelmingly support the majority's interpretation.]

. . .

The . . . analysis of the language, structure, and legislative history of the 1866 Civil Rights Act shows, I believe, that the Court's thesis that the Act was meant to extend to purely private action is open to the most serious doubt, if indeed it does not render that thesis wholly untenable. Another, albeit less tangible, consideration points in the same direction. Many of the legislators who took part in the congressional debates inevitably must have shared the individualistic ethic of their time, which emphasized personal freedom and embodies a distaste for governmental interference which was soon to culminate in the era of laissez-faire. It seems to me that most of these men would have regarded it as a great intrusion on individual liberty for the Government to take from a man the power to refuse for personal reasons to enter into purely private transaction involving the disposition of property, albeit those personal reasons might reflect racial bias. It should be remembered that racial prejudice was not uncommon in 1866, even outside the South. Although Massachusetts had recently enacted the Nation's first law prohibiting racial discrimination in public accommodations, Negroes could not ride within Philadelphia streetcars or attend public schools with white children in New York City. Only five States accorded equal voting rights to Negroes, and it appears that Negroes were allowed to serve on juries only in Massachusetts. Residential segregation was the prevailing pattern almost everywhere in the North. There were no state "fair housing" laws in 1866, and it appears that none has ever been proposed. In this historical context, I cannot conceive that a bill thought to prohibit purely private discrimination not only in the sale or rental of housing but in *all* property transactions would not have received a great deal of criticism explicitly directed to this feature. The fact that the 1866 Act received *no* criticism of this kind is for me strong additional evidence that it was not regarded as extending so far.

In sum, the most which can be said with assurance about the intended impact of the 1866 Civil Rights Act upon purely private discrimination is that the Act probably was envisioned by most members of Congress as prohibiting official, community-sanctioned discrimination in the South, engaged in pursuant to local "customs" which in the recent time of slavery probably were embodied in laws or regulations. . . .Adoption of a "state action" construction of the Civil Rights Act would therefore have the additional merit of bringing its interpretation into line with that of the Fourteenth Amendment, which this Court has consistently held to reach only "state action." This seems especially desirable in light of the Fourteenth Amendment, at least in the minds of its congressional proponents, was to assure that the rights conferred by the then recently enacted Civil Rights Act could not be taken away by a subsequent Congress.

The foregoing, I think, amply demonstrates that the Court has chosen to resolve this case by according to a loosely worded statute a meaning which is open to the strongest challenge in light of the statute's legislative history.

. . .

The fact that a case is "hard" does not, of course, relieve a judge of his duty to decide it. Since, the Court did vote to hear this case, I normally would consider myself obligated to decide whether the petitioners are entitled to relief on either of the grounds on which they rely. After mature reflection, however, I have concluded that this is one of those rare instances in which an event which occurs after the hearing of argument so diminishes a case's public significance, when viewed in light of the difficulty of the questions presented as to justify this Court in dismissing the writ as improvidently granted.

The occurrence to which I refer is the recent enactment of the Civil Rights Act of 1968. . . . Title VIII of that Act contains comprehensive "fair housing" provisions, which by the terms of Sec. 803 will become applicable on January 1, 1969, to persons who, like the petitioners, attempt to buy houses from developers. Under those provisions, such persons will be entitled to injunctive relief and damages from developers who refuse to sell to them on account of race or color, unless the parties are able to resolve their dispute by other means. Thus, the type of relief which the petitioners seek will be available within seven months time under the terms of a presumptively constitutional Act of Congress. In these circumstances, it seems obvious that the case has lost most of its public importance, and I believe that it would be much the wiser course for this Court to refrain from deciding it. I think it particularly unfortunate for the Court to persist in deciding this case on the basis of a highly questionable interpretation of a sweeping, century-old statute which, as the Court acknowledges . . . contains none of the exemptions which the Congress of our own time found it necessary to

include in a statute regulating relationships so personal in nature. In effect, this Court, by its construction of Sec. 1982, has extended the coverage of federal "fair housing" laws far beyond that which Congress in its wisdom chose to provide in the Civil Rights Act of 1968. The political process now having taken hold again in this very field, I am at a loss to understand why the Court should have deemed it appropriate or, in the circumstances of this case, necessary to proceed with such precipitous and insecure strides.

I am not dissuaded from my view by the circumstance that the 1968 Act was enacted after oral argument in this case, at a time when the parties and *amici curiae* had invested time and money in anticipation of a decision on the merits, or by the fact that the 1968 Act apparently will not entitle these petitioners to the relief which they seek. For the certiorari jurisdiction was not conferred upon this Court "merely to give the defeated party in the . . . Court of Appeals another hearing," *Magnum Co.* v. *Coty,* 262 U.S. 159, 164, or "for the benefit of the particular litigants," *Rice* v. *Sioux City Cemetery,* 349 U.S. 70, 74, but to decide issues, "the settlement of which is important to the public as distinguished from . . . the parties," *Layne & Bowler Corp.* v. *Western Well Works, Inc.,* 261 U.S. 387, 393. I deem it far more important that this Court should avoid, if possible, the decision of constitutional and unusually difficult statutory questions than that we fulfill the expectations of every litigant who appears before us.

# GOMILLION v. LIGHTFOOT

364 U. S. 339; 5 L. Ed. 2d 110; 81 S. Ct. 125 (1960)

MR. JUSTICE FRANKFURTER *delivered the opinion of the Court.*

This litigation challenges the validity, under the United States Constitution, of Local Act No. 140, passed by the Legislature of Alabama in 1957, redefining the boundaries of the City of Tuskegee. Petitioners, Negro citizens of Alabama who were, at the time of this redistricting measure, residents of the City of Tuskegee, brought an action in the United States District Court for the Middle District of Alabama for a declaratory judgment that Act 140 is unconstitutional, and for an injunction to restrain the Mayor and officers of Tuskegee and the officials of Macon County, Alabama, from enforcing the Act against them and other Negroes similarly situated. Petitioners' claim is that enforcement of the statute . . . will constitute a discrimination against them in violation of the Due Process and Equal Protection Clauses of the Fourteenth Amendment to the Constitution and will deny them the right to vote in defiance of the Fifteenth Amendment.

The respondents moved for dismissal of the action for failure to state a claim upon which relief could be granted and for lack of jurisdiction of the District Court. The court granted the motion, stating, "This Court has no control over, no supervision over, and no power to change any boundaries of municipal corporations fixed by a duly convened and elected legislative body, acting for the people of the State of Alabama." . . . On appeal, the Court of Appeals for the Fifth Circuit, affirmed the judgment, one judge dissenting. . . . We brought the case here since serious questions were raised concerning the power of a State over its municipalities in relation to the Fourteenth and Fifteenth Amendments. . . .

. . . The sole question is whether the allegations entitle . . . [petitioners] to make good on their claim that they are being denied rights under the United States Constitution. The complaint . . . allege[s] the following facts: Prior to Act 140 the City of Tuskegee was square in shape; the Act transformed it into a strangely irregular twenty-eight-sided figure. . . . The essential inevitable effect of this redefinition of Tuskegee's boundaries is to remove from the city all save only four or five of its 400 Negro voters while not removing a single white voter or resident. The result of the Act is to deprive the Negro petitioners discriminatorily of the benefits of residence in Tuskegee, including, inter alia, the right to vote in municipal elections.

These allegations, if proven, would abundantly establish that Act 140 was not an ordinary geographic redistricting measure even within familiar abuses of gerrymandering. If these allegations upon a trial remained uncontradicted or unqualified, the conclusion would be irresistible, tantamount for all practical purposes to a mathematical demonstration, that the legislation is solely concerned with segregating white and colored voters by fencing Negro citizens out of town so as to deprive them of their preexisting municipal vote.

It is difficult to appreciate what stands in the way of adjudging a statute having this inevitable effect invalid in light of the principles by which this Court must judge, and uniformly has judged, statutes that, however speciously defined, obviously discriminate against colored citizens. "The (Fifteenth) Amendment nullifies sophisticated as well as simple-minded modes of discrimination." *Lane* v. *Wilson*, 307 U.S. 268, 275. . . .

The complaint amply alleges a claim of racial discrimination. Against this claim the respondents have never suggested, either in their brief or in oral argument, any countervailing municipal function which Act 140 is designed to serve. The respondents invoke generalities expressing the State's unrestricted power—unlimited, that is, by the United States Constitution—to establish, destroy, or reorganize by contraction or expansion its political subdivisions, to wit, cities, counties, and other local units. We freely recognize the breadth and importance of this aspect of the State's political power. To exalt this power into an absolute is to misconceive the reach and rule of this Court's decisions. . . .

. . .

. . . [T]he cases that have come before this Court regarding legislation by States dealing with their political subdivisions fall into two classes: (1) those in which it is claimed that the State, by virtue of the prohibition against impairment of the obligation of contract (Art 1, Sec. 10) and of the Due Process Clause of the Fourteenth Amendment, is without power to extinguish, or alter the boundaries of, an existing municipality; and (2) in which it is claimed that the State has no power to change the identity of a municipality whereby citizens of a pre-existing municipality suffer serious economic disadvantages.

Neither of these claims is supported by such a specific limitation upon State power as confines the States under the Fifteenth Amendment. As to the first category, it is obvious that the creation of municipalities— clearly a political act—does not come within the conception of a contract under the Dartmouth College Case. . . . As to the second, if one principle clearly emerges from the numerous decisions of this Court dealing with taxation it is that the Due Process Clause affords no immunity against mere inequalities in tax burdens, nor does it afford protection against their increase as an indirect consequence of a State's exercise of its political powers.

Particularly in dealing with claims under broad provisions of the Constitution, which derive content by an interpretive process of inclusion and exclusion, it is imperative that generalizations, based on and qualified by the concrete situations that gave rise to them, must not be applied out of context in disregard of variant controlling facts. Thus, a correct reading of . . . kindred cases is not that the State has plenary power to manipulate in every conceivable way, for every conceivable purpose, the affairs of its municipal corporations, but rather that the State's authority is unrestrained by the particular prohibitions of the Constitution considered in those cases.

. . .

. . . [T]he Court has never acknowledged that the States have power to do as they will with municipal corporations regardless of consequences. Legislative control of municipalities, no less than other state power, lies within the scope of relevant limitations imposed by the

United States Constitution.

. . .

The respondents find another barrier to the trial of this case in *Colegrove* v. *Green,* 328 U.S. 549. . . . In that case the Court passed on an Illinois law governing the arrangement of congressional districts within that State. The complaint rested upon the disparity of population between the different districts which rendered the effectiveness of each individual's vote in some districts far less than in others. This disparity came to pass solely through shifts in population between 1901, when Illinois organized its congressional districts, and 1946, when the complaint was lodged. During this entire period elections were held under the districting scheme devised in 1901. The Court affirmed the dismissal of the complaint on the ground that it presented a subject not meet for adjudication. The decisive facts in this case . . . are wholly different from the considerations found controlling in *Colegrove.*

. . . The petitioners here complain that affirmative legislative action deprives them of their votes and the consequent advantages that the ballot affords. When a legislature thus singles out a readily isolated segment of a racial minority for special discriminatory treatment, it violates the Fifteenth Amendment. In no case involving unequal weight in voting distribution that has come before the Court did the decision sanction a differentiation on racial lines whereby approval was given to unequivocal withdrawal of the vote solely from colored citizens. Apart from all else, these considerations lift this controversy out of the so-called "political" arena and into the conventional sphere of constitutional litigation.

. . . A statute which is alleged to have worked unconstitutional depriva-

tions of petitioners' rights is not immune to attack simply because the mechanism employed by the legislature is a redefinition of municipal boundaries. According to the allegations here made, the Alabama Legislature has not merely redrawn the Tuskegee city limits with incidental inconvenience to the petitioners; it is more accurate to say that it has deprived the petitioners of the municipal franchise and consequent rights and to that end it has incidentally changed the city's boundaries. While in form this is merely an act redefining metes and bounds, if the allegations are established, the inescapable human effect of this essay is to despoil colored citizens and only colored citizens, of their theretofore enjoyed voting rights. That was not *Colegrove* v. *Green.*

When a State exercises power wholly within the domain of state interest, it is insulated from federal judicial view. But such insulation is not carried over when the state power is used as an instrument for circumventing a federally protected right. . . .

For these reasons, the principal conclusions of the District Court and the Court of Appeals are clearly erroneous and the decision below must be reversed.

Mr. Justice Whittaker, *concurring.*

I concur in the Court's judgment, but not in the whole of its opinion. It seems to me that the decision should be rested not on the Fifteenth Amendment, but rather on the Equal Protection Clause of the Fourteenth Amendment to the Constitution. I am doubtful that the averments of the complaint, taken for present purposes to be true, show a purpose by

Act No. 140 to abridge petitioners' "right . . . to vote," in the Fifteenth Amendment sense. It seems to me that the "right . . . to vote" that is guaranteed by the Fifteenth Amendment is but the same right to vote as is enjoyed by all others within the same election precinct, ward or other political division. And, inasmuch as no one has the right to vote in a political division, or in a local election concerning only an area in which he does not reside, it would seem to follow that one's right to vote in Division A is not abridged by a redistricting that places his residence in Division B *if* he there enjoys the same voting privileges as all others in that Division, even though the redistricting was done by the State for the purpose of placing a racial group of citizens in Division B rather than A.

But it does seem clear to me that accomplishment of a State's purpose— to use the Court's phrase—of "fencing Negro citizens out of" Division A and into Division B is an unlawful segregation of races of citizens, in violation of the Equal Protection Clause of the Fourteenth Amendment . . . and, . . . I would think the decision should be rested on that ground. . . .

## SOUTH CAROLINA v. KATZENBACH

383 U. S. 301; 15 L. Ed. 769; 86 S. Ct. 803 (1966)

MR. CHIEF JUSTICE WARREN *delivered the opinion of the Court.*

By leave of the Court . . . South Carolina has filed a bill of complaint, seeking a declaration that selected provisions of the Voting Rights Act of 1965 violate the Federal Constitution, and asking for an injunction against enforcement of these provisions by the Attorney General. . . .

Recognizing that the questions presented were of urgent concern to the entire country, we invited all of the States to participate in this proceeding as friends of the Court. A majority responded by submitting or joining in briefs on the merits, some supporting South Carolina and others the Attorney General.* Seven of these

States also requested and received permission to argue the case orally at our hearing. Without exception, despite the emotional overtones of the proceeding, the briefs and oral arguments were temperate, lawyerlike and constructive. . . .

The Voting Rights Act was designed by Congress to banish the blight of racial discrimination in voting, which has infected the electoral process in parts of our country for nearly a century. The Act creates stringent new remedies for voting discrimination where it persists on a pervasive scale, and in addition the statute strengthens existing remedies for pockets of voting discrimination elsewhere in the country. Congress assumed the power to prescribe these

* States supporting South Carolina: Alabama, Georgia, Louisiana, Mississippi, and Virginia. States supporting the Attorney General: California, Illinois, and Massachusetts, joined by Hawaii, Indiana, Iowa, Kansas, Maine, Maryland, Michigan, Montana, New Hampshire, New Jersey, New York, Oklahoma, Oregon, Pennsylvania, Rhode Island, Vermont, West Virginia, and Wisconsin.

remedies from section 2 of the Fifteenth Amendment, which authorizes the National Legislature to effectuate by "appropriate" measures the constitutional prohibition against racial discrimination in voting. We hold that the sections of the Act which are properly before us are an appropriate means for carrying out Congress' constitutional responsibilities and are consonant with all other provisions of the Constitution. We therefore deny South Carolina's request that enforcement of these sections of the Act be enjoined.

The constitutional propriety of the Voting Rights Act of 1965 must be judged with reference to the historical experience which it reflects. Before enacting the measure, Congress explored with great care the problem of racial discrimination in voting. . . . At the close of . . . deliberations, the verdict of both chambers was overwhelming. The House approved the bill by a vote of 328–74, and the measure passed the Senate by a margin of 79–18.

Two points emerge vividly from the voluminous legislative history of the Act contained in the committee hearings and the floor debates. First: Congress felt itself confronted by an insidious and pervasive evil which had been perpetuated in certain parts of our country through unremitting and ingenious defiance of the Constitution. Second: Congress concluded that the unsuccessful remedies which it had prescribed in the past would have to be replaced by sterner and more elaborate measures in order to satisfy the clear commands of the Fifteenth Amendment. . . .

[Here followed a review of Congressional remedies from 1870 to 1964.]

. . .

Despite the earnest efforts of the Justice Department and of many federal judges, these new laws [enacted in 1956, 1960 and 1964] have done little to cure the problem of voting discrimination. According to estimates by the Attorney General during hearings on the Act, registration of voting-age Negroes in Alabama rose only from 14.2% to 19.4% between 1958 and 1964; in Louisiana it barely inched ahead from 31.7% to 31.8% between 1956 and 1965; and in Mississippi it increased only from 4.4% to 6.4% between 1954 and 1964. In each instance, registration of voting-age whites ran roughly 50 percentage points or more ahead of Negro registration.

The previous legislation has proved ineffective for a number of reasons. Voting suits are unusually onerous to prepare, sometimes requiring as many as 6,000 man-hours spent combing through registration records in preparation for trial. Litigation has been exceedingly slow, in part because of the ample opportunities for delay afforded voting officials and others involved in the proceedings. Even when favorable decisions have finally been obtained, some of the States affected have merely switched to discriminatory devices not covered by the federal decrees or have enacted difficult new tests designed to prolong the existing disparity between white and Negro registration. Alternatively, certain local officials have defied and evaded court orders or have simply closed their registration offices to freeze the voting rolls. The provision of the 1960 law authorizing registration by federal officers has had little impact on local maladministration because of its procedural complexities.

. . .

The Voting Rights Act of 1965 reflects Congress' firm intention to rid the country of racial discrimination in voting. The heart of the Act is a complex scheme of stringent remedies aimed at areas where voting discrimination has been most flagrant. Section 4(a)–(d) lays down a formula defining the States and political subdivision to which these new remedies apply. The first of the remedies, contained in section 4(a), is the suspension of literacy tests and similar voting qualifications for a period of five years from the last occurrence of substantial voting discrimination. Section 5 prescribes a second remedy, the suspension of all new voting regulations pending review by federal authorities to determine whether their use would perpetuate voting discrimination. The third remedy, covered in sections 6(b), 7, 9, and 13(a), is the assignment of federal examiners on certification by the Attorney General to list qualified applicants who are thereafter entitled to vote in all elections.

Other provisions of the Act prescribe subsidiary cures for persistent voting discrimination. Section 8 authorizes the appointment of federal poll-watchers in places to which federal examiners have already been assigned. Section 10(d) excuses those made eligible to vote in sections of the country covered by section 4(b) of the Act from paying accumulated past poll taxes for state and local elections. Section 12(e) provides for balloting by persons denied access to the polls in areas where federal examiners have been appointed.

The remaining remedial portions of the Act are aimed at voting discrimination in any area of the country where it may occur. Section 2 broadly prohibits the use of voting rules to abridge exercise of the franchise on racial grounds. Sections 3, 6(a), and 13(b) strengthen existing procedures for attacking voting dis-

crimination by means of litigation. Section 4(e) excuses citizens educated in American schools conducted in a foreign language from passing English-language literacy tests. Section 10(a)–(c) facilitates constitutional litigation challenging the imposition of all poll taxes for state and local elections. Sections 11 and 12(a)–(d) authorize civil and criminal sanctions against interference with the exercise of rights guaranteed by the Act.

. . . The only sections of the Act to be reviewed at this time are sections 4(a)–(d), 5, 6(b), 7, 9, 13(a), and certain procedural portions of section 14, all of which are presently in actual operation in South Carolina. We turn now to a . . . description of these provisions and their present status.

### COVERAGE FORMULA

The remedial sections of the Act assailed by South Carolina automatically apply to any State, or to any separate political subdivision such as a county or parish, for which two findings have been made: (1) the Attorney General has determined that on November 1, 1964, it maintained a "test or device," and (2) the Director of the Census has determined that less than 50% of its voting-age residents were registered on November 1, 1964, or voted in the presidential election of 1964. These findings are not reviewable in any court and are final upon publication in the Federal Register.

. . .

South Carolina was brought within the coverage formula of the Act on August 7, 1965, pursuant to appropriate administrative determinations which have not been challenged in this proceeding. On the same day, coverage was also extended to Alabama, Alaska, Georgia, Louisiana,

Mississippi, Virginia, 26 counties in North Carolina, and one county in Arizona. Two more counties in Arizona, one county in Hawaii, and one county in Idaho were added to the list on November 19, 1965. Thus far Alaska, the three Arizona counties, and the single county in Idaho have asked the District Court for the District of Columbia to grant a declaratory judgment terminating statutory coverage.

## SUSPENSION OF TESTS

In a State or political subdivision covered by section 4(b) of the Act, no person may be denied the right to vote in any election because of his failure to comply with a "test or device." Secton 4(a).

On account of this provision, South Carolina is temporarily barred from enforcing the portion of its voting laws which requires every applicant for registration to show that he:

Can both read and write any section of [the State] Constitution submitted to [him] by the registration officer or can show that he owns, and has paid all taxes collectible during the previous year on, property in this State assessed at three hundred dollars or more. SC Code Ann. section 23-62(4) (1965 Supp.).

The Attorney General has determined that the property qualification is inseparable from the literacy test, and South Carolina makes no objection to this finding. Similar tests and devices have been temporarily suspended in the other sections of the country listed above.

## REVIEW OF NEW RULES

In a State or political subdivision covered by section 4(b) of the Act, no person may be denied the right to vote in any election because of his failure to comply with a voting qualification or procedure different from those in force on November 1, 1964. This suspension of new rules is terminated, however, under either of the following circumstances: (1) if the area has submitted the rules to the Attorney General, and he had not interposed an objection within 60 days, or (2) if the area has obtained a declaratory judgment from the District Court for the District of Columbia, determining that the rules will not abridge the franchise on racial grounds. . . .

South Carolina altered its voting laws in 1965 to extend the closing hour at polling places from 6 P.M. to 7 P.M. . . . the Attorney General . . . does not challenge the amendment. There are indications in the record that other sections of the country listed above have also altered their voting laws since November 1, 1964.

## FEDERAL EXAMINERS

In any political subdivision covered by section 4(b) of the Act, the Civil Service Commission shall appoint voting examiners whenever the Attorney General certifies either of the following facts: (1) that he has received meritorious written complaints from at least 20 residents alleging that they have been disenfranchised under color of law because of their race, or (2) that the appointment of examiners is otherwise necessary to effectuate the guarantees of the Fifteenth Amendment. In making the latter determination, the Attorney General must consider, among other factors, whether the registration ratio of non-whites to whites seems reasonably attributable to racial discrimination, or whether there is substantial evidence of good-faith efforts to comply with the Fifteenth Amendment. . . .

. . . Any person who meets the voting requirements of state law, insofar as these have not been suspended by the Act, must promptly be placed on a list of eligible voters. . . . Any person listed by an examiner is entitled to vote in all elections held more than 45 days after his name has been transmitted. . . .

On October 30, 1965, the Attorney General certified the need for federal examiners in two South Carolina counties, and examiners appointed by the Civil Service Commission have been serving there since November 8, 1965. Examiners have also been assigned to 11 counties in Alabama, five parishes in Louisiana, and 19 counties in Mississippi. . . .

These provisions of the Voting Rights Act of 1965 are challenged on the fundamental ground that they exceed the powers of Congress and encroach on an area reserved to the States by the Constitution. South Carolina and certain of the amici curiae also attack specific sections of the Act for more particular reasons. They argue that the coverage formula prescribed in section 4(a)–(d) violates the principle of the equality of States, denies due process by employing an invalid presumption and by barring judicial review of administrative findings, constitutes a forbidden bill of attainder, and impairs the separation of powers by adjudicating guilt through legislation. They claim that the review of new voting rules required in section 5 infringes Article III by directing the District Court to issue advisory opinions. They contend that the assignment of federal examiners authorized in section 6(b) abridges due process by precluding judicial review of administrative findings and impairs the separation of

powers by giving the Attorney General judicial functions; also that the challenge procedure prescribed in section 9 denies due process on account of its speed. Finally, South Carolina and certain of the amici curiae maintain that sections 4(a) and 5, buttressed by section 14(b) of the Act, abridge due process by limiting litigation to a distant forum.

. . . The objections to the Act which are raised under these provisions may . . . be considered only as additional aspects of the basic question presented by the case: Has Congress exercised its powers under the Fifteenth Amendment in an appropriate manner with relation to the States?

The ground rules for resolving this question are clear. The language and purpose of the Fifteenth Amendment, the prior decisions construing its several provisions, and the general doctrines of constitutional interpretation, all point to one fundamental principle. As against the reserved powers of the States, Congress may use any rational means to effectuate the constitutional prohibition of racial discrimination in voting. . . .

Section 1 of the Fifteenth Amendment declares that "[t]he right of citizens of the United States to vote shall not be denied or abridged by the United States or by any State on account of race, color, or previous condition of servitude." This declaration has always been treated as self-executing and has repeatedly been construed, without further legislative specification, to invalidate state voting qualifications or procedures which are discriminatory on their face or in practice. . . . [S]tates "have broad powers to determine the conditions under which the right of suffrage may be exercised." [However,] [t]he gist of the matter is that the Fifteenth

Amendment supersedes contrary exertions of state power. "When a State exercised power wholly within the domain of state interest, it is insulated from federal judicial review. But such insulation is not carried over when state power is used as an instrument for circumventing a federally protected right." *Gomillion* v. *Lightfoot*, 364 U.S., at 347. . . .

South Carolina contends that the [previous] cases are precedents only for the authority of the judiciary to strike down state statutes and procedures—that to allow an exercise of this authority by Congress would be to rob the courts of their rightful constitutional role. On the contrary, section 2 of the Fifteenth Amendment expressly declares that "Congress shall have power to enforce this article by appropriate legislation." By adding this authorization, the Framers indicated that Congress was to be chiefly responsible for implementing the rights created in section 1. "It is the power of Congress which has been enlarged. Congress is authorized to *enforce* the prohibitions by appropriate legislation. Some legislation is contemplated to make the [Civil War] amendments fully effective." *Ex parte Virginia*, 100 U.S. 339, 345. . . . Accordingly, in addition to the courts, Congress has full remedial powers to effectuate the constitutional prohibition against racial discrimination in voting.

Congress has repeatedly exercised these powers in the past, and its enactments have repeatedly been upheld. . . .

The basic test to be applied in a case involving section 2 of the Fifteenth Amendment is the same as in all cases concerning the express powers of Congress with relation to the reserved powers of the States. Chief Justice Marshall laid down the classic formulation, 50 years before the Fifteenth Amendment was ratified:

Let the end be legitimate, let it be within the scope of the constitution, and all means which are appropriate, which are plainly adapted to that end, which are not prohibited, but consist with the letter and spirit of the constitution, are constitutional. *McCulloch* v. *Maryland*, 4 Wheat 316, 421. . . .

The Court has subsequently echoed his language in describing each of the Civil War Amendments:

Whatever legislation is appropriate, that is, adapted to carry out the objects the amendments have in view, whatever tends to enforce submission to the prohibitions they contain, and to secure to all persons the enjoyment of perfect equality of civil rights and the equal protection of the laws against State denial or invasion, if not prohibited, is brought within the domain of congressional power. *Ex parte Virginia,* 100 U.S., at 345.

. . .

Congress exercised its authority under the Fifteenth Amendment in an inventive manner when it enacted the Voting Rights Act of 1965. First: The measure prescribes remedies for voting discrimination which go into effect without any need for prior adjudication. This was clearly a legitimate response to the problem, for which there is ample precedent under other constitutional provisions. . . . Congress had found that case-by-case litigation was inadequate to combat widespread and persistent discrimination in voting, because of the inordinate amount of time and energy required to overcome the obstructionist tactics invariably encountered in these lawsuits. After enduring nearly a century of systematic resistance to the Fifteenth Amendment, Congress might well decide to shift the advantage of time and inertia from the perpetrators of the evil to its victims. . . .

Second: The Act intentionally confines these remedies to a small number of States and political subdivisions which in most instances were familiar to Congress by name. This, too, was a permissible method of dealing with the problem. Congress had learned that substantial voting discrimination presently occurs in certain sections of the country, and it knew no way of accurately forecasting whether the evil might spread elsewhere in the future. In acceptable legislative fashion, Congress chose to limit its attention to the geographic areas where immediate action seemed necessary.

. . .

After enduring nearly a century of widespread resistance to the Fifteenth Amendment, Congress has marshalled an array of potent weapons against the evil, with authority in the Attorney General to employ them effectively. Many of the areas directly affected by this development have indicated their willingness to abide by any restraints legitimately imposed upon them. We here hold that the portions of the Voting Rights Act properly before us are a valid means for carrying out the commands of the Fifteenth Amendment. Hopefully, millions of non-white Americans will now be able to participate for the first time on an equal basis in the government under which they live. We may finally look forward to the day when truly "[t]he right of citizens of the United States to vote shall not be denied or abridged by the United States or by any State on account of race, color, or previous condition of servitude."

The bill of complaint is

*Dismissed.*

MR. JUSTICE BLACK, *concurring and dissenting.*

. . .

Though . . . I agree with most of the Court's conclusions, I dissent from its holding that every part of section 5 of the Act is constitutional. Section 4(a), to which section 5 is linked, suspends for five years all literacy tests and similar devices in those States coming within the formula of section 4(b). Section 5 goes on to provide that a State covered by section 4(b) can in no way amend its constitution or laws relating to voting without first trying to persuade the Attorney General of the United States or the Federal District Court for the District of Columbia that the new proposed laws do not have the purpose and will not have the effect of denying the right to vote to citizens on account of their race or color. I think this section is unconstitutional on at least two grounds.

The Constitution gives federal courts jurisdiction over cases and controversies only. If it can be said that any case or controversy arises under this section which gives the District Court for the District of Columbia jurisdiction to approve or reject state laws or constitutional amendments, then the case or controversy must be between a State and the United States Government. But it is hard for me to believe that a justiciable controversy can arise in the constitutional sense from a desire by the United States Government or some of its officials to determine in advance what legislative provisions a State may enact or what constitutional amendments it may adopt. If this dispute between the Federal Government and the States amounts to a case or controversy it is a far cry from the traditional constitutional notion of a case or controversy as a dispute over the meaning of enforceable laws or the manner in which they are applied. And if by this section Congress has created a case or controversy, and I do not believe it has, then it seems to me that the most appropriate judicial forum for settling these important questions is this Court acting under its original Art. III, section 2, jurisdiction to try cases in which a State is a party. At least a trial in this Court would treat the States with dignity to which they should be entitled as constituent members of our Federal Union.

The form of words and the manipulation of presumptions used in section 5 to create the illusion of a case or controversy should not be allowed to cloud the effect of that section. By requiring a State to ask a federal court to approve the validity of a proposed law which has in no way become operative, Congress had asked the State to secure precisely the type of advisory opinion our Constitution forbids. . . .

My second and more basic objection to section 5 is that Congress has here exercised its power under section 2 of the Fifteenth Amendment through the adoption of means that conflict with the most basic principles of the Constitution. As the Court says the limitations of the power granted under section 2 are the same as the limitations imposed on the exercise of any of the powers expressly granted Congress by the Constitution. . . . Section 5, by providing that some of the States cannot pass state laws or adopt state constitutional amendments without first being compelled to beg federal authorities to approve their policies, so distorts our constitutional structure of government as to render any distinction drawn in the Constitution between state and federal power almost meaningless. One of the most basic premises upon which our structure of government was founded was that the Federal Govern-

ment was to have certain specific and limited powers and no others, and all other power was to be reserved either "to the States respectively, or to the people." Certainly if all the provisions of our Constitution which limit the power of the Federal Government and reserve other power to the States are to mean anything, they mean at least that the States have power to pass laws and amend their constitutions without first sending their officials hundreds of miles away to beg federal authorities to approve them. Moreover, it seems to me that section 5 which gives federal officials power to veto state laws they do not like is in direct conflict with the clear command of our Constitution. that "The United States shall guarantee to every State in this Union a Republican Form of Government." I cannot help but believe that the inevitable effect of any such law which forces any one of the States to entreat federal authorities in faraway places for approval of local laws before they can become effective is to create the impression that the State or States treated in this way are little more than conquered provinces. And if one law concerning voting can make the States plead for this approval by a distant federal court or the United States Attorney General, other laws on different subjects can force the States to seek the advance approval not only of the Attorney General but of the President himself or any other chosen members of his staff. It is inconceivable to me that such a radical degradation of state power was intended in any of the provisions of our Constitution or its Amendments. Of course I do not mean to cast any doubt whatever upon the indisputable power of the Federal Government to invalidate a state law once enacted and operative on the ground that it intrudes into the area of supreme federal power. But the Federal Government has heretofore always been content to exercise this power to protect federal supremacy by authorizing its agents to bring lawsuits against state officials once an operative state law has created an actual case and controversy. A federal law which assumes the power to compel the States to submit in advance any proposed legislation they have for approval by federal agents approaches dangerously near to wiping the States out as useful and effective units in the government of our country. I cannot agree to any constitutional interpretation that leads inevitably to such a result.

. . .

In this and other prior Acts Congress has quite properly vested the Attorney General with extremely broad power to protect voting rights of citizens against discrimination on account of race or color. Section 5 viewed in this context is of very minor importance and in my judgment is likely to serve more as an irritant to the States than as an aid to the enforcement of the Act. I would hold section 5 invalid for the reasons stated above with full confidence that the Attorney General has ample power to give vigorous, expeditious and effective protection to the voting rights of all citizens.

## LOVING v. COMMONWEALTH OF VIRGINIA

### 388 U. S. 1; 18 L. Ed. 2d 1010; 87 S. Ct. 1817 (1967)

MR. CHIEF JUSTICE WARREN *delivered the opinion of the Court.*

This case presents a constitutional question never addressed by this Court: whether a statutory scheme adopted by the State of Virginia to prevent marriages between persons solely on the basis of racial classifications violates the Equal Protection and Due Process Clauses of the Fourteenth Amendment. For reasons which seem to us to reflect the central meaning of those constitutional commands, we conclude that these statutes cannot stand consistently with the Fourteenth Amendment.

In June 1958, two residents of Virginia, Mildred Jeter, a Negro woman, and Richard Loving, a white man, were married in the District of Columbia pursuant to its laws. Shortly after their marriage, the Lovings returned to Virginia and established

their marital abode in Caroline County. At the October Term, 1958, of the Circuit Court of Caroline County, a grand jury issued an indictment charging the Lovings with violating Virginia's ban on interracial marriages. On January 6, 1959, the Lovings pleaded guilty to the charge and were sentenced to one year in jail, however, the trial judge suspended the sentence for a period of 25 years on the condition that the Lovings leave the State and not return to Virginia together for 25 years, stating that:

Almighty God created the races white, black, yellow, malay, and red, and he placed them on separate continents. And but for the interference with his arrangement there would be no cause for such marriages. The fact that he separated the races shows that he did not intend for the races to mix.

After their convictions, the Lovings took up residence in the District of Columbia. On November 8, 1963, they filed a motion in the state trial court to vacate the judgment and set aside the sentence on the ground that the statutes which they had violated were repugnant to the Fourteenth Amendment. The motion not having been decided by October 28, 1964, the Lovings instituted a class action in the United States District Court for the Eastern District of Virginia requesting that a three-judge court be convened to declare the Virginia antimiscegenation statutes unconstitutional and to enjoin state officials from enforcing their convictions. On January 22, 1965, the state trial judge denied the motion to vacate the sentences, and the Lovings perfected an appeal to the Supreme Court of Appeals of Virginia. On February 11, 1965, the three-judge District Court continued the case to allow the Lovings to present their constitutional claims to the highest state court.

The Supreme Court of Appeals upheld the constitutionality of the antimiscegenation statutes and, after modifying the sentence, affirmed the convictions. . . .

. . . The Lovings were convicted of violating Sec. 20–58 of the Virginia Code:

*Leaving State to evade law.* If any white person and colored person shall go out of this State, for the purpose of being married, and with the intention of returning, and be married out of it, and afterwards return to and reside in it, cohabiting as man and wife, they shall be punished as provided in Sec. 20-59, and the marriage shall be governed by the same law as if it had been solemnized in this State. The fact of their cohabitation here as man and wife shall be evidence of their marriage. . . .

The Lovings have never disputed in the course of this litigation that Mrs. Loving is a "colored person" or that Mr. Loving is a "white person" within the meanings given those terms by the Virginia statutes.

Virigina is now one of 16 States which prohibit and punish marriages on the basis of racial classifications. Penalties for miscegenation arose as an incident to slavery and have been common in Virginia since the colonial period.

In upholding the constitutionality of these provisions in the decision below, the Supreme Court of Appeals of Virginia referred to its 1955 decision in *Naim* v. *Naim,* 197 Va. 80, 87 S.E. 2d 739, as stating the reasons supporting the validity of these laws. In *Naim,* the state court concluded that the State's legitimate purposes were "to preserve the racial integrity of its citizens," and to prevent "the corruption of blood," "a mongrel breed of citizens," and "the obliteration of racial pride," obviously an endorsement of the doctrine of White Supremacy. . . . The court also reasoned that marriage has traditionally been subject to state regulation without federal intervention, and consequently, the regulation of marriage should be left to exclusive state control by the Tenth Amendment.

While the state court is no doubt correct in asserting that marriage is a social relation subject to the State's police power, . . . the State does not contend in its argument before this Court that its powers to regulate marriage are unlimited notwithstanding the commands of the Fourteenth Amendment. . . . Instead, the State argues that the meaning of the Equal Protection Clause, as illuminated by the statements of the Framers, is only that state penal laws containing an interracial element as part of the definition of the offense must apply equally to whites and Negroes in the sense that members of each race are punished to the same degree. Thus, the State contends that, because its miscegenation statutes punish equally both the white and the Negro participants in an interracial marriage, these statutes, despite their reliance on racial classifications do not constitute an invidious discrimination upon race. The second argument is that, if the Equal Protection clause does not outlaw miscegenation statutes because of their reliance on racial classifications, the question of constitutionality would thus become whether there was any rational basis for a State to treat interracial marriages differently from other marriages. On this question, the State argues, the scientific evidence is substantially in doubt and, consequently, this Court should defer to the wisdom of the state legislature in adopting its policy of discouraging interracial marriages.

Because we reject the notion that the mere "equal application" of a statute containing racial classifications is enough to remove the classifications from the Fourteenth Amendment's proscription of all invidious racial discriminations, we do not accept the State's contention that these statutes should be upheld if there is any possible basis for concluding that they serve a rational purpose. The mere fact of equal application does not mean that our analysis of this statute should follow the approach we have taken in cases involving no racial discrimination where the Equal Protection Clause has been arrayed against a statute discriminating between the kinds of advertising which may be displayed on trucks in New York City, *Railway Express Agency, Inc.* v. *People of State of New York,* 336 U.S. 106, . . . or an exemption in Ohio's ad valorem tax for mer-

chandise owned by a non-resident in a storage warehouse, *Allied Stores of Ohio, Inc.* v. *Bowers,* 358 U.S. 522. . . . In these cases, involving distinctions not drawn according to race, the Court has merely asked whether there is any rational foundation for the discriminations, and has deferred to the wisdom of the state legislatures. In the case at bar, however, we deal with statutes containing racial classifications, and the fact of equal application does not immunize the statute from the very heavy burden of justification which the Fourteenth Amendment has traditionally required of state statutes drawn according to race.

The State argues that statements in the Thirty-ninth Congress about the time of the passage of the Fourteenth Amendment indicate that the Framers did not intend the Amendment to make unconstitutional state miscegenation laws. . . . While these statements have some relevance to the intention of Congress in submitting the Fourteenth Amendment, it must be understood that they pertained to the passage of specific statutes and not to the broader, organic purpose of a constitutional amendment. As for the various statements directly concerning the Fourteenth Amendment, we have said in connection with a related problem, that although these historical sources "cast some light" they are not sufficient to resolve the problem; "[a]t best, they are inconclusive. The most avid proponents of the post-War Amendments undoubtedly intended them to remove all legal distinctions among 'all persons born or naturalized in the United States.' Their opponents, just as certainly, were antagonistic to both the letter and the spirit of the Amendments and wished them to have the most limited effect." *Brown et al.* v. *Board of Education of Topeka et al.,*

347 U.S. 483. . . . We have rejected the proposition that the debates in the Thirty-ninth Congress or in the state legislatures which ratified the Fourteenth Amendment supported the theory advanced by the State, that the requirement of equal protection of the laws is satisfied by penal laws defining offenses based on racial classifications so long as white and Negro participants in the offense were similarly punished. *McLaughlin et al.* v. *State of Florida,* 379 U.S. 184. . . .

There can be no question but that Virginia's miscegenation statutes rest solely upon distinctions drawn according to race. The statutes proscribe generally accepted conduct if engaged in by members of different races. Over the years, this Court has consistently repudiated "[d]istinctions between citizens solely because of their ancestry" as being "odious to a free people whose institutions are founded upon the doctrine of equality." *Hirabayashi* v. *United States,* 320 U.S. 81, 100. At the very least, the Equal Protection Clause demands that racial classifications, especially suspect in criminal statutes, be subjected to the "most rigid scrutiny," . . . and, if they are ever to be upheld, they must be shown to be necessary to the accomplishment of some permissible state objective, independent of the racial discrimination which it was the object of the Fourteenth Amendment to eliminate. Indeed, two members of this Court have already stated that they "cannot conceive of a valid legislative purpose . . . which makes the color of a person's skin the test of whether his conduct is a criminal offense." *McLaughlin* v. *Florida, supra,* 379 U.S. at 198. . . . (Stewart, J., joined by Douglas, J., concurring).

There is patently no legitimate overriding purpose independent of invidious racial discrimination which justifies this classification. The fact that Virginia only prohibits interracial marriages involving white persons demonstrates that the racial classifications must stand on their own justification, as measures designed to maintain White Supremacy. We have consistently denied the constitutionality of measures which restrict the rights of citizens on account of race. There can be no doubt that restricting the freedom to marry solely because of racial classifications violates the central meaning of the Equal Protection Clause.

These statutes also deprive the Lovings of liberty without due process of law in violation of the Due Process Clause of the Fourteenth Amendment. The freedom to marry has long been recognized as one of the vital personal rights essential to the orderly pursuit of happiness by free men.

Marriage is one of the "'basic civil rights of man," fundamental to our very existence and survival. . . . To deny this fundamental freedom on so unsupportable a basis as the racial classifications embodied in these statutes, classifications so directly subversive of the principle of equality at the heart of the Fourteenth Amendment, is surely to deprive all of the State's citizens of liberty without due process of law. The Fourteenth Amendment requires that the freedom of choice to marry not be restricted by invidious racial discrimination. Under our Constitution, the freedom to marry or not marry, a person of another race resides with the individual and cannot be infringed by the State.

These convictions must be reversed. It is so ordered.

*Reversed.*

Mr. Justice Stewart, *concurring.*

I have previously expressed the belief that "it is simply not possible for a state law to be valid under our Constitution which makes the criminality of an act depend upon the race of the actor." *McLaughlin* v. *State of Florida,* 379 U.S. 184, 198 . . . 222 (concurring opinion). Because I adhere to that belief, I concur in the judgment of the Court.

## SELECTED REFERENCES

Barker, Lucius J., "Third Parties in Litigation: A Systemic View of the Judicial Function," 29 *Journal of Politics* 41 (1967).

Blumrosen, A. W., "Duty of Fair Recruitment Under the Civil Rights Act of 1964," 22 *Rutgers Law Review* 465 (1968).

Carmichael, Stokley and Charles Hamilton, *Black Power: The Politics of Liberation in America* (New York: Random House, Inc., 1967).

Clark, Leroy D. and W. Haywood Burns, "The Realpolitik of Racial Segregation in Northern Schools: Some Pragmatic Approaches," 14 *Howard Law Journal* 217 (1968).

Grier, William H. and Price M. Cobbs, *Black Rage* (New York: Basic Books, Inc., 1968).

Jenkins, Timothy L., "Study of Federal Effort to End Job Bias: A History, A Status Report, and A Prognosis," 14 *Howard Law Journal* 259 (1968).

Larson, Arthur, "The New Law of Race Relations," 1969 *Wisconsin Law Review* 470 (1969) .

Matthews, Donald R. and James W. Prothro, *Negroes and the New Southern Politics* (New York: Harcourt, Brace & World, Inc., 1966).

Miller, Loren, *The Petitioners: The Story of the Supreme Court of the United States and the Negro* (Cleveland: The World Publishing Company, 1966).

Peltason, Jack W., *Fifty-eight Lonely Men: Southern Federal Judges and School Desegregation* (New York: Harcourt, Brace & World, Inc., 1961).

Pritchett, C. Herman, "Equal Protection and the Urban Majority," 58 *American Political Science Review* 869 (1964).

*Report of the National Advisory Commission on Civil Disorders* (Washington: U.S. Government Printing Office, 1968).

Ryan, Phillip Scott, "Decent Housing As A Constitutional Right—42 U.S.C. Sec. 1983—Poor People's Remedy for Deprivation," 14 *Howard Law Journal* 338 (1968).

Steel, Lewis M., "A Critic's View of the Warren Court—Nine Men in Black Who Think White," *New York Times Magazine* (October 13, 1968) pp. 56 ff.

Symposium "Anatomy of a Riot: An Analytical Symposium of the Causes and Effects of Riots," 45 *Journal of Urban Law* 499 (1968).

United States Commission on Civil Rights, Periodic Reports of the Commission (Washington: U.S. Government Printing Office, 1959–1968).

Wilson, James Q., "Why We Are Having a Wave of Violence," *New York Times Magazine* (May 19, 1968) pp. 23 ff.

Woodward C. Vann, *The Strange Career of Jim Crow* (New York: Oxford University Press, Inc., 1966).

# Index

\* Asterisks mark those decisions that appear in this book, on the italicized pages.

469